America

A CONCISE HISTORY

Volume 1: To 1877

SECOND EDITION

America

A CONCISE HISTORY

Volume 1: To 1877

James A. Henretta
University of Maryland

David Brody
University of California, Davis

Lynn Dumenil
Occidental College

BEDFORD/ST. MARTIN'S
Boston • New York

For Bedford/St.Martin's
Publisher of History: Patricia A. Rossi
Developmental Editors: Gretchen Boger, Jessica Angell
Production Editor: Bridget Leahy
Senior Production Supervisor: Joe Ford
Marketing Manager: Jenna Bookin Barry
Copyeditor: Rosemary Winfield
Text Design: Wanda Kossak
Advisory Editor for Cartography: Michael P. Conzen, University of Chicago
Indexer: Melanie Belkin
Cover Design: Donna Lee Dennison
Cover Art: Hudson Highlands, by Thomas Chambers, ca. 1840. Courtesy of the Ralph Brill
   Hudson River Collection
Composition: TechBooks
Printing and Binding: R.R. Donnelley & Sons Company

President: Charles H. Christensen
Editorial Director: Joan E. Feinberg
Director of Marketing: Karen Melton
Director of Editing, Design, and Production: Marcia Cohen
Managing Editor: Elizabeth M. Schaaf

Library of Congress Control Number: 2001087440

Manufactured in the United States of America.

6   5   4   3   2   1
f   e   d   c   b   a

For information, write: Bedford/St. Martin's, 75 Arlington Street, Boston, MA 02116
(617-399-4000)

ISBN: 0–312–25612–4 (combined edition)
       0–312–25613–2 (Vol. 1)
       0–312–25614–0 (Vol. 2)

For Ellie,
Susan,
Janet, Michael, & Emily

PREFACE

This is the second edition of *America: A Concise History.* In the first edition, our main task was to shorten our comprehensive text, *America's History,* by 40 percent—in effect, to make six words do the work of ten—without compromising the balanced coverage and explanatory power of the original text. Not an easy task, but we are satisfied that *America: A Concise History* met that challenge. In this second edition, our starting point is the concise version itself. And the question we face is the one always confronting textbook authors when they contemplate a new edition: how do we improve on what we have already written? At this juncture, we aspire to make this concise edition a more compelling *narrative* text. What would most please us as authors would be for students to regard *America: A Concise History* as a book to be read, not as a set of assignments to be gotten through.

We remain committed, however, to the historical perspective that has informed this textbook project from its inception. We are bent on a democratic history, one that captures the experiences of ordinary people even as it records the achievements of the great and powerful. Throughout the book, we focus not only on the marvelous diversity of peoples who became Americans but also on the institutions—political, economic, social, and cultural—that forged a common national identity. We want to show how people of all classes and groups make their own history while simultaneously being influenced and constrained by circumstances, by the customs and institutions inherited from the past, and by the distribution of power in the present. We are writing narrative history harnessed to historical argument—not simply a retelling of "this happened and then that happened." The story, we hope, tells not only what happened but *why* it happened.

Features

Accomplishing these goals means first of all grounding *America: A Concise History* in a clear chronology and a strong conceptual framework. Each of the two volumes is divided into three parts, with each corresponding to a distinct phase of development.

Every part begins at a crucial turning point in American history, such as the American Revolution or the cold war, and emphasizes the dynamic forces at work. Part openers contain **Thematic Timelines** that highlight key developments and **Part Essays** that focus on the crucial engines of historical change that create new conditions of life. This part organization helps students to understand the major themes in each period of American history and the larger patterns of development that lend significance to the bits and pieces of historical data.

To put a human face on historical experience, each chapter contains two **American Voices,** first-person excerpts from letters, diaries, autobiographies, and public testimony that paint a vivid picture of the social or political life of the time. One-third of these are new to this edition, including reactions to the contested 2000 presidential election. Each chapter is enhanced by a selection of maps and contemporary illustrations, vibrantly displayed in an all-new four-color design. Coupled with generous margins and a new typeface, this second edition has the feel of a trade book.

America: A Concise History's map and graph program, the most extensive of any brief text, aids students in capturing aspects of American life geographically and in drawing sound conclusions based on statistical analysis. Full-color art, 60 percent of it new to this edition, reinforces students' understanding of history via striking images from the period being discussed. Detailed captions give students context for the images and allow the visual material to extend the text discussion in a substantive and engaging manner. Also new to this edition is **For Further Exploration,** a brief bibliographical essay at the close of each chapter designed to pique the student's interest in reading further. To assist instructors and advanced students, a full bibliography is available on the web at <www.bedfordstmartins.com/henrettaconcise>.

Taken together, these documents and illustrations provide instructors with a trove of teaching materials and allow students to enter the life of the past and see it from within.

Textual Changes

Good narrative history is primarily a product of good sentences and good paragraphs. So our labors have been mostly in the trenches in a line-by-line striving toward the vividness and human presence that are the hallmarks of narrative history. But larger strategies also have been called into play. We have doubled the length of the essays opening each part to afford us more scope for setting the thematic stage for our story. Each chapter now begins with an anecdote or scene selected to capture the reader's interest and establish the chapter's main ideas and topics. Our chapter endings eschew the usual textbook summary in favor of apt statements bringing the discussion to a satisfying close and opening the way for what follows. Within chapters we have been especially attentive to chronology, which sometimes involved, as in Chapters 18 and 19, major reordering of sections. We have also reduced the numbers of chapters from 33 to 31 to correspond more closely with the academic calendar. Former Chapters 13 (on sectionalism) and 14 (on the crisis of union) have been combined, with much of Chapter 13's treatment of southern society, industrialization, and the West shifted to earlier chapters, while former Chapter 30 (on the politics of the 1960s) has been incorporated into the surrounding chapters. Changes of this magnitude have a bracing effect, and we are hopeful that by being forced to think hard about how to organize materials, we have come up with a stronger periodization and clearer thematic development.

The revising process is also an opportunity to incorporate new scholarship. In this second edition we have expanded the treatment of Native Americans in the colonial era, and we have been more attentive to the role of gender and the emergence of a distinctive southern social order before 1820. Our treatment of the coming of the Industrial Revolution shifts the emphasis from industrialization as such to the extension of markets, in keeping with new scholarship on the market revolution. We have drawn on recent Reconstruction scholarship that sees the transition from slavery to freedom in large part as a battle over labor systems. We have improved our analysis of Native Americans in the Great Depression and postwar years and expanded our account of the New Right in the 1970s. The final chapter not only updates political developments but also discusses the economic prosperity of the late 1990s.

A new feature of this edition of *America: A Concise History* is the Epilogue, which deals with some of the open, still unresolved questions of our own time and how the historian thinks about them. The Epilogue invites the student to enter the historian's world—to participate with us in the act of interpretation that lies behind every historical text, including this one.

Supplements

Since the first edition of *America: A Concise History*, we have been working with instructors from around the country to determine how we can improve our ancillary package. Instructors stress the growing demand for online resources, particularly for students, and now more than ever our supplements reflect that request.

ONLINE STUDY GUIDE FOR STUDENTS

By Michael Goldberg, University of Washington, Bothell

We are pleased to offer a new *Online Study Guide* that features up-to-date technology to present students with attractive and highly effective presentations and learning tools. Written by Michael Goldberg of the University of Washington, Bothell, this interactive resource has unique self-assessment capabilities. As a student completes a practice test, the *Online Study Guide* immediately assesses her performance, targets the subject areas that need review, and refers the student back to the appropriate portions of the text. Through a series of multiple-choice, fill-in-the-blank, short-answer, and essay questions, students can gauge whether they have mastered the chapter's key events and themes. Exercises on the maps and on special features in the book encourage critical thinking. This resource is located at <www.bedfordstmartins.com/henrettaconcise>.

DOCUMENTS COLLECTION

Volume 1 by David L. Carlton (Vanderbilt University) and Volume 2 by Samuel T. McSeveny (Vanderbilt University)

This affordable two-volume *Documents Collection* offers students over 350 primary-source readings on topics covered in *America: A Concise History.* The documents emphasize contested issues in American history that will spark critical thinking and class discussions. Sets of documents highlight different perspectives on the same issue, while added attention has been given to America in the context of the larger world. Each document is preceded by a brief introduction and followed by questions for further thought.

INSTRUCTOR'S RESOURCE MANUAL

By Bradley T. Gericke (United States Military Academy)

Instructors, too, will benefit from our ancillary package. Bradley Gericke's *Instructor's Resource Manual,* provided free of charge with adoption of the book, offers an extensive collection of tools to aid both first-time and experienced teachers in structuring and customizing the American history course. The *Instructor's Resource Manual* has been revised and expanded to include informative and guiding chapter outlines, lecture strategies, questions to prompt class discussion, and writing assignments involving our American Voices features. This resource also includes map exercises, an extensive film guide, and historiographical essays on topics of particular interest.

TEST BANK

Volume 1 by Thomas L. Altherr (Metropolitan State College of Denver) and Volume 2 by Adolph Grundman (Metropolitan State College of Denver)

Our *Test Bank* now places a greater emphasis on thematic concerns within American history. What patterns in religious, cultural, political, and economic history do we see develop over time? How is a specific incident representative of a larger trend? *Test Bank* authors Thomas L. Altherr and Adolph Grundman have revised our first edition with these questions in mind. They have included multiple-choice, fill-in-the-blank, short-answer, essay, and map questions for each chapter. To provide greater ease in using this resource, it is now available on CD-ROM.

TRANSPARENCIES

An expanded set of over 150 full-color acetate transparencies, free to adopters, includes all maps and many tables, graphs, and images from the text.

CD-ROM WITH PRESENTATION MANAGER PRO

For teachers who wish to use electronic media in the classroom, this CD-ROM includes images, maps, graphs, and tables from *America: A Concise History* as well as sound recordings and a collection of supplementary images, in an easy-to-use format that allows instructors to customize their own presentations. The CD-ROM may be used with Presentation Manager Pro or with PowerPoint.

USING THE BEDFORD SERIES IN THE U.S. HISTORY SURVEY, SECOND EDITION

By Scott Hovey

Recognizing that many instructors use a survey text in conjunction with supplements, Bedford/St. Martin's has made the Bedford series volumes available at a discount to adopters of *America: A Concise History.* This short guide gives practical suggestions for using the more than fifty volumes from The Bedford Series in History and Culture and the Historians at Work series with a core text. The guide not only supplies connections between the text and the supplements but also provides ideas for starting discussions focused on a single primary-source volume.

Acknowledgments

The scholars and teachers who reviewed *America: A Concise History* made suggestions that we gratefully incorporated in the new edition. All of our reviewers have used concise texts in their courses, and their classroom experience has helped us to craft a book that meets the needs of today's diverse students. Thanks are due to Michael Goldberg, University of Washington, Bothell; David F. Krugler, University of Wisconsin–Platteville; Connie L. Lester, Mississippi State University; Carl H. Moneyhon, University of Arkansas at Little Rock; Katherine M. B. Osburn, Tennessee Technological University; Glenna R. Schroeder-Lein, University of Tennessee, Knoxville; and Nancy Shoemaker, University of Connecticut.

As the authors of *America: A Concise History,* we know how much this book is the work of other hands and minds. We are grateful to Katherine E. Kurzman and Patricia A. Rossi, who oversaw the project, and Gretchen Boger, who did a splendid job as our history editor (before departing for the Dominican Republic to serve in the Peace Corps). Elizabeth M. Welch offered invaluable insight and guidance along the way. Charles H. Christensen and Joan E. Feinberg have been generous in providing the resources we needed to produce the second edition. Elizabeth M. Schaaf, Joe Ford, and Bridget Leahy have done an outstanding job overseeing the production of the book. Karen Melton and Jenna Bookin Barry in the marketing department have been instrumental in helping this book reach the classroom. We also thank the rest of our editorial and production team for their dedicated efforts: Jessica Angell, Sarah Barrash, Rose Corbett Gordon, William Lombardo, Pembroke Herbert and Sandi Rygiel at Picture Research Consultants, Sandy Schechter, and Rosemary Winfield. Finally, we want to express our appreciation for the invaluable assistance of Patricia Deveneau, Stephanie Murvachik, Norman S. Cohen, and Anastasia Christman, whose work contributed in many ways to the intellectual vitality of this new edition of *America: A Concise History*.

James A. Henretta
David Brody
Lynn Dumenil

CONTENTS

Part Two
THE NEW REPUBLIC, 1775–1820   **156**

CHAPTER 6
WAR AND REVOLUTION, 1775–1783   160

CHAPTER 7
THE NEW POLITICAL ORDER, 1776–1800   189

LIST OF MAPS

Seattle
Olympia ★
WASHINGTON
Spokane

Columbia R.
Portland ★
Salem ★
OREGON

Great Falls ●
Helena ★
MONTANA

Missouri R.

Yellowstone R.
Billings ●

NORTH
DAKOTA

Bismarck ★

SOUTH
DAKOTA

Pierre ★

Boise ★
IDAHO

Snake R.

R
O
C
K
Y
WYOMING

M
O
U
N
T
A
I
N
S

Cheyenne ★

NEBRASKA

North Platte R.
Platte R.

45°

40°

35°

30°

Reno ●
NEVADA
Carson City ●

Sacramento ★
San Francisco ● Oakland ●
San Jose ●

SIERRA NEVADA

Fresno ●

CALIFORNIA

San Joaquin R.

Great
Salt Lake

Salt Lake City ●

UTAH

Green R.

Colorado R.

South Platte R.
Denver ★
COLORADO
Colorado ●
Springs

KANSAS

Las Vegas ●

Los ●
Angeles

San Diego ●

ARIZONA

Phoenix ★

Tucson ●

Santa Fe ★

Albuquerque ●

NEW MEXICO

Amarillo ●

TEXAS

El Paso ●

Rio Grande

Colorado R.

Pecos R.

Nueces R.

Pacific Ocean

22°

Honolulu ★

Pacific
Ocean

HAWAII

20°

0   100
Miles

160°   155°

70°

RUSSIA

BROOKS RANGE

Yukon R.

ALASKA

ALASKA RANGE

Anchorage ●

60°

CANADA

MEXICO

Juneau ★

International Date Line

50°

Bering Sea

Gulf of Alaska

0   500
Miles

175°   175°   165°   155°   145°   135°

CANADA

Red River of the North

Fargo
Duluth
MINNESOTA

MICHIGAN

L. Superior

L. Huron

MAINE

Augusta

Burlington
Montpelier VT. N.H.
Concord
Manchester
Portland

St. Paul
Minneapolis

Wisconsin R.

WISCONSIN

L. Michigan

Lansing

Detroit

L. Ontario

Buffalo

NEW YORK

Albany

Boston

MASS.
Providence

Hartford
CONN. R.I.

Sioux Falls

Milwaukee
Madison

Mississippi R.

Chicago

L. Erie

Cleveland

Allegheny R.

PENNSYLVANIA
Harrisburg

Newark
New York

Trenton

NEW
JERSEY

IOWA

Des Moines

Illinois R.

Gary

Wabash R.

OHIO
Columbus

Wheeling

Pittsburgh

Baltimore

Philadelphia
Dover

DELAWARE

Omaha
Lincoln

INDIANA
Indianapolis

Springfield

Cincinnati

WEST
VIRGINIA

MD.
Annapolis

WASHINGTON D.C.

Charleston

Richmond

Topeka

Kansas
City

St. Louis

Frankfort

Ohio R.

Louisville

Norfolk

Potomac R.

VIRGINIA

Missouri R.

Jefferson
City

ILLINOIS

KENTUCKY

Cumberland R.

Roanoke R.

Raleigh

Wichita

MISSOURI

Knoxville
Nashville

NORTH
CAROLINA

Charlotte

Cape Fear R.

Oklahoma
City

Canadian R.

ARKANSAS

Memphis

TENNESSEE

APPALACHIAN MOUNTAINS

SOUTH
CAROLINA

Columbia

Atlantic Ocean

Arkansas R.

Little Rock

Tennessee R.

Birmingham

Atlanta

Charleston

Santee R.

OKLAHOMA

Mississippi R.

Jackson

ALABAMA
Montgomery

GEORGIA

Chattahoochee R.

Dallas
Fort
Worth

LOUISIANA

MISSISSIPPI

Alabama R.

Jacksonville

Red R.

Baton Rouge

Tallahassee

Austin
Houston

Sabine R.

Trinity R.

Brazos R.

New Orleans

FLORIDA

San Antonio

Gulf of Mexico

BAHAMAS

Miami

CUBA

67° *Atlantic 66°
Ocean*

San Juan

PUERTO RICO
Ponce

18°

*Caribbean
Sea*

0   500
Miles

Elevation

Feet		Meters
9,843		3,000
6,562		2,000
3,281		1,000
1,640		500
656		200
0		0
Below sea level		Below sea level

0   200   400
Miles

95°   90°   85°   80°   75°

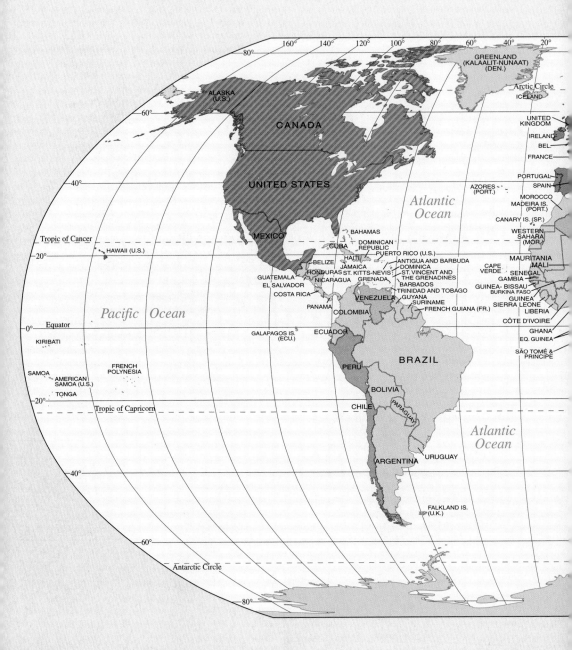

80°   160°   140°   120°   100°   80°   60°   40°   20°

GREENLAND
(KALAALIT-NUNAAT)
(DEN.)

Arctic Circle
ICELAND

60°

ALASKA
(U.S.)

CANADA

UNITED
KINGDOM

IRELAND

BEL.

FRANCE

40°

UNITED STATES

Atlantic
Ocean

PORTUGAL

AZORES
(PORT.)

SPAIN

MOROCCO

MADEIRA IS.
(PORT.)

CANARY IS. (SP.)

Tropic of Cancer

MEXICO

BAHAMAS

WESTERN
SAHARA
(MOR.)

20°   HAWAII (U.S.)

CUBA

DOMINICAN
REPUBLIC

PUERTO RICO (U.S.)

MAURITANIA

MALI

HAITI

BELIZE

JAMAICA

ANTIGUA AND BARBUDA

DOMINICA

CAPE
VERDE

SENEGAL

GUATEMALA

HONDURAS ST. KITTS-NEVIS

ST. VINCENT AND
THE GRENADINES

GAMBIA

EL SALVADOR

NICARAGUA

GRENADA

BARBADOS

GUINEA- BISSAU

BURKINA FASO

COSTA RICA

TRINIDAD AND TOBAGO

GUINEA

PANAMA

VENEZUELA

GUYANA

SIERRA LEONE

LIBERIA

COLOMBIA

SURINAME

FRENCH GUIANA (FR.)

CÔTE D'IVOIRE

GHANA

Equator   0°

GALAPAGOS IS.
(ECU.)

ECUADOR

EQ. GUINEA

KIRIBATI

SÃO TOMÉ &
PRINCIPE

PERU

BRAZIL

SAMOA

FRENCH
POLYNESIA

AMERICAN
SAMOA (U.S.)

BOLIVIA

TONGA

20°

CHILE

PARAGUAY

Tropic of Capricorn

Pacific Ocean

Atlantic
Ocean

URUGUAY

40°

ARGENTINA

FALKLAND IS.
(U.K.)

60°

Antarctic Circle

80°

Political divisions as of January 2001

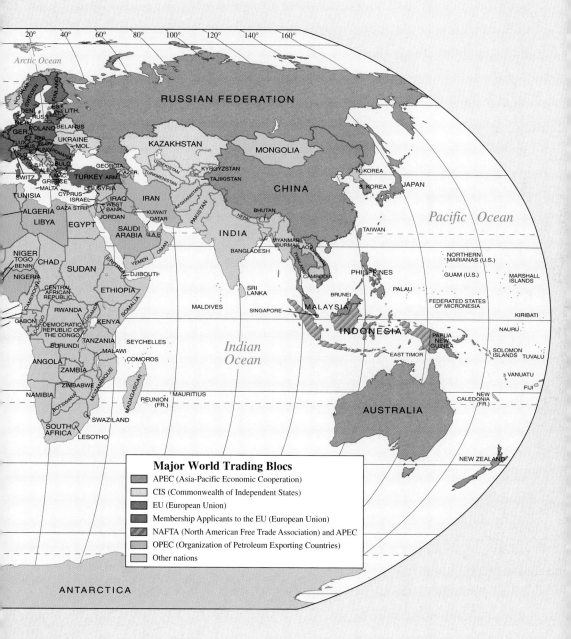

20°   40°   60°   80°   100°   120°   140°   160°

Arctic Ocean

RUSSIAN FEDERATION

NORWAY
SWEDEN
FINLAND
DEN.
NETH.
RUSS.
EST
LAT.
LITH.
GER.
POLAND
BELARUS
LUX.
CZ. REP.
SLOV.
UKRAINE
B.H.
HUNG.
SLO.
MOL.
SCR.
ALB.
MAC.
ROMANIA
BULG.
GREECE
SWITZ.
MALTA
TURKEY
ARM.
CYPRUS
LEB.
SYRIA
ISRAEL
GAZA STRIP
WEST BANK
JORDAN
TUNISIA
ALGERIA
LIBYA
EGYPT
SAUDI ARABIA
U.A.E.

KAZAKHSTAN
MONGOLIA
UZBEKISTAN
KYRGYZSTAN
TURKMENISTAN
TAJIKISTAN
GEORGIA
AZER.
IRAQ
IRAN
KUWAIT
QATAR
AFGHANISTAN
PAKISTAN
NEPAL
BHUTAN
INDIA

CHINA

N. KOREA
S. KOREA
JAPAN

Pacific   Ocean

TAIWAN

NIGER
TOGO
BENIN
CHAD
SUDAN
NIGERIA
CENTRAL AFRICAN REPUBLIC
ETHIOPIA
CAMEROON
RWANDA
GABON
DEMOCRATIC REPUBLIC OF THE CONGO
KENYA
UGANDA
BURUNDI
TANZANIA
SEYCHELLES
MALAWI
COMOROS
ANGOLA
ZAMBIA
ZIMBABWE
MOZAMBIQUE
MADAGASCAR
NAMIBIA
BOTSWANA
MAURITIUS
REUNION (FR.)
SOUTH AFRICA
SWAZILAND
LESOTHO

YEMEN
ERITREA
DJIBOUTI
OMAN
SOMALIA

BANGLADESH
MYANMAR (BURMA)
LAOS
THAILAND
CAMBODIA
VIETNAM
PHILIPPINES
BRUNEI
SRI LANKA
MALDIVES
SINGAPORE
MALAYSIA
INDONESIA
EAST TIMOR
PAPUA NEW GUINEA

PALAU

NORTHERN MARIANAS (U.S.)
GUAM (U.S.)
FEDERATED STATES OF MICRONESIA
MARSHALL ISLANDS
KIRIBATI
NAURU
SOLOMON ISLANDS
TUVALU
VANUATU
FIJI
NEW CALEDONIA (FR.)

Indian Ocean

AUSTRALIA

NEW ZEALAND

Major World Trading Blocs

APEC (Asia-Pacific Economic Cooperation)
CIS (Commonwealth of Independent States)
EU (European Union)
Membership Applicants to the EU (European Union)
NAFTA (North American Free Trade Association) and APEC
OPEC (Organization of Petroleum Exporting Countries)
Other nations

ANTARCTICA

ABOUT THE AUTHORS

James A. Henretta is Priscilla Alden Burke Professor of American History at the University of Maryland, College Park. He received his undergraduate education at Swarthmore College and his Ph.D. from Harvard University. He has taught at the University of Sussex, England; Princeton University; UCLA; Boston University; as a Fulbright lecturer in Australia at the University of New England; and at Oxford University as the Harmsworth Professor of American History. His publications include *The Evolution of American Society, 1700–1815: An Interdisciplinary Analysis;* *"Salutary Neglect": Colonial Administration under the Duke of Newcastle; Evolution and Revolution: American Society, 1600–1820;* and *The Origins of American Capitalism.* Recently he co-edited and contributed to a collection of original essays, *Republicanism and Liberalism in America and the German States, 1750–1850,* as part of his larger research project on "The Rise and Transformation of the Liberal State: New York, 1820–1940."

David Brody is Professor Emeritus of History at the University of California, Davis. He received his B.A., M.A., and Ph.D. from Harvard University. He has taught at the University of Warwick in England, at Moscow State University in the former Soviet Union, and at Sydney University in Australia. He is the author of *Steelworkers in America; Workers in Industrial America: Essays on the 20th Century Struggle;* and *In Labor's Cause: Main Themes on the History of the American Worker.* He has been awarded fellowships from the Social Science Research Council, the Guggenheim Foundation, and the National Endowment for the Humanities. He is past president (1991–1992) of the Pacific Coast Branch of the American Historical Association. His current research is on industrial labor during the Great Depression.

Lynn Dumenil is Robert Glass Cleland Professor of American History at Occidental College in Los Angeles. She is a graduate of the University of Southern California and received her Ph.D. from the University of California, Berkeley. She has written *The Modern Temper: American Culture and Society in the 1920s* and *Freemasonry and American Culture: 1880–1930.* Her articles and reviews have appeared in the *Journal of American History, the Journal of American Ethnic History, Reviews in American History,* and *the American Historical Review.* She has been a historical consultant to several documentary film projects and is on the Council of the Pacific Coast Branch of the American Historical Association. Her current work, for which she received a National Endowment for the Humanities Fellowship, is on World War I, citizenship, and the state. In 2001–2002 she will be at the University of Helsinki as the Bicentennial Fulbright Chair in American Studies.

SECOND EDITION

America

A CONCISE HISTORY

Part One

THE CREATION OF AMERICAN SOCIETY
1450–1775

THEMATIC TIMELINE

	ECONOMY	SOCIETY	GOVERNMENT
	FROM STAPLE CROPS TO INTERNAL GROWTH	ETHNIC, RACIAL, AND CLASS DIVISIONS	FROM MONARCHY TO REPUBLIC
1450	• Native American subsistence economy • Europeans fish off North American coast.	• Sporadic warfare among Indian peoples • Spanish conquest of Mexico (1519–1521)	• Rise of monarchical nation-states in Europe
1600	• First staple crops: furs and tobacco	• English-Indian warfare • African servitude begins in Virginia (1619).	• James I rules by "divine right" in England. • Virginia House of Burgesses (1619)
1640	• New England trade with sugar islands • Mercantilist regulations: first Navigation Act (1651)	• White indentured servitude in the Chesapeake • Indians retreat inland.	• Puritan Revolution • Stuart restoration (1660) • Bacon's rebellion (1675)
1680	• Tobacco trade stagnates. • Rice cultivation expands.	• Indian slavery in the Carolinas • Ethnic rebellion in New York (1689)	• Dominion of New England (1686–1689) • Glorious Revolution (1688–1689)
1720	• Mature agricultural economy in North • Imports from Britain increase.	• Scots-Irish and German migration • Growing rural inequality	• Rise of the representative assembly • Challenge to "deferential" politics
1760	• Trade boycotts encourage domestic manufacturing.	• Uprisings by tenants and backcountry farmers • Artisan protests	• Ideas of popular sovereignty • Battles of Lexington and Concord (1775)

RELIGION	CULTURE
FROM HIERARCHY TO PLURALISM	THE CREATION OF AMERICAN IDENTITY
• Protestant Reformation begins (1517).	• Diverse Native American cultures in eastern Woodlands
• Persecuted English Puritans and Catholics migrate to America.	• Puritans implant Calvinism, education, and freehold ideal.
• Established churches in Virginia and Massachusetts • Roger Williams creates religious liberty in Rhode Island.	• Aristocratic aspirations in the Chesapeake
• Religious freedom in Quaker Pennsylvania	• Emergence of African American language and culture
• German and Scots-Irish Pietists in mid-Atlantic region • Great Awakening	• Emergence of regional cultures • Franklin and the American Enlightenment
• Evangelical Baptists in Virginia • Quebec Act allows Catholicism (1774).	• Emergence of "American" identity • Republican innovations in political theory

Societies are made, not born. They are the creation of generations of human endeavor and experience. Many centuries ago hunting and gathering peoples who migrated to the Western Hemisphere from Asia formed the first American societies. Over many generations these migrants—called the Native Americans—came to live in a wide variety of environments and cultures. In much of North America they developed kinship-based societies that relied on hunting and farming. But in the lower Mississippi Valley, Native Americans developed a hierarchical social order similar to that of the great civilizations of the Aztecs, Mayas, and Incas of Mesoamerica.

The coming of the Europeans and their diseases tore the fabric of most Native American cultures into shreds. Indian peoples increasingly confronted a *new* American society that included thousands of enslaved Africans and was dominated by even greater numbers of settlers of European ancestry. Most of the Europeans attempted to transplant their traditional societies to America—their farming practices, their social hierarchies, their culture and heritage, and their religious ideas. But in learning to live in the new land, the Europeans who settled Britain's North

American colonies eventually created societies that were distinctly different from those of their homelands in their economies, social character, political systems, religion, and culture.

Many of the new settlements compiled an impressive record of economic achievement. Traditional Europe was made up of poor and unequal societies periodically racked by famine. But in the bountiful natural environment of North America, plenty replaced poverty, and the settlers created a bustling economy and many prosperous communities of independent farm families. Indeed, England's northern mainland colonies became "the best poor man's country" for migrants from the British Isles and Germany.

However, some of the new settlements became places of oppressive captivity for Africans. Aided by African slavers, Europeans transported hundreds of thousands of Africans, from many peoples, to the West Indies and the southern mainland colonies and forced them to work as slaves on sugar, tobacco, and rice plantations. Although their labor produced vast quantities of valuable export crops, these enslaved Africans lived from one generation to the next in abject poverty and without civil or political rights.

At the same time the Europeans who lived in the emerging American societies created an increasingly free and competitive political system. The first English settlers brought many authoritarian institutions with them, and the English government attempted to impose tight control over their lives. But after 1689 authoritarian customs and controls gradually gave way to governments based in part on representative assemblies. Eventually, the growth of self-rule in these colonies led to demands for political independence from Britain.

The American experience profoundly changed religious institutions and values. Many migrants came to America in the wake of the conflicts of Europe's Protestant Reformation seeking to practice their religion without interference. The societies they created became increasingly religious, especially after the evangelical revivals of the 1740s. By this time many Americans had rejected the harshest tenets of Calvinism (a strict Protestant doctrine), and others had embraced the rationalist view of the European Enlightenment. As a result, American Protestant Christianity became increasingly tolerant, democratic, and optimistic.

Finally, the new American society was marked by changes in the family, the local community, and the broader culture. The first English settlers lived in patriarchal families ruled by dominant fathers and in communities controlled by men of high status. By 1750, however, many American fathers no longer strictly managed their children's lives. Geographic and economic expansion helped to create more open and diverse communities in which many white men—and some women—began to enjoy greater personal independence. These communities formed part of an increasingly pluralistic society that by the eighteenth century was composed of various European migrants—English, Scots, Scots-Irish, Dutch, and German—as well as enslaved West Africans and many different Native American peoples. As these migrants settled in distinct American environments, four regional cultures developed: in New England, the mid-Atlantic colonies, the Chesapeake, and the lower South. Consequently an American identity—based on the English language, British legal and political institutions, and shared experiences—emerged very slowly.

The story of the colonial experience is historically and morally complex—a multifaceted world that brought oppression to some and opportunity to others. The European intruders warred with Native Americans and condemned most Africans to bondage, even as their new society offered a continuing stream of European migrants rich possibilities for economic security, political freedom, and spiritual fulfillment.

Chapter 1

WORLDS COLLIDE: EUROPE, AFRICA, AND AMERICA
1450–1620

Soon there will come from the rising sun a different kind of man from any you have yet seen. . . . [After that,] the world will fall to pieces.

A SPOKANE INDIAN PROPHET

"Before the French came among us," an elder of the Natchez people of Mississippi exclaimed in 1728, "we were men . . . and we walked with boldness every road." "But now," he lamented, "we walk like slaves, which we shall soon be, since the French already treat us . . . as they do their black slaves." Before the 1420s the Indian peoples of the Western Hemisphere knew absolutely nothing about the French inhabitants of Europe and the dark-skinned peoples of Africa, and those peoples knew only a little bit about each other. Then a few Europeans, hungry for the trade and riches of Asia, sailed along the west coast of Africa and were soon involved in the long-established trade in African slaves. By 1492 Christopher Columbus, another European searching for a sea route to Asia, had encountered the lands and peoples of the Americas. The destinies of three continents quickly became intertwined. In 1493, on his second voyage to the Western Hemisphere, Columbus carried a cargo of enslaved Africans, beginning the centuries-long process that created a multitude of triracial societies in the Americas.

As the Natchez elder well knew, the resulting mixture of peoples from the three continents was based not on equality but on exploitation. In 1728 he was urging his people to fight the encroachment of Europeans, but resistance by then was useless. Within a decade, 250 years after the strangers had first arrived in the Americas, Europeans and their Indian allies had killed hundreds of Natchez and sold many of the survivors into slavery in the West Indies.

The fate of the Natchez was not new. Over the course of the three centuries following Columbus's voyage, many Native American peoples came under the domination of the Europeans—Spanish, Portuguese, French, English, Dutch—who had colonized the Western Hemisphere and now worked its plantations with enslaved Africans. How did Europeans become leaders in world trade and extend their influence across the Atlantic? What was the character of the Native Americans' life and culture, and what made their societies vulnerable to conquest by European adventurers? And what led to the transatlantic trade in African slaves? In the answers to these questions lie the origins of the United States.

Native American Worlds

When the Europeans arrived, the great majority of Native Americans—about 40 million—lived in Mesoamerica (present-day Mexico and Guatemala), and another 15 million resided in lands to the north (present-day United States and Canada). Some lived in simple hunter-gatherer or agricultural communities governed by kin ties, but the majority resided in societies ruled by warrior-kings and priests. In Mesoamerica and Peru Indian peoples created civilizations whose art, religion, society, and economy were as complex as those of Europe and the Mediterranean.

THE FIRST AMERICANS

For the Navajo people, history began when their ancestors emerged from under the earth; for the Iroquois, the story of their Nations began when people fell from the sky. However, most anthropologists and historians believe that the first people to live in the Western Hemisphere were migrants from Asia. Some might have come by water, but most probably came by land. Strong archaeological evidence suggests that during the last Ice Age, which began about 30,000 years ago, small bands of hunters followed herds of game across a land bridge between Siberia and Alaska. A tale of the Tuscarora Indians, who lived in present-day North Carolina, tells of a famine in the old world and a journey over ice toward where "the sun rises," a trek that brought their ancestors to a lush forest with abundant food and game. Most anthropologists believe that this migratory stream continued for about 20,000 years, until the glaciers melted and the rising ocean waters submerged the land bridge and created the Bering Strait. Then the people of the Western Hemisphere, who by that time had moved as far south as the tip of South America and as far east as the Atlantic coast of North America, were cut off from the rest of the world for 400 generations.

For many centuries the first Americans lived as hunter-gatherers, subsisting on the abundant wildlife and vegetation. But about 3000 B.C. some Native American peoples began to develop horticulture, most notably in the area of present-day Mexico. These inventive farmers planted avocado, chili peppers, and cotton and learned how to breed maize, or Indian corn, as well as tomatoes, potatoes, and manioc—crops that would eventually enrich the food supply of the entire world. Over the centuries the Indian peoples bred maize into a much larger, extremely nutritious plant that was hardier, had more varieties, and had a higher yield per

Gold Piece from Peru

Skilled Inca artisans created gold jewelry of striking beauty. Note the intricate detail on the head-dress and the stylized treatment of the face.

(Dumbarton Oaks Research Library and Collections, Washington, DC)

acre than wheat, barley, and rye, the staple cereals of Europe. They also learned to cultivate beans and squash and plant them together with corn, creating a mix of crops that provided a nutritious diet and preserved soil fertility, allowing intensive farming and high yields. The resulting agricultural surplus laid the economic foundation for populous and wealthy societies in Mexico, in Peru, and in the Mississippi River Valley.

THE MAYAS AND THE AZTECS

The flowering of civilization in Mesoamerica began among the Mayan peoples of the Yucatan Peninsula of Mexico and the neighboring rain forests of Guatemala (see Map 1.1). The Mayas built large religious centers, urban communities with elaborate systems of water storage and irrigation. By A.D. 300 the Mayan city of Tikal had at least 20,000 inhabitants, mostly farmers who worked the nearby fields and whose labor was used to build huge stone temples. An elite class claiming descent from the gods ruled Mayan society, living in splendor on goods and taxes extracted from peasant families. Drawing on religious and artistic traditions that stretched back to the Olmec people, who had lived along the Gulf of Mexico around 700 B.C., skilled Mayan artisans decorated temples and palaces with art depicting warrior-gods and complex religious rituals. Mayan astronomers created a calendar that recorded historical events and predicted eclipses of the sun and the moon with remarkable accuracy. The Mayas also developed hieroglyphic writing to record royal lineages and noteworthy events, including wars.

Beginning around A.D. 800, Mayan civilization declined. Some evidence suggests that a two-century-long dry period caused a decline in population and an economic crisis that prompted overtaxed peasants to desert the temple cities and retreat into the countryside. By A.D. 900 many religious centers had been abandoned, but some Mayan city-states lasted until the Spanish invasion in the 1520s.

As the Mayan peoples flourished in the Yucatan, a second major Mesoamerican civilization developed in the central highlands of Mexico around the city of

MAP 1.1
Native American Peoples, 1492

Native Americans populated the entire Western Hemisphere at the time of Columbus's arrival. Having learned how to live in many environments, they created diverse cultures that ranged from the centralized agriculture-based empires of the Mayas and the Aztecs to seminomadic tribes of hunter-gatherers. The sheer diversity among Indians—of culture, language, and tribal identity—inhibited united resistance to the European invaders.

Teotihuacán, with its magnificent Pyramid of the Sun. At its zenith about A.D. 500 Teotihuacán had more than 100 temples, about 4,000 apartment buildings, and a population of at least 100,000. By A.D. 800 Teotihuacán had also declined, probably because of a long-term drop in rainfall and recurrent invasions by seminomadic warrior peoples. Eventually one of these peoples, the Aztecs, established an even more extensive empire.

The Aztecs entered the highlands of Mexico from the north and settled on an island in Lake Texcoco. There, in A.D. 1325, they began to build a new city, Tenochtitlán (present-day Mexico City). They learned the settled ways of the resident peoples, mastered their complex irrigation systems, and established an elaborate culture with a hierarchical social order. Priests and warrior nobles ruled over twenty clans of free Aztec commoners who farmed communally owned land, and the nobles used huge numbers of non-Aztec slaves and serfs to labor on their private estates. Artisans worked in stone, pottery, cloth, leather, and especially obsidian (hard volcanic glass used to make sharp-edged weapons and tools).

The Aztecs remained an aggressive tribe and soon subjugated most of central Mexico. Their rulers demanded both economic and human tribute from scores of subject tribes, gruesomely sacrificing untold thousands of men and women to ensure agricultural fertility and the daily return of the sun. Aztec merchants created far-flung trading routes and imported furs, gold, textiles, food, and obsidian. By A.D. 1500, when the Spanish arrived in the Caribbean, Tenochtitlán had grown into a great metropolis with splendid palaces and temples and over 200,000 inhabitants. The Aztecs' wealth, strong institutions, and military power posed a formidable challenge to any adversary, at home or from afar.

THE INDIANS OF THE NORTH

The Indians who resided north of the Rio Grande were fewer in number and lived in less coercive societies. In A.D. 1500 these Indians lived in dispersed communities of a few thousand people and spoke many different languages—no fewer than sixty-eight east of the Mississippi River (see Map 1.1). Most were organized in self-governing tribes composed of clans—groups of related families that had a common identity and a real or legendary common ancestor. The tribes were led by local chiefs who, aided by the clan elders, conducted ceremonies and regulated personal life. For example, elders encouraged individuals to share food and other scarce goods, promoting an ethic of reciprocity rather than one of accumulation. "You are covetous, and neither generous nor kind," the Micmac Indians of Nova Scotia told French fur traders around 1600. "As for us, if we have a morsel of bread, we share it with our neighbor." The individual ownership of land was virtually unknown in Indian culture, although elders granted families exclusive use-rights over certain planting grounds and hunting areas. Clan leaders also resolved personal feuds, disciplined individuals who violated customs, decided whether to go to war, and banned marriage between members of the same clan, a rule that helped prevent inbreeding. However, their power was far less than that of the Mayan and Aztec nobles because their kinship-based system of government was locally based and worked by consensus, not by coercion.

Over the centuries some of these tribes exerted influence over their immediate neighbors through trade or conquest. The earliest expansive Indian cultures appeared in the eastern woodlands of North America as the inhabitants increased the food supply by domesticating plants and were thus able to settle in large villages. By A.D. 100 the vigorous Hopewell people in the area of present-day Ohio had spread their influence through trade from Wisconsin to Louisiana, importing obsidian from the Yellowstone region of the Rocky Mountains, copper from the Great Lakes, and pottery and marine shells from the Gulf of Mexico. They built large burial mounds and surrounded them with extensive circular, rectangular, or octagonal earthworks that in some cases still survive. The Hopewell people buried their dead with striking ornaments fashioned by their craftsmen: copper beaten into elaborate designs, crystals of quartz, mica cut into the shapes of serpents and human hands, and stone pipes carved to represent frogs, hawks, bears, and other animals. For unknown reasons, their elaborate trading network gradually collapsed around A.D. 400.

A second complex culture developed among the Pueblo peoples of the Southwest. By A.D. 600 Mogollon peoples in the highland region along the border of present-day Arizona and New Mexico were using irrigation to grow two crops a year, fashioning fine pottery, and worshipping their gods on platform mounds; by A.D. 1000, they were living in elaborate multiroom stone structures (or pueblos). In the north of present-day New Mexico, the Anasazi culture developed around

Casas Grandes Pot

The artistically and architecturally talented Mogollon and Anasazi peoples of Arizona and New Mexico took utilitarian objects—such as this ordinary pot—and decorated them with black-on-white designs. Their cultures flourished from 600 to 1150, after which they slowly declined.

(The Amerind Foundation, Dragoon, AZ. Photo by Robin Stancliff)

A.D. 900. The Anasazis were master architects, building residential-ceremonial villages in steep cliffs and a pueblo in Chaco Canyon that housed 1,000 people. Over 400 miles of straight roads radiated out of Chaco Canyon, making it a center for trade. But the culture of the Anasazis and the Mogollons (as well as that of the neighboring Hohokam people) gradually collapsed after A.D. 1150 as long periods of drought disrupted food production and prompted the abandonment of Chaco Canyon and other long-established communities. The descendants of these Pueblo peoples—including the Zunis and the Hopis—later built strong but smaller and more dispersed village societies.

The last large-scale culture to emerge north of the Rio Grande was the Mississippian civilization. Beginning about A.D. 700, the advanced farming technology of Mesoamerica spread into the Mississippi River Valley, perhaps carried by emigrants fleeing from warfare among the Mayas. The resident peoples planted new strains of maize and beans on fertile river bottomland, providing a protein-rich diet and creating an agricultural surplus. A robust culture based on small, fortified temple cities quickly emerged. By A.D. 1150 the largest city, Cahokia (near present-day St. Louis), had a population of 15,000 to 20,000 and more than 100 temple mounds, one of them as large as the great Egyptian pyramids. As in Mesoamerica, the tribute paid by peasant cultivators supported a privileged class of nobles and priests who waged war against neighboring chiefdoms, patronized skilled artisans, and may have been worshipped as deities.

However, by A.D. 1350 this 600-year-old Mississippian civilization was in rapid decline, undermined by warfare over fertile bottomlands and by urban diseases such as tuberculosis. Nonetheless, the values and institutions of this culture endured for centuries in the lands to the east of the Mississippi River and help to account for the fierce resistance of the inhabitants to Spanish and French invaders. When the Spanish invaded northern Florida in the 1540s, they found the Apalachee and Timucua Indians living in permanent settlements and planting and harvesting their fields twice a year. A century and a half later French traders and priests who encountered the Natchez people in the area of present-day Mississippi found a society rigidly divided among hereditary chiefs, two groups of nobles and honored people, and a bottom class of peasants. Undoubtedly influenced by Mayan or Aztec rituals, the Natchez practiced human sacrifice; the death of a chief called for the sacrifice of his wives and the enlargement of a ceremonial mound to bury their remains (see American Voices, "The Customs of the Natchez"). Like the Indians of Mesoamerica, the peoples of this region (such as the Choctaws, Creeks, Chickasaws, Cherokees, and Seminoles) developed a stable, agricultural-based way of life, prompting eighteenth-century British settlers to call them the Civilized Tribes.

Although farming in Mesoamerica was the province of both sexes, among peoples who lived in the eastern woodlands of North America it became the work of women. Over the centuries Indian women became adept horticulturists, using flint hoes and more productive strains of corn, squash, and beans to reduce the

The Customs of the Natchez

FATHER LE PETITE

B *eliefs and institutions from the earlier Mississippian culture* (A.D. *1000–1450) lasted for centuries among the Natchez, who lived in the area of present-day Mississippi. This letter was written around 1730 by Father le Petite, a Jesuit priest who lived among the Natchez after their uprising against the French. Here, Father le Petite accurately describes many Indian customs but misinteprets the rules governing the succession of the chief, which simply followed the normal practice of descent and inheritance in a matrilineal society.*

My Reverend Father, The peace of Our Lord.

This Nation of Savages inhabits one of the most beautiful and fertile countries in the World, and is the only one on this continent which appears to have any regular worship. Their Religion in certain points is very similar to that of the ancient Romans. They have a Temple filled with Idols, which are different figures of men and of animals, and for which they have the most profound veneration. Their Temple in shape resembles an earthen oven, a hundred feet in circumference. They enter it by a little door about four feet high, and not more than three in breadth. Above on the outside are three figures of eagles made of wood, and painted red, yellow, and white. Before the door is a kind of shed with folding-doors, where the Guardian of the Temple is lodged; all around it runs a circle of palisades, [pointed wooden stakes], on which are seen exposed the skulls of all the heads which their Warriors had brought back from the battles in which they had been engaged with the enemies of their Nation. . . .

The Sun is the principal object of veneration to these people; as they cannot conceive of anything which can be above this heavenly body, nothing else appears to them more worthy of their homage. It is for the same reason that the great Chief of this Nation, who knows nothing on the earth more dignified than himself, takes the title of brother of the Sun, and the credulity of the people maintains him in the despotic authority which he claims. To enable them better to converse together, they raise a mound of artificial soil, on which they build his cabin, which is of the same construction as the Temple.

The old men prescribe the Laws for the rest of the people, and one of their principles is . . . the immortality of the soul, and when they leave this world they go, they say, to live in another, there to be recompensed or punished.

In former times the Nation of the *Natchez* was very large. It counted sixty Villages and eight hundred Suns or Princes; now it is reduced to six little Villages and eleven Suns. [Its] Government is hereditary; it is not, however, the son of the reigning Chief who succeeds his father, but the son of his sister, or the first Princess of the blood. This policy is founded on the knowledge they have of the licentiousness of their women. They are not sure, they say, that the children of the chief's wife may be of the blood Royal, whereas the son of the sister of the great Chief must be, at least on the side of the mother.

SOURCE: Reuben Gold Thwaites, ed., *The Jesuit Relations and Allied Documents* (Cleveland: Murrow Brothers, 1900), vol. 68: pp. 121–35.

Timucuan Women at Work in the Field

As suggested in this engraving by the European artist De Bry, Indian women took the major responsibility for growing corn, beans, and other food crops. But there are many inaccuracies in the portrait. Indians did not use plows (and so there should be no furrows), and though men removed trees and brush from the fields, they did not usually wield hoes.

(Courtesy of the John Carter Brown Library at Brown University)

dependence of their peoples on gathering and hunting. In the summer many tribes lived in semipermanent villages of domed wigwams where women cultivated fields, passing the right to use them to their daughters. Because of the importance of farming, a matrilineal inheritance system developed among many eastern Indians, including the Five Nations of the Iroquois. The ritual lives of these peoples also focused on religious ceremonies related to the agricultural cycle, such as the Iroquois green corn and strawberry festivals. Indian peoples ate better as a result of these advances in farming, but they enjoyed few material comforts, and their populations grew slowly.

In A.D. 1500 most Indians north of the Rio Grande had resided on the same lands for generations, but the elaborate civilizations that had once flourished in the Southwest and in the great river valleys in the heart of the continent had vanished. Consequently, when the European adventurers, traders, and settlers came ashore from the Atlantic, there were no great Indian empires or religious centers that could lead a campaign of military and spiritual resistance against the invaders.

Traditional European Society in 1450

In A.D. 1450 few observers would have predicted that the European peoples would become the overlords of the Western Hemisphere. A thousand years after the fall of the Roman empire Europe remained a backward society. Most Europeans, like most Native Americans, were exploited peasants or poor farmers who had little knowledge of the wider world. Their lives and those of their descendants who would migrate to the Americas were shaped by the cultural and religious values of the traditional rural world.

THE PEASANTRY

There were only a few large cities in Western Europe before A.D. 1450—only Paris, London, and Naples had 100,000 residents and thus equaled the size of Teotihuacán at its zenith. More than 90 percent of the population consisted of peasants living in small rural communities. Peasant families usually owned or leased a small dwelling in the village center and had the right to farm strips of land in the surrounding fields. The fields were not divided by fences or hedges, making cooperative farming a necessity. Because there were few merchants or good roads, most families exchanged surplus grain and meat with their neighbors or bartered their farm products for the services of local millers, weavers, and blacksmiths. Most peasants yearned to be yeomen, who were under no obligation to a landlord and owned enough land to support a family in comfort, but relatively few achieved that goal.

As among the Native Americans, many aspects of European peasant life followed a seasonal pattern. The agricultural year began in March or April, when the ground thawed and dried, allowing the villagers to begin the exhausting work of spring plowing and the planting of wheat, rye, and oats. During these busy months men sheared the thick winter wool of their sheep, which the women washed and spun into yarn. Peasants cut the first crop of hay in June and stored it as winter fodder for their livestock. In the summer life became more relaxed, and families mended their fences or repaired their barns. August and September often were marked by grief as infants and old people succumbed to epidemics of fly-borne dysentery. Fall brought the strenuous harvest time, followed by solemn feasts of thanksgiving and riotous bouts of merrymaking. As winter approached, peasants slaughtered excess livestock and salted or smoked the meat. During the cold months they completed the tasks of threshing grain and weaving textiles and had time to visit friends and relatives in nearby villages. Many rural people died in January and February, victims of viral diseases and the cold. Then, just before the agricultural cycle began again in the spring, rural residents held carnivals to celebrate with drink and dance the end of the long winter night.

For most peasants survival required unremitting labor, and the margin of existence was thin, corroding family relations. Malnourished mothers fed their babies sparingly, calling them "greedy and gluttonous," and many newborn girls were "helped to die" so that their older brothers would have enough to eat. About half of all peasant children died before the age of twenty-one. Violence—assault, murder, rape—was much more prevalent than in the modern world, and hunger and disease were constant companions. "I have seen the latest epoch of misery," a French doctor reported as famine and plague struck. "The inhabitants . . . lie down in a meadow to eat grass, and share the food of wild beasts."

Often destitute, usually exploited and dominated by landlords and aristocrats, many peasants simply accepted their condition, but others did not. It would be the deprived rural classes of Britain, Spain, and Germany, hoping for a better life for themselves and their children, who would supply the majority of white migrants to the Western Hemisphere.

HIERARCHY AND AUTHORITY

In the traditional European social order, as among the Aztec and Mayan peoples, authority came from above. Kings and princes owned vast tracts of land, conscripted men for military service, and lived in splendor off the labor of the peasantry. Yet rulers were far from supreme, given the power of the nobles, each of whom also owned large estates and controlled hundreds of peasant families. Collectively, these noblemen had the power to challenge royal authority. They had their own legislative institutions, such as the French parlements and the English House of Lords, and enjoyed special privileges, such as the right to a trial before a jury of other noblemen. But after 1450 kings began to undermine the power of the nobility and create more centralized states, laying the basis for overseas expansion.

Just as kings and nobles ruled the state, so the men in peasant families ruled their women and children. The man was the head of the house, his power justified by the teachings of the Christian Church. As one English clergyman put it, "The woman is a weak creature not embued with like strength and constancy of mind"; law and custom consequently "subjected her to the power of man." On marriage, an English woman assumed her husband's surname and was required (under the threat of legally sanctioned physical "correction") to submit to his orders. Moreover, she surrendered to her husband the legal right to all her property; on his death she received a dower, usually the use during her lifetime of one-third of the family's land and goods.

A father controlled the lives of his children with equal authority, demanding that they work for him until their middle or late twenties. Then a landowning peasant would try to provide land to sons and dowries to daughters and choose marriage partners of appropriate wealth and status for them. In many regions fathers bestowed most of the land on the eldest son, an inheritance practice known as primogeniture, forcing many younger children to join the ranks of the roaming poor. In such a society few men—and even fewer women—had much personal freedom or individual identity.

Hierarchy and authority prevailed in the traditional European social order both because of the power of established institutions and because, in a violent and unpredictable world, they offered ordinary people a measure of security. These values, which migrants carried with them to America, would shape the character of family life and the social order there well into the eighteenth century.

THE POWER OF RELIGION

The Roman Catholic Church served as one of the great unifying forces in Western European society. By A.D. 1000 virtually all of pagan Europe had adopted Christianity. The pope, as head of the Catholic Church, directed a vast hierarchy of cardinals, bishops, and priests. Latin, the language of scholarship, was preserved by Catholic priests and monks, and Christian dogma provided a common understanding of God, the world, and human history. Equally important, the Church provided another bulwark of authority and discipline in society. Every village had a church, and holy shrines dotted the byways of Europe.

Christian doctrine penetrated deeply into the everyday lives of peasants. Over the centuries the Church had devised a religious calendar that followed the

Christ's Crucifixion

This graphic portrayal of Christ's death on the cross, by the German painter Grünewald, reminded believers of the reality of death and the need for repentance.

(Isenheim Altarpiece, Colmar, Musée Unterlinden, Giraudon/Art Resource)

agricultural cycle and transformed pagan festivals into Christian holy days. Thus the winter solstice, which for pagans marked the return of the sun and the victory of light over darkness, became the feast of Christmas. This merging of the sacred and the agricultural cycle endowed all worldly events with meaning. Few Christians believed that events occurred by chance; they were the result of God's will. To avert famine and plague, peasants turned to priests for spiritual guidance and offered prayers to Christ and the saints.

The Church taught that Satan constantly challenged God by tempting people into evil. If prophets spread unusual doctrines, or "heresies," they were surely the tools of Satan. If a devout Christian fell mysteriously ill, the sickness might be the result of an evil spell cast by a witch in league with Satan. Crushing other religions and suppressing false doctrines (heresies) among Christians was an obligation of rulers and a principal task of the new orders of Christian knights. Between A.D. 1096 and 1291 successive armies of Christians, led by European kings and nobles, embarked on a series of Crusades to expel Arab Muslims—followers of the Islamic religion—from the Holy Land where Jesus had lived.

The crusaders temporarily gained control of much of Palestine, but the impact of the Crusades on Europe was more profound. Religious warfare reinforced and intensified its Christian identity, resulting in renewed persecution of Jews and their expulsion from many European countries. The Crusades also broadened the intellectual and economic horizons of the privileged classes of Western Europe, bringing them into contact with the Arab peoples of the Mediterranean region of North Africa, who controlled the trade among Europe, Asia, and Africa and led the world in scholarship.

Europe Encounters Africa and the Americas, 1450–1550

Around A.D. 1400 Europeans shook off the lethargy of their traditional agricultural society with a major revival of learning, the Renaissance (from the French word for "rebirth"). Inspired by new knowledge and a new optimism, the rulers of Portugal and Spain commissioned Italian navigators to find new trade routes to India and China. These maritime adventurers soon brought Europeans into direct contact with the peoples of Africa, Asia, and the Americas, beginning a new era in world history.

THE RENAISSANCE

Stimulated by the wealth and learning of the Arab world, first Italy and then the countries of northern Europe experienced the rebirth of learning and cultural life now known as the Renaissance. Arab traders had access to the fabulous treasures of the East, such as silks and spices, and Arab societies had acquired magnetic compasses, water-powered mills, and mechanical clocks. In great cultural centers such as Alexandria and Cairo in Egypt, Arab scholars carried on the legacy of Christian Byzantine civilization, which had preserved the great achievements of the Greeks and Romans in religion, medicine, philosophy, mathematics, astronomy, and geography. Through Arab learning, the peoples of Europe reacquainted themselves with their own classical heritage.

The Renaissance had the most profound impact on the upper classes. Merchants from the Italian city-states of Venice, Genoa, and Pisa dispatched ships to Alexandria, Beirut, and other eastern Mediterranean ports, where they purchased goods from China, India, Persia, and Arabia and sold them throughout Europe. The enormous profits from this commerce created a new class of merchants, bankers, and textile manufacturers who conducted trade, lent vast sums of money, and spurred technological innovation in silk and wool production. This moneyed elite ruled the republican city-states of Italy and created the concept of civic humanism, an ideology that celebrated public virtue and service to the state and would profoundly influence European and American conceptions of government.

Drawing inspiration from classical Greek and Roman (rather than Christian) sources, Renaissance intellectuals were optimistic in their view of human nature and celebrated individual potential. They saw themselves not as prisoners of blind fate or victims of the forces of nature but as many-sided individuals with the capacity to change the world.

This energetic view appealed to Renaissance rulers. In *The Prince* (1513), Niccolò Machiavelli provided unsentimental advice on how monarchs could increase their political power. The kings of Western Europe followed his advice, creating royal law courts and bureaucracies to reduce the power of the landed classes and seeking alliances with merchants and urban artisans. Monarchs allowed merchants to trade throughout their realms and granted privileges to artisan guilds, encouraging both domestic manufacturing and foreign trade. In return, these rulers extracted taxes from towns and loans from merchants to support their armies and officials. This alliance of monarchs, merchants, and royal bureaucrats challenged the power of the agrarian nobility, while the increasing wealth of monarchical nation-states such as Spain and Portugal propelled Europe into its first age of overseas expansion.

Under the direction of Prince Henry (1394–1460), Portugal led the great surge of maritime commercial expansion. Henry was at once a Christian warrior and a Renaissance humanist. As a general of the Crusading Order of Christ, he had fought the Muslims in North Africa, an experience that reinforced his desire to extend the bounds of Christendom—and Portuguese power. As a humanist, Henry patronized Renaissance thinkers and relied on Arab and Italian geographers for the latest knowledge about the shape and size of the continents. Imbued with the spirit of the Renaissance, he tried to fulfill the mission assigned to him by an astrologer: "to engage in great and noble conquests and to attempt the discovery of things hidden from other men."

Because Arab and Italian merchants dominated trade in the Mediterranean, Henry sought an alternate oceanic route to the wealth of Asia. In the 1420s he established a center for exploration and ocean mapping near Lisbon and sent ships to sail the African coast. His seamen soon discovered and settled the islands of Madeira and the Azores. By 1435 Portuguese sea captains were roaming the coast of West Africa, seeking ivory and gold in exchange for salt, wine, and fish. By the 1440s, they were trading in humans as well, the first Europeans to engage in the African slave trade.

WEST AFRICAN SOCIETY AND SLAVERY

Vast and diverse, West Africa stretches from present-day Senegal to Cameroon and then extends southward to Congo and Angola. In the 1400s tropical rain forest covered much of the coast, but a series of great rivers—the Senegal, Gambia, Volta, Niger, and Congo—provided relatively easy access to the woodlands, plains, and savanna of the interior (see Map 3.2, p. 76).

Most of the people of West Africa farmed small plots and lived in extended families in small villages. Normally, men cleared the land, and women planted and harvested the crops. On the plains of the savanna, millet, cotton, and livestock were the primary products, while the forest peoples grew yams and harvested oil-rich palm nuts. Forest dwellers exchanged kola nuts, a mild stimulant, for the textiles and leather goods produced by savanna dwellers. Similarly, salt produced along the seacoast was traded for iron or gold mined in the hills of the interior.

West Africans spoke many different languages and had formed hundreds of distinct cultural and political groups. A majority of the people lived in hierarchical, socially stratified societies ruled by princes. Others resided in stateless societies organized by family and lineage (much like those of the Woodland Indians of eastern North America). Both women and men had secret societies that united people from different lineages and clans and that exercised political influence by checking the powers of rulers in princely states. These societies provided sexual education for the young, conducted adult initiation ceremonies, and, by shaming individuals and officials, enforced codes of public conduct and private morality.

Spiritual beliefs varied greatly. Although some West Africans had been converted to the Muslim faith and believed in a single god, most recognized a variety of deities—ranging from a remote creator-god who seldom interfered in human affairs to numerous spirits that lived in the earth, animals, and plants. Africans treated their ancestors with great respect, for they were believed to inhabit a spiritual world from which they could intercede on behalf of their descendants. Royal families in particular paid elaborate homage to their ancestors, hoping to give themselves an aura of divinity.

At first European traders had a positive impact on life in West Africa by introducing new plants and animals. Portuguese merchants carried coconuts from East Africa, oranges and lemons from the Mediterranean, pigs from Western Europe, and (after 1500) maize, manioc, and tomatoes from the Americas. Portuguese merchants also expanded existing trade networks, stimulating the African economy.

European iron bars and metal products joined kola nuts and salt moving inland; grain, gold, ivory, and cotton textiles flowed to the coast to provision European ships. Because of disease, this inland trade remained in the hands of Africans; Europeans who lived in West Africa were quickly stricken by yellow fever, malaria, and dysentery, and their death rate was more than 50 percent a year.

However, Europeans soon joined in the long-established trade in humans. Unfree status had existed for many centuries in West Africa. Some people were held in bondage as security for debts; others were sold into servitude by their kin, often in exchange for food in times of famine; still others were war captives. Although treated as property and exploited as agricultural laborers, slaves usually were considered members of the society that had enslaved them and sometimes were treated as kin. Most retained the right to marry, and their children were often free. A small proportion of unfree West Africans were "trade slaves," sold from one kingdom to another or carried overland to the Mediterranean region, mostly by Arab traders. Thus, the first Portuguese in Senegambia found that the Wolof king

> supports himself by raids which result in many slaves from his own as well as neighboring countries. He employs these slaves in cultivating the land allotted to him; but he also sells many to the Azanaghi [Arab] merchants in return for horses and other goods, and also to the Christians, since they have begun to trade with these blacks.

Initially, Portuguese traders carried a few thousand African slaves each year to sugar plantations in Madeira and the Azore Islands and also to Lisbon, which soon had a black population of 9,000. From this small beginning the maritime slave trade expanded enormously, especially after 1550 when Europeans set up sugar plantations in Brazil and the West Indies. By 1700 slave traders were carrying hundreds of thousands of slaves to toil and die on American plantations.

EUROPE REACHES THE AMERICAS

As they traded with Africans, Portuguese adventurers continued to look for a direct ocean route to Asia. In 1488 Bartholomeu Dias rounded the Cape of Good Hope, the southern tip of Africa, and ten years later Vasco da Gama reached India (see Map 1.2). Although the Arab, Indian, and Jewish merchants who controlled the trade along India's Malabar Coast tried to exclude him, da Gama acquired a highly profitable cargo of cinnamon and pepper—spices that were especially valuable because they could be used to flavor and preserve meat. To capture the trade in spices and Indian textiles for Portugal, da Gama returned to India in 1502 with twenty-one fighting vessels, which outmaneuvered and outgunned the Arab fleets. Soon the Portuguese government set up fortified trading posts for its merchants at key points around the Indian Ocean and opened trade routes from Africa to Indonesia and up the coast of Asia to China and Japan. In a momentous transition,

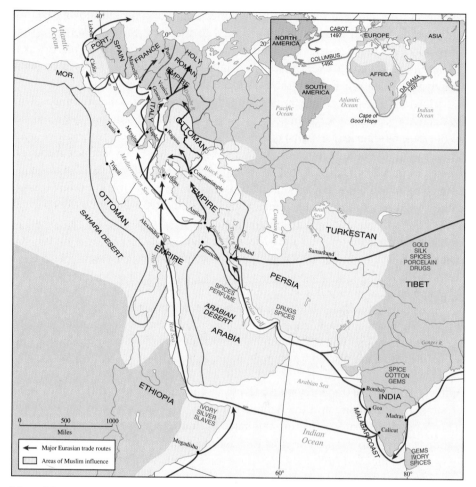

M A P 1.2

Europeans Seek Control of World Trade, 1460–1560

For centuries the Mediterranean Sea was the meeting point for the commerce of Europe, northern Africa, and southern Asia. Beginning in the 1490s, Portuguese, Spanish, and Dutch adventurers and merchants opened up new trade routes, challenging the primacy of the Muslim-dominated Mediterranean.

Portuguese replaced Arabs as the leaders in world commerce and the trade in African slaves.

Spain quickly followed Portugal's example. As Renaissance rulers, King Ferdinand of Aragon and Queen Isabella of Castile saw national unity and commerce as the keys to power and prosperity. Married in their teens in an arranged match, the young rulers (r. 1474–1516) combined their kingdoms and completed the centuries-long campaign known as the *reconquista* to oust the Muslims from their realm. In 1492 their armies reconquered Granada, the last outpost of Islam in Western Europe. Continuing their effort to use the Catholic religion to build a sense of "Spanishness," Ferdinand and Isabella launched a brutal Inquisition against suspected Christian heretics and expelled or forcibly converted thousands of Jews. Simultaneously they sought new opportunities for trade and empire.

Because Portugal controlled the southern, or African, approach to Asia, Isabella and Ferdinand listened with interest to proposals for an alternate, western route to the riches of the East. The main advocate for such a route was Christopher Columbus, a struggling Genoese sea captain who was determined to become rich and famous. Misinterpreting the findings of Italian geographers, Columbus believed that the Atlantic Ocean, long feared by Arab sailors as an endless "green sea of darkness," was little more than a narrow channel of water separating Europe from Asia. Dubious at first about Columbus's theory, Ferdinand and Isabella finally agreed to arrange financial backing from Spanish merchants. They charged Columbus with the task of discovering a new trade route to China and, in an expression of the crusading mentality of the *reconquista,* of carrying Christianity to the peoples of Asia.

Columbus set sail with three small ships on August 3, 1492. Six weeks later, after a perilous voyage of 3,000 miles, he finally found land, disembarking on one of the islands of the present-day Bahamas on October 12, 1492. Although surprised by the rude living conditions of the natives, Columbus expected them to "easily be made Christians, for it appeared to me that they had no religion." With ceremony and solemnity, he claimed the islands for Spain and for Christendom.

Believing he had reached Asia—"the Indies," in fifteenth-century parlance—Columbus called the native inhabitants Indians and the islands the West Indies. He then explored the neighboring Caribbean islands, demanding gold from the local Taino, Arawak, and Carib peoples. Buoyed by the natives' stories of rivers of gold lying "to the west," Columbus left forty men on the island of Hispaniola (present-day Haiti and Santo Domingo) and returned triumphantly to Spain, taking several Tainos to display to Isabella and Ferdinand.

Although Columbus brought back no gold, the Spanish monarchs were sufficiently impressed by his discovery to support three more voyages over the next twelve years. During those expeditions Columbus began the colonization of the West Indies, transporting more than a thousand settlers and hundreds of domestic animals. He also began the transatlantic slave trade, carrying hundreds of Indians to bondage in Europe and importing black slaves from Africa to work as artisans and farmers in the new Spanish settlements. However, Columbus failed to find either golden treasures or great kingdoms, and his death in 1506 went virtually unrecognized. Ignoring Columbus, a German geographer gave the new continents the name of a Florentine merchant, Amerigo Vespucci, who had traveled to South America around 1500 and called it a *nuevo mundo,* a New World. For its part, the Spanish crown was determined to make it a Spanish world.

THE SPANISH CONQUEST

Columbus and other Spanish adventurers ruled the peoples of the Caribbean islands with an iron hand, seizing their goods and exploiting their labor. After subduing the Arawak and Taino on Hispaniola, the Spanish probed coastal settlements on the mainland in search of booty. In 1513 Juan Ponce de León searched for gold and slaves along the coast of Florida and gave the peninsula its name. That same year Vasco Núñez de Balboa crossed the Isthmus of Darien (Panama), becoming the first European to see the Pacific Ocean basin. Although these greedy adventurers found no gold, rumors of riches to the west encouraged others to launch an invasion of the interior. These men were not explorers or merchants but hardened veterans of the wars against the Muslims who were eager to do battle and get rich. The Spanish crown offered them plunder, estates in the conquered territory, and titles of nobility in return for creating an empire.

The first great success of the Spanish conquistadors (conquerors) occurred in present-day Mexico (see Map 1.3). In 1519 Hernando Cortés landed on the Mexican

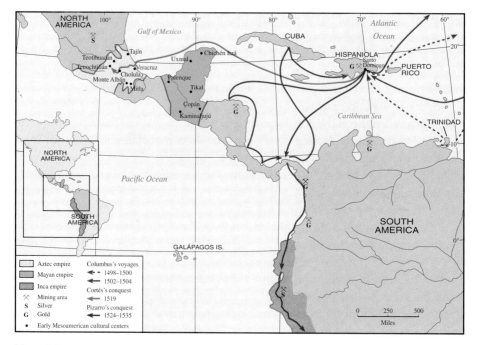

M A P 1.3
The Spanish Conquest, 1492–1535

The Spanish first invaded the islands of the Caribbean. Rumors of a magnificent golden civilization led to Cortés's invasion of the Aztec empire in 1519. By 1535, other Spanish conquistadors had conquered the Mayan temple cities and the Inca empire in Peru, completing one of the great conquests in world history.

coast with 600 men and marched toward the Aztec capital of Tenochtitlán. Fortu-itously for the Spaniards, Cortés arrived in the very year in which Aztec mythology had predicted the return of the god Quetzalcoatl to his earthly kingdom. Believing that Cortés might be the returning god, Moctezuma, the Aztec ruler, acted indeci-sively. After the failure of an ambush against the conquistadors, he allowed Cortés to proceed without challenge to Tenochtitlán and received him with great ceremony, only to become his captive. When Moctezuma's forces finally attempted to expel the invader, they were confronted by superior European military technology. The sight of the Spaniards in full armor, with cannon that shook the heavens, made a deep impression on the Aztecs, who had learned how to purify gold and fashion it into ornate religious objects but did not produce iron tools or weapons. Moreover, the Aztecs had no wheeled carts or cavalry, and their warriors, fighting on foot with flint- or obsidian-tipped spears and arrows, were no match for mounted Spanish conquistadors, wielding steel swords and protected by heavy armor. Although heav-ily outnumbered and suffering great losses, Cortés and his men were able to fight their way out of the Aztec capital.

At this point, the vast population of the Aztec empire could easily have crushed the European invaders if the Indian peoples had remained united. But Cortés ex-ploited the widespread resentment against the Aztecs, forming military alliances and raising thousands of troops from subject peoples who had seen their wealth expropriated by Aztec nobles and their people sacrificed to the Aztec sun god. The Aztec empire collapsed, the victim not of superior Spanish military technology but of a vast internal rebellion of Indian peoples (see American Voices, "Aztec Elders Describe the Spanish Conquest").

As the Spanish sought to impose their dominion over the peoples of the Aztec empire, they had a silent ally—disease. Separated from Eurasia for thousands of years, the inhabitants of the Western Hemisphere had no immunities to common European diseases. A massive smallpox epidemic lasting seventy days ravaged Tenochtitlán following the Spanish exodus, "striking everywhere in the city," ac-cording to an Aztec source, killing Moctezuma's brother and "a vast number of our people." Subsequent outbreaks of smallpox, influenza, and measles killed hundreds of thousands of the highland peoples and sapped the morale of the survivors. Ex-ploiting this demographic weakness, Cortés quickly extended Spanish rule over the entire highland region, and his lieutenants then moved against the Mayan city-states in the Yucatan Peninsula, eventually conquering them as well.

In 1524 the Spanish conquest entered a new phase, when Francisco Pizarro led a military expedition to the mountains of Peru, home of the rich and powerful Inca empire. By the time Pizarro and his small force of 168 men and 67 horses reached Peru, half of the Inca population had died from European diseases, which had been spread by Indian traders. Weakened militarily and fighting over succession to the throne, the Inca nobility was easy prey for Pizarro's army. In little more than a decade Spain had become the master of the wealthiest and most populous regions of the Western Hemisphere.

Aztec Elders Describe the Spanish Conquest

FRIAR BERNARDINO DE SAHAGÚN

*D*uring the 1550s Friar Bernardino de Sahagún published the *Florentine Codex: General History of New Spain. According to Sahagún, the authors of the* Codex *were Aztec elders who lived through the Conquest. Here the elders describe their reaction to the invading Europeans and the devastating impact of smallpox. They speak in a repetitive style, using the conventions of Aztec oral histories.*

Moctezuma enjoyed no sleep, no food, no one spoke to him. Whatsoever he did, it was as if he were in torment. Ofttimes it was as if he sighed, became weak, felt weak. . . . Wherefore he said, "What will now befall us? Who indeed stands [in charge]? Alas, until now, I. In great torment is my heart; as if it were washed in chili water it indeed burns." . . . And when he had so heard what the messengers reported, he was terrified, he was astounded. . . . Especially did it cause him to faint away when he heard how the gun, at [the Spaniards'] command, discharged: how it resounded as if it thundered when it went off. It indeed bereft one of strength; it shut off one's ears. And when it discharged, something like a round pebble came forth from within. Fire went showering forth; sparks went blazing forth. And its smoke smelled very foul; it had a fetid odor which verily wounded the head. And when [the shot] struck a mountain, it was as if it were destroyed, dissolved . . . as if someone blew it away.

All iron was their war array. In iron they clothed themselves. With iron they covered their heads. Iron were their swords. Iron were their crossbows. Iron were their shields. Iron were their lances. And those which bore them upon their backs, their deer [horses], were as tall as roof terraces.

And their bodies were everywhere covered; only their faces appeared. They were very white; they had chalky faces; they had yellow hair, though the hair of some was black. . . . And when Moctezuma so heard, he was much terrified. It was as if he fainted away. His heart saddened; his heart failed him. . . .

[Soon] there came to be prevalent a great sickness, a plague. It was in Tepeilhuitl that it originated, that there spread over the people a great destruction of men. Some it indeed covered [with pustules]; they were spread everywhere, on one's face, on one's head, on one's breast. There was indeed perishing; many indeed died of it. No longer could they walk; they only lay in their abodes, in their beds. No longer could they move. . . . And when they bestirred themselves, much did they cry out. There was much perishing. Like a covering, covering-like, were the pustules. Indeed, many people died of them, and many just died of hunger. There was death from hunger; there was no one to take care of another; there was no one to attend to another.

SOURCE: Friar Bernardino de Sahagún, *Florentine Codex: General History of New Spain*, trans. Arthur J. O. Anderson and Charles E. Dibble (Santa Fe, NM, and Salt Lake City: The School of American Research and University of Utah Press, 1975), book 12: pp. 17–20, 26, 83.

The Spanish invasion and European diseases changed life forever throughout the Americas. Virtually the entire Indian population of Hispaniola—several million people—was wiped out by disease and warfare. Mesoamerica as a whole in 1500 had probably 40 million Indians; by 1650 that region had only 3 million Native Americans. In Peru the population plummeted from 9 million in 1530 to fewer than half a million a century later. In the present-day United States, diseases introduced by early Spanish expeditions inflicted equally catastrophic losses on the Pueblo peoples of the Southwest and the Mississippian chiefdoms of present-day Florida and the Southeast.

Once the conquistadors had triumphed, the Spanish government quickly created an elaborate bureaucratic empire, headed in Madrid by the Council of the Indies, which issued laws and decrees to viceroys and other Spanish-born officials in America. However, the conquistadors remained powerful because they had military and legal control of the native population. They ruthlessly exploited the surviving Native Americans, forcing them to work on vast plantations to raise crops for local consumption and cattle whose hides were exported to Europe. The Spaniards also altered the natural environment by introducing grains and grasses that supplanted the native flora. Horses, first brought to the mainland by Cortés, gradually spread throughout the Western Hemisphere and in the following centuries dramatically changed the way of life of many Indian peoples, especially on the Great Plains of the United States.

The Spanish invasion of the Americas had a significant impact on life in Europe and Africa as well. In a process of transfer known as the Columbian Exchange, the food products of the Western Hemisphere—maize, tomatoes, potatoes, cassava (manioc)—became available to the peoples of other continents, increasing agricultural yields and stimulating the growth of population. Similarly, the crops—and human diseases—of African and Eurasian lands became part of the lives of residents of the Americas. Nor was that all. The gold and silver that had honored Aztec gods flowed into the countinghouses of Spain and into the treasury of its monarchs, making that nation the most powerful in Europe.

By 1550 the once magnificent civilizations of Mexico and Peru lay in ruins. "Of all these wonders"—the great city of Tenochtitlán, rich orchards, overflowing markets—"all is overthrown and lost, nothing left standing," recalled Bernal Díaz, who had been a young soldier in Cortés's army. Moreover, those Native Americans who survived had lost vital parts of their cultural identity. Spanish priests had suppressed their worship of traditional gods and converted them to Catholicism; as early as 1531 an Indian convert reported a vision of a dark-skinned Virgin Mary, later known as the Virgin of Guadalupe. Soon Spanish bureaucrats imposed taxes and supervised the lives of the Indians, and no fewer than 450,000 Spanish migrants settled on their lands between 1500 and 1650. Because nearly 90 percent of the Spanish settlers were men who took Indian women as wives or mistresses, the result was a substantial mestizo (mixed-race) population. Around 1800, at the end of the colonial era, Spanish America had about 17 million people: 7.5 million Indians, 3.2 million Europeans, 1 million enslaved Africans, and 5.5 million people of mixed race and cultural heritage.

Some Indians resisted assimilation by retreating into the mountains, but they lacked the numbers or the power to oust the Spanish invaders or their descendants. Today only a single Indian tongue, Guarani in Paraguay, is a recognized national language, and no Native American state has representation in the United Nations. For the original Americans the consequences of the European intrusion in 1492 were tragic and irreversible.

The Protestant Reformation and the Rise of England, 1500–1620

Religious fervor had played an important role in the expansionary policies of Portugal and Spain, but after 1517 Christianity was no longer a unifying force in European society. New religious doctrines preached by Martin Luther and other reformers divided Christians into armed camps of Catholics and Protestants. In the 1560s a Protestant rebellion in the Spanish Netherlands drained the newfound American wealth of the Spanish crown. Meanwhile, England was undergoing a major economic transformation that would give it the resources to expand into North America—bringing about a new collision of European and Indian peoples.

THE PROTESTANT MOVEMENT

Over the centuries the Catholic Church had become a large and wealthy institution, controlling vast resources throughout Europe. Renaissance popes and cardinals were among the leading patrons of the arts, but some also misused the Church's wealth. Pope Leo X (r. 1513–1521) was the most notorious, receiving half a million ducats a year from the sale of religious offices. Ordinary priests and monks regularly used their authority to obtain economic or sexual favors. One English reformer denounced the clergy as a "gang of scoundrels" who should be "rid of their vices or stripped of their authority," but he was ignored. Other reformers, such as Jan Hus of Bohemia, were tried and executed as heretics.

In 1517 Martin Luther, a German monk and professor at the university in Wittenberg, nailed his famous Ninety-five Theses to the door of the castle church. That widely reprinted document condemned the sale of indulgences—church certificates that pardoned a sinner from punishments in the afterlife. Luther argued that redemption could come only from God through grace, not from the church for a fee. He was excommunicated by the pope and threatened with punishment by King Charles I of Spain, who in 1519 became head of the Holy Roman Empire, which embraced most of Germany. Northern German princes, who were resisting the emperor's authority for political reasons, embraced Luther's teachings and protected him from arrest.

Luther broadened his attack, articulating positions that differed from Roman Catholic doctrine in three major respects. First, Luther rejected the doctrine that Christians could win salvation through good deeds, arguing that people could be saved only by grace, which came as a gift from God. Second, he downplayed the role of clergymen and the pope as mediators between God and the people, proclaiming, "Our baptism consecrates us all without exception and makes us all priests." Third, Luther said that believers must look to the Bible (not church doctrine) as the ultimate authority in matters of faith. So that every German-speaking believer could read the Bible, he translated it from Latin into German.

Peasants as well as princes heeded Luther's attack on authority and, to his dismay, mounted protests of their own. In 1524 some German peasants rebelled against their manorial lords and were ruthlessly suppressed. Fearing social revolution, Luther urged obedience to established political institutions and condemned the teachings of new groups of religious dissidents, such as the Anabaptists (so called because they rejected infant baptism).

Embracing Luther's views, most princes in northern Germany broke from Rome, in part because they wanted the power to appoint bishops and control the Church's property. In response, Emperor Charles dispatched armies to Germany to restore his political authority and Catholicism, unleashing a generation of warfare. Eventually the Peace of Augsburg (1555) restored order by allowing princes to decide the religion of their subjects. Most southern German rulers installed Catholicism as the official religion, while those in the north made Lutheranism the state creed.

The most rigorous Protestant doctrine was established in Geneva, Switzerland, under the leadership of the French theologian John Calvin. Even more than Luther, Calvin stressed the omnipotence of God and the corruption of human nature. His *Institutes of the Christian Religion* (1536) depicted God as an awesome and absolute sovereign who governed the "wills of men so as to move precisely to that end directed by him." Calvin preached the doctrine of predestination—the idea that God had chosen certain people for salvation even before they were born, condemning the rest to eternal damnation. In Geneva he set up a model Christian community, eliminating bishops and placing spiritual power in the hands of ministers chosen by the members of each congregation. These ministers and pious laymen ruled the city, prohibiting frivolity and luxury. Despite widespread persecution, Calvinists won converts all over Europe. Calvinism was adopted by the Huguenots in France, by reformed churches in Belgium and Holland, and by Presbyterians and Puritans in Scotland and England.

In England, King Henry VIII (r. 1509–1547) initially opposed the spread of Protestantism in his kingdom. But when the pope denied his request for an annulment of his marriage to Catherine of Aragon, Henry broke with Rome in 1534 and made himself the head of a national Church of England (which promptly granted the annulment). Although Henry made few changes in church doctrine, organization, and ritual, his daughter, Queen Elizabeth I (r. 1558–1603) approved a Protestant confession of faith that incorporated both the Lutheran doctrine of salvation by grace and the Calvinist belief in predestination. To mollify traditionalists Elizabeth retained the Catholic ritual of Holy Communion—now conducted in English rather than in Latin—as well as the hierarchy of bishops and archbishops.

Elizabeth's compromises angered radical Protestants, who condemned the power of bishops as "anti-Christian and devilish and contrary to the Scriptures" and demanded major changes in church organization. Many of these reformers took inspiration from the Presbyterian system pioneered in Calvin's Geneva and developed fully by John Knox for the Church of Scotland; in Scotland local congregations elected lay elders (presbyters), who assisted ministers in running the church. By 1600, 500 ministers in the Church of England wanted to eliminate bishops and install a presbyterian form of church government.

Other radical English Protestants were calling themselves "unspotted lambs of the Lord" or "Puritans." To a greater extent than most Protestants they wanted to "purify" the church of "false" teachings and practices. Following radical Calvinist principles, Puritans condemned many traditional religious rites as magical or idolatrous. Puritan services avoided appeals to dead saints or the burning of incense and instead focused on a carefully argued sermon on ethics or dogma. Puritans also placed special emphasis on the idea of a "calling," the duty to serve God in one's work. To ensure that all men and women had access to God's commands, they encouraged everyone to read the Bible, thus promoting widespread literacy. Finally, most Puritans wanted authority over spiritual and financial matters to rest primarily with the local congregation, not with bishops or even Presbyterian synods. Eventually thousands of Puritan migrants to America would establish churches based on these radical Protestant doctrines.

THE DUTCH AND THE ENGLISH CHALLENGE SPAIN

Luther's challenge to Catholicism in 1517 came just two years before Cortés conquered the Aztec empire, and the two events remained linked. Gold and silver from Mexico and Peru made Spain the wealthiest nation in Europe and King Philip II (r. 1556–1598), the successor to Charles I, its most powerful ruler. In addition to Spain, Philip presided over wealthy city-states in Italy, the commercial and manufacturing provinces of the Spanish Netherlands (present-day Holland and Belgium), and, after 1580, Portugal and all its possessions in America, Africa, and the East Indies.

Philip, an ardent Catholic, tried to root out Protestantism in the Netherlands, which had become wealthy from trade with the vast Protuguese empire and from the weaving of wool and linen. To protect their Calvinist faith and political liberties, the Dutch and Flemish provinces revolted in 1566, and in 1581 the seven northern provinces declared their independence, becoming the Dutch Republic (or Holland). When Elizabeth I of England dispatched 6,000 troops to assist the Dutch cause, Philip found a new enemy. In 1588 he sent the Spanish Armada—130 ships and 30,000 men—against England. Philip planned to reimpose Catholicism in England and then wipe out Calvinism in Holland. But the Armada failed utterly, as English ships and a fierce storm destroyed the Spanish fleet. Philip continued to spend his American gold on foreign wars, undermining the Spanish economy and prompting the migration of hundreds of thousands of Spaniards to America. By the time of his death in 1598, Spain was in serious decline.

As Spain faltered, Holland prospered, the economic miracle of the seventeenth century. Amsterdam emerged as the financial capital of northern Europe, and the Dutch Republic became the leading commercial power of Europe, replacing Portugal as the dominant trader in Asia and coastal Africa. The Dutch also looked across the Atlantic, creating the West India Company, which invested in sugar plantations in Brazil and the Caribbean and established fur-trading posts in North America.

Elizabeth I (r. 1558–1603)

Attired in richly decorated clothes to symbolize her power, Queen Elizabeth I relishes the destruction of the Spanish Armada (pictured in background) and proclaims her nation's imperial ambitions. The Queen's hand rests on a globe, asserting England's claims in the Western Hemisphere.

England also emerged as an important European state, its economy stimulated by a rise in population from 3 million in 1500 to 5 million in 1630. An equally important factor was the state-supported expansion of the merchant community. English merchants had long supplied high-quality wool to European weavers, and around 1500 they created their own system of textile production. In this *outwork* (or *putting-out*) system merchants bought wool and provided it to landless peasants, who spun and wove the wool into cloth. The merchants then sold the finished product in English and foreign markets. The government helped manufacturers to expand production by setting low rates for wages and assisted merchants to increase exports by granting special monopoly privileges to the Levant Company (Turkey) in 1581, the Guinea Company (Africa) in 1588, and the East India Company in 1600.

This system of state-supported manufacturing and trade became known as *mercantilism*. Mercantilist-minded monarchs like Elizabeth encouraged merchants to invest in domestic manufacturing, thereby increasing exports and reducing imports, in order to give England a favorable balance of trade. The queen and her advisors wanted gold and silver to flow into the country in payment for English manufactures, stimulating further economic expansion and enriching the merchant community. Increased trade also meant higher revenues from import duties, which swelled the royal treasury and enhanced the power of the national government. By 1600 the success of these merchant-oriented policies made overseas colonization possible. The English (as well as the Dutch) now had the merchant fleets and economic wealth needed to challenge Spain's monopoly in the Western Hemisphere.

THE SOCIAL CAUSES OF ENGLISH COLONIZATION

Other economic changes in England (as well as continuing religious conflict) provided a large body of willing settlers. The massive expenditure of American gold and silver by Philip II had doubled the money supply of Europe and sparked a major inflation—known today as the Price Revolution—that brought about profound social changes.

In England, the nobility were the first casualties of the Price Revolution. Aristocrats had customarily rented out their estates on long leases for fixed rents, gaining a secure income and plenty of leisure. As one English nobleman put it, "We eat and drink and rise up to play and this is to live like a gentleman." Then inflation struck. In two generations the price of goods tripled, but the nobility's income from the rents on its farmlands barely increased. As the wealth and status of the aristocracy declined, that of the gentry and the yeomen rose. The gentry (substantial landholders) kept pace with inflation by renting land on short leases at higher rates. Yeomen, described by a European traveler as "middle people of a condition between gentlemen and peasants," owned small amounts of land that they worked with family help. As wheat prices tripled, yeomen used the profits to build larger houses and provide their children with land.

Economics influenced politics. As aristocrats lost wealth, their branch of Parliament, the House of Lords, declined in influence. At the same time, members of the rising gentry entered the House of Commons, the political voice of the propertied classes. Supported by the yeomen, the gentry demanded new rights and powers for the Commons, such as control of taxation. Thus the Price Revolution encouraged the rise of governing institutions in which rich commoners and small property owners had a voice, a development with profound consequences for English—and American—political history.

Peasants and farm laborers made up three-fourths of the population of England, and their lives also were transformed by the Price Revolution. Many of these rural folk lived in open-field settlements, but the rise of domestic manufacturing increased the demand for wool, prompting profit-minded landlords and wool merchants to persuade Parliament to pass enclosure acts. These acts allowed owners to fence in open fields and put sheep to graze on them. Thus dispossessed of their land, peasant families lived on the brink of poverty, spinning and weaving wool or working as wage laborers on large estates. Wealthy men had "taken farms into their hands," an observer noted in 1600, "and rent them to those that will give most, whereby the peasantry of England is decayed and become servants to gentlemen."

These changes set the stage for a substantial migration to America. As land prices continued to rise, thousands of yeomen families looked across the Atlantic for land for their children. The enclosure movement created an even greater number of impoverished peasants, who were prepared to go to America as indentured servants. This migration of English men and women would bring about a new collision between the European and Native American worlds and, eventually, a new plantation society worked by enslaved Africans.

Before 1450 the peoples of Africa, Europe, and the Americas had lived in different worlds. But the fate of the three continents became intertwined once Spanish conquistadors vanquished the Aztec, Maya, and Inca empires and Portuguese merchants began to carry African slaves across the Atlantic. Just as the intrusion of the Spanish and Portuguese had changed forever the history of Mesoamerica and Brazil, the coming of the English—and Dutch and French—among the Indians of eastern North America after 1600 would produce a similar spectacle of disease, war, religious conversion, and cultural conflict.

T I M E L I N E

30,000– 10,000 B.C.	Settlement of the Americas	1400– 1550	Renaissance invigorates European society.
3000– 2000 B.C.	Indians begin maize cultivation.	1492	Christopher Columbus's first voyage to America
		1513	Juan Ponce de León explores Florida.
A.D. 100– 400	Hopewell culture in the Ohio region	1517	Martin Luther starts the Protestant Reformation.
300– 900	Height of Mayan and Teotihuacán civilizations in Mesoamerica	1519	Hernando Cortés begins the conquest of the Aztec empire.
600– 1150	Pueblo cultures flourish in Southwest.	1524	Francisco Pizarro marches to the Inca empire in Peru.
700– 1100	Spread of Arab Muslim civilization	1534	Henry VIII establishes Protestantism in England.
700– 1350	Mississippian societies; great temples at Cahokia	1536	John Calvin publishes his doctrine of predestination.
1055– 1492	*Reconquista* expels Muslims from Portugal and Spain.	1550– 1630	Price Revolution in Europe disrupts society. English mercantilism prepares the way for colonization.
1096– 1291	European Crusaders encounter Muslim civilization.		Enclosure movement creates potential American migrants.
1325	Aztecs establish a capital at Tenochtitlán.	1560s	English Puritan movement begins.
1440s	Portugal joins the trade in African slaves.	1588	The defeat of the Spanish Armada pre- serves Protestantism in England and Holland.

For Further Exploration

Alvin M. Josephy Jr., ed., *America in 1492: The World of the Indian Peoples Before the Arrival of Columbus* (1991), offers a panorama of the indigenous societies of the Americas in a nicely illustrated collection of essays. Recent scholarship on the prehistoric Indians of the United States is brought to life by Brian M. Fagan, *The Great Journey: The People of Ancient America* (1987). For the European background of colonization, begin with George Huppert, *After the Black Death* (2nd ed., 1998), a short and highly readable introduction of Western Europe's recovery from the devastating epidemic of the mid-fourteenth century. William D. Phillips with Carla Rahn Phillips continue the story of European expansion in *The Worlds of Christopher Columbus* (1992), an engaging biography that places Columbus's voyages in the larger context of European exploration and describes their enormous consequences.

Peter Laslett, *The World We Have Lost* (3rd ed., 1984), offers a vivid portrait of society in seventeenth-century England, while Susan Doran and Christopher Durston, *Princes, Pastors, and People: The Church and Religion in England, 1529–1689* (1991), discuss the impact of the Protestant Reformation on theology, the role of the clergy, and church services.

Two interesting Public Broadcasting Service (PBS) videos examine the ancient civilizations of MesoAmerica: *Odyssey: Maya Lords of the Jungle* (1 hour) and *Odyssey: The Incas* (1 hour). For additional information log on to "1492: An Ongoing Voyage" at <http://lcweb.loc.gov/exhibits/1492/intro.html>, which provides a survey of the native cultures of the Western Hemisphere, the impact of discovery, and full-color images of artifacts and art. Material on an early Indian civilization in the southwestern United States is available at "Sipapu: The Anasazi Emergence into the Cyber World," <http://sipapu.ucsb.edu/index.html>. "Martin Luther" at <http://www.luther.de/e/index.html> offers biographies of the leading figures of the Protestant Reformation and striking images of the era.

Chapter 2

THE INVASION AND SETTLEMENT OF NORTH AMERICA
1550–1700

Human life is reduced to real suffering, to hell, only when . . . cultures and religions overlap.

ALBRECHT VON HALLER

Establishing colonies in the distant land of North America was not for the faint of heart. First came a long voyage in small ships over stormy, dangerous waters. Then the migrants, weakened by weeks of travel, spoiled food, and shipboard diseases, faced the challenges of life in an alien land inhabited by potentially hostile Indian peoples. "We neither fear them or trust them," Puritan Francis Higginson reported, but rely for protection on "our musketeers." Although the risks were great and the rewards uncertain, tens of thousands of Europeans crossed the Atlantic during the seventeenth century, driven by poverty and persecution at home or drawn by the lures of the New World: land, gold, and—as another Puritan settler put it—the hope of "propagating the Gospel to these poor barbarous people."

For Native Americans, the European invasion was nothing short of catastrophic. "You know our fathers had plenty of deer and skins, . . . and our coves were full of fish and fowl," the Narragansett chief Miantonomi warned the neighboring Montauk people in 1642, "but these English having gotten our land . . . their cows and horses eat the grass, and their hogs spoil our clam banks, and we shall all be starved." Whether they came as settlers or missionaries or fur traders, the white-skinned people spread havoc, bringing new diseases and religions and threatening Indian peoples with the loss of their cultures, lands, and lives. As a Narragansett warrior put it, European-style warfare "slays too many men." The first century of cultural contact foretold the course of North American history: the advance of the invaders, the dispossession of the Indian peoples, and the importation of enslaved Africans to work the lands.

Imperial Conflicts and Rival Colonial Models

In Mesoamerica the Spanish colonial regime forced the Indians to convert to Catholicism and to work digging gold and farming large estates. But in the sparsely populated lands north of the Rio Grande, other Europeans founded different types of colonies. In the fur-trading empires created by the French and the Dutch, the native peoples retained their lands and political autonomy, while in the quickly growing English settler-colonies, Indians were simply not welcome and were pushed ever farther to the west. Despite the differing goals of these colonial regimes—the exploitation of native labor by the Spanish, the trading of furs by the French and Dutch, the creation of farming communities by the English—nearly everywhere the Indian peoples eventually rose in revolt.

NEW SPAIN: COLONIZATION AND CONVERSION

In their ceaseless quest for gold, Spanish adventurers became the first Europeans to explore the southern and western United States. In 1540 Francisco Vásquez de Coronado searched in vain for the fabled seven golden cities of Cíbola, said to lie north of present-day Albuquerque. Continuing his search, he dispatched expeditions that discovered the Grand Canyon in Arizona, the Pueblo peoples of New Mexico, and the grasslands of central Kansas. Simultaneously, Hernando de Soto and a force of 600 adventurers cut a bloody swath across the densely populated Southeast, doing battle with the Apalachee of northern Florida and the Coosa of northern Alabama but finding no gold and few other riches.

By the 1560s few Spanish officials still dreamed of finding rich Indian empires north of Mexico. Now their main goal was to prevent other European nations from establishing settlements. Roving English "sea dogs" were already plundering Spanish possessions in the Caribbean, and French corsairs were attacking Spanish treasure ships, halving the Spanish crown's revenue. Equally ominously, French Protestants began to settle in Florida, long claimed by Spain. In response King Philip II ordered that the Frenchmen in Florida, be "cast . . . out by the best means," and Spanish troops massacred 300 members of the "evil Lutheran sect."

To safeguard Florida, in 1565 Spain established a fort at St. Augustine, the first permanent European settlement in the future United States. It also founded a dozen other military outposts and religious missions, one as far north as Chesapeake Bay, but these were soon destroyed by Indian attacks. Spain also confronted a new threat from the Atlantic. In 1586 the English sea captain Sir Francis Drake sacked the important port city of Cartagena (in present-day Colombia) and nearly wiped out St. Augustine.

These military setbacks prompted the Spanish crown to adopt a new policy toward Native Americans. The Comprehensive Orders for New Discoveries, issued in 1573, placed the "pacification" of new lands primarily in the hands of missionaries, not conquistadors. Franciscan friars promptly established missions in the Pueblo world visited by Coronado two generations before, naming the area Nuevo México (see Map 2.1). The friars built their missions and churches near existing Indian pueblos and farming villages and often learned Indian languages. Protected by Spanish soldiers, the robed and sandaled Franciscans smashed the religious idols of the native Americans and, to win their allegiance to the Christian god, dazzled them with rich vestments, gold crosses, and silver chalices.

For the Franciscans, religious conversion and cultural assimilation went hand in hand. They introduced the European practice of having men instead of women grow most of the crops and encouraged the Indians to talk, cook, dress, and walk like Spaniards. Spanish rule was hardly benevolent. Sexual sinners and spirit worshipers were whipped, and monks and settlers alike systematically ignored Spanish laws intended to protect the native peoples from coerced labor. Franciscan missions depended on Indian workers, who grew the crops and carried them to market,

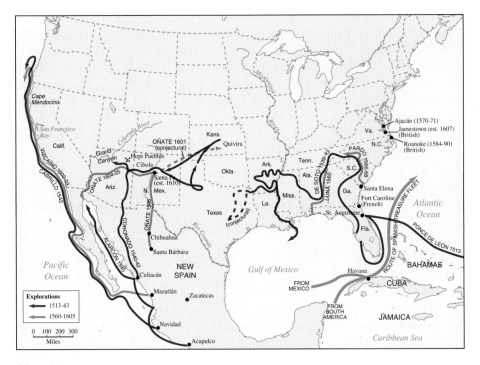

M A P 2.1
New Spain Looks North, 1513–1610

The quest for gold drew Spanish adventurers deep into North America. Cortés himself dispatched the first expeditions along the Pacific coast, and Hernando de Soto and Francisco Vásquez de Coronado led wide-ranging expeditions in the 1540s, but the first permanent settlement to the north of New Spain came only in 1565, at St. Augustine in present-day Florida. A generation later, following the explorations of Juan de Oñate, the Spanish founded Santa Fe in New Mexico.

often on their backs. Privileged Spanish landowners (*encomenderos*) collected tribute from the native population, both in goods and through forced labor. They also "ransomed" Native American women and children who had been captured by nomadic Indians and forced them to work as slaves. Most Native Americans tolerated the Franciscans out of fear of military reprisals or in hopes of learning their spiritual secrets. But when Christian prayers failed to prevent European diseases, drought, and Apache raids from devastating their communities, many Indians returned to their ancestral religions and began to question Spanish rule.

Then in 1598 Juan de Oñate led an expedition of 500 Spanish soldiers and settlers into New Mexico to establish a fort and a trading villa. Oñate's men seized corn and clothing from the Pueblo peoples and murdered or raped those who resisted. When Indians of the Acoma pueblo killed 11 soldiers, the remaining troops destroyed the pueblo, killing 500 men and 300 women and children. Faced by now-hostile Indian peoples, most of the settlers withdrew. In 1610 the Spanish returned, founding the town of Santa Fe and reestablishing the system of missions and forced labor.

By 1680 nearly a hundred years of European diseases, forced tribute, drought, and raids by Navajos and Apache threatened many pueblos in New Mexico with extinction. Their population, which had numbered 60,000 in 1600, had declined to a mere 17,000. In 1680, led by Popé, an Indian shaman (priest), the peoples of two dozen pueblos mounted a carefully coordinated rebellion, killing over 400 Spaniards and forcing the remaining 2,000 colonists to flee 300 miles down the Rio Grande to El Paso. Rejecting Christianity, the Pueblo peoples desecrated churches and tortured and killed twenty-one missionaries. Reconquered a decade later, they rebelled again in 1696, only to be subdued. Exhausted by war but now able to practice their own religion and avoid forced labor, the Pueblo peoples accepted their dependent position, joining with the Spanish to defend their lands against attacks by nomadic Indians.

With great difficulty Spain had managed to maintain its northern empire but had largely failed to achieve its goals of religious conversion and cultural assimilation. Taken aback by the costs of expansion, Spanish officials decided not to undertake the settlement of the distant region of California, delaying until 1769 the permanent European occupation of that area. For the time being, Florida and New Mexico stood as the defensive outposts of Spain's American empire.

NEW FRANCE: FURS AND SOULS

In the 1530s Jacques Cartier had claimed the lands bordered by the Gulf of St. Lawrence for France, but the first permanent settlement came only in 1608, when Samuel de Champlain founded Quebec. Even then, few French men and women migrated to America. Unlike the English peasantry, many held strong legal rights to their village lands in France and thus successfully resisted dispossession. Moreover, the government wanted an ample supply of farm laborers and military recruits in France and offered few incentives to migrants. Finally, the Catholic monarchs barred Huguenots (French Protestants) from Quebec, fearing they would not be loyal to the government. Consequently, New France did not develop as a settler-colony; in 1698 its European population was only 15,200, compared with 100,000 settlers in the English colonies.

Instead, New France became a vast fur-trading enterprise, and French explorers traveled deep into the continent to seek new suppliers. In return for French support against the Five Nations of the Iroquois, the Huron Indians (who lived just to the north of the Great Lakes) allowed Champlain, the founder of Quebec, and other fur traders into their territory. By 1673 another French explorer, Jacques Marquette, reached the Mississippi River in present-day Wisconsin and traveled as far south as Arkansas. Exploration of the majestic river was completed in 1681 by Robert de La Salle, who sought fortune as well as fame. As a French priest noted with disgust, La Salle's expedition hoped "to buy all the Furs and Skins of the remotest Savages, who, as they thought, did not know their Value; and so enrich themselves in one single voyage." To honor Louis XIV, the Sun King, La Salle named the region Louisiana; soon it included the thriving port of New Orleans on the Gulf of Mexico.

Despite their small numbers, French traders and explorers had a disastrous impact on Native Americans living near the Great Lakes. By introducing European diseases, they unwittingly triggered epidemics that killed 25 to 90 percent of the native population, including thousands of their Huron allies. Moreover, by providing a market for deerskins and beaver pelts, the French set in motion a devastating series of Indian wars. Beginning in the 1640s, the New York Iroquois seized control of the fur trade by launching aggressive wars against the Huron, forcing them to migrate to the north and west.

While French traders amassed furs, French priests sought converts among both the defeated Huron and the belligerent Iroquois. Between 1625 and 1763 hundreds of Jesuit priests lived among the Indians and, to a greater extent than the Spanish Franciscans, came to understand their values. One Jesuit reported a Huron belief that "our souls have desires which are inborn and concealed, yet are made known by means of dreams"; he then used this belief to explain the Christian doctrines of immortality and salvation to the native peoples. Indians at first welcomed the "Black Robes" as powerful spiritual beings with magical secrets, such as the ability to forge iron, but, as in New Mexico, skepticism grew when prayers to the Christian god did not protect them from disease and enemy attack. A Peoria chief charged that the priest's "fables are good only in his own country; we have our own [religious beliefs], which do not make us die as his do."

Unlike the Spanish Franciscans, the French missionaries did not use Indians for forced labor and tried to keep alcoholic beverages, which wreaked havoc among Indian peoples, from becoming a bargaining item in the French fur trade. Moreover, the French Jesuits won converts by addressing Indian needs. In the 1690s young women of the Illinois people in the Mississippi River Valley embraced the cult of the Virgin Mary, using its emphasis on chastity to assert the Algonquian belief that unmarried women were "masters of their own body." Still, the French colonial system—which brought only a few Jesuits and traders into Indian territory—allowed most Native Americans to retain their traditional beliefs, and many chose to do so.

NEW NETHERLAND: COMMERCE

Unlike the French and Spanish, the Dutch in North America had little interest in religious conversion. Their eyes were fastened on commerce, for the Dutch Republic was the trading hub of Europe. In 1609 Henry Hudson, an Englishman employed by the Dutch East India Company, found and named the Hudson River in the area of present-day New York, and a few years later the Dutch established fur-trading posts on Manhattan Island and at Fort Orange (present-day Albany). In 1621 the Dutch government chartered the West India Company, giving it a trade monopoly in West Africa and exclusive authority to establish outposts in America. Three years later the company "purchased" Manhattan Island from the Indians, founding the town of New Amsterdam as the capital of New Netherland.

These wilderness outposts attracted few Dutch settlers, and their small size made them vulnerable to invasion by rival European nations. To encourage migration, the West India Company granted huge estates along the Hudson River to wealthy Dutchmen, stipulating that each proprietor settle fifty tenants on his land within four years or lose it; by 1646 only one proprietor, Kiliaen Van Rensselaer, had succeeded. The population in Dutch North America remained small, reaching only 1,500 in 1664.

Although New Netherland failed as a settler colony, it flourished briefly as a fur-trading enterprise. In 1633 Dutch traders at Fort Orange exported 30,000 beaver and otter pelts. Subsequently, the Dutch seized prime farming land from the Algonquian-speaking peoples and took over their trading network, in which corn and wampum from Long Island were exchanged for furs from Maine. The Algonquians responded with force. By the end of a bloody two-year war more than 200 Dutch residents and 1,000 Indians had been killed, many in brutal massacres of women, children, and elderly men. After the war the Dutch traders expanded their profitable links with the Mohawk, one of the Iroquois Nations of New York, exchanging guns and other manufactures for furs. However, the West India Company now largely ignored its crippled North American settlement, concentrating instead on the profitable importation of African slaves to its sugar plantations in Brazil.

Moreover, Dutch officials in New Amsterdam ruled shortsightedly. Governor Peter Stuyvesant rejected the demands of English settlers on Long Island for a representative system of government, alienating the colony's increasingly diverse population of Dutch, English, and Swedish migrants. Consequently, in 1664, during an Anglo-Dutch war, the population of New Amsterdam offered little resistance to an English invasion and subsequently accepted English rule. For the rest of the century the renamed towns of New York and Albany remained small fur-trading centers, Dutch-English outposts in a region still dominated by Native Americans.

THE FIRST ENGLISH MODEL: TOBACCO AND SETTLERS

The first English ventures in North America, all in the 1580s, were abject failures. Sir Humphrey Gilbert's settlement in Newfoundland collapsed for lack of financing, and Sir Ferdinando Gorges's colony along the coast of Maine foundered because of inadequate supplies and the harsh climate. Sir Walter Raleigh's three expeditions to North Carolina likewise ended in disaster when the famous "lost" colony of Roanoke vanished without a trace. After these failures, merchants replaced minor gentry as the leaders of English expansion, and, initially, trade rather than settlement became the main goal. To provide adequate funding, the merchants formed joint-stock companies, which sold shares to many investors. In 1606 a group of ambitious London merchants received a charter from the new monarch, King James I (r. 1603–1625), that granted them the right to exploit North America from present-day North Carolina to southern New York. To honor the memory of Elizabeth I, the "Virgin Queen," the company's directors named the region Virginia.

Carolina Indians, 1585

The artist John White traveled with the first English settlers to Sir Walter Raleigh's colony on Roanoke Island (in present-day North Carolina) and, before returning to England, painted a series of watercolors that provide a rich visual record of Native American life. Here the Indians of Albemarle Sound are harvesting a protein-rich diet of fish from its shallow waters.

(Trustees of the British Museum)

They promised to settle the land and "propagate the *Christian* religion" among the "infidels and Savages."

But trade for gold and other valuable goods was the main goal of the Virginia Company, and the first expedition in 1607 included no settlers, ministers, or women. The company retained ownership of all the land and appointed a governor and a small council to direct the migrants, who were its employees or "servants." They were expected to procure their own food and ship anything of value—gold, exotic crops, and Indian merchandise—to England. The traders were unprepared for the challenges they would face. Some were young gentlemen with personal ties to the shareholders of the Company but no experience in living off the land: a bunch of "unruly Sparks, packed off by their Friends to escape worse Destinies at home." The rest were cynical adventurers bent on seizing gold from the Indians or turning a quick profit from trade in English cloth and metalware. Arriving in Virginia after a hazardous four-month voyage, the newcomers settled on a swampy peninsula on a river. They named both their new home (Jamestown) and the waterway (James River) after their new sovereign.

The adventurers were immediately confronted by the Pamumkey chief Powhatan, the leader of the Algonquian-speaking tribes of the region, some 14,000 people in all. Powhatan, whom Governor John Smith described as a "grave majestical man," willingly exchanged corn for English cloth and iron hatchets and pots but treated the English as one of the dependent peoples of his chiefdom.

For their part, the English adventurers did not want to plant crops and raise food for themselves. All they wanted, as one of them said, was to "dig gold, refine gold, load gold." But there was no gold and not much food. Of the 120 Englishmen who embarked on the expedition, only 38 were alive nine months later, and death continued to take a high toll. By 1611 the Virginia Company had sent 1,200 settlers to Jamestown, but fewer than half had survived. "Our men were destroyed with cruell diseases, as Swellings, Fluxes, Burning Fevers, and by warres," one of the leaders reported, "but for the most part they died of meere famine."

Although Powhatan accused the English of coming "not to trade but to invade my people and possess my country," he eventually ceased his efforts to evict them and acquiesced in the marriage of his daughter Pocahontas to the adventurer John Rolfe in 1614. Rolfe played a leading role in the colony until his death in 1622. After importing seeds from the West Indies, he began to cultivate tobacco, which was already popular in England as a result of imports from Spanish America, and soon became the basis of economic life in Virginia.

As tobacco exports rose, the Virginia Company instituted a new and far-reaching set of policies. In 1617 it allowed individual settlers to own land, granting 100 acres to every freeman in Virginia, and established a *headright* system in which every incoming head of a household had a right to 50 acres of land and 50 additional acres for every adult family member or servant. The company also approved a system of representative government. The House of Burgesses, which first convened in Jamestown in 1619, had the authority to make laws and levy taxes, although its legislative acts could be vetoed by the governor or nullified by the company. By 1622 these incentives of land ownership and local self-government had attracted about 4,500 new English recruits. Virginia was on the verge of becoming a settler colony.

The influx of settlers sparked all-out war with the Indians. Land-hungry farmers demanded access to land that the native Americans had cleared and were using, alarming Opechancanough, Powhatan's brother and successor. Mobilizing the peoples of many Chesapeake tribes, in 1622 Opechancanough launched a surprise attack, killing nearly a third of the white population and vowing to drive the rest into the ocean. The English retaliated by harvesting the Indians' cornfields, providing food for themselves while depriving their enemies of sustenance, a strategy that gradually secured the safety of the colony.

The cost of the war was high for both sides. The Indians killed many settlers and destroyed much property, but Opechancanough's strategy had failed; rather than ending the invasion of the English, it accelerated their expansion. As one English militiaman put it, "[We now felt we could] by right of Warre, and law of Nations, invade the Country, and destroy them who sought to destroy us; whereby wee shall enjoy their cultivated places . . . possessing the fruits of others' labour." Soon the invaders excluded the Indian peoples from huge areas and sold captured warriors into slavery. By 1630 the English settlement in the region of Chesapeake Bay was well established.

The Chesapeake Experience

The English colonies in the Chesapeake brought wealth to some settlers but poverty and moral degradation to many more. Settlers forcefully dispossessed Indians of their lands, and prominent families ruthlessly pursued their dreams of wealth by exploiting the labor of English indentured servants and enslaved African laborers.

SETTLING THE TOBACCO COLONIES

Distressed by the Indian uprising of 1622, James I dissolved the Virginia Company, accusing its directors of mismanagement, and created a royal colony in 1624. Under the terms of the charter, the king and his ministers appointed the governor and a small advisory council. The House of Burgesses was retained, but any legislation it enacted required ratification by the king's Privy Council. James also legally established the Church of England in Virginia, so that all property owners had to pay taxes to support the clergy. These institutions—a royal governor, an elected assembly, and an established Anglican church—became the model for royal colonies throughout English America.

However, a second tobacco-growing settler colony, which developed in neighboring Maryland, had a different set of institutions. Maryland was owned by an aristocrat, Cecilius Calvert, who carried the title Lord Baltimore. In 1632 King Charles I (r. 1625–1649), the successor to James I, gave Baltimore a charter that made him the proprietor of the territory bordering the vast Chesapeake Bay. Baltimore could sell, lease, or give this land away as he wished. He also had the authority to appoint public officials and to found churches and appoint ministers.

Baltimore wanted Maryland to become a refuge from persecution for his fellow English Catholics. He therefore devised a policy of religious toleration intended to minimize confrontations between Catholics and Protestants, instructing the governor (his brother, Leonard Calvert) to allow "no scandall nor offence to be given to any of the Protestants" and to "cause All Acts of Romane Catholicque Religion to be done as privately as may be." In 1634, 20 gentlemen (mostly Catholics) and 200 artisans and laborers (mostly Protestants) established St. Mary's City overlooking the mouth of the Potomac River. The population grew quickly, for the Calvert family carefully planned and supervised the colony's development, hiring skilled artisans and offering ample grants of land to wealthy migrants. However, political and religious conflict threatened Maryland's stability. When Governor Leonard Calvert tried to govern without the "Advice, Assent, and Approbation" of the freemen of the colony, as the charter specified, a representative assembly elected by the freemen insisted on the right to initiate legislation, which Lord Baltimore grudgingly granted. Uprisings by Protestant settlers also threatened Maryland's religious mission. To protect his Catholic coreligionists, who remained a minority, Lord Baltimore managed to persuade the Assembly to enact a Toleration Act (1649) that granted religious freedom to all Christians.

In Maryland, as in Virginia, tobacco was the basis of the economy. Indians had long used tobacco leaves as a medicine and a stimulant. By the 1620s English men and women began to crave tobacco and the nicotine it contained, smoking, chewing, and snorting it with abandon. Initially James I condemned the use of this "vile Weed" and warned that its "black stinking fumes" were "baleful to the nose, harmful to the brain, and dangerous to the lungs." But his attitude changed as revenues from an import tax on tobacco filled the royal treasury.

European demand for tobacco set off a forty-year economic boom in the Chesapeake, attracting thousands of profit-hungry migrants. "All our riches for the present do consist in tobacco," a planter remarked in 1630. Exports rose from about 3 million pounds in 1640 to 10 million pounds in 1660. Planters moved up the river valleys, establishing large farms (plantations) that were distant from one another but easily reached by water. The scarcity of towns meant a much weaker sense of community than that existing in the open-field villages of rural England.

Unfortunately, mosquitoes as well as tobacco flourished in the mild Chesapeake climate, spreading malaria and weakening people's resistance to other diseases. Pregnant women were especially hard hit. Many died after bearing a first or second child,

The Tobacco Economy

The owners of large plantations used indentured servants and slaves to grow and process tobacco. Workers cured the tobacco by hanging it for several months in a well-ventilated shed; then they stripped the leaves off the stalks and packed them tightly into large plantation-made barrels, or "hogsheads," for shipment to Europe.
(Library of Congress)

and so settler families were small. More than 15,000 settlers arrived in Virginia between 1622 and 1640, but the population rose only from 2,000 to 8,000.

For most of the seventeenth century life in the Chesapeake colonies remained harsh and short. Most men never married because there were few women settlers. Families often were disrupted by early death; in Middlesex County in Virginia 61 percent of children lost one or both of their parents by the time they were thirteen. Orphaned children and unmarried young men constituted much of the population, making Chesapeake society very different from that in England.

MASTERS, SERVANTS, AND SLAVES

Despite the dangers, the prospect of owning land continued to lure migrants to the Chesapeake region. By 1700 over 80,000 English settlers had moved to Virginia, and another 20,000 had arrived in Maryland, the great majority not as free men and women but as indentured servants. English shipping registers provide insight into the background of these servants. Three-quarters of the 5,000 migrants from the port of Bristol were young men, many of whom had traveled hundreds of miles searching for work. Once in Bristol, these penniless wanderers were persuaded by merchants and sea captains to sign labor contracts called *indentures* and embark for the Chesapeake. The indentures bound them to work in return for room and board for a period of four or five years, after which they would be freemen, able to plant corn for sustenance and tobacco for sale.

For merchants, servants represented valuable cargo because their contracts fetched high prices from local planters in the labor-starved Chesapeake. For plantation owners, they were an incredible bargain. During the tobacco boom a male indentured servant could produce five times his purchase price in a year. Furthermore, servants were counted as household members, and so planters in Virginia received 50 acres of land for each one they imported.

Most masters ruled their servants with an iron hand, beating them for bad behavior and withholding permission to marry. If a servant ran away or became pregnant, a master went to court to increase the term of service. Female servants were especially vulnerable to abuse. As a Virginia law of 1692 stated, "dissolute masters have gotten their maids with child; and yet claim the benefit of their service." Planters got rid of uncooperative servants by selling their contracts to new masters. As an Englishman remarked in disgust, in Virginia "servants were sold up and down like horses."

For most indentured servants this ordeal did not provide the escape from poverty they had sought (see American Voices, "Hard Times in Early Virginia"). Half the men died before receiving their freedom, and another quarter remained poor. The remaining quarter benefited from their ordeal, acquiring property and respectability. If they survived, female servants generally fared better because men in the Chesapeake had grown "very sensible of the Misfortune of Wanting Wives." Many such servants married their masters or other well-established men. By migrating to the Chesapeake, these few—and very fortunate—men and women escaped a life of landless poverty in England.

The first African workers fared worse. In 1619 John Rolfe noted, "a Dutch man of warre . . . sold us twenty Negars," but for a generation the numbers of Africans remained small. About 400 Africans lived in the Chesapeake colonies in 1649, making up 2 percent of the population, and by 1670 the proportion of blacks had reached only 5 percent. Although many of these Africans served their masters for life, they were not legally enslaved. English common law acknowledged indentured servitude but not chattel slavery—the ownership of one human being by another. Consequently, a significant number of black workers escaped bondage after working for a number of years or by converting to Christianity. Some African Christian freemen even purchased slaves, bought the labor contracts of white servants, and married English women, suggesting that at this time religion and personal initiative were as important as race in determining social status. By becoming a

AMERICAN VOICES

Hard Times in Early Virginia

RICHARD FRETHORNE

The lot of an indentured servant in Virginia was always hard, especially before 1630, when food was scarce and Indians were a constant danger. In 1623 Richard Frethorne begged his parents to buy out the remaining years of his labor contract so that he could return to England.

Loving and kind father and mother . . . this is to let you understand that I your child am in a most heavy case by reason of the nature of the country . . . it causes much sickness, as the scurvy and the bloody flux [severe dysentery], and diverse other diseases, which make the body very poor and weak, and when we are sick there is nothing to comfort us. For since I came out of the ship, I never ate anything but peas and loblollie [gruel]. As for deer or venison I never saw any since I came into this land. There is indeed some fowl, but we are not allowed to go and get it, but must work hard both early and late for a mess of water gruel and a mouthful of bread and beef.

People cry out day and night, Oh that they were in England without their limbs and would not care to lose any limb to be in England again . . . we live in fear of the enemy every hour. . . . We are in great danger, for our plantation is very weak, by reason of the dearth, and sickness of our company. . . .

I have nothing to comfort me, nor there is nothing to be gotten here but sickness and death, except that one had money to lay out in some things for profit; but I have nothing at all, no not a shirt to my back, but two rags nor no clothes, but one poor suit, nor but one pair of shoes . . . my cloak is stolen by one of my own fellows, and to his dying hours would not tell me what he did with it, but some of my fellows saw him have butter and beef out of a ship, which my cloak [no] doubt paid for. . . .

SOURCE: Susan M. Kingsbury, ed., *The Records of the Virginia Company of London* (Washington, DC: Library of Congress, 1935), vol. 4: pp. 58–60.

Christian and a planter, an enterprising African could aspire to near equality with the English settlers.

Beginning in the 1660s, for reasons that are not clear, legislatures in the Chesapeake colonies enacted laws that lowered the status of Africans. Perhaps the English-born elite grew more conscious of race as the number of Africans increased. By 1671 the Virginia House of Burgesses had forbidden Africans to own guns or join the militia. It had also barred them—"tho baptized and enjoying their own Freedom"—from buying the labor contracts of white servants and specified that conversion to Christianity did not qualify Africans for eventual freedom. Being black was becoming a mark of inferior legal status, and being a slave was becoming a permanent and hereditary condition.

THE SEEDS OF SOCIAL REVOLT

By the 1660s the growing size of the Chesapeake tobacco crop triggered a collapse of the market. During the boom years of the 1620s tobacco sold for 24 pence a pound; forty years later it was fetching barely one-tenth as much. As the economic boom turned into a "bust," long-standing social conflicts flared up in political turmoil.

Political decisions in England had a lot to do with the decline of tobacco prices. In 1651, in an effort to exclude Dutch ships and merchants from England's overseas possessions, Parliament passed an Act of Trade and Navigation. Revised and extended in 1660 and 1663, the Navigation Acts permitted only English or colonial-owned ships to enter American ports. They also required the colonists to ship certain "enumerated articles," including tobacco, only to England. Thus, Chesapeake planters could no longer legally trade with Dutch merchants, who paid the highest prices. Moreover, to increase royal revenues the English monarchs continually raised the import duty on tobacco, thereby increasing the price to consumers and stifling growth of the market. As a result, by the 1670s planters got only one penny a pound for their crop.

Nonetheless, the number of planters in Virginia and Maryland grew, and tobacco exports continued to increase from 20 million pounds annually in the 1670s to 41 million pounds between 1690 and 1720. But profit margins were now thin, and the Chesapeake ceased to be a land of upward social mobility. Yeomen families grew about 10,000 tobacco plants each year but earned just enough to scrape by, and many fell into debt. Even harder hit were newly freed indentured servants. Low tobacco prices made it nearly impossible for them to pay the necessary fees to claim the 50 acres of land to which they were entitled and buy the tools and seed needed to plant it. Consequently, most former servants had to sell their labor again, signing new indentures or becoming wage workers or tenant farmers.

Gradually the Chesapeake colonies came to be dominated by an elite of planter-landlords and merchants. Landowners prospered by dividing their ample estates and leasing small plots to the growing army of former servants. They also lent money at high interest rates to hard-pressed yeomen families. Some well-to-do planters became commercial middlemen, setting up small retail stores or charging a commission for storing the tobacco of their poorer neighbors and selling it to English merchants. In Virginia this elite accumulated nearly half the land by soliciting favors from royal governors. In Maryland well-connected Catholic planters were equally dominant; by 1720 Charles Carroll owned 47,000 acres of land, farmed by scores of tenants and bound workers.

As these aggressive entrepreneurs confronted a growing number of young landless laborers, social divisions intensified, reaching a breaking point in Virginia during the corrupt regime of Governor William Berkeley. Berkeley first served as governor of Virginia between 1642 and 1652, and he won fame in 1644 by putting down the second major Indian revolt led by Opechancanough. Serving as governor again beginning in 1660, he made large land grants to himself and to members of his council, who exempted their own lands from taxation and appointed friends as county judges and local magistrates. Berkeley suppressed dissent in the House of Burgesses by assigning land grants to friendly legislators and appointing their relatives to the posts of sheriff, tax collector, and justice of the peace. Social and political unrest increased when the corrupt Burgesses changed the voting system to exclude landless freemen, who constituted half of all adult white males. Property-holding yeomen retained the vote, and—distressed by tobacco prices, rising taxes, and political corruption—some of them now rose in a rebellion against the planter elite.

BACON'S REBELLION

An Indian conflict in the summer of 1675 sparked Bacon's rebellion. By this time the Indians in Virginia were few and weak, their numbers having dwindled from 30,000 in 1607 to a mere 3,500, as compared to 38,000 Europeans and about 2,500 Africans. Most Indians lived along the frontier on lands guaranteed by treaty. Hundreds of poor freeholders and aspiring tenants who wanted cheap land insisted that the Indians be expelled or exterminated. But wealthy planters on the seacoast, who wanted a ready supply of labor, opposed expansion into Indian territory, as did the planter-merchants who traded with the Native Americans for furs.

Fighting broke out when a band of Virginia militiamen murdered thirty Indians. Defying orders from Governor Berkeley, a larger force of 1,000 militiamen then surrounded a fortified Susquehannock village and killed five chiefs who had come out to negotiate. The outraged Susquehannocks, who had recently migrated from the north, retaliated by killing 300 whites in raids on outlying plantations. Berkeley did not want war, which would disrupt the fur trade, and proposed a defensive military policy, asking the House of Burgesses in March 1676 to raise money to build a series of frontier forts. Western settlers dismissed this strategy as useless, a plot by planters and merchants to impose high taxes and, in the words of one yeoman, to take "all our tobacco into their own hands."

Nathaniel Bacon emerged as the leader of the protesters. A wealthy and bold man, he had recently arrived from England and settled on a frontier estate. Although he was only twenty-eight, Bacon commanded the respect of his neighbors because of his vigor and his high status as a member of the governor's council. When Berkeley refused to grant Bacon a military commission, Bacon marched his frontiersmen against the Indians anyway, slaughtering some of the peaceful Doeg people and triggering a political upheaval. Condemning the frontiersmen as "rebels and mutineers," Berkeley expelled Bacon from the council and placed him under arrest. Then, realizing the rebel leader's military power, the governor agreed to legislative elections and accepted the far-reaching political reforms enacted by the new House of Burgesses that curbed the powers of the governor and the council and restored voting rights to landless freemen.

These much-needed reforms did not end the rebellion. Bacon was bitter about Berkeley's arbitrary actions, and the poor farmers and indentured servants in his army were resentful of exploitation by the political elite and eager to flaunt their power. Backed by 400 armed men, Bacon seized control of the colony and issued a "Manifesto and Declaration of the People," demanding the death or removal of all Indians and an end to the rule of wealthy "parasites." "All the power and sway is got into the hands of the rich," Bacon proclaimed, as his army burned Jamestown to the ground and plundered the plantations of Berkeley's allies. When Bacon died suddenly from dysentery in October 1676, the governor took his revenge, dispersing the rebel army, seizing the estates of well-to-do rebels, and hanging twenty-three men.

Bacon's rebellion was a pivotal event in the history of Virginia. Although planter-merchants continued to dominate the colony, they limited the governor's authority and found public positions for substantial and politically ambitious property owners like Bacon. The planter-merchant elite also appeased the lower social orders by cutting their taxes and supporting the expansion of English settlement onto Indian lands. The uprising also contributed to the expansion of African slavery. To forestall another rebellion planters in Virginia and Maryland sought to limit the number of freed white servants in the colony. Instead they enacted laws explicitly legalizing slavery and imported thousands of Africans, committing their descendants to a social system based on racial exploitation.

Puritan New England

The Puritan exodus to America from 1620 to 1640 was both a worldly quest for land and a spiritual effort to preserve the "pure" Christian faith. By creating a Holy Commonwealth in the new world, these pious migrants hoped to promote reform within the established Church of England. By gaining access to land, they hoped to build a society of independent property-owning farm families. By defining their mission in spiritual terms, the Puritans gave a moral dimension to American history.

THE PURITAN MIGRATION

From the beginning New England differed from other European settlements. New Spain and Jamestown were populated initially by unruly male adventurers, and New France and New Netherland by commercial-minded fur traders. By contrast Plymouth, the first permanent community in New England, was settled by women and children as well as men, and its leaders were pious Protestants—the Pilgrims.

The Pilgrims were Puritans who had left the Church of England, thus earning the name "Separatists." When King James I embraced traditional religious doctrines in the 1610s and threatened to harry Puritans "out of the land, or else do worse," the Pilgrims left England and settled among like-minded Dutch Calvinists in Holland. Subsequently, thirty-five of them decided to migrate to America, where they hoped to maintain their English identity. Led by William Bradford and joined by sixty-seven other migrants from England, they sailed to America aboard the *Mayflower* in 1620 (see Map 2.2).

Before their departure, the Pilgrims had organized themselves into a joint-stock corporation with backing from sympathetic Puritan merchants. Arriving in America without a royal charter, they created their own covenant of government, the Mayflower Compact, to "combine ourselves together into a civill body politick." This document was the first "constitution" adopted in North America and used the Puritan model of a self-governing religious congregation as the blueprint for political society.

The first winter in America tested the Pilgrims. As in Jamestown, hunger and disease took a heavy toll; of the 102 migrants who arrived in November, only half survived until the spring. Thereafter the Plymouth colony—unlike Virginia—

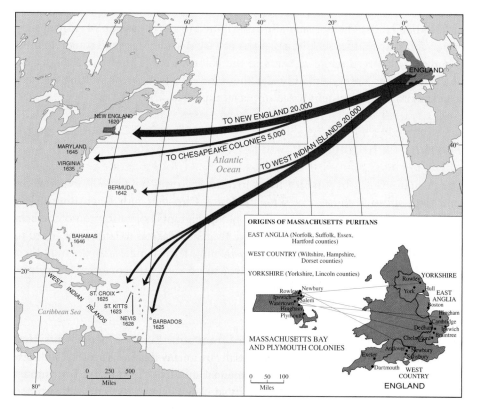

M A P 2.2
The Puritan Migration to America, 1620–1640

Nearly 50,000 Puritans left England between 1620 and 1640. In New England migrants from the three major areas of English Puritanism—Yorkshire, East Anglia, and the West Country—commonly settled among those from their own region. They named American communities after their English towns of origin and transplanted regional customs, such as the open-field agriculture practiced in Rowley in Yorkshire and Rowley in Massachusetts Bay.

became a healthy and thriving community. The cold climate inhibited the spread of mosquito-borne diseases, and the Pilgrims' religious discipline established a strong work ethic. Moreover, because a severe epidemic in 1618 had killed 90 percent of the local Wampanoag people, the migrants faced few external threats. The Pilgrims quickly built solid houses, planted ample crops, and entered the fur trade. Their numbers grew rapidly, to 3,000 by 1640, prompting the creation of ten new towns with extensive powers of self-government. A new legal code established in 1636 provided for a colonywide system of representative self-government, guaranteed various political rights, and provided for the separation of church and state by forbidding government interference in spiritual matters.

Meanwhile, England was plunging deeper into religious turmoil. King Charles I (r. 1625–1649) supported the Church of England but personally repudiated some Protestant doctrines, such as justification by faith. The Puritans, who had gained many seats in Parliament, accused the king of "popery"—holding Catholic beliefs. Charles's response was to dissolve Parliament in 1629, claiming that he ruled by "divine right," and to raise money through royal edicts, customs duties, and the sale of monopolies. The king's arbitrary rule struck at the power of the landed gentry, who expected to exercise authority through the House of Commons, and cut away at the profits of the merchant community, a stronghold of Puritanism. Then in 1633 the king chose William Laud, who loathed Puritans, to head the Church of England. Laud removed hundreds of Puritan ministers and forced Anglican rituals on their congregations, prompting thousands of Puritans to seek refuge in America.

In 1630, 900 Puritans boarded eleven ships and sailed across the Atlantic under the leadership of John Winthrop, a well-educated country squire. Winthrop believed that England was morally corrupt and "overburdened with people." He sought land and opportunity for his children and a place in history for his people. "We must consider that we shall be as a City upon a Hill," Winthrop told his fellow passengers aboard the ship *Arbella* in 1630. "The eyes of all people are upon us." Like the Pilgrims, the Puritans envisioned a reformed Christian society, a genuinely "New" England. Many Puritans saw themselves as a "saving remnant" chosen by God to preserve the true faith in America and inspire religious change in England.

Once in America, Winthrop and his associates established the Massachusetts Bay colony in the area around Boston and transformed their joint-stock business corporation, the General Court of shareholders, into a colonial legislature. Over the next decade about 10,000 Puritans migrated to the Massachusetts Bay colony, along with 10,000 others fleeing hard times in England. The Puritans created representative political institutions that were locally based, with the governor as well as the assembly and council elected by the colony's freemen. However, to ensure rule by the godly the Puritans limited the right to vote and hold office to men who were Puritan church members. Eschewing the religious toleration of the Pilgrims, they established Puritanism as the state-supported religion and barred members of other faiths from conducting services. Massachusetts Bay became a religious commonwealth with the Bible as its legal as well as spiritual guide. For example, following a biblical rule Puritans there divided inheritances among all children in a given family, with a double portion going to the oldest son. "Where there is no Law," the colony's government advised local magistrates, they should rule "as near the law of God as they can."

RELIGION AND SOCIETY, 1630–1670

In establishing their churches, the Puritans in New England tried to re-create the simplicity of the first Christians. They eliminated bishops and devised a democratic church structure controlled by the laity, or the ordinary members of the congregation—hence their name, Congregationalists. Influenced by John Calvin, Puritans embraced predestination, believing that God had decided, or "predestined," the fates of all people before they were born, choosing a few "elect" men and women (the Saints) for salvation and condemning the rest to damnation. Most congregations set extraordinarily high standards for church membership, rigorously examining those who applied. Even so, many Saints lived in great anxiety, for they could never be sure that God had predestined them for salvation.

Puritans dealt with the uncertainties of divine election in three ways. Some congregations stressed the conversion experience: when God infused a soul with grace, the person was "born again" and knew that salvation was at hand. Other Puritans stressed "preparation," the confidence in redemption that came from years of spiritual guidance and church discipline. Still others believed that God had entered into a *covenant*, or contract, with them, promising to treat them as a divinely "chosen people" as long as they lived according to His laws.

To maintain God's favor, the Puritan magistrates of Massachusetts Bay felt they must purge their society of religious dissidents. One target was Roger Williams, who in 1634 had become the minister of the Puritan church in Salem. Williams preferred the Pilgrims' separation of church and state in Plymouth Colony and condemned the legal establishment of Congregationalism in Massachusetts Bay. He taught that political magistrates should have authority over only the "bodies, goods, and outward estates of men," not their spiritual lives. Moreover, he questioned the Puritans' right to seize (rather than buy) Indian lands. In response, the Puritan magistrates banished him from Massachusetts Bay in 1635.

Williams and his followers resettled in Rhode Island in 1636, founding the town of Providence on land acquired from the Narragansett Indians. Other religious dissidents founded Portsmouth and Newport. In 1644 these towns obtained a corporate charter from the English Parliament that granted them full authority "to rule themselves." In Rhode Island as in Plymouth there was no legally established church; every congregation was autonomous, and individual men and women could worship God as they pleased.

Puritan magistrates also felt threatened by Anne Hutchinson, the wife of a merchant and a mother of seven who worked as a midwife. Hutchinson held weekly prayer meetings in her house—attended by as many as sixty women—in which she

Changing Images of Death

Death—sudden and arbitrary—was a constant presence in the preindustrial world. Pre-1700 New England gravestones often depicted death as a frightening skull, warning sinners to repent of their sins. After 1700 a smiling cherub adorned many gravestones, suggesting a more optimistic view of the afterlife.

(Peabody Essex Museum)

accused certain Boston clergymen of placing undue emphasis on church laws and good behavior. In words that recalled Martin Luther's rejection of indulgences, Hutchinson argued that salvation was not something that people could earn through good deeds; there was no "covenant of works." Instead, salvation was bestowed by God through the "covenant of grace." Hutchinson stressed the importance of revelation: the direct communication of truth by God to the individual believer. Since this doctrine diminished the role of ministers and, indeed, of all established authority, Puritan magistrates found it heretical.

The magistrates also resented Hutchinson because of her sex. Like other Christians, Puritans believed in the equality of souls: both men and women could be saved. When it came to matters concerning the governance of church and state, however, women were seen as being clearly inferior to men. As the Pilgrim minister John Robinson put it, women "are debarred by their sex from ordinary prophesying, and from any other dealing in the church wherein they take authority over the man." Puritan women could never be ministers, lay preachers, or even voting members of the congregation.

In 1637 the Massachusetts Bay magistrates put Hutchinson on trial for heresy, accusing her of believing that inward grace freed an individual from the rules of the church. Hutchinson defended her views with great skill and tenacity, and even Winthrop admitted that she was "a woman of fierce and haughty courage." But the judges found her guilty and berated her for not attending to "her household affairs, and such things as belong to women." Banished, she followed Roger Williams into exile in Rhode Island.

The coercive policies of the magistrates, along with the desire for better land, prompted some Puritans to leave Massachusetts Bay. In 1636 Thomas Hooker led a hundred settlers to the Connecticut River Valley, where they established the town of Hartford. Others followed, settling along the river at Wethersfield and Windsor. In 1639 the Connecticut Puritans adopted the Fundamental Orders, a plan of government that included a representative assembly and a popularly elected governor. Connecticut was patterned after Massachusetts Bay, with a firm union of church and state and a congregational system of church government, but voting rights were extended to most property-owning men—not just church members.

As Puritans established themselves in America, England fell into a religious war. When Archbishop Laud imposed a new Church of England prayer book on Presbyterian Scotland, a Scottish army invaded England. In 1642 thousands of English Puritans rose up in revolt, demanding greater authority for Parliament and reform of the established church. Hundreds of Puritans returned from America to join the conflict. After four years of civil war the Parliamentary forces led by Oliver Cromwell were victorious. In 1649 Parliament executed Charles I, proclaimed a republican commonwealth, and reformed the Church of England by eliminating bishops and elaborate rituals.

The Puritan triumph was short-lived. Popular support for the Commonwealth quickly ebbed, especially when Cromwell took dictatorial control of the government in 1653. After his death a repentant Parliament summoned the son of Charles I to the throne, restoring the monarch and the power of bishops in the Church of England. For many Puritans, Charles II's accession in 1660 represented the victory of the Antichrist—the false prophet described in the last book of the New Testament.

For the Puritans in Massachusetts, the restoration of the monarchy began a new phase of their "errand into the wilderness." They had come to New England to preserve the "pure" Christian church, expecting to return in triumph to a Europe ready to receive the true Gospel. Since that sacred mission had been dashed by the failure of the English Revolution, Puritan ministers articulated a new vision: they exhorted their congregations to create a permanent new society in America based on their faith and ideals.

THE PURITAN IMAGINATION AND WITCHCRAFT

Like the Native Americans they encountered in New England, the Puritans thought that the physical world was full of supernatural forces. This belief in "spirits" stemmed in part from Christian teachings, such as the Catholic belief in miracles and the Protestant faith in the powers of "grace." Devout Christians saw signs of God's (or Satan's) power in blazing stars, deformed births, and other unusual events. Noting that "more Ministers' Houses than others proportionally had been smitten with Lightning," Cotton Mather, a prominent Massachusetts minister, wondered "what the meaning of God should be in it."

The Puritans' respect for spiritual "forces" also reflected certain pagan assumptions that were held by all sections of society. When Samuel Sewall, a Puritan merchant and judge, moved into a new house, he tried to fend off evil spirits by driving a metal pin into the floor. And thousands of ordinary Puritans followed pagan astrological charts printed in farmers' almanacs to determine the best times to plant crops, marry off their children, and make other important decisions.

Zealous ministers attacked many of these beliefs and practices as a return to "superstition" and condemned "cunning" individuals who claimed to have special powers as healers or prophets. Many Christians looked on folk doctors or conjurers as "wizards" or "witches" who acted at the command of Satan. The people of Andover, Massachusetts "were much addicted to sorcery," claimed one observer, and "there were forty men in it that could raise the Devil as well as any astrologer." Between 1647 and 1662 civil authorities in Massachusetts and Connecticut hanged fourteen people for witchcraft, mostly older women who, their accusers claimed, were "double-tongued" or "had an unruly spirit."

The most dramatic episode of witch-hunting took place in Salem, Massachusetts, in 1692. The causes were complex and are still hard to fathom. Some historians stress group rivalries, pointing out that many of the accusers were the daughters and young female servants of poor farmers in a rural area of Salem, whereas many of the accused were wealthier church members or their friends. Things got out of hand when judges allowed the introduction of "spectral" evidence, visions seen only by the accusers. Soon Massachusetts authorities had arrested 175 people and executed 20 of them. Because 19 of those killed were women, other historians argue that the incident was part of a systematic attempt to intimidate women, especially those who had inherited property, and make certain they remained subordinate "helpmates" to their husbands. Other scholars have called attention to the fears raised by recent Indian attacks along the nearby frontier in Maine, attacks that took the lives of the parents of the young girls whose accusations sparked the Salem prosecutions.

The Salem episode marked a turning point for New England. Popular revulsion against the executions dealt a blow to the traditional dominance of religion in public life; there would be no more legal prosecutions for witchcraft. The European Enlightenment, a major intellectual movement that began around 1675, also promoted a more rational view of the world. Increasingly, educated people explained accidents and sudden deaths through theories about natural forces, not through religion, astrology, or witchcraft. In contrast to Cotton Mather (who died in 1728), well-read men of the next generation—such as Benjamin Franklin—would conceive of lightning as a natural phenomenon rather than a supernatural sign.

A YEOMAN SOCIETY, 1630–1700

In creating New England communities, Puritans consciously avoided the worst features of traditional Europe. They did not wish to live in a society dominated by a few wealthy landowners or under a distant government that levied oppressive taxes. Consequently, they instituted land-distribution policies that encouraged the development of self-governing communities composed primarily of property-owning families. Instead of granting thousands of acres to wealthy planters (as occurred in the Chesapeake colonies), the General Courts of Massachusetts Bay and Connecticut bestowed the title to a township on a group of settlers, or proprietors, who distributed the land among themselves. The title was given in *fee simple,* which meant that the proprietors' families held the land outright, free from manorial obligations or feudal dues; they could sell, lease, or rent it as they pleased.

Widespread ownership of land did not imply equality of wealth or status. Like most seventeenth-century Europeans, Puritans believed in a social and economic hierarchy. "God had Ordained different degrees and orders of men," proclaimed the wealthy Boston merchant John Saffin, "some to be Masters and Commanders, others to be Subjects, and to be commanded." Consequently, town proprietors normally bestowed the largest plots of land on men of high social status, who often became political leaders. However, all male heads of families received some land, laying the basis for a society of independent yeomen farmers, and all of them had a voice in the town meeting, the main institution of local government.

Local communities in New England had much more political power than did most peasant villages in Europe. Each year the town meeting chose selectmen to manage town affairs. It also levied taxes; enacted ordinances regarding fencing, lot sizes, and road building; and regulated the use of common fields for grazing livestock and cutting firewood. Beginning in 1634 each town in Massachusetts Bay elected its own representatives to the General Court. As the number of towns increased, their representatives in General Court gained authority at the expense of the governor and magistrates, further enhancing local control.

Over time the farming communities of New England became more socially divided. The larger proprietors owned enough land to divide among all their sons (usually three or four). Smallholders could provide land for only some of their sons, which forced the rest to become propertyless laborers. Newcomers who lacked the rights of proprietors were the least well off, for they had to buy land or work as tenants or laborers. By 1702 in Windsor, Connecticut, landless sons and newcomers accounted for no less than 30 percent of the male taxpayers. It would take years of saving or migration to a new town for these men and their families to become freeholders.

Despite these inequalities, nearly all New Englanders had an opportunity to acquire property, and even those at the bottom of the social scale enjoyed some economic security. When he died in the 1690s, Nathaniel Fish was one of the poorest men in Barnstable, Massachusetts, yet he owned a two-room cottage, 8 acres of land, an ox, and a cow. For him and thousands of other settlers New England had proved to be the promised land, a new world of opportunity.

The Indians' New World

Native Americans on the eastern seaboard were also living in a new world, but for them it was a bleak, dangerous, and conflict-ridden place. Some Indian peoples, like the Pequots, resisted the invaders by force. Others retreated into the Appalachian Mountains to preserve their traditional culture or to band together in new tribes.

PURITANS AND PEQUOTS

Seeing themselves as God's chosen people, the Puritans attempted to justify their intrusions on Native American lands from a moral perspective. "By what right or warrant can we enter into the land of the Savages," they asked themselves while still in England, "and take away their rightfull inheritance from them?" John Winthrop thought that a disastrous smallpox epidemic of 1633, which reduced the Indian population from 13,000 to 3,000, provided a clear answer. "If God were not pleased with our inheriting these parts," he pointed out, "why doth he still make roome for us by diminishing them as we increase?" Citing the Book of Genesis, the magistrates of Massachusetts Bay declared that the Indians had not "subdued" their land and therefore had no "just right" to it.

Imbued with moral righteousness, the Puritans often treated Native Americans with a brutality equal to that of the Spanish conquistadors and Nathaniel Bacon's frontiersmen. In 1636 when Pequot warriors attacked English farmers who had intruded onto their lands, Puritan militiamen and their Indian allies led a surprise attack on a Pequot village and massacred about 500 men, women, and children. "God laughed at the Enemies of his People," one soldier boasted, "filling the Place with Dead Bodies." Many of the survivors were ruthlessly tracked down and sold into slavery in the Caribbean.

Like most Europeans, English Puritans viewed the Indians as "savages," culturally inferior people who did not deserve civilized treatment. But the Puritans were not racist as the term is understood today. To them, Native Americans were not genetically inferior—they were white people with sun-darkened skins—and "sin," rather than race, accounted for their degenerate condition. "Probably the devil" delivered these "miserable savages" to America, wrote the Puritan minister Cotton Mather, "in hopes that the gospel of the Lord Jesus Christ would never come here to destroy or disturb his absolute empire over them."

This interpretation inspired attempts at conversion by John Eliot, who translated the Bible into Algonquian and undertook missions to Indians in eastern Massachusetts. Because Puritans demanded that Indians master Puritan theology, only a few Native Americans became full members of Puritan congregations. However, the Puritans created "praying towns" that, like the Spanish Franciscans' missions in New Mexico, sought to supervise the Indian population. Soon more than 1,000 Indians lived in fourteen special mission towns. By 1670 a combination of European diseases, military force, and Christianization had pacified most of the Algonquian-speaking peoples who lived along the seacoast of New England, guaranteeing, at least temporarily, the safety of the white settlers.

METACOM'S WAR

By the 1670s the white population of New England had reached 55,000 while the Indian population had declined from an estimated 120,000 in 1570, to 70,000 in 1620, to barely 16,000 in 1670. Like Opechancanough in Virginia and Popé in New Mexico, Metacom, leader of the Wampanoag tribe, concluded that only united resistance could stop the relentless advance of the European invaders. In 1675 Metacom forged a military alliance with the Narragansett and Nipmuck peoples and attacked white settlements throughout New England. Bitter fighting continued into 1676, ending only when Indian warriors ran short of guns and powder and Mohawks hired by the Massachusetts Bay government ambushed and killed Metacom. The war was a deadly affair. The Indians burned 20 percent of the English towns in Massachusetts and Rhode Island and killed 1,000 whites, about 5 percent of the adult population. But their own losses—from famine and disease as well as battle—were much larger: as many as 4,500, or 25 percent of an already diminished population. Many survivors were sold into slavery in the Caribbean, including Metacom's wife and nine-year-old son.

Many of the defeated New England Algonquian peoples migrated into the backcountry, where they intermarried with other tribes tied to the French. They had suffered a double tragedy, losing both their land and the integrity of their traditional cultures. Over the next century, these displaced peoples would take their revenge, allying with the French to attack their Puritan enemies (see American Voices, "The Unredeemed Captive").

THE FUR TRADE AND THE INLAND PEOPLES

Until well after 1700 the Indian peoples who lived near the Appalachian Mountains and in the great forested areas beyond remained independent, but few were able to maintain their customary way of life. The greatest threat to their cultures came from

***Metacom (King Philip),
Chief of the Wampanoag***

The Indian uprising of 1675 left an indelible mark on the historical memory of New England. This painting, done on semitransparent cloth and lit from behind for dramatic effect, was used by traveling performers during the 1850s to tell the story of King Philip's War. (Shelburne Museum)

the wars and epidemics brought by the fur trade. Yet many inland tribes were eager to control the fur trade to obtain European guns and goods. The militarily aggressive and diplomatically astute Iroquois peoples had the best chance. From their location in central New York, Iroquois warriors could move quickly to the east and south along the Mohawk, Hudson, Delaware, and Susquehanna Rivers to exchange goods with (or threaten) the English and Dutch colonies. They could also travel north via Lake Champlain and the Richelieu River to French traders in Quebec, and west by means of the Great Lakes and the Allegheny-Ohio river system to the rich fur-bearing lands of the Mississippi Valley. In 1600 the Iroquois in the area of present-day New York numbered about 30,000 and lived in large towns of 500 to 2,000 inhabitants. Two decades later they had organized themselves in a great "longhouse" confederation of the Five Nations: the Senecas, Cayugas, Onondagas, Oneidas, and Mohawks.

AMERICAN VOICES

The Unredeemed Captive

PETER SCHULYER

A decade and a half after Metacom's War, Indians mounted new attacks against Massachusetts frontier settlements. In 1704 Mohawk Indians devastated the town of Deerfield and took back to French Canada 112 prisoners, including seven-year-old Eunice Williams. Most of the captives were returned or ransomed, and in 1713 Peter Schulyer, an Albany fur trader, sought the return of Eunice Williams, who was now sixteen.

I arrived from Albany at Mont Reall [Montreal] on ye 15th of April. . . . Monsr. De Vaudruille [Vaudrieuil], Governor and Chief of Canada . . . gave me all the Encouragement I could immagine for her to go home. . . . Accordingly I went to the ffort of Caghenewaga [Kahnawake] being accompanied by one of the Kings officers and a ffrench Interpreter [and] likewise another of the Indian language. . . .

I thought fitt first to apply mySelf to the priests. . . . And [as I] was informed before that this infant (As I may say) was married to a young Indian, I therefore proposed to know the Reason why this poor captive should be Married to an Indian being a Christian born . . . said he they came to me to Marry them. . . . And if he would not marry them they matter'd not, for they were resolved never to leave the other. . . . He sent for her, who presently came with the Indian She was married to both together. She looking very poor in body, bashfull in the face, but proved harder than Steel in her breast. . . .

I first Spoak to her in English, Upon wch she did not Answr me; And I believe She did not understand me, she being very Young when she was taken. . . . I Imployed my Indian Languister to talk to her . . . but could not get one word from her. . . . And I could not prevail wth her to go home . . . that she might only go to see her father, And directly return hither again. . . .

And these two words ["Jaghte oghte, a plaine denyall"] were all we could gett from her; in allmost two hours time that we talked with her . . . and the time growing late and I being very Sorrowfull, that I could not prevail upon nor get one word more from her I took her by the hand and left her in the priest's house.

[Eunice Williams remained among the Mohawk, bore two daughters, twice visited her English brothers and sisters in Massachusetts, and died in Canada in 1785, aged eighty-nine.]

SOURCE: John Demos, *The Unredeemed Captive: A Family Story from Early America* (New York: Knopf, 1994), pp. 101–08.

Although their numbers were cut by a third by a virulent smallpox epidemic in 1633, the Iroquois waged a successful series of wars against the Iroquoian-speaking Hurons (1649), Neutrals (1651), Eries (1657), and Susquehannocks. These victories gave the Iroquois control of the fur trade with the French in Quebec and the Dutch in New York and enabled them to replenish their depleted ranks by incorporating war captives. By 1667 half the population of many Mohawk towns consisted of adopted prisoners. Following these victories, the Five Nations made peace with their traditional French foes and allowed a considerable number of Jesuit missionaries in Iroquoia. Soon about 20 percent of the Five Nations were Christians, some living under French protection in separate mission-towns.

In 1680 the Iroquois renewed their struggle for control of the western fur trade to maintain their supply of guns and goods from the English in New York. Warriors of the Five Nations pushed a dozen Algonquian-speaking peoples who were allied with the French—the Ottawas, Foxes, Sauks, Kickapoos, Miamis, Illinois—out of their traditional lands north of the Ohio River and into a newly formed multitribal region (present-day Wisconsin) west of Lake Michigan. After suffering heavy losses—half of their 2,200 warriors—the Iroquois again made peace with French.

These wars and contact with European traders transformed the character of Indian society. Most tribes became smaller as European diseases devastated their peoples, and the rum and corn liquor sold by fur traders took their toll. "Strong spirits . . . Causes our men to get very sick," a Catawba leader protested, "and many of our people has Lately Died by the Effects of that Strong Drink." Many Indian peoples also lost their economic and cultural independence. As they exchanged furs for European-made iron utensils and cloth blankets, they neglected traditional artisan skills—making fewer flint hoes, clay pots, and skin garments. As a Cherokee chief complained in the 1750s, "Every necessity of life we must have from the white people." Moreover, as French missionaries won converts among the Hurons, Iroquois, and inland peoples, they divided communities into hostile religious factions.

The fur trade created other conflicts as well. The commitment to constant warfare altered tribal politics by increasing the influence of those who made war, shifting political power from cautious elders, the sachems, to headstrong young warriors. The sachems, one group of Seneca warriors said with scorn, "were a parcell of Old People who say much but who Mean or Act very little." Equally important, the position and status of women changed in complex and contradictory ways. Traditionally, the eastern Woodland women had asserted authority as the chief providers of food and hand-crafted goods, roles that were undermined because of the influx of trade goods and the disruptive impact of warfare on agricultural production. Yet the influence of women in victorious tribes increased as they assumed responsibility for assimilating captive peoples into the culture.

Finally, the sheer extent of the fur industry—the trapping and killing of hundreds of thousands of beaver, deer, otter, and other animals—profoundly altered the environment. Streams ran faster because there were fewer beaver dams, and the winter hunt for food became more arduous and less fruitful. Death from trapping and hunting had decimated the animal population of North America, just as death from disease and warfare had cut down its native peoples.

All of the European invaders—Dutch and French fur traders no less than French Jesuits, Spanish conquistadors, and English settlers—undermined traditional Native

Algonquian Beaver Bowl

Because of the impor-
tance to the fur trade, the
beaver played a significant
role in Native American
economic and cultural
life. This beaver-shaped
bowl, carved from the
root of an ash tree, was
the work of an eighteenth-
century Algonquian arti-
san in present-day Ohio
or Illinois.
(Peabody Museum, Harvard
University. Photograph by Hillel
Burger)

American societies, forcing Indians to fashion new ways of life. Among the English
migrants, Puritans tried consciously to create a different world in America, a "New"
England dedicated to the doctrines of a radical Protestant Christianity. In the Chesapeake the planters' quest for wealth likewise produced a new model of society—
one based on the naked exploitation of white indentured servants and, especially
after 1700, of enslaved African laborers. America had become a new world for all
of its peoples.

For Further Exploration

For a comprehensive and insightful narrative of the Spanish exploration and settlement of
the lands to the north of the Rio Grande, consult David Weber, *The Spanish Frontier in North
America* (1992). Bernard Bailyn, *The Peopling of British North America: An Introduction*
(1986), presents a brief, vivid history of English migration and settlement. In *American
Slavery, American Freedom* (1975) Edmund Morgan offers a compelling portrayal of white
servitude and black slavery in early Virginia, while John Demos, *The Unredeemed Captive:
A Family Story from Early America* (1994), relates the gripping tale of Eunice Williams, a
captured Puritan girl who lived her life among the Mohawks. Another fine study of Native
American life is James Merrell, *The Indians' New World: Catawbas and Their Neighbors from
European Contact Through the Era of Removal* (1989). William Cronon, *Changes in the Land:
Indians, Colonists, and the Ecology of New England* (1983), is a succinct analysis of the im-
pact of the Indians and the English on the ecology of New England. Arthur Quinn, *A New
World: An Epic of Colonial America from the Founding of Jamestown to the Fall of Quebec*
(1994), is a lively narrative filled with portraits of important political figures, macabre events,
and high hopes that end disastrously.

TIMELINE

1530s	Jacques Cartier claims Gulf of St. Lawrence lands for France.	1622	Opechancanough's uprising
		1624	Virginia becomes a royal colony.
1540s	Francisco Vásquez de Coronado and Hernando de Soto seek gold in the present-day United States.	1630	Puritans found Massachusetts Bay colony.
1565	Spain establishes St. Augustine, Florida.	1634	Maryland settled as a Catholic refuge.
1580s	Failure of Roanoke and other English settlements	1636	Roger Williams, expelled from Massachusetts Bay, founds Rhode Island.
1598	Acoma War in New Mexico	1637	Pequot War. Anne Hutchinson banished
1607	Powhatan confronts the English at Jamestown in Virginia.	1640s	Five Iroquois Nations go to war over fur trade. Puritan Revolution in England
1608	Samuel de Champlain founds Quebec.		
1619	The first Africans arrive in Chesapeake. The Virginia House of Burgesses convened.	1660s–1720	Low tobacco prices spark social conflict.
		1664	England conquers New Netherland.
1620	Pilgrims found Plymouth colony.	1675–1676	Bacon's rebellion in Virginia. Metacom's (King Philip) uprising in New England
1620s–1660s	Tobacco boom in Chesapeake colonies. Growth of English servitude and African slavery in Chesapeake	1680	Popé's Rebellion in New Mexico
1621	Dutch West India Company settles New Netherland.	1692	Salem witchcraft trials

A PBS video, *Surviving Columbus* (2 hours), traces the experiences of the Pueblo Indians over 450 years. "First Nations Histories," at <http://www.dickshovel.com/Compacts.html>, presents short histories of many North American Indian peoples and information on their politics, language, culture, and demography. A highly acclaimed site on the Pilgrims at Plymouth is "Caleb Johnson's Mayflower Web Pages," at <http://members.aol.com/calebj/mayflower.html>. "Colonial Williamsburg," at <http://www.history.org/>, offers an extensive collection of documents, illustrations, and secondary texts about colonial life, as well as information about the archeological excavations at Williamsburg. Extensive materials on the Salem witchcraft episode can be viewed at <http://etext.lib.virginia.edu/salem/witchcraft/>.

Chapter 3

THE BRITISH EMPIRE IN AMERICA
1660–1750

> The Planters in General have throve and grown Rich . . . by the help and Labour of their Slaves.
>
> RICHARD HILL, 1743

In 1660 England was a second-class commercial power, picking up the crumbs left by Dutch merchants who dominated the Atlantic. As the Duke of Albemarle lamented, "What we want is more of the trade the Dutch now have." To achieve that goal the English government passed the Navigation Acts, which excluded Dutch merchants from its American colonies, and then went to war against the Dutch to enforce the new legislation. By the 1720s the newly unified kingdom of Great Britain (comprising England and Scotland) controlled the North Atlantic trade. "We have within ourselves and in our colonies in America," a British pamphleteer declared, "an inexhaustible fund to supply ourselves, and perhaps Europe." A generation later most British officials celebrated trade with their American possessions as a leading source of the nation's prosperity. As the ardent imperialist Malachy Postlethwayt proclaimed in 1745, the British empire "was a magnificent superstructure of American commerce and naval power on an African foundation."

The rise of the British empire in America is a central story of the period from 1660 to 1750. As Postlethwayt observed, the wealth of the empire was the direct result of the trade in African slaves and the profits generated by slave labor, primarily on the sugar plantations of the West Indies. To protect Britain's increasingly valuable sugar colonies from European rivals—the Dutch in New Netherland, the French in Quebec and the West Indies, and the Spanish in Florida—British officials expanded the navy and repeatedly went to war during these decades. The British empire was the product of calculated diplomatic and military policy, not chance.

This period also saw the beginning of a long struggle for British administrative control over its American settlements. To profit from the products and commerce of the colonies, the home government successfully imposed the economic controls of the Navigation Acts and, with less success, tried to subordinate colonial political institutions to imperial direction. These commercial, military, and administrative policies made Britain a dominant power in Europe and brought at least modest prosperity to most of the white colonists, even as they condemned hundreds of thousands of enslaved Africans to brutal work and early death.

The Politics of Empire, 1660–1713

In the first decades of settlement the Chesapeake and New England colonies were governed in a haphazard fashion. Taking advantage of the upheaval produced by religious conflict and civil war in England, local oligarchies of Puritan magistrates and tobacco-growing planters governed as they wished. However, with the restoration of the monarchy in 1660 royal bureaucrats imposed order on the unruly settlements and, with the aid of Indian allies, went to war aginst rival European powers.

THE RESTORATION COLONIES

In 1660 Charles II ascended to the English throne. A generous but extravagant man who was always in debt, Charles rewarded the aristocrats who had supported his return to power with millions of acres of American land. In 1663 he gave the Carolinas, an area long claimed by Spain and populated by thousands of Indians, to eight aristocratic friends. In 1664 he granted all the territory between the Delaware and Connecticut Rivers to his brother James, the Duke of York. In that same year James took possession of the conquered province of New Netherland, renaming it New York after himself, and passed on the ownership of the adjacent lands to two of the Carolina proprietors, who established the province of New Jersey.

In one of the great land grabs in history, a few English aristocrats had won title to vast provinces. Like Maryland, their new colonies were proprietorships; the aristocrats owned all the land and could rule as they wished as long as the laws conformed broadly to those of England. Most proprietors sought to create a traditional social order presided over by a gentry class and a legally established Church of England. Thus, the Fundamental Constitutions of Carolina (1669) prescribed a manorial system with a powerful nobility and a mass of serfs.

This aristocratic scheme was pure fantasy. The first settlers in North Carolina, poor families from Virginia, refused to work on large manors and chose to live on modest farms, raising grain and tobacco. Indeed, farmers in Albemarle County, inspired by Bacon's rebellion in Virginia and angered by taxes on tobacco exports, rebelled in 1677. They deposed the governor and forced the proprietors to abandon most of their financial claims.

The colonists of South Carolina, many of whom had come from Barbados (which became an overcrowded sugar-producing island during the 1660s), refused to accept the Fundamental Constitutions. Rather, they imposed their own design on the colony, bringing enslaved Africans from Barbados and using them to raise cattle and food crops for export to the West Indies. They also opened a lucrative trade with Native Americans, exchanging English manufactured goods for furs and Indian slaves. The growing demand for Indian slaves encouraged attacks against Indian settlements in Florida and the backcountry, raising the threat of war with Spain and in 1715 prompting a brutal war with the resident Yamasee people, which took the lives of 400 settlers. Until the 1720s South Carolina remained an ill-governed, violence-ridden frontier settlement.

In dramatic contrast to the Carolinas, the proprietary colony of Pennsylvania (which included present-day Delaware) pursued a pacifistic policy toward native Americans and quickly became prosperous. In 1681 Charles II bestowed the colony on William Penn in payment of a large debt owed to Penn's father. Born to wealth and seemingly destined for courtly pursuits, the younger Penn had converted to the Society of Friends (Quakers), a radical Protestant sect, and used his prestige to spread its influence. He designed Pennsylvania as a refuge for Quakers, who were persecuted in England because they refused to serve in the army and would not pay taxes to support the Church of England.

Like the Puritans, the Quakers wanted to restore the simplicity and spiritual-ity of early Christianity. But Quakers were not like Puritans or other Calvinists, who restricted salvation to a small elect. Rather, Quakers followed the teachings of the English visionaries George Fox and Margaret Fell, who argued that all men and women had been imbued by God with an inner "light" of grace or understanding. In Quaker meetings for worship there were no ministers or sermons; members sat in silence until moved to speak by the inner light.

Penn's Frame of Government (1681) extended Quaker radicalism into politics. In a world dominated by established churches, it guaranteed religious freedom to Christians of all denominations, allowing all property-owning men to vote and hold office. Thousands of Quakers, primarily from the middling classes of northwestern England, settled along the Delaware River in or near the city of Philadelphia, which Penn himself planned. The proprietor sold land at low prices and, to attract other Protestant settlers, advertised the advantages of his colony in Dutch and German. In 1683 migrants from the German province of Saxony founded Germantown (just outside Philadelphia) and were soon joined by thousands of other Germans at-tracted by fertile land and the prospect of freedom from religious warfare and per-secution. Ethnic diversity, pacifism, and freedom of conscience made Pennsylvania the most open and democratic of the Restoration colonies.

FROM MERCANTILISM TO DOMINION

In the 1650s the English government began to control the external trade of its colonies to increase England's wealth. It imposed a set of policies—known as *mercantilism*—that regulated colonial commerce and manufacturing. According to mercantilist theory, the American colonies were to produce agricultural goods and raw materials, which English merchants would carry to the home country, where they would be reexported or manufactured into finished products. Consequently, the Navigation Act of 1651 sought to oust Dutch merchants from the colonial trade and give English traders a monopoly by requiring that goods imported into England or its American settlements be carried on English-owned ships. New parliamentary acts in 1660 and 1663 strengthened the ban on foreign merchants trading with the colonies and stipulated that colonial sugar, tobacco, and indigo could be shipped only to England. To provide even more business for English merchants, the acts also required that European exports to America pass through England. To enforce these mercantilist laws and raise money, the Revenue Act of 1673 imposed a "plantation duty" on sugar and tobacco exports and created a staff of customs officials to collect it.

The English government backed its mercantilist policy with force. In three commercial wars between 1652 and 1674 the English navy drove the Dutch from New Netherland and ended Dutch supremacy in the West African slave trade. Meanwhile, English merchants expanded their fleets and dominated Atlantic commerce.

Many Americans resisted these mercantilist laws as burdensome and intrusive. Edward Randolph, an English customs official in Massachusetts, reported that the colony's Puritan-dominated government took "no notice of the laws of trade," welcoming Dutch merchants, importing goods from the French sugar islands, and claiming that its royal charter exempted it from most of the new regulations. Outraged, Randolph called for English troops to "reduce Massachusetts to obedience." Instead of using force, English officials pursued a punitive legal strategy. In 1679 they denied the claim of Massachusetts Bay to the adjoining province of New Hampshire and created a separate colony there with a royal governor. To bring the Puritans in Massachusetts Bay directly under their control, in 1684 English officials persuaded the English Court of Chancery to annul the colony's charter on the grounds that the Puritan government had virtually outlawed the Church of England and violated the Navigation Acts.

The accession to the throne of James II (r. 1685–1688), an admirer of France's authoritarian Louis XIV and of "divine-right" monarchy, prompted English officials to create a centralized imperial system in America. Backed by the king, in 1686 they revoked the corporate charters of Connecticut and Rhode Island and merged them with the Massachusetts Bay and Plymouth colonies to form a new royal province, the Dominion of New England. Two years later the home government added New York and New Jersey to the Dominion, creating a single colony that stretched from the Delaware River to Maine.

This administrative innovation went far beyond mercantilism, which had respected the political autonomy of the various colonies while regulating their trade, and extended to America the authoritarian model of colonial rule imposed on Catholic Ireland. James II appointed Sir Edmund Andros, a former military officer, as governor of the Dominion and empowered him to abolish the existing colonial legislative assemblies and rule by decree. In Massachusetts Andros advocated public worship in the Church of England, offending Puritan Congregationalists, and banned town meetings, angering villagers who prized local self-rule. Even worse, the new governor challenged all land titles granted under the original Massachusetts charter. He offered to provide new deeds but only if the colonists would agree to pay a small annual fee. The Puritans protested to the king, but James refused to restore the old charter.

THE GLORIOUS REVOLUTION OF 1688

Fortunately for the colonists, James II angered English political leaders as much as Andros alienated the Americans. The king revoked the charters of many English towns, rejected the advice of Parliament, and aroused popular opposition by openly practicing Roman Catholicism. Then in 1688 James's foreign-born Catholic wife gave birth to a son, raising the prospect of a Catholic heir to the throne. In response Protestant parliamentary leaders carried out a quick and bloodless coup known as the Glorious Revolution. Backed by popular protests and the army they forced James into exile and enthroned Mary, his Protestant daughter by his first wife, and her Protestant Dutch husband, William of Orange. Queen Mary II and King William III agreed to rule as constitutional monarchs, accepting a Bill of Rights that limited royal prerogatives and increased personal liberties and parliamentary powers.

To justify their coup parliamentary leaders relied on the political philosopher John Locke. In his *Two Treatises on Government* (1690) Locke rejected divine-right theories of monarchical rule; he argued that the legitimacy of government rests on the consent of the governed and that individuals have inalienable natural rights to life, liberty, and property. Locke's celebration of individual rights and representative government had a lasting influence in America, where many political leaders wanted to expand the powers of the colonial assemblies.

More immediately, the Glorious Revolution sparked rebellions by colonists in Massachusetts, Maryland, and New York in 1689. When the news of the coup reached Boston in April 1689, Puritan leaders seized Governor Andros and shipped him back to England. Responding to American protests the new monarchs broke up the Dominion of New England. However, they refused to restore the old Puritan-dominated government, creating instead a new royal colony of Massachusetts (which included Plymouth and Maine). According to the new charter of 1692, the king would appoint the governor (as well as naval officers who were charged with enforcing customs regulations), and members of the Church of England would enjoy religious freedom. The charter restored the Massachusetts assembly but stipulated that it be elected by all male property owners (not just Puritan church members).

The uprising in Maryland had both economic and religious causes. Since 1660 tobacco prices had been falling, threatening the livelihoods of smallholders, tenant farmers, and former indentured servants, most of whom were Protestants. They resented the rising taxes and the high fees imposed by wealthy proprietary officials, who were primarily Catholics. When Parliament ousted James II, a Protestant Association in Maryland quickly removed the Catholic officials appointed by Lord

Baltimore. The Lords of Trade suspended Baltimore's proprietorship, imposed royal government, and established the Church of England as the colony's official church. This settlement lasted until 1715, when Benedict Calvert, the fourth Lord Baltimore, converted to the Anglican faith and the crown restored the proprietorship to the Calvert family.

In New York the rebellion against the Dominion of New England was led by English settlers angered by James's prohibition of representative institutions and was strongly supported by Dutch Protestants, who welcomed the succession of Queen Mary and her Dutch husband. Dutch artisans in New York City ousted Lieutenant Governor Nicholson, an Andros appointee and an alleged Catholic sympathizer, and rallied behind a new government led by Jacob Leisler, a migrant German soldier who had married into a prominent Dutch merchant family. At first Leisler won the support of all classes and ethnic groups. But when he freed debtors from prison and championed a more democratic town-meeting form of government, most wealthy merchants (who had traditionally controlled the city

A Prosperous Dutch Farmstead

Many Dutch farmers in the Hudson River Valley prospered because they enjoyed easy access to markets and exploited the labor of African American slaves (shown here tending chickens and sheep). To record his success, Martin Van Bergen of Leeds, New York, had this mural painted over his mantelpiece.

(New-York State Historical Association, Cooperstown, NY. Photo by Richard Walker.)

government) turned against him. In 1691 a newly appointed royal governor took control of New York from Leisler, instituted a representative assembly, and supported the wealthy merchants against the Dutch artisans. He had Leisler indicted for treason, and the former governor was convicted by an English-dominated jury, hanged, and then decapitated. A new merchant-dominated Board of Aldermen passed ordinances that lowered artisans' wages, ending the social uprising.

In both America and England the Glorious Revolution of 1688 and 1689 began a new phase in imperial history. The uprisings in Boston and New York toppled the authoritarian Dominion of New England and restored internal self-government. In England, the new constitutional monarchy promoted an empire based on commerce, launching a period of "salutary neglect" that gave free rein to enterprising merchants and financiers who developed the American colonies as a source of trade. Although Parliament created a new Board of Trade (1696) to supervise the American settlements, it had little success. Settlers and proprietors resisted the Board's attempt to install royal governors in every colony, as did many English political leaders, who feared an increase in royal power. Consequently, the empire remained diverse. Colonies that were of minor economic and political importance retained their corporate governments (Connecticut and Rhode Island) or proprietary institutions (Pennsylvania, Maryland, and the Carolinas) while royal governors ruled the lucrative staple-producing settlements in the West Indies and Virginia.

IMPERIAL WARS AND NATIVE PEOPLES

Between 1689 and 1815 Britain and France vied for dominance in western Europe in a series of wars. As these wars spread to the Western Hemisphere, they involved increasing numbers of Native American warriors, who were now armed with European guns and steel knives and hatchets. Many Indian people were also familiar enough with European goals and diplomacy to turn the fighting to their own advantage.

The first significant fighting in North America occurred during the War of the Spanish Succession (1702–1713), which pitted Britain against France and Spain. The English settlers in the Carolinas tried to protect their growing settlements by launching an attack against Spanish Florida. Seeking allies, the Carolinians armed the Creeks, a 9,000-member agrarian people who lived in matrilineal clans on the fertile lands along the present-day Georgia-Alabama border. A joint English-Creek expedition burned the town of St. Augustine but failed to capture the Spanish fort. Fearing that future Carolinian-backed Indian raids would endanger its colony of Florida and pose a threat to Havana in nearby Cuba, the Spanish reinforced St. Augustine and launched unsuccessful attacks against Charleston, South Carolina.

The Creeks had their own quarrels to settle with the pro-French Choctaws to the west and the Spanish-allied Apalachees to the south, and they took this opportunity to become the dominant tribe in the region. During the 1710s a force of Creek warriors destroyed the remaining Franciscan missions in northern Florida, attacked the Spanish settlement at Pensacola, and massacred the Apalachees, selling 1,000 Apalachee prisoners to South Carolina as slaves. Subsequently, a Carolina-supplied and Creek-led army attacked the Tuscarora people of North Carolina, killing 1,400 and selling another 1,000 into slavery. The Tuscaroras who survived migrated to the north and joined the Iroquois, who now became the Six Nations.

Native Americans also played a central role in the fighting in the northeast, where French Catholics from Canada confronted English Puritans from New England. Aided by the French, Abnaki and Mohawk warriors took revenge on their Puritan enemies. They destroyed English settlements along the coast of Maine and in 1704 attacked the western Massachusetts town of Deerfield, where they killed 48 residents and carried 112 into captivity ("The Unredeemed Captive," p. 62 in Chapter 2). New England responded to these raids by launching attacks against French settlements, joining with British naval forces and troops in 1710 to seize Port Royal in Nova Scotia. However, in the following year a major British-American expedition against the French stronghold at Quebec failed miserably.

The New York frontier remained quiet because France and England did not want to disrupt the lucrative fur trade and because most of the Iroquois nations had adopted a new policy of "aggressive neutrality." In 1701 the Iroquois peoples concluded a peace with France. Simultaneously, they reinterpreted their "covenant chain" of military alliances with the English governors of New York and the Algonquin tribes of New England. For the next half century the Iroquois exploited their central geographic location by trading with the English and the French but refusing to fight for either side. The Delaware leader Teedyuscung explained this strategy by showing his people a pictorial message from the Iroquois: "You see a Square in the Middle, meaning the Lands of the Indians; and at one End, the Figure of a Man, indicating the English; and at the other End, another, meaning the French. Let us join together to defend our land against both."

Despite the military stalemate in the colonies, Britain used victories in Europe to win major territorial and commercial concessions in the Americas in the Treaty of Utrecht (1713). From France, Britain obtained Newfoundland, Acadia (Nova Scotia), the Hudson Bay region of northern Canada, and access to the western Indian trade (see Map 3.1). From Spain, Britain acquired the strategic fortress of Gibraltar at the entrance to the Mediterranean and commercial privileges in Spanish America. These gains solidified Britain's commercial supremacy and brought peace to eastern North America for a generation.

The Imperial Slave Economy

Britain's increasing administrative and military interest in American affairs reflected the growing importance of its Atlantic trade in slaves and staple crops. European merchants had created a new agricultural and commercial order—the South Atlantic system, as historians call it—that produced sugar, tobacco, rice, and other

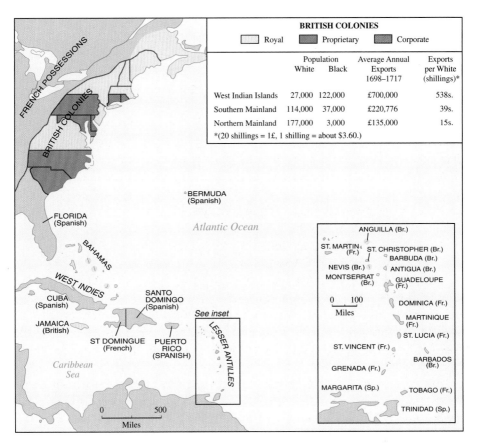

BRITISH COLONIES			
☐ Royal	■ Proprietary	■ Corporate	
	Population White Black	Average Annual Exports 1698–1717	Exports per White (shillings)*
West Indian Islands	27,000 122,000	£700,000	538s.
Southern Mainland	114,000 37,000	£220,776	39s.
Northern Mainland	177,000 3,000	£135,000	15s.
*(20 shillings = 1£, 1 shilling = about $3.60.)			

M A P 3.1
Britain's American Empire, 1713

Britain's West Indian possessions were small—mere dots on the Caribbean Sea. However, in 1713 they were by far the most valuable parts of the empire. Their sugar crops brought wealth to English merchants, trade to the northern colonies, and a brutal life (and early death) to African workers.

subtropical products. At the core of the new productive regime stood plantations staffed by enslaved labor from Africa.

THE SOUTH ATLANTIC SYSTEM

The components of the South Atlantic system were lands seized from Indians, laborers purchased from Africans, and capital invested by Europeans. Primarily in Brazil and the West Indies—but elsewhere as well—European adventurers and settlers took Indian lands to grow sugar and other valuable crops. Then European merchants and investors provided the organizational skill, ships, and money needed to

MAP 3.2
Africa in the Eighteenth Century

The tropical rain forest region of West Africa was home to scores of peoples and dozens of kingdoms. Some states, such as Dahomey, became aggressive slavers, taking tens of thousands of war captives and funneling them to the seacoast, where they were purchased by European traders. About 15 percent of the enslaved Africans died on the transatlantic voyage, the feared "Middle Passage"; most of the survivors labored on sugar plantations in Brazil and the British and French West Indies.

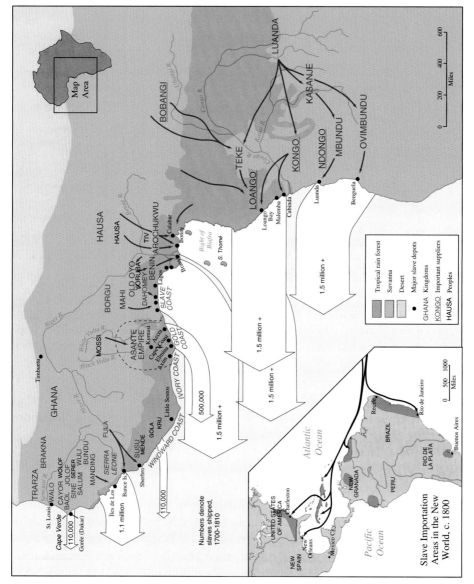

Map Area

BOBANGI

LUANDA

KASANJE

TEKE

LOANGO

KONGO

NDONGO

MBUNDU

OVIMBUNDU

HAUSA

HAUSA

TIV

AROCHUKWU

Calabar

BENIN

OLD OYO

YORUBA

DAHOMEY

MAHI

BORGU

Bonny

Bight of Biafra

S. Thomé

Lagos

Badagri

SLAVE COAST

Cape Coast

GOLD COAST

ASANTE EMPIRE

Kumasi

MOSSI

Accra

Elmina

Axim

IVORY COAST

Little Sestos

KRU

GOLA

MENDE

SUSU

SIERRA LEONE

FULA

WINDWARD COAST

Sherbro

Bance Is.

Îles de Los

GHANA

BRAKNA

TRARZA

St. Louis

BACOL

WALO

CAYOR

WOLOF

JOLOF

SINE

SERER

SALUM

WULI

BUNDU

MANDING

Cape Verde

Gorée (Dakar)

Timbuktu

110,000

1.1 million

110,000

500,000

1.5 million +

1.5 million +

1.5 million +

1.5 million +

1.5 million +

Loango Bay
Maleba
Cabinda

Luanda

Benguela

Niger R.

White Volta R.

Black Volta R.

Benue R.

Congo R.

Kasai R.

Kwango R.

Ubangi R.

Numbers denote slaves shipped, 1700–1810

0   200   400   600
Miles

Tropical rain forest
Savanna
Desert
Major slave depots
GHANA Kingdoms
KONGO Important suppliers
HAUSA Peoples

Slave Importation Areas in the New World, c. 1800

UNITED STATES OF AMERICA

Charleston

NEW ORLEANS

NEW SPAIN

Mexico City

NEW GRANADA

PERU

BRAZIL

Recife

Rio de Janeiro

RIO DE LA PLATA

Buenos Aires

Atlantic Ocean

Pacific Ocean

0   500   1000
Miles

market the crops and to supply the sugar-growing plantations with European tools and equipment. To provide labor for the plantations, the merchants relied primarily on slaves from Africa. Between 1550 and 1700 Portuguese and Dutch traders annually transported about 10,000 Africans across the Atlantic. Subsequently British and French merchants took over this commerce, developing African-run slave-catching systems that extended far into the interior. Between 1700 and 1810 they carried about 7 million Africans—800,000 in the 1780s alone—to toil in the Americas (see Map 3.2).

Sugar was the cornerstone of the South Atlantic system, and its cultivation created a craving among Europeans—whose sweeteners had previously been limited to honey and fruit juices. Imitating Dutch and Portuguese planters in Brazil, English and French merchants developed sugar plantations in the West Indies, beginning with Barbados around 1650. By 1700 they were investing heavily in the Leeward Islands and Jamaica; by 1750 Jamaica, the largest island in the British West Indies, had 700 large sugar plantations worked by more than 105,000 enslaved Africans.

Sugar production required fertile land, many laborers to plant and cut the cane, and heavy equipment to process it into raw sugar and molasses. Because only wealthy merchants or landowners had the capital to outfit a plantation, a planter-merchant elite financed the sugar industry and drew annual profits of more than 10 percent on investments. As the Scottish economist Adam Smith declared in his famous treatise *The Wealth of Nations* (1776), sugar was the most profitable crop in Europe and America.

The South Atlantic system brought wealth to the entire European economy. To take England as an example, the owners of most of the plantations in the British West Indies lived as "absentees" in England, spending their profits there. Moreover, the British Navigation Acts required that American sugar be sold to English consumers or sent through England to continental markets, thus raising the level of trade. By 1750 reexports of American sugar and tobacco accounted for half of all British exports. Substantial profits also came from the slave trade, for the Royal African Company and other English traders sold male slaves in the West Indies for five times what it paid for them in Africa. Finally, the trade in American sugar and tobacco stimulated manufacturing. To transport slaves (and machinery and settlers) to America, English shipyards built hundreds of vessels. Thousands of English and Scottish men and women worked in related industries: building port facilities and warehouses, refining sugar and tobacco, distilling rum from molasses (a by-product of sugar), and manufacturing textiles and iron products for the growing markets in Africa and America. Commercial expansion also provided a supply of experienced sailors, helping to make the Royal Navy the most powerful fleet in Europe.

As the South Atlantic system enhanced prosperity in Europe, it brought economic and human tragedy to West Africa and the parts of East Africa, such as Madagascar, where slavers were also active. Between 1550 and 1870 the Atlantic slave trade uprooted about 15 million Africans, diminishing the wealth and population of the continent and provoking untold human misery. Overall, the iron, tinware,

AMERICAN VOICES

The Slave Trade in Africa

VENTURE SMITH

The demand for black laborers in the Americas disrupted African society, encouraging wars among peoples and forever changing millions of lives. The narrative of Venture Smith, who escaped slavery and lived out his life in London, describes the impact of African slaving on his own family and community.

I was born at Dukandarra, in Guinea, about the year 1729. My father's name was Saungm Furro, Prince of the tribe of Dukandara. My father had three wives. Polygamy was not uncommon in that country, especially among the rich, as every man was allowed to keep as many wives as he could maintain. By his first wife he had three children. The eldest of them was myself, named by my father, Broteer. . . .

The first thing worthy of notice which I remember was, a contention between my father and mother, on account of my father marrying his third wife without the consent of his first and eldest, which was contrary to the custom generally observed among my countrymen. In consequence of this rupture, my mother left her husband and country, and travelled away with her three children to the eastward. I was then five years old . . . ; [a year later] the difference between my parents had been made up . . . and I was once more restored to my paternal dwelling in peace and happiness. . . .

[Shortly afterwards] my father learned that the place had been invaded by a numerous army, from a nation not far distant, . . . instigated by some white nation who equipped them [with guns] and sent them to subdue and possess the country. . . . The army of the enemy was large, I should suppose consisting of about six thousand men. Their leader was called Baukurre. After destroying the old prince [my father], they decamped and immediately marched towards the sea, lying to the west, taking with them myself and the women prisoners. . . .

All of us were then put into the castle, and kept for market. On a certain time I and other prisoners were . . . rowed to a vessel belonging to Rhode Island. . . . I was brought on board by one Robertson Mumford, steward of said vessel, for four gallons of rum, and a piece of calico, and called VENTURE, on account of his having purchased me with his own private venture. Thus I came by my name. All the slaves that were bought for that vessel's cargo, were two hundred and sixty.

SOURCE: John Bayles, ed., *Black Slave Narratives* (New York: Macmillan, 1970), pp. 36–44.

rum, cloth, and other European products that entered the African economy in exchange for slaves were worth from one-tenth (in the 1680s) to one-third (by the 1780s) as much as the goods those slaves subsequently produced in America.

In addition, the slave trade changed the nature of West African society by promoting centralized states and military conquest. In 1739 an observer noted that "whenever the King of Barsally wants Goods or Brandy . . . the King goes and ransacks some of his enemies' towns, seizing the people and selling them." War and slaving became a way of life in Dahomey, where the royal house made the sale of slaves a state monopoly and used the resulting access to European guns to create a regime of military despotism. Dahomey's army, which included a contingent of 5,000 women, systematically raided the interior for captives, exporting thousands of slaves each year (see Map 3.2 and American Voices, "The Slave Trade in Africa"). The Asante kings also used the firearms and wealth acquired through the Atlantic trade to create a bureaucratic empire of 3 million to 5 million people. Yet slaving remained a choice for Africans, not a necessity. The old and still powerful Kingdom of Benin, famous for its cast bronzes and carved ivory, resolutely opposed the slave trade, prohibiting the export of male slaves for over a century.

The trade in humans changed many aspects of African life. Class divisions hardened as people of noble birth enslaved and sold those of lesser status. Gender relations shifted as well. Men constituted two-thirds of the slaves sent across the Atlantic both because European planters paid more for men and because African traders directed women captives into local slave markets. The resulting imbalance between the sexes allowed some African men to take several wives, changing the

An African King

This striking bronze plaque, circa 1550–1680, from Benin, an important kingdom in West Central Africa, depicts a mounted king, his attendants, and (probably) his children. (The Metropolitan Museum of Art. The Michael C. Rockefeller Collection)

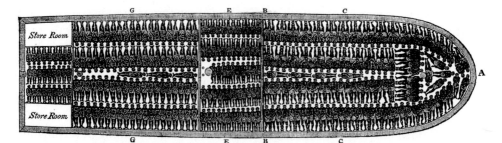

Two Views of the Middle Passage

As the slave trade boomed during the eighteenth century, ship designers packed in more and more human cargo, treating enslaved Africans with no more respect than hogsheads of sugar or tobacco. By contrast, a watercolor of 1846, painted by a ship's officer on a voyage to Brazil captures the humanity and dignity of the enslaved Africans.

(Top: Royal Albert Memorial Museum, Exeter, England; bottom: Peabody Essex Museum)

nature of marriage. Most important, the Atlantic trade prompted harsher forms of slavery in Africa, eroding the dignity of human life there as well as in the Western Hemisphere.

But those Africans sold into the heart of the South Atlantic system had the bleakest fate. Torn from their village homes, captives were marched in chains to coastal ports such as Elmina on the Gold Coast. From there they made the perilous Middle Passage to the New World in hideously overcrowded ships. There was little to eat and drink, and the stench of excrement was nearly unbearable. Some captives jumped overboard, choosing to drown rather than endure more suffering. Nearly a million (15 percent of the 8 million who crossed the Atlantic between 1700 and 1810) died on the journey, mostly from dysentery, smallpox, or scurvy.

For the survivors of the Middle Passage, life only got worse on arrival in northwest Brazil or the West Indies because plantation society was based on relentless exploitation and systematic violence. Planting and harvesting sugarcane required intense labor under a tropical sun, with a pace set by the overseer's whip. With sugar prices high and the cost of slaves low, many planters worked slaves to death and then imported more. Between 1708 and 1735 about 85,000 Africans were brought into Barbados, where they constituted nearly 90 percent of the inhabitants, but the black population increased only from 42,000 to 46,000 during these decades.

SLAVERY IN THE CHESAPEAKE AND SOUTH CAROLINA

As the British slave trade increased after 1700, planters in Virginia and Maryland imported thousands of Africans and created a "slave society." By 1720 Africans numbered 20 percent of the Chesapeake population, and slavery had become a defining principle of the social order, not just one of several forms of labor. Equally important, slavery was increasingly defined in racial terms. A Virginia law of 1692 prohibited sexual intercourse between English and Africans, and in 1705 another statute explicitly defined virtually all resident Africans as slaves: "All servants imported or brought into this country by sea or land who were not Christians in their native country shall be accounted and be slaves."

Living conditions in Maryland and Virginia were much less severe than in the West Indies, and slaves lived relatively long lives. In terms of labor to produce a harvest, tobacco was not as physically demanding a crop as sugar. Slaves planted the young seedlings in the spring, hoed and weeded the crop throughout the summer, and in the fall picked and hung up the leaves to cure over the winter. Epidemic diseases did not spread easily because the plantations were small and dispersed. Also, because tobacco profits were low, planters could not constantly buy new slaves and therefore treated those they had less harshly. Some tobacco planters attempted to increase their workforce through reproduction, purchasing a higher proportion of female slaves than sugar planters did and encouraging large families. In 1720 women made up about a third of the African population of Maryland, and the black population had begun to increase naturally. One absentee owner instructed his plantation agent "to be kind and indulgent to the breeding wenches, and not to force them when with child upon any service or hardship that will be injurious to them." And, he added, "the children are to be well looked after." By midcentury American-born slaves formed a majority among Chesapeake blacks.

Slaves in South Carolina labored under much more oppressive conditions. The colony had grown slowly until 1700, when Africans from rice-growing societies, who knew how to plant, harvest, and process that nutritious grain, turned it into a profitable export crop. To expand rice production, white planters imported tens of thousands of slaves. By 1720 Africans made up a majority of the population of South Carolina, with 80 percent of those living in the rice-growing areas, where many of them met an early death. Mosquito-borne epidemic diseases swept through the swampy lowlands, taking thousands of African lives. Overwork killed many more slaves because moving tons of dirt to build irrigation works was brutally hard labor. As in the West Indies, there were many deaths and few births, and the importation of new slaves constantly "re-Africanized" the black population.

South Carolina slaveowners preferred laborers from the Gold Coast and Gambia, who had a reputation as hard workers with farming experience (see Map 3.2). But as African sources of slaves shifted southward after 1730, more than 30 percent of the colony's workforce came from the Congo and Angola. As a result of such changes in the slave trade, there were no American colonies in which any African people or language group became dominant. Moreover, many white planters consciously enhanced this cultural diversity to prevent slave revolts. "The safety of the Plantations," declared a widely read English pamphlet, "depends upon having Negroes from all parts of Guiny, who do not understand each other's languages and Customs and cannot agree to Rebel."

AFRICAN AMERICAN COMMUNITY

In fact, slaves initially did not regard each other as "Africans" or "blacks" but as members of a specific people: Mende, Hausa, Ibo, Yoruba. Gradually, however, enslaved peoples found it in their interest to transcend these cultural barriers. In the West Indies and also in the lowlands of South Carolina, the largely African-born population created new languages that combined English and African words in an African grammatical structure. Thus, South Carolina blacks created the Gullah dialect. In the Chesapeake, where there were more American-born blacks (and in the northern colonies, which had small numbers of slaves), many Africans gradually gave up their native tongues for English. A European visitor to mid-eighteenth century Virginia reported with surprise that "all the blacks spoke very good English."

The acquisition of a common language, whether Gullah or English, was a prerequisite for the creation of an African American community. A more equal sex ra-

Slave Dwellings at Mulberry Plantation

Most pictures of plantations depict the imposing mansions of the slaveowners. However, this view of Mulberry plantation in South Carolina steals a look behind the big house to the meager dwellings of the slaves, whose labor produced the wealth of the plantation.

(The Gibbes Museum of Art, Carolina Art Association)

tio, which would encourage stable families, was another. In South Carolina a high death rate undermined ties of family and kinship, but after 1725 blacks in the Chesapeake colonies created strong nuclear families and extended kin relationships. These "African Americans" gradually developed a culture of their own, passing on family names, traditions, and knowledge to the next generation.

As enslaved blacks forged an identity in an alien land, their lives continued to be shaped by their African past. This heritage took tangible form in wood carvings inspired by African motifs, the large wooden mortars and pestles that slaves used to hull rice, and the design of shacks, which often had rooms arranged from front to back in a distinctive "I" pattern (not side by side, as was common in English houses). Traditional African values also persisted, as some slaves retained Muslim religious beliefs, and many more relied on the spiritual powers of conjurers, who knew the ways of African gods. Other slaves adopted Protestant Christianity but reshaped its doctrines, ethics, and rituals to fit their needs and create a spiritually rich and long-lasting religious culture of their own.

Yet there were drastic limits on African American creativity because slaves were denied education and accumulated few material goods. A well-traveled European who visited a slave hut in Virginia in the late eighteenth century found it to be

> more miserable than the most miserable of the cottages of our peasants. The husband and wife sleep on a mean pallet, the children on the ground; a very bad fireplace, some utensils for cooking. . . . They work all week, not having a single day for themselves except for holidays.

Slaves resisted the rigorous work routine at their peril. To punish slaves who disobeyed, refused to work, or ran away, planters resorted to the lash and the amputation of fingers, toes, and ears. Declaring the chronic runaway Ballazore an "incorrigeble rogue," Robert "King" Carter of Virginia ordered all his toes cut off: "nothing less than dismembering will reclaim him." Thomas Jefferson, who witnessed such cruelty on his father's plantation in mid-eighteenth-century Virginia, noted that each generation of whites was "nursed, educated, and daily exercised in tyranny," for the relationship "between master and slave is a perpetual exercise of the most unremitting despotism on the one part, and degrading submission on the other."

The extent of violence by whites depended on the size and density of the slave population. Because their numbers were so small, blacks in rural areas of New York, Pennsylvania, and other northern colonies endured low status but little violence. Conversely, assertive slaves in the predominantly African West Indian islands routinely suffered branding with hot irons. In the lowlands of South Carolina, where Africans outnumbered Europeans eight to one, black workers were forbidden to leave the plantation without special passes and risked punishment from rural patrols if they did. Slaves dealt with their plight in a variety of ways. Some newly arrived Africans fled to the frontier, where they tried to establish African villages or, more often, married into Indian tribes. Blacks familiar with white ways, especially those fluent in English, fled to towns, where they tried to pass as free blacks. But the great majority of African Americans worked out their destinies as enslaved laborers on rural plantations through a process of continual negotiation with their owners. Sometimes they agreed to do extra work in return for better food and clothes; at other times they seized a small privilege and dared the master to revoke it; or they protested their bondage silently by working slowly or stealing. Still others attacked their owners or overseers when provoked beyond endurance, even though this was punishable by mutilation or death. And despite the fact that whites were armed and, outside of coastal South Carolina, more numerous than Africans, some blacks plotted rebellion.

Predictably, South Carolina became the setting for the largest slave uprising of the eighteenth century—the Stono rebellion. The governor of Spanish Florida instigated the revolt in the late 1730s by promising freedom and land to slaves who ran away from their English owners. By February 1739 at least sixty-nine slaves had escaped to St. Augustine, and rumors circulated "that a Conspiracy was formed by Negroes in Carolina to rise and make their way out of the province." When war between England and Spain broke out later that year, seventy-five Africans—some of them Portuguese-speaking Christians from the African Kingdom of Kongo—killed a number of whites near the Stono River, stole guns and ammunition, and marched south toward Florida "with Colours displayed and two Drums beating." Unrest swept the countryside, but the white militia killed many of the Stono rebels and dispersed the rest, preventing a general uprising. Frightened whites imported fewer new slaves and tightened plantation discipline. For Africans the price of active resistance was high.

THE SOUTHERN GENTRY

As the southern colonies became full-fledged slave societies, the character of life changed for whites as well as blacks. As settlement in the Chesapeake region moved inland after 1675, away from the disease-ridden swampy lowlands, English migrants lived much longer and formed stable families and communities. Similarly, many white planters in South Carolina improved their health by transferring their residence to Charleston during the hot, mosquito-ridden summer months. As their longevity increased, men reassumed their customary control of family property. When death rates had been high, many husbands had named their wives as executors of their estates and legal guardians of their children and had given their widows large inheritances. After 1700 most wealthy planters named male kin as executors and guardians and once again gave priority to male children with respect to inheritance, limiting a widow's portion to the traditional one-third share during her lifetime.

The reappearance of strict patriarchy within the family mirrored broader social developments. The planter elite now stood at the top of a social hierarchy very much like that of Europe, exercising authority over a small yeoman class, a much larger group of white tenant farmers, and a growing host of enslaved black laborers—the American equivalent of oppressed peasants and serfs. Wealthy planters used Africans to grow food as well as tobacco; build houses, wagons, and tobacco casks; and make shoes and clothes. By increasing the self-sufficiency of their plantations, the planter elite survived the depressed tobacco market between 1660 and 1720. Small-scale planters who used family labor to grow tobacco fared less well, falling deeper into debt to their creditors among the elite.

To prevent another rebellion like Bacon's uprising, the southern gentry paid attention to the concerns of middling and poor whites. They urged smallholders to become slaveowners, and by 1770 no less than 60 percent of the English families in the Chesapeake owned at least one slave, giving them a personal stake in this exploitative labor system. In addition, the gentry gradually reduced the taxes paid by poorer whites; in Virginia the annual poll tax paid by every free man fell from 45 pounds of tobacco in 1675 to 5 pounds in 1750. And the political elite allowed poor yeomen and some tenants to vote. The strategy of the leading families—the Carters, Lees, Randolphs, Robinsons—was to curry favor with these voters at election time, bribing them with rum, money, and the promise of favorable legislation. In return, they expected yeomen and tenants to elect them to political office and defer to their authority. This "horse-trading" solidified the social authority of the planter elite, which used its control of the House of Burgesses to cut the political power of the royal governor—bargaining with him over patronage and land grants.

Even as the expansion of voting and slaveholding created new ties between rich and poor whites, wealthy Chesapeake planters set themselves apart from their less affluent neighbors. Until the 1720s the ranks of the gentry were filled with boisterous, aggressive men who enjoyed many of the amusements of common folk—from hunting, hard drinking, and gambling on horse races to sharing tales of their manly prowess in seducing female servants and slaves. As time passed, however, affluent Chesapeake planters took on the trappings of wealth, modeling themselves after the English aristocracy. Beginning in the 1720s they replaced their modest wooden houses with mansions of brick and mortar and sent their sons to London to be educated as lawyers and gentlemen. Most of the southern men who were educated in England returned to America, married, and followed in their fathers' footsteps, managing plantations, socializing with other members of the gentry class, and participating in politics.

Wealthy Chesapeake and South Carolina women also emulated the elegant and refined ways of the English gentry. They read English newspapers and fashionable magazines, wore English clothes, and dined in the English fashion, with an elaborate afternoon tea. To improve their daughters' chances of finding a desirable marriage partner, they hired English tutors to teach them etiquette. Once married, affluent gentry women deferred to their husbands' authority, reared pious children, and maintained elaborate social networks—gradually creating the new ideal of the southern genteel woman. Using the profits of the South Atlantic system, the planter elite formed an increasingly well-educated, refined, and stable ruling class.

THE NORTHERN MARITIME ECONOMY

The South Atlantic system had a broad geographic reach. As early as the 1640s, New England farmers provided bread, lumber, fish, and meat to the sugar islands. As a West Indian explained in 1647, planters in the islands "had rather buy food at very dear rates than produce it by labour, so infinite is the profit of sugar works." By 1700 the economies of the West Indies and New England were tightly interwoven. After 1720 farmers and merchants in New York, New Jersey, and Pennsylvania entered the West Indian trade, shipping wheat, corn, and bread to the sugar islands.

The South Atlantic system tied the whole British empire together economically. In return for the sugar they exported to England, West Indian planters received bills of exchange (credit slips) from London merchant houses. The planters used those bills to buy slaves from transatlantic slavers and also to reimburse North American

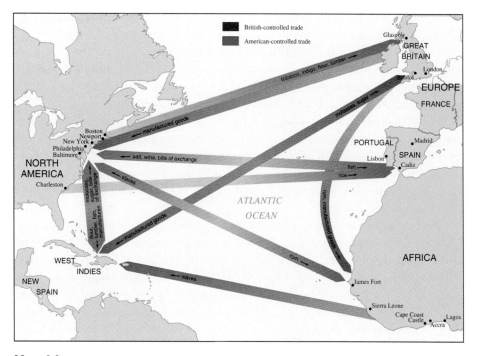

M A P 3.3
The Rise of the American Merchant, c. 1750

In accordance with mercantilist doctrine, British merchants controlled most of the transatlantic commerce in manufactures, sugar, tobacco, and slaves. However, American merchants seized control of other routes, dominating the trade between the mainland and West Indies, importing African slaves into Rhode Island, and carrying fish and rice to southern Europe.

farmers and merchants for their provisions and shipping services. Farmers and merchants then exchanged the bills for British manufactures, primarily textiles and iron goods, thus completing the cycle (see Map 3.3).

The West Indian trade created the first American merchant fortunes and the first urban industries. Merchants in Boston, Newport, Providence, Philadelphia, and New York invested their profits from the West Indian trade in new ships and in factories that refined raw sugar into finished loaves (which previously had been imported from England) and distilled West Indian molasses into rum. By the 1740s Boston distillers were exporting more than half a million gallons of rum annually. In addition, merchants in smaller ports, such as Salem and Marblehead, built a major fishing industry, providing salted mackerel and cod to feed the slaves of the sugar islands and to export to southern Europe. Southern merchants transformed Baltimore into a major port by developing a bustling trade in wheat, while Charleston traders exported deerskins, indigo, and rice to European markets.

The expansion of Atlantic commerce in the eighteenth century fueled rapid growth in American port cities and coastal towns. By 1750 Newport, Rhode Island,

and Charleston, South Carolina, had nearly 10,000 residents apiece, Boston had 15,000, and New York had almost 18,000. The largest port was Philadelphia, whose population reached 30,000 by 1776, the size of a large European provincial city. Smaller coastal towns emerged as centers of the shipbuilding and lumber industries. By the 1740s seventy sawmills dotted the Piscataqua River in New Hampshire, providing low-cost wood for homes, warehouses, and especially shipbuilding. Taking advantage of the Navigation Acts, which allowed colonists to build and own trading vessels, scores of shipwrights turned out ocean-going ships, while hundreds of other artisans made ropes, sails, and metal fittings for the new fleet. Shipyards in Boston and Philadelphia launched about 15,000 tons of ocean-going vessels annually; eventually colonial-built ships made up about one-third of the British merchant fleet.

The impact of the South Atlantic system extended into the interior of North America. A small fleet of trading vessels sailed back and forth between Philadelphia and the villages along the Delaware Bay, exchanging cargoes of European goods for barrels of flour and wheat for sale in both the West Indies and Europe. By the 1750s hundreds of professional teamsters in Maryland moved 370,000 bushels of wheat and corn and 16,000 barrels of flour to market each year—over 10,000 wagon trips. To service this traffic entrepreneurs and artisans set up taverns, horse stables, and barrel-making shops in small towns along the wagon roads, providing additional jobs. The prosperous interior town of Lancaster, Pennsylvania boasted more than 200 artisans, both German and English. The South Atlantic system thus provided not only markets for farmers (by far the largest group of northern residents) but also opportunities for merchants, artisans, and workers in country towns and seaport cities.

At the top of seaport society stood a small group of wealthy landowners and prosperous merchants. By 1750 about forty merchants controlled over 50 percent of Philadelphia's trade and had taxable assets averaging £10,000, a huge sum at the time. Like the Chesapeake gentry, these urban merchants imitated the British upper classes, importing design books from England and building Georgian-style mansions to showcase their wealth. Their wives created a genteel culture, decorating their houses with fine furniture and entertaining guests at elegant dinners.

Artisan and shopkeeper families formed the middle ranks of seaport society and numbered nearly half the population. Innkeepers, butchers, seamstresses, shoemakers, weavers, bakers, carpenters, masons, and dozens of other specialists socialized among themselves, formed mutual self-help societies, and worked to gain a "competency"—an income sufficient to maintain their families in modest comfort and dignity. Wives and husbands often worked as a team, teaching the "mysteries of the craft" to their children. Some artisans aspired to wealth and status, an entrepreneurial ethic that prompted them to hire apprentices and expand production, and the most prosperous owned their own houses and shops (sometimes run by widows continuing a family business). However, most craft workers were not well-to-do, and many of them were quite poor. In his entire lifetime a tailor was lucky to accumulate £30 worth of property—far less than the £2,000 owned by an ordinary merchant or the £300 accumulated by a successful blacksmith.

Laboring men and women formed the lowest ranks of urban society. Merchants needed hundreds of dockworkers to unload manufactured goods and molasses from inbound ships and reload the ships with barrels of wheat, fish, and rice for export. They often filled these demanding jobs with black slaves—who numbered 10 percent of the workforce in Philadelphia and New York City—or they hired unskilled men who worked for wages. Poor women—whether single, married, or widowed—could eke out a living by washing clothes, spinning wool, or working as servants or prostitutes. To make ends meet, most laboring families sent their children out to work at an early age. Indispensable to the economy yet without homes of their own, these urban laborers lived in crowded tenements in back alleys. In good times hard work brought family security or enough money to drink cheap New England rum in waterfront taverns.

Periods of stagnant commerce affected everyone, threatening merchants with bankruptcy and artisans with irregular work. For laborers and seamen, whose household budgets left no margin for sickness or unemployment, depressed trade meant hunger, dependence on charity handed out by town-appointed overseers of the poor, and—for the most desperate—a life of petty thievery. Involvement in the South Atlantic system between 1660 and 1750 brought economic uncertainty as well as jobs and opportunities to northern workers and farmers.

The New Politics of Empire, 1713–1750

The triumph of the South Atlantic system of production and trade changed the politics of empire. British ministers, pleased with the prosperous commerce in staple crops, were content to rule the colonies with a gentle hand. The colonists enjoyed a significant degree of self-government and economic autonomy, which put them in a position to challenge the rules of the mercantilist system.

THE RISE OF COLONIAL ASSEMBLIES

Before 1689 the authority of the representative assemblies in most colonies was weak. Political power rested in the hands of proprietors, royal governors, and authoritarian elites, reflecting the traditional view that "Authority should Descend from Kings and Fathers to Sons and Servants," as a royal-minded political philosopher put it. In the Glorious Revolution of 1688 the political faction known as the Whigs challenged that hierarchical outlook in England, winning the fight for a constitutional monarchy that limited the authority of the crown. English Whigs did not advocate democracy but did believe that the substantial property owners represented by the House of Commons should have some political power, especially over the levying of taxes. When Whig politicians forced William and Mary to accept a Declaration of Rights in 1689, they strengthened the powers of the Commons at the expense of the crown.

American representative assemblies also wished to limit the powers of the crown and insisted on maintaining their authority over taxes, refusing to fund military projects and other programs advocated by royal governors. Gradually the colonial legislatures won partial control of the budget and the appointment of local officials, angering imperial bureaucrats and absentee proprietors. "The people in power in America," complained the proprietor William Penn during a struggle with the Pennsylvania Assembly, "think nothing taller than themselves but the Trees." In Massachusetts during the 1720s the assembly refused repeatedly to obey the king's instructions to provide a permanent salary for the royal governor; subsequently legislatures in North Carolina, New Jersey, and Pennsylvania declined to pay their governors any salary for several years.

The rising power of the colonial assemblies created an elitist rather than a democratic political system. Although most property-owning white men had the right to vote after 1700, only men of considerable wealth and status stood for election. In Virginia in the 1750s seven members of the influential slaveowning Lee family sat in the House of Burgesses and, along with other powerful families, dominated its major committees. In New England descendants of the original Puritans had intermarried and formed a core of political leaders. "Go into every village in New England," John Adams said in 1765, "and you will find that the office of justice of the peace, and even the place of representative, have generally descended from generation to generation, in three or four families at most."

However, neither elitist assemblies nor wealthy property owners could impose unpopular edicts on the people. The crowd actions that had overthrown the Dominion of New England in 1689 were a regular part of political life in America and were used to enforce community values. In New York mobs closed houses of prostitution, while in Salem, Massachusetts, they ran people with infectious diseases out of town. In Boston in 1710 crowds prevented merchants from exporting grain during a wartime shortage, and in New Jersey in the 1730s and 1740s angry mobs obstructed proprietors who were forcing tenants from disputed lands. When officials in Boston attempted to restrict the sale of farm produce to a designated public marketplace, a crowd destroyed the building and defied the authorities to arrest them. "If you touch One you shall touch All," an anonymous letter warned the sheriff, "and we will show you a Hundred Men where you can show one" (see American Voices, "A 'Leveling' Spirit in the Colonies").

Such expressions of popular power, combined with the growing power of the assemblies, undermined the old authoritarian system. By the 1750s most colonies had representative political institutions that were broadly responsive to popular pressure and increasingly immune to British control.

AMERICAN VOICES
A "Leveling" Spirit in the Colonies
GOVERNOR JOSEPH DUDLEY AND JOHN WINCHESTER

In 1705 legal authorities in Massachusetts prosecuted two woodcutters, John Winchester and Thomas Trowbridge, for insubordination for defying Royal Governor Joseph Dudley. The following extracts from the court testimony serve to illustrate both upper-class disdain for ordinary folk and popular resistance to arbitrary authority.

Account of Governor Joseph Dudley:

The Charet [coach] wherein the Governour was had three sitters and their Servants . . . drawn by four horses, one very unruly, & was attended only at that instant by Mr. William Dudley, the Governour's son.

When the Governour saw the two carts approaching he directed his son to bid them to give him the way. . . . Who accordingly did Ride up & told them the Govr was there, & they must give way. Immediately upon it the second Carter came up to ye first . . . & one of them says aloud he would not go out the way for the Governour whereupon the Govr came out of the Charet and told Winchester he must give way to the Charet. Winchester answered boldly . . . I am as good flesh & blood as you. I will not give way. You may go out the way, & came towards the Governour. Whereupon the Governour drew his sword to secure himself & command the Road & went forward . . . and again commanded them to give way. Winchester answered that he was a Christian & would not give way & as the Governour came toward him he advanced & at length laid hold of the Govr & broke the sword in his hands. . . . And this is averred upon the honour of the Governour. . . .

Then came up John Winchester . . . who gives the following account.

. . . I left my cart and . . . asked Mr. William Dudley why he was so rash. He replied this dog [Trowbridge] won't turn out the way for the Governor. . . . I then told his excellency, if he would have patience a minute or two I would clear that way for him. . . . The Governour followed me with his drawn sword and said run the dogs through and with his naked sword stabbed me in the back. I facing about, he struck me on the head . . . giving me there a bloody wound. . . . I caught hold of his sword and broke it.

SOURCE: David Brion Davis and Steven Mintz, *The Boisterous Sea of Liberty: A Documentary History of America from Discovery Through the Civil War* (New York: Oxford University Press, 1998), pp. 105–06.

SALUTARY NEGLECT

British colonial policy during the reigns of George I (r. 1714–1727) and George II (r. 1727–1760) contributed significantly to the rise of American self-government. Royal bureaucrats relaxed their supervision of internal colonial affairs, focusing in-

Sir Robert Walpole, the King's Minister

All eyes are on Walpole (left) as he offers advice to the Speaker of the House of Commons. A brilliant politician, Walpole used patronage to command a majority in the Commons and to win the support of George I and George II—the German-speaking monarchs from the duchy of Hanover. Walpole's personal motto, "Let sleeping dogs lie," helps to explain his colonial policy of salutary neglect. (National Trust Photographic Library/John Hammond)

stead on defense and trade. Two generations later the British political philosopher Edmund Burke would praise this strategy as "salutary [healthy] neglect."

Salutary neglect was a by-product of the political system developed by Sir Robert Walpole, the leader of the British Whigs in the House of Commons and the king's chief minister between 1720 and 1742. By strategically dispensing appointments and pensions in the name of the king, Walpole won parliamentary support for his policies. But Walpole's politically driven use of patronage weakened the imperial system by filling the Board of Trade and the royal governorships with men of little talent. When Governor Gabriel Johnson went to North Carolina in the 1730s, he vowed to curb the powers of the assembly and "make a mighty change in the face of affairs." However, Johnson was soon discouraged by the lack of support from the Board of Trade. Forsaking reform, Johnson decided "to do nothing which can be reasonably blamed, and leave the rest to time, and a new set of inhabitants."

Walpole's tactics also weakened the empire by undermining faith in the integrity of the political system. Radical-minded English Whigs were the first to raise the alarm. They argued that Walpole had betrayed the constitutional monarchy established by the Glorious Revolution by using patronage and bribery to create a strong Court (or crown) Party. A Country Party of landed gentlemen likewise warned that Walpole's policies of high taxes and a bloated royal bureaucracy threatened the liberties of the British people. Politically minded colonists adopted these arguments as their own, maintaining that royal governors likewise abused their patronage powers. To preserve American liberty, they tried to enhance the powers of the provincial representative assemblies, thus preparing the way for later demands for political equality within the British empire.

PROTECTING THE MERCANTILE SYSTEM OF TRADE

Walpole's main preoccupation was to protect British commercial interests in America from the military threats posed by the Spanish and French colonies and from the economic dangers posed by the unwillingness of the American colonists to abide by the Acts of Trade and Navigation.

One of Walpole's major initiatives was to provide a subsidy for the new colony of Georgia, chartered in 1732. In the early 1730s General James Oglethorpe and social reformers seeking a refuge for Britain's poor won King George II's support for a colony south of the Carolinas. Envisioning a society of small farms worked by independent landowners and white indentured servants, the trustees of Georgia limited most land grants to 500 acres and initially outlawed slavery.

Walpole arranged for Parliament to subsidize Georgia because he wanted to protect the valuable rice colony of South Carolina. Spain had long resented the British presence in Carolina and was outraged by the expansion into Georgia, where Spanish Franciscans had Indian missions. In addition, English merchants had steadily increased their trade in slaves and manufactured goods to Spain's colonies in Mesoamerica, eventually controlling two-thirds of that trade. To resist Britain's commercial and geographic expansion, in 1739 Spanish naval forces sparked the so-called War of Jenkins' Ear by mutilating Robert Jenkins, an English sea captain who was trading illegally with the Spanish West Indies.

Yielding to Parliamentary pressure Walpole used this provocation to launch a predatory war against Spain's American empire. In 1740 British regulars commanded by Governor Oglethorpe attacked St. Augustine without success, in part because South Carolina whites—still shaken by the Stono Revolt—refused to commit militia units to the expedition. In 1741 the governors of the other mainland colonies raised 2,500 volunteers, who joined a British naval force in an assault on the prosperous Spanish seaport of Cartagena (in present-day Colombia). The attack failed, and instead of enriching themselves with Spanish booty hundreds of colonial troops died of tropical diseases.

The War of Jenkins' Ear became part of a general European conflict, the War of the Austrian Succession, bringing a new threat from France. French naval forces roamed the West Indies, seeking without success to conquer a British sugar-producing island, but initially there was little fighting along the long frontier between the Anglo-American colonies and French Canada. Then in 1745, 3,000 New England militiamen, supported by a British naval squadron, captured the powerful French naval fortress of Louisbourg, which protected the entrance into the St. Lawrence River. The Treaty of Aix-la-Chapelle (1748) returned Louisbourg to France, but the war secured the territorial integrity of Georgia by reaffirming British military superiority over Spain.

At the same time, Walpole and other British officials confronted an unexpected American threat to British economic ascendancy. According to the mercantilist Navigation Acts, the colonies were expected to produce agricultural goods and other raw materials that British merchants would carry to England and Scotland, where they would be consumed, exported to Europe, or turned into manufactured goods. To enforce the monopoly enjoyed by British manufacturers, Parliament passed a series of acts that prohibited Americans from selling colonial-made textiles (1699), hats (1732), and iron products such as plows, axes, and skillets (1750).

However, the Navigation Acts had a major loophole because they allowed Americans to own ships and transport goods. Colonial merchants exploited those provisions, securing 95 percent of the commerce between the mainland and the West Indies and 75 percent of the trade in manufactures shipped from London and Bristol. Quite unintentionally, the Atlantic trade had created a dynamic community of colonial merchants (see Map 3.3).

Moreover, by the 1720s the British sugar islands could not use all of the flour, fish, and meat produced by the rapidly growing mainland colonies, and so colonial merchants sold them in the French West Indies. These supplies helped French planters produce low-cost sugar, enabling them to undercut British sales in Europe. When American rum distillers began to buy cheap French molasses rather than molasses from the British sugar islands, planters petitioned Parliament for help. The resulting Molasses Act of 1733 permitted the mainland colonies to export fish and farm products to the French islands but—to enhance the competitiveness of British molasses—placed a high tariff on imports of French molasses. American merchants and public officials protested that the act would cut farm exports and cripple their distilling industry, making it more difficult for colonists to purchase British goods. When Parliament ignored their petitions, American merchants turned to smuggling, importing French molasses and bribing customs officials to ignore the new tax. Luckily for the Americans, sugar prices rose sharply in the late 1730s, enriching planters in the British West Indies, so the act was not enforced.

The lack of adequate currency in the colonies led to another confrontation. American merchants sent most of the gold and silver coins and bills of exchange they earned in the West Indian trade to Britain to pay for manufactured goods, draining the domestic money supply. To remedy this problem, the assemblies of ten colonies established "land banks" that lent paper money to farmers, taking their land as collateral. Farmers used the paper money to buy tools or livestock or to pay their creditors, thereby stimulating trade. But some assemblies, such as that of Rhode Island, issued large amounts of currency, causing it to fall in value, and required merchants to accept it as legal tender. Creditors, especially English merchants, rightly complained that they were being forced to accept worthless currency. In 1751 Parliament passed a Currency Act that prevented all the New England colonies from establishing new land banks and prohibited the use of public currency to pay private debts.

These economic conflicts and the growing assertiveness of the colonial assemblies angered a new generation of British political leaders, who believed that the colonies already had too much autonomy. In 1749 Charles Townshend of the Board of Trade charged that American assemblies had assumed many of the "ancient and established prerogatives wisely preserved in the Crown." Townshend and other officials were determined to replace salutary neglect with a more rigorous system of imperial control.

The wheel of empire had come full circle. In the 1650s England set out to build a centralized colonial empire and, over the course of a century, achieved the economic part of that goal through the use of sweeping mercantilist legislation, warfare against the Dutch, French, and Spanish, and the forced labor of more than a million African slaves. However, as the result of the Glorious Revolution and the era of salutary neglect that followed, the empire unexpectedly devolved into a group of politically self-governing colonies linked together primarily by trade. And so in the 1740s British officials vowed once again to create a politically centralized colonial system.

For Further Exploration

The best short overview of England's empire is Michael Kammen, *Empire and Interest: The American Colonies and the Politics of Mercantilism* (1970), while a clearly written study of the multicultural tensions resulting from the quest for American possessions is Joyce Goodfriend, *Before the Melting Pot: Society and Culture in Colonial New York City, 1664–1730*. Two fine portrayals of imperial military and political affairs in the eighteenth century are Fred Anderson, *A People's Army: Massachusetts Soldiers and Society in the Seven Years' War* (1984), a compelling picture of army life, and Richard Bushman, *King and People in Provincial Massachusetts* (1985), a nicely crafted story of the decline of British authority in New England.

Betty Wood, *Origins of American Slavery* (1998), offers a survey of this important topic. For a lucid discussion of the diversity and evolving character of African bondage, see Ira Berlin, *Many Thousands Gone: The First Two Centuries of Slavery in North America* (1998). Peter Wood, *Black Majority: Negroes in Colonial South Carolina Through the Stono Rebellion* (1974), presents a rich analysis of the skills and culture of enslaved West Africans in South Carolina. Olaudah Equiano, *The Interesting Narrative of the Life of Olaudah Equiano* (originally published 1789; Bedford/St. Martin's, 1995), provides a powerful first-person account of a child's life in Africa, his kidnapping and sale into slavery in America, and his odyssey toward freedom and fame.

T I M E L I N E

1651	First Navigation Act creates an English monopoly of trade with American colonies.	1720–1742	Sir Robert Walpole chief minister
1660	Restoration of Charles II	1720–1750	Dahomey becomes a "slaving" state.
1660s	Barbados becomes a sugar-producing island. New Navigation Acts extend the English control of American trade.		Chesapeake slaves increase through reproduction. Rice exports from South Carolina soar. Africans in South Carolina create the Gullah language. Rise of planter aristocracy in southern colonies Growth of Atlantic seaport cities
1664	New Netherland is captured and becomes New York.		
1681	William Penn founds Pennsylvania.	1732	Georgia chartered
1686–1689	Dominion of New England	1733	Molasses Act places a high tariff on imported French molasses.
1688	The Glorious Revolution in England deposes James II.	1739	Stono rebellion War of Jenkins' Ear
1689	Rebellions in Massachusetts, Maryland, and New York	1750	Iron Act prohibits colonists from manufacturing iron products.
1690	John Locke's *Two Treatises on Government* rejects divine-right rule.	1751	Currency Act prevents New England colonies from creating land banks and using paper money as legal tender.
1705	Virginia legally defines resident Africans as slaves.		
1714–1750	British policy of "salutary neglect" Rise of colonial assemblies		

The PBS video *Africans in America, Part 1: Terrible Transformation, 1450–1750* (1.5 hours) covers the African American experience in the colonial period; the website at <http://www.pbs.org/wgbh/aia/part1/title.html> contains a wide variety of pictures, historical documents, and scholarly commentary. "Excerpts from Slave Narratives" at <http://vi.uh.edu/pages/mintz/primary.htm> presents materials selected by Steven Mintz from forty-six accounts, arranged in eleven chronological and thematic categories.

Chapter 4

GROWTH AND CRISIS IN COLONIAL SOCIETY
1720–1765

The thirst after Indian lands, is become almost universal.

SIR WILLIAM JOHNSON TO THE EARL OF SHELBURNE, 1766

In 1736 Alexander MacAllister left the Highlands of Scotland to settle in the backcountry of North Carolina, where he was soon joined by his wife
and three sisters. Over the years MacAllister prospered as a landowner and mill
proprietor and had only praise for his new home. Carolina was "the best poor
man's country I have heard in this age," he wrote to his brother Hector, urging him
to "advise all poor people . . . to take courage and come." There were no landlords
to keep "the face of the poor . . . to the grinding stone," and so many Highlanders
were arriving that "it will soon be a new Scotland." Here, on the margin of the
British empire, people could "breathe the air of liberty, and not want the neces-
sarys of life." Tens of thousands of European migrants—Highland Scots, English,
Scots-Irish, German—heeded such advice, helping to swell the size of Britain's
North American settlements from 400,000 people in 1720 to almost 2 million by
1765.

The rapid and continuous increase in the number of settlers—and slaves—
transformed the character of life in every region of British America. Long-settled
towns in New England became overcrowded, antagonistic ethnic and religious communities jostled uneasily with one another in the Mid-Atlantic region, and the influx of the MacAllisters and thousands of other settlers into the backcountry altered
the traditional dynamics of southern politics. Moreover, in every region the impact
of a European spiritual movement called Pietism changed the tone of religious life.
Finally, as the new immigrants and the landless children of long-settled families
moved inland, they reignited conflict with native peoples and with the other
European powers contesting for dominance of North America—France and Spain.
A generation of growth produced a decade of crisis.

Freehold Society in New England

In the 1630s the Puritans had migrated from a country where a handful of nobles and gentry owned 75 percent of the arable land and farmed it by using servants, leaseholding tenants, and wage laborers. In their new home they consciously created a yeoman society composed of independent farm families who owned their lands as freeholders—without feudal dues or leases. By 1750, however, the rapidly growing population outstripped the supply of easily farmed land, posing a severe challenge to the freehold ideal.

FARM FAMILIES: WOMEN'S PLACE

The Puritans' commitment to equality did not extend to the family, which by law and custom remained a patriarchy. Men claimed power in the state and authority in the family. As the Reverend Benjamin Wadsworth of Boston advised women in *The Well-Ordered Family* (1712), being richer, more intelligent, or of higher social status than their husbands mattered little: "Since he is thy Husband, God has made him the head and set him above thee." Therefore, Wadsworth concluded, it was their duty "to love and reverence him."

Throughout their lives women saw firsthand that their role was a subordinate one. Small girls watched their mothers defer to their fathers. As young adults they learned that their marriage portions would be inferior in kind and size to those of their brothers; usually daughters received not highly prized land but rather livestock or household goods. Thus Ebenezer Chittendon of Guilford, Connecticut, left all his land to his sons, decreeing that "Each Daughter have half so much as Each Son, one half in money and the other half in Cattle."

In rural New England—indeed, throughout the colonies—women were raised to be dutiful helpmeets (helpmates) to their husbands. Farmwives spun thread and yarn from flax or wool and wove it into shirts and gowns. They knitted sweaters and stockings, made candles and soap, churned milk into butter and pressed curds into cheese, fermented malt for beer, preserved meats, and mastered dozens of other household tasks. The most exemplary or "notable" practitioners of these domestic arts won praise from the community, for their labor was crucial to the rural household economy.

Bearing and rearing children were also central tasks. Most women married in their early twenties; by their early forties they had given birth to six or seven children, usually delivered with the assistance of midwives. A large family sapped a woman's physical and emotional strength, focusing her energies on domestic activities for about twenty of her most active years. A Massachusetts mother explained that she had less time than she would have liked for religious activities because "the care of my Babes takes up so large a portion of my time and attention." Yet more women than men joined the churches of New England, so "that their children may be baptized," as the revivalist Jonathan Edwards explained, and because they feared the dangers of childbirth.

A gradual reduction in farm size in long-settled communities prompted many couples to have fewer children. After 1750 women in Andover, Massachusetts, bore an average of only four children and thus gained the time and energy to pursue other tasks. Farm women made extra yarn, cloth, or cheese to exchange with neighbors or sell to shopkeepers, enhancing their families' standard of living. Or like Susan Huntington of Boston (the wife of a prosperous merchant), they spent more time in "the care & culture of children, and the perusal of necessary books, including the scriptures."

Yet women's lives remained tightly bound by a web of legal and cultural restrictions. While ministers often praised the piety of the women, they excluded them from church governance. When Hannah Heaton grew dissatisfied with her Congregationalist minister, thinking him unconverted and a "blind guide," she sought out one of the few sects (mostly Quaker or Baptist) that welcomed questioning women and allowed them to become spiritual leaders. But Heaton was an exception. Willingly or not, most New England women lived according to the conventional view that, as Timothy Dwight put it, they should be "employed only in and about the house and in the proper business of the sex."

The Character of Family Life: The Cheneys

Life in a large colonial-era family was very different from that in a small modern one. Mrs. Cheney's face shows the rigors of having borne ten children, a task that occupied her entire adult life. Her children grew up with many older (or younger) siblings, which blurred differences between the generations.

(National Gallery of Art, Washington; Gift of Edgar William and Bernice Chrysler Garbisch)

FARM PROPERTY: INHERITANCE

By contrast European men who migrated to the colonies escaped many traditional constraints, including the curse of landlessness. "The hope of having land of their own & becoming independent of Landlords is what chiefly induces people into America," an official noted in the 1730s. But acquiring a farmstead was only the first step toward family security because most migrating Europeans wanted to provide land for the next generation. Parents with small farms often indentured their sons and daughters as servants and laborers in more prosperous households, where they would have enough to eat. When the indentures ended at age eighteen or twenty-one, the more ambitious young men would begin the slow ten- to twenty-year climb up the agricultural ladder, from laborer to tenant and finally to freeholder.

Luckier sons and daughters in successful farm families received a marriage portion when they reached marriageable age—usually twenty-three to twenty-five. The marriage portion—land, livestock, or farm equipment—repaid children for their past labor and allowed parents to choose their children's partners, which they did not hesitate to do because the family's prosperity and the parents' security during old age depended on a wise choice. Normally, children had the right to refuse an unacceptable match, but they did not have the luxury of "falling in love" with whomever they pleased.

Marriage under English common law was hardly a contract between equals. A bride relinquished to her husband the legal ownership of her land and personal property. After his death, she received the right to use (but not to sell) a third of the family's estate. Her own death or remarriage canceled this use-right, and the widow's portion was divided among the children. In this way the widow's property rights were subordinated to those of the family "line," which stretched, through the children, across the generations.

It was the cultural duty of the father to provide inheritances for his children, and men who failed to do so lost status in the community. Some fathers willed the family farm to a single son, providing their other children with money, apprenticeship contracts, or uncleared land along the frontier, or requiring the inheriting son to do so. Alternatively, yeomen moved their families to the New England frontier or to other unsettled regions, where life was hard but land for the children was cheap and abundant. "The Squire's House stands on the Bank of the Susquehannah," the traveler Philip Fithian reported from the Pennsylvania backcountry in the early 1760s. "He tells me that he will be able to settle all his sons and his fair Daughter Betsy on the Fat of the Earth."

The historic accomplishment of these farmers was the creation of whole communities composed of independent property owners. A French visitor remarked on the sense of personal worth and dignity in this rural world, which contrasted sharply with European peasant life. Throughout the northern colonies, he wrote, he had found "men and women whose features are not marked by poverty, by lifelong deprivation of the necessities of life, or by a feeling that they are insignificant subjects and subservient members of society."

THE CRISIS OF FREEHOLD SOCIETY

With each generation the population of New England doubled, mostly as a result of natural increase. The Puritan colonies had about 100,000 people in 1700, 200,000 in 1725, and almost 400,000 in 1750. In long-settled areas farms had been divided and subdivided, leaving parents in a quandary. In the 1740s the Reverend Samuel Chandler of Andover, Massachusetts, was "much distressed for land for his children," seven of whom were boys. A decade later in the neighboring town of Concord, about 60 percent of farmers owned less land than their fathers had.

Because parents had less to give their children, they had less control over their children's lives. The system of arranged marriages broke down as young people engaged in premarital sex and used the urgency of pregnancy to win their fathers' permission to marry. Throughout New England the number of firstborn children conceived before marriage rose spectacularly, from about 10 percent in the 1710s to 30 percent or more in the 1740s. Given another chance, young people "would do the same again," an Anglican minister observed, "because otherwise they could not obtain their parents' consent to marry."

New England families met the threat to the freeholder ideal through a variety of strategies. Many parents chose to have smaller families by using primitive methods of birth control. Others joined with neighbors to petition the provincial government for land grants, moving inland to central Massachusetts and western Connecticut—and eventually into New Hampshire and the future Vermont—and hacking new farms out of the forest. Still other farmers learned to use their small plots more productively, replacing the traditional English crops of wheat and barley with high-yielding potatoes and Indian corn. Corn offered a hearty food for humans, and its leaves furnished feed for cattle and pigs, which in turn provided milk and meat. New England developed a livestock economy, becoming the major supplier of salted and pickled meat to the West Indies.

Finally, New England farmers made do on their smaller farms by exchanging goods and labor, developing the full potential of what one historian has called the "household mode of production." Men lent each other tools, draft animals, and grazing land. Women and children joined other families in spinning yarn, sewing quilts, and shucking corn. Farmers plowed fields owned by artisans and shopkeepers, who repaid them with shoes, furniture, or store credit. Typically, no money changed hands; instead, farmers, artisans, and shopkeepers recorded their debts and credits in personal account books and every few years "balanced" the books by transferring small amounts of cash. The system of exchange allowed households—and the entire economy—to achieve maximum output, thereby preserving the freehold ideal.

The Mid-Atlantic: Toward a New Society, 1720–1765

Unlike New England, which was settled mostly by English Puritans, the Mid-Atlantic colonies of New York, New Jersey, and Pennsylvania became home to peoples of differing origins, languages, and religions. These settlers—Scots-Irish Presbyterians, English and Welsh Quakers, German Lutherans, Dutch Reformed Protestants, and others—created ethnic and religious communities that coexisted uneasily with one another.

ECONOMIC GROWTH AND SOCIAL INEQUALITY

Ample fertile land and a long growing season attracted migrants to the Mid-Atlantic, and profits from wheat financed its settlement. Between 1720 and 1770 wheat prices doubled in Western Europe because of a population explosion, and American farmers increased their exports of wheat, corn, flour, and bread to meet the demand. This boom in exports helped the combined population of New York, New Jersey, and Pennsylvania surge from 50,000 in 1700 to 120,000 in 1720 and 350,000 in 1765.

As the population rose, so did the demand for land. Nonetheless, many migrants refused to settle in New York's Hudson River Valley, where long-established Dutch families presided over manors created by the Dutch West India Company, and wealthy British families, such as the Clarke and Livingston clans, dominated vast tracts granted by English governors between 1700 and 1714 (see Map. 4.1). Like the slaveowning planters in the Chesapeake, these landlords tried to live like European gentry by dominating a dependent peasantry, but few migrants were interested in becoming their tenants. However, as freehold land became scarce in eastern New York, manorial lords attracted tenants by granting them long leases and the right to sell any improvements they made to the next tenant. Thus, the number of tenants on the vast Rensselaer estate rose from 82 in 1714, to 345 in 1752, and nearly 700 by 1765.

Most tenant families hoped that with hard work and luck they could save enough to acquire freehold farmsteads. However, they rarely produced enough grain to do so because preindustrial technology limited their output during the crucial harvest season. As the wheat ripened, a worker with a hand sickle could reap only half an acre a day; any ripe uncut grain promptly sprouted and became useless. The cradle scythe, an agricultural tool introduced during the 1750s, doubled or tripled the amount of grain a worker could cut. Even so, a family with two adult workers could not harvest more than about 12 acres of wheat, a yield of perhaps 150 to 180 bushels of wheat and rye. After family needs were met, the remaining grain might be worth £15—enough to buy salt and sugar, tools, cloth.

Unlike New York, rural Pennsylvania and New Jersey were initially marked by relative economic equality because the original migrants arrived with approximately equal resources. They lived simply in small houses with one or two rooms, a sleeping loft, a few benches or stools, some wooden trenchers (platters), and a few

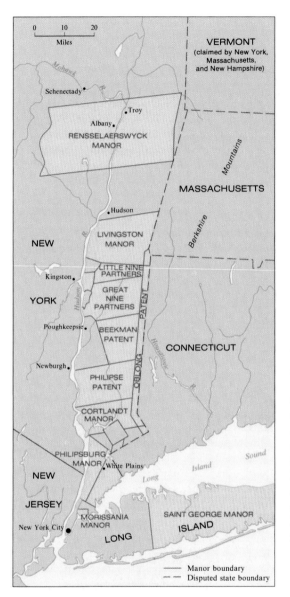

M A P 4.1

The Hudson River Manors, c. 1765

Dutch and English manorial lords dominated the fertile eastern shores of the Hudson River Valley—leasing small farms to German tenant families and refusing to sell land to migrants from overcrowded New England. This powerful landowning elite produced Patriot leaders, such as Robert Livingston and Gouverneur Morris, and leading American families, such as the Roosevelts.

wooden noggins (cups). Only the wealthiest families ate off pewter or ceramic plates imported from England or Holland. The rise of the wheat trade and an influx of poor settlers introduced marked social divisions. By the 1760s some farmers in eastern Pennsylvania had grown wealthy by buying slaves and hiring propertyless laborers to raise large quantities of wheat for market sale (see American Voices, "Runaway Servants and Slaves"). Others had become successful entrepreneurs, providing newly arrived settlers with land, equipment, goods, and services. Gradually a new class of wealthy agricultural capitalists—large-scale farmers, rural landlords,

AMERICAN VOICES

Runaway Servants and Slaves

B etween 1720 and 1775 thousands of poor Europeans came to the mainland colonies as indentured servants and redemptioners and were sold to the highest bidder. "They sell the servants here as they do their horses, and advertise them as they do their beef and oatmeal," wrote an astonished British officer. Many of these servants labored side by side with enslaved Africans, and, as shown by these newspaper advertisements from the Pennsylvania Gazette, the two groups found that they shared a passion for freedom.

October 12, 1752

Run away from doctor Thomas Graeme's plantation, in Horsham township, Philadelphia county, a Molatto slave, named Will, about 29 years of age, approaching very near the Negroe complexion, being of a Negroe father, and Indian mother, about five feet eight inches high, of an open bold countenance, somewhat pitted with the small-pox, speaks both English and Dutch, and is a very cunning sensible fellow. There went with him, a labouring man, that work'd by the day or month, called Thomas Stillwell, a tall smooth fac'd fair complexion'd fellow, with pale strait hair. . . . The said Stillwell is supposed to countenance the escape of the Molatto, by assuming the character of his master, or some such false pretence.

May 21, 1761

FIVE POUNDS Reward

Run away from the Subscribers, living at Little-Elk, Caecil County, Maryland, a Servant Woman named Margaret Sliter (but probably will change her Name) about 28 Years old, fresh colour, darkish brown Hair, born in England; had on when she ran away, two Bed-Gowns, one blue and white, the other dark Brown, both Callicoe. . . . Also a Negroe Man, named Charles, a lusty able Fellow, about 29 Years of Age, pitted with the Small-Pox, speaks good English, talks fast, is apt to get drunk, and pretends to be married to the aforesaid Margaret Sliter; had on when he ran away, a Pair of Thickset Breeches . . . a light coloured Jacket, an old brown Body-coat. . . .

Virginia, Lancaster County, Sept. 22, 1752

RUN away from the subscriber . . . on the 4th of May, A convict servant woman, named Sarah Knox (alias Howard, alias Wilson) of a middle size, brown complexion, short notes, talks broad, and said she was born in Yorkshire . . . and is a very deceitful, bold, insinuating woman, and a great liar. . . . I find [in the *Gazette*] an extract of a letter from Chester, in Pennsylvania, mentioning a quack Doctor, by the name of Charles Hamilton . . . who turns out to be a woman in mens cloaths, and now assumes the name of Charlotte Hamilton. . . . If she talks broad, I have reason to believe that she is the very servant who belongs to me.

SOURCE: Billy G. Smith and Richard Wojtowicz, *Blacks Who Stole Themselves: Advertisements for Runaways in the* Pennsylvania Gazette, *1728–1790* (Philadelphia: University of Pennsylvania Press, 1989), pp. 35, 50, 164.

speculators, storekeepers, and gristmill operators—accumulated estates that included mahogany tables, four-poster beds, couches, table linen, and imported Dutch dinnerware.

By 1760 there were many more people at the bottom of the Mid-Atlantic social order, for half of all white men were propertyless. Some landless men were the sons of property owners and would eventually inherit at least part of the family estate, but just as many were Scots-Irish *inmates*—single men or families "such as live in small cottages and have no taxable property, except a cow." In the predominantly German settlement of Lancaster, Pennsylvania, a merchant noted an "abundance of Poor people" who "maintain their Families with great difficulty by day Labour." Although Scots-Irish and German migrants hoped to become tenants and eventually landowners, sharply rising land prices prevented many from realizing their dreams.

Merchants and artisans took advantage of the ample supply of labor by organizing an "outwork" system. They bought wool or flax from large-scale producers and paid propertyless workers and subsistence farm families to spin it into yarn or weave it into cloth. In the 1760s an English traveler reported that hundreds of Pennsylvanians had turned "to manufacture, and live upon a small farm, as in many parts of England." Indeed, in many places the colonies had become as crowded and socially divided as rural England, and many farm families feared—with good reason—a return to the lowly status of the European peasant.

CULTURAL DIVERSITY

The middle colonies were not a melting pot in which European cultures blended into a homogeneous "American" society; rather, they were a patchwork of ethnically and religiously diverse communities. A traveler in Philadelphia in 1748 found no fewer than twelve religious denominations, including Anglicans, Quakers, Swedish and German Lutherans, Scots-Irish Presbyterians, and even Roman Catholics.

Migrants usually tried to preserve their cultural identities, marrying within their own ethnic groups or maintaining the customs of their native lands. The major exception was the Huguenots—Calvinists who were expelled from Catholic France. They settled in New York and various seacoast cities and gradually lost their French ethnic identity by intermarrying with other Protestants. More typical were the Welsh Quakers. Seventy percent of the children of the original Welsh migrants to Chester County, Pennsylvania, married other Welsh Quakers, as did 60 percent of the third generation.

Members of the Society of Friends (Quakers) became the dominant social group in Pennsylvania, at first because of their numbers and later because of their wealth and influence. Quakers controlled Pennsylvania's representative assembly until the 1750s and exercised considerable power in New Jersey as well. Because Quakers were pacifists, they dealt peaceably with Native Americans, negotiating treaties and buying land rather than seizing it by force. These conciliatory policies enabled Pennsylvania to avoid a major Indian war until the 1750s. Some Quakers extended the egalitarian values emphasized by their faith to their relations with blacks. After 1750 most Quaker meetings condemned the institution of slavery, and some expelled members who continued to keep slaves.

The Quaker vision of a "peaceable kingdom" attracted many German settlers who were fleeing war, religious persecution, and poverty. First to arrive, in 1683, was a group of religious dissenters—the Mennonites—attracted by a pamphlet promising religious freedom. In the 1720s religious upheaval and population growth in southwestern Germany and Switzerland stimulated another wave of migrants. "Wages were far better" in Pennsylvania, Heinrich Schneebeli reported to his friends in Zurich after an exploratory trip, and "one also enjoyed there a free unhindered exercise of religion." Beginning in 1749 thousands of Germans and Swiss fled their overcrowded societies; by 1756, 37,000 of these migrants had landed in Philadelphia. Some of these newcomers were redemptioners—a type of indentured servant—but many more were propertied farmers and artisans, who migrated to improve the lives of their children.

German settlements soon dominated certain areas of Pennsylvania, and thousands of Germans moved down the Shenandoah Valley into the western parts of Maryland, Virginia, and the Carolinas. They guarded their language and cultural heritage carefully, encouraging their American-born children to marry within the

A German Farm in Western Maryland

Beginning in the 1730s wheat became a major export crop in Maryland and Virginia. This engraving probably depicts a German farm because the harvesters are using oxen, not horses, and women are working in the field alongside men. (Library of Congress)

community. A minister in North Carolina admonished his congregation "not to contract any marriages with the English or Irish," explaining that "we owe it to our native country to do our part that German blood and the German language be preserved in America." Thus, these migrants and their descendants spoke German, read German-language newspapers, conducted church services in German, and preserved German agricultural practices, with women taking an active part in plowing and harvesting. English travelers remarked that German women were "always in the fields, meadows, stables, etc. and do not dislike any work whatsoever." Most German migrants felt at ease living in a British-controlled colony, for few of them came from the governing classes and many rejected political activism on religious grounds. They engaged in politics only to protect their religious liberty and property rights—insisting, for example, that as in Germany, married women should have property rights.

Emigrants from Ireland formed the largest group of incoming Europeans, some 150,000 in number. Some were Catholic but most were the descendants of the Presbyterian Scots who had been sent to Ireland between 1608 and 1650 to bolster English control of its Catholic population. In Ireland the Scots faced discrimination and economic regulation. The Irish Test Act of 1704 excluded Scottish Presbyterians as well as Irish Catholics from holding public office; English mercantilist regulations placed heavy import duties on the woolen goods produced by Scots-Irish weavers; and Scots-Irish farmers faced heavy taxes. "Read this letter, Rev. Baptist Boyd," a New York settler wrote back to his minister, "and tell all the poor folk of ye place that God has opened a door for their deliverance . . . all that a man works for is his own; there are no revenue hounds [tax collectors] to take it from us here." Lured by such reports, after 1720 thousands of Scots-Irish sailed for Philadelphia and then migrated to central Pennsylvania and southward down the Shenandoah Valley into Maryland and Virginia backcountry. Like the Germans, the Scots-Irish were determined to keep their culture. They held to their Presbyterian faith and promoted marriage within the church.

RELIGIOUS IDENTITY AND POLITICAL CONFLICT

In Western Europe government authorities condemned religious diversity, and in America many ministers remained committed to an established church and the state's enforcement of religious rules. Consequently, ministers criticized the separation of church and state in Pennsylvania. "The preachers do not have the power to punish anyone, or to force anyone to go to church," complained the minister Gottlieb Mittelberger. As a result, "Sunday is very badly kept. Many people plough, reap, thresh, hew or split wood and the like." Thus, Mittelberger concluded, "Liberty in Pennsylvania does more harm than good to many people, both in soul and body."

Mittelberger ignored the fact that religious sects in Pennsylvania enforced moral behavior among their members through communal self-discipline. For example, each Quaker family attended a weekly worship meeting and a monthly discipline meeting. Four times a year a committee met with each family to make certain the children were receiving proper religious instruction. The committee also reported on the moral behavior of adults; a Chester County meeting disciplined one of its members "to reclaim him from drinking to excess and keeping vain company." Quaker meetings gave permission to marry only to couples with sufficient land and livestock to support a family. As a result, the children of well-to-do Friends usually married within the sect; those who lacked resources remained unmarried or married without permission—in which case they were usually barred from Quaker meetings. In these various ways communal sanctions effectively sustained a self-contained and prosperous Quaker community.

In the 1750s Quaker dominance in Pennsylvania came under attack. Scots-Irish Presbyterians who migrated to frontier settlements west of the Susquehanna River challenged the pacifism of the Quaker-dominated assembly by demanding a more aggressive Indian policy. Many of the newer German migrants also opposed the Quakers; they wanted laws that respected their inheritance customs and representation in the provincial assembly in proportion to their numbers. As a European visitor noted, Scots-Irish Presbyterians, German Baptists, and German Lutherans had begun to form "a general confederacy" against the Quakers, but they found it difficult to unite because of "a mutual jealousy, for religious zeal is secretly burning." During the 1760s and again during the War for Independence, these latent religious and ethnic passions would disrupt Pennsylvania politics, but the Quaker-inspired experiment would survive the American Revolution and become a model for the future. In the centuries to come cultural pluralism, an open political order, and passionate ethnic and social conflicts would characterize much of American society.

The Enlightenment and the Great Awakening, 1740 – 1765

Two great European cultural movements reached America between the 1720s and the 1760s: the Enlightenment and Pietism. The *Enlightenment,* which emphasized the power of human reason to shape the world, appealed especially to well-educated men and women from merchant or planter families and to urban artisans. *Pietism,* an emotional, evangelical religious movement that stressed a Christian's personal relation to God, attracted many adherents, especially among farmers and urban laborers. The two movements promoted independent thinking in different ways; together they transformed American intellectual and cultural life.

THE ENLIGHTENMENT IN AMERICA

Most early Americans relied on religious teachings or folk wisdom to explain the workings of the natural world. Thus, Swedish settlers in Pennsylvania attributed medicinal powers to the great white mullein, a common wildflower, tying the leaves around their feet and arms when they had a fever. Even educated people believed that events occurred for reasons that today would be considered magical. When a measles epidemic struck Boston in the 1710s, the Puritan minister Cotton Mather thought that only God could end it. Like most Christians, Mather believed that the earth stood at the center of the universe and that God intervened directly in human affairs.

Early Americans held to these beliefs despite the scientific revolution of the sixteenth and seventeenth centuries, which had challenged both traditional Christian and folk worldviews. As early as the 1530s the astronomer Copernicus had observed that the earth traveled around the sun rather than vice versa, implying a more modest place for humans in the universe. Other scholars had conducted experiments using empirical methods—actual observed experience—to learn about the natural world. Eventually the English scientist Isaac Newton, in his *Principia Mathematica* (1687), used mathematics to explain the movement of the planets around the sun. Newton's laws of motion and concept of gravity described how the universe could operate without God's constant intervention, undermining traditional Christian explanations of the cosmos.

In the century between the publication of Newton's book and the outbreak of the French Revolution in 1789, the philosophers of the European Enlightenment applied scientific reasoning to all aspects of life, including social institutions and human behavior. Enlightenment thinkers believed that men and women could observe, analyze, understand, and improve their world. They advanced four fundamental principles: the lawlike order of the natural world, the power of human reason, the natural rights of individuals (including the right to self-government), and the progressive improvement of society.

In his *Essay Concerning Human Understanding* (1690), the English philosopher John Locke emphasized the impact of environment, experience, and reason on human behavior, proposing that the character of individuals and societies was not fixed by God's will but could be changed through education and purposeful action. Locke's *Two Treatises on Government* (1690) advanced the revolutionary theory that political authority was not given by God to monarchs (as kings such as James II had insisted) but was derived from "social compacts" that people made to preserve their "natural rights" to life, liberty, and property. In Locke's view, the people should have the right to change governmental policies—or even their form of government—through the decision of a majority.

The ideas of Locke and other Enlightenment thinkers came to America through books, travelers, and educated migrants and quickly affected the beliefs of influential colonists about religion, science, and politics. As early as the 1710s the Reverend John Wise of Ipswich, Massachusetts, used Locke's political principles to defend the decision to vest power in the ordinary members of Congregational churches. Wise argued that just as the "social compact" formed the basis of political society, the religious covenant made the congregation—not the bishops of the Church of England—the proper interpreter of religious truth. And when a smallpox epidemic threatened Boston in the 1720s, Cotton Mather sought a scientific rather than a

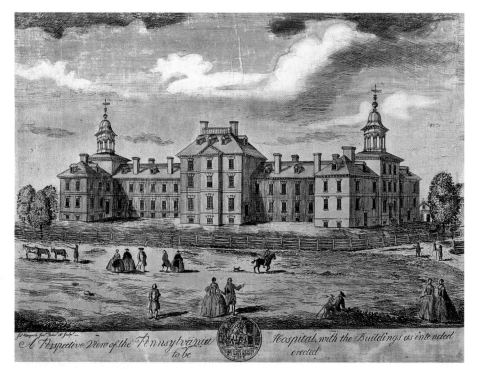

A Perspective View of the Pennsylvania Hospital, with the Buildings as intended to be erected

Enlightenment Philanthropy: The Philadelphia Hospital

This imposing structure, built in 1753 with public funds and private donations, embodied two Enlightenment principles—that purposeful action could improve society and that the world should express reason and order, exhibited here in the symmetrical façade. Etchings of the hospital and other important Philadelphia buildings circulated widely, bolstering the city's reputation as the center of the American Enlightenment. (Historical Society of Pennsylvania)

religious remedy, joining with a prominent Boston physician to support the new technique of inoculation.

Benjamin Franklin was the epitome of the American Enlightenment. Born in Boston in 1706 to a devout Calvinist family and apprenticed to a printer as a youth, Franklin was a self-made, self-taught man. As a tradesman, printer, and journalist in Philadelphia he formed "a club of mutual improvement" that met weekly to discuss "Morals, Politics, or Natural Philosophy." These discussions and Enlightenment literature, rather than the Bible, shaped Franklin's imagination. As Franklin explained in his *Autobiography* (1771), "from the different books I read, I began to doubt of Revelation [God-revealed truth] itself." Like many urban artisans, wealthy Virginia planters, and affluent seaport merchants, Franklin became a *deist*. Influenced by Enlightenment science, deists believed that God had created the world but allowed it to operate in accordance with the laws of nature. The deists' God was a rational being, a divine "watchmaker" who did not intervene directly in history or in people's lives. Rejecting the authority of the Bible, deists relied on people's "natural reason" to define a moral code. Adherence to the code, they believed, would be rewarded after death.

Franklin popularized the practical outlook of the Enlightenment in *Poor Richard's Almanac* (1732–1757), which was read by thousands. In 1743 he helped found the American Philosophical Society, an institution devoted to "the promotion of useful knowledge," and proceeded to invent bifocal lenses for eyeglasses, an improved stove (the Franklin stove), and the lightning rod. Franklin's book on electricity, first published in England in 1751, was praised by the English scientist Joseph Priestley as the greatest contribution to science since Newton. In Philadelphia and other American cities ambitious printers published newspapers and gentleman's magazines, the first significant nonreligious publications to appear in the colonies. Thus, the European Enlightenment added a secular dimension to colonial intellectual life, preparing the way for the great American contributions to republican political theory by John Adams, James Madison, and other Patriots during the Revolutionary era.

PIETISM IN AMERICA

As a few influential Americans—merchants and wealthy Virginia planters—and various urban artisans turned to deism, many other colonists embraced the European devotional movement known as Pietism. Pietists emphasized devout, or "pious," behavior, emotional church services, and striving for a mystical union with God—appealing to the hearts, rather than the minds, of their congregations. Their teachings came to America with German migrants in the 1720s and sparked a religious revival among many farmers, artisans, and laborers. In Pennsylvania and New Jersey the Dutch minister Theodore Jacob Frelinghuysen moved from church to church, preaching rousing, emotional sermons to German settlers. In private prayer meetings he encouraged lay members to preach a message of spiritual urgency to growing congregations. A decade later William Tennent and his son Gilbert, Presbyterian clergymen who copied Frelinghuysen's approach, led revivals among Scots-Irish migrants in the same area.

Simultaneously, a native-born pietistic movement appeared in Puritan New England. Puritanism had begun in England during the 1580s as part of an earlier pietistic upsurge, but over the decades many Puritan congregations had lost their religious zeal. In the 1730s the minister Jonathan Edwards restored spiritual enthusiasm to the Congregational churches in the Connecticut River Valley. An accomplished philosopher as well as an effective preacher, Edwards urged his hearers—especially young men and women—to commit themselves to a life of piety and prayer.

George Whitefield, a young English revivalist with what one historian has called a "flamboyant, highly sexualized style," transformed the local revivals into a "Great Awakening" that spanned the mainland settlements. Whitefield had experienced conversion after reading German pietistic tracts and had worked with John Wesley, the founder of English Methodism, who combined enthusiastic preaching with disciplined "methods" of worship. In 1739 Whitefield carried Wesley's style to America and over the next two years preached to huge crowds of "enthusiasts" from Georgia to Massachusetts. "Religion is become the Subject of most Conversations," the *Pennsylvania Gazette* reported. "No books are in Request but those of Piety and Devotion." The usually skeptical and restrained Benjamin Franklin was so impressed by Whitefield's oratory that when the preacher asked for contributions, Franklin emptied his pockets "wholly into the collector's dish, gold and all." By the time the

George Whitefield, c. 1742

No painting completely captured Whitefield's magical appeal. When Whitefield spoke to a crowd near Philadelphia, an observer noted, his words were "sharper than a two-edged sword. . . . Some of the people were pale as death; others were wringing their hands . . . and most lifting their eyes to heaven and crying to God for mercy." (National Portrait Gallery, London)

The Power of a Preacher

NATHAN COLE

*G*eorge Whitefield's reputation as an inspired preacher drew thousands to his sermons, including Nathan Cole, a Connecticut farmer, and his wife. Cole recorded his impressions in a journal that relates his intense struggles with feelings of religious "unworthiness"— an internal conflict that was sparked by Whitefield and lasted for many years.

Now it please God to Send Mr. Whitefield into this land; and my hearing of his preaching at Philadelphia, like one of the old apostles . . . I felt the Spirit of God drawing me by conviction; I longed to see and hear him and wished he would come this way. . . . Then of a sudden, in the morning about 8 or 9 of the clock there came a messenger and said Mr. Whitefield . . . is to preach at Middletown this morning at ten of the clock. . . .

And when we came within about half a mile of the road that comes down . . . to Middletown, on high land I saw before me a cloud or fog rising . . . [and] a noise something like a low rumbling thunder and presently found it was the noise of horses' feet coming down the road, and this cloud was a cloud of dust made by the horses' feet . . . and as I drew nearer it seemed like a steady stream of horses and their riders. . . . And when we got to Middletown old meeting house there was a great multitude, it was said to be 3 or 4000 of people, assembled together. . . .

When I saw Mr. Whitefield come upon the scaffold, he looked almost angelical; a young slim, slender youth before some thousands of people with a bold undaunted countenance. And my hearing how God was with him everywhere as he came, it solemnized my mind and put me into a trembling fear before he began to preach; for he looked as if he was clothed with authority from the Great God, and a sweet solemnity sat upon his brow, and my hearing him preach gave me a heart wound. By God's blessing my old foundation was broken up, and I saw that my righteousness would not save me.

SOURCE: Merrill Jensen, ed., *American Colonial Documents to 1776*, vol. 9, *English Historical Documents* (New York: Oxford University Press, 1955), pp. 544–45.

evangelist reached Boston, the Reverend Benjamin Colman reported, the people were "ready to receive him as an angel of God."

Whitefield owed his appeal partly to his compelling personal presence. "He looked almost angelical; a young, slim, slender youth . . . cloathed with authority from the Great God," wrote a Connecticut farmer (see American Voices, "The Power of a Preacher"). Like most evangelical preachers, Whitefield did not read his sermons but spoke from memory as if inspired, raising his voice for dramatic effect, gesturing eloquently, making striking use of biblical metaphors, and even at times assuming a female persona—as a woman in labor struggling to deliver the word of God. The young preacher evoked a deep emotional response, telling his listeners they had all sinned and must seek salvation. Hundreds of men and women suddenly felt the "new light" of God's grace within them. Afterward, strengthened and self-confident, these New Lights were prepared to follow in Whitefield's footsteps.

RELIGIOUS UPHEAVAL IN THE NORTH

Like all cultural explosions, the Great Awakening was controversial. Conservative (or "Old Light") ministers such as Charles Chauncy of Boston condemned the "cryings out, faintings and convulsions" produced by emotional preaching. In Connecticut the Old Lights persuaded the legislative assembly to prohibit traveling preachers from speaking to established congregations without the ministers' permission. When Whitefield returned to Connecticut in 1744, he found many pulpits closed to him. But the New Lights resisted attempts by civil authorities to silence them: "I shall bring glory to God in my bonds," a dissident preacher wrote from jail. Dozens of farmers, women, and artisans roamed the countryside, condemning the Old Lights as "unconverted" sinners.

As the Awakening proceeded, it undermined support for traditional churches and challenged the authority of governments to impose taxes that supported them. In New England many New Lights left the established Congregational Church; by 1754 they had founded 125 "separatist" churches, supporting their ministers through voluntary contributions. Other religious dissidents joined Baptist congregations, which favored a greater separation of church and state. According to the Baptist preacher Isaac Backus, "God never allowed any civil state upon earth to impose religious taxes." In New York and New Jersey the Dutch Reformed Church split in two, as New Lights resisted conservative church authorities in the Netherlands.

The Awakening also challenged the authority of ministers, whose education and biblical knowledge had traditionally commanded respect. In an influential pamphlet, *The Dangers of an Unconverted Ministry* (1740), Gilbert Tennant maintained that the minister's authority came not from theological training but through the conversion experience. Reasserting Martin Luther's commitment to the priesthood of all believers, Tennent suggested that anyone who had experienced the saving grace of God could speak with ministerial authority. Not long afterward, Isaac Backus celebrated this spiritual democracy, noting that "the common people now claim as good a right to judge and act in matters of religion as civil rulers or the learned clergy."

Religious revivalism carried a social message, reaffirming the communal ethic of many farm families and questioning the growing competition and pursuit of wealth that accompanied the expansion of the American economy. "In any truly Christian society," Tennent explained, "mutual *Love* is the *Band* and *Cement*"—not the mercenary values of the marketplace. Suspicious of merchants and land speculators and dismayed by the erosion of traditional morality, Jonathan Edwards spoke for many rural Americans when he charged that a "private niggardly [miserly] spirit" was more suitable "for wolves and other beasts of prey, than for human beings."

As religious enthusiasm spread, churches founded new colleges to educate their youth and train ministers. New Light Presbyterians established the College of New Jersey (Princeton) in 1746, and New York Anglicans founded King's College (Columbia) in 1754. Baptists set up the College of Rhode Island (Brown) and the Dutch Reformed Church subsidized Queen's College (Rutgers) in New Jersey. The true intellectual legacy of the Awakening, however, was not education for the few but a new sense of religious authority among the many.

SOCIAL AND RELIGIOUS CONFLICT IN THE SOUTH

In the southern colonies religious enthusiasm also sparked social conflict. In Virginia the Church of England was the legally established religion, supported by public taxes. However, Anglican ministers generally ignored the spiritual needs of African Americans (about 40 percent of the population), and landless whites (another 20 percent) attended irregularly. Middling white freeholders, who accounted for about 35 percent of the population, formed the core of most Anglican congregations. But prominent planters and their families (a mere 5 percent of the population) held real power in the church and used their control of parish finances to discipline Anglican ministers. One clergyman complained that dismissal awaited any minister who "had the courage to preach against any Vices taken into favor by the leading Men of his Parish."

The Great Awakening challenged both the Church of England and the power of the southern planter elite. In 1743 the bricklayer Samuel Morris, inspired by his reading of George Whitefield's sermons, led a group of Virginia Anglicans out of the established church. Seeking a more vital religious experience, Morris and his followers invited New Light Presbyterian ministers from Scots-Irish settlements along the Virginia frontier to lead their prayer meetings. Soon these Presbyterian revivals spread across the backcountry and into the so-called Tidewater region along the Atlantic coast, threatening the social authority of the Virginia gentry. Planters and their well-dressed families were accustomed to arriving at Anglican services in elaborate carriages drawn by well-bred horses, and they often flaunted their power by marching in a body to their seats in the front pews. These potent reminders of the gentry's social superiority would vanish if freeholders attended New Light Presbyterian rather than Church of England services. Moreover, religious pluralism would threaten the government's ability to tax the population to support the established church.

To prevent the spread of New Light doctrines, Virginia's governor denounced them as "false teachings," and Anglican justices of the peace closed down Presbyterian meetinghouses. This harassment kept most white yeomen families and poor tenants within the Church of England, as did the fact that most Presbyterian ministers were highly educated and sought converts mainly among skilled workers and propertied farmers.

Baptists succeeded where Presbyterians failed. The evangelical Baptist preachers who came to Virginia in the 1760s drew their congregations primarily from the poor by offering them solace and hope in a troubled world. Their central ritual was adult baptism, often involving complete immersion in water. Once men and women had experienced the infusion of grace—had been "born again"—they were baptized in an emotional public ceremony that celebrated the Baptists' shared fellowship. During the 1760s thousands of yeomen and tenant farm families in Virginia were drawn to revivalist meetings by the enthusiasm and democratic ways of Baptist preachers.

Even slaves were welcome at Baptist revivals. As early as 1740 George White-field had openly condemned the brutality of slaveholders and urged that blacks be brought into the Christian fold. In South Carolina and Georgia a handful of New Light planters had taken up this challenge, but the hostility of the white population and the commitment of many Africans to their ancestral religions kept the number of converts low. Virginia in the 1760s witnessed the first significant conversion of slaves to Christianity, as second- and third-generation African Americans who knew the English language and English ways responded positively to the Baptist message that all people were equal in God's eyes.

The ruling planters reacted violently to the Baptists, who posed a threat to the social authority and way of life of the gentry. The Baptists emphasized equality by calling one another "brother" and "sister," and their preachers condemned the customary pleasures of Chesapeake planters—gambling, drinking, whoring, and cockfighting. To maintain the social hierarchy Anglican sheriffs and justices of the peace broke up Baptist services by force. In Caroline County, Virginia, an Anglican posse attacked a prayer meeting led by Brother Waller, who, a fellow Baptist reported, "was violently jerked off the stage; they caught him by the back part of his neck, beat his head against the ground, and a gentleman gave him twenty lashes with his horsewhip." Despite such attacks, about 20 percent of Virginia's whites and hundreds of enslaved blacks had joined Baptist churches by 1775. In the south as in the north, Protestant revivalism was on the way to becoming a powerful American religious movement.

Although the revival did not significantly undermine the political power of Anglican slaveholders in Virginia, it gave spiritual meaning to the lives of poor yeoman and tenant families and, by creating a sense of community, assisted them to assert their social values and economic interests. Moreover, as Baptist ministers spread Christianity among slaves, the cultural gulf between blacks and whites shrank, undermining one justification for slavery and giving blacks a new sense of spiritual identity. Within a generation African Americans would develop their own versions of Protestant Christianity.

The Midcentury Challenge: War, Trade, and Social Conflict, 1750–1765

Between 1750 and 1765 colonial life was transformed not only by Pietism and the Enlightenment but also by war, economic change, and frontier violence. First, Britain embarked on a war in America, the French and Indian War, which became a worldwide conflict—the Great War for Empire. Second, the expansion of transatlantic trade increased colonial prosperity but put Americans into debt to British creditors. Third, a great westward migration led to new battles with the Indians, armed conflicts between settlers and landowners, and frontier rebellions against eastern governments.

THE FRENCH AND INDIAN WAR

In 1750 the interior of North America was still controlled by Indian peoples. Most French settlers lived along the St. Lawrence River, near the fur-trading centers of Montreal and Quebec (see Map 4.2). The more numerous British inhabitants had not ventured across the Appalachian Mountains, both because there were few natural transportation routes and because of Indian resistance. For more than a generation the Iroquois and other Native Americans had used their control of the fur trade to bargain for guns and subsidies from British and French officials and had firmly resisted the intrusion of white settlers. However, this strategy of playing off the French against the British was breaking down as European governments refused to pay the rising cost of "gifts" of arms and money and as the Indian alliances crumbled. Along the upper Ohio River the Delawares and Shawnees declared that they would no longer abide by Iroquois policies.

Moreover, the escalating Anglo-American demand for Indian lands, a result of colonial population growth and European migration, was eliciting strong resistance among Indian peoples. The Mohawks rebuffed attempts by Sir William Johnson, a British Indian agent and land speculator, to settle Scottish migrants west of Albany. To the south, the Iroquois were infuriated when Governor Dinwiddie of Virginia and a group of prominent planters laid plans to settle the upper Ohio River Valley, an area that they had traditionally controlled. Supported by influential London merchants, the Virginia speculators formed the Ohio Company in 1749 and obtained a royal grant of 200,000 acres along the upper Ohio River. "We don't know what you Christians, English and French intend," the outraged Iroquois complained, "we are so hemmed in by both, that we have hardly a hunting place left."

To shore up the alliance with the Iroquois Nations, the British Board of Trade, the body charged with supervising American affairs, called for a great intercolonial meeting with the Indians at Albany, New York, in June 1754. At the meeting the American delegates assured the Iroquois that they had no designs on their lands and asked for their assistance against the French. To bolster colonial defenses, Benjamin Franklin proposed a Plan of Union among the colonies with a continental assembly that would manage all western affairs: trade, Indian policy, and defense. But neither the Albany Plan nor a similar proposal by the Board of Trade for a political "union between ye Royal, Proprietary, & Charter Governments" ever materialized because both the provincial assemblies and the imperial government feared that collaboration would undermine their authority.

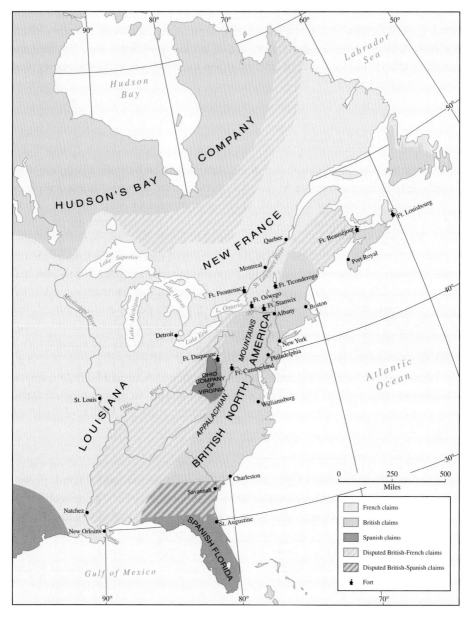

M AP 4.2
European Spheres of Influence, 1754

France and Spain laid claim to vast areas of North America and relied on Indian allies to combat the numerical superiority of British settlers. For their part, Native American peoples played off one European power against another. As a British official noted: "To preserve the Ballance between us and the French is the great ruling Principle of Modern Indian Politics." By expelling the French from North America, the Great War for Empire disrupted this system, leaving Indian peoples on their own in resisting Anglo-American settlers.

Britain's movement into the Ohio River Valley alarmed the French, who countered by constructing a series of forts, including Fort Duquesne at the point where the Monongahela and Allegheny Rivers join to form the Ohio (present-day Pittsburgh). The confrontation escalated when Governor Dinwiddie dispatched an expedition led by Colonel George Washington, a young planter and Ohio Company stockholder, to support the Company's claims. In July 1754 French troops seized Washington and his men, prompting expansionists in Virginia and Britain to demand war. But the British prime minister, Henry Pelham, urged calm: "There is such a load of debt, and such heavy taxes already laid upon the people, that nothing but an absolute necessity can justifie our engaging in a new War."

Pelham could not control the march of events. In Parliament William Pitt, a rising British statesman, and Lord Halifax, the new head of the Board of Trade, strongly advocated a policy of expansionism in the colonies. They persuaded Pelham to dispatch naval and military forces to America, where they joined with colonial militia in attacking French forts. In June 1755 British and New England troops captured Fort Beauséjour in Nova Scotia (Acadia) and deported nearly 10,000 French residents, some of whom eventually settled in Louisiana. In July as 1,400 British regulars and Virginia militiamen advanced on Fort Duquesne, they were surprised by a small force of French and a larger group of Delawares and Shawnees, who had decided to side with the French. In the ensuing battle the British commander, General Edward Braddock, lost his life and nearly two-thirds of his troops. "We have been beaten, most shamefully beaten, by a handfull of Men," Washington complained bitterly as he led the militiamen back to Virginia.

THE GREAT WAR FOR EMPIRE

By 1756 the fighting in America had spread to Europe, where the conflict aligned Britain and Prussia against France and Austria and was known as the Seven Years' War. When Britain decided to mount major offensives in India and West Africa as well as in North America and the West Indies, the conflict became a great war for empire. Britain had reaped unprecedented profits from its overseas trading empire and was determined to crush France, the main obstacle to further expansion.

William Pitt, who was appointed Secretary of State in 1757, was the grandson of the East Indies merchant "Diamond" Pitt and a committed expansionist. A haughty man, Pitt was constantly at odds with his colleagues. "I know that I can save this country and that I alone can," he declared. Indeed, Pitt was a master of strategy, both commercial and military, and planned to cripple France by attacking its colonies. In designing the critical campaign against New France, Pitt exploited a demographic advantage: on the North American mainland, Britain's 2 million subjects outnumbered the French by fourteen to one. To mobilize the colonists, Pitt agreed to pay half the cost of their troops and supply them with arms and equipment, an expenditure in America of nearly £1 million a year. He then committed a major British fleet and 30,000 British regulars to the American conflict, appointing three young officers—James Wolfe, Jeffrey Amherst, and William Howe—as the top commanders.

In 1758 the British forced the French to abandon Fort Duquesne (which they renamed Fort Pitt) and then captured Louisbourg at the mouth of the St. Lawrence River. The following year Wolfe sailed down the St. Lawrence to attack Quebec, the heart of France's American empire. After several failed attacks, 4,000 British troops scaled the high cliffs protecting the city and defeated the French. Quebec's fall was the turning point of the war. The Royal Navy prevented French reinforcements from crossing the Atlantic, and when British forces captured Montreal in 1760, the conquest of Canada was complete.

Elsewhere the British went from success to success. Fulfilling Pitt's dream, the East India Company captured French commercial outposts and took control of trade in large sections of India. British forces seized French Senegal in West Africa, the French sugar islands of Martinique and Guadeloupe, and the Spanish colonies of Cuba and the Philippine Islands. The Treaty of Paris of 1763 confirmed this triumph, granting Britain sovereignty over half the continent of North America, including French Canada, all French territory east of the Mississippi River, and Spanish Florida. Spain received

Pontiac

This portrait depicts Pontiac as both an Indian, symbolized by the necklace of bear claws, and a European-style ruler with a regal demeanor and a flowing robe. Pontiac did indeed partake of two worlds, absorbing French culture as he asserted his Indian identity. (Stock Montage, Inc.)

Louisiana west of the Mississippi, along with the restoration of Cuba and the Philippines. The French empire in North America was reduced to a handful of sugar islands in the West Indies and two rocky islands off the coast of Newfoundland.

As British armies and traders occupied French forts, Indian peoples from New York to Michigan grew increasingly concerned. Fearing an influx of Anglo-American settlers, the Ottawa chief Pontiac hoped for a return of the French, declaring, "I am French, and I want to die French." Neolin, a Delaware prophet, went further, teaching that the suffering of the Indian peoples stemmed from their dependence on the Europeans and their goods, guns, and rum. He called for the expulsion of all Europeans. Inspired by Neolin's vision and his own anti-British sentiments, in 1763 Pontiac led a group of loosely confederated tribes in a major uprising, capturing nearly every British garrison west of Fort Niagara, besieging the fort at Detroit, and killing or capturing over 2,000 frontier settlers. But the Indian alliance gradually weakened, and British military expeditions defeated the Delawares near Fort Pitt and broke the siege of Detroit. In the peace settlement that followed, Pontiac and his allies accepted the British as their new political "fathers." In return, the British addressed some of the Indians' concerns, temporarily barring Anglo-Americans from settling west of the Appalachians by establishing the Proclamation Line of 1763. Thus, the war for empire won Canada for the British crown but did not provide land for the expansion-minded American colonists.

BRITISH ECONOMIC GROWTH AND THE CONSUMER REVOLUTION

Britain owed its military and diplomatic success in large part to its unprecedented economic resources. Since 1700, when it had wrested control of many oceanic trade routes from the Dutch, Britain had been the dominant commercial power. By 1750 it was becoming the first country to undergo industrialization. Its new technology and work discipline made Britain the first—and for over a century the most powerful—industrial nation in the world.

The new machines and new business practices of the Industrial Revolution allowed Britain to produce more wool and linens, more iron tools, paper, chinaware, and glass than ever before—and to sell those goods at lower prices. British artisans had designed and built water- and steam-driven machines that powered lathes for shaping wood, jennies and looms for spinning and weaving textiles, and hammers for forging iron. The new machines produced goods far more rapidly than human hands could. Furthermore, the entrepreneurs who ran the new factories drove their employees hard, forcing them to keep pace with the machines and work long hours. To market the resulting products, English and Scottish merchants launched aggressive campaigns in the rapidly growing mainland colonies, extending a full year's credit to American traders instead of the traditional six months.

This first "consumer revolution" raised the living standard of many Americans, who soon were purchasing 20 percent of all British exports and paying for them by increasing their exports of wheat, rice, and tobacco. For example, Scottish merchants financed the settlement of the Virginia Piedmont, a region of plains and rolling hills just inland from the Tidewater counties. They granted planters and Scots-Irish migrants ample credit to purchase land, slaves, and equipment and took their tobacco crop in payment, exporting it to expanding markets in France and central Europe. In South Carolina planters supported their luxurious lifestyle by developing indigo plantations. By the 1760s they were exporting large quantities of the deep-blue dye to English textile factories as well as exporting about 65 million pounds of rice a year to Holland and southern Europe. Simultaneously, New York, Pennsylvania, Maryland, and Virginia became the breadbasket of the Atlantic world, supplying Europe's exploding population with wheat at ever-increasing profits. In Philadelphia wheat prices jumped almost 50 percent between 1740 and 1765.

This first American spending binge, like most subsequent splurges, landed many consumers in debt. Even during the boom times of the 1750s and early 1760s exports paid for only 80 percent of imported British goods. The remaining 20 percent—millions of pounds—was financed by Britain, both by the extension of credit and by Pitt's military expenditures in the colonies. As the war wound down, the loss of military supply contracts and cash subsidies made it more difficult for Americans to purchase British goods. Colonial merchants looked anxiously at their overstocked warehouses and feared bankruptcy. "I think we have a gloomy prospect before us," a Philadelphia trader noted in 1765, "as there are of late some Persons failed, who were in no way suspected." The increase in transatlantic trade had raised living standards but also had made Americans more dependent on overseas creditors and international economic conditions.

LAND CONFLICTS

In good times and bad the colonial population continued to grow, causing increased conflicts over land rights. The families who founded the town of Kent, Connecticut, in 1738 had lived in the colony for a century. Each generation their sons and daughters had moved westward to establish new farms, but now they lived at the generally accepted western boundary of the colony. To provide for the next generation, Kent families joined other Connecticut farmers in 1749 to form the Susquehanna Company to settle the Wyoming Valley in northeastern Pennsylvania, petitioning the legislature to assert jurisdiction over that region on the basis of Connecticut's "sea-to-sea" royal charter. But this land had also been granted by English kings to the Penn family, which invoked its proprietary rights and issued its own land grants. Soon settlers from Connecticut and Pennsylvania were burning down one another's houses. To avert further violence the two governments referred the dispute to the authorities in London, where it remained undecided at the time of independence.

Simultaneously, three different land disputes broke out in the Hudson River Valley. First, groups of Massachusetts settlers moved across the imprecise border with New York and claimed freehold estates on manor lands controlled by the Van Rensselaer and Livingston families. Second, the Wappinger Indians reasserted their ownership of land granted by English governors to various manorial lords. Finally, Dutch and German tenants asserted ownership rights to farms they had long held by lease and, when the landlords ignored their claims, refused to pay rent. By 1766 the tenants in Westchester, Dutchess, and Albany counties were in open rebellion against their landlords and used mob violence to close the courts. At the behest of the royal governor, General Thomas Gage and two British regiments joined local sheriffs and manorial bailiffs to suppress the tenant uprising, intimidate the Wappinger Indians, and evict the Massachusetts squatters.

Other land disputes erupted in New Jersey and the southern colonies, where resident landowners and English aristocrats successfully asserted legal claims based on long-dormant seventeenth-century charters. For example, one court decision upheld the right of Lord Granville, an heir of one of the original Carolina proprietors, to collect an annual tax on land in North Carolina; another decision awarded ownership of the entire northern neck of Virginia (along the Potomac) to Lord Fairfax.

This revival of proprietary power underscored the growing strength of the landed gentry and the increasing resemblance between rural societies in Europe and America. High-quality land east of the Appalachians was getting more expensive, and English aristocrats, manorial landlords, and wealthy speculators controlled much of it. Tenants and even yeomen farmers feared they soon might be reduced to the status of European peasants and searched for cheap freehold land in the west.

WESTERN UPRISINGS

Movement to the western frontier created new disputes over Indian policy, political representation, and debts. During the war, Delaware and Shawnee warriors had attacked farms throughout central and western Pennsylvania, destroying property and killing and capturing hundreds of residents. Subsequently, the Scots-Irish who lived along the frontier wanted to push the Indians out of the colony, but pacifistic Quakers prevented such military action. In 1763 a band of Scots-Irish farmers known as the Paxton Boys took matters into their own hands and massacred twenty members of the Conestoga tribe. When Governor John Penn tried to bring the murderers to justice, about 250 armed Scots-Irish advanced on Philadelphia. Benjamin Franklin intercepted the angry mob at Lancaster and arranged a compromise, narrowly averting a battle. Prosecution of the accused men failed for lack of witnesses. Although the Scots-Irish dropped their demand for the expulsion of the Indians, the episode left a legacy of racial hatred and political resentment.

Violence also broke out in the backcountry of South Carolina, where land-hungry whites had clashed repeatedly with Cherokees during the war with France. After the war ended in 1763, a group of landowning vigilantes, the Regulators, tried to suppress outlaw bands of whites that were roaming the countryside and stealing cattle and other property. The Regulators wanted greater political rights for their region and demanded that the eastern-controlled government provide them with more local courts, fairer taxes, and greater local representation in the provincial assembly. The government, which was dominated by lowland rice planters, wanted to suppress the Regulators but decided to compromise because it feared slave revolts if the militia were away in the backcountry. In 1767 the assembly agreed to create locally controlled courts in the west and reduce the fees for legal documents. However, it refused to reapportion the assembly or lower western taxes. Eventually a rival group, the Moderators, raised an armed force of its own and forced the Regulators to accept the authority of the colonial government. Like the Paxton Boys in Pennsylvania, the South Carolina Regulators attracted attention to western needs but ultimately failed to wrest power from the eastern elite.

In 1766 another Regulator movement arose in the newly settled backcountry of North Carolina. After the Great War for Empire tobacco prices plummeted, forcing many debt-ridden farmers into court. Eastern judges directed sheriffs to seize the property of bankrupt farmers and auction it off to pay creditors and court costs. Backcountry farmers resented merchants' lawsuits, not just because they generated high fees for lawyers and court officials but also because they violated local custom. As in rural New England farmers made loans among neighbors on trust and often allowed the loans to remain unpaid for years.

To save their farms, North Carolina debtors joined together in a Regulator movement that intimidated judges, closed down courts, and broke into jails to free their comrades. Their leader, Herman Husband, told his followers not to vote for "any Clerk, Lawyer, or Scotch merchant. We must make these men subject to the laws or they will enslave the whole community." But the North Carolina Regulators also proposed a coherent program of reforms, demanding passage of a law allowing them to pay their taxes in the "produce of the country" rather than in cash. They insisted on lower legal fees, greater legislative representation, and fairer taxes, so that each person would be taxed "in proportion to the profits arising from his estate." In 1771 the royal governor mobilized the eastern militia and defeated a large Regulator force at the Alamance River; seven insurgent leaders were summarily executed. Not since Leisler's revolt in New York in 1689 (see Chapter 3) had a domestic political conflict caused so much bloodshed in America.

In 1771 as in 1689, colonial conflicts became intertwined with imperial politics. In Connecticut the Reverend Ezra Stiles defended the Regulators. "What shall an injured & oppressed people do," he asked, when faced with "Oppression and tyranny (under the name of Government)?" Stiles's remarks reflected growing resistance to British imperial control, a result of the profound changes that had occurred in the mainland colonies between 1720 and 1765. America was still a dependent society closely tied to Britain by trade, culture, and politics, but it was also an increasingly complex society with the potential for an independent existence. British policies would determine the direction the maturing colonies would take.

T I M E L I N E

1700–1714	New Hudson River manors created	1743	Benjamin Franklin founds the American Philosophical Society.
1710s–1730s	Enlightenment ideas spread from Europe to America. Deists rely on "natural reason" to define a moral code.	1749	Virginia speculators create the Ohio Company. Connecticut farmers form the Susquehanna Company.
1720s	Germans and Scots-Irish settle in the Mid-Atlantic colonies. Theodore Jacob Frelinghuysen preaches Pietism to German migrants.	1750s	Industrial Revolution begins in England. "Consumer revolution" increases American imports and debt to Britain.
1730s	William and Gilbert Tennent lead Presbyterian revivals among Scots-Irish migrants. Jonathan Edwards preaches in New England.	1754	French and Indian War begins. Meeting of Iroquois and Americans at Albany; Plan of Union
		1756	Britain begins a Great War for Empire.
1739	George Whitefield sparks the Great Awakening.	1759	Britain captures Quebec.
1740s–1760s	Growing shortage of farmland in New England Religious and ethnic pluralism in the Mid-Atlantic colonies Rising grain and tobacco prices Increasing rural inequality	1760s	Land conflict along the border between New York and New England Regulator movements in the Carolinas suppress outlaw bands. Baptist revivals in Virginia
		1763	Pontiac's uprising leads to the Proclamation of 1763. Treaty of Paris ends the Great War for Empire.
1740s	The Great Awakening sparks conflict between Old Lights and New Lights. Colleges established by religious denominations.		Scots-Irish Paxton Boys massacre Indians in Pennsylvania.

For Further Exploration

The social history of eighteenth-century America comes alive in studies of individual lives. In *Good Wives: Image and Reality in the Lives of Women in Northern New England, 1650–1750* (1982), Laurel Thatcher Ulrich paints a vivid picture of the everyday lives of women as they assumed a variety of roles. Benjamin Franklin's *Autobiography* (available in many editions) provides an entertaining look at the bustling city of Philadelphia and demonstrates Franklin's Enlightenment sensibility and his pursuit of wealth and influence. A less successful quest for self-betterment is the subject of another autobiography, *The Infortunate: The Voyage and Adventures of William Moraley, an Indentured Servant,* edited by Susan E. Klepp and Billy G. Smith (1992). Harry S. Stout's *The Divine Dramatist: George Whitefield and the Rise of Modern Evangelicalism* (1991) shows how the charismatic preacher's flair for theatrics and self-promotion enabled him to preach effectively and fulfill his sense of duty to God.

Other well-written social histories are Rhys Isaac, *The Transformation of Virginia, 1740–1790* (1982); Patricia U. Bonomi, *A Factious People: Politics and Society in Colonial New York* (1971); and Fred Anderson, *A People's Army: Massachusetts Soldiers and Society in the Seven Years' War* (1984).

For insight into the day-to-day lives of women, see the PBS video *A Midwife's Tale* (1.5 hours), which tells the story of Martha Ballard, who lived at the end of the eighteenth century; additional materials on Ballard's experiences are available at <http://www.pbs.org/amex/midwife> and <http://www.DoHistory.org>. On day-to-day economic life, see the "Colonial Currency and Colonial Coin" site at <http://www.coins.nd.edu:8002/>, which contains detailed essays as well as pictures of colonial money. Franklin's life and times are presented at "The Electric Franklin," <http://www.ushistory.org/franklin/index/htm>. "Jonathan Edwards On-Line" at <http://www.JonathanEdwards.com/> provides access to the writings of the great philosopher and preacher, but note that this site uses Edwards's arguments to advance one side of a present-day theological debate.

Chapter 5

TOWARD INDEPENDENCE: YEARS OF DECISION
1763–1775

The said [Stamp] act is contrary to the rights of mankind, and subversive of the English Constitution.

TOWN MEETING OF LEICESTER, MASSACHUSETTS, 1765

As the Great War for Empire ended in 1763, Seth Metcalf and many other American colonists rejoiced over the triumph of British arms. A Massachusetts veteran just returned from the war, Metcalf thanked "the Great Goodness of God" for the "General Peace" that was so "perculary Advantageous to the English Nation." Two years later, God's dialogue with his chosen Puritan people seemed to carry a very different message. As Metcalf wrote in his journal: "God is angry with us of this land and is now Smiting with his Rod Especially by the hands of our [British] Rulers."

The rapid disintegration of the bonds uniting Britain and America—events that Metcalf explained in terms of Divine Providence—mystified many Americans. How had it happened, asked the president of King's College in New York in 1775, that such a "happily situated" people had armed themselves and were ready to "hazard their Fortunes, their Lives, and their Souls, in a Rebellion"? Unlike other colonial peoples of the time, the majority of Americans had enjoyed life in a prosperous and relatively free society with a strong tradition of self-government. They had little to gain and much to lose by rebelling.

Or so it seemed in 1765, before the British government attempted to reform the imperial system. The long overdue but disastrous administrative reforms prompted a violent response, beginning a downward spiral of ideological debate and political conflict that ended in civil war. Yet this course of events was far from inevitable. Careful British statecraft could have saved the empire. Instead, inflexible responses to passionate Patriot agitation brought about its demise.

The Imperial Reform Movement, 1763–1765

The Great War for Empire had a mixed legacy. By driving the French out of Canada, Britain had achieved dominance over eastern North America (see Map 5.1). But the cost of the triumph was high: a mountain of debt that prompted the British ministry to impose new taxes on its American possessions. More fundamentally, it prompted Parliament to redefine the character of the empire, moving from one based on self-government and trade to one centered on rule by imperial officials.

THE LEGACY OF WAR

The war fundamentally changed the relationship between Britain and its American colonies—and the nature of British public life. The fighting revealed basic social and administrative conflicts between the home country and the colonies. As British regiments set up quarters, Americans were shocked by the arrogance of the officers. A Massachusetts militiaman wrote in his diary that British soldiers "are but

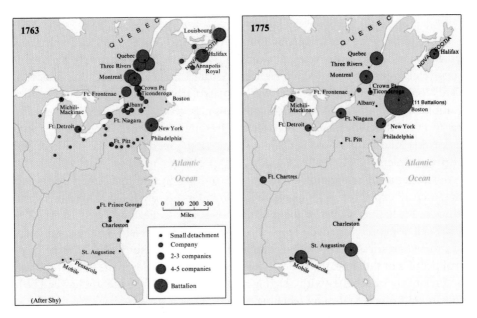

M AP 5.1
British Troop Deployments, 1763 and 1775

As the imperial crisis deepened, British military priorities changed. In 1763 most British battalions (the large circles representing 350 men) were stationed in Canada to deter French Canadian revolts and Indian attacks. Following the Stamp Act riots of 1765, the British moved more troops to the seaboard cities. By 1775 eleven battalions of British regulars occupied Boston, the center of the American Patriot movement.

little better than slaves to their officers." The disdain was mutual. General James Wolfe complained that colonial troops were drawn from the dregs of society and that "there was no depending on them in action."

The war also exposed the weak position of British royal governors and other officials, prompting immediate administrative reforms. In theory governors had extensive political powers, including command of the provincial militia, but in reality they had to share power with the colonial assemblies. Britain's Board of Trade complained that in Massachusetts "almost every act of executive and legislative power is ordered and directed by votes and resolves of the General Court." To enhance the authority of the crown in America, British officials began a strict enforcement of the Navigation Acts. Before the war colonial merchants had routinely bribed customs officials to avoid paying the duties imposed by the Molasses Act of 1733. To curb such corruption, in 1762 Parliament passed a Revenue Act that tightened the customs service. In addition, the ministry instructed the Royal Navy to seize vessels that were carrying goods between the mainland colonies and the French islands. The fact that French armies attempting "to Destroy one English province, are actually supported by Bread raised in another" was absurd, declared an outraged British politician.

The victory over France provoked a fundamental shift in imperial military policy in 1763, with the deployment of a large peacetime army of about 10,000 men in North America. The decision stemmed from a variety of motives. The ministry wanted to discourage rebellion by the 60,000 French residents of the newly captured province of Quebec and to protect Florida, which Spain wanted back. Moreover, Pontiac's rebellion had underscored the need for a substantial military garrison along the frontier both to restrain the Indians and to deter land-hungry whites from settling west of the Proclamation Line of 1763. Finally, some British politicians worried that Americans who no longer needed protection from an invasion from Canada would seek greater freedom from imperial control. As Henry Knox, a Treasury official who once had served the crown in Georgia, put it: "The main purpose of Stationing a large Body of Troops in America is to secure the Dependence of the Colonys on Great Britain." By stationing an army in America, the British ministry was indicating its willingness to use force to preserve its authority.

Yet another significant result of the war was the rapid increase in Britain's national debt, which soared from £75 million in 1754 to £133 million in 1763, and the consequent changes in government policies. To pay the rising interest charges, Lord Bute, the new prime minister, needed to raise taxes—certainly in Britain and perhaps in America as well. Treasury officials advised against increasing the British land tax, which was paid by the influential propertied classes, so Bute imposed higher import duties on tobacco and sugar, which manufacturers passed on to British consumers in the form of higher prices. The ministry also increased excise levies—essentially sales taxes—on goods such as salt, beer, and distilled spirits, once again passing on the costs of the war to the king's ordinary subjects. Left unresolved for the moment was question of imposing taxes on the colonies.

To collect these taxes and duties, the British government doubled the size of its bureaucracy and increased its powers. Customs agents and informers patrolled the coasts of southern Britain, arresting smugglers and seizing tons of goods, such as French wines and Flemish textiles, on which import duties had not been paid. Convicted smugglers faced heavy penalties, including death or "transportation" to America as indentured servants.

The price of empire abroad had turned out to be debt and a more powerful government at home. The appearance of a big and expensive government confirmed the predictions of the opposition, the Radical Whigs and Country Party landlords. They pointed out that the huge war debt had left the Treasury at the mercy of the "monied interest," the banks and financiers who were reaping millions of pounds in interest from government bonds. Moreover, the expansion of the tax bureaucracy had created thousands of patronage positions that were filled with "worthless pensioners and placemen." To reverse these developments, reformers demanded that Parliament be made more representative of the property-owning classes. The Radical Whig John Wilkes called for an end to "rotten boroughs"—tiny districts whose voters were controlled by wealthy aristocrats and merchants. In domestic affairs as in colonial policy, the war had transformed British political life, creating a more active and intrusive government.

THE SUGAR ACT AND COLONIAL RIGHTS

As the war ended, a new generation of British officials undertook a systematic reform of the imperial system. The first to act was George Grenville, who became prime minister in 1763. Grenville quickly won Parliamentary approval of a Currency Act (1764) that protected British merchants by banning the use of paper money (which was often worth less than its face value) as legal tender; colonists would have to pay their debts in gold or silver coin. Then he proposed a new Navigation Act, the Sugar Act of 1764, to replace the widely evaded Molasses Act of 1733. Treasury officials who understood the pattern of colonial trade convinced Grenville that the mainland settlers had to sell some of their wheat, fish, and lumber in the French islands. Without the molasses, sugar, and bills of exchange those sales brought, they pointed out, the colonists would lack the funds to buy British manufactured goods. Therefore, Grenville resisted demands from British sugar planters for a duty of 6 pence per gallon that would cut off colonial imports of French molasses. Instead, he settled on a smaller duty of 3 pence per gallon, arguing that it would allow British molasses to compete with the cheaper French product without destroying the trade of the North American mainland colonies or their distilling industry.

This carefully crafted policy garnered little support in America. Many New England merchants, such as John Hancock of Boston, had made their fortunes by smuggling French molasses and thus had never paid the duty. Their profits would be cut severely if the new regulations were enforced. These merchants and New

George Grenville, Architect of the Stamp Act

As prime minister from 1764 to 1766, Grenville assumed leadership of the movement for imperial reform and taxation. This portrait of 1763 suggests Grenville's energy and ambition. As events were to show, the new minister was determined to reform the imperial system and ensure that the colonists shared the cost of the empire. (The Earl of Halifax, Garrowby, Yorkshire)

England distillers, who feared a rise in the price of molasses, campaigned publicly against the Sugar Act, claiming that the new tax would wipe out trade with the French islands. Privately, they vowed to evade the duty by smuggling or by bribing officials.

More important, the merchants and their allies raised constitutional objections to the new legislation. The speaker of the Massachusetts House of Representatives argued that the duties constituted a tax, making the Sugar Act "contrary to a fundamental Principall of our Constitution: That all Taxes ought to originate with the people." The Sugar Act raised other constitutional issues as well. Merchants accused of violating the Act would be tried by vice-admiralty courts—maritime tribunals composed only of a judge—and not by a local common-law jury. For half a century colonial legislatures had vigorously opposed vice-admiralty courts, expanding the jurisdiction of colonial courts to cover customs offenses occurring in the seaports. As a result, most merchants charged with violating the Navigation Acts were tried in common-law courts and were often acquitted by local juries. By extending the jurisdiction of vice-admiralty courts to all customs offenses, the Sugar Act closed this loophole.

The new powers given to the vice-admiralty courts revived old American fears and complaints. For a century, the influential Virginia planter Richard Bland reminded his fellow settlers, the colonies had been subject to the Navigation Acts, which restricted their manufactures and commerce. But, he protested, the colonists "were not sent out to be the Slaves but to be the Equals of those that remained behind." John Adams, a young Massachusetts lawyer who was defending merchant John Hancock on a charge of smuggling, similarly condemned the new vice-admiralty courts, saying that they "degrade every American . . . below the rank of an Englishman."

While the logic of these arguments was compelling, some of the facts were wrong. The Navigation Acts certainly discriminated against the colonists, but the new vice-admiralty legislation did not—because those in Britain had long been subject to the same rules. The real issue was the new spirit of reform among British officials and the growing administrative power of the British state. Having lived for decades under a policy of salutary neglect, Americans were quick to charge that the new British policies challenged the existing constitutional structure of the empire. As a committee of the Massachusetts House put it, the Sugar Act and other British edicts "have a tendency to deprive the colonies of some of their most essential Rights as British subjects."

For their part, British officials insisted on the supremacy of Parliamentary laws and denied that the colonists were entitled to special privileges or even the traditional legal rights of Englishmen. When Royal Governor Francis Bernard of Massachusetts heard that the Massachusetts assembly had objected to the Sugar Act, claiming no taxation without representation, he asserted that Americans did not have that constitutional right. "The rule that a British subject shall not be bound by laws or liable to taxes, but what he has consented to by his representatives," Bernard argued, "must be confined to the inhabitants of Great Britain only." In the eyes of most British officials and politicians, Americans were second-class subjects of the king, their rights limited by the Navigation Acts and the national interests of the British state, as determined by Parliament.

AN OPEN CHALLENGE: THE STAMP ACT

The issue of taxation sparked the first great imperial crisis. When Grenville introduced the Sugar Act in 1764, he also intended to seek a stamp tax the following year to cover part of the cost of keeping 10,000 British troops in America—some £200,000 per year (about $20 million today). The new tax would raise revenue by requiring small embossed markings (somewhat like today's postage stamps) on all court documents, land titles, contracts, playing cards, newspapers, and other printed items. A similar tax in England was yielding an annual revenue of £290,000; Grenville hoped the American levy would raise at least £60,000 a year. The prime minister knew that some Americans would object to the tax on constitutional grounds, and so he asked explicitly whether any member of the House of Commons doubted "the power and sovereignty of Parliament over every part of the British dominions, for the purpose of raising or collecting any tax." No one rose to object.

Confident of Parliament's support, Grenville then vowed to impose a stamp tax in 1765 unless the colonists would tax themselves. This challenge threw the London representatives of the colonial legislatures into confusion because they did not see how the American assemblies could collectively raise and apportion their defense budget. Colonial officials had met together only once, at the Albany Congress of 1754, and not a single assembly had accepted that body's proposals. Benjamin Franklin, representing the Pennsylvania assembly, proposed another solution to Grenville's challenge: American representation in Parliament. "If you chuse to tax us," he suggested to an influential British friend, "give us Members in your Legislature, and let us be one People." With the exception of William Pitt, British politicians rejected Franklin's radical idea. They argued that the colonists were already "virtually" represented in the home legislature by the merchants who sat in Parliament and by other members with interests in America. Colonial leaders were equally skeptical. Americans were "situate at a great Distance from their Mother Country," the Connecticut assembly declared, and therefore "cannot participate in the general Legislature of the Nation." Influential merchants in Philadelphia, worried that a handful of colonial delegates would be powerless in Parliament, warned Franklin "to beware of any measure that might extend to us seats in the Commons."

The way was now clear for Grenville to introduce the Stamp Act. His goal was not only to raise revenue but also to assert a constitutional principle: "the Right of Parliament to lay an internal Tax upon the Colonies," as his chief assistant declared. The ministry's plan worked smoothly. The House of Commons refused to accept American petitions opposing the act and passed the new legislation by an overwhelming vote of 205 to 49. At the request of General Thomas Gage, commander of British military forces in America, Parliament also passed a Quartering Act directing colonial governments to provide barracks and food for the British troops stationed in the colonies. Finally, Parliament approved Grenville's proposal that violations of the Stamp Act be tried in vice-admiralty courts.

The design was complete. Using the doctrine of Parliamentary supremacy, Grenville had begun to fashion a genuinely imperial administrative system run by British officials without regard for the American assemblies. He thus provoked a constitutional confrontation not only on the specific issues of taxation, jury trials, and quartering of the military but also on the fundamental question of representative self-government.

The Dynamics of Rebellion, 1765–1766

Grenville had thrown down the gauntlet to the Americans. Although the colonists had often opposed unpopular laws and arbitrary governors, they had never before faced a reform-minded ministry and Parliament. But Patriots—as the defenders of

American rights came to be called—took up Grenville's challenge, organizing protest meetings, rioting in the streets, and articulating an ideology of resistance.

THE CROWD REBELS

In May 1765 the eloquent young Patrick Henry addressed the Virginia House of Burgesses and blamed the new king, George III (1760–1820) for naming—and supporting—the ministers who designed the new legislation. Comparing George to the tyrannical Charles I, Henry seemed to call for a new republican revolution. Although the Burgesses were dismayed by Henry's remarks against the king (which bordered on treason), they endorsed his attack on the Stamp Act, declaring that any attempt to tax the colonists without their consent "has a manifest Tendency to Destroy American freedom." In Massachusetts, James Otis, another republican-minded firebrand, persuaded the House of Representatives to call for a general meeting of all the colonies "to implore Relief" from the act.

Nine colonial assemblies sent delegates to the Stamp Act Congress, which met in New York City in October. The Congress issued a set of Resolves protesting against the loss of American "rights and liberties," especially trial by jury. The Resolves also challenged the constitutionality of the Stamp and Sugar Acts, declaring that only the colonists' elected representatives could impose taxes on them. However, most

The Intensity of Patrick Henry

This portrait, painted in 1795 when Henry was in his sixties, captured his lifelong seriousness and intensity. As an orator, Henry drew on evangelical Protestantism to create a new mode of political oratory. "His figures of speech . . . were often borrowed from the Scriptures," a contemporary noted, and the content of his speeches mirrored "the earnestness depicted in his own features."

(Mead Art Museum, Amherst College)

of the delegates were moderate men who sought compromise, not confrontation. They concluded by assuring Parliament that Americans "glory in being subjects of the best of Kings" and humbly petitioning for repeal of the Stamp Act. Other influential Americans advocated nonviolent resistance through a boycott of British goods.

Popular resentment was not so easily contained. When the act went into effect on November 1, disciplined mobs went into action. Led by men who called themselves the Sons of Liberty, the mobs demanded the resignation of newly appointed stamp-tax collectors, most of whom were native-born colonists. In Boston the Sons of Liberty made an effigy of the collector Andrew Oliver, which they beheaded and burned; then they destroyed a new brick building he owned. Two weeks later Bostonians attacked the house of Lieutenant Governor Thomas Hutchinson, a defender of social privilege and imperial authority, breaking the furniture, looting the wine cellar, and burning the library (see American Voices, "The Threat of Mob Rule").

In nearly every colony similar crowds of angry people—the "rabble," as their detractors called them—intimidated royal officials. Near Wethersfield, Connecticut, 500 farmers and artisans held tax collector Jared Ingersoll as a captive until he resigned his office. This was "the Cause of the People," shouted one rioter, and he would not "take Directions about it from any Body." In New York nearly 3,000 shopkeepers, artisans, laborers, and seamen marched through the streets, breaking street lamps and windows and crying "Liberty!"

Although the strength of the Liberty mobs was surprising, such plebeian crowd actions were a fact of life in both Britain and America. Every November 5 Protestant mobs burned an effigy of the pope to celebrate the failure in 1605 of a plot by Guy Fawkes and other English Catholics to blow up the Houses of Parliament. Colonial mobs regularly destroyed houses used as brothels and rioted to protest the impressment of merchant seamen by the Royal Navy.

If rioting was traditional, its political goals were new. The leaders of the Sons of Liberty in New York City were minor merchants, such as Isaac Sears and Alexander McDougall, who were Radical Whigs. They tried to direct the raw energy of the crowd against the new tax measures, but the mobs drew support from established artisans, struggling journeymen, and poor laborers and seamen who had their own agendas. Some artisans joined the crowds because imports of low-priced British shoes and other manufactured goods threatened their livelihood, and they feared the additional burden of a stamp tax. Unlike "the Common people of England," a well-traveled colonist observed, "the people of America ... never would submitt to be taxed that a few may be loaded with palaces and Pensions and riot in Luxury and Excess, while they themselves cannot support themselves and their needy offspring with Bread."

Other members of the crowd were stirred by the religious passions of the Great Awakening. As evangelical Protestants who led disciplined, hardworking lives, they resented the arrogance of British military officers and the corruption of royal bureaucrats. In New England, some protesters looked back to the English Puritan

AMERICAN VOICES
The Threat of Mob Rule
JOSIAH QUINCY JR.

A *lthough crowd actions were a familiar aspect of English and colonial life, they were of-* *ten condemned. To Josiah Quincy Jr., a Boston gentleman, the destruction of the house* *of Chief Justice Thomas Hutchinson by the Sons of Liberty in August 1765 was an unjust at-* *tack against a loyal American and an example of "lawless despotism."*

There cannot, perhaps, be found in the records of time a more flagrant instance to what a pitch of infatuation an incensed populace may arise than the last night afforded. . . . The populace of Boston . . . assembled in King's Street; where, after having kindled a fire, they proceeded, in two separate bodies, to attack the houses of two gentlemen of distinction . . . and did great damage in destroying their houses, furniture, &c., and irreparable damage in destroying their papers. Both parties . . . then unitedly proceeded to the Chief-Justice's house, who, not expecting them, was unattended by his friends who might have assisted, or proved his innocence. . . .

This rage-intoxicated rabble . . . beset the house on all sides, and soon destroyed every thing of value. . . . The destruction was really amazing. . . .

The distress a man must feel on such an occasion can only be conceived by those who the next day saw his Honor the Chief-Justice come into court . . . with tears starting from his eyes, and a countenance which strongly told the inward anguish of his soul.

> GENTLEMEN [he said]: There not being a quorum of the court without me, I am obliged to appear. Some apology is necessary for my dress: indeed, I had no other. Destitute of every thing. . . .

> I call my Maker to witness, that I never, in New England or Old, in Great Britain or America, neither directly nor indirectly, was aiding, assisting, or supporting— in the least promoting or encouraging—what is commonly called the Stamp Act; but, on the contrary, did all in my power, and strove as much as in me lay, to prevent it. . . .

Who, that marks the riotous tumult, confusion, and uproar of a democratic . . . state [would not fly] . . . to that best asylum, that glorious medium, the British Constitution? . . . May ye never lose it through a licentious abuse of your invaluable rights.

SOURCE: Jack P. Greene, ed., *Colonies to Nation: 1763–1789* (Baltimore: John Hopkins University Press, 1967), pp. 61–63.

revolution, reviving antimonarchial and prorepublican sentiments of their great-grandparents. A letter sent to a Boston newspaper promising to save "all the Freeborn Sons of America" from "tyrannical ministers" was signed "Oliver Cromwell," the English republican revolutionary of the 1640s. Finally, the mobs included apprentices,

The Bostonian's Paying the EXCISE-MAN, or TARRING & FEATHERING

Plate I.

A British View of American Mobs

This satiric attack on the Sons of Liberty questions their brutal treatment of John Malcolm, the Commissioner of the Customs in Boston, who was tarred and feathered and forced to drink huge quantities of tea. The Liberty Tree in the background raises the question: Does liberty mean anarchy? (Courtesy of the John Carter Brown Library at Brown University)

journeymen, day laborers, and unemployed sailors—young men seeking adventure and excitement who, when fortified by drink, were ready to resort to violence.

Throughout the colonies popular resistance nullified the Stamp Act. Fearing a massive assault on Fort George on Guy Fawkes Day (November 5, 1765), New York Lieutenant Governor Cadwallader Colden called on General Gage to use his small military force to protect the stamps stored in the fort. Gage refused. "Fire from the Fort might disperse the Mob, but it would not quell them," he told Colden, and the result would be "an Insurrection, the Commencement of Civil War." Frightened collectors gave up their stamps, and angry Americans coerced officials into accepting legal documents without them. This popular insurrection gave a democratic cast to the emerging American Patriot movement, extending it far beyond the ranks of merchants, lawyers, and elected officials. "Nothing is wanting but your own Resolution," a New York Son of Liberty declared during the upheaval, "for great is the Authority and Power of the People."

Slow communication across the Atlantic meant that the ministry's response to the Stamp Act Congress and the Liberty mobs would not be known until the following spring. But it was already clear that royal officials could no longer count on the deferential political behavior that had ensured the empire's stability for three generations. As the collector of the customs in Philadelphia lamented, "What can a Governor do without the assistance of the Governed?"

IDEOLOGICAL ROOTS OF RESISTANCE

Initially the American resistance movement had no acknowledged leaders and no central organization. It had arisen spontaneously in the seaport cities because urban residents were directly affected by British policies. The Stamp Act taxed the newspapers and documents used by merchants and lawyers, the Sugar Act raised the cost of molasses to distillers, and the flood of British manufactures threatened the livelihood of urban artisans. As urban merchants and lawyers protested the new measures, they found some allies in the colonial assemblies—the traditional defenders of American interests—but the movement was slow to develop a coherent outlook and organization.

Consequently, the first protests focused narrowly on particular economic and political matters. One pamphleteer complained that colonists were being compelled to give the British "our money, as oft and in what quantity they please to demand it." Other writers alleged that the British had violated specific "liberties and privileges" embodied in colonial charters. But American Patriot publicists gradually focused the debate by defining "liberty" as an abstract ideal—a "natural right" of all people—rather than a set of historical privileges. As pamphlets of remarkable political sophistication circulated throughout the colonies, they provided the resistance movement with an intellectual rationale, a political agenda, and a visible cadre of leaders.

Patriot publicists drew on three intellectual traditions. The first was English common law—the centuries-old body of legal rules and procedures that protected the king's subjects against arbitrary acts by the government. In 1761 the Boston lawyer James Otis had cited English legal precedent in the famous Writs of Assistance case, in which he disputed the constitutionality of a general search warrant permitting customs officials to inspect the property and possessions of any and all persons. Similarly, in demanding a jury trial for John Hancock, John Adams invoked common-law tradition. "This 29th Chap. of Magna Charta," Adams argued, referring to an ancient English document that had established the right to trial by jury, "has for many Centuries been esteemed by Englishmen, as one of the ... firmest Bulwarks of their Liberties." Other lawyers protested when the terms of appointment for colonial judges were altered from "during good behavior" to "at the pleasure" of the royal governor, arguing that the change in wording compromised the independence of the judiciary.

A second major intellectual resource for educated Americans was the rationalist thought of the Enlightenment. Unlike American common-law attorneys, who used legal precedents to criticize British measures, the Virginia planter Thomas Jefferson invoked Enlightenment philosophers, such as David Hume and Francis Hutcheson, who questioned the past and relied on reason to discover and correct social ills. Jefferson and other Patriot authors also drew on the political philosopher John Locke, who argued that all individuals possessed certain "natural rights," such as life, liberty, and property, which government was responsible for protecting. And they celebrated the French theorist Montesquieu, who devised institutional curbs to prevent the arbitrary exercise of political power.

The republican and Whig strands of the English political tradition provided the third ideological basis for the American Patriot movement. In some places, particularly Puritan New England, Americans had long venerated the Commonwealth era—the brief period between 1649 and 1660 when England was a republic. After the Glorious Revolution of 1688, many colonists had welcomed the constitutional restrictions placed on the monarchy by English Whigs, such as the ban on royally imposed taxes. Later, educated Americans such as Samuel Adams of Boston absorbed the arguments of Radical Whig spokesmen who denounced political corruption. "Bribery is so common," John Dickinson of Pennsylvania had complained during a visit to London in the 1750s, "that there is not a borough in England where it is not practiced." These republican and Radical Whig sentiments made many Americans suspicious of royal officials. Joseph Warren, a physician and Patriot, reported that many Bostonians believed the Stamp Act was intended "to force the colonies into rebellion," after which the ministry would use "military power to reduce them to servitude."

These writings—swiftly disseminated thanks to the power of the printing press—provided the developing Patriot movement with a sense of identity and an ideological agenda, turning a series of impromptu riots and tax protests into a coherent political coalition.

PARLIAMENT COMPROMISES, 1766

In Britain, Parliament was in turmoil, with different political factions advocating radically different responses to the American challenge. George III had replaced Grenville with a new prime minister, Lord Rockingham, who was allied with the Old Whigs and opposed Grenville's tough policies toward the colonies. But hardliners in Parliament, outraged by the popular rebellion in America, demanded that imperial reform continue. They wanted to dispatch British soldiers to suppress the riots and force the Americans to submit to the constitutional supremacy of Parliament. "The British legislature," declared Chief Justice Sir James Mansfield, "has authority to bind every part and every subject, whether such subjects have a right to vote or not."

Three factions were willing to repeal the Stamp Act, but for different reasons. The Old Whigs advocated repeal for reasons of policy: they believed that America was more important for its "flourishing and increasing trade" than its tax revenues.

Some Old Whigs even agreed with the colonists that the new tax was unconstitutional. British merchants favored repeal out of self-interest because the American boycott of British goods had caused a drastic fall in their sales. In January 1766 the leading commercial centers of London, Liverpool, Bristol, and Glasgow deluged Parliament with petitions, pointing out the threat to their prosperity. "The Avenues of Trade are all shut up," a Bristol merchant with large inventories on hand complained. "We have no Remittances and are at our Witts End for want of Money to fulfill our Engagements with our Tradesmen." Finally, former Prime Minister William Pitt demanded that "the Stamp Act be repealed absolutely, totally, and immediately" as a failed policy. Pitt's view of the constitutional issues was confusing; he argued that Parliament could not tax the colonies but that British authority over America was "sovereign and supreme, in every circumstance of government and legislation whatsoever."

Rockingham gave each group just enough to feel satisfied. To assist British merchants and mollify colonial opinion, he repealed the Stamp Act and ruled out the use of troops against colonial crowds. He also modified the Sugar Act, reducing the duty on French molasses from 3 pence to 1 penny a gallon but extending it to British molasses as well. Thus, the revised Sugar Act regulated foreign trade, which most American officials accepted, but it also taxed a British product, which some colonists saw as unconstitutional. Finally, Rockingham pacified imperial reformers and hardliners with the Declaratory Act of 1766, which explicitly reaffirmed the British Parliament's "full power and authority to make laws and statutes . . . to bind the colonies and people of America . . . in all cases whatsoever."

Because the Stamp Act crisis ended quickly, it might have been forgotten just as quickly. As of 1766 political positions had not yet hardened. Leaders of goodwill could still hope to work out an imperial relationship that was acceptable to British officials and American colonists.

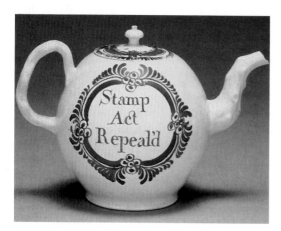

Mixing Business and Politics, 1766

Hurt by the colonists' trade boycott, British manufacturers campaigned for repeal of the Stamp Act. To celebrate the repeal—and expand the market for its teapots in America—the Cockpit Hill factory in Derby quickly produced a commemorative design.

(Courtesy of the Peabody Essex Museum, Salem, MA)

The Growing Confrontation, 1767–1770

The compromise of 1766 was short-lived. Within a year political rivalries in Britain sparked a new and more prolonged struggle with the American provinces, reviving the passions of 1765. The newfound ideological rigidity of key British ministers and American officials aggravated the conflict and dashed prospects for a quick resolution.

THE TOWNSHEND INITIATIVES

Often the course of history is changed by a small event—a leader's illness, a personal grudge, a chance remark. So it was in 1767, when Rockingham's Old Whig ministry collapsed and George III named William Pitt to head the new ministry. Pitt, the master strategist of the Great War for Empire, was chronically ill with gout and frequently missed Parliamentary debates, leaving Chancellor of the Exchequer Charles Townshend in command. Pitt was sympathetic toward America; Townshend was not. So when Grenville attacked Townshend's military budget in 1767, demanding that the colonists pay for the British troops in America, Townshend made an unplanned, fateful policy decision. Long convinced of the necessity of imperial reform and eager to reduce the English land tax, he promised that he would find a new source of revenue in America.

The new tax legislation, known as the Townshend Act of 1767, was intended to free royal officials in the colonies from financial dependence on the American legislatures, enabling them to enforce Parliamentary laws and royal directives. The tax imposed duties on paper, paint, glass, and tea imported into the colonies and was expected to raise about £40,000 a year. To pacify Grenville, part of the revenue would defray military expenses, but the major part would be used to pay the salaries of colonial governors, judges, and other imperial officials. To increase royal power, Townshend also devised the Revenue Act of 1767. The new act created a Board of American Customs Commissioners in Boston and vice-admiralty courts in Halifax, Boston, Philadelphia, and Charleston. These administrative innovations posed a greater threat to American autonomy than did the small sums raised by the import duties.

New York prompted Townshend to raise a new threat to the colonial assemblies when it refused to comply with the Quartering Act of 1765. Fearing an unlimited drain on its treasury, the New York legislature first denied General Gage's requests for barracks and supplies and then limited its assistance. In response, the British ministry instructed New York to pay the entire cost of its defense against Indian raids. If the assembly refused, some members of Parliament threatened to impose a special duty on New York's imports and exports. The earl of Shelburne, the new secretary of state, went even further, suggesting the appointment of a military governor with authority to seize funds from New York's treasury to pay for quartering the troops and "to act with Force or Gentleness as circumstances might make necessary." Townshend decided on a less provocative measure, the Restraining Act of 1767, which suspended the New York assembly until it submitted to the Quartering Act. Faced with the loss of self-government, New Yorkers appropriated the required funds.

The Restraining Act was of great significance because it threatened Americans with the loss of their representative governments. The British Privy Council had always supervised the assemblies, invalidating about 5 percent of all colonial laws (such as those establishing land banks or vesting new powers in the assemblies). Townshend's Restraining Act went much further by declaring American governmental institutions to be completely dependent on Parliamentary favor.

AMERICA AGAIN DEBATES AND RESISTS

The Townshend duties revived the constitutional debate over taxation. During the Stamp Act crisis some Americans had suggested that "external" duties on trade, which Britain had always regulated, were acceptable but that direct or "internal" taxes, which had never before been levied, were not. Townshend thought this distinction between internal and external taxes "perfect nonsense" but told Parliament that "since Americans were pleased to make that distinction, he was willing to indulge them [and] . . . to confine himself to regulations of Trade." Most colonial leaders refused to accept the legitimacy of Townshend's measures, however. They agreed with John Dickinson, author of *Letters from a Farmer in Pennsylvania* (1768), that the real issue was not whether the tax was internal or external but the intention of the legislation. Because the Townshend duties were really designed to raise revenue, they amounted to taxes imposed without consent.

Townshend's measures reinvigorated the American resistance movement. In February 1768 the Massachusetts House of Representatives sent a letter to the other assemblies condemning the Townshend Act, and by the summer Boston and New York merchants had begun a new boycott of British goods. Philadelphia merchants, sailors, and dockworkers, who were more directly involved in trade with Britain, refused to join the movement, believing they had too much to lose. Nonetheless, public support for nonimportation gradually emerged in the smaller port cities of Salem, Newport, and Baltimore and in the countryside. In Puritan New England, ministers and public officials supported the boycott by condemning the use of "foreign superfluities" and promoting the domestic manufacture of necessities such as cloth (Table 5.1).

American women, ordinarily excluded from public affairs, became crucial to the nonimportation movement through their production of "homespun" textiles. During the Stamp Act boycott of English manufactured goods, the wives and daughters of Patriot leaders had increased their output of yarn and cloth. Resistance to the Townshend duties mobilized a much broader group of women, including pious farmwives who assembled to spin yarn at the homes of their ministers. Some gatherings were openly patriotic, such as one in Berwick, Maine, where "true

TABLE 5.1
Patriot Resistance, 1762–1775

British Action	Date	Patriot Response
Revenue Act	1762	Merchants complain privately
Proclamation Line	1763	Land speculators voice discontent
Sugar Act	1764	Protests by merchants and Massachusetts House
Stamp Act	1765	Riots by Sons of Liberty / Stamp Act Congress / First nonimportation movement
Quartering Act	1765	New York Assembly refuses to implement until 1767
Townshend Duties	1767	Second nonimportation movement / Harassment of pro-British merchants
Troops occupy Boston	1768	Boston Massacre of 1770
Gaspée affair	1772	Committees of Correspondence created
Tea Act	1773	Widespread resistance / Boston Tea Party
Coercive Acts and Quebec Act	1774	First Continental Congress / Third nonimportation movement
British raids on Lexington and Concord	1775	Armed resistance by Minutemen / Second Continental Congress

Daughters of Liberty" celebrated American goods, "drinking rye coffee and dining on bear venison." Many more women's groups combined support for nonimportation with charitable work by spinning flax and wool to donate to the needy.

Newspapers celebrated these women as Patriots, prompting thousands to redouble their efforts at the spinning wheel and loom. One Massachusetts town proudly claimed an annual output of 30,000 yards of cloth; East Hartford, Connecticut, reported 17,000 yards. Although this surge in domestic production did not compensate for the loss of British imports, which had averaged about 10 million yards a year, it inspired support for nonimportation in hundreds of communities.

Indeed, the boycott united thousands of Americans in a common political movement. The Sons of Liberty published the names of merchants who imported British goods, broke their store windows, and harassed their employees. In March 1769 most Philadelphia merchants finally responded to public pressure and joined the nonimportation movement. Two months later the members of the Virginia House of Burgesses agreed not to buy dutied articles, luxury goods, or slaves imported by British merchants. "The whole continent from New England to Georgia seems firmly fixed," the *Massachusetts Gazette* proudly announced; "like a strong, well-constructed arch, the more weight there is laid upon it, the firmer it stands;

and thus with America, the more we are loaded, the more we are united." Reflecting colonial self-confidence, Benjamin Franklin called for a return to the pre-1763 mercantilist system and proposed a "plan of conciliation" that was really a demand for British capitulation: "repeal the laws, renounce the right, recall the troops, refund the money, and return to the old method of requisition."

But American resistance only increased British determination. When a copy of the Massachusetts House's letter opposing the Townshend duties reached London in the late spring of 1768, Lord Hillsborough, the secretary of state for American affairs, branded it as "unjustifiable opposition to the constitutional authority of Parliament." To strengthen the "Hand of Government" in Massachusetts and assist the Commissioners of the Customs, who had been forced by a mob to take refuge on a British naval vessel, Hillsborough dispatched four regiments of troops to Boston. By the end of 1768, 4,000 British regulars were encamped in Boston, and military coercion was a very real prospect. General Gage accused public leaders in Massachusetts of "Treasonable and desperate Resolves" and advised the ministry to "Quash this Spirit at a Blow." Parliament responded by threatening to appoint a special commission to hear evidence of treason, and Hillsborough tried to win support for a plan that would isolate Massachusetts from the other colonies and then use the British army to bring the rebellious New Englanders to their knees.

The stakes had risen. In 1765 American resistance to taxation had provoked a Parliamentary debate. In 1768 it produced a plan for military coercion.

LORD NORTH COMPROMISES, 1770

At this critical moment the British ministry's resolve faltered. A food shortage in Britain caused riots across the countryside; in the highly publicized "Massacre of Saint George Fields," troops killed seven demonstrators. The Radical Whig John Wilkes, supported by associations of merchants, tradesmen, and artisans, stepped up his attacks on government corruption and won election to Parliament. Overjoyed, American Patriots drank toasts in Wilkes's honor and purchased thousands of teapots and drinking mugs emblazoned with his picture. Riots in Ireland over the growing military budget there added to the ministry's difficulties.

The American trade boycott also began to hurt. Normally the colonies had an annual trade deficit of £500,000, but in 1768 they imported less from Great Britain, cutting the deficit to £230,000. In 1769 the boycott had a major impact. By continuing to export tobacco, rice, fish, and other goods to Britain while refusing to buy its manufactured goods, Americans accumulated a trade surplus of £816,000. To revive their flagging fortunes, British merchants and manufacturers petitioned Parliament for repeal of the Townshend duties. British government revenues, which were heavily dependent on excise taxes and duties on imported goods, had also suffered. By late 1769 merchants' petitions had persuaded some ministers that the Townshend duties were a mistake, and the king had withdrawn his support for Hillsborough's coercive military plans.

Early in 1770 Lord North became prime minister and arranged a new compromise. Arguing that it was foolish to tax British exports to America, raising their price and decreasing consumption, North persuaded Parliament to repeal the duties on glass, paper, paint, and other manufactured items. But he retained the tax on tea as a symbol of Parliament's supremacy. Gratified, merchants in New York and Philadelphia rejected pleas from Patriots in Boston to continue the boycott. Indeed, most Americans did not contest the symbolic levy on tea but simply avoided the tax by drinking smuggled tea.

Even violence in New York City and Boston did not rupture the compromise. During the boycott New York artisans and workers had taunted British troops, mostly with words but occasionally with stones and fists. In retaliation the soldiers tore down a Liberty Pole (a Patriot flagpole), setting off a week of street fighting. In Boston friction between the residents and British soldiers over constitutional principles and everyday issues, such as competition for part-time jobs, sparked the "Boston Massacre." In March 1770, a group of soldiers fired into a rowdy crowd, killing five men, including one of the leaders, Crispus Attucks, an escaped slave who was working as a seaman. A Radical Whig pamphlet accused the British of deliberately planning the massacre.

Although most Americans remained loyal to the empire, five years of conflict over taxes and constitutional principles had taken its toll. In 1765 American public leaders had accepted Parliament's authority; the Stamp Act Resolves had opposed only certain "unconstitutional" legislation. By 1770 the most outspoken Patriots—Benjamin Franklin in Pennsylvania, Patrick Henry in Virginia, and Samuel Adams in Massachusetts—had repudiated Parliamentary supremacy, claiming equality for the American assemblies. Franklin wanted to create a looser form of empire, with Britain and the colonies as "distinct and separate states" united under "the same Head, or Sovereign, the King." His proposal horrified Thomas Hutchinson, the American-born royal governor of Massachusetts, who rejected the idea of "two independent legislatures in one and the same state." For Hutchinson, the British empire was a single whole, its sovereignty indivisible. "I know of no line," he told the Massachusetts House of Representatives, "that can be drawn between the supreme authority of Parliament and the total independence of the colonies."

There the matter rested. The British had twice tried to impose taxes on the colonies, and American Patriots had twice forced them to retreat. If Parliament insisted on exercising its claim to sovereignty, at least some Americans would have to be subdued by force. Fearful of civil war, the ministry hesitated to take the final fateful step.

The Road to War, 1771–1775

The repeal of the Townshend duties in 1770 restored harmony to the British empire. For the next three years most disputes were resolved peacefully. Yet below the surface lay strong fears and passions and mutual distrust. Suddenly, in 1773 those undercurrents erupted, overwhelming any hope for compromise. In less than two years the Americans and the British stood on the brink of war.

THE TEA ACT: THE COMPROMISE IGNORED

Radical Boston Patriots who wanted greater rights for the colonies continued to warn Americans of the dangers of imperial domination. In November 1772 Samuel Adams persuaded the Boston town meeting to establish a Committee of Correspondence to write to Patriots in other towns and colonies in order "to state the Rights of the Colonists of this Province." Within a few months eighty Massachusetts towns had similar committees. Other colonies copied the practice when the British government set up a royal commission to investigate the burning of the *Gaspée*, a British customs vessel, in Rhode Island. The commission's powers, particularly its authority to send Americans to Britain for trial, first aroused the Virginia House of Burgesses, which created a Committee of Correspondence "to communicate with the other colonies" about the situation in Rhode Island. By July 1773 committees had sprung up in Connecticut, New Hampshire, and South Carolina.

Parliament's passage of a Tea Act in May 1773 initiated the chain of events that led directly to civil war. Lord North had designed the act to provide financial relief for the British East India Company, which was deeply in debt because of military expeditions undertaken to extend British trade in India. The Tea Act provided the company with a government loan and, more important, relieved the Company of paying tariffs on the tea it imported into Britain or exported to the colonies. Only the American consumers would pay the duty.

Lord North failed to understand how unpopular the Tea Act would be in America. Since 1768, when the Townshend Act had placed a duty of 3 pence a pound on tea, the colonies had evaded the tax by illegally importing tea from Dutch sources. However, by relieving the East India Company of English tariffs, the Tea Act was designed to make its tea cheaper than Dutch tea—and thus encourage Americans to pay the Townshend duty on tea. Consequently, radical Patriots accused the ministry of bribing Americans to give up their principled opposition to British taxation. As an anonymous woman wrote in the *Massachusetts Spy*, "the use of [British] tea is considered not as a private but as a public evil . . . a handle to introduce a variety of . . . oppressions amongst us." In addition to taxation, another such oppression was the East India Company's decision to distribute the tea directly to shopkeepers, a tactic that would exclude most colonial merchants from the profits of the trade. "The fear of an Introduction of a Monopoly in this Country," General Haldimand reported from New York, "has induced the mercantile part of the Inhabitants to be very industrious in opposing this Step and added Strength to a Spirit of Independence already too prevalent."

The newly formed Committees of Correspondence took the lead in organizing resistance to the Tea Act. They held public bonfires at which they persuaded their fellow citizens (sometimes gently, sometimes not) to consign British tea to the flames. The Sons of Liberty also prevented East India Company ships from landing new supplies. By forcing the Company's captains to return the tea to Britain or store it in public warehouses, the Patriots effectively nullified the legislation.

Governor Thomas Hutchinson of Massachusetts was determined to uphold the Tea Act and hatched a scheme to land the tea and collect the tax. When a shipment of tea arrived on the *Dartmouth*, he had the ship passed through customs immediately so that the Sons of Liberty could not prevent its landing. If necessary, he was prepared to use the British army to unload the tea and supervise its sale by auction. But Patriots foiled the governor's plan by raiding the *Dartmouth*: a group of artisans and laborers disguised as Indians boarded the ship, broke open the 342 chests of tea (valued at about £10,000, or roughly $800,000 today), and threw them into the harbor. "This destruction of the Tea is so bold and it must have so important Consequences," John Adams wrote in his diary, "that I cannot but consider it as an Epoch in History."

The British Privy Council was outraged, as was the king. "Concessions have made matters worse," George III declared. "The time has come for compulsion." Early in 1774 Parliament decisively rejected a proposal to repeal the duty on American tea; instead, it enacted four Coercive Acts to force Massachusetts into submission. A Port Bill closed Boston Harbor until the East India Company received payment for the destroyed tea. A Government Act annulled the Massachusetts charter and prohibited most local town meetings. A new Quartering Act required the colony to build barracks or accommodate soldiers in private houses. To protect royal officials from Patriot-dominated juries in Massachusetts, a Justice Act allowed the transfer of trials for capital crimes to other colonies or to Britain.

In response, Patriot leaders throughout the mainland colonies condemned these "Intolerable Acts" and rallied support for Massachusetts. In far-off Georgia, a Patriot warned the "Freemen of the Province" that "every privilege you at present claim as a birthright, may be wrested from you by the same authority that blockades the town of Boston." "The cause of Boston," George Washington declared from Virginia, "now is and ever will be considered as the cause of America." The activities of the Committees of Correspondence had created a firm sense of unity.

In 1774 Parliament passed the Quebec Act, which heightened the sense of common danger among Americans of European Protestant descent who lived in the seaboard colonies. The law extended the boundaries of Quebec into the Ohio River Valley, thus restricting the western boundaries of Virginia and other coastal colonies and angering influential land speculators and politicians with western land claims (see Map 5.2). It also gave legal recognition in Quebec to Roman Catholicism, a humane concession to the colony's predominantly French Catholics but one that aroused old religious hatreds, especially in New England, where Puritans associated Catholicism with arbitrary royal government and popish superstition. Although the ministry had not intended the Quebec Act as a coercive measure, many colonial leaders saw it as another demonstration of Parliament's power to intervene in American domestic affairs.

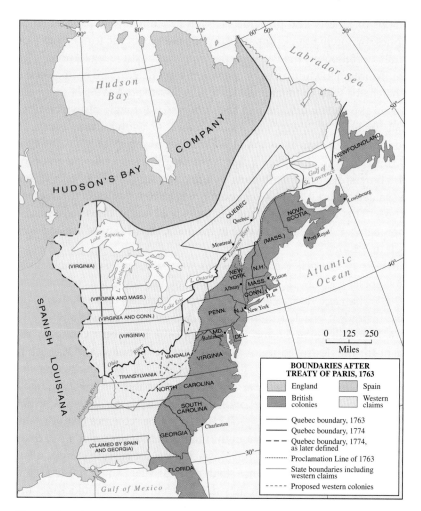

M AP 5.2
British Western Policy, 1763–1774

The Proclamation Line of 1763 prohibited white settlement west of the Appalachian Mountains. Nevertheless, colonial land speculators planned the new colonies of Vandalia and Tran-
sylvania. However, the Quebec Act of 1774 designated these western lands as Indian reserves
and, by vastly increasing the boundaries of Quebec, eliminated the sea-to-sea land claims of
many eastern colonies. The act angered many Americans: settlers and land speculators, New
England Protestants who feared Catholicism in Quebec, and Patriots who condemned its failure to provide a representative assembly in Quebec.

THE CONTINENTAL CONGRESS RESPONDS

American leaders called for a new all-colony assembly, the Continental Congress.
The newer colonies—Florida, Quebec, Nova Scotia, and Newfoundland—did not
attend, nor did Georgia, whose legislature was effectively controlled by a royal gov-

Religion and Rebellion

Many American Protestants hated bishops and the ecclesiastical power they represented. This cartoon warned that the Quebec Bill of 1774, which allowed the practice of Catholicism in Canada, was part of a plot by the hierarchy of the Church of England to impose bishops on the American colonies. (Courtesy of the John Carter Brown Library at Brown University, Providence, RI)

ernor. But delegates chosen by the other twelve mainland assemblies met in Philadelphia in September 1774. New England delegates advocated political union and defensive military preparations. Southern leaders had long resented the Navigation Acts and feared a British plot "to overturn the constitution and introduce a system of arbitrary government." They favored a new economic boycott, but many delegates from the middle colonies held out for a political compromise.

Led by Joseph Galloway of Pennsylvania, these men of "loyal principles" outlined a scheme for a new imperial system that resembled the Albany Plan of Union of 1754. Under Galloway's proposal, America would have a legislative council selected by the colonial assemblies and a president-general appointed by the king. The new council would have veto power over Parliamentary legislation that affected America. Despite this feature, however, the delegates refused to endorse Galloway's plan. With British troops occupying Boston, it was thought to be too conciliatory.

Instead, the First Continental Congress passed a Declaration of Rights and Grievances that condemned the Coercive Acts and demanded their repeal. It also repudiated the Declaratory Act of 1766, which had proclaimed Parliament's supremacy over the colonies, and demanded that Britain restrict its supervision of American affairs to matters of external trade. Finally, the Congress began a program of economic retaliation, beginning with nonimportation and nonconsumption agreements that would take effect in December 1774. If Parliament did not repeal the Intolerable Acts by September 1775, virtually all colonial exports to

Britain, Ireland, and the British West Indies would be cut off. Ten years of constitutional conflict had culminated in a threat of all-out commercial warfare.

Even at this late date a few British leaders hoped for compromise. In January
1775 the earl of Chatham (William Pitt) asked that Parliament give up its claim to
tax the colonies and recognize the Continental Congress as a lawful body. In return
for these and other concessions, he suggested, the Congress should acknowledge
Parliamentary supremacy and grant a continuing revenue to help defray the British
national debt.

The British ministry rejected Chatham's plan. Twice it had backed down in the
face of colonial resistance; a third retreat was impossible. The honor of the nation
was at stake. Branding the Continental Congress an illegal assembly, it dismissed
Lord Dartmouth's proposal to send commissioners to America to negotiate a settlement. Instead, Lord North unilaterally set stringent terms: Americans must pay
for their own defense and administration and acknowledge Parliament's authority
to tax them. To put teeth in these demands, North imposed a naval blockade on
American trade with foreign nations and ordered General Gage to suppress dissent
in Massachusetts. "Now the case seemed desperate," the prime minister told former
Massachusetts Governor Thomas Hutchinson, who was living in exile in London.
"Parliament would not—could not—concede. For aught he could see it must come
to violence."

THE RISING OF THE COUNTRYSIDE

Ultimately, the success of the urban-led Patriot movement would depend on the
actions of the large rural population. At first most farmers had little interest in
imperial issues. Their lives were deeply rooted in the soil, and their prime allegiance
was to family and community. But the French and Indian War intruded into their
lives, taking their sons for military duty and raising their taxes. In Newtown, Long
Island, farmers had paid an average of 10 shillings a year in taxes until 1754; by
1756 their wartime taxes had jumped to 30 shillings. Peace brought only slight relief, for in 1771 the British-imposed Quartering Act cost each Newtown resident 20
shillings in taxes. These levies angered rural Americans, though in fact they paid
much lower taxes than did most Britons.

The urban-led nonimportation movements of 1765 and 1769 also raised the
political consciousness of many rural Americans. When the Continental Congress
declared a new economic boycott of British goods in 1774, it easily established a
network of local Committees of Safety and Inspection to support it. Appealing to
rural thriftiness, the Congress condemned those who wore expensive imported
clothes to funerals, approving only "a black crape or ribbon on the arm or hat for
gentlemen, and a black ribbon and necklace for ladies." In Concord, Massachusetts,
80 percent of male heads of families and a number of single women signed a Solemn
League and Covenant vowing support for nonimportation.

Patriots also appealed to the yeoman tradition of agricultural independence, which was everywhere under attack. Arable land had become scarce and expensive in long-settled regions; in many new communities merchants were seizing farmsteads for delinquent debts. The new demands of the British government would further drain "this People of the Fruits of their Toil," complained the town meeting of Petersham, Massachusetts. "The duty on tea," added a Patriot pamphlet, "was only a prelude to a window-tax, hearth-tax, land-tax, and poll-tax, and these were only paving the way for reducing the country to lordships." By the 1770s many northern yeomen felt personally threatened by British imperial policy.

Despite their much higher standard of living, southern slaveowners had similar fears. Many influential Virginia Patriots—including Patrick Henry, George Washington, and Thomas Jefferson—were speculators in western lands and reacted angrily when first the Proclamation Line of 1763 and then the Quebec Act of 1774 invalidated their claims and their hopes of great fortunes. Moreover, many Chesapeake planters had fallen deeply into debt to British merchants, usually because of extravagant spending. "I must return again to a low and less expensive Prudence," planter Landon Carter vowed unsuccessfully in 1771. As Washington noted, Carter and other planters wanted to live "genteely and hospitably" and were "ashamed" to adopt frugal ways. Accustomed to being masters on their plantations, they resented their financial dependence and feared the prospect of political dependence. Once Parliament used the Coercive Acts to subdue Massachusetts, the planters feared, it might seize control of Virginia's county courts and House of Burgesses, depriving the gentry of its political power. This threat moved Patriot planters to action, closing the courts so that yeomen could bargain with Scottish merchants over tobacco prices without risking suits for debt. "The spark of liberty is not yet extinct among our people," one planter declared, "and if properly fanned by the Gentlemen of influence will, I make no doubt, burst out again into a flame."

While many wealthy planters and affluent merchants supported the Patriot cause, other prominent Americans worried that resistance to Britain would destroy respect for all political institutions, ending in mob rule. Their fears increased when the Sons of Liberty turned to violence to enforce nonimportation. As a well-to-do New Yorker complained, "No man can be in a more abject state of bondage than he whose Reputation, Property and Life are exposed to the discretionary violence . . . of the community." As the crisis continued, these men rallied to the support of the royal governors.

Other social groups also refused to support the resistance movement. In regions where many wealthy landlords became Patriots, such as the Hudson Valley of New York, tenant farmers supported the crown because they hated their landlords. Similar social divisions prompted some Regulators in the North Carolina backcountry and many farmers on the eastern shore of Chesapeake Bay in Maryland to oppose the policies advocated by the local Patriot gentry. A group of enslaved blacks in Virginia, James Madison reported in November 1774, planned to flee from their Patriot owners and had chosen "a leader who was to conduct them when the English troops should arrive." Many Quakers and Germans in Pennsylvania and New Jersey tried to remain neutral because of pacifist religious principles and fear of political change.

Beginning in 1774, prominent Americans of "loyal principles"—mostly royal officials, merchants with military contracts, clergy of the Church of England, and well-established lawyers—denounced the Patriot movement, accusing it of seeking independence. They formed an articulate pro-British party, but one that remained small and ineffective. A Tory Association started by Governor Wentworth of New Hampshire drew only fifty-nine members, fourteen of whom were the governor's relatives. At this crucial juncture Americans who favored resistance to British rule commanded the allegiance—or at least the acquiescence—of the majority of white Americans.

THE FAILURE OF COMPROMISE

When the Continental Congress met in September 1774, New England was already in open defiance of British authority. In August 150 delegates had gathered in Concord, Massachusetts, for a Middlesex County Congress. This illegal convention had advised Patriots to close the royal courts of justice and transfer their political allegiance to the popularly elected House of Representatives. Following the congress, armed crowds harassed Loyalists and ensured Patriot rule in most of New England.

General Thomas Gage, by then the military governor of Massachusetts, tried desperately to maintain imperial power. In September 1774 he ordered British troops in Boston to seize Patriot armories and storehouses at Charlestown and Cambridge. In response, 20,000 colonial militiamen mobilized to safeguard military supply depots in Concord and Worcester. The Concord town meeting voted to raise a defensive force, the famous Minutemen, to "Stand at a minutes warning in Case of alarm." Increasingly, Gage's authority was limited to Boston, where it rested primarily on the bayonets of his 3,500 troops. Meanwhile, the Massachusetts House met on its own authority, issued regulations for the collection of taxes, strengthened the militia, and assumed the responsibilities of government.

Even before the news of Massachusetts's defiance reached London, the colonial secretary, Lord Dartmouth, had proclaimed the colony to be in a state of "open rebellion." Declaring that "force should be repelled by force," he ordered Gage to march quickly against the "rude rabble." On the night of April 18, 1775, Gage dispatched 700 soldiers to capture colonial leaders and supplies at Concord. But Paul Revere and two other Bostonians warned the Patriots, and at dawn on April 19 local militiamen met the British first at Lexington and then at Concord. The skirmishes took a dozen lives. As the British retreated along the narrow roads to Boston, they were repeatedly ambushed by militiamen from neighboring towns. By the end of the day, 73 British soldiers were dead, 174 wounded, and 26 missing. British fire had killed 49 American militiamen and wounded 39 (see American Voices, "A British View of Lexington and Concord").

AMERICAN VOICES

A British View of Lexington and Concord

LIEUTENANT-COLONEL FRANKLIN SMITH

O n April 26, 1775, the Patriot-controlled Provincial Congress issued what it called a "true, and authentic account" of the battles at Lexington and Concord, declaring that at Lexington "the regulars rushed on with great violence and first began the hostilities" and that in the retreat of the British troops "women in child-bed were driven by soldiery naked in the streets, old men peaceably in their houses were shot dead." British Lieutenant-Colonel Franklin Smith offered a very different account of those events.

At Lexington . . . [we] found on a green close to the road a body of the country people drawn up in military order, with arms and accoutrements, and, as appeared afterward, loaded. . . . Our troops advanced towards them, without any intention of injuring them . . . ; but they in confusion went off, principally to the left, only one of them fired before he went off, and three or four more jumped over a wall and fired from behind it among the soldiers; on which the troops returned it, and killed several of them. They likewise fired on the soldiers from the Meeting and dwelling-houses. . . .

While at Concord we saw vast numbers assembling in many parts; at one of the bridges they marched down, with a very considerable body, on the light infantry posted there. On their coming pretty near, one of our men fired on them, which they returned; on which an action ensued and some few were killed and wounded. In this affair, it appears that, after the bridge was quitted, they scalped and otherwise ill treated one or two of [our] men who were either killed or severely wounded. . . .

On our leaving Concord to return to Boston they began to fire on us from behind walls, ditches, trees, &c., which, as we marched, increased to a very great degree, and continued . . . for, I believe, upwards of eighteen miles; so that I can't think but it must have been a preconcerted scheme in them, to attack the King's troops the first favorable opportunity that offered; otherwise, I think they could not, in such a short a time from our marching out, have raised such a numerous body.

SOURCE: Massachusetts Historical Society, *Proceedings, 1876* (Boston, 1876), pp. 350ff.

In the aftermath of the Stamp Act and Townshend duties, political leaders had fashioned compromises that patched up the fabric of empire. By the time of the Tea Act, neither the British ministry nor the Patriot leadership was prepared to give way, and the extent of the fighting in Massachusetts settled the issue. Too much blood had now been spilled to allow another compromise. Twelve years of economic conflict and constitutional debate had ended in civil war.

T I M E L I N E

1754–1763	Seven Years (French and Indian) War. British national debt doubles.	1768	Second nonimportation movement begins. Daughters of Liberty make homespun cloth. British army occupies Boston.
1760	George III becomes king.		
1763	Proclamation Line restricts western settlement. Peacetime army in America Grenville becomes prime minister.	1770	North compromises: repeals most Townshend duties. Boston Massacre
1764	Sugar Act Colonists oppose vice-admiralty courts. Franklin proposes American representation in Parliament.	1772	*Gaspée* affair prompts creation of Committees of Correspondence.
		1773	Tea Act leads to Boston Tea Party.
		1774	Coercive Acts punish Massachusetts. Quebec Act First Continental Congress meets. Third nonimportation movement Loyalists organize.
1765	Stamp Act Stamp Act Congress and riots led by Sons of Liberty		
1765–1766	First nonimportation movement	1775	Ministry orders Gage to suppress rebellion in Massachusetts. Battles of Lexington and Concord
1766	Parliament compromises: repeals Stamp Act and enacts Declaratory Act.		
1767	Townshend duties Restraining Act in New York		

For Further Exploration

Two stimulating overviews of the prerevolutionary years are A. J. Langguth's *Patriots: The Men Who Started the American Revolution* (1988), a suspenseful story of such famous figures as George Washington, John Adams, Samuel Adams, and Patrick Henry, and Edward Countryman's *The American Revolution* (1985), which focuses on ordinary people. Edmund Morgan and Helen Morgan also use the experience of individual colonists to tell the story of *The Stamp Act Crisis* (1953). Philip Lawson's *George Grenville* (1984) offers a sympathetic biography of a reform-minded prime minister. The coming of the revolution is covered in three lucidly written and broadly conceived studies. Hiller B. Zobel's *The Boston Massacre* (1970) captures the social unrest and latent violence of these years, while Benjamin Labaree's *The Boston Tea Party* suggests how one "small" event altered the course of history. The rise of the Radical Patriots and the outbreak of the fighting in Massachusetts is captivatingly retold in David Hackett Fischer's *Paul Revere's Ride* (1994). For events in Virginia, see the exciting study by Woody Holton, *Forced Founders: Indians, Debtors, Slaves, & the Making of the American Revolution in Virginia* (1999).

Liberty! The American Revolution (6 hours), a six-part video available through PBS, provides a coherent narrative of the movement for independence. Contrasting firsthand accounts of Boston Massacre are available on the website "From Revolution to Reconstruction" at the University of Groningen, available at <http://odur.let.rug.nl/~usa/D/1751 -1775/bostonmassacre/prest.htm>, which also contains other materials on the revolutionary era. The website of the National Gallery of Art, available at <http://www.nga.gov>, has an interesting section devoted to American paintings of the colonial and revolutionary periods, including a detailed analysis of a work by Jonathan Copley. See its "Index of American Design" for a collection of eighteenth-century German-American folk art.

Part Two

THE NEW REPUBLIC
1775–1820

THEMATIC TIMELINE

	GOVERNMENT	DIPLOMACY	ECONOMY
	CREATING REPUBLICAN INSTITUTIONS	EUROPEAN ENTANGLEMENTS	EXPANDING COMMERCE AND MANUFACTURING
1775	• State constitutions devised and implemented	• Independence declared (1776) • French alliance (1778)	• Wartime expansion of manufacturing
1780	• Articles of Confederation ratified (1781) • Philadelphia convention drafts U.S. Constitution (1787).	• Treaty of Paris (1783) • British trade restrictions in West Indies • U.S. government signs treaties with Indian peoples.	• Bank of North America (1781) • Commercial recession (1783–1789) • Western land speculation
1790	• Bill of Rights (1791) • First national parties: Federalists and Republicans	• Wars of the French Revolution • Jay's and Pinckney's treaties (1795) • Undeclared war with France (1798)	• First Bank of the United States (1792–1812) • States charter business corporations. • Outwork expands.
1800	• Revolution of 1800 • Activist state legislatures • Chief Justice Marshall asserts judicial power.	• Napoleonic wars (1802–1815) • Louisiana Purchase (1803) • Embargo of 1807	• Cotton expands into Old Southwest. • Farm productivity improves. • Embargo encourages U.S. manufacturing.
1810	• Triumph of Republican Party • State constitutions democratized	• War of 1812 • Treaty of Ghent (1816) ends war.	• Second Bank of the United States (1816–1836) • Supreme Court protects business. • Emergence of a national economy

SOCIETY		CULTURE
DEFINING LIBERTY AND EQUALITY		**PLURALISM AND NATIONAL IDENTITY**
• Emancipation of slaves begins in the North.		• Paine's *Common Sense* calls for a republic.
• Virginia Statute of Religious Freedom (1786) • Idea of republican motherhood		• Land ordinances create a national domain in the West.
• French Revolution sparks ideological debate. • Sedition Act limits freedom of the press (1798).		• Indians form Western Confederacy. • Sectional divisions emerge between South and North.
• Young choose own marriage partners. • New Jersey ends woman suffrage (1807). • Atlantic slave trade legally ended (1808)		• African Americans absorb Protestant Christianity. • Tenskwatawa and Tecumseh revive Indian identity.
• Expansion of suffrage for white men • New England abolishes established church (1820s).		• War of 1812 tests national unity. • Second Great Awakening shapes American culture.

"The American war is over," the Philadelphia Patriot Benjamin Rush declared in 1787, "but this is far from being the case with the *American revolution*. On the contrary, nothing but the first act of the great drama is closed. It remains yet to establish and perfect our new forms of government." The job was even greater than Rush imagined, for the republican revolution of 1776 challenged nearly all the values and institutions of the colonial social order, forcing changes not only in politics but also in economic, religious, and cultural life.

The first and most fundamental task was to devise a republican system of government. In 1775 no one in America knew how the new state governments should be organized and if there should be a permanent central authority along the lines of the Continental Congress. It would take time and experience to find out. It would take even longer to come to terms with a new institution, the political party. Yet by 1820 American political leaders had fashioned a successful republican system on both the state and national levels. This system of political authority had three striking characteristics: popular sovereignty—government of the people; activist legislatures that pursued

157

the public good—government for the people; and democratic decision making by most white adult men—government by the people.

To create and preserve their new republic, Americans of European descent had to fight two wars against Great Britain, an undeclared war against France, and many battles with Indian peoples and confederations. The wars against Britain divided the country into bitter factions—Patriots versus Loyalists in 1776 and prowar Republicans against antiwar Federalists in 1812—and expended much blood and treasure. Tragically, the settlement of the trans-Appalachian West by white Americans brought cultural disaster to many Indian peoples, whose lives were destroyed by European diseases and alcohol and whose lands were seized by gun-toting settlers. Whatever the costs, by 1820 the United States had emerged as a strong independent state, free from a half-century of entanglement in the wars and diplomacy of Europe and prepared to exploit the riches of the continent.

By this time the expansion of commerce and the market system had laid the foundations for a strong national economy. Beginning in the 1780s merchants financed commercial banks and organized a rural-based system of manufacturing, while state governments used charters and legal incentives to provide improved transportation. Southern planters carried slavery west to Alabama and Mississippi and grew rich by exporting a new crop—cotton—to markets in Europe and the North. Simultaneously northern farm families settled new lands in the Midwest where they grew bountiful crops of wheat and corn, produced raw materials such as leather and wool for the new manufacturing enterprises, and undertook additional labor as handicraft workers. As a result of these efforts, by 1820 the new American republic was on the verge of achieving economic as well as political independence.

As Americans defined the character of their new republican society, they divided along lines of gender, race, religion, and class. They also held differing views on many fundamental questions—legal equality for women, the status of slavery, the meaning of religious liberty, and the public's responsibility to address social inequality. Public sentiment and responsive political leaders resolved some of these issues, moving to end slavery in the North and to eliminate the system of state-sponsored churches. But Americans continued to argue over southern slavery, distinctions of wealth and status, and the nature of family relations in a republican society.

The final task Americans faced—creating a distinct culture and identity—was complicated by the diversity of peoples and regions. Native Americans still lived in their own clans and nations, while black Americans, one-fifth of the enumerated population, were developing a new, African American culture. The white inhabitants created vigorous regional cultures and preserved parts of their ancestral heritage—English, Scottish, Scots-Irish, German, and Dutch. Nevertheless, political institutions began to unite Americans, as did their increasing participation in the market economy and in evangelical Protestant churches. By 1820 to be an American meant, for the dominant white population, being a republican, a Protestant, and an enterprising individual in a capitalist-run market system.

Chapter 6

WAR AND REVOLUTION
1775–1783

A government of our own is our natural right . . . 'TIS TIME TO PART.
—Thomas Paine, 1776

When the Patriots of Frederick County, Maryland, demanded loyalty to the American cause in 1776, Robert Gassaway would have none of it. "It was better for the poor people to lay down their arms and pay the duties and taxes laid upon them by King and Parliament," he told local Council of Safety, "than to be . . . commanded and ordered about." The story was much the same in Farmington, Connecticut, where Nathaniel Jones and seventeen other men were imprisoned for a month for "remaining neutral" and failing to join their militia unit in opposing a British raid. Everywhere, the logic of events was forcing families to choose sides. In this battle for the allegiance of ordinary men and women, the Patriots' control of local governments gave them the edge. Combining physical threats with monetary incentives, they built loyal militia units and an effective Continental army. "I admire the American troops tremendously!" exclaimed a French officer toward the end of the war. "It is incredible that soldiers composed of every age, even children of fifteen, of whites and blacks, almost naked, unpaid, and rather poorly fed, can march so well and withstand fire so steadfastly."

Military mobilization created political commitment. By forcing ordinary Americans to support the war—as soldiers, taxpayers, or loyal residents—Patriots prompted some to turn to Loyalism and many more to become active republicans. "From subjects to citizens the difference is immense," remarked the South Carolina physician and Patriot David Ramsay. "Each citizen of a free state contains . . . as much of the common sovereignty as another." By repudiating aristocratic and monarchical rule and raising a democratic army, the Patriots placed sovereignty in the people, launching the age of democratic revolutions.

Toward Independence, 1775–1776

The Battle of Concord was fought on April 19, 1775, but fourteen months would elapse before the rebels formally broke with Britain. In the meantime Patriot legislators in most of the thirteen colonies stretching from New Hampshire to

Georgia threw out their royal governors and created the two essentials for independence: a government and an army.

THE SECOND CONTINENTAL CONGRESS AND CIVIL WAR

Armed struggle in Massachusetts lent urgency to the Second Continental Congress, which met in Philadelphia in May 1775. Soon after the Congress opened, more than 3,000 British troops attacked new American fortifications on Breed's Hill and Bunker Hill overlooking Boston. After three assaults and 1,000 casualties they finally dislodged the Patriot militia. Inspired by his countrymen's valor, John Adams exhorted the Congress to rise to the "defense of American liberty" by creating a Continental army headed by George Washington of Virginia. More cautious delegates and those with Loyalist sympathies warned that these measures would commit the colonists irretrievably to rebellion. After bitter debate Congress approved the proposals—but as Adams lamented, only "by bare majorities."

Despite the blood that had been shed, a majority in Congress still hoped for reconciliation with Britain. Led by John Dickinson of Pennsylvania, these moderates passed an Olive Branch petition, expressing loyalty to George III and requesting the repeal of oppressive parliamentary legislation. But zealous Patriots such as Samuel Adams of Massachusetts and Patrick Henry of Virginia mobilized anti-imperial sentiment by winning passage of a Declaration of the Causes and Necessities of Taking Up Arms. Americans dreaded the "calamities of civil war," it asserted, but were "resolved to die Freemen rather than to live [as] slaves." The king decided the issue by refusing to receive the moderates' petition and in August 1775 issuing a Proclamation for Suppressing Rebellion and Sedition.

In September the radicals in Congress won support for an invasion of Canada that they hoped would unleash a popular uprising and add a fourteenth colony to the rebellion. Patriot forces easily took Montreal, but in December they failed to capture Quebec. To aid the Patriot cause American merchants waged financial warfare, implementing the resolution of the First Continental Congress to cut off all exports to Britain and its West Indian sugar islands. By ending the tobacco trade and disrupting sugar production, they hoped to undermine the British economy. Parliament retaliated at the end of 1775 with a Prohibitory Act outlawing all trade with the rebellious colonies.

Meanwhile, skirmishes between Patriots and Loyalists broke out in Virginia. In June 1775 the Patriot-dominated House of Burgesses forced the royal governor, Lord Dunmore, to take refuge on a British warship in Chesapeake Bay. Branding the Patriots "traitors," the governor organized two military forces—one white, the Queen's Own Loyal Virginians, and one black, the Ethiopian Regiment, enlisting about 1,000 slaves who had fled from their Patriot owners. Then in November Dunmore issued a controversial proclamation, offering freedom to slaves and indentured servants who joined the Loyalist cause. White planters denounced Dunmore's "Diabolical scheme" as "pointing a dagger to their Throats, thru the hands of their slaves." Faced with black unrest and pressed by yeoman and tenant farmers demanding independence, Patriot planters called for a final break with Britain.

In North Carolina as well, military conflict increased demands for independence. Early in 1776 North Carolina's royal governor, Josiah Martin, raised a force of 1,500 Scottish Highlanders from the Carolina backcountry. In response, low-country Patriots mobilized the militia and in February defeated Martin's army at the Battle of Moore's Creek Bridge, capturing more than 800 Highlanders (see American Voices, "The Meaning of War"). By April radical Patriots had transformed the North Carolina assembly into an independent Provincial Congress, which instructed its representatives in Philadelphia "to concur with the Delegates of other Colonies in declaring Independency, and forming foreign alliances." Virginia followed suit. In May, led by James Madison, Edmund Pendleton, and Patrick Henry, Virginia Patriots met in convention and resolved unanimously to support independence.

COMMON SENSE

Resolutions favoring independence came slowly because most Americans retained a deep loyalty to the crown. Joyous crowds had toasted the health of George III following repeal of the Stamp Act, and even as the imperial crisis worsened, Benjamin Franklin had proposed that the king rule over autonomous American assemblies. The very structure of American society supported this loyalty to the crown. Americans used the same metaphors of age and family to describe both social authority and imperial rule. They often pictured the colonies as the dependent children of Britain, the "mother country." Just as the settlers respected male elders in town meetings, churches, and families, so they obeyed the king as the father of his people. Denial of the king's legitimacy might threaten all paternal authority and disrupt the hierarchical social order.

Nonetheless, by 1775 many Americans responded to escalating conflict by accusing George III of supporting oppressive legislation and ordering military retaliation against them. Surprisingly, agitation against the king became especially intense in Philadelphia, the largest but hardly the most tumultuous seaport city. Because Philadelphia merchants harbored Loyalist sympathies, the city had been slow to join the boycott against the Townshend duties. But artisans, who accounted for about half the city's population, had become a powerful force in the Patriot movement. Worried that British imports threatened their small-scale manufacturing enterprises, they organized a Mechanics Association to protect America's "just Rights and Privileges." By February 1776 forty artisans sat with forty-seven merchants on the Philadelphia Committee of Resistance, the extralegal body that enforced the latest trade boycott.

Many Scots-Irish artisans and laborers in Philadelphia became Patriots for religious reasons. They came from Presbyterian families who had fled British-controlled northern Ireland to escape economic and religious discrimination.

AMERICAN VOICES

The Meaning of War

MARY HOOKS SLOCUMB

F or sixteen-year-old Mary Hooks Slocumb, the outbreak of fighting in 1776 had personal significance: it threatened the safety of her husband, a member of the North Carolina Light Horse Rangers.

The men all left on Sunday morning. More than eighty went from this house with my husband. . . . I kept thinking where they had got to—how far; where and how many of the regulars and tories they would meet; [that night] . . . I had a dream. . . . I saw distinctly a body wrapped in my husband's guard cloak—bloody—dead; and others dead and wounded on the ground around him. . . . If ever I felt fear it was at that moment. . . . I went to the stable, saddled my mare—as fleet and easy a nag as ever travelled; and in one minute we were tearing down the road at full speed. . . .

When day broke I was some thirty miles from home. . . . The blind path I had been following brought me into the Wilmington road leading Moore's Creek Bridge. . . . a few yards from the road, under a cluster of trees were lying perhaps twenty men. . . . In an instant my whole soul was centered in one spot; for there, wrapped in his bloody guard-Cloak, was my husband's body! . . . I remember uncovering his head and seeing a face clothed with gore from a dreadful wound across the temple. I put my hand on the bloody face; 'twas warm; and an *unknown voice* begged for water. . . . I brought it; poured some in his mouth; washed his face; and behold—it was Frank Cogdell. He soon revived and could speak. I was washing the wound in his head. Said he, "It is not that; it is that hole in my leg that is killing me." A puddle of blood was standing on the ground around his feet. I took his knife, cut away his trousers and stocking, found the blood came from a shot-hole through and through the fleshy part of his leg. I looked about and could see nothing that looked as if it would do for dressing wounds but some heart-leaves. I gathered a handful and bound them tight to the holes; and the bleeding stopped. . . . I dressed the wounds of many a brave fellow who did good fighting long after that day! . . . Just then I looked up, and my husband, as bloody as a butcher, and as muddy as a ditcher, stood before me.

"Why Mary," he exclaimed, "What are you doing there?" . . . I would not tell my husband what brought me there. . . . In the middle of the night I again mounted my mare and started for home. . . . What a happy ride I had back! and with what joy did I embrace my child as he ran to meet me!

SOURCE: Elizabeth F. Ellet, *The Women of the American Revolution* (1850; New York: Haskell House, 1969), vol. 1: pp. 316–21.

Moreover, many of them had embraced the egalitarian message preached by Gilbert Tennent and other New Light ministers. As pastor of Philadelphia's Second Presbyterian Church, Tennent had told his congregation that all men and women were equal before God. Applying that idea to politics, New Light Presbyterians shouted in street demonstrations that they had "no king but King Jesus." Republican ideas derived from the European Enlightenment also circulated freely in Pennsylvania. Well-educated scientists and statesmen such as Benjamin Franklin and Benjamin Rush questioned not only the wisdom of George III but also the idea of monarchy itself.

At this pivotal moment with popular sentiment in flux, a single pamphlet tipped the balance. In January 1776 Thomas Paine published *Common Sense,* a call for independence and republicanism phrased in language that aroused the general public. Paine had been fired from the English Customs Service for protesting low wages. In 1774, with a letter of introduction from Benjamin Franklin, he had migrated to Philadelphia, where he met Benjamin Rush and others who shared his republican sentiments. In *Common Sense* Paine called George III "the hard hearted sullen Pharaoh of England" and blasted the British system of "mixed government," which yielded only "monarchical tyranny in the person of the King and aristocratical tyranny in the persons of the peers." Almost overnight *Common Sense* turned thousands of ordinary Americans against British rule. "There is abundance talked about independency," a Virginia conservative lamented, "it is all from Mr. Common sense." Paine's message was clear: reject the arbitrary powers of king and Parliament and create independent republican states.

INDEPENDENCE DECLARED

Throughout the colonies Patriot conventions, inspired by Paine's arguments and beset by armed Loyalists, called urgently for a break from Britain. In June 1776 Richard Henry Lee presented the Virginia Convention's resolution to the Continental Congress: "That these United Colonies are, and of right ought to be, free and independent states . . . absolved from all allegiance to the British Crown." Faced with certain defeat, staunch Loyalists and anti-independence moderates withdrew from the Congress, leaving committed Patriots to take the fateful step. On July 4, 1776, the Congress approved a Declaration of Independence.

The main author of the Declaration was Thomas Jefferson, a young Virginia planter and legislative leader who had mobilized resistance to the Coercive Acts with the pamphlet *A Summary View of the Rights of British America.* To persuade Americans and foreign observers of the need to create an independent republic, Jefferson justified the revolt by blaming the rupture on George III rather than on Parliament: "He has plundered our seas, ravaged our coasts, burned our towns, and destroyed the lives of our people. . . . A prince, whose character is thus marked by every act which may define a tyrant, is unfit to be the ruler of a free people."

Jefferson, who was steeped in the ideas and rhetoric of the European Enlightenment, preceded these accusations with a proclamation of "self-evident" truths:

"that all men are created equal"; that they possess the "unalienable rights" of "Life, Liberty, and the pursuit of Happiness"; that government derives its "just powers from the consent of the governed" and can rightly be overthrown if it "becomes destructive of these ends." By linking these doctrines of individual liberty and popular sovereignty with independence, Jefferson established revolutionary republicanism as a defining value of the new nation.

For Jefferson as for Paine the pen proved mightier than the sword. In rural hamlets and seaport cities crowds celebrated the Declaration by burning George III in effigy and toppling statues of the king. These acts of destruction broke the Patriots' psychological ties to the mother country and the father monarch. Americans were ready to create republics, state governments that would derive their authority from the people.

The Trials of War, 1776–1778

The Declaration of Independence coincided with Britain's decision to launch a full-scale military assault against the Patriots. For the next two years British forces outfought the Continental army commanded by George Washington, winning nearly every battle. A few inspiring American victories kept the rebellion alive, but in late 1776 and during the winter of 1777 to 1778 at Valley Forge the Patriot cause hung in the balance.

WAR IN THE NORTH

When the British resorted to military force to crush the American revolt, few observers gave the rebels a chance. Great Britain had 11 million people, compared with the colonies' 2.5 million, nearly 20 percent of whom were enslaved Africans. The British also had a profound economic advantage in the immense profits created by the South Atlantic system and the emerging Industrial Revolution. These financial resources paid for the most powerful navy in the world, a standing army of 48,000 men, and thousands of German mercenaries. British military officers had been tested in combat, and their soldiers were well armed. Finally, the imperial government had the support of tens of thousands of American Loyalists as well as many Indian tribes hostile to white expansion.

By contrast, the rebellious Americans were militarily weak. They had no navy, and General Washington's poorly trained army consisted of about 18,000 troops, mostly short-term militiamen hastily recruited by state governments in Virginia and New England. The Patriots could field thousands more militiamen but only for short periods and only near their own farms and towns. Although many American officers were capable veterans of the French and Indian War, even the most experienced had never commanded a large force or faced a disciplined army skilled in the intricate maneuvers of European warfare.

To exploit this military advantage Britain's prime minister, Lord North, responded quickly to the unexpected American invasion of Canada in 1775. He assembled a large invasion force and selected General William Howe, a veteran of the French and Indian War, to lead it. North ordered him to capture New York City and seize control of the Hudson River, hoping to isolate the radical Patriots in New England from the other colonies. In July 1776, as the Continental Congress was declaring independence in Philadelphia, Howe was beginning to land 32,000 troops—British regulars and German mercenaries—outside New York City.

British superiority was immediately apparent. In August 1776 Howe attacked the Americans in the Battle of Long Island and forced their retreat to Manhattan Island. There Howe outflanked Washington's troops, nearly trapping them on several occasions. Outgunned and outmaneuvered, the Continental army again retreated, first to Harlem Heights, then to White Plains, and finally across the Hudson River to New Jersey. By December the British army had pushed the rebels out of New Jersey and across the Delaware River into Pennsylvania, forcing Congress to flee from Philadelphia to Baltimore (see Map 6.1).

From the Patriots' perspective winter came just in time, for the overconfident British halted their campaign for the cold months, according to eighteenth-century military custom. The respite allowed the Americans to catch them off guard and score a few triumphs. On Christmas night in 1776 Washington crossed the Delaware River and staged a surprise attack on Trenton, New Jersey, forcing the surrender of 1,000 German mercenaries (Hessians). Then in early January 1777 the Continental army won a small engagement at nearby Princeton, raising Patriot morale and allowing the Continental Congress to return to Philadelphia. Bright stars in a dark night, these minor triumphs could not mask British military superiority. These are the times, wrote Tom Paine, that "try men's souls."

ARMIES AND STRATEGIES

Throughout 1776 Howe's strategy had been to use his superior military power to convince the Continental Congress that resistance was futile. In 1774 he had opposed the Coercive Acts, calling them too harsh, and now as British commander he hoped to negotiate a compromise with the rebels. Howe's cautious military policy also reflected the conventions of eighteenth-century warfare, which focused on winning the surrender of opposing forces rather than destroying them. The British general was also well aware that his troops were 3,000 miles from home; in case of a major defeat he could not replenish his force for six months. Although Howe's tactics were understandable, they cost the British the opportunity to nip the rebellion in the bud.

Howe's failure to win a decisive victory was paralleled by Washington's success in avoiding a major defeat. He too was cautious, challenging Howe on occasion but retreating in the face of superior strength. As Washington advised Congress, "On our Side the War should be defensive." His strategy was to draw the

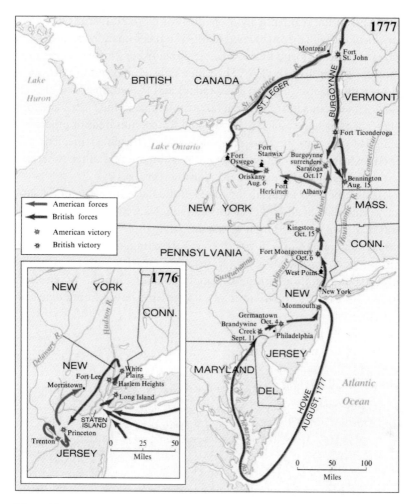

MAP 6.1
The War in the North, 1776–1777

In 1776 the British army drove Washington's forces across New Jersey into Pennsylvania. The Americans counterattacked at Trenton and Princeton, winning minor victories. In 1777 General Howe attacked Philadelphia from the south and easily captured it. Simultaneously, General Burgoyne and Colonel St. Leger launched invasions of New York from bases in Canada. Aided by thousands of New England militia Continental army forces commanded by General Horatio Gates defeated Burgoyne at Bennington (Vermont) and then at Saratoga (New York), the military turning point of the war.

British away from the seacoast, extend their lines of supply, and sap their morale while keeping the Continental army intact as a symbol and instrument of American resistance.

Congress had promised Washington a regular force of 75,000 men, but the Continental army never reached a third of that number. Yeomen preferred to serve in the local militia, and so the regular army drew most of its recruits from the lower ranks of society. General William Smallwood of Maryland commanded soldiers who were either poor American-born youths or older foreign-born men—British ex-convicts and former indentured servants. Such men enlisted not out of patriotism but for a bonus of $20 in cash (about $2,000 today) and the promise of 100 acres of land. Molding such recruits into a fighting force took time. In the face of a British artillery bombardment or flank attack many men panicked; hundreds of others deserted, unwilling to submit to the discipline and danger of military life. The soldiers who stayed resented the contemptuous way Washington and other American officers treated the women who fed and cared for the recruits.

Such personal support was crucial, for the Continental army was poorly supplied and faintly praised. Radical Whig Patriots had long viewed a peacetime standing army as a threat to liberty, and even in wartime they preferred the militia to a professional force. General Philip Schuyler of New York complained that his troops were "weak in numbers, dispirited, naked, destitute of provisions, without camp equipage, with little ammunition, and not a single piece of cannon." Given these handicaps, Washington was fortunate to have escaped an overwhelming defeat in the first year of the war.

A British Camp, circa 1778

While American troops at Valley Forge huddled from the cold in thin tents, British troops stationed just outside New York City (on upper Manhattan Island) lived in simple but well-constructed and warm log cabins. Each hut housed either a few officers or as many as ten soldiers of the 17th Regiment of Foot. This painting, based on careful archaeological fieldwork, was executed in 1915 by John Ward Dunsmore. (The New-York Historical Society)

American Militiamen

Because of the shortage of cloth the Patriot army dressed in many fabrics and fashions. This German engraving, based on a drawing by a German officer, shows two barefoot American militiamen arrayed in hunting shirts and trousers made of ticking, a strong woven linen fabric that was often used as the coverings for mattresses and pillows.

(Anne S. K. Brown Military Collection, Brown University)

VICTORY AT SARATOGA

Howe's failure to achieve a quick victory dismayed Lord North and his colonial secretary, Lord George Germain. Accepting the challenge of a long-term military commitment, the British ministry increased the land tax to finance the war and prepared to mount a major campaign in 1777.

The isolation of New England remained the primary British goal and was to be achieved by a three-pronged attack converging on Albany, New York. General John Burgoyne was to lead a large contingent of British regulars from Quebec to Albany. A second, smaller force of Iroquois warriors (who had allied themselves with the British to protect their land from American settlers) would attack from the west under Colonel Barry St. Leger. To assist Burgoyne from the south, Germain ordered Howe to dispatch a force northward from New York City (see Map 6.1).

Howe had a different scheme. He wanted to attack Philadelphia, the home of the Continental Congress, and end the rebellion with a single victory over Washington's army. With Germain's apparent approval, Howe set his plan in motion.

Rather than march overland through New Jersey, British troops sailed south from New York then up the Chesapeake Bay. Approaching Philadelphia from the south, Howe's troops easily outflanked the American positions along Brandywine Creek in Delaware and forced Washington to withdraw. On September 26 the British marched triumphantly into Philadelphia, hoping that the capture of the rebels' capital would end the uprising. But the Continental Congress fled into the interior, determined to continue the struggle.

The British paid a high price for Howe's victory in Philadelphia, for it contributed directly to Burgoyne's defeat. Initially Burgoyne's troops had sped across Lake Champlain, overwhelming the American defenses at Fort Ticonderoga and driving toward the upper reaches of the Hudson River. Then they stalled, for Burgoyne—"Gentleman Johnny," as he was called—fought with style, not speed, weighed down by comfortable tents and ample stocks of food and wine. Burgoyne's progress was further impeded by General Horatio Gates, whose troops felled trees across the crude wagon trail Burgoyne was following and raided his long supply lines to Canada.

By the end of the summer Burgoyne's army—6,000 regulars (half of them German mercenaries) and 600 Loyalists and Indians—was in trouble, bogged down in the wilderness near Saratoga, New York. In August 2,000 American militiamen left their farms to fight a bitter battle at nearby Bennington, Vermont, that cost Burgoyne 900 casualties and deprived him of much-needed supplies of food and horses. Meanwhile, Patriot forces in the Mohawk Valley forced St. Leger and the Iroquois to retreat. To make matters worse, the British commander in New York City recalled the 4,000 troops he had sent toward Albany and dispatched them to Howe in Philadelphia. While Burgoyne waited for help, thousands of Patriot militiamen from Massachusetts, New Hampshire, and New York joined Gates's forces. They "swarmed around the army like birds of prey," an alarmed English sergeant wrote in his journal, and in October 1777 forced Burgoyne to surrender.

The battle at Saratoga proved to be the turning point of the war. The Americans captured more than 5,000 British troops and their equipment. Their victory virtually ensured the success of American diplomats in Paris, who were seeking a military alliance with France. Patriots on the home front were delighted, though their joy was muted by wartime difficulties.

SOCIAL AND FINANCIAL PERILS

The war exposed tens of thousands of civilians to deprivation, displacement, and death. "An army, even a friendly one, are a dreadful scourge to any people," a Connecticut soldier wrote from Pennsylvania. "You cannot imagine what devastation and distress mark their steps." New Jersey was particularly hard hit by the fighting, as British and American armies marched back and forth across the state. Families with reputations as Patriots or Loyalists fled their homes to escape arrest—or worse. Soldiers and partisans looted farms, seeking food or political revenge. Wherever the armies went, drunk and disorderly troops harassed and raped women and girls. Families lived in fear of their approach.

Indeed, the War of Independence became a bloody partisan conflict. In New England mobs of Patriot farmers beat suspected Tories or destroyed their property. "Every Body submitted to our Sovereign Lord the Mob," a Loyalist preacher lamented. Patriots organized local Committees of Safety to collect taxes, send food and clothing to the Continental army, and impose fines or jail sentences on those who failed to support the cause.

These local initiatives reflected the weakness of the new state governments, which teetered on the brink of bankruptcy. To feed, clothe, and pay their troops, state officials borrowed gold, silver, or British currency from wealthy individuals. When those funds ran out, Patriot officials were afraid to raise taxes, knowing how unpopular that would be. Instead, individual states printed paper money, issuing a total of $260 million in currency and transferable bonds. Theoretically, the new notes could be redeemed in gold or silver, but since they were printed in huge quantities and were not backed by tax revenues or mortgages on land, many Americans refused to accept them at face value. North Carolina's paper money came to be worth so little even the state government's tax collectors refused it.

The finances of the Continental Congress collapsed too, despite the efforts of the Philadelphia merchant Robert Morris, the government's chief treasury official. The Congress lacked the authority to impose taxes and so depended on funds requisitioned from the states, which frequently paid late or not at all. Congress therefore borrowed $6 million in specie from France, using it as security to encourage wealthy Americans to purchase $27 million in Continental loan certificates. When those funds and other French and Dutch loans were exhausted, Congress followed the lead of the states and printed currency and bills of credit. Between 1775 and 1779 it issued notes with a face value of $191 million, but when funds received from the states retired only $3 million, the actual value of the bills fell dramatically.

Indeed, the excess of currency helped to spark the worst inflation in American history. The amount of goods available for purchase—both domestic foodstuffs and foreign manufactures—had shrunk significantly because of the fighting and the British naval blockade, while the money in circulation had multiplied. Because more currency was chasing fewer goods, prices rose rapidly. In Maryland a bag of salt that had cost $1 in 1776 sold for $3,900 in currency a few years later. Unwilling to accept nearly worthless currency, farmers refused to sell their crops, even to the Continental army. Instead, merchants and farmers turned to barter—trading wheat for tools or clothes—or sold goods only to those who could pay in gold or silver. The result was social upheaval. In Boston a mob of women accused merchant Thomas Boyleston of hoarding goods, "seazd him by his Neck," and forced him to sell—at the traditional prices. In rural Ulster County, New York, women surrounded the Patriot Committee of Safety, demanding steps to end the food shortages; otherwise, they said, "their husbands and sons shall fight no more." Civilian morale and social cohesion crumbled, causing some Patriot leaders to doubt that the rebellion could succeed.

Fears reached their peak during the winter of 1777 to 1778. Howe camped in Philadelphia and with his officers partook of the finest wines, foods, and entertainment the city could offer. Washington's army retreated to Valley Forge, some 20 miles to the west, where about 12,000 soldiers and hundreds of camp followers suffered horribly. "The army . . . now begins to grow sickly," a surgeon confided to his diary. "Poor food—hard lodging—cold weather—fatigue—nasty clothes—nasty cookery. . . . Why are we sent here to starve and freeze?" Nearby farmers refused to help. Some were pacifists—Quakers and German sectarians—unwilling to support either side. Others were self-interested, hoarding their grain in hopes of higher prices in the spring or willing to accept only the gold and silver offered by British quartermasters. "Such a dearth of public spirit, and want of public virtue," Washington complained—but to no effect. By spring a thousand of his hungry soldiers had vanished into the countryside, and another 3,000 had died from malnutrition and disease. One winter at Valley Forge took as many American lives as had two years of fighting against General Howe.

The Path to Victory, 1778–1783

The Patriots' prospects improved dramatically in 1778, when the United States formed a military alliance with France, the most powerful European nation. The alliance brought the Americans money, troops, and supplies and changed the conflict from a colonial rebellion to an international war.

THE FRENCH ALLIANCE

France and America were unlikely partners. France was Catholic and a monarchy; the United States, largely Protestant and a federation of republics. The two peoples had been on opposite sides in wars from 1689 to 1763. But France was intent on avenging its loss of Canada in the French and Indian War. In 1776 the Comte de Vergennes, the French foreign minister, persuaded King Louis XVI to extend a secret loan to the rebellious colonies and supply them with gunpowder. Early in 1777 Vergennes opened official commercial and military negotiations with Benjamin Franklin and two other American diplomats. When news of the American victory at Saratoga reached Paris in December 1777, Vergennes sought a formal alliance with the Continental Congress.

Franklin and his associates craftily exploited the rivalry between France and Britain, using the threat of a negotiated settlement with Britain to win an explicit French commitment to American independence. The Treaty of Alliance of February 1778 specified that once France had entered the war against Great Britain, neither partner would sign a separate peace before the "liberty, sovereignty, and independence" of the United States were ensured. The American diplomats pledged that their government would recognize any French conquests in the West Indies.

The alliance with France gave new life to the Patriots' cause. With access to military supplies and European loans, the American army soon strengthened and hopes soared. "There has been a great change in this state since the news from France," a Patriot soldier reported from Pennsylvania; farmers—"mercenary wretches," he called them—"were as eager for Continental Money now as they were a few weeks ago for British gold."

With renewed energy and purpose the Congress addressed the demands of the officer corps for pensions. Most officers came from the upper ranks of society and had used their own funds to equip themselves and sometimes their men as well. In return they demanded lifetime military pensions at half pay. John Adams condemned the petitioners for "scrambling for rank and pay like apes for nuts," but General Washington urged Congress to grant the pensions, warning the lawmakers that "the salvation of the cause depends upon it." Congress reluctantly agreed to grant the officers half pay after the war but only for seven years.

Meanwhile, the war was becoming increasingly unpopular in Britain. Radical agitators and republican-minded artisans supported American demands for greater rights and campaigned for political reform at home, including broadened voting rights and more equitable representation for cities in Parliament. The landed gentry and urban merchants protested increases in the land tax and new levies on carriages, wine, and imported goods. "It seemed we were to be taxed and stamped ourselves instead of inflicting taxes and stamps on others," a British politician complained.

But George III remained determined to crush the rebellion. If America won independence, he warned Lord North, "the West Indies must follow them. Ireland would soon follow the same plan and be a separate state, then this island would be reduced to itself, and soon would be a poor island indeed." Following the British defeat at Saratoga the king assumed a more pragmatic attitude. To head off an American alliance with France, the king authorized North to seek a negotiated settlement. In February 1778 North persuaded Parliament to repeal the Tea and Prohibitory Acts and in an amazing concession to renounce its power to tax the colonies. The prime minister then opened discussions with the Continental Congress, offering a return to the constitutional "condition of 1763," before the Sugar and Stamp Acts. But the Patriots, now allied with France, rejected the overture.

WAR IN THE SOUTH

The French alliance expanded the war but did not rapidly conclude it. When France entered the conflict in June 1778, it hoped to capture a rich sugar island and therefore concentrated its naval forces in the West Indies. Spain, which joined the war in 1779, also had its own agenda: in return for naval assistance to France, it wanted to regain Florida and Gibraltar.

The British ministry, by 1778 beset by war on many fronts, settled on a modest strategy in North America. It would use its army to recapture the rich tobacco- and rice-growing colonies of Virginia, the Carolinas, and Georgia and rely on local Loyalists to hold and administer them. The British knew that Scottish Highlanders in North Carolina retained a strong allegiance to the crown and hoped to recruit other Loyalists from the ranks of the Regulators, the enemies of the low-country Patriot planters. The ministry also hoped to take advantage of racial divisions in the South. In 1776 over 1,000 slaves had fought for Lord Dunmore under the banner "Liberty to Slaves!"; a British military offensive might prompt thousands more to flee from their Patriot owners. In fact, because African Americans formed 30 to 50 percent of the population, planters were afraid that allowing their sons or white overseers to leave the plantations and join the Continental forces would encourage slave revolts.

Implementing this southern strategy became the responsibility of Sir Henry Clinton. In June 1778 Clinton moved the main British army from Philadelphia to more secure quarters in New York. In December he launched his southern campaign, capturing Savannah, Georgia, and mobilizing hundreds of blacks to build barricades and unload supplies. Then Clinton moved inland, capturing Augusta early in 1779. By the end of the year, with the help of local Loyalists, Clinton's forces had reconquered Georgia, and 10,000 troops were poised for an assault on South Carolina. To counter this threat the Continental Congress suggested that South Carolina raise 3,000 black troops, but the state assembly overwhelmingly rejected the proposal.

During most of 1780 British forces marched from victory to victory (see Map 6.2). In May Clinton forced General Benjamin Lincoln and his 5,000 troops to surrender at Charleston, South Carolina. Shortly afterward Lord Cornwallis assumed control of the British forces and sent out expeditions to secure the countryside. In August Cornwallis routed an American force commanded by General Horatio Gates, the hero of Saratoga. Only about 1,200 Patriot militiamen joined Gates at the battle in Camden—a fifth of the number at Saratoga, and many of them panicked, handing the British control of South Carolina. Hundreds of African Americans fled to freedom in British-controlled Florida, while hundreds more found refuge with the British army, providing labor in return for their liberty.

Then the tide of battle turned. The Dutch declared war against Britain, and France finally dispatched troops to America. The French decision was partly the work of the Marquis de Lafayette, a republican-minded aristocrat who had long supported the American cause. In 1780 Lafayette persuaded Louis XVI to send General Comte de Rochambeau and 5,500 men to Newport, Rhode Island.

As the French army threatened the British in New York City, Washington called on General Nathanael Greene to recapture the Carolinas. To make use of local militiamen, who were "without discipline and addicted to plundering," Greene devised a new military strategy. He divided the militia into small groups with strong leaders and directed them to harass the less mobile British forces. In October 1780 a

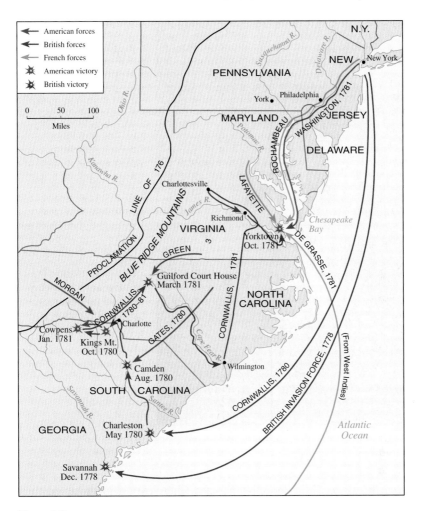

M A P 6.2
Campaigns in the South, 1778–1781

In 1778 the British ministry's southern strategy started well as its military forces captured
Savannah in December 1778 and Charleston in May 1780. Over the next eighteen months
brutal warfare raged in the interior, fought mostly by small bands of irregulars. When
Cornwallis's army carried the battle into Virginia in late 1781, a Franco-American force
led by Washington and Lafayette surrounded his troops at Yorktown, aided by the French
fleet under Admiral de Grasse.

militia force of Patriot farmers defeated a regiment of Loyalists at King's Mountain,
South Carolina, taking about 1,000 prisoners. Led by the "Swamp Fox," General
Francis Marion, American guerrillas won a series of small but fierce battles in South
Carolina, while General Daniel Morgan led another band to a bloody victory at
Cowpens, South Carolina, in January 1781. But Loyalist garrisons and militia

Lafayette at Yorktown

This contemporary painting, executed by the French artist J. B. Le Paon in 1780, shows the Marquis de Lafayette and James Armistead, an enslaved African American who served as a spy for the Patriot army commanded by the French general. Receiving his freedom as a reward for exploits as a spy, James took Lafayette's surname, becoming James Lafayette. The two Lafayettes met again in 1824 when the Frenchman visited the United States.

(Lafayette College Art Collection, Easton, PA. Gift of Mrs. John Hubbard)

remained powerful, assisted by the well-organized Cherokees, who protected their lands by attacking American settlers and troops. "We fight, get beaten, and fight again," General Greene declared doggedly. In March 1781 Greene's soldiers fought Cornwallis's seasoned army to a draw at North Carolina's Guilford Court House.

Weakened by this war of attrition, Cornwallis decided to concede the southernmost states to Greene and seek a decisive victory in Virginia. Aided by reinforcements from New York, the British general invaded Virginia's Tidewater region. There Benedict Arnold, the infamous traitor to the Patriot cause, led British troops up and down the James River, where they met only slight resistance from an American force commanded by Lafayette. Then in May 1781, as the two armies sparred near the York Peninsula, France ordered its large fleet from the West Indies to North America.

Emboldened by the naval forces at his disposal, Washington launched a well-coordinated attack. Feinting an assault on New York City, he secretly marched General Rochambeau's army from Rhode Island to Virginia, where it joined his Continental army. Simultaneously, the French fleet massed off the coast, establishing control of Chesapeake Bay. By the time the British discovered Washington's audacious plan, Cornwallis was surrounded, his 9,500-man army outnumbered two to one on land and cut off from reinforcement or retreat by sea. Abandoned by the British navy, Cornwallis surrendered at Yorktown in October 1781.

The Franco-American victory at Yorktown broke the resolve of the British government. "Oh God! It is all over!" Lord North exclaimed when he heard the news. The combined French and Spanish fleet was menacing the British sugar islands, Dutch merchants were capturing European markets from British traders, and a group of European states—the League of Armed Neutrality—was demanding an end to Britain's commercial blockade of France. Isolated diplomatically in Europe, stymied militarily in America, and lacking public support at home, the British ministry gave up active prosecution of the war.

THE PATRIOT ADVANTAGE

Angry members of Parliament demanded an explanation. How could mighty Britain, victorious in the Great War for Empire, be defeated by a motley group of colonists? The ministry blamed the military leadership, pointing with some justification to a series of blunders. Why had Howe not been more ruthless in pursuing Washington's army in 1776? How could Howe and Burgoyne have failed to coordinate the movement of their armies in 1777? Why had Cornwallis marched deep into the Patriot-dominated state of Virginia in 1781?

Historians have also criticized these blunders while emphasizing the high odds against British success, given broad-based American support for the rebel cause. Although only a third of the white colonists were zealous Patriots, another third were supportive enough to pay the taxes imposed by state governments. Unlike most revolutionaries the Patriots were led by experienced politicians who commanded public support. And even though the Continental army had to be built from scratch and was never very large, it was fighting on its own territory with the assistance of thousands of militiamen. The more than 55,000 Tories and thousands of native Americans who fought for the British could not offset these advantages. Once the rebels had the financial and military support of France, they could reasonably hope for victory.

While Britain suffered mediocre generals, Americans had the inspired leadership of George Washington as commander of the Continental army. An astute politician, Washington deferred to the civil authorities, winning respect and support from the Congress and the state governments alike. Confident of his own abilities, he recruited outstanding military officers to instill discipline in the ranks of the fledgling Continental army and turn it into a respectable fighting force.

But Washington also had a greater margin for error than the British generals did because Patriots controlled local governments and at crucial moments could mobilize the militia to assist his Continental army. Thousands of militiamen had besieged General Gage in Boston in 1775, surrounded Burgoyne at Saratoga in 1777, and forced Cornwallis from the Carolinas in 1781. In the end the American people decided the outcome of the conflict. Preferring Patriot rule, they refused to support Loyalist forces or accept imperial control in British-occupied areas. Consequently, while the British won many military victories, they achieved little, and their defeats at Saratoga and Yorktown proved catastrophic.

DIPLOMATIC TRIUMPH

After Yorktown diplomats took two years to conclude the war. Peace talks began in Paris in April 1782, but the French and Spanish stalled for time, hoping for a major naval victory or territorial conquest. Their delaying tactics infuriated the American diplomats—Benjamin Franklin, John Adams, and John Jay—who feared that France might sacrifice American interests. For this reason the Americans negotiated secretly with the British, prepared if necessary to cut their ties to France and sign a separate peace. The British ministry was also eager to obtain a quick settlement, for the war had little support in Parliament and officials feared the loss of a rich West Indian sugar island.

Exploiting the rivalry between Britain and France, the American diplomats finally secured peace on very favorable terms. In the Treaty of Paris, signed in September 1783, Great Britain formally recognized the independence of its seaboard colonies and, while retaining Canada, also relinquished its claims to all the lands south of the Great Lakes between the Appalachian Mountains and the Mississippi River—the domain of undefeated, pro-British Indian peoples. Leaving the Native Americans to their fate, the British negotiators did not insist on a separate Indian territory and promised to withdraw their garrisons "with all convenient speed." "In endeavouring to assist you," a Wea Indian complained to a British general, "it seems we have wrought our own ruin." Other treaty provisions granted Americans fishing rights off Newfoundland and Nova Scotia, forbade the British from "carrying away any negroes or other property," and guaranteed freedom of navigation on the Mississippi to both British subjects and American citizens "forever." In its only concessions the American government promised to allow British merchants to recover prewar debts and to encourage the state legislatures to return confiscated property to Loyalists and grant them citizenship.

In the Treaty of Versailles, signed at the same time as the Treaty of Paris, Britain made peace with France and Spain. Neither American ally gained very much. Spain reclaimed Florida from Britain but failed in its main objective of retaking Gibraltar. France had the pleasure of reducing British power, but its only territorial gain was the Caribbean island of Tobago. Moreover, the war had quadrupled France's national debt; only six years later cries for tax relief and political liberty would spark the French Revolution. Only Americans profited handsomely from the treaties, which gave them independence from Britain and opened up the interior of the North American continent for settlement.

Republicanism Defined and Challenged

From the moment they became revolutionary republicans, Americans began to define the character of their new social order. In the Declaration of Independence Thomas Jefferson had turned to John Locke, the philosopher of private liberty, when he declared a universal human right to "Life, Liberty, and the pursuit of Happiness." But Jefferson and many other Americans also lauded "republican virtue," an enlightened quest for the public good. As the New Hampshire constitution phrased it, "Government [was] instituted for the common benefits, protection, and security of the whole community." The tension between self-interest and the public interest would shape the future of the new nation.

REPUBLICAN IDEALS UNDER WARTIME PRESSURES

Simply put, a republic is a state without a monarch and with a representative system of government. Yet for many Americans republicanism was also a social philosophy. "The word republic" in Latin, wrote Thomas Paine, "means the public good," which citizens have a duty to secure. "Every man in a republic is public property," asserted the Philadelphia Patriot Benjamin Rush, who eventually extended the notion to include women as well. "His time and talents—his youth—his manhood—his old age—nay more, life, all belong to his country." Reflecting this sense of community, members of the Continental Congress praised the militiamen who fought and fell at Lexington and Concord, Saratoga and Camden. And they applauded Henry Laurens of South Carolina, who condemned as a "total loss of virtue" the wartime demand by Continental officers for lifetime pensions. Raised as gentlemen, officers were supposed to be exemplars of virtue who gave freely to the republic.

As the war continued, military self-sacrifice declined. During the winters of 1779 and 1780 Continental troops stationed at Morristown in New Jersey mutinied, unwilling any longer to endure low pay and sparse rations. To restore military authority Washington ordered the execution of several leaders of the revolt but urged Congress to pacify the soldiers with back pay and new clothing. Later in the war unrest among officers erupted at Newburgh, New York, and Washington had to use his personal authority to thwart a dangerous challenge to the Congress's policies.

Meanwhile, economic distress tested the republican virtue of ordinary citizens. The British naval blockade had disrupted the New England fishing industry and cut the supply of European manufactures. British occupation of Boston, New York, and Philadelphia had also trimmed domestic trade and manufacturing. As unemployed shipwrights, dock laborers, masons, coopers, and bakers deserted the cities and drifted into the countryside, New York City's population declined from 21,000 residents in 1774 to less than half that number by the war's end. In the Chesapeake the British blockade deprived tobacco planters of European markets, forcing them to cultivate grain, which could be sold to the contending armies.

In those difficult times Patriot women contributed both to the war effort and the well-being of their families by increasing their production of homespun cloth. One Massachusetts town produced 30,000 yards of homespun, while women in Elizabeth, New Jersey, promised "upwards of 100,000 yards of linnen and woolen cloth." Other women assumed the burdens of farm production while their men were away at war. Some went into the fields, plowing, harvesting, and loading grain, while others supervised hired laborers or slaves, in the process acquiring a taste for decision making. "We have sow'd our oats as you desired," Sarah Cobb Paine wrote to her absent husband; "had I been master I should have planted it to Corn." Taught from childhood to value the welfare of their fathers, brothers, and husbands above their own, women were expected to act "virtuously" and often did so. Their wartime efforts not only increased farm household productivity but also boosted their self-esteem and prompted some to claim greater rights in the new republican society.

Despite the women's efforts goods were in short supply, bringing a sharp rise in prices and widespread appeals for government regulation. Hard-pressed consumers decried merchants and traders as "enemies, extortioners, and monopolizers." But in 1777, when a convention of New England states limited price increases to 75 percent, many farmers and artisans refused to sell their goods at the set prices. In the end, a government official admitted, consumers had to pay the much higher market price "or submit to starving." In civilian life as in the military, self-interest tended to triumph over republican virtue.

Spiraling inflation posed a severe challenge to American families and the notion of public virtue. By 1778 so much currency had been printed that a family needed $7 in Continental bills to buy goods worth $1 in gold or silver. The ratio steadily escalated—to 42 to 1 in 1779, 100 to 1 in 1780, and 146 to 1 in 1781, when not even the most dedicated Patriots would accept paper money. To restore the value of Continental currency, the Congress asked the states to accept tax payments in depreciated Continental bills (with $40 in paper money counting as $1 in specie). This plan redeemed $120 million in Continental bills, but at the end of the war speculators still held $71 million in currency, hoping they could eventually redeem it at face value. "Private Interest seemed to predominate over the public weal," a leading Patriot complained.

Ultimately, this currency inflation transferred most of the costs of the war to ordinary Americans. The tens of thousands of farmers and artisans who received Continental bills as payment for supplies and the soldiers who took them as pay found that the currency literally depreciated in their pockets. Every time they received a paper dollar and kept it for a week, the money lost value and could buy less, thus imposing a hidden "currency tax" on them. Each individual "tax" was small—a few pennies on each dollar they handled. But taken together—as millions of dollars changed hands multiple times—these currency taxes paid the huge cost of the war.

THE LOYALIST EXODUS

As the war turned in favor of the Patriots, more than 100,000 Loyalists, fearing for their lives, emigrated to the West Indies, Britain, and Canada. The exodus disrupted the social hierarchy in many communities because a significant minority of Loyalists came from the ranks of wealthy merchants, lawyers, and landowners of high status. Although some angry Patriots demanded that the state governments seize the property of these "traitors," most public officials argued that confiscation would be contrary to Patriot principles. In Massachusetts officials cited the state's Constitution of 1780, which declared that every citizen should be protected "in the enjoyment of his life, liberty, and property, according to the standing laws."

Thus, there was no government-led social revolution. Most states seized only a limited amount of Loyalist property and usually sold it to the highest bidder, who was often a wealthy Patriot rather than a yeoman or foot soldier. But in a few cases confiscations did produce a democratic result. In North Carolina about half the new owners of Loyalist lands were small-scale farmers. And on the former Philipse manor in New York many Patriot tenants used their hard-earned savings to buy the seized land and become fee-simple owners. When Philipse tried to reclaim his land, former tenants told him they had "purchased it with the price of their best blood" and "will never become your vassals again." But in general the revolutionary upheaval did not drastically alter the structure of rural society.

Social turmoil was greater in the cities, as Patriot merchants replaced Tories at the top of the economic ladder. In Massachusetts the Lowell, Higginson, Jackson, and Cabot families moved their trading enterprises to Boston to fill the vacuum created by the departure of the Loyalist Hutchinsons and Apthorps. In Philadelphia, small-scale traders stepped into the vacancies created by the collapse of Anglican and Quaker mercantile firms. In the countinghouses as on the battlefield, Patriots emerged triumphant. The War of Independence replaced a tradition-oriented economic elite—one that invested its profits from trade in real estate, becoming landlords—with a group of entrepreneurial-minded republican merchants who promoted new trading ventures and domestic manufacturing.

THE PROBLEM OF SLAVERY

Slavery revealed a contradiction in the Patriots' republican ideology. "How is it that we hear the loudest yelps for liberty among the drivers of Negroes?" the British author Samuel Johnson chided the rebellious white Americans, a point some Patriots took to heart. "I wish most sincerely there was not a Slave in the province," Abigail Adams wrote to her husband, John, as Massachusetts went to war. "It always appeared a most iniquitous Scheme to me—to fight ourselves for what we are daily robbing and plundering from those who have as good a right to freedom as we have."

In fact, the struggle of white Patriots for their independence from Britain raised the prospect of freedom for enslaved Africans. Many hoped for a British invasion that would free them. When the war began, a black preacher in Georgia told his fellow slaves that King George III "came up with the Book [the Bible], and was about to alter the World, and set the Negroes free." Similar rumors circulated among slaves in Virginia and the Carolinas, prompting thousands of African Americans to seek freedom by fleeing behind British lines. Two neighbors of Richard Henry Lee, the Virginia Patriot, lost "every slave they had in the world," as did many other planters. When the British army evacuated Charleston, more than 6,000 former slaves went with them; another 4,000 left from Savannah. Hundreds of these black Loyalists settled permanently in Canada. Over 1,000 others, poorly treated by British officials and settled on inferior land in Nova Scotia, sought a better life in the abolitionist settlement in Sierra Leone, West Africa.

For a variety of reasons thousands of African Americans decided to serve the Patriot cause. Knowing firsthand the meaning of slavery and anxious to raise their status in society, free blacks in New England volunteered for military service in the First Rhode Island Company and the Massachusetts "Bucks." In Maryland a large number of slaves also took up arms for the Patriot cause in return for a promise of freedom. Elsewhere in the South slaves struck informal bargains with their Patriot masters, trading loyalty in wartime for a promise of eventual liberty. In 1782 the Virginia assembly passed an act allowing manumission (liberation); within a decade planters had freed 10,000 slaves.

The Quakers, whose belief in religious and social equality had made them sharp critics of many inequities, took the lead in condemning slavery. Beginning in the 1750s the Quaker evangelist John Woolman had urged Friends to free their slaves, and during the war many did so. Other rapidly growing pietistic groups, notably

Symbols of Slavery—and Freedom

The scar on the forehead of this black woman, widely known as "Mumbet," symbolized the cruelty of slavery. Winning emancipation through a legal suit in Massachusetts, she chose a name befitting her new status: Elizabeth Freeman. This watercolor, by Susan Sedgwick, was painted in 1811.
(Massachusetts Historical Society)

the Methodists and the Baptists, also advocated emancipation and admitted both enslaved and free blacks to their congregations. In 1784 a conference of Virginia Methodists declared that slavery was "contrary to the Golden Law of God on which hang all the Law and Prophets."

Enlightenment philosophy also worked to undermine slavery and racism. John Locke had argued that ideas were not innate but stemmed from a person's experiences in the world. Accordingly, Enlightenment thinkers suggested that the oppressive conditions of slavery, not inherent inferiority, accounted for the debased situation of Africans in the Western Hemisphere. As one American put it, "A state of slavery has a mighty tendency to shrink and contract the minds of men." Anthony Benezet, a Quaker philanthropist who funded a school for blacks in Philadelphia, defied popular opinion in declaring that African Americans were "as capable of improvement as White People."

By 1784 Massachusetts had abolished slavery outright, and three other states— Pennsylvania, Connecticut, and Rhode Island—had provided for its gradual termination. Within another twenty years every state north of Delaware had enacted similar laws. Gradual emancipation laws compensated white owners by requiring more years—even decades—of servitude while promising blacks eventual freedom. Thus, the New York Emancipation Act of 1799 granted freedom only to the children of slaves and then only at age twenty-five. As late as 1810, 30,000 blacks in the northern states—nearly a fourth of their African American residents—were still enslaved. Emancipation came slowly because whites feared competition for jobs and housing and the prospect of race melding. To keep the races separate in 1786 Massachusetts reenacted an old law prohibiting whites from marrying blacks, Indians, or mulattos (see American Voices, "The Character of Northern Slavery").

The tension between the republican values of liberty and property was greatest in the South, where slaves made up 30 to 60 percent of the population and represented a huge financial investment. Some planters, moved by religious principles or oversupplied with workers on declining tobacco plantations, allowed blacks to buy their freedom through paid work as artisans or laborers. Manumission and self-purchase gradually freed about a third of the African Americans in Maryland, but in 1792 the Virginia legislature made manumission more difficult. Following the lead of Thomas Jefferson, who owned more than 100 slaves, the Chesapeake gentry argued that slavery was a "necessary evil" required to maintain white supremacy and the luxurious planter lifestyle. Resistance to freedom for blacks was even greater in North Carolina, where the legislature condemned Quaker manumissions as "highly criminal and reprehensible." And the rice-growing states of South Carolina and Georgia rejected emancipation out of hand.

The debate over emancipation among southern whites ended in 1800, when Virginia authorities thwarted an uprising planned by the enslaved artisan Gabriel Prosser and hanged him and thirty of his followers. "Liberty and equality have brought the evil upon us," a letter to the *Virginia Herald* proclaimed, for such doctrines are "dangerous and extremely wicked in this country, where every white man

AMERICAN VOICES

The Character of Northern Slavery

ALEXANDER COVENTRY

A lexander Coventry migrated from Scotland to New York in 1785 and recorded his daily experiences in a journal. The selections below provide insight into the condition of New York's rural African Americans, most of whom were owned by farmers of Dutch descent. His comments indicate that slavery in the rural North was very different from that on the plantations of the South.

2 February 1787 Rode through the Cocksaxie settlement. . . . The houses are substantially built of Lime-stone, and are generally 1½ stores high; the barns are capacious. . . . Cocksaxie farmers are supposed to be the most opulent in the state. Their fertile soil, and its convenience to market, being much in their favor. The tact [area of land] is almost exclusively inhabited by the low Dutch . . . and each farmer has a number of Negro slaves . . . who did all the work on the farm, and in the house. . . . Although the blacks were slaves, yet I feel warranted in asserting that the laboring class in no country lived more easy, were better clothed and fed, or had more of life, than these slaves.

2 April 1787 [Went with] William Van Valkenburg to see his brother John, who has received a stab in his thigh about 5 inches deep. He received the wound from a negro, whom his former master and John went to take. The negro and his wench had run away, and escaped into Boston state (Massachusetts) where negroes are free.

9–11 April 1789 Van Curen's negro Cuff came here and wanted W.C. [William Coventry, Alexander's cousin] to buy him . . . but Van Curen and W.C. could not agree, therefore I told him if the negro would agree to live with me, I would buy him. He asked 77 pounds. I offered 76 pounds. We tossed up and he won. . . . I asked Cuff if he would live with me. He said he would; he helped to drive the cows home to fodder. . . . Cuff wanted two days next week to keep Paas [Easter Sunday]. I told him to return on Wednesday morning, which he said he would do.

4 April 1790 While foddering, Thursday, before sunrise, a man and woman passed, the man was black, and asked the road to Hudson. Heard since that it was a negro run off with a white woman.

21 December 1791 Went over to Jacobus Legat's to see whether he would sell his Wench, Cuff's wife. Legat offered her, with her youngest child for £45. I offered him £40 and so we parted [without a sale].

3 February 1792 Cornelius Van Curen here; wants to buy Cuff back again, but Cuff won't go to him again.

SOURCE: Coventry Manuscript Diary, New-York Historical Society.

is a master, and every black man is a slave." To preserve their privileged social position, whites would redefine republicanism so that it applied only to the master race.

A REPUBLICAN RELIGIOUS ORDER

Political revolution broadened the appeal of religious liberty, forcing Patriot lawmakers to devise a new relationship between church and state. During the colonial era only the Quaker- and Baptist-controlled governments of Pennsylvania and Rhode Island had repudiated the idea of an established church. Then in 1776 James Madison and George Mason of Virginia used Enlightenment principles to undermine the traditional commitment to a single state-supported church. They persuaded the Virginia constitutional convention to issue a Declaration of Rights that guaranteed to all Christians the "free exercise of religion." To win broad support for the war, the Virginia Anglican elite carried this doctrine into practice, accepting the legitimacy of the dissenting Presbyterian and Baptist churches that they had previously persecuted. In 1778 Virginia Anglicans launched their own religious revolution by severing their ties with the hierarchy of the Church of England in London and creating the Protestant Episcopal Church of America.

After the Revolution an established church and compulsory religious taxes were no longer the norm in the United States. Baptists in particular opposed the use of taxes to support religion. In Virginia their political influence prompted lawmakers to reject a bill supported by George Washington and Patrick Henry, which would have imposed a general tax to fund all Christian churches. Instead, in 1786 the Virginia legislature enacted Thomas Jefferson's Bill for Establishing Religious Freedom, which made all churches equal before the law and granted direct financial support to none. In New York and New Jersey the sheer number of churches—Episcopalian, Presbyterian, Dutch Reformed, Lutheran, and Quaker, among others—prevented legislative agreement on an established church or compulsory religious taxes. However, in New England Congregationalist ministers preserved an official state church until the 1830s by allowing Baptists and Methodists to pay religious taxes to their own churches.

Still, many Americans felt that firm connections between church and state were necessary to promote morality and respect for authority. "Pure religion and civil liberty are inseparable companions," a group of North Carolinians advised their minister. "It is your particular duty to enlighten mankind with the unerring principles of truth and justice, the main props of all civil government." Accepting this premise, most state governments provided churches with indirect aid by exempting their property and ministers from taxation. Thus, the separation of church and state was never complete.

Freedom of conscience proved equally difficult to achieve. In Virginia Jefferson's Bill for Establishing Religious Freedom instituted the principle of liberty of conscience by outlawing religious requirements for political and civil posts. But many other states enforced religious criteria for voting and office holding, penalizing individuals who dissented from the doctrines of Protestant Christianity. The North Carolina constitution of 1776 disqualified from public office any citizen "who shall deny the being of God, or the Truth of the Protestant Religion, or the Divine Authority of the Old or New Testament." New Hampshire's constitution contained a similar provision until 1868.

Americans influenced by the Enlightenment and by evangelical Protestantism condemned such restrictions on freedom of conscience but for different reasons. Leading American intellectuals, including Thomas Jefferson and Benjamin Franklin, argued that God had given humans the power of reason so that they could determine moral truths for themselves. To protect society from "ecclesiastical tyranny," they demanded complete freedom of expression. Many evangelical Protestants also wanted religious liberty, but their goal was to protect their churches from the government. The New England minister Isaac Backus warned Baptists not to incorporate their churches under the law or accept public funds because that might lead to state control. In Connecticut a devout Congregationalist welcomed "voluntarism" (the voluntary funding of churches by their members) for another reason: it allowed the laity to control the clergy, furthering "the principles of republicanism."

In religion as in politics, independence provided Americans with the opportunity to fashion a new institutional order. In each case they repudiated the hierarchical ways of the past—monarchy and establishment—in favor of a republican alternative. These choices reflected the outlook and increased influence of ordinary citizens, who had fought and financed the long, difficult military struggle. True to the prediction of a wealthy Virginia planter in April 1776, independence and revolution had allowed yeomen to promote "their darling Democracy."

For Further Exploration

In *Angel in the Whirlwind: The Triumph of the American Revolution* (1997), Benson Bobrick presents the break with England as a grand epic stretching from the French and Indian War to Washington's inauguration. A compelling fictional account of the life of Tom Paine is Howard Fast, *Citizen Tom Paine* (1943). Pauline Maier, *American Scripture: Making the Declaration of Independence* (1997), explains the background of the Declaration and shows how it has been redefined over the past two centuries. For some vivid firsthand accounts of the military conflict, see John C. Dann, ed., *The Revolution Remembered: Eyewitness Accounts of the War for Independence* (1980). James L. Stokesbury, *A Short History of the American Revolution* (1991), suggests parallels between the British defeat and the American failure in Vietnam. Barbara Graymont, *The Iroquois in the American Revolution* (1972), offers an assessment of the war from an Indian perspective. In *Liberty's Daughters: The Revolutionary Experience of American Women, 1750–1800* (1980), Mary Beth Norton portrays both the continuities and the changes in women's lives. Sylvia R. Frey, *Water from the Rock: Black Resistance in a Revolutionary Age* (1991), traces the impact of the revolution on African Americans and their adaptations of republican ideology and Christian beliefs.

T I M E L I N E

1775	Battle of Concord (April 19)	**1778**	Franco-American alliance (February 6)
	Second Continental Congress meets in Philadelphia (May).		Congress rejects negotiations with Britain.
	Battle of Bunker Hill		Britain begins a southern strategy and captures Savannah (December).
	Continental army is created and headed by George Washington.	**1779**	Spain declares war against Britain.
	Olive Branch petition is passed by moderates in Continental Congress.	**1780**	The British capture Charleston (May).
	Lord Dunmore's proclamation offers freedom to slaves and indentured servants (November).		The French army lands in Rhode Island.
	American invasion of Canada	**1781**	Cornwallis invades Virginia (April).
1776	Patriots and Loyalists battle in the south.		Cornwallis surrenders at Yorktown (October).
	Thomas Paine's *Common Sense* (January)		Large-scale Loyalist emigration
	Declaration of Independence (July 4)	**1782**	Peace talks begin in Paris (April).
	General Howe forces Washington to retreat from New York and New Jersey (December).		Virginia passes an act allowing slave manumission (reversed in 1792).
			Gradual emancipation laws in northern states
1777	Women begin to increase textile output.	**1783**	Britain signs the Treaty of Paris (September).
	Price inflation begins.	**1786**	Virginia Bill for Establishing Religious Freedom
	Howe occupies Philadelphia (September).		
	Gates defeats Burgoyne at Saratoga (October).	**1800**	Gabriel Prosser's slave rebellion is thwarted in Virginia.
	Continental army suffers at Valley Forge (December).		

Liberty! The American Revolution (PBS video; 6 hours) and the companion website at <http:/www.pbs.org/liberty> cover the war and the making of the Constitution. The "Virtual Marching Tour of the Philadelphia Campaign 1777" at <http://www.ushistory.org/brandywine/index.html> offers an interesting multimedia view of Howe's attack on Philadelphia and subsequent events. A fine, data-rich source on the black experience is "Africans in America: Revolution" at <http://www.pbs.org/wgbh/aia/part2/title.html>; other parts of this site cover the entire African American experience. To explore the political philosophy of Thomas Jefferson, log on to "Quotations from the Writings of Thomas Jefferson" at <http://etext.virginia.edu/jefferson/quotations>, a site that is conveniently arranged by topic.

Chapter 7

THE NEW POLITICAL ORDER
1776–1800

But where, say some, is the king of America? . . . in America the law
is king.

—THOMAS PAINE, 1778

Like an earthquake the American Revolution shook the foundations
of the traditional European political order, and its aftershocks were felt far into the
nineteenth century. By "creating a new republic based on the rights of individual,
the North Americans introduced a new force into the world," the great German historian Leopold von Ranke explained to the king of Bavaria in a private lecture in
1854, warning that the ideology of republicanism might cost the monarch his
throne:

> This was a revolution of principle. Up to this point, a king who ruled by the
> grace of God had been the center around which everything turned. Now the
> idea emerged that power should come from below [from the people]. . . . These
> two principles are like opposite poles, and it is the conflict between them that
> determines the course of the modern world.

Previous revolutions—such as that of the Puritan Commonwealth in England
in the 1650s—had ended in political chaos and military rule, and many Europeans
expected the new American republic to experience the same fate. But General
George Washington stunned the world in 1783 when he voluntarily left public life
to return to his plantation, leaving power in the hands of elected Patriot leaders.
"Tis a Conduct so novel," the American painter Jonathan Trumbull reported from
London, "so inconceivable to People [here], who, far from giving up powers they
possess, are willing to convulse the empire to acquire more."

Fashioning republican institutions absorbed the energy and intellect of an entire generation. Between 1776 and 1800 Americans wrote new state and federal constitutions and devised a system of politics that was responsive to the popular will.
When a bill was introduced into a state legislature, conservative Ezra Stiles grumbled, every elected official "instantly thinks how it will affect his constituents" rather
than its impact on the welfare of the public as a whole. What Stiles criticized as an

excess of democracy, most ordinary Americans welcomed. For the first time the interests of ordinary citizens were represented in the halls of government, and the monarchs of Europe trembled.

Creating Republican Institutions, 1776–1787

Now that independence had been won, a Philadelphia newspaper observed, "the contest was no longer that of resistance against foreign rule but which of us shall be the rulers?" Where would power reside, in the national government or the states? Who would control the new republican institutions, traditional elites or ordinary citizens?

THE STATE CONSTITUTIONS: HOW MUCH DEMOCRACY?

In May 1776 the Continental Congress had urged Americans to suppress royal authority and establish new governing institutions. Most states quickly complied. Within six months Virginia, Maryland, North Carolina, New Jersey, Delaware, and Pennsylvania had written new constitutions, and Connecticut and Rhode Island had transformed their colonial charters into republican documents by deleting references to the king.

The Declaration of Independence had stated the principle of popular sovereignty: governments derive "their just powers from the consent of the governed." In the heat of revolution many Patriots gave this clause a democratic twist. In North Carolina the backcountry farmers of Mecklenburg County instructed their delegates to the state's constitutional convention to "oppose everything that leans to aristocracy or power in the hands of the rich and chief men exercised to the oppression of the poor." In Virginia voters elected a new assembly that, an observer remarked, "was composed of men not quite so well dressed, nor so politely educated, nor so highly born," while Delaware's constitution declared that "the Right of the People to participate in the Legislature, is the Foundation of Liberty and of all free government."

This democratic outlook received its fullest expression in Pennsylvania, thanks to a coalition of Scots-Irish farmers, Philadelphia artisans, and Enlightenment-influenced intellectuals. Pennsylvania's constitution abolished property owning as a test of citizenship and granted all men who paid taxes the right to vote and hold office. It also created a unicameral (one-house) legislature with complete power. No council or upper house was reserved for the wealthy, and no governor exercised veto power. Other constitutional provisions mandated an extensive system of elementary education, protected citizens from imprisonment for debt, and called for a society of economically independent freemen.

Pennsylvania's democratic constitution alarmed many leading Patriots, who believed that voting and especially officeholding should be restricted to "men of learning, leisure and easy circumstances." Jeremy Belknap of New Hampshire insisted that "the people be taught . . . that they are not able to govern themselves." He and other conservative Patriots feared that popular rule would lead to ordinary citizens using their numerical advantage to tax the rich.

From Boston John Adams denounced Pennsylvania's unicameral legislature as "so democratical that it must produce confusion and every evil work." To counter its appeal Adams published his *Thoughts on Government* in 1776 and sent the treatise to friends at constitutional conventions in other states. Adams adapted the British Whig theory of mixed government (in which power was shared by the king, lords, and commons) to a republican society. To preserve liberty his system dispersed authority by assigning the different functions of government—lawmaking, administering, and judging—to separate branches. Thus, legislatures would make the laws, and the executive and the judiciary would enforce them. Adams also called for a bicameral (two-house) legislature in which the upper house would be restricted to men who owned substantial property and would check the power of popular majorities in the lower house. As a further curb on democracy, he proposed an elected governor with the power to veto laws and an appointed—not elected—judiciary to review them. Adams argued that his plan was republican because the people would elect both the chief executive and the legislature.

Leading Patriots endorsed Adams's scheme because it preserved representative government while restricting popular power. Consequently, most state constitutions provided for bicameral legislatures in which membership in both houses was elective. However, only three constitutions gave the veto power to governors because many Patriots recalled the arbitrary conduct of royal governors. In line with Adams's suggestions, many states retained property qualifications for voting. In New York 90 percent of white men could vote in assembly elections, but only 40 percent could vote for the governor and the upper house. The most flagrant use of property to maintain the power of the elite occurred in South Carolina, where the 1778 constitution required candidates for governor to have a debt-free estate of £10,000 (about $600,000 today), senators to be worth £2,000, and assemblymen to own property valued at £1,000. These provisions ruled out officeholding for about 90 percent of white men.

Nonetheless, post-Revolutionary politics had a democratic tinge. The legislature emerged as the dominant branch of government, and state constitutions apportioned seats on the basis of population, giving farmers in rapidly growing western areas the representation they had long demanded. Indeed, because of backcountry pressure some legislatures moved the state capital from merchant-dominated seaports such as New York City and Philadelphia to inland cities such as Albany and Harrisburg. Even conservative South Carolina moved its seat of government inland, from Charleston to Columbia.

Most of the state legislatures were filled by new sorts of political leaders. Rather than electing their social "betters" to office, ordinary citizens increasingly chose men of "middling circumstances" who knew "the wants of the poor." By the mid-1780s

middling farmers and urban artisans controlled the lower houses in most northern states and formed a sizable minority in southern assemblies. These middling
men took the lead in opposing the collection of back taxes and other measures that
tended "toward the oppression of the people."

The political legacy of the Revolution was complex. Only in Pennsylvania and
Vermont were radical Patriots able to take power and create democratic institutions.
Yet everywhere representative legislatures had more power, and the day-to-day
politics of electioneering and interest-group bargaining became much more
responsive to the demands of ordinary citizens.

The extraordinary excitement of the Revolutionary era also tested the dictum
that only men could engage in politics. While men continued to control all public
institutions—legislatures, juries, government offices—upper-class women entered
into political debate, filling their letters and diaries (and undoubtedly their conversations) with opinions on public issues. "The men say we have no business [with
politics]," Eliza Wilkinson of South Carolina complained in 1783. "They won't even
allow us liberty of thought, and that is all I want" (see American Voices, "Women
and Republicanism").

These American women did not insist on complete equality with men, but they
wanted to eliminate certain restrictive customs and laws. Abigail Adams demanded
equal legal rights for married women, pointing out that under existing common
law they could not own most forms of property and could not enter into a contract or initiate a lawsuit without their husbands' action. "Men would be tyrants"
if they continued to hold such power over women, Adams declared to her husband,
criticizing him and other Patriots for "emancipating all nations" from monarchical
despotism while "retaining absolute power over Wives."

Most men paid little attention to women's requests, and most husbands remained patriarchs, dominating their households. Even young men who embraced
the republican ideal of "companionate" marriage did not support reform of the
common law or a public role for their wives and daughters. With the partial exception of New Jersey, which until 1807 granted the vote to unmarried and widowed women of property, women remained second-class citizens, unable to
participate directly in American political and economic life.

The republican quest for an educated citizenry provided the avenue for the
most important advances made by American women. In her 1779 essay "On the
Equality of the Sexes" (published in 1790), Judith Sargent Murray compared the intellectual faculties of men and women, arguing that women had an equal capacity
for memory and superior imagination. Murray conceded that most women were
inferior to men in judgment and reasoning, but only because of a lack of training:
"We can only reason from what we know," she argued, and most women had been
denied "the opportunity of acquiring knowledge." To remedy this situation, the attorney general in Massachusetts persuaded a jury in the 1790s that girls had an
equal right to schooling under the state constitution. With greater access to public
elementary schools and the creation of female academies (private high schools),

Women and Republicanism

ELIZA WILKINSON

*I*n 1780 Eliza Wilkinson was a young widow managing one of her parents' plantations on the South Carolina Sea Islands, when the islands were invaded by the British. In this letter to a friend, Wilkinson casts herself as a "female patriot" and claims the right to express political opinions.

The land of Liberty! how sweet the sound! . . . O! Americans—Americans! strive to retain the glorious privilege which your virtuous ancestors left you. . . . ; and let not the blood of your brave countrymen, who have so lately (in all the States) died to defend it, be spilt in vain. Pardon this digression, my dear Mary—my pen is inspired with sympathetic ardor, and has run away with my thought before I was aware. I do not live to meddle with political matters; the men say we have no business with them, it is not in our sphere! . . . but I must beg pardon—I won't have it thought, that because we are the weaker sex as to *bodily* strength, my dear, we are capable of nothing more than minding the dairy, visiting the poultry-house, and all such domestic concerns; our thoughts can soar aloft, we can form conceptions of things of a higher nature; and have as just a sense of honor, glory, and great actions as these "lords of the Creation." . . . They won't even allow us the liberty of thought and that is all I want. I should not wish that we should meddle in what is unbecoming female delicacy, but surely we may have sense enough to give our opinions. . . .

 Word was brought that a party of the enemy were at a neighboring plantation, not above two miles off, carrying provisions away. In an instant the men were under arms . . . they did not stay out long; but returned with seven [British] prisoners, four whites and three blacks. . . . Blush, O Britons, and be confounded! . . . an Almighty arm has visibly supported us; or a raw, undisciplined people, with so many disadvantages too on their side, could ever have withstood, for so long a time, an army which has repeatedly fought and conquered. . . .

SOURCE: Nancy Wolock, ed., *Early American Women: A Documentary History, 1600–1900* (Belmont, CA: Wadsworth, 1992), pp. 169–70.

many young women became literate and knowledgeable. By 1850 as many women as men in the northeastern states would be able to read and write, and literate women would challenge their subordinate legal and political status.

THE ARTICLES OF CONFEDERATION

As the Patriots moved toward independence in 1776, they envisioned a central government with limited powers. Carter Braxton of Virginia thought the Continental Congress should have the power to "regulate the affairs of trade, war, peace, alliances,

&c." but "should by no means have authority to interfere with the internal police [governance] or domestic concerns of any Colony."

This localistic outlook informed the Articles of Confederation, passed by Congress in November 1777. As the first national constitution, this document provided for a loose confederation in which "each state retains its sovereignty, freedom, and independence" as well as all powers and rights not "expressly delegated" to the United States. The Articles gave the confederation government the authority to declare war and peace, make treaties with foreign nations, adjudicate disputes between the states, borrow and print money, and requisition funds from the states "for the common defense or general welfare." These powers were to be exercised by a central legislature, the Congress, in which each state had one vote regardless of its wealth or population. There was no separate executive branch or judiciary. Important laws needed approval by at least nine of the thirteen states, and changes in the Articles required unanimous consent.

Because of disputes over western lands the Articles were not ratified by all the states until 1781. States with no claims to land in the West, such as Maryland and Pennsylvania, refused to accept the Articles until Virginia and other states that did have such claims (based on royal charters in which boundaries stretched to the Pacific Ocean) agreed to relinquish them to Congress to create a common national domain in the West. Threatened by Cornwallis's army in 1781, Virginia finally agreed to give up its land claims (Map 7.1 shows the dates of the actual cessions), and Maryland, the last holdout, then ratified the Articles.

Judith Sargent (Murray), Age Nineteen

The well-educated daughter of a wealthy Massachusetts merchant, Judith Sargent enjoyed a privileged childhood. But she endured a difficult seventeen-year marriage to John Stevens, a bankrupt who fled from his creditors and died in the West Indies. In 1788 she wed the Reverend John Murray, who became a leading American Universalist. Her portrait, painted around 1771 by the renowned artist John Singleton Copley, captures Murray's skeptical view of the world, an outlook that enabled her to question customary gender roles.
(Private collection. Photo courtesy Frick Art Reference Library)

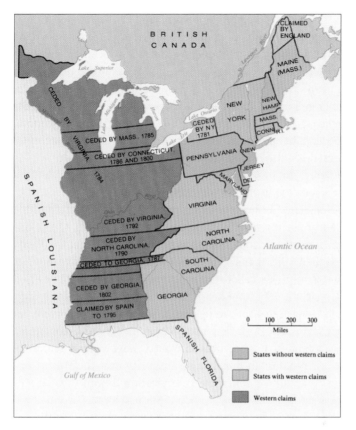

M A P 7.1
The Confederation and Western Land Claims

The Confederation Congress resolved the overlapping western land claims of the states by creating a "national domain" to the west of the Appalachian Mountains. Between 1781 and 1802
all the seaboard states with western land claims ceded them to the national government. The
Confederation Congress established territories with representative political institutions and declared them to be open to settlement by citizens from all the states.

Formal approval of the Articles was anticlimactic. The Congress had been exercising de facto constitutional authority for four years, raising the Continental
army and negotiating with foreign nations. Despite its successes the Confederation
had a major weakness. Congress lacked the authority to impose taxes and therefore
had to requisition funds from the state legislatures and hope they would pay, which
they usually failed to do. Faced with the prospect of the Confederation's bankruptcy
in 1780, General Washington called urgently for a national system of taxation, warning Patriot leaders that otherwise "our cause is lost."

In response, nationalist-minded members of Congress tried to expand the
Confederation's authority. Robert Morris, who became superintendent of finance
in 1781, persuaded Congress to charter the Bank of North America, a private

institution in Philadelphia, hoping to use its notes to stabilize the inflated Continental currency. Morris also developed a comprehensive financial plan that apportioned some war expenses among the states while centralizing control of army expenditures and foreign debt. He hoped that the existence of a national debt would underline the Confederation's need for an import duty. But some state legislatures refused to support an increase in the Confederation's powers, which required the unanimous consent of the states. In 1781 Rhode Island rejected Morris's proposal for an import duty of 5 percent, and two years later New York refused to accept a similar plan, pointing out that it had opposed British-imposed import duties and would not accept them from Congress.

Despite its limited powers, the Congress successfully planned the settlement of the trans-Appalachian West. The Congress asserted the Confederation's title to the West in order to sell it and raise revenue for the government. Thus, in 1783 Congress began to negotiate with Indian tribes, hoping to persuade them that the Treaty of Paris had extinguished their land rights. The Congress also bargained with white squatters—"white savages," John Jay called them—allowing them to stay only if they paid for their lands. Given the natural barrier of the Appalachian Mountains, many members of Congress feared that westerners might establish separate republics and export their crops via the Mississippi River and Spanish-controlled Louisiana. The danger was real: in 1784 settlers in what is now eastern Tennessee organized the new state of Franklin. To preserve its authority over the West, Congress refused to recognize Franklin or consider its application to join the Confederation. Instead, the delegates directed the states of Virginia, North Carolina, and Georgia to administer the process of creating new states south of the Ohio River, a decision that indirectly allowed the expansion of slavery into that region.

To the north of the Ohio Congress established the Northwest Territory and issued three ordinances affecting the settlement and administration of western lands. The Ordinance of 1784, written by Thomas Jefferson, called for the admission of states carved out of the territory as soon as their populations equaled that of the smallest existing state. To deter squatters the Land Ordinance of 1785 established a grid surveying system and required that the lands be surveyed before settlement. It also specified a minimum price of $1 per acre and required that 50 percent of the townships be sold in single blocks of 23,040 acres each, which only large-scale investors and speculators could afford, and the rest in parcels of 640 acres each, which only well-to-do farmers could manage to buy (see Map 7.2).

Finally, the Northwest Ordinance of 1787 provided for the creation of three to five territories that would eventually become the states of Ohio, Indiana, Illinois, Michigan, and Wisconsin. Reflecting the Enlightenment social philosophy of Jefferson and other Patriots, the ordinance prohibited slavery in those territories and earmarked funds from the sale of some land for the support of schools. It also specified that initially Congress should appoint a governor and judges to administer a new territory. Once the number of free adult men reached 5,000, settlers could elect their own legislature. When the population grew to 60,000, residents could

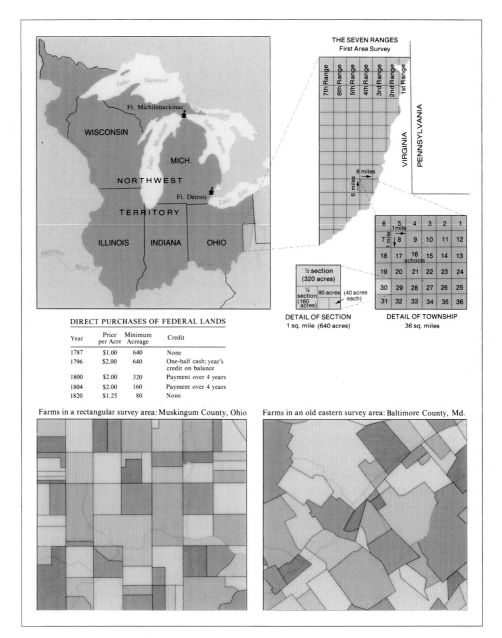

THE SEVEN RANGES
First Area Survey

7th Range | 6th Range | 5th Range | 4th Range | 3rd Range | 2nd Range | 1st Range

VIRGINIA

PENNSYLVANIA

6 miles

6 miles

½ section
(320 acres)

¼
section
(160
acres) | 80 acres | (40 acres
each)

6	5 1mile	4	3	2	1
7	8	9	10	11	12
18	17	16 schools	15	14	13
19	20	21	22	23	24
30	29	28	27	26	25
31	32	33	34	35	36

DETAIL OF SECTION
1 sq. mile (640 acres)

DETAIL OF TOWNSHIP
36 sq. miles

Lake Superior

Ft. Michilimackinac

WISCONSIN

MICH.

NORTHWEST

Ft. Detroit

Lake Erie

TERRITORY

ILLINOIS | INDIANA | OHIO

Missouri River

DIRECT PURCHASES OF FEDERAL LANDS

Year	Price per Acre	Minimum Acreage	Credit
1787	$1.00	640	None
1796	$2.00	640	One-half cash; year's credit on balance
1800	$2.00	320	Payment over 4 years
1804	$2.00	160	Payment over 4 years
1820	$1.25	80	None

Farms in a rectangular survey area: Muskingum County, Ohio

Farms in an old eastern survey area: Baltimore County, Md.

M A P 7.2
Land Divisions in the Northwest Territory

The ordinances of 1785 and 1787 divided the Northwest Territory into uniform sections or townships. The townships were about the same size as New England communities, 36 square miles, and were divided into thirty-six sections of 1 square mile, or 640 acres, surveyed in a grid pattern. The ordinances favored speculators over yeomen by requiring that half the townships be sold in single blocks of 23,040 acres.

write a republican constitution and apply to join the Confederation. On admission a new state would enjoy all the rights and privileges of the existing states.

The ordinances of the 1780s were a great and enduring achievement. They provided for the orderly settlement of the West while reducing the prospect of secessionist movements and preventing the emergence of dependent "colonies." The ordinances also added a new "western" dimension to the national identity. The United States was no longer confined to thirteen governments on the eastern seaboard. It had space to expand.

SHAYS'S REBELLION

However bright the futures of the western states, in the East postwar conditions were grim. Peace had brought a recession rather than a return to prosperity. The war had destroyed many American merchant ships and disrupted the export of tobacco and other farm goods. And now the British Navigation Acts, which had nurtured colonial commerce, barred Americans from trading with the British West Indies. Moreover, low-priced British manufactures flooded American markets, driving many artisans and wartime textile firms out of business.

State governments emerged from the war with large debts and worthless currencies. Speculators—mostly wealthy merchants and landowners—who had purchased state debt certificates for far less than face value advocated high taxes so that the bonds could be redeemed quickly at full value. But yeomen farmers and artisans, hard hit by the postwar recession, demanded tax relief. To assist debtors many states enacted laws allowing them to pay creditors in installments. Other states printed more paper currency in an effort to extend credit. Although wealthy men deplored these actions as destructive of "the just rights of creditors," the stopgap measures probably prevented a major social upheaval.

In Massachusetts the lack of debtor-relief legislation provoked the first armed uprising in the new nation. Merchants and creditors had persuaded the legislature to impose taxes to repay the state's war debt and not to issue more paper currency. When cash-strapped farmers could not pay their debts, creditors hauled them into court, taking their property and saddling them with high legal fees. In 1786 residents of central and western counties called extralegal meetings to protest the taxes and property seizures, and bands of angry farmers closed the courts by force. The resistance gradually grew into a full-scale revolt led by Captain Daniel Shays, a former Continental army officer.

As a struggle against taxes imposed by the distant state government in Boston, Shays's Rebellion resembled colonial resistance to the British Stamp Act. "The people have turned against their teachers the doctrines which were inculcated to effect the late revolution," complained the conservative Massachusetts political leader Fisher Ames (see American Voices, "An Anti-Shaysite Interviews the Rebels"). But even the Radical Patriots of 1776 condemned the Shaysites as anti-republican. "Those Men, who . . . would lessen the Weight of Government lawfully exercised

An Anti-Shaysite Interviews the Rebels

A fter Shays's Rebellion, both sides sought to justify their cause. This clever piece was pub- lished in the Massachusetts Centinel, *an anti-Shaysite newspaper. Unlike most other contributors to the* Centinel, *who explicitly condemned the rebels, this author indicates the nature of the rebels' grievances but subtly emphasizes their selfish motives, portraying them as a mob ("the mobility") intent on avoiding taxes and contesting all authority.*

What influenced them to thus rise and oppose government? What did they aim at thereby? . . . I was present with them at the late rising . . . conversed with almost every one, and penetrated to the secret recesses of their souls. . . . I inquired of an old plough jogger [plow- man or farmer] the confessed aim of the people of that assembly. He said, "To get redress of grievances." I asked, "What grievances?"

He said, "We have grievances enough; I can tell you mine. I have labored hard all my days, and fared hard. I have been greatly abused, been obliged to do more than my part in the war, been loaded down with [many taxes:] class-rates, town-rates, province-rates, con- tinental-rates, and all rates, lawsuits, and have been pulled and hauled by sheriffs, consta- bles, and collectors, and had my cattle sold for less than they were worth. I have been obliged to pay, and nobody will pay me . . . and the great men are going to get all we have, and I think it is time for us to rise and put a stop to it, and have no more courts, nor sher- iffs, nor collectors, nor lawyers. I design to pay no more. . . .

I next asked a pert lad . . . (who fancied himself a deep politician) [and he] made a long harangue upon governors, and jobbers [traders or speculators], and lawyers and judges . . . and salaries, and fees, and pensions, and such has ten times too much, and such has five times too much, and . . . the great men pocket up all the money and live easy, and we work hard, and we can't pay it, and we won't pay it. . . .

Thus I went from rank to rank, through all the mobility. . . . I got the secrets of their hearts. . . .

SOURCE: Linda R. Monk, ed., *Ordinary Americans: U.S. History Through the Eyes of Everyday People* (Alexandria, VA: Close Up, 1994), pp. 42–43.

must be Enemies to our happy Revolution and Common Liberty," charged one- time revolutionary Samuel Adams. To preserve its authority the Massachusetts leg- islature passed a Riot Act outlawing illegal assemblies. Governor James Bowdoin, supported by eastern merchants, equipped a strong fighting force to put down the rebellion and called for additional troops from the Continental Congress. But Shays's army dwindled during the winter of 1786–87, falling victim to freezing weather and inadequate supplies, and Bowdoin's military force easily dispersed the rebels.

"Gen. *Daniel Shays,* Col. *Job Shattuck*"

This woodcut was published in *Bickerstaff's Boston Almanack* for 1787 by "Friends of Government," who attacked the rebel leaders as upstarts and demagogues. "Liberty is still the object I have in view," a Shaysite declared in reply, but the former radical Sam Adams would have none of it: "The man who dares to rebel against the laws of a republic ought to suffer death." Shattuck was sentenced to death for treason but then pardoned; Shays fled to New York State, where he died in 1821, still a poor farmer.
(National Portrait Gallery, Smithsonian Institution/Art Resource, NY)

The collapsed rebellion provided graphic proof that the costs of war and the fruits of independence were not being shared evenly. Many ordinary families who had suffered while supporting the struggle for independence felt they had exchanged one tyranny for another. Angry Massachusetts voters turned Governor Bowdoin out of office, and debt-ridden farmers in New York, northern Pennsylvania, Connecticut, and New Hampshire closed courthouses, demanding economic relief. As British officials in Canada predicted the imminent demise of the United States, many Americans feared for the fate of their republican experiment. At this dire moment nationalists redoubled their efforts to create a central government equal to the challenges facing the new republic.

The Constitution of 1787

From the moment of its creation, the Constitution was a controversial document. Some Americans took issue with the startling ways it redefined republicanism and created a more centralized government, whereas other citizens questioned the motives of its authors.

THE RISE OF A NATIONALIST FACTION

Money questions—debts, taxes, and tariffs—dominated the postwar agenda, and men who had served the Confederation government during the war as military officers, diplomats, and officials looked at them from a "national" rather than a "state" perspective. General Washington, the financier Robert Morris, and the diplomats Benjamin Franklin, John Jay, and John Adams became advocates of a stronger central government with the power to control foreign commerce and impose tariffs. They knew that without tariff revenue Congress would be unable to pay the interest on the foreign debt and the nation's credit would collapse. However, key commercial states in the North—New York, Massachusetts, Pennsylvania—resisted national tariffs because they had devised trade policies that subsided local merchants and imposed state tariffs on imported goods. Most southern planters also opposed tariffs on cheap British textiles and ironware, which they were eager to import.

Some of the planters who opposed tariffs had other reasons for taking a nationalist stance. By 1786 many wealthy southerners were worried about the financial policies of the state governments. Legislatures in Virginia and other southern states had granted tax relief to various groups of citizens, diminishing public revenue and delaying the redemption of state debts. Taxpayers were being led to believe they would "never be compelled to pay" the public debt, lamented Charles Lee of Virginia, a wealthy bondholder. Private creditors had similar complaints. "While men are madly accumulating enormous debts, their legislators are making provisions for their nonpayment," a South Carolina creditor complained.

Nationalists took the initiative in 1786, when James Madison persuaded the Virginia legislature to call a special convention to discuss tariff and taxation policies. Twelve men representing only five states met in Annapolis, Maryland; they called for another meeting in Philadelphia to undertake an even broader review of the Confederation. Nationalists in Congress, frightened by Shays's Rebellion, secured a resolution supporting the Philadelphia convention and calling for a revision of the Articles of Confederation "adequate to the exigencies of government and the preservation of the Union." "Nothing but the adoption of some efficient plan from the Convention," a fellow nationalist wrote to James Madison, "can prevent anarchy first & civil convulsions afterwards."

THE PHILADELPHIA CONVENTION

In May 1787 fifty-five delegates arrived in Philadelphia, representing every state except Rhode Island, whose legislature opposed any increase in central authority. Some delegates, such as Benjamin Franklin of Pennsylvania, had been early leaders of the independence movement. Others, including George Washington and Robert Morris, had become prominent during the war. Several famous Patriots missed the convention. John Adams and Thomas Jefferson were in Europe, serving as the American ministers to Britain and France. The radical Samuel Adams had not been chosen as a delegate by the Massachusetts legislature, while the firebrand Patrick Henry refused to attend because he favored a strictly limited national government. Their places were taken by capable younger men such as James Madison and Alexander Hamilton; both believed that the decisions of the convention would "decide for ever the fate of Republican Government."

Most delegates to the Philadelphia convention were merchants, slaveholding planters, or "monied men." There were no artisans, backcountry settlers, or tenants and only a single yeoman farmer. Consequently, most delegates supported creditors' property rights and favored a central government that would protect the republic from "the imprudence of democracy," as Hamilton put it.

The delegates elected Washington as the presiding officer and, to forestall popular opposition, decided to deliberate behind closed doors. They agreed that each state would have one vote, as in the Confederation, and that a majority of states would decide an issue. Then the delegates exceeded their mandate to revise the Articles of Confederation and considered the Virginia Plan, a scheme for a truly national government devised by James Madison. Madison had arrived in Philadelphia determined to fashion a new political order run by men of high character. A graduate of Princeton, he had read classical and modern political theory and served in both the Confederation Congress and the Virginia assembly. His experience in Virginia had convinced him of the "narrow ambition" and lack of public virtue of many state political leaders.

Madison's Virginia Plan differed from the Articles of Confederation in three crucial respects. First, it rejected state sovereignty in favor of the "supremacy of national authority." The central government would have the power not only to "legislate in all cases to which the separate States are incompetent" but also to overturn state laws. Second, the plan called for a national republic that drew its authority directly from all the people and had direct power over them. As Madison explained, the new central government would bypass the states, operating directly "on the individuals composing them." Third, the plan created a three-tier national government with a lower house elected by voters, an upper house elected by the lower house, and an executive and judiciary chosen by the entire legislature.

From a political perspective Madison's plan had two fatal flaws. First, state politicians and citizens would strongly oppose the provision allowing the national government to veto state laws. Second, by assigning great power to the lower house, whose composition was based on population, Madison's plan increased the influence of voters who lived in the large states. Consequently, delegates from small states rejected the plan, fearing, as a Delaware delegate put it, that the states with many inhabitants would "crush the small ones whenever they stand in the way of their ambitious or interested views."

Delegates from the small states rallied behind the New Jersey Plan devised by William Paterson. This plan strengthened the Confederation by giving the central government the power to raise revenue, control commerce, and make binding requisitions on the states. But it preserved the states' control over their own laws and guaranteed their equality: each state would have one vote in a unicameral legislature, as in the Confederation. Delegates from the larger states rejected this provision and, after a month of debate, mustered a bare majority in favor of the principles of the Virginia Plan.

This decision raised the prospect of a dramatically new constitutional system. During the hot, humid summer of 1787 the delegates met six days a week, debating high principles and considering a multitude of technical details. Experienced and realistic politicians, they knew that their final plan had to be acceptable to existing political interests and powerful social groups. Pierce Butler of South Carolina invoked a classical Greek precedent: "We must follow the example of Solon, who gave the Athenians not the best government he could devise but the best they would receive."

Representation remained the central problem. To satisfy both large and small states the Connecticut delegates suggested amending the Virginia Plan so that the upper house, the Senate, would always seat two members from each state, while seats in the lower chamber, the House of Representatives, would be apportioned on the basis of population. The size of the states' delegations would be altered every ten years on the basis of a national census. This "Great Compromise" was accepted but only after bitter debate; to some it seemed less a compromise than a victory for the smaller states.

Other state-related matters were quickly settled. One delegate objected to establishing national courts within the states, warning that "the states will revolt at such encroachments." The convention therefore defined the judicial power of the United States in broad terms, vesting it "in one supreme Court" and leaving the new national legislature to decide whether to establish lower courts within the states. The convention also decided against requiring voters to own a certain amount of land. "Eight or nine states have extended the right of suffrage beyond the freeholders [landowners]," George Mason of Virginia pointed out. "What will people there say if they should be disfranchised?" The convention also placed the selection of the president in an electoral college chosen on a state-by-state basis and specified that state legislatures, not the voters at large, would elect members of the U.S. Senate. By giving state governments an important role in the new constitutional system, the delegates encouraged them to accept a reduction in their sovereignty.

Slavery was not a prominent issue at the convention, but its consideration revealed an important threefold regional division. Speaking for many northerners Gouverneur Morris of New York condemned slavery as "a nefarious institution" and hoped for its eventual demise. Reflecting the outlook of many Chesapeake planters, who wanted to retain the institution but had ample numbers of slaves, George Mason of Virginia advocated an end to Atlantic slave trade. But delegates from the rice-growing states of South Carolina and Georgia insisted that slave imports continue, warning that otherwise their states "shall not be parties to the Union."

For the sake of national unity, the delegates treated slavery as a political rather than a moral issue. To satisfy Georgia and South Carolina they denied Congress the power to regulate slave imports for twenty years, and to discourage slaves from fleeing they agreed to a "fugitive" clause that allowed masters to reclaim enslaved blacks (or white indentured servants) who took refuge in other states. To mollify the northern states the delegates did not mention slavery explicitly in the Constitution (referring instead to citizens and "all other Persons"), thus denying the institution national legal status. They also refused southern demands to count slaves and citizens equally in determining states' representation in Congress, accepting a compromise proposal in which a slave would be counted as three-fifths of a free person for purposes of representation and taxation.

Having allayed the concerns of small states and slave states, the delegates proceeded to create a powerful, procreditor national government. The finished document declared that the Constitution and all national legislation and treaties made under its authority would be the "supreme" law of the land. It gave the national government broad powers over taxation, military defense, and external commerce as well as the authority to make all laws "necessary and proper" to implement those and other provisions. To protect creditors and establish the fiscal integrity of the new government, the Constitution mandated that the United States honor the existing national debt. Finally, it restricted the ability of state governments to assist debtors by forbidding the states to issue money or enact any "Law impairing the Obligation of Contracts."

The proposed Constitution was not a "perfect production," Benjamin Franklin admitted on September 17, 1787, as he urged the forty-one delegates still present to sign it. Yet the great diplomat confessed his astonishment at finding "this system approaching so near to perfection as it does." His colleagues apparently agreed; all but three signed the document.

THE PEOPLE DEBATE RATIFICATION

The delegates hesitated to submit the Constitution to the state legislatures for their unanimous consent, as required by the Articles of Confederation, because they knew that Rhode Island (and perhaps a few other states) would reject it. So they specified that the Constitution would go into effect on ratification by special conventions in at least nine of the thirteen states. Because of its nationalist sympathies the Confederation Congress winked at this extralegal procedure.

As a great national debate began, the nationalists seized the initiative with two bold moves. First, they called themselves "Federalists," a term that suggested a loose, decentralized system of government and partially obscured their quest for a strong central authority. Second, they launched a coordinated political campaign, publishing dozens of pamphlets and newspaper articles supporting the proposed Constitution.

The opponents of the Constitution, who became known as Antifederalists, had diverse backgrounds and motives. Some, like Governor George Clinton of New York, feared losing their power at the state level. Others were rural democrats who feared that a powerful central government controlled by merchants and creditors would produce a new aristocracy. "These lawyers and men of learning and monied men expect to be managers of this Constitution," worried a Massachusetts farmer, "and get all the power and all the money into their own hands and then they will swallow up all of us little folks . . . just as the whale swallowed up Jonah." They pointed out that the Constitution, unlike most state constitutions, lacked a declaration of individual rights.

Well-educated Americans with a traditional republican outlook also opposed the new system. To keep government "close to the people," they wanted the nation to remain a collection of small sovereign republics tied together only for trade and defense—not the "United States" but the "States United." Citing the French political philosopher Montesquieu, Antifederalists argued that republican institutions were best suited to cities or small states. Thus Melancton Smith of New York warned that the large electoral districts prescribed by the Constitution would encourage the election of a few wealthy upper-class men, whereas the smaller state districts produced "a representative body, composed principally of respectable yeomanry." Patrick Henry predicted the Constitution would recreate the worst features of British rule: high taxes, an oppressive bureaucracy, a standing army, and a "great and mighty President . . . supported in extravagant munificence."

In New York, where ratification was hotly contested, James Madison, John Jay, and Alexander Hamilton countered these arguments in a series of newspaper articles published in 1787 and 1788 and collectively called *The Federalist*. They stressed the need for a strong government to conduct foreign affairs and denied that it would foster domestic tyranny. Citing Montesquieu's praise for "mixed government" (and drawing on John Adams's *Thoughts on Government*), the authors of *The Federalist* pointed out that national authority would be divided among a president, a bicameral legislature, and a judiciary. Each branch of government would "check and balance" the others, thus preserving liberty.

Indeed, in *The Federalist*, No. 10, Madison maintained that the size of the national republic would be its greatest protection against tyranny. It was "sown in the nature of man," Madison wrote, that individuals would seek power and form factions to advance their interests. Indeed, "a landed interest, a manufacturing interest, a mercantile interest, a moneyed interest, with many lesser interests, grow up of necessity in civilized nations." He argued that a free society should not suppress those groups but simply prevent any one of them from becoming dominant—an end best achieved in a large republic. "Extend the sphere," Madison concluded, "and you take in a greater variety of parties and interests; you make it less probable that a majority of the whole will have a common motive to invade the rights of other citizens."

The delegates who met at the state ratifying conventions between December 1787 and June 1788 represented a wide spectrum of Americans, from untutored farmers and middling artisans to well-educated gentlemen. Generally, delegates from the backcountry were Antifederalists, whereas those from the seacoast were Federalists. Thus, a coalition of merchants, artisans, and commercial farmers from Philadelphia and its vicinity spearheaded an easy Federalist victory in Pennsylvania. Other early Federalist successes came in the less populous states of Delaware, New Jersey, Georgia, and Connecticut, where delegates counted on a strong national government to offset the power of their larger neighbors.

The Constitution's first real test came in January 1788 in Massachusetts, one of the most populous states and a hotbed of Antifederalist sentiment (see Map 7.3). Influential Patriots, including Samuel Adams and Governor John Hancock, opposed the new constitution, as did Shaysite sympathizers in the west. But Boston artisans, who wanted tariff protection from British imports, supported ratification. Astute Federalist politicians finally persuaded wavering delegates by promising that the new government would consider a national guarantee of individual rights. By a close vote of 187 to 168, the Federalists carried the day.

Spring brought new Federalist victories in Maryland and South Carolina. When New Hampshire ratified by the narrow margin of fifty-seven to forty-seven in June, the required nine states had approved the Constitution. Still, the essential states of Virginia and New York had not yet acted. Writing in *The Federalist*, Madison, Jay, and Hamilton used their superb rhetorical skills to win support in those states. Addressing a powerful Antifederalist argument, leading Federalists reiterated their promise to amend the Constitution with a bill of rights. In the end the Federalists won narrowly in Virginia, eighty-nine to seventy-nine, and that success carried them to victory in New York by the even smaller margin of thirty to twenty-seven. Suspicious of centralized power, the yeomen of North Carolina and Rhode Island ratified only in 1789 and 1790, respectively.

Ratification of the Constitution brought an end to the Revolutionary era and the temporary ascendancy of the democratically inclined state legislatures. Working against great odds the Federalists had created a national republic that restored the political authority of established leaders. To celebrate their victory Federalists organized great processions in the seaport cities. By marching in orderly fashion (a sharp contrast to the riotous Revolutionary mobs) the citizenry affirmed its commitment to a self-governing republican community based on law. Floats carried the Constitution on an "altar of liberty," using sacred symbols to endow the new national regime with moral legitimacy and lay the foundations for a secular "civil religion."

THE FEDERALISTS IMPLEMENT THE CONSTITUTION

The Constitution expanded the dimensions of American political life, allowing voters to fill national as well as local and state offices. The Federalists swept the elec-

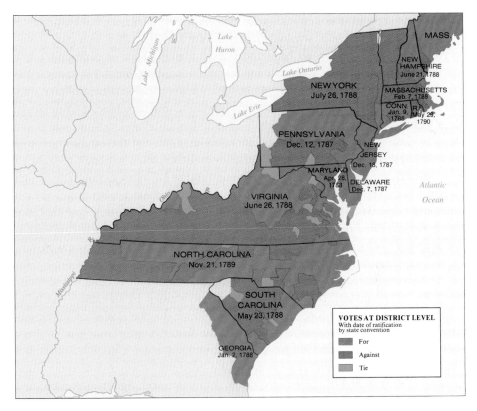

M A P 7.3
Ratifying the Constitution

In 1907 the geographer Owen Libby plotted the votes of the state ratification conventions on a map. Looking at the pattern of voting he suggested that most delegates who favored the Constitution came from commercial farming districts, while those who opposed it came primarily from subsistence regions. Subsequent research has confirmed Libby's socioeconomic interpretation in North and South Carolina and Massachusetts; however, other factors influenced delegates in some states with backcountry districts, such as Georgia, where the Constitution was ratified unanimously.

tion of 1788, placing forty-four supporters in the first Congress; only eight Antifederalists were elected. As expected, members of the Electoral College chose George Washington as president. John Adams received the second highest number of electoral votes and became vice president. The two men took up their posts in New York City, the temporary home of the national government.

Washington, the military savior of his country, became its political father as well. At fifty-seven he was a man of great personal dignity and influence. Instinctively cautious he generally followed the administrative practices of the Confederation, asking Congress to reestablish the existing executive departments: Foreign Affairs (State), Finance (Treasury), and War. The Constitution gave the president the power to appoint major officials with the consent of the Senate, but Washington insisted that only he could remove them, thus ensuring the chief executive's control over the bureaucracy. To head the Department of State Washington chose Thomas Jefferson, a fellow Virginian and an experienced diplomat. For secretary of the Treasury he turned to Alexander Hamilton, a lawyer and wartime military aide. The new president designated Jefferson, Hamilton, and Secretary of War Henry Knox as his cabinet, or advisory body.

The Constitution had created a Supreme Court but left the establishment of the court system to Congress. Because the Federalists wanted national institutions to act directly on individual citizens, they enacted the Judiciary Act of 1789, which created a hierarchical federal court system with thirteen district courts, one for each state, and three circuit courts to hear appeals. As the Constitution specified, the Supreme Court had the final say. Moreover, the Judiciary Act permitted appeals to the Supreme Court of constitutional matters that arose in the state courts, ensuring that national judges would decide contested issues.

The Federalists kept their promise to add a declaration of rights to the Constitution. Drawing on proposed lists of rights submitted by the states' ratifying conventions, James Madison, who had been elected to the House of Representatives, submitted nineteen amendments to the first Congress, and ten of them were approved by the first Congress and ratified by the states in 1791. These ten amendments, which became known as the Bill of Rights, safeguarded certain fundamental personal rights, such as freedom of speech and religion, and mandated certain legal procedures that protected the individual, such as trial by jury. The Second Amendment gave the people the right to bear arms so that they might serve in the militia and defend their liberties, while the Tenth Amendment limited the authority of the national government by reserving powers not otherwise addressed to the states or the people. In addressing Antifederalists' concerns through the Bill of Rights, Congress secured the legitimacy of the new government and ensured broad political support for the Constitution.

The Political Crisis of the 1790s

The final decade of the century brought fresh political challenges. The Federalists divided into two irreconcilable factions over financial policy, and the ideological impact of the French Revolution widened this split. In the course of these struggles Alexander Hamilton and Thomas Jefferson defined contrasting views of the American future.

HAMILTON'S FINANCIAL PROGRAM

One of George Washington's most important decisions was his choice of Alexander Hamilton as secretary of the Treasury. An ambitious self-made man of great charm and intelligence, Hamilton had served as Washington's personal aide during the war. He married the daughter of a wealthy Hudson River landowner and during the 1780s became a leading lawyer in New York City. At the Philadelphia convention Hamilton condemned the "amazing violence and turbulence of the democratic spirit," calling for an authoritarian government headed by a president with nearly monarchical powers.

As Treasury secretary Hamilton devised bold policies to enhance the authority of the national government and favor financiers and seaport merchants. He outlined his plans in three path-breaking and interrelated reports to Congress: on public credit (January 1790), a national bank (December 1790), and manufactures (December 1791).

The financial and social implications of Hamilton's "Report on the Public Credit" made it instantly controversial. It asked Congress to buy ("redeem") at face value the millions of dollars in securities issued by the Confederation, a redemption plan that would bolster the government's credit but also provide windfall profits to speculators. For example, the merchant firm of Burrell & Burrell had paid about $600 for Confederation notes with a face value of $2,500; their redemption at full value would bring the firm an enormous profit of $1,900. Equally controversial, Hamilton proposed to create a permanent national debt to pay the Burrells and other noteholders. In return for their Confederation notes they would receive new government-issued securities bearing the relatively high interest rate of 6 percent.

Hamilton's plan for a permanent national debt funded by wealthy men reawakened Radical Whig and republican fears of scheming British financiers. Speaking for the Virginia House of Burgesses Patrick Henry condemned the plan, arguing that "in an agricultural country like this, to erect, and concentrate, and perpetuate a large monied interest [must prove] . . . fatal to the existence of American liberty." Challenging the morality of Hamilton's proposal, James Madison asked Congress to assist the thousands of shopkeepers, farmers, and soliders who had accepted Confederation securities during the dark days of the war and then sold them to speculators. Madison proposed giving the present bondholders only "the highest price which has prevailed in the market" and distributing the remaining funds to the original owners. But identifying the original owners would have been difficult, and nearly half the members of the House of Representatives owned Confederation securities and would personally profit from Hamilton's plan. Melding practicality with self-interest the House rejected Madison's proposal.

Hamilton then advanced a second proposal that favored wealthy creditors, a plan by which the national government would take over ("assume") the war debts of the states. This assumption plan unleashed a flurry of speculation and some governmental corruption. Before Hamilton's announcement Assistant Secretary of the Treasury William Duer used insider knowledge to buy up the depreciated war bonds of southern states; if Congress approved the assumption plan, Duer and his speculator associates would reap an enormous profit. To win support for assumption in the House of Representatives among the delegations from Virginia and Maryland, which had already paid off part of their war debt, Hamilton agreed to repay those states and back their bid to locate the national capital along the banks of the Potomac.

In December 1790 Hamilton, bolstered by the passage of his funding and re-demption/assumption bills, asked Congress to charter a national financial institu-tion, the Bank of the United States. The Bank would be jointly owned by private stockholders and the national government. Hamilton argued that the Bank, by mak-ing loans to merchants, handling government funds, and issuing financial notes, would provide a respected currency for the specie-starved American economy and make the new national debt easier to fund. These benefits persuaded Congress to enact Hamilton's bill and send it to the president for approval.

At this critical juncture Secretary of State Thomas Jefferson joined ranks with Madison against Hamilton. Jefferson had condemned the shady dealings in southern war bonds and the "corrupt squadron of paper dealers" who had arranged them. Now he charged that Hamilton's scheme for a national bank was unconstitutional. "The incorporation of a Bank," Jefferson told President Washington, was not a power "delegated to the United States by the Constitution." Giving a *strict* interpretation to the national charter, Jefferson maintained that the central government had only the limited powers explicitly assigned to it. In response, Hamilton articulated a *loose* interpretation, noting that Article 1, Section 8, empowered Congress to make "all Laws which shall be necessary and proper" to carry out the Constitution's provisions. Washington agreed with his Treasury secretary and signed the legisla-tion creating the bank.

Hamilton turned now to the final element of his financial system: a national rev-enue that would be used to pay the annual interest on the permanent debt. At Hamil-ton's insistence in 1792 Congress imposed a variety of domestic excise taxes, including a duty on whiskey distilled in the United States. But the revenue from those taxes was small, and so the Treasury secretary proposed to raise tariffs on foreign imports. Although his "Report on Manufactures" (1791) called for a nation that was self-sufficient in manufactured goods, he did not ask Congress to impose high "protec-tive" tariffs that would exclude foreign products. Such tariffs would cut trade, and so Hamilton settled for a modest increase in customs duties, a tariff for "revenue."

Hamilton's carefully designed plan worked brilliantly. As American trade in-creased, customs revenue rose steadily (providing about 90 percent of the U.S. gov-ernment's income from 1790 to 1820), allowing the Treasury to pay for the redemption and assumption programs. In less than two years Hamilton had de-vised a strikingly modern fiscal system that provided the new national government with financial stability.

JEFFERSON'S AGRARIAN VISION

Hamilton paid a high price for this success. By the time Washington began his sec-ond four-year term in 1793, Hamilton's financial measures had split the Federalists who wrote and ratified the Constitution into irreconcilable factions. Most north-

Two Visions of America

Thomas Jefferson and Alexander Hamilton confront each other in these portraits, as they did during the political battles of 1790s. Jefferson was pro-French; Hamilton, pro-British. Jefferson favored farmers and artisans; Hamilton supported merchants and financiers. Jefferson believed in democracy and rule by legislative majorities; Hamilton argued for a strong executive and judicial review. But Hamilton's timely intervention in 1800 secured the presidency for his longtime political foe.

(Jefferson by Rembrandt Peale, The White House Collection, copyright White House Historical Association; Hamilton by John Trumbull, 1792, Yale University Art Gallery, Mabel Brady Garven Collection)

ern Federalists adhered to the political alliance led by Hamilton, and most southerners to a rival group headed by Madison and Jefferson. By the elections of 1794 the two factions had acquired names. Hamilton's supporters retained their original name: Federalists; Madison's and Jefferson's supporters were called Democratic-Republicans or simply Republicans.

The southern planters and western farmers who became Republicans rejected Hamilton's economic and social philosophy. Thomas Jefferson, a man of great learning, spoke for them. Well read in architecture, natural history, scientific farming, and political theory, Jefferson embraced the optimistic spirit of the Enlightenment, declaring his belief in the "improvability of the human race." But he knew that progress was not inevitable and deplored both the long-standing speculative practices of merchants and financiers and the emerging social divisions of an urban industrial economy. Having seen the masses of propertyless laborers in the manufacturing regions in Britain, Jefferson had concluded that workers who depended on wages lacked the economic independence required to sustain a republic.

Jefferson's vision of the American future was agrarian and democratic. Although he had grown up (and remained) a privileged slaveowner, he understood the needs of yeomen farmers and other ordinary white Americans. His vision took form in his *Notes on the State of Virginia* (1785): "Those who labor in the earth are the chosen people of God," he wrote. When Jefferson drafted the Ordinance of 1784, he had pictured a West settled by productive yeomen farm families. Their grain and meat would feed European nations, which "would manufacture and send us in exchange our clothes and other comforts."

During the 1790s Jefferson's vision was fulfilled as turmoil in Europe created new opportunities for American farmers. The French Revolution began in 1789, and four years later France's new republican government went to war against a British-led coalition of monarchical states. As warfare disrupted European farming, wheat prices leapt from 5 to 8 shillings a bushel and remained high for twenty years, bringing substantial profits to export-minded Chesapeake and Middle Atlantic farmers. Simultaneously, a boom in the export of raw cotton, fueled by the invention of the cotton gin and mechanization of cloth production in Britain, boosted the economy of Georgia and South Carolina. As Jefferson had hoped, European markets brought prosperity to American farmers and planters.

THE FRENCH REVOLUTION DIVIDES AMERICANS

American merchants profited even more handsomely from the European war because President Washington issued a Proclamation of Neutrality that allowed U.S. citizens to trade with both sides. As neutral carriers American ships claimed the right to pass through the British naval blockade along the French coastline and soon took over the lucrative trade between France and its West Indian sugar islands. The American merchant fleet became one of the largest in the world, increasing from 355,000 tons in 1790 to more than 1.1 million tons in 1808. Commercial earnings rose spectacularly, averaging $20 million annually in the 1790s—twice the value of cotton and tobacco exports. To keep up with demand, shipowners invested in new vessels, providing work for thousands of shipwrights, sail makers, laborers, and seamen. Hundreds of carpenters, masons, and cabinetmakers found work building warehouses and elegant Federal-style town houses for newly affluent merchants.

Even as they prospered from the European struggle, Americans argued passionately over its ideologies. Most Americans had welcomed the French Revolution of 1789 because it abolished feudalism and established a constitutional monarchy. But the creation of the democratic French republic in 1792 and the execution of King Louis XVI the following year divided public opinion. Many American artisans praised the egalitarianism of the radical French Jacobins and followed their example, addressing each other as "citizen" and founding political clubs, most of which supported Jefferson's Republican Party. But most wealthy Americans and many of those with strong Christian beliefs denounced the Terror (the executions of Louis XVI and his aristocratic supporters) and condemned the new French regime for abandoning Christianity in favor of atheism.

Federalist Gentry

A prominent New England Federalist, Oliver Ellsworth served as Chief Justice of the United
States (1796–1800), while Abigail Wolcott Ellsworth was the daughter of a Connecticut governor. In 1792 the portraitist Ralph Earl captured the aspirations of the Ellsworths by giving
them an aristocratic demeanor and prominently displaying their mansion (in the window).
Like other Federalists who tried to reconcile their wealth and social authority with republican
values, Ellsworth dressed with restraint and his manners, remarked Timothy Dwight, were
"wholly destitute of haughtiness and arrogance." (Wadsworth Atheneum, Hartford)

These ideological conflicts sharpened the debate over Hamilton's economic
policies and even helped foment a domestic insurrection. In 1794 farmers in western Pennsylvania mounted the Whiskey Rebellion to protest Hamilton's excise tax
on spirits, which had raised the price—and thus cut the demand—for the corn
whiskey they sold locally and bartered for eastern manufactures. Like the Sons of
Liberty of 1765 and the Shaysites of 1786, the Whiskey rebels attacked both local
tax collectors and the authority of a distant government. But these protesters also
waved banners proclaiming the French revolutionary slogan "Liberty, Equality, and
Fraternity!" To uphold national authority (and deter secessionist movements along
the frontier) President Washington raised an army of 12,000 troops that soon
suppressed the rebels.

Britain's maritime strategy also widened the growing political divisions in the United States. In November 1793 the Royal Navy began to prey on American ships bound for France from the West Indies, seizing more than 250 vessels and confiscating their sugar cargoes. To avoid war President Washington sent John Jay to Britain. Jay returned in 1795 with a treaty that required the U.S. government to make "full and complete compensation" to British merchants for all pre–Revolutionary War debts owed by American citizens. The treaty also acknowledged Britain's right to remove French property from neutral ships, overturning the American merchants' claim that "free ships make free goods." In return, the agreement allowed American merchants to submit claims of illegal seizure to arbitration and required the British to remove their military garrisons from the Northwest Territory and to end their aid to the Indians there. Jefferson and other Republicans attacked Jay's Treaty as too conciliatory, and the Senate ratified it only by the bare two-thirds majority required by the Constitution. As long as Hamilton and his Federalist allies were in power, the United States would have a pro-British foreign policy.

THE RISE OF POLITICAL PARTIES

The appearance of Federalists and Republicans marked a new stage in American politics. Although colonial legislatures had often divided into temporary factions based on family alliances, ethnicity, or region, they lacked well-organized parties. The new state and national constitutions made no provision for organized political bodies because their framers considered parties unnecessary and dangerous. Following classical republican principles, they wanted voters and legislators to act independently and in the interest of the public—not a party.

But the revolutionary ideology of popular sovereignty had drawn ordinary citizens into politics, and the financial and ideological conflicts of the 1790s created a competitive party system. Merchants and creditors favored Federalist policies, as did wheat-exporting slaveholders in the Tidewater districts of the Chesapeake. The emerging Republican coalition was more diverse and drew supporters from across the social spectrum. It included farmers in the South and the West, artisans in the seaport cities, and many Germans and Scots-Irish.

Party identity crystallized during the election of 1796. To prepare for the election Federalist and Republican leaders called legislative caucuses in Congress and conventions in the states to discuss policies and nominate candidates. To mobilize the citizenry the parties organized public festivals and processions, with the Federalists celebrating Washington's achievements and the Republicans invoking the egalitarian principles of the Declaration of Independence.

Federalist candidates triumphed in the 1796 election, winning a majority in Congress and electing John Adams as the new president. Adams continued Hamilton's pro-British foreign policy and reacted sharply when the French navy seized American merchant ships. When the French foreign minister Talleyrand solicited a loan and a bribe from American diplomats to stop the seizures, Adams urged Congress to prepare for war. He charged that Talleyrand's agents, whom he dubbed X, Y, and Z, had insulted the honor of the United States. Responding to the "XYZ Affair," the Federalist-controlled Congress cut off trade with France in 1798 and authorized American privateers to seize French ships. Party conflict, which had begun over Hamilton's financial policies, now extended to foreign affairs.

CONSTITUTIONAL CRISIS, 1798–1800

For the first time in American history (but not the last) a controversial foreign policy prompted domestic protest and governmental repression. As the United States fought an undeclared maritime war against France, pro-Republican immigrants from Ireland vehemently attacked Adams's foreign policy. Some Federalists responded in kind: "Were I president, I would hang them for otherwise they would murder me," declared a Philadelphia Federalist pamphleteer. To silence its critics, in 1798 the administration enacted a series of coercive measures. The Naturalization Act increased the residency requirement for American citizenship from five to fourteen years; the Alien Act authorized the deportation of foreigners; and the Sedition Act prohibited the publication of ungrounded or malicious attacks on the president or Congress. "He that is not for us is against us," thundered the Federalist *Gazette* of the United States. Prosecutors arrested more than twenty Republican newspaper editors and politicians, accused them of sedition, and imprisoned some of them.

The Federalists' actions created a constitutional crisis. Republicans charged that the Sedition Act violated the First Amendment's prohibition against "abridging the freedom of speech, or of the press." However, they did not appeal to the Supreme Court, both because the Court's power to review congressional legislation had not been established and because the Court was packed with Federalists. Instead, Madison and Jefferson took the fight to the state legislatures. At their urging in 1798 the Kentucky legislature declared the Alien and Sedition Acts to be "unauthoritative, void, and of no force." The Kentucky legislators justified their rejection of this national legislation by arguing that the states had created the national government and therefore had a "right to judge" the constitutionality of its laws. The Virginia legislature passed a similar resolution, also setting forth a "states' rights" interpretation of the Constitution.

The debate over the Sedition Act set the stage for the election of 1800. Jefferson, once opposed in principle to political parties, now saw them as a valuable way "to watch and relate to the people" the activities of a repressive government. Republicans strongly supported Jefferson's bid for the presidency, pointing to the wrongful imprisonment of newspaper editors and championing states' rights. President Adams responded to these attacks by reevaluating his foreign policy. Rejecting the advice of Hamilton and other Federalists to declare war against France (and benefit from an upsurge in patriotism), Adams put country ahead of party and entered into diplomatic negotiations that brought an end to the fighting.

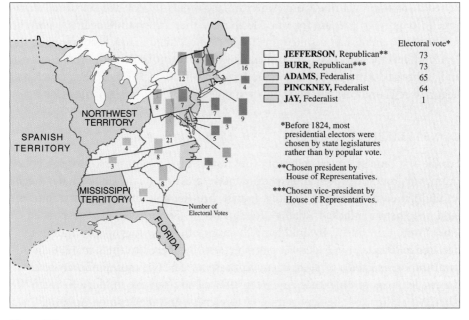

Electoral vote*

☐ **JEFFERSON**, Republican**   73
☐ **BURR**, Republican***   73
☐ **ADAMS**, Federalist   65
☐ **PINCKNEY**, Federalist   64
☐ **JAY**, Federalist   1

*Before 1824, most
presidential electors were
chosen by state legislatures
rather than by popular vote.

**Chosen president by
House of Representatives.

***Chosen vice-president by
House of Representatives.

MAP 7.4
The Election of 1800

Voting in the election of 1800 followed regional lines. John Adams of Massachusetts carried every New England state and, reflecting Federalist strength in maritime and commercial areas, the eastern districts of various mid-Atlantic states. But the Republicans led by Thomas Jefferson of Virginia eked out a narrow victory by winning most of the electoral votes of the South and, thanks to the efforts of vice-presidential candidate Aaron Burr, the twelve votes of the pivotal state of New York.

Nonetheless, the election of 1800 was the first "dirty" political campaign. The Federalists attacked Jefferson's character, branding him as an irresponsible pro-French radical, "the arch-apostle of irreligion and free thought," and both parties forced changes in state election laws to favor their candidates. A low Federalist turnout in Virginia and Pennsylvania and the three-fifths rule (which boosted the voting power of white southerners) gave Jefferson a narrow seventy-three to sixty-five victory in the electoral college (see Map 7.4). But the Republican electors unexpectedly also gave seventy-three votes to Aaron Burr of New York (Jefferson's choice for vice president), throwing the presidential election into the House of Representatives. (The Twelfth Amendment, ratified in 1804, would remedy this constitutional defect by requiring electors to vote separately for president and vice president.)

Ironically, as the era of Federalism and its aristocratic outlook came to an end, Alexander Hamilton ushered in a more democratic era. For thirty-five ballots

T I M E L I N E

1776	Pennsylvania approves a democratic constitution.		James Madison, Alexander Hamilton, and John Jay's *The Federalist*
	John Adams's *Thoughts on Government*	1789	Judiciary Act establishes a federal court system.
	Propertied women allowed to vote in New Jersey (retracted in 1807)		
1777	Articles of Confederation (ratified 1781)	1790– 1792	Hamilton wins enactment of his financial program.
1779	Judith Sargent Murray's "On the Equality of the Sexes" (published in 1790)	1791	Bill of Rights ratified
		1794	Madison and Jefferson found the Democratic-Republican Party.
1780s	Postwar commercial recession Creditor-debtor conflicts in the states		Whiskey Rebellion in western Pennsylvania
1781	Bank of North America chartered by Congress	1795	Jay's Treaty resolves many conflicts between United States and Britain.
1785	Thomas Jefferson's *Notes on the State of Virginia*	1798	XYZ Affair (1797) sparks undeclared war against France.
1786	Annapolis commercial convention Shays's Rebellion in Massachusetts		Alien Act, Sedition Act, and Naturalization Act
1787	Northwest Ordinance		Kentucky and Virginia resolutions condemn the Alien and Sedition Acts.
	Constitutional convention in Philadelphia	1800	Jefferson elected in "Revolution of 1800"
1787– 1788	Ratification conventions in the states		

Federalists in the House of Representatives blocked Jefferson's election. Then the former Treasury secretary intervened. Calling Burr an "embryo Caesar" and the "most unfit man in the United States for the office of president," Hamilton persuaded key Federalists to permit Jefferson's selection. The Federalists' concern for political stability also played a role. As Senator James Bayard of Delaware explained, "It was admitted on all hands that we must risk the Constitution and a Civil War or take Mr. Jefferson."

Jefferson called the election the "Revolution of 1800," and so it was. The bloodless transfer of power demonstrated that governments elected by the people could be changed in an orderly way, even in times of bitter partisan conflict and foreign crisis. In his inaugural address in 1801 Jefferson praised this achievement, declaring: "We are all Republicans, we are all Federalists." Despite the predictions of European conservatives, new republican constitutional order of 1776 had survived a quarter-century of economic and political turmoil.

For Further Exploration

For a lively, drama-filled retelling of the Constitutional Convention, see Catherine Drinker Bowen's *Miracle at Philadelphia: The Story of the Constitutional Convention, May to September 1787* (1966). Jack Rakove's *Original Meanings: Politics and Ideas in the Making of the Constitution* (1996) is a more complex analysis that shows the divergent perspectives of the Framers and how they compromised their differences. Michael Kammen, *A Machine That Would Go by Itself: The Constitution in American Culture* (1986), explains the changing reputation of the founding document, while David Waldstreicher, *In the Midst of Perpetual Fetes: The Making of American Nationalism, 1776–1820* (1997), presents a fascinating analysis of the links between public celebrations and the emergence of an American national identity.

James Roger Sharp offers an engaging study of the near-disintegration of the new nation in the 1790s in *American Politics in the Early Republic: The New Nation in Crisis* (1993). A detailed study of one of the major crises of these years, Thomas P. Slaughter's *The Whiskey Rebellion* (1986), shows how this uprising reflected the localistic, antitax outlook of the Revolutionary era. Rosemarie Zagarri suggests the impact of republicanism on women and provides a concise biography of an important Patriot in *A Woman's Dilemma: Mercy Otis Warren and the American Revolution* (1995). The strong political and leadership abilities of the first president is a central theme of William Martin's fictionalized biography of *Citizen Washington* (1999); Martin also wrote the documentary *George Washington: The Man Who Wouldn't Be King* (PBS video, 1 hour). Additional material, including Washington's published correspondence, is available online at "The Papers of George Washington," <http://www.virginia.edu/gwpapers/>. For more information on Thomas Jefferson consult the PBS website "Thomas Jefferson" at <http://www.pbs.org/jefferson>, which contains information on the documentary (PBS video, 3 hours), transcripts of interviews with Jefferson scholars, and a good collection of documents relating to Jefferson's personal and public life.

Chapter 8

WESTWARD EXPANSION AND A NEW POLITICAL ECONOMY

1790–1820

It is a country in flux. That which is true today as regards its population, its establishments, its prices, its commerce will not be true six months from now.

—Duc de La Rochfoucauld-Liancourt, 1799

M any generations in the past, Shawnee diplomats told American officials in 1803, their ancestors had stood on the shores of the Atlantic Ocean and seen a strange object. "At first they took it for a great bird, but they soon found it to be a monstrous canoe filled with . . . white people." Soon the white people robbed the Shawnees of their wisdom, the diplomats explained, and then "usurped their land," purchasing it with goods that "were more the property of the Indians than the white people because the knowledge which enabled them to manufacture these goods actually belonged to the Shawnees."

Whatever the truth of this legend, the young American republic was a threat to the Shawnees and other native peoples. "The thirst after Indian lands, is become almost universal," an observer had noted as early as 1766. So when the Treaty of Paris in 1783 gave the United States access to the trans-Appalachian West, hundreds of thousands of extraordinarily self-confident Americans trekked into the interior and imposed a new system of economic production on the land.

The votes of western farmers helped to ensure the political ascendancy of the Republican Party and its western-oriented policies. To provide even more land for American farmers President Thomas Jefferson doubled the country's size through the Louisiana Purchase in 1803. Less than a decade later, western Republicans led the nation into war against Great Britain in part because of British support for the Western Indian Confederacy.

While Republican policy encouraged homesteading in the West, state legislatures in the East promoted banking, manufacturing, and commercial growth. As a result beginning around 1800 per capita income in the United States increased by more than 1 percent per year—over 30 percent in a single generation. By the 1820s this extraordinary productivity heralded a new economic order. After half a century

"The Fairview Inn" by Thomas Cole Ruckle

Scores of inns dotted the roads of the new republic, providing food, accommodations, and livery services for settlers moving west and for cattle drovers and teamsters taking western produce to eastern markets. Although executed in 1889, this painting accurately depicts the architecture of an early nineteenth-century Maryland inn and captures the character of its workforce—with free and enslaved African Americans driving cattle and tending to horses. (Maryland Historical Society)

of political independence the nation was well on its way to becoming a republic that was continental in scope and capitalist in character.

Westward Expansion

In 1790 the United States contained 3.9 million people, both white and black, but only 200,000 Americans lived west of the Appalachian Mountains. During the next thirty years the West grew much more rapidly than the rest of the nation. By 1820 there were 9.6 million white and black Americans, and 2 million of them inhabited nine new states and three new territories west of the Appalachians. The country was moving West at an astonishing pace.

NATIVE AMERICAN RESISTANCE

In the Treaty of Paris of 1783 Great Britain relinquished its claims to the trans-Appalachian region and, as one British statesman put it, left the Indian nations "to the care of their [American] neighbours." "Care" was hardly the right term, for some influential Americans advocated exterminating the natives. "Cut up every Indian Cornfield and burn every Indian town," proclaimed William Henry Drayton of South Carolina, so that their "nation be extirpated and the lands become the property of the public." Many others, including Henry Knox, President Washington's first secretary of war, favored assimilating the Indians into American society. Knox wanted commonly held tribal lands to become the private property of individual Indian families, who would become citizens of the various states, a policy that most Indians rejected out of hand.

Not surprisingly, the major struggle between Indians and whites concerned land rights. Invoking the Paris treaty and claiming that pro-British Indians were conquered peoples, the United States government asserted ownership over all Indian lands in the West. Native Americans rejected this claim, pointing out that they had not signed the treaty and had never been conquered. The Confederation Congress and the state governments brushed aside those arguments. In 1784 U.S. commissioners used military threats to force pro-British Iroquois peoples—the Mohawks, Onondagas, Cayugas, and Senecas—to sign the Treaty of Fort Stanwix and relinquish much of their land in New York and Pennsylvania. New York officials and land speculators used liquor and bribes to take title to additional millions of acres. By 1800 the once powerful Iroquois were confined to relatively small reservations.

American negotiators employed similar tactics farther to the west. In 1785 they induced the Chipewyans, Delawares, Ottawas, and Wyandots to sign away most of the future state of Ohio. The tribes quickly repudiated the agreements, claiming—justifiably—that they were made under duress. Those peoples, and the Shawnees, Miamis, and Potawatomis, formed a Western Confederacy to defend themselves against aggressive settlers. Led by Little Turtle, a Miami chief, they defeated American armies in 1790 and again in 1791.

Fearing an alliance between the Western Confederacy and the British in Canada, President Washington doubled the size of the U.S. Army and ordered General "Mad Anthony" Wayne to lead a new expedition. In August 1794 Wayne defeated the Indians in the Battle of Fallen Timbers (near present-day Toledo, Ohio). Nevertheless, the Western Confederacy remained strong, forcing a compromise peace in the Treaty of Greenville (Ohio) in 1795. American negotiators acknowledged Indian ownership rights in the trans-Appalachian West, while the Confederacy accepted American political sovereignty over the entire region and agreed to place themselves "under the protection of the United States, and no other Power whatever." In practice this agreement encouraged American officials and settlers to pressure native Americans to give up their lands, while enabling Indian peoples to demand money or goods in return. Indeed, at Greenville the Indians ceded ownership of most of

Ohio and certain strategic areas along the Great Lakes, including Detroit and the future site of Chicago (see Map 8.1). Recognizing the gains made by the United States, Britain cut some of its trading ties with the Indians and, in Jay's Treaty of 1795, reaffirmed its (still unfulfilled) obligation under the Treaty of Paris to remove its military garrisons from the region.

American westward migration increased as soon as the fighting ended. In 1805 the two-year-old state of Ohio had more than 100,000 residents. Thousands more farm families moved into the future states of Indiana and Illinois, sparking new conflicts with native peoples over land and hunting rights. As a Delaware Indian declared, "The Elks are our horses, the buffaloes are our cows, the deer are our

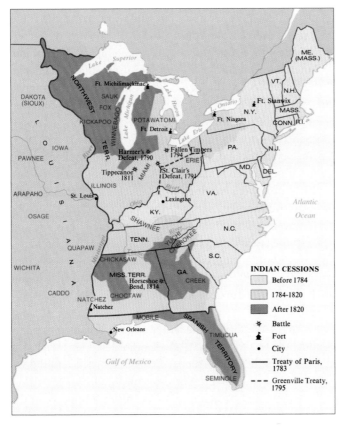

M A P 8.1
Military and Diplomatic Expansion, to 1840

The United States claimed sovereignty over the entire trans-Appalachian West by virtue of the Treaty of 1783 with Britain. When the Western Confederacy contested this claim, the American government sent armies into the West during the 1790s and again during the War of 1812. By the 1830s the continuation of this armed diplomacy had forced Native American peoples to cede by treaty most of their lands east of the Mississippi River.

sheep, & the whites shan't have them." To alleviate these tensions the U.S. government continued to encourage Native Americans to become farmers and assimilate into white society. The goal, as one Kentucky Protestant minister put it, was to make the Indian "a farmer, a citizen of the United States, and a Christian."

Most Native Americans resisted these attempts to destroy their traditional tribal cultures. Many Indian peoples drove out white missionaries and forced converts to Christianity to participate in tribal rites. As a Munsee prophet put it, "There are two ways to God, one for the whites and one for the Indians." Among the Senecas of New York the prophet Handsome Lake tried to find a middle way, from 1801 to 1807 promoting traditional ceremonies in which celebrants gave thanks to the earth, plants, animals, water, and sun and incorporating some Christian beliefs, such as heaven and hell, into his teachings. But Handsome Lake's rejection of some Indian beliefs and his support of Quaker missionaries divided the tribe into hostile religious factions. The more conservative Senecas, led by Chief Red Jacket, condemned Indians who accepted white ways and beliefs and demanded a return to ancestral customs.

Most Indian women also rejected European farming practices. Among the Iroquois, women had long been responsible for growing staple foods and, as a result, controlled the inheritance of cultivation rights and exercised considerable political power. Shawnee women had even more authority, as women "war" chiefs decided whether to dispatch a war party or to torture captives. Even those Indians who embraced Christian teachings retained many traditional values. To view themselves as individuals, as the Europeans demanded, meant repudiating the clan, the essence of Indian life.

THE CHANGING AGRICULTURAL ECONOMY

Between 1790 and 1820 more than 250,000 white and black migrants crossed the Appalachians into Kentucky and Tennessee and moved along the coastal plain of the Gulf of Mexico into the future states of Alabama and Mississippi. Most migrants who flocked through the Cumberland Gap into Kentucky and Tennessee were white tenant farmers and struggling yeomen families. They were fleeing the depleted soils and planter elite of the Chesapeake region, confident that they would prosper by growing cotton and hemp, which were in great demand.

First they had to gain title to the land. Those without ready cash based their claims for free land on "the ancient cultivation law" governing frontier tracts. Invoking the argument of the North Carolina Regulators (see Chapter 4), they argued that poor settlers had a customary right "from time out of Mind" to occupy "back waste vacant Lands" sufficient "to provide a subsistence for themselves and their posterity." The Virginia government, which administered the Kentucky Territory, had a more elitist vision. While it allowed settlers to purchase up to 1,400 acres of land at reduced prices, it also dispensed grants of 20,000 to 200,000 acres to scores of wealthy individuals and partnerships. Consequently, when Kentucky became a state in 1792, a handful of speculators owned one-fourth of the state, whereas half the adult white men owned no land and lived as squatters or tenants.

The rest of the southern frontier became a stronghold of racial slavery. Until the 1810s, wealthy planters and up-and-coming young men from the Chesapeake and the Lower South set up new slave plantations in the interior of Georgia and South Carolina and then they moved into the Old Southwest—the future states of Alabama, Mississippi, and Louisiana (see American Voices, "Settling the Southwestern Frontier"). They carried some slaves with them and imported more from Africa. Between 1776 and 1809, when Congress cut off the Atlantic slave trade, these planters bought about 115,000 African slaves. The black population also grew through reproduction, increasing from a half million in 1775 to 1.8 million in 1820.

Although many enslaved African Americans still toiled in tobacco and rice fields of the Chesapeake and South Carolina, it was a new crop—cotton—that financed the expansion of slavery into the Old Southwest. After 1750 technological breakthroughs such as water-powered spinning jennies and weaving mules boosted European textile production and greatly increased the demand for raw wool and cotton. By the 1790s American inventors—including Connecticut-born Eli

A Slave Auction in Charleston, South Carolina, 1833

As one slave departs with his new master (far right), the auctioneer tries to interest the assembled planters in his next sale item, a black family. The artist, a British Canadian named Henry Byam Martin, showed his disdain for these proceedings both visually (compare the family's dignified bearing with the planters' slouching posture) and verbally, giving the sketch a sarcastic title: "The Land of the Free and the Home of the Brave."
(National Archives of Canada/C-115001)

Settling the Southwestern Frontier

REUBEN DAVIS

*B*orn around 1810, Reuben Davis grew up on the southwestern frontier, where his slave-*
owning father had migrated to find land and opportunities for his many children. Davis
eventually became a lawyer in Mississippi and in 1890 published a memoir that describes—
in a partly realistic, partly romantic fashion—the interaction among whites, Indians, and
African Americans in early Alabama.

My father was one of the earliest settlers in this country. He was a man of limited means, and though of strong and vigorous intellect, had only the imperfect education of the pioneers of that day. His chief study was the Bible and a few volumes of history, which formed his only library. Although a Baptist minister of high standing, he occupied himself, during the week, with ordinary farm labor, and could never be induced to accept any compensation for his services in the church. . . .

Both my parents were born in Virginia, and remained there after marriage until ten children were added to their family. They then removed to Tennessee [and later] . . . to North Alabama. The land had been recently purchased from the Indians, and many of them yet roamed the dense forests of that section. I well remember how I hunted with these wild companions, and was taught by them to use the bow and arrow. . . . Occasional deeds of frightful atrocity were committed in the immediate neighborhood. Long before I was competent to reason on it, the problem of race-hatred was forced upon my observation. The fierce antagonism of one race for another and the frequent rising of the conquered against the conqueror were met then as practical questions,—as the fashion of the day was,—without much speculation or moralizing. . . .

At that time the country was as wild and unsettled as possible; there were no laws, no schools, and no libraries. Every man did what was right in his own eyes, but in spite of general recklessness and lawlessness, there was a rough code of honor and honesty which was rarely broken. The settlers lived a life of great toil and many privations, but they were eminently social, kindly, and friendly. . . .

Clearing land and opening a farm required constant and severe labor, and I, with my five brothers, performed our full share. . . . My brothers and myself, assisted by six colored hands, cultivated the land, and attended school only about three months in the year. In this way we learned to read and write, as well as the rudiments of arithmetic and a little Latin. . . .

There was this great advantage that, while none were very wealthy, few were poor enough to suffer actual want. . . . The simple habits of the laboring man were not shamed by the ostentation of his more prosperous neighbor; and there was none of that silent, perpetual contrast of luxury and penury, which now adds bitterness to class hatreds.

SOURCE: Reuben Davis, *Recollections of Mississippi and Mississippians* (Boston: Houghton, Mifflin, 1890), pp. 2–4.

Whitney—had developed machines (called *gins*) that efficiently extracted the seeds from the strands of cotton, and thousands of white planters in South Carolina and Georgia began growing the crop. During the 1810s planters—and their slaves— carried cotton production into Alabama and Mississippi, which entered the Union in 1817 and 1819, respectively.

As slaveowning cotton planters moved south and west, a new wave of yeoman farm families flowed out of Massachusetts and Connecticut (see Map 8.2). Previous generations had moved north and east, settling New Hampshire, Vermont, and Maine, but many towns in Massachusetts and Connecticut remained overcrowded, their lands subdivided into small, depleted farmsteads. To provide land for the four or five children who survived to adulthood, thousands of families packed their wagons with tools and household goods and migrated into New York. By 1820 nearly 800,000 New England migrants lived in a string of settlements that stretched from Albany to Buffalo. Thousands more moved on to Ohio and Indiana.

This vast migration was organized not by governments or joint-stock companies but by the settlers themselves, who often moved in large groups linked by family and religion. As a traveler reported from central New York, "The town of Herkimer is entirely populated by families come from Connecticut. We stayed at Mr. Snow's who came from New London with about ten male and female cousins." When 176 residents of Granville, Massachusetts, moved to Ohio, they transplanted their Congregational ministers and elders along with their system of freehold agriculture. Throughout the northern trans-Appalachian West many "new" communities were actually old communities that had moved inland.

In New York, as in Kentucky, well-connected speculators snapped up much of the best land. In the 1780s the financier Robert Morris acquired 1.3 million acres in the Genesee region of central New York, where the Wadsworth family also bought thousands of acres of prime land and created leasehold farms similar to those on Hudson river valley manors. To attract tenants the Wadsworths leased farms rent-free for the first seven years, after which they charged rents. Many New England yeomen preferred to sign agreements with the Dutch-owned Holland Land Company because these contracts allowed them to buy the land as they worked it. But high interest rates and the lack of markets mired thousands of these aspiring freeholders deeply in debt. As one pioneer recalled, "In the early years, there was none but a home market and that was mostly barter—it was so many bushels of wheat for a cow; so many bushels for a yoke of oxen." Fleeing declining prospects in the East these farmers found themselves at the bottom of the economic ladder in the West.

The settlement of western lands prompted changes in eastern agriculture. As low-cost western wheat began to flow to eastern markets, farmers in New England planted different crops, such as potatoes, which were nutritious and high yielding. To compensate for the lost labor of sons and daughters, Middle Atlantic farmers replaced metal-tipped wooden plows with cast-iron models that dug deeper and required a single yoke of oxen instead of two or three. These improvements allowed them to maintain production levels even with fewer laborers.

Easterners also took advantage of the progressive farming methods recently publicized by wealthy British agricultural reformers. "Improvers" rotated their crops to maintain soil fertility, planting nitrogen-rich clover to offset nutrient-hungry crops of wheat and corn. In Pennsylvania crop rotation doubled the average wheat yield per acre. Yeomen diversified production, raising sheep and selling the wool to textile manufacturers. Many farmers adopted a year-round planting cycle, sowing wheat in the winter for market and corn in the spring for animal fodder. Women and girls milked the family cows and sold butter and cheese in the growing towns and cities.

MAP 8.2
Regional Cultures Move West, 1720–1820

By 1720 four distinct "core" cultures had developed along the Atlantic seaboard. By 1775 settlers from the Middle Atlantic and Chesapeake regions had carried their customs and institutions into the southern backcountry. Between 1780 and 1820 the descendants of these migrants moved into the trans-Appalachian West, while Carolinians transplanted their slave society to the Old Southwest and New Englanders transmitted their customs to upstate New York and the Old Northwest.

In this new agricultural economy families worked harder and longer, but their efforts were rewarded with higher output and a better standard of living. Whether hacking fields out of western forests or carting manure to replenish eastern soils, farm families increased their productivity. Westward migration had boosted the entire American economy.

THE TRANSPORTATION BOTTLENECK

American geography threatened to cut short this economic advance: water transport was the quickest and cheapest way to get goods to market, but no rivers cut through the Appalachian Mountains. It had cost eighteenth-century Pennsylvania farmers as much to send crops 30 miles by road to Philadelphia as to ship them from Philadelphia to London. Without access to waterways or other cheap means of transportation, settlers west of the Appalachian Mountains would be unable to send goods to markets in the East, Europe, and the West Indies.

Improved inland trade therefore became a high priority for the new state governments, which actively encouraged transportation ventures. Between 1793 and 1812 the Pennsylvania legislature granted fifty-five corporate charters to private turnpike companies, and Massachusetts chartered over a hundred. Turnpike companies built level gravel roads that significantly reduced travel time and transport costs and charged tolls for their use. State governments and private entrepreneurs constructed even more cost-efficient inland waterways, dredging rivers to make them navigable and constructing short canals to bypass waterfalls or rapids. By 1816 the United States had about 100 miles of canals, but only three were more than 2 miles long and none breached the great Appalachian barrier. Only after 1819, when the Erie Canal began to connect the central and western counties of New York to the Hudson River, could inland farmers sell their produce in eastern markets (see Chapter 10).

For farmers further west the great streams that connected to the Mississippi River represented the great hope. Western settlers paid premium prices for land along navigable rivers, while speculators bought up property in growing towns—such as Cincinnati, Louisville, Chattanooga, and St. Louis—along the Ohio, Tennessee, and Mississippi Rivers. Western farmers and merchants built barges to float cotton and surplus grain and meat down this interconnected river system to the port of New Orleans, which by 1815 was processing about $5 million in agricultural products yearly.

But many isolated western settlers in the trans-Appalachian West had no choice but to be self-sufficient. "A noble field of Indian corn stretched away into the forest on one side," an English visitor to an Ohio farm in the 1820s noted, "and immediately before the house was a small potato garden, with a few peach and apple trees. The woman told me that they spun and wove all the cotton and woollen garments of the family, and knit all the stockings; her husband, though not a shoemaker by trade, made all the shoes. She manufactured all the soap and candles they use." Self-sufficiency meant a low standard of living. As late as 1840 per capita in-

"View of Cincinnati," by John Casper Wild, 1835

Thanks to its location on the Ohio River, Cincinnati quickly became one of the major commercial cities of the trans-Appalachian West. By the 1820s passenger steamboats as well as freight barges connected the city with Pittsburgh to the north and the ocean port of New Orleans, far to the south. (M. and M. Karolik Collection. Courtesy Museum of Fine Arts, Boston)

come in states formed out of the Northwest Territory was only 70 percent of the national average.

Despite these financial hardships and transportation bottlenecks white Americans continued to migrate westward. They knew it would take a generation to clear land, build houses, barns, and roads and plant orchards, and yet they were confident that their sacrifices and the expansion of the canal and road system would yield future security for themselves and their children. The humble achievements of thousands of yeomen and tenant families slowly transformed the landscape of the interior of the continent, turning forests into farms and crossroads into communities.

The Republicans' Political Revolution

Agricultural expansion was a central policy of the Republican Party and accounted for much of its appeal. From 1801 to 1825 three Republicans from Virginia—Thomas Jefferson, James Madison, and James Monroe—served two terms each as president. Supported by voters in the new western states and strong majorities in Congress, this "Virginia Dynasty" reversed many Federalist policies, completing what Jefferson called the Revolution of 1800. Western issues such as Indian policy and territorial disputes with Spain and Britain occupied the attention of politicians and, together with maritime disputes in the Atlantic, precipitated the War of 1812.

THE JEFFERSONIAN PRESIDENCY

Thomas Jefferson was an accomplished and versatile statesman, an insightful political philosopher, and a superb politician. On assuming the presidency in 1801 Jefferson became the first chief executive to hold office in the District of Columbia, the new national capital. However, his administration did not begin with a clean slate. After a dozen years of Federalist presidents the federal judiciary was filled with their appointees. The most important was the formidable John Marshall of Virginia, who presided over the Supreme Court. Moreover, in 1801 the outgoing Federalist-controlled Congress had passed a Judiciary Act. It created sixteen new judgeships and six additional circuit courts, which, along with a variety of existing patronage posts, President Adams had filled with "midnight appointments" just before he left office. The Federalists "have retired into the judiciary as a stronghold," Jefferson complained, "and from that battery all the works of Republicanism are to be beaten down and destroyed."

To bolster their political position Republicans in Congress repealed the Judiciary Act, and James Madison, the new secretary of state, refused to commission William Marbury, one of Adams's midnight appointees, as a justice of the peace in the District of Columbia. Marbury promptly petitioned the Supreme Court to compel delivery of his commission. However, in *Marbury v. Madison* (1803) John Marshall declared that while Marbury had a right to his commission, the Court did not have the constitutional power to enforce that right. By using this reasoning Marshall cleverly condemned Madison's action and asserted the Court's power to review laws (*judicial review*) while avoiding a direct confrontation with the Republican administration.

For his part Jefferson challenged many Federalist policies. Charging the Federalists with grossly expanding the national government's size and power, he led Republican efforts to shrink it back. When the Alien and Sedition Acts expired in 1801, the Republican Congress did not reenact them, branding the acts as politically motivated and unconstitutional. It also amended the Naturalization Act to permit resident aliens to become citizens after five years. But Jefferson governed tactfully, appointing some Federalists to government posts and allowing competent Federalist bureaucrats to remain in their jobs. During eight years as chief executive he removed only 109 of 433 Federalist officeholders, and forty of those were Adams's "midnight appointees."

In foreign affairs Jefferson faced an immediate crisis. In the 1790s the Barbary States of North Africa had systematically raided American merchant ships, and Federalist officials had paid an annual bribe ("tribute") to buy their protection. Initially Jefferson reversed this policy, declaring in 1801 that the United States would no longer pay tribute. When the Barbary "pirates" renewed their assaults, he ordered the U.S. Navy to retaliate. But Jefferson wanted to avoid all-out war, which would increase taxes and the national debt. So he accepted a diplomatic solution that granted a reduced tribute.

In domestic matters Jefferson set a clearly Republican course. He abolished all internal taxes, including the excise tax that had sparked the Whiskey Rebellion of 1794. Addressing his party's fears of a military takeover, Jefferson reduced the size of the permanent army. He tolerated the economically important Bank of the United States (which he had condemned as unconstitutional in 1791), but he chose Albert Gallatin, a fiscal conservative who believed that the national debt was "an evil of the first magnitude," as secretary of the treasury. By carefully controlling government expenditures and using customs revenues to redeem government bonds, Gallatin reduced the debt from $83 million in 1801 to $45 million in 1808. With Jefferson and Gallatin at the helm the nation was no longer run in the interests of northeastern creditors and merchants.

JEFFERSON AND THE WEST

Long before he became president Jefferson championed the settlement of the West. He celebrated the yeoman farmer in *Notes on the State of Virginia* (1785), helped compose the Confederation's western land ordinances, and strongly supported Pinckney's Treaty of 1795, which allowed settlers to ship crops down the Mississippi River for export through the Spanish-held port of New Orleans.

As president Jefferson seized the opportunity to increase the flow of settlers to the West. During the 1790s the Federalist-dominated Congresses had refused to amend the Land Ordinance of 1785 to make it easier for migrating families to buy a farm in the national domain. In fact, the Federalist Land Act of 1796 doubled the minimum price to $2 per acre. Because Jefferson wanted to see the West populated with yeomen farm families, the Republicans in Congress passed laws in 1800 and 1804 reducing the minimum allotment first to 320 and then to 160 acres. Eventually the Land Act of 1820 cut the minimum purchase to 80 acres and the price to $1.25 per acre, enabling a farmer with only $100 in cash to buy a western farm.

International events challenged Jefferson's vision for the West. In 1799 Napoleon Bonaparte seized power in France and began an ambitious campaign to establish a French empire both in Europe and America. In 1801 Napoleon coerced Spain into signing a secret treaty that returned to France its former colony of Louisiana. A year later he directed Spanish officials in Louisiana to restrict American access to New Orleans, thus violating the terms of Pinckney's Treaty of 1795. Meanwhile, Napoleon planned an invasion to restore French rule in Haiti (then called Saint-Domingue), a rich sugar island seized in 1793 by rebellious black slaves led by Toussaint L'Ouverture.

Napoleon's aggressive actions prompted Jefferson to question his party's traditionally pro-French foreign policy. Any nation that denied Americans access to the port of New Orleans, Jefferson declared, must be "our natural and habitual enemy." To avoid hostilities with France Jefferson instructed Robert R. Livingston, the American minister in Paris, to negotiate the purchase of New Orleans. Simultaneously, Jefferson sent James Monroe to Britain to seek its assistance in case of war. "The day that France takes possession of New Orleans," the president warned, "we must marry ourselves to the British fleet and nation."

Jefferson's diplomacy yielded a magnificent prize: the entire territory of Louisiana. By 1802 the French invasion of Haiti was faltering, a new war threatened in Europe, and Napoleon feared an American invasion of Louisiana. With characteristic decisiveness, in April 1803 the French ruler offered to sell not only New Orleans but also the entire territory of Louisiana. For about $15 million ($450 million today), Livingston and Monroe concluded what became known as the Louisiana Purchase (see Map 8.3). "We have lived long," Livingston remarked to Monroe, "but this is the noblest work of our lives."

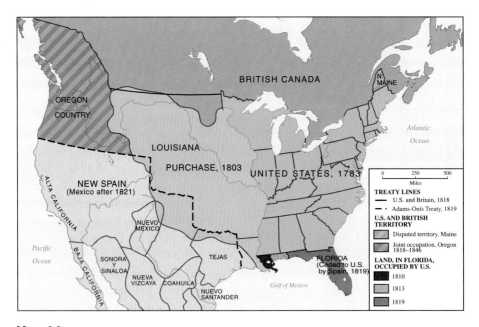

M A P 8.3
Defining the National Boundaries, to 1840

After the War of 1812 John Quincy Adams negotiated treaties with Great Britain and Spain that made Florida and northern Maine part of the United States and defined the American boundaries with Canada and New Spain (which in 1821 became the independent nation of Mexico). These treaties eliminated the threat of war until the 1840s, providing the young American nation with a much needed period of peace.

The Louisiana Purchase forced the president to reconsider his interpretation of the Constitution. Jefferson had always been a strict constructionist, maintaining that the national government possessed only the powers "expressly" delegated to it in the Constitution. There was no provision in the Constitution for adding new territory, however, so to fulfill his dreams for the West Jefferson pragmatically accepted a loose interpretation of the Constitution.

A scientist as well as a statesman, Jefferson wanted detailed information about the physical features of the new territory and its plant and animal life. In 1804 he sent his personal secretary, Meriwether Lewis, to explore the region with William Clark, an army officer. Aided by Indian guides Lewis and Clark and their group of American soldiers and frontiersmen traveled up the Missouri River, across the Rocky Mountains, and (venturing beyond the Purchase) down the Columbia River to the Pacific Ocean. After two years they returned with the first maps of the immense wilderness and vivid accounts of its natural resources and inhabitants.

The Louisiana Purchase intensified existing political conflicts. New England Federalists, fearing that western expansion would diminish their power, talked openly of leaving the Union. When Alexander Hamilton refused to support their plan for a separate Northern Confederacy, the secessionists turned to Aaron Burr, the ambitious vice president, who was seeking election as governor of New York. In July 1804 Hamilton accused Burr of participating in a conspiracy to destroy the Union, and Burr challenged him to a pistol duel. Hamilton died by gunshot in the illegal confrontation, and state courts in New York and New Jersey indicted Burr for murder.

After his vice-presidential term ended early in 1805, Burr moved West to avoid prosecution. There he conspired with General James Wilkinson, the military governor of the Louisiana Territory. Their plan remains a mystery, but it probably involved either the capture of territory in New Spain or a rebellion to establish Louisiana as a separate nation headed by Burr. Wilkinson betrayed Burr, however, and arrested him for treason as the former vice president led an armed force down the Ohio River. In a highly politicized trial presided over by Chief Justice John Marshall, the jury acquitted Burr of treason. The verdict was less important than the dangers to national unity that it revealed. The Republicans' policy of western expansion had increased sectional tension and party conflict, giving new life to states' rights sentiment and secessionist schemes.

CONFLICT WITH BRITAIN AND FRANCE

As the Napoleonic Wars ravaged Europe between 1802 and 1815, they threatened the commercial interests of the American republic. Great Britain and France, the major belligerents, refused to respect the neutrality of American merchant vessels. Napoleon imposed the "Continental System" on European ports under French control, requiring customs officials to seize neutral ships that had stopped in Britain. For its part, the British ministry set up a naval blockade, seizing ships carrying goods to Europe, including American vessels filled with sugar and molasses from the French West Indies. The British Navy also searched American ships for British deserters and impressed (or forced) them back into service. Between 1802 and 1811 British officers seized nearly 8,000 sailors, many of whom were American citizens. American resentment turned to outrage in 1807, when a British warship attacked the U.S. Navy vessel *Chesapeake,* killing or wounding twenty-one men and seizing four alleged deserters. "Never since the battle of Lexington have I seen this country in such a state of exasperation as at present," Jefferson declared.

To protect American interests while avoiding war Jefferson pursued a policy of peaceful coercion. Working closely with Secretary of State James Madison, the president devised the Embargo Act of 1807, which prohibited American ships from leaving their home ports until Britain and France repealed their restrictions on U.S. trade. Though the embargo was a creative diplomatic measure—an economic weapon similar to the nonimportation movements between 1765 and 1775—it overestimated the dependence of France and Britain on American shipping and underestimated resistance from New England merchants, who feared it would ruin them.

The embargo caused American exports to plunge from $108 million in 1806 to $22 million in 1808, hurting farmers as well as merchants and prompting Federalists to demand its repeal. When the Republican Congress passed a Force Act giving customs officials extraordinary powers to prevent smuggling into Canada, Federalists railed against government tyranny. "Would to God," exclaimed one Federalist, "that the Embargo had done as little evil to ourselves as it has done to foreign nations."

Despite discontent over the embargo voters elected James Madison, one of its authors, to the presidency in 1808. As the main architect of the Constitution, an advocate of the Bill of Rights, and a prominent congressman and party leader, Madison had served the nation well. As president Madison acknowledged the embargo's failure and replaced it with a series of new economic restrictions, none of which succeeded in persuading France and Britain to respect America's neutral rights. "The Devil himself could not tell which government, England or France, is the most wicked," an exasperated congressman declared.

Republican congressmen from the West—the future "war hawks" of 1812—thought Britain was the major offender, pointing in particular to its assistance to the Indians in the Ohio River Valley. Bolstered by British guns and supplies, in 1809 the Shawnee chief Tecumseh, assisted by his brother, the Prophet Tenskwatawa, had revived the Western Confederacy of the 1790s. Their goal was to exclude whites from all lands west of the Appalachian Mountains. Responding to this threat expansionists in Congress condemned British support of Tecumseh and threatened to invade Canada. In 1811, following a series of clashes between settlers and the Confederacy, William Henry Harrison, the governor of the Indiana Territory, led an army against Tenskwatawa's village of Prophetstown (on the Wabash River in present-day Indiana). After fending off the Confederation's warriors at the Battle of Tippecanoe, Harrison burned the village to the ground (see American Voices, "The Battle of Tippecanoe").

AMERICAN VOICES

The Battle of Tippecanoe

CHIEF SHABONEE

In this interview with a newspaper reporter, the Potawatomi chief Shabonee recalls the events surrounding the Battle of Tippecanoe in 1811 and offers a penetrating view of reality: the unfaithfulness of allies, the confidence and impulsiveness of youth, and the false promises of war leaders.

It was fully believed among the Indians that we should defeat General Harrison, and that we should hold the line of the Wabash and dictate terms to the whites. The great cause of our failure, was the Miamies, whose principal country was south of the river, and they wanted to treat with the whites so as to retain their land, and they played false to their red brethren and yet lost all. They are now surrounded and will be crushed. . . .

Our young men said: We are ten to their one. If they stay upon the other side, we will let them alone. If they cross the Wabash, we will take their scalps or drive them into the river. They cannot swim. Their powder will be wet. The fish will eat their bodies. The bones of the white men will lie upon every sand bar. Their flesh will fatten buzzards. These white soldiers are not warriors. Their hands are soft. Their faces are white. One half of them are calico peddlers. The other half can only shoot squirrels. They cannot stand before men. . . .

Such were the opinions and arguments of our warriors. They did not appreciate the great strength of the white men. I knew their great war chief, and some of his young men. He was a good man, very soft in his words to his red children, as he called us; and that made some of our men with hot heads mad. I listened to his soft words, but I looked into his eyes. They were full of fire. I knew that they would be among his men like coals of fire in the dry grass. The first wind would raise a great flame. I feared for the red men that might be sleeping in its way. . . .

Our women and children were in the town only a mile from the battle-field waiting for victory and its spoils. They wanted white prisoners. The Prophet [Tenskwatawa, the Shawnee religious leader] had promised that every squaw of any note should have one of the white warriors to use as her slave, or to treat as she pleased. Oh how these women were disappointed! Instead of slaves and spoils of the white men coming into town with the rising sun, their town was in flames and women and children were hunted like wolves and killed by hundreds or driven into the river and swamps to hide. With the smoke of that town and the loss of that battle I lost all hope of the red men being able to stop the whites.

SOURCE: Wesley Whickar, ed., "Shabonne's Account of Tippecanoe," *Indiana Magazine of History* 18 (December 1921), pp. 355–59.

Henry Clay of Kentucky, the new speaker of the House of Representatives, and John C. Calhoun, a rising young congressman from South Carolina, pushed Madison toward war with Great Britain. Southern and western Republican congressmen eyed new territory in British Canada and Spanish Florida, part of which had already been seized by American militia. They also hoped that war would discredit the Federalists, who had long pursued a pro-British foreign policy. With national elections approaching, Madison demanded British respect for American sovereignty in the West and neutral rights on the Atlantic. When the British did not respond quickly, Madison asked Congress for a declaration of war. In June 1812 a sharply divided Senate voted nineteen to thirteen for war, and the House of Representatives concurred, seventy-nine to forty-nine. To mobilize support for the war, Republicans emphasized Britain's disregard for American rights. As President Madison put it, "National honor is national property of the highest value."

The underlying causes of the War of 1812 have been much debated. Officially, the United States went to war because of violations of its neutral rights: the seizure of its ships and the impressment of its sailors. But the Federalists who represented merchants' and seamen's interests in Congress voted against the war declaration, and in the subsequent election voters in New England and the Middle Atlantic states cast their ballots (and eighty-nine electoral votes) for the Federalist candidate for president, De Witt Clinton of New York. Madison amassed most of his 128 electoral votes in the South and West, where Republican congressmen and their constituents supported the war. Because of this regional split, more than one historian has argued that the conflict was "a western war with eastern labels."

THE WAR OF 1812

The War of 1812 was a near disaster for the United States, both militarily and politically. Predictions of an easy victory over British forces in Canada ended when a first invasion resulted in a hasty American retreat back to Detroit. But Americans stayed on the offensive in the West, as Commodore Oliver Hazard Perry defeated a small British flotilla on Lake Erie. Then in October 1813 General William Henry Harrison triumphed over a combined British and Indian force at the Battle of the Thames, killing Tecumseh, who had become a general in the British army. Another American expedition burned York (present-day Toronto) but lacking sufficient men and supplies quickly withdrew.

Political divisions in the United States prevented a major invasion of Canada in the East. New Englanders opposed the war and prohibited their militias from fighting outside their states. Boston merchants and banks declined to lend money to the federal government, making the war difficult to finance. In Congress Daniel Webster, a dynamic young representative from New Hampshire, led Federalist opposition to higher taxes and tariffs and to the national conscription of state militiamen.

By 1813 the tide of battle had begun to turn in Britain's favor. Initially the British had lost scores of merchant vessels to American privateers, but the Royal Navy redeployed its forces and British commerce moved in relative safety. Now a flotilla of British warships moved up and down the American coastline, harassing American shipping and threatening seaport cities. In 1814 a British fleet sailed up

Chesapeake Bay and attacked the District of Columbia, burning government buildings. Then the troops advanced on Baltimore, where they were finally repulsed at Fort McHenry. After two years of sporadic warfare the United States had made little military progress along the Canadian frontier and was on the defensive along the Atlantic, with its new capital city in ruins. The only positive news came from the Southwest. There a rugged slaveowning planter named Andrew Jackson led an army of militiamen from Tennessee to victory over the British-supported Creek Indians in the Battle of Horseshoe Bend (1814), forcing the Indians to cede 23 million acres of land.

American military setbacks strengthened opposition to the war, especially in New England. In 1814 Federalists in the Massachusetts legislature called for a convention "to lay the foundation for a radical reform in the National Compact," and in December New England Federalists met in Hartford, Connecticut, to discuss strategy. Some delegates to the Hartford Convention proposed secession by their states, but the majority favored revising the Constitution. To end domination of the presidency by Virginians the delegates proposed a constitutional amendment that would limit the office to a single four-year term and require it to rotate among citizens from different states. Other delegates suggested amendments restricting commercial embargoes to sixty days and requiring a two-thirds' majority in Congress to declare war, prohibit trade, or admit a new state to the Union.

As a minority party in Congress and the nation, the Federalists could prevail only if the war continued to go badly—a very real prospect. In late summer of 1814 a planned British invasion of the Hudson River Valley was narrowly averted by an American naval victory at the Battle of Lake Champlain. Then while the Federalists were meeting in Hartford in December, thousands of seasoned British troops landed at New Orleans, threatening to cut off western access to the sea. The United States was under military pressure from both north and south.

Fortunately for the young American republic, Britain wanted peace. The twenty-year struggle against France had sapped its wealth and energy, and so it entered into negotiations with the United States in Ghent, Belgium. At first the American commissioners—John Quincy Adams, Albert Gallatin, and Henry Clay—demanded territory in Canada and Florida, and British diplomats insisted on an Indian buffer state between the United States and Canada. Ultimately, both sides realized that small concessions won at the bargaining table were not worth the costs of prolonged warfare. The Treaty of Ghent, signed on Christmas Eve 1814, restored the prewar borders of the United States.

This result hardly justified three years of fighting, but a final victory in combat lifted Americans' morale. Before news of the Treaty of Ghent reached the United States, newspaper headlines proclaimed an "ALMOST INCREDIBLE VICTORY!! GLORIOUS NEWS": on January 8, 1815, General Andrew Jackson's troops (including a contingent of French-speaking black Americans, the Corps d'Afrique) crushed the British forces attacking New Orleans. British losses totaled 700 dead and 2,000 wounded or taken prisoner. By contrast the Americans sustained only 13 dead and 58 wounded. The victory made Jackson a national hero and a symbol of the emerging West. It also redeemed the nation's battered pride and, together with the coming of peace, undercut the demands of the Hartford Convention.

Just as Jackson emerged as a war hero, John Quincy Adams rose to national prominence for his diplomatic efforts at Ghent and his subsequent success in resolving boundary disputes. The son of Federalist president John Adams, John Quincy had joined the Republican Party before the war, and in 1817 became secretary of state under President James Monroe (1817–1825). In 1817 Adams negotiated the Rush-Bagot Treaty with Great Britain that limited both nations' naval forces on the Great Lakes; the following year he concluded another agreement that set the border between the Louisiana Purchase and British Canada at the forty-ninth parallel. Then in 1819 Adams persuaded Spain to cede Florida to the United States in the Adams-Onís Treaty. In return the American government took responsibility for its citizens' financial claims against Spain, renounced Jefferson's earlier claim to Spanish Texas, and agreed on a compromise boundary between New Spain and the Louisiana Purchase (see Map 8.3). As a result of Adams's efforts the United States gained undisputed possession of nearly all the land south of the forty-ninth parallel and between the Mississippi River and the Rocky Mountains.

The Capitalist Commonwealth

The increasing size of the American republic was paralleled by the growth of its economic institutions and wealth. Before 1790 the United States was an agricultural society, dependent on Great Britain for markets, credit, and manufactured goods. Over the next generation the nation gradually developed a more diverse economy as some rural Americans became manufacturers, bankers supplied credit to expand industry and trade, merchants developed regional markets, and state governments actively encouraged economic development.

The emerging American economic order was capitalist in character because it was based on private property and market exchanges and because capitalists—financiers, bankers, and wealthy entrepreneurs—shaped many of its political and economic policies. But this capitalist political economy was still influenced by the political ideology of the republican commonwealth, which elevated the public good over private gain.

A MERCHANT-BASED ECONOMY: BANKS, MANUFACTURING, AND MARKETS

America was "a Nation of Merchants," a British visitor reported from Philadelphia in 1798, "always alive to their interests; and keen in the pursuit of wealth in all the various modes of acquiring it." And acquire it they did, especially during the European wars that dragged on from 1792 to 1815. Entrepreneurs such as the fur trader John Jacob Astor and the merchant Robert Oliver became the nation's first millionaires. Migrating from Germany to New York in 1784, Astor became wealthy by carrying furs from the Pacific Northwest to markets in China. He soon became the largest landowner in New York City. Oliver started in Baltimore as an agent for Irish linen merchants and then opened his own mercantile firm. Exploiting the wartime shipping boom, he reaped enormous profits in the West Indian coffee and sugar trade.

To finance such enterprises Americans needed a banking system. Before 1776 ambitious colonists found it difficult to secure loans. Farmers relied on government-sponsored land banks, while merchants arranged partnerships, borrowed funds from other merchants, or obtained credit from British suppliers. Then in 1781 Philadelphia merchants persuaded the Confederation Congress to charter the Bank of North America to provide short-term commercial loans; traders in Boston and New York founded similar banks in 1784.

In 1791, on Alexander Hamilton's initiative, Congress chartered the First Bank of the United States. The bank had the power to issue notes and make commercial loans, and although the bank's managers used their lending powers cautiously, profits still averaged a handsome 8 percent annually. By 1805, in response to the continuing demand for commercial credit, the bank had branches in eight major cities. Despite this success the First Bank of the United States did not survive. Jeffersonians accused the bank of encouraging "a consolidated, energetic government supported by public creditors, speculators, and other insidious men lacking in public spirit of any kind." When the bank's charter expired in 1811, President Madison did not seek renewal, forcing merchants, artisans, and farmers to ask their state legislatures to charter new banks. By 1816, when Madison adopted a more "national" stance with respect to economic policy and signed the congressional legislation creating the Second Bank of the United States, there were 246 state-chartered banks.

Many state banks were shady operations, issuing notes without adequate specie reserves and making ill-advised loans to insiders. Such poorly managed state banks were one cause of the Panic of 1819, a credit crisis sparked by a sharp drop in world agricultural prices. As farm income plummeted by one-third, many farmers could not pay their bills, causing bankruptcies among local storekeepers, wholesale merchants, and overextended state banks. The Panic gave Americans their first taste of the business cycle—the periodic expansion and contraction of profits and employment that is an inherent part of a market economy.

The Panic also revealed that artisans and yeomen as well as merchants now depended on regional or national markets. Before 1790 most artisans in New England and the Mid-Atlantic region sold their handicrafts locally or bartered them with neighbors. But others—shipbuilders in seacoast towns, iron smelters in Pennsylvania and Maryland, and shoemakers in Lynn, Massachusetts—sold their products in far-flung markets. Subsequently, a small group of merchant-entrepreneurs developed a rural-based manufacturing system similar to the European outwork, or putting-out, system (see Chapter 1) and sold its products in all parts of the nation.

Merchants stood at the center of this system, buying raw materials, organizing workers, and selling finished products. At the periphery were hundreds of thousands of farm families that supplied the labor. When a French traveler visited central Massachusetts in 1795, he found "almost all these houses . . . inhabited by men who are both cultivators and artisans; one is a tanner, another a shoemaker, another sells goods, but all are farmers."

By the 1820s thousands of New England farm families produced shoes, brooms, palm-leaf hats, and tinware—baking pans, cups, utensils, lanterns. Merchants shipped these products to cities and slave plantations, while New England peddlers, equipped "with a horse and a cart covered with a box or with a wagon," blanketed the South and acquired a reputation as crafty, hard-bargaining "Yankees." The success of these peddlers and merchants expanded the capitalist sector of the American domestic economy.

This economic advance stemmed initially from innovations in organization and marketing rather than in technology. Water-powered machines—the product of the Industrial Revolution in Britain—were adopted slowly in America, beginning in the textile industry. In the 1780s merchants built small mills along the waterways

The Yankee Peddler, c. 1830

Even in the 1830s most Americans lived too far from market towns to go there regularly to buy needed goods. Instead they purchased most of their tinware, clocks, textiles, and other manufactures from peddlers, often from New England, who traveled far and wide in small horse-drawn vans (such as that pictured in the doorway). (Courtesy IBM Corporation, Armonk, NY)

of New England and the Mid-Atlantic states. They installed water-powered machines and hired workers to card and comb wool—and later cotton—into long strands. For several decades the next steps in the manufacturing process were accomplished under the outwork system rather than in water-powered factories. Wage-earning farm women and children spun the strands into yarn by hand, and men in other households used foot-powered looms to weave the yarn into cloth. In his *Letter on Manufactures* (1810) Secretary of the Treasury Albert Gallatin estimated that there were 2,500 outwork weavers in New England. A decade later more than 12,000 household workers in that region wove woolen cloth, which then went to water-powered fulling mills to be pounded flat and finished smooth.

The penetration of the market economy into rural areas motivated farmers to produce more goods. Ambitious farm families switched from mixed-crop agriculture to raising dairy cows for cheese making; as a Polish traveler in central Massachusetts reported in 1798, "Along the whole road from Boston, we saw women engaged in making cheese" for sale in cities. "Straw hats and Bonnets are manufactured by many families," a Maine official commented, while another observer noted that "probably 8,000 females" in the vicinity of Foxborough, Massachusetts, braided rye straw into hats for market sale. Other farm families expanded the size of their cattle herds, selling hides to the booming shoe industry, and their sheep flocks, providing wool to textile manufacturers. Processing these raw materials brought prosperity and new businesses to many farming towns. In 1792 Concord, Massachusetts, had one slaughterhouse and five small tanneries; a decade later the town had eleven slaughterhouses and six large tanneries. Foul odors from the stockyards and tanning pits wafted over Concord, but its residents were able to acquire more goods and live more comfortably.

At first, barter transactions were a central feature of the emergent market system. When Ebenezer and Daniel Merriam of Brookfield, Massachusetts, began selling books to publishing houses in New York City, Philadelphia, and Boston in the 1810s, they received neither cash nor credit in return but other books, which they had to exchange with local storekeepers to get supplies for their business. The Merriams also paid their employees on a barter basis; a journeyman printer received a third of his "wages" in books, which he had to peddle himself. Gradually a cash economy replaced this complex barter system. As farm families joined the outwork system, they stopped making their own textiles and bought them instead, using the cash or store credit they had earned in the outwork system.

The new capitalist-run market economy had some drawbacks. Rural parents and their children now worked longer and harder, making specialized products during the winter and farming during the warmer seasons. Perhaps more important, they lost some of their economic independence. Instead of working solely for themselves as yeomen farm families, they toiled as part-time wage earners for merchants and manufacturers. The new market system decreased the self-sufficiency of families and communities even as it made them more productive. But the tide of change was unstoppable.

PUBLIC POLICY: THE COMMONWEALTH SYSTEM

Throughout the nineteenth century state governments were the most important political institutions in the United States. Beginning in the late 1810s many states decreased the property requirements for voting, reapportioned legislatures, and increased the number of elected (rather than appointed) officials. State legislatures also took the lead in regulating social life. They abolished slavery in the North but upheld it in the South, enacted laws governing criminal and civil affairs, established taxation systems, and oversaw county, city, and town officials. Consequently, state governments had a much greater impact on the day-to-day lives of Americans than did the national government.

As early as the 1790s many state legislatures devised an American plan of mercantilism, known to historians as the "commonwealth" system (because its goal was to increase the common wealth of the society). Just as the British Parliament had promoted the imperial economy through the Navigation Acts (1651–1696), state legislatures enacted measures to stimulate commerce and economic development. In particular, they granted hundreds of corporate charters to private businesses to build roads, bridges, and canals. For example, in 1794 the Pennsylvania assembly chartered the Lancaster Turnpike Company to lay a graded gravel road between Lancaster and Philadelphia, a venture that made a modest profit for the investors but greatly enhanced the regional economy by allowing a rapid movement of goods and people. "The turnpike is finished," noted a farm woman, "and we can now go to town at all times and in all weather." A boom in turnpike construction soon connected dozens of inland market centers to seaport cities.

By 1800 state governments had granted more than 300 corporate charters. Incorporation often included a grant of *limited liability* that made it easier to attract investors; in the event the business failed, the personal assets of the shareholders could not be seized to pay the corporation's debts. Most transportation charters also included the power of *eminent domain,* giving turnpike, bridge, and canal corporations the use of the judicial system to force the sale of privately owned land along proposed routes.

To some critics such uses of state power by private companies ran contrary to republicanism, "which does not admit of granting peculiar privileges to any body of men." Charters not only violated the "equal rights" of all citizens, opponents argued, but also restricted the sovereignty of the people. As a Pennsylvanian put it, "Whatever power is given to a corporation, is just so much power taken from the State" and therefore the citizenry. Nonetheless, state courts consistently upheld corporate charters and routinely approved grants of eminent domain to private corporations. "The opening of good and easy internal communications is one of the highest duties of government," a New Jersey court declared.

State mercantilism soon encompassed much more than transportation. Following the Embargo of 1807, which cut off goods and credit from Europe, New England states awarded charters to 200 iron-mining, textile-manufacturing, and banking firms, and the Pennsylvania legislature granted more than 1,100. Thus by 1820 innovative state governments had created a new political economy: the commonwealth system. The use of state incentives to encourage business and improve the general welfare would continue for another generation.

FEDERALIST LAW: JOHN MARSHALL AND THE SUPREME COURT

Both Federalists and Republicans endorsed the commonwealth idea but in different ways. Federalists looked to the national government for economic leadership and supported Hamilton's program of national mercantilism: a funded debt, tariffs, and a central bank. Jeffersonian Republicans generally opposed such policies, relying instead on state legislatures to promote economic development.

The difference between Federalist and Jeffersonian Republican conceptions of public policy emerged during John Marshall's tenure on the Supreme Court. Appointed Chief Justice of the Court by President Adams in January 1801, Marshall was a committed Federalist who upheld nationalist principles until his death in 1835. His success stemmed not from a mastery of legal principles and doctrines but from the power of his logic and the force of his personality. By winning the support of Joseph Story and other nationalist-minded Republican judges on the court, Marshall shaped constitutional interpretation on the crucial issues of judicial review, federal-state relations, and property rights.

The Marshall Court's first major decision involved judicial review. In 1798, during the dispute over the Alien and Sedition Acts, Republican-dominated legislatures in Kentucky and Virginia had asserted their authority to determine the constitutionality of national laws. However, the Constitution stated that "the judicial Power shall extend to all Cases . . . arising under this Constitution [and] the Laws of the United States," implying that the Supreme Court held the final power of judicial review over such legislation. But before 1803, when Marshall composed the decision in *Marbury v. Madison,* the Supreme Court had never overturned a national law or explicitly claimed the power of judicial review. In deciding that the Judiciary Act of 1789 violated the Constitution, the Chief Justice did both. "It is emphatically the province and duty of the judicial department to say what the law is," Marshall declared.

Thereafter, the doctrine of judicial review evolved slowly. During the first half of the nineteenth century the Supreme Court and the state courts used it sparingly and then only to overturn state laws that clearly conflicted with constitutional principles. Not until the *Dred Scott* decision of 1857 would the Supreme Court void another law passed by Congress (see Chapter 13).

The position of the Marshall Court on federal-state relations was most eloquently expressed in *McCulloch v. Maryland* (1819). In 1816 Congress created the Second Bank of the United States, giving it authority to handle the notes of

John Marshall, by Chester Harding, c. 1830

Even at age seventy-five, John Marshall (1755–1835) had a commanding personal presence. On becoming Chief Justice of the United States Supreme Court in 1801, Marshall elevated the court from a minor department of the national government into a major institution in American legal and political life. His constitutional decisions dealing with judicial review, contract rights, the regulation of commerce, and national banking permanently shaped the character of American law. (The Boston Athenaeum)

state-chartered banks and thus to monitor their financial reserves. To preserve the independence and competitive position of its state banks, the Maryland legislature passed a statute imposing an annual tax of $15,000 on notes issued by the Baltimore branch office of the Second Bank. The Second Bank contested the constitutionality of the Maryland law, claiming that it infringed on the powers of the national government. In response, lawyers for the state of Maryland adopted Jefferson's argument against the First Bank of the United States, maintaining that Congress lacked the constitutional authority to charter a national bank. Even if such a bank could be created, the lawyers argued, Maryland had a right to tax its activities within the state.

Marshall and the nationalist-minded Republicans on the Court firmly rejected both arguments. The Second Bank was constitutional, said the Chief Justice, because it was "necessary and proper," given the national government's responsibility to control currency and credit. Like Alexander Hamilton and other Federalists, Marshall preferred a loose construction of the Constitution. If the goal of a law is "legitimate [and] ... within the scope of the Constitution," he wrote, then "all means which are appropriate" to secure that goal are also constitutional, even if they are not explicitly mentioned in the Constitution. As for Maryland's right to tax the national bank, the Chief Justice stated that "the power to tax involves the power to destroy," suggesting that Maryland's bank tax would render the national government "dependent on the states"—an outcome that "was not intended by the American people" who ratified the Constitution.

The Marshall Court asserted the dominance of national statutes over state legislation again in *Gibbons v. Ogden* (1824), which struck down a monopoly that the New York legislature had granted to Aaron Ogden for steamboat passenger service across the Hudson River to New Jersey. Asserting that the Constitution gave the federal government the authority to regulate interstate commerce, the Chief Justice sided with Thomas Gibbons, who held a federal license to transport people and goods between the two states.

Marshall also turned to the Constitution to uphold his view of property rights. To protect individuals' property from government interference, Marshall seized on the contract clause of the Constitution (Article 1, Section 10), which prohibits the states from passing any law "impairing the obligation of contracts." Delegates at the Philadelphia convention in 1787 had included this clause primarily to allow creditors to overturn state laws that protected debtors, but Marshall expanded the scope of the contract clause by using it to defend other property rights.

To do this Marshall gave a broad definition to the term *contract,* extending it to embrace state grants and charters. The case of *Fletcher v. Peck* (1810) involved a large grant of land made by the Georgia legislature to the Yazoo Land Company. A newly elected state legislature canceled the grant, and speculators who had already purchased Yazoo lands appealed to the Supreme Court to uphold their titles. Marshall ruled that the purchasers held valid contracts that could not be later voided by the legislature. This far-reaching decision not only gave constitutional protection to those who purchased state-owned lands but also promoted the development of a national capitalist economy by protecting out-of-state investors.

The court extended its defense of property rights even further in *Dartmouth College v. Woodward* (1819). Dartmouth College was a private institution established by a charter granted by King George III. In 1816 the Republican-dominated legislature of New Hampshire tried to convert the college into a public university that would educate more of the state's citizens, thereby enhancing the commonwealth. The Dartmouth trustees resisted the legislature and engaged Daniel Webster, a great constitutional lawyer as well as a leading politician, to plead their case. Webster argued that the royal charter constituted a contract and therefore could not be tampered with by the New Hampshire legislature. Accepting Webster's argument, Marshall and Story upheld the rights of the college.

Marshall's triumph seemed complete. Many Federalist principles, such as judicial review and corporate rights, had been permanently incorporated into the American legal system. Yet when Marshall announced the *Dartmouth* and *McCulloch* decisions in 1819, the political fortunes of the Federalist Party were in severe decline. Nationalist-minded Republicans had won the allegiance of many Federalists in the East, while Jeffersonian Republicans commanded the support of most western farmers and southern planters. "No Federal character can run with success," Gouverneur Morris of New York lamented, and the election results of 1818 bore out his pessimism. Following the election Republicans outnumbered Federalists 37 to 7 in the Senate and 156 to 27 in the House of Representatives. Westward expansion and the transformation in American government begun by Jefferson's Revolution of 1800 had brought the tumultuous era of Federalist-Republican conflict to an end.

T I M E L I N E

1783	Treaty of Paris gives Americans access to the trans-Appalachian West.	1804–1806	Lewis and Clark's expedition explores Louisiana Purchase.
1790s	State mercantilism: states grant corporate charters. Entrepreneurs build turnpikes and short canals. Merchants create a rural outwork system, especially for shoes and textiles.	1807	Embargo Act cripples American shipping.
		1809	Tecumseh and Tenskwatawa mobilize Indians. Congress bans importation of slaves.
1790–1791	Little Turtle defeats American armies.	1810	*Fletcher v. Peck* extends contract clause.
1791	First Bank of the United States founded (dissolved in 1811)	1810s	Expansion of slavery into the Old Southwest
1792	Kentucky joins Union; Tennessee follows (1796).	1811	Battle of Tippecanoe
		1812–1815	War of 1812
1794	Battle of Fallen Timbers	1817	Rush-Bagot Treaty limits U.S. and British naval forces in the Great Lakes.
1795	Treaty of Greenville acknowledges Indian land rights in the trans-Appalachian West.	1817–1825	Era of Good Feeling
1801	Federalist John Marshall becomes Chief Justice.	1818	U.S. and British treaty sets the Canadian border.
1801–1808	Treasury Secretary Albert Gallatin reduces national debt. Handsome Lake leads revival among Iroquois.	1819	Adams-Onís Treaty annexes Florida and defines the Texas boundary. *McCulloch v. Maryland* enhances the power of the national government. *Dartmouth College v. Woodward* protects property rights.
1803	Louisiana Purchase asserts judicial review in *Marbury v. Madison*.		

The decline of political controversy prompted contemporary observers to dub James Monroe's two terms as president (1817–1825) the Era of Good Feeling. Actually, national political harmony was more apparent than real, for the Republican Party was now divided into a "national" faction and a Jeffersonian (or "state"-oriented) faction. The two groups fought over patronage and policy, especially the issue of federal support for internal improvement projects such as roads and canals. As the aging Jefferson himself complained about the National Republicans, "You see so many of these new republicans maintaining in Congress the rankest doctrines of the old federalists." With this division in the Republican Party, the cycle of American politics and economic debate was about to enter a new phase.

For Further Exploration

For a fine overview of the spiritual beliefs and political strategies of four Indian nations, see Gregory Evans Dowd, *A Spirited Resistance: The North American Indian Struggle for Unity, 1745–1815* (1992). Alan Taylor, *William Cooper's Town: Power and Persuasion on the Frontier of the Early American Republic* (1995), captures the feel of the European American frontier experience in New York.

Ralph Louis Ketcham's *Presidents Above Party: The First American Presidency, 1789–1829* (1984) portrays the evolving political ideology of the early republic, while Gore Vidal's *Burr: A Novel* (1973) offers an entertaining narrative of the life and times of Aaron Burr. Donald R. Hickey's *The War 1812: A Forgotten Conflict* places the war in its economic and diplomatic context. Thomas C. Cochran, *Frontiers of Change: Early Industrialism in America* (1981), is a short, engaging synthesis of industrial development from the Revolutionary era to the Civil War.

Lewis and Clark: The Journey of the Corps of Discovery (PBS video: 4 hours) tells the story of the initial European exploration of the Louisiana Purchase; the companion website at <http://www.pbs.org/lewisandclark/> contains a rich body of material on the explorers and the Indian peoples of the region. Compiled by K. M. Armstrong, the "Chickasaw Historical Research Page," at <http://home.flash.net/~kma/>, contains letters written by or about Chickasaw Indians between 1792 and 1849, the texts of more than thirty treaties, and other documents. *The Duel* (PBS Video: 1 hour) reenacts the confrontation between Alexander Hamilton and Aaron Burr, while "A Century of Lawmaking for a New Nation," at <http://memory.loc.gov/ammem/amlaw/lawhome.html>, part of the Library of Congress's American Memory project, contains congressional documents and debates, including discussions of the Northwest Ordinance, the ban on slave imports, the Embargo of 1807, and the decision for war in 1812. The site also contains information and maps of "Indian Land Cessions, 1784–1894."

Chapter 9

THE QUEST FOR A REPUBLICAN SOCIETY
1790–1820

The women in every free country, have an absolute control of manners [customs]: and . . . in a republic, manners are of equal importance with laws.

—JAMES TILTON, 1790

By the 1820s a sense of optimism pervaded white American society. "The temperate zone of North America already exhibits many signs that it is the promised land of civil liberty, and of institutions designed to liberate and exalt the human race," a Kentucky judge declared in a Fourth of July speech. Not even the deaths on July 4, 1826, of both John Adams and Thomas Jefferson shook people's optimism. Two great founding fathers had died, but the republic lived on.

There were good reasons for this enthusiasm. A half century after independence white Americans lived in a self-governing society that was free from both arbitrary taxes and a dogmatic, established church. Moreover, many citizens had come to consider themselves "republicans" not simply in their constitutional system of representative government and guaranteed individual rights but also in their political outlook, social behavior, and culture. However, Americans defined republicanism in different ways. Many white Americans in the North subscribed to "democratic republicanism," an ideology that encouraged individuals to aspire to greater equality in politics and within the family. By contrast, articulate southerners devised an "aristocratic republican" ideology that mirrored the hierarchical class and racial divisions of their society. Yet a third group of Americans—white and black, southern and northern—imbibed a "religious republicanism" that both transcended and enhanced sectional divisions. Swept up in the Second Great Awakening, they saw the United States as the republican seedbed of a new Christian civilization.

Democratic Republicanism

After independence, leading Americans developed a political system based on the principle of "ordered liberty," which in practice meant rule by the traditional elite. Gradually, white men of modest means deserted these elite political leaders and embraced the republican doctrines of political equality and social mobility. These citizens also reorganized traditional institutions such as families and schools, pursuing more egalitarian marriages and more affectionate ways of rearing and educating their children.

SOCIAL AND POLITICAL EQUALITY FOR WHITE MEN

Between 1780 and 1820 hundreds of well-educated Europeans visited the United States. Coming from countries with monarchical governments, established churches, male-dominated families, and profound divisions between social classes, they thought that the American republic represented a genuinely different and more just social order. In his famous *Letters from an American Farmer* (1782) the French-born essayist St. Jean de Crèvecoeur wrote that European society was composed "of great lords who possess everything, and of a herd of people who have nothing." America, by contrast, had "no aristocratical families, no courts, no kings, no bishops."

This absence of a hereditary aristocracy encouraged Americans to condemn inherited social privilege, and republican ideology proclaimed legal equality for all free men. "The law is the same for everyone both as it protects and as it punishes," noted one European traveler. Yet Americans accepted social divisions if they were based on personal achievement. As one letter to a newspaper put it, people should be valued not for their "wealth, titles, or connections" but for their "talents, integrity, and virtue." As individuals gained wealth, they gained a higher social standing, a result that astounded some Europeans. "In Europe to say of someone that he rose from nothing is a disgrace and a reproach," remarked an aristocratic Polish visitor. "It is the opposite here. To be the architect of your own fortune is honorable. It is the highest recommendation."

Changes in the legal profession exemplify the popular belief in the superiority of a competitive, achievement-oriented society. During the Revolutionary era American attorneys had won legislation that prevented untrained lawyers from practicing law. By 1800 most states required at least three years of formal schooling or apprenticeship, training only available to young men from well-established families. As legal rules became more central to American life, the legal profession grew in importance, and critics attacked what they called the "professional aristocracy" of lawyers. They demanded regulation of attorneys' fees, the creation of courts in which ordinary citizens could represent themselves, and easier standards for admission to the bar. By the 1820s only eleven of the twenty-six states required a fixed period of legal education. These changes probably lowered the intellectual quality of the legal profession, but they made it more democratic in composition and spirit.

Some Americans from long-distinguished families questioned the morality of a social order based on mobility and financial success. "The aristocracy of Kingston [New York] is more one of money than any village I have ever seen," complained Nathaniel Booth, whose family had once ruled Kingston but had now lost its prominence. "Man is estimated by dollars," he lamented; "what he is worth determines his character and his position at once." For most white men such a system meant the opportunity to better themselves.

By the 1810s republicanism also meant voting rights for all free white men. As early as 1776 the state constitutions of Pennsylvania and Vermont allowed all taxpayers to vote, undermining the traditional rule that political participation hinged on property ownership. By 1810 Maryland and South Carolina had extended the vote to all adult white men, and the new states of Indiana (1816), Illinois (1818), and Alabama (1819) provided for a broad male franchise in their constitutions. Within another decade fifteen states allowed all white male taxpayers to vote, and another seven had instituted universal white manhood suffrage, leaving only three states with property qualifications (see Map 9.1).

The changing tone of politics reflected the expansion of the suffrage. Increasingly, Americans rejected the deferential political views of Federalists such as Samuel Stone, who had called for "a speaking aristocracy in the face of a silent democracy." They refused to vote for politicians who flaunted their high social status, with their "top boots, breeches, and shoe buckles," their hair in "powder and queues." Instead, voters elected politicians who dressed simply, even if they still favored policies that benefited the economic elite.

As the political power of middling and poor white men grew, the rights and status of white women and free blacks declined. In 1802 Ohio disfranchised blacks, and in 1821 New York kept property-holding requirements for black voters while eliminating them for whites. The most striking case was New Jersey, where the state constitution of 1776 had granted suffrage to all property holders. As Federalists and Republicans competed for votes after 1800, they encouraged property-owning blacks and unmarried women to vote, challenging political custom. In 1807 New Jersey legislature closed this loophole, defining full citizenship (and therefore voting rights) as an attribute of males only. To justify the exclusion of women, legislators invoked both biology and tradition. As one letter to a newspaper put it, "Women, generally, are neither by nature, nor habit, nor education, nor by their necessary condition in society fitted to perform this duty with credit to themselves or advantage to the public."

REPUBLICAN MARRIAGE AND MOTHERHOOD

European and American husbands had long dominated their wives and controlled the family's property. But as John Adams had lamented in 1776, the revolutionary

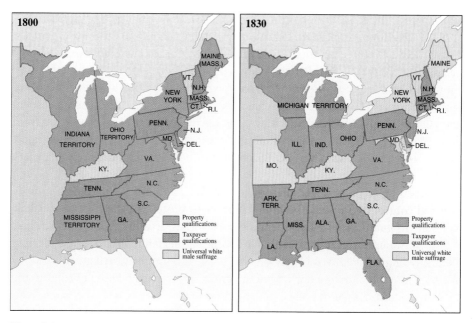

M A P 9.1
The Expansion of Voting Rights for White Men, 1800–1830

Between 1800 and 1830 the United States moved steadily toward political democracy for white men. Many existing states revised their constitutions, replacing property ownership with tax-paying or militia service as a qualification for voting, and some newly admitted western states extended the suffrage to all adult white men. As political parties competed for votes, they created an open and competitive political system that reflected the interests of ordinary people—and the patronage demands of party officials.

doctrine of political equality had "spread where it was not intended," encouraging some white women to demand the right to control their inheritances or speak out on public matters. These women argued that the subordination of women was at odds with a belief in equal natural rights. Patriarchy was not "natural" and could be justified only "for the sake of order in families," as the Patriot writer Mercy Otis Warren put it.

Economic and cultural changes also eroded customary paternal authority. Traditionally, fathers used the promise of future substantial land inheritance as a way of controlling their offspring, particularly their children's selection of a spouse. As land holdings were repeatedly divided in long-settled rural communities, parents could no longer use this incentive, and young men and women began to choose their own marriage partners. Many were influenced by European *sentimentalism*, which by 1820 had touched all classes of American society. Dripping from the pages of German and English literary works, falling from the lips of actors in popular tear-jerking melodramas, and infusing the rhetoric of revivalist preachers, sentimentalism celebrated the importance of "feeling"—that is, a physical, sensuous appreciation of God, nature, and other human beings.

As the passions of the heart overwhelmed the cool logic of the mind, a new marriage system appeared. Parents had always considered physical attraction and emotional compatibility in arranging marriages for their children, but they were more concerned with the personal character and financial resources of a prospective son- or daughter-in-law. Now magazines promoted marriages "contracted from motives of affection, rather than of interest"; this outlook encouraged a young person to seek a spouse who was, as Eliza Southgate of Maine put it, "calculated to promote my happiness."

As young people arranged their own marriages, fathers gave up the goal of patriarchal control and instead became paternalists, protecting the interests of their children. To guard against free-spending sons-in-law, wealthy fathers placed their daughters' inheritances in legal trust—out of their husbands' control. As a Virginia planter wrote to his lawyer, "I rely on you to see the property settlement properly drawn before the marriage, for I by no means consent that Polly shall be left to the Vicissitudes of Life."

Young adults who chose partners unwisely were severely disappointed when their spouses failed as providers or faithful companions, and a few sought divorces. Before 1800 most petitioners for divorce had charged their spouses with neglect,

The Wedding, 1805

The unknown artist who painted this watercolor depicts the bride and groom staring intently into each other's eyes as they exchange marriage vows, suggesting that their union stems from love rather than economic calculation. Given the plain costumes and sparse furnishings, this may be a rural Quaker wedding.

(Philadelphia Museum of Art. The Edgar and Bernice Chrysler Garbisch Collection)

abandonment, or adultery—serious offenses against the moral order of society. After 1800 emotional grounds dominated divorce petitions. One woman complained that her husband had "ceased to cherish her," and one man lamented that his wife had "almost broke his heart." Reflecting these changed cultural values, some states made divorce somewhat easier and expanded the legal grounds for divorce to include personal cruelty and drunkenness.

Theoretically the new republican ideal of "companionate" marriage gave wives "true equality, both of rank and fortune" with their husbands, as one Boston man suggested. However, husbands continued to occupy a privileged position because of deeply ingrained habits and laws that gave them control of the family's property. The new marriage system also discouraged parents from becoming involved in children's married lives, making young wives more dependent on their husbands than their mothers had been. And, as one lawyer noted, governments accepted no obligation to protect a woman who would rather "starve than submit" to the orders of her husband. The marriage contract "is so much more important in its consequences to females than to males," a young man at the Litchfield Law School in Connecticut concluded in 1820, "for besides leaving everything else to unite themselves to one man, they subject themselves to his authority. He is their all—their only relative—their only hope."

Once women were married, their main responsibilities were to run the household and to bear and raise children. However, by the 1790s the birth rate in the northern seaboard states was dropping dramatically. In the farm village of Sturbridge, Massachusetts, women who had married around 1750 had an average of eight or nine children, whereas women who married around 1810 had only about six. There was an even greater decline in urban areas, where native-born white women bore an average of only four children.

The United States was one of the first countries in the world to experience this sharp decline in the birth rate. There were several causes. Beginning in the 1790s thousands of young men migrated to the trans-Appalachian West, leaving some women without partners and delaying the marriage of many more. Women who married later had fewer children. Also, thousands of white American couples in the emerging middle class deliberately limited the size of their families. After having four or five children, they used birth control or abstained from sexual intercourse. Fathers wanted to provide each of their children with an adequate inheritance and so favored smaller families; mothers, affected by new ideas of individualism and self-achievement, were no longer willing to spend all of their active years bearing and rearing children.

As women looked for new opportunities they found support from changes in Christian thought. Traditionally, most religious writers had viewed women as morally inferior to men—as sexual temptresses or witches, but by 1800 Protestant ministers had begun to place responsibility for sexual misconduct primarily on men. In fact, Christian moralists now claimed that modesty and purity were inherent in woman's nature, making women uniquely qualified to educate the spirit.

Reflecting this sentiment, political leaders called on women to become "republican wives" and "republican mothers" who would correctly shape the characters of American men. In *Thoughts on Female Education* (1787) the Philadelphia physician Benjamin Rush argued that a young woman should receive intellectual training so that she would be "an agreeable companion for a sensible man" and ensure "his perseverance in the paths of rectitude." Rush also called for loyal "republican mothers" who would instruct "their sons in the principles of liberty and government." As the author of a list of "Maxims for Republics" commented, "Some of the first patriots of ancient times were formed by their mothers."

Christian ministers readily embraced the idea of republican motherhood. "Preserving virtue and instructing the young are not the fancied, but the real 'Rights of

Republican Motherhood

Art often reveals cultural values. In this painting executed in 1795 the artist James Peale (brother of the famous portraitist Charles Wilson Peale) depicts himself with his wife and children. The mother stands in the foreground, offering advice to her eldest daughter; the father, who was usually the center of attention in colonial era portraits (see p. 99), stands in the rear, giving pride of place to his wife and children. (Courtesy of the Pennsylvania Academy of the Fine Arts, Philadelphia. Gift of John Frederick Lewis)

Women,'" the Reverend Thomas Bernard told the Female Charitable Society of Salem, Massachusetts. He urged his audience to dismiss the public roles advocated by English women's rights advocate Mary Wollstonecraft and others. Instead, women should be content to care for their children, a responsibility that gave them "an extensive power over the fortunes of man in every generation." A few ministers went further and envisioned a public role for women based on their domestic virtues. As South Carolina minister Thomas Grimké asserted, "Give me a host of educated pious mothers and sisters and I will revolutionize a country, in moral and religious taste."

RAISING AND EDUCATING REPUBLICAN CHILDREN

Republican social thought also altered assumptions about inheritance and child rearing. Under English common law property owned by a father who died without a will passed to his eldest son, a practice known as *primogeniture*. In most American states legislators enacted statutes that required the estate of a man who died without a will to be divided among all his children (while continuing the traditional common-law dower right of his widow to use one-third of the estate during her lifetime). Most American parents supported these statutes because they had already begun to treat all of their children as equals.

Foreign visitors suggested that republicanism encouraged American parents to relax parental discipline and give their children greater freedom. Because of the "general ideas of Liberty and Equality engraved on their hearts," suggested a Polish aristocrat who traveled through the United States around 1800, American children had "scant respect" for their parents. Several decades later a British traveler was dumbfounded when an American father excused his son's "resolute disobedience" with a smile and the remark, "a sturdy republican, sir." The traveler guessed that American parents encouraged such independence to enable young people to "go their own way" in the world.

However, these childrearing habits were not universal. Foreign critics interacted primarily with well-to-do Americans, who were often members of Episcopal or Presbyterian churches. These parents followed the teachings of religious writers influenced by John Locke and the Enlightenment. In their minds children were "rational creatures" who should be encouraged to act correctly by means of praise, advice, and reasoned restraint. Training should develop the children's consciences and stress self-discipline so that young people would learn to control their own behavior and to think and act responsibly.

By contrast, many yeomen and tenant farmers influenced by the Second Great Awakening were much stricter and more authoritarian parents, especially in Calvinist-oriented families. Evangelical Baptists and Methodists believed that infants were "full of the stains and pollution of sin" and needed strict discipline. Fear was a "useful and necessary principle in family government," the minister John Abbott advised parents; a child "should submit to your authority, not to your arguments or persuasions." Abbott told parents to instill humility in children and to teach them to subordinate their personal desires to God's will.

The values transmitted within families were crucial because until the 1820s most education still took place within the household. In New England locally funded public schools provided most boys and some girls with basic instruction in reading and writing. In other regions fewer white children and virtually no African American children received schooling; about a quarter of the boys and perhaps 10 percent of the girls attended privately funded schools or had personal tutors. Even in New England only a small fraction of the men and almost no women went on to grammar (high) school. Only 1 percent of men graduated from college.

In the 1790s Bostonian Caleb Bingham, an influential textbook author, called for "an equal distribution of knowledge to make us emphatically a 'republic of letters.'" Thomas Jefferson and Benjamin Rush separately proposed ambitious schemes for a comprehensive system of primary and secondary schooling, followed by college attendance for young men. They also advocated the establishment of a university in which distinguished scholars would lecture on law, medicine, theology, and political economy.

To ordinary citizens such ideas smacked of elitism. Farmers, artisans, and laborers looked to schools for basic instruction in the "three R's": reading, 'riting, and 'rithmetic. They supported public funding for primary schools but not for secondary schools or colleges, which were of no use to their teenage children. "Let anybody show what advantage the poor man receives from colleges," an anonymous "Old Soldier" wrote to the *Maryland Gazette*. "Why should they support them, unless it is to serve those who are in affluent circumstances, whose children can be spared from labor, and receive the benefits?"

Although constitutions of many states encouraged the use of public resources to fund primary schools, there was not much progress until the 1820s. Then a new generation of reformers, primarily led by merchants and manufacturers, successfully campaigned to raise standards by certifying qualified teachers and appointing state superintendents of education. To instill self-discipline and individual enterprise in the students, the reformers chose textbooks, such as *The Life of George Washington* by "Parson" Mason Weems, that praised honesty and hard work while condemning gambling, drinking, and laziness. They also required the study of American history, believing that patriotic instruction would foster shared cultural ideals. As Thomas Low, a New Hampshire schoolboy, recalled "we were taught every day and in every way that ours was the freest, the happiest, and soon to be the greatest and most powerful country of the world."

The author Noah Webster had long championed the goal of American intellectual greatness. Asserting that "America must be as independent in literature as she is in politics," he called on his fellow citizens to detach themselves "from the dependence on foreign opinions and manners, which is fatal to the efforts of genius in this country." Webster's *Dissertation on the English Language* (1789) introduced American spelling (such as *labor* for the British *labour*) and defined words according to American usage. His "blue-backed speller," first published in 1783, sold 60 million copies over the next half-century and helped give Americans of all backgrounds a common vocabulary and grammar. "None of us was 'lowed to see a book," an enslaved African American recalled, "but we gits hold of that Webster's old blue-back speller and we . . . studies [it]."

Ironically, the most accomplished and successful writer in the new republic was Washington Irving, an elitist-minded Federalist in politics and an expatriate. His essays and histories, including *Salmagundi* (1807) and *Diedrich Knickerbocker's History of New York* (1809), had substantial American sales and won fame abroad. Impatient with the slow pace of American literary development, Irving lived in Europe for seventeen years, drawn to its aristocratic manners and intense intellectual life.

Apart from Irving no American author was well known in Europe, partly because most American writers followed primary careers as planters, merchants, or lawyers. "Literature is not yet a distinct profession with us," Thomas Jefferson told an English friend. "Now and then a strong mind arises, and at its intervals from business emits a flash of light. But the first object of young societies is bread and covering." Not until the 1830s and 1840s, in the works of Ralph Waldo Emerson and novelists of the American Renaissance, would American-born authors make a real contribution to the great literature of the Western world (see Chapter 12).

Aristocratic Republicanism and African American Culture

Both in theory and in practice republicanism in the South differed significantly from that in the North. Although nearly all free white southern men had the right to vote, they had relatively little political power and few opportunities for social mobility. An elite group of white planters had grown rich by exploiting the labor of enslaved African Americans—one-third of the South's population—and used their wealth to rule over dependent white tenants and independent yeomen. For their part yeomen farmers dominated the lives of their wives and children.

THE NORTH AND THE SOUTH GROW APART

"When I was in Congress," Timothy Bloodworth of North Carolina recalled in 1789, there were distinct "Southern and Northern" differences over slavery and other issues. After 1800 these regional differences increased as the northern states ended slavery and the South expanded its slave-based agricultural economy. As the invention of the cotton gin and British demand drove up the price of cotton, farmers planted the nutrient-hungry crop year after year, quickly exhausting the soil and denuding the land. Less than a generation after they had been settled, the farms of Georgia's eastern plantation belt were described as "red old hills stripped of their native growth and virgin soil, and washed with deep gullies." Armed with British capital planters looked to the west for fertile lands.

As southern whites carried plantation agriculture into states of the lower Mississippi Valley, they tore apart hundreds of black communities in the states of the Chesapeake and the Carolinas. Between 1790 and 1820 whites relocated more than 250,000 African Americans. Some migrating slaves—perhaps as many as one-half—moved with relatives and friends when their owners sold their old plantations and began anew on the fertile plains of Alabama and Mississippi. Many other African Americans were "sold South" through a new domestic slave trade that provided tobacco and cotton planters in Maryland, Virginia, and other long-settled regions with a major source of income (see Map 9.2).

The expansion of slavery into the Southwest dashed the hope of many northerners that slavery would "die a natural death" following the demise of the Atlantic slave trade and the decline of the tobacco economy. Antislavery advocates grew increasingly concerned during the 1810s when Louisiana, Mississippi, and Alabama joined the Union with state constitutions permitting slavery. When Missouri applied for admission to the Union as a slave state in 1819, antislavery forces rose in opposition. Congressman James Tallmadge of New York proposed a ban on the importation of slaves into Missouri and the gradual emancipation of its black inhabitants. When Missouri whites rejected those conditions, the northern majority in the House of Representatives blocked the territory's admission to the Union. Southerners retaliated by using their power in the equally divided Senate

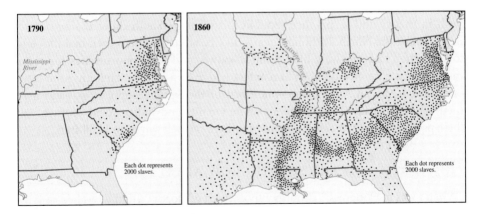

MAP 9.2
Distribution of the Slave Population, 1790–1860

The cotton boom shifted enslaved African Americans to the Mississippi Valley. In 1790 most slaves lived and worked on the tobacco plantations of the Chesapeake and in the rice and indigo areas of South Carolina. By 1860 hundreds of thousands were laboring on the cotton and sugar lands of the lower Mississippi Valley and along an arc of fertile cotton land—the "black belt"—sweeping from Mississippi through Georgia.

The Internal Slave Trade

Mounted whites escort a convoy of slaves from Virginia to Tennessee in Louis Miller's *Slave Trader, Sold to Tennessee*. For white planters the trade was a lucrative one, pumping money into the declining Chesapeake economy and providing workers for the expanding plantations of the cotton belt. For blacks it was a traumatic journey, a new Middle Passage that broke up families and communities. (Abby Aldrich Rockefeller Folk Art Museum)

to withhold statehood from Maine, which was seeking to separate itself from Massachusetts.

Controversy raged for two years before Henry Clay of Kentucky and others put together a series of agreements known collectively as the Missouri Compromise. This legislation allowed Maine to enter the Union as a free state in 1820 and Missouri to be admitted as a slave state in 1821. The compromise preserved the existing balance between North and South in the Senate and set a precedent for the future admission of states in pairs—one free and one slave. To mollify antislavery sentiment in the House of Representatives southern congressmen accepted the prohibition of slavery in the rest of the Louisiana Purchase north of latitude 36°30′, the southern boundary of Missouri (see Map 9.3).

Just as in the Constitutional Convention of 1787, white leaders in both the North and South had given first priority to the Union, finding complex but workable ways to reconcile regional interests. But the task had become more difficult. The Philadelphia delegates had resolved their sectional differences in two months; Congress took two years to work out the Missouri Compromise, with no guarantee that it would work. The fate of the western lands, the Union, and the black race had become inextricably intertwined and had raised the specter of civil war. As the aging

MAP 9.3
The Missouri Compromise, 1820–1821

The Missouri Compromise resolved for a generation the issue of slavery in the lands of the Louisiana Purchase. Slavery was forbidden north of the compromise line, 36°30′ north latitude, with the exception of Missouri, which entered the Union as a slave state. The compromise provided for the nearly simultaneous admission of Maine, maintaining an equal number of free and slave states in the Senate.

Thomas Jefferson exclaimed at the time of the Missouri controversy, "This momentous question, like a fire-bell in the night, awakened and filled me with terror."

THE SOUTHERN SOCIAL ORDER

After independence, white society in the South became increasingly hierarchical. During the 1770s nearly 60 percent of white families in the Chesapeake region owned at least one slave, yet within a few generations only about 25 percent of white families in the South held slaves, with the top 2 percent of southern whites owning about half of all slaves and much of the most fertile land. Wealthy, socially influential, and politically powerful, this planter elite dominated society and gave an aristocratic republican definition to politics and culture.

Members of the slaveholding elite described themselves as natural aristocrats and indulged in displays of conspicuous consumption. They married their children to one another, and their sons and daughters became commercial and cultural leaders—the men working as planters, merchants, lawyers, newspaper editors, and ministers and the women hosting plantation balls and church bazaars. John Henry Hammond, a leading South Carolina planter and politician, inhabited a Greek Revival mansion with a center hall 53 feet by 20 feet, its floor embellished with stylish Belgian tiles and expensive Brussels carpets. "Once a year, like a great feudal landlord," a guest recounted, Hammond "gave a fete or grand dinner to all the country people."

The planters justified their power by endowing it with moral purpose, a task more difficult after the Revolution when Quakers and other antislavery advocates in the North called for an end to human bondage. In the 1810s southern apologists defended slavery as a "necessary evil" to maintain white living standards and prevent racial warfare; subsequently they relied increasingly on religious justifications, pointing out that the Hebrews, God's chosen people, had owned slaves and that Christ had never condemned slavery. As Hammond told a British abolitionist in 1845: "What God ordains and Christ sanctifies should surely command the respect and toleration of man." Some defenders of slavery also depicted planters as aristocratic models of "disinterested benevolence" whose workers were adequately fed, housed, and provided for in old age. Southern writers praised planters' wives as household managers and nurses who cared for the sick and the elderly. These views helped the planter elite to see itself as a republican aristocracy, maintaining a stable, orderly society. To retain the allegiance of ambitious men from modest backgrounds, Hammond and other planters encouraged them to buy slaves and grow rich as they had.

Indeed, many proslavery apologists argued that the only genuine republic was one founded on slavery because it made all white men equal in the public sphere and preserved property rights and liberty by excluding the dangerous propertyless classes from the political process. In fact, white politics and society in the South remained deeply divided along the lines of class and region. As the system of cotton production expanded, some white yeomen became the tenants of wealthy landlords and others scraped by on small farms, growing foodstuffs for sustenance and a few bales of cotton for cash. Drawing on the patriarchal ideology of the planter class, they asserted traditional male authority over their wives and children, ruling the small world of the household with a firm hand. Other yeomen farmers retreated into the backcountry near the Appalachian Mountains, hoping to maintain economic independence and control local county governments. Owning hilly farms of 50 to 100 acres, these families grew some cotton but primarily raised corn and livestock, especially hogs. Their goal was modest: to preserve their holdings and secure enough new land or goods to set up all of their children as farmers.

These yeomen—and those who lived in the plantation belt—had to contend with the wealthy slave owners who dominated the state legislatures. By the 1830s in Alabama only 30 percent of the electorate owned slaves, but 75 percent of the legislators did; one-quarter of the legislators owned fifty or more slaves. Slaveowners used their political power to enhance their own welfare, exempting slave property from taxation. They also imposed land taxes by acreage rather than by value, thereby imposing relatively high taxes on subsistence farms in the backcountry. In addition, planters enacted laws that forced yeomen to "fence in" their livestock, sparing themselves the cost of building fences around their large properties. Finally, legislatures forced all white men—whether they owned slaves or not—to serve in patrols and militias that deterred slaves from running away or rising in rebellion. They warned tenants and yeomen that they had to support slavery or face economic competition and race warfare with freed African Americans. John Henry Hammond told his poor white neighbors, "In a slave country every freeman is an aristocrat."

Few yeomen became aristocrats or even well to do because the character of the southern economy limited their opportunities. The wealthy planters who controlled southern society wanted a compliant labor force, content with the drudgery of agricultural work. Consequently, they trained most of their slaves as field hands (allowing only a few to learn the arts of the blacksmith, carpenter, or bricklayer), and they made little or no effort to provide ordinary whites with elementary instruction in reading or arithmetic. Even as the cotton boom of the 1820s and 1830s increased the prosperity of slave owners, over one-third of white southerners could not read or write, compared to less than 1 percent of New Englanders. The illiterate signed legal documents such as wills and marriage licenses with an *X* or other mark.

In addition, planters discouraged the growth of manufacturing by concentrating their resources in cotton and slaves. As a result the percentage of southerners who lived in towns and worked in factories remained small. The only major cities in the South were the old seaports of Baltimore, Charleston, and New Orleans, which remained predominantly commercial centers. Lacking cities, factories, and educated workers, the South could not provide a majority of its people with a rising standard of living. Enslaved African Americans and white tenant farmers had little or no property, and landholding yeomen in the backcountry lacked access to profitable markets. Prosperity was limited primarily to the 25 percent of the white population that owned plantations and slaves. The political and social equality hoped for during the Revolutionary era was dashed by the South's aristocratic republican social order.

SLAVE SOCIETY AND CULTURE

As planters imposed their values on white society, three developments helped to create a distinct—and a more unified—culture among enslaved African Americans. First, the end of the transatlantic slave trade in 1809 gradually created an entirely American-born black population. Even in South Carolina—the destination of most of the slaves imported since independence—in 1820 only about 20 percent of the black inhabitants had been born in Africa. Second, the movement of slavery into the Mississippi Valley slowly reduced cultural differences among slaves. For example, the Gullah dialect spoken by slaves from the Carolina low country gradually died out on the cotton plantations of Alabama and Mississippi, replaced by the black English spoken by slaves from the Chesapeake. Third, in both southern and northern cities, free blacks consciously created a distinct African American community.

Even as the black population became more homogeneous, African cultural elements remained important. At least one-third of the slaves who entered the United States between 1776 and 1809 were from the Congo region of west-central Africa, and they brought their culture with them. As the traveler Isaac Holmes reported in 1821, "In Louisiana, and the state of Mississippi, the slaves . . . dance for several hours during Sunday afternoon. The general movement is in what they call the Congo dance." Similar descriptions of blacks who "danced the Congo and sang a purely African song to the accompaniment of . . . a drum" appeared as late as 1890.

Enslaved blacks in South Carolina and elsewhere continued to respect African incest taboos, shunning marriage between cousins. On the Good Hope plantation in South Carolina nearly half of the slave children born were related by blood to one another, yet only one marriage took place between cousins. (By contrast, many wealthy planter families in South Carolina and Georgia encouraged cousin marriages to keep inherited property in the family.)

However, southern state legislatures and law courts prohibited legal marriages between slaves, so that they could be sold without breaking a legal bond. African Americans therefore devised their own marriage rituals, first asking their parents' consent to marry and then seeking their owner's permission to live together. Following African custom many couples symbolized their married state by jumping over a broomstick together in a public ceremony. Christian slaves often had a religious service performed by a white or black preacher, but these rites never ended with the customary phrase "until death do you part." Everyone knew that black marriages could end with the sale of one or both of the spouses.

Separation was a common experience among many African American families. In 1790 many of the slaves on the Tayloe plantation in Virginia came from families who had lived there since the 1720s. Over the decades more slaves were born than the plantation could employ, so in 1792 John Tayloe III sold fifty slaves, separating husbands from their wives and children from their parents. Over the next two generations Tayloe and his sons moved 180 other slaves to new plantations in Alabama, where they worked "from day clean to first dark" clearing land and planting cotton. Other planters remained on their estates in Virginia, the Carolinas, and Georgia and sold their "surplus" blacks to slave traders. "I am Sold to a man by the name of Peterson a trader," lamented a Georgia slave. "My Dear wife for you and my Children my pen cannot Express the griffe I feel to be parted from you all." Some of these slaves forever lost touch with their families. "Dey sole [sold] my sister Kate," Anna Harris remembered decades later, ". . . and I ain't seed or heard of her since."

Although forced separations split many black families, the majority of slave marriages were stable. On the Good Hope plantation in South Carolina about 70 percent of the women had all their children by their husbands. On Louisiana plantations family ties were much more fragile because the dangerous disease environment and the demanding work of growing sugarcane took many black men's lives. Thirty percent of the slave women on one Louisiana plantation lived alone with their children, who were fathered by a succession of men.

To maintain their cultural identity recently imported slaves often gave their children African names. Males born on Friday were often called Cuffee—the name of that day in several west African languages. Most Chesapeake slaves chose names of British origin and named sons after fathers, uncles, or grandfathers and daughters after grandmothers. Like incest rules and marriage rituals these naming patterns solidified kinship ties, creating order in a harsh and arbitrary world.

By forming stable families and strong communities, African Americans were better able to control their own lives. In the rice-growing lowlands of South Carolina blacks won the right to labor by the task rather than work under constant supervision. Each day a worker had to complete a precisely defined task—for example, turn over a quarter acre of land, hoe half an acre, or pound seven mortars of rice. By working hard many finished their tasks "by one or two o'clock in the afternoon," a Methodist preacher reported, and had "the rest of the day for themselves, which they spend in working their own private fields . . . planting rice, corn, potatoes, tobacco &c. for their own use and profit." These private efforts provided slaves with better clothes and food, and on some large plantations planters gave decent health care to children, the sick, and the elderly. But few enslaved African Americans enjoyed a comfortable standard of living, and slaves clearly understood that planters gave them material favors not out of benevolence but to protect their investment (see American Voices, "A Child Learns the Meaning of Slavery").

In theory white masters had virtually unlimited power over their slaves. By law enslaved individuals were personal property, subject to discipline at the will of their owners and bought and sold as if they were horses. As Thomas Ruffin, a justice of the North Carolina Supreme Court, declared in a court decision in 1829, "The power of the master must be absolute to render the submission of the slave perfect." In practice both social conventions and black resistance limited the power of masters. Before 1800 the slave population was diverse and ill organized, and owners abused slaves without much fear of retribution. Although sexual assault, branding, and mutilation did not stop after 1800, they were questioned more often. Politicians and community leaders condemned rape as an aristocratic vice ill suited to a republican society, and the spread of evangelical Christianity prompted many masters to treat slaves more humanely.

But planters were never able to turn slaves into willing workers. "Should any owner increase the work beyond what is customary," a rice planter in South Carolina warned around 1800, "he subjects himself . . . to such discontent amongst his slaves as to make them of little use to him." To increase output, profit-conscious owners devised a new gang-labor system. Planters with twenty or more slaves organized disciplined teams, or "gangs," supervised by black "drivers" or white overseers and assigned them specific tasks. They instructed drivers and overseers to use the lash to work the gangs at a steady pace, clearing and plowing new land or hoeing and picking cotton. A traveler glimpsed two gangs returning from work in Mississippi:

A Child Learns the Meaning of Slavery

JACOB STROYER

Jacob Stroyer was born into slavery in South Carolina around 1800 but was emancipated and moved to Massachusetts, where he became a minister. In My Life in the South *(1855) Stroyer relates an incident that dramatically revealed his parents' subordinate, powerless status.*

Father . . . used to take care of horses and mules. I was around with him in the barnyard when but a small boy; of course that gave me an early relish for the occupation of hostler [stable boy], and soon I made known my preference to Colonel Singleton, who was a sportsman and had fine horses. . . . Hence I was allowed to be numbered among those who took care of the fine horses, and learned to ride. . . .

It was not long after I had entered my new work before they put me upon the back of a horse which threw me to the ground almost as soon as I reached his back. . . . When I got up there was a man standing near with a switch in hand, and he immediately began to beat me. . . . This was the first time I had been whipped by anyone except Mother and Father, so I cried out in a tone of voice as if I would say, this is the first and last whipping you will give me when Father gets hold of you.

When I got away from him I ran to Father with all my might, but soon my expectation was blasted, as Father very coolly said to me, "Go back to your work and be a good boy, for I cannot do anything for you." But that did not satisfy me, so I went on to Mother with my complaint and she came out to the man who whipped me. He was a groom, a white man whom master hired to train his horses . . . [and] he took a whip and started for her, and she ran from him, talking all the time. . . .

Then the idea first came to me that I, with my dear father and mother and the rest of my fellow Negroes, was doomed to cruel treatment through life and was defenseless. . . .

SOURCE: Linda R. Monk, ed., *Ordinary Americans: U.S. History Through the Eyes of Everyday People* (Alexandria, VA: Close Up Publications, 1994), pp. 71–72.

First came, led by an old driver carrying a whip, forty of the largest and strongest women I ever saw together; they were all in a simple uniform dress of a bluish check stuff, the skirts reaching little below the knee; their legs and feet were bare; they carried themselves loftily, each having a hoe over the shoulder, and walking with a free, powerful swing.

Next marched the plow hands with their mules, "the cavalry, thirty strong, mostly men, but a few of them women." Finally, "a lean and vigilant white overseer, on a brisk pony, brought up the rear."

Harvesting Sugarcane

Growing sugar was arduous work and took the lives of thousands of slaves. In both the West Indies and Louisiana sugar planters used gang labor to ditch and drain marshlands and plant cane seedlings in long ditches. Harvesting the mature cane and carrying it to the plantation's mill was equally strenuous and, as this watercolor by Franz Holzlhuber shows, was the work of women as well as men. (Collection of the Glenbow Museum, Calgary, Alberta, Canada)

To resist gang labor and other controls, slaves slowed the pace of work by feigning illness and were deliberately careless with the master's property, losing or breaking tools and setting fire to houses and barns. They also challenged the arbitrary breakup of communities, insisting that people be sold "in families" and defying their masters when they were not. One Maryland slave, faced with transport to Mississippi and separation from his wife (who was owned by another master), "neither yields consent to accompany my people, or to be exchanged or sold," his owner reported. Masters ignored such resistance at their peril because a slave's relatives might retaliate with arson, poison, or destruction of crops or equipment.

A few blacks, such as Gabriel and Martin Prosser in Virginia (1800) and Denmark Vesey in South Carolina (1822), plotted mass uprisings and murders. But in most areas blacks accounted for less than half the population, and everywhere they lacked the strong institutions—such as the communes of free peasants or serfs in Europe—needed to organize a successful rebellion. Moreover, whites were well armed, unified, and militant. Escape was equally problematic. Blacks in the lower South could seek freedom in Spanish Florida until 1819, when the United States annexed the territory. Nonetheless hundreds of blacks continued to flee to Florida, where they intermarried with the Seminole Indians. Elsewhere in the South small groups of escaped slaves eked out a living in deserted marshy areas or in mountain valleys, hoping that they would not be killed, enslaved, or returned by Indian warriors. Given these limited options most slaves had no choice but to build the best possible lives for themselves on the plantations where they lived.

THE FREE BLACK POPULATION

Meanwhile, between 1790 and 1820 the number of free blacks rose steadily from 8 percent of the total African American population to about 13 percent. About half of all free blacks lived in the North, where they performed the most menial and low-paying work and were treated as second-class citizens. In rural areas free blacks worked as farm laborers or tenant farmers; in towns and cities, as domestic servants, laundresses, or day laborers. They were usually forbidden to vote, attend public schools, or sit next to whites in churches. Of the states admitted to the Union between 1790 and 1821 only Vermont and Maine extended the vote to free blacks, and they could testify against whites in court only in Massachusetts. The federal government did not allow free African Americans to work for the postal service, claim public lands, or hold a U.S. passport.

Nonetheless, a few free blacks in the North were able to make full use of their talents, and some achieved great distinction. The mathematician and surveyor Benjamin Banneker published an almanac and helped lay out the new national capital in the District of Columbia. Joshua Johnston, a skilled painter, won praise for his portraiture, and merchant Robert Sheridan acquired a small fortune from his business enterprises. More impressive and enduring were the community institutions created by this first generation of free African Americans. In many northern communities they founded schools, mutual-benefit organizations, and fellowship societies. Discriminated against in white Protestant churches, they also formed their own congregations and an independent religious denomination—the African Methodist Episcopal (AME) Church. These institutions gave free African Americans a sense of cultural, if not political, autonomy.

Most free blacks in slave states lived in the upper South. In Maryland a quarter of the black population was free by 1820; in Delaware free blacks outnumbered slaves by three to one. Free blacks accused of crimes were often denied a jury trial, and many others had to contend with vagrancy and apprenticeship laws intended to force them back into slavery. To prove their free status blacks had to carry manumission documents and in some states needed official permission to travel across county lines. Even with valid papers free African Americans in the South had to be careful; kidnapping and sale were constant threats. Yet the shortage of skilled workers in southern cities did create opportunities for a few. Trained African American carpenters, blacksmiths, barbers, butchers, and shopkeepers in Baltimore, Richmond, Charleston, and New Orleans formed benevolent societies and churches, providing education, recreation, and social welfare programs for their communities.

As a privileged group among African Americans free blacks felt both loyalty to the welfare of their families, which often meant assimilating white culture, and loyalty to their race, which meant identification with the great mass of enslaved African Americans. Some wealthier free blacks, particularly the mulatto children of white masters and black women, drew apart from common laborers and field hands and adopted the outlook of the planter class. In New Orleans a few free African Americans even owned slaves.

Generally, however, both free and enslaved African Americans saw themselves as one people. "We's different [from whites] in color, in talk and in 'ligion and beliefs," as one put it. Knowing their own freedom was not secure as long as slavery existed, free blacks sought to win freedom for all those of African ancestry. Free southern blacks aided fugitive slaves, while free black northerners supported the antislavery movement. In the rigid caste system of American race relations free blacks stood as symbols of hope to enslaved African Americans and as omens of danger to the majority of whites.

Protestant Christianity as a Social Force

Beginning in 1790 a series of religious revivals planted the values of Protestant Christianity deep in the national character and gave a spiritual definition to American republicanism. The revivals also created new public roles for women, especially in the North, and changed African American life. Free and enslaved blacks became Christians, absorbing the faith of white Baptists and Methodists and creating a distinctive and powerful institution—the black church.

THE SECOND GREAT AWAKENING

The revivals that began around 1790 were much more complex than those of the First Great Awakening. In the 1740s most revivals had occurred in existing congregations; fifty years later they took place in frontier camp meetings as well and often involved the creation of new churches and denominations. More striking, the Second Great Awakening spawned new organizations dedicated to social and political reform.

Churches that prospered in the new nation were those that adopted a republican outlook, proclaiming doctrines of spiritual equality. Because the Roman Catholic Church was dominated by bishops and priests, it attracted few converts among Protestants, who adhered to Luther's doctrine of the priesthood of all believers, or among the unchurched, who feared clerical power. Likewise, few ordinary Americans joined the Episcopal Church (created by former members of the Church of England), which had a similar hierarchical structure and was dominated by its wealthiest members. The Presbyterian Church was more popular, in part because ordinary members elected laymen to the synods (congresses) where doctrine and practice were formulated. Methodists and Baptists attracted even more Americans because most of their preachers were fervent evangelists and promoted an egalitarian religious culture, encouraging lay preaching and communal singing.

A continuous wave of revivalism fueled the expansion of Protestant Christianity. Beginning in the 1790s Baptists and Methodists evangelized the cities and the backcountry of New England. A new sect of Universalists, who repudiated the Calvinist doctrine of predestination and preached universal salvation, attracted thousands of converts, especially in northern New England. After 1800 enthusiastic camp-meeting revivals swept the frontier regions of South Carolina, Kentucky, Tennessee, and Ohio (see American Voices, "A Camp Meeting in Indiana").

When frontier preachers got together at a revival meeting, they were electrifying. James McGready, a Scots-Irish Presbyterian preacher, "could so array hell before the wicked," an eyewitness reported, "that they would tremble and Quake, imagining a lake of fire and brimstone yawning to overwhelm them." James Finley described the Cane Ridge, Kentucky, revival of 1802:

> The noise was like the roar of Niagara. The vast sea of human beings seemed to be agitated as if by a storm. I counted seven ministers, all preaching at one time, some on stumps, others on wagons. . . . Some of the people were singing, others praying, some crying for mercy.

Because of their emotional message, revivalists were particularly successful in attracting the unchurched—the great number of Americans who had never belonged to churches. Their promise of religious fellowship also appealed to young men and women and geographically mobile families who had few social ties in their new communities.

The Second Great Awakening changed the denominational base of American religion. The leading churches of the colonial period—the Congregationalists, Episcopalians, and Quakers—declined in relative membership because they were content to maintain existing congregations or to grow slowly through natural increase. Because of their evangelism and democratic outlook Methodist and Baptist churches grew spectacularly. By the early nineteenth century they had become the largest religious denominations in the United States. In the South and West, Baptist and Methodist preachers traveled constantly. A Methodist cleric followed a circuit, "riding a hardy pony or horse . . . with his Bible, hymn-book, and Discipline." These "circuit riders" established new churches by searching out devout families, bringing them together for worship, and then appointing lay elders to lead the congregation and enforce moral discipline until the circuit rider returned.

Evangelical ministers copied the techniques of George Whitefield and other eighteenth-century revivalists, codifying their methods in manuals on "practical preaching." To attract converts preachers were cautioned to emphasize piety over theology; extemporaneous speech was deemed more powerful than a written

A Camp Meeting in Indiana

FRANCES TROLLOPE

Frances Trollope, a successful English author, resided in the United States during the late 1820s, living for a time in Cincinnati. Her critical and at times acerbic Domestic Manners of the Americans (1832) achieved wide popularity in Europe and the United States. Here she provides her readers with a vivid description of a revivalist meeting in Indiana around 1830.

We reached the ground about an hour before midnight, and the approach to it was highly picturesque. The spot chosen was the verge of an unbroken forest, where a space of about twenty acres appeared to have been partially cleared for the purpose. Tents of different sizes were pitched very near together in a circle round the cleared space. . . .

Four high frames, constructed in the form of altars, were placed at the four corners of the inclosure; on these were supported layers of earth and sod, on which burned immense fires of blazing pine-wood. On one side a rude platform was erected to accommodate the preachers, fifteen of whom attended this meeting, and with very short intervals for necessary refreshment and private devotion, preached in rotation, day and night, from Tuesday to Saturday.

When we arrived, the preachers were silent; but we heard issuing from nearly every tent mingled sounds of praying, preaching, singing, and lamentation. . . . The floor [of one of the tents] was covered with straw, [which was covered by a] close-packed circle of men and women who knelt on the floor.

Out of about thirty persons thus placed, perhaps half a dozen were men. One of these [was] a handsome-looking youth of eighteen or twenty. . . . His arm was encircling the neck of a young girl who knelt beside him, with her hair hanging dishevelled upon her shoulders, and her features working with the most violent agitation; soon after they both fell forward on the straw, as if unable to endure in any other attitude the burning eloquence of a tall grim figure in black, who, standing erect in the center, was uttering with incredible vehemence an oration that seemed to hover between praying and preaching. . . .

At midnight, a horn sounded through the camp, which, we were told, was to call the people from private to public worship. . . . There were about two thousand persons assembled. One of the preachers began in a low nasal tone, and, like all other Methodist preachers, assured us of the enormous depravity of man. . . . Above a hundred persons, nearly all females, came forward, uttering howlings and groans so terrible that I shall never cease to shudder when I recall them. They appeared to drag each other forward, and on the word being given, "let us pray," they fell on their knees . . . and they were soon all lying on the ground in an indescribable confusion of heads and legs.

SOURCE: Frances Trollope, *Domestic Manners of the Americans* (London: Whittaker, Treacher, 1832), pp. 139–42.

sermon. "Preach without papers," advised one minister, "seem earnest & serious; & you will be listened to with Patience, & Wonder; both of your hands will be seized, & almost shook off as soon as you are out of the Church."

Beginning in the 1790s evangelical white Baptists and Methodists won the conversion of slaves and free blacks, who absorbed their teachings and adapted them to their needs. Black Christians generally preferred to envision God as a warrior who had liberated the Jews, his chosen people. Their cause was similar to the Israelites', Martin Prosser told his fellow slave conspirators as they plotted rebellion in Virginia in 1800. "I have read in my Bible where God says, if we worship him, we should have peace in all our land and five of you shall conquer a hundred and a hundred of you a hundred thousand of our enemies." Confident of their special relationship with God, the slaves prepared themselves spiritually for emancipation, which they saw as deliverance to the Promised Land.

Blacks generally ignored the doctrines of original sin and predestination as well as biblical passages that encouraged unthinking obedience to authority or portrayed the church as a lawgiver. When a white minister urged slaves in Liberty County, Georgia, to obey their masters, he noted that "one half of my audience deliberately rose up and walked off." Slaves identified with the persecuted Christ, who had suffered and died so that his followers might gain salvation. By offering eventual liberation from life's sorrows the Christian message helped many slaves endure their bondage. Amid the manifest injustice of their own lives African Americans used Christian principles to affirm their equality with whites in the eyes of God and to hope for ultimate justice in the afterlife. Black Christianity thus developed as a religion of emotional fervor and stoical endurance.

Like African Americans whites also were influenced by the times to emphasize certain Christian doctrines over others. The Calvinist preoccupation with human depravity and weakness had shaped the thinking of many earlier writers, teachers, and statesmen. By the early nineteenth century ministers (whether or not they were revivalists) had begun to place greater stress on human ability and individual free will, making the religious culture of the United States more optimistic and more compatible with republican doctrines of liberty and equality.

In New England many educated, well-off Congregationalists reacted against the emotionalism of Methodist and Baptist services by stressing the power of human reason. Rejecting the concept of the Trinity—God the Father, Son, and Holy Spirit— they worshipped an indivisible and "united" God, hence their name: Unitarians. "The ultimate reliance of a human being is, and must be, on his own mind," argued the famous Unitarian minister William Ellery Channing, "for the idea of God is the idea of our own spiritual nature, purified and enlarged to infinity." This emphasis on a believer's reason, a legacy of the Enlightenment, gave Unitarianism a humanistic and individualistic aspect.

Lyman Beecher, the preeminent New England Congregationalist clergyman, accepted the doctrine of universal salvation. Although Beecher continued to believe that humans had a natural tendency to sin, he retreated from the Calvinist doctrine of predestination, declaring that men and women had the capacity to choose God. In emphasizing choice—the free will of the believer—Beecher testified to the growing confidence in the power of human action.

For many in the years after 1800 individual salvation became linked with social reform through the concept of *religious benevolence*—the practice of disinterested virtue. According to the New York Presbyterian minister John Rodgers fortunate individuals who had received God's sanctifying grace had a duty "to dole out charity to their poorer brothers and sisters." Heeding this message pious merchants founded the New York Humane Society and other charitable organizations. By the 1820s some conservative church leaders were complaining that lay men and women were devoting themselves to secular reforms, such as the prevention of pauperism, to the neglect of spiritual goals. Their criticism underlined a key element of the new religious outlook: its emphasis on improving society. It was her belief, the social reformer Lydia Maria Child later recalled, that "the *only* true church organization [is] when heads and hearts unite in working for the welfare of the human-race."

Unlike the First Great Awakening of the 1740s, which split churches into factions, the Second Great Awakening fostered cooperation among the denominations. Five interdenominational societies were founded between 1815 and 1826: the American Education Society (1815), the American Bible Society (1816), the American Sunday School Union (1824), the American Tract Society (1824), and the American Home Missionary Society (1826). Each year these societies dispatched hundreds of missionaries to small towns and rural villages and distributed tens of thousands of religious pamphlets, organizing thousands of church members in a great collective undertaking and diminishing the importance of differences over religious doctrine. Many congregations abandoned books and pamphlets that took controversial stances on old theological debates over predestination and replaced them, a layman explained, with publications that would not give "offense to the serious Christians of any denomination."

This unity among Protestants had a galvanizing effect, as men and women scattered across the vast nation saw themselves as part of a single religious movement that could change the course of history. To do so they turned to politics. On July 4, 1827, the Reverend Ezra Stiles Ely called on the members of the Seventh Presbyterian Church in Philadelphia to begin a "Christian party in politics." In his sermon entitled "The Duty of Christian Freemen to Elect Christian Rulers," Ely set out for the American republic a new religious goal—one that the recently deceased Thomas Jefferson and John Adams would have found strange if not troubling. The two founders had believed that America's mission was to spread political republicanism. In contrast Ely urged the United States to become an evangelical Christian nation, dedicated to religious conversion at home and abroad. As Ely put it, "All our rulers ought in their official capacity to serve the Lord Jesus Christ."

WOMEN'S NEW RELIGIOUS ROLES

Pious women assumed a new leading role in many Protestant churches in the North and even founded new sects. Mother Ann Lee organized the Shaker sect in Britain and migrated in 1774 to America, where she and a handful of followers attracted numerous recruits; by the 1820s Shaker communities dotted the American countryside from New Hampshire to Kentucky and Indiana. In 1776 in Rhode Island, Jemima Wilkinson, a young Quaker woman stirred by reading the sermons of George Whitefield, had a vision that her body was infused by the "Spirit of Light." Repudiating her birth name, Wilkinson declared herself to be the Publick Universal Friend and won scores of converts to her new religion, which blended the Calvinist warning of "a lost and guilty, gossiping, dying World" with Quaker-inspired plain dress, pacifism, and abolitionism.

Far more important were the activities undertaken by women in mainstream churches. To give but a few examples, in New Hampshire women managed more than fifty local "cent" societies to raise funds for the Society for Promoting Christian Knowledge. Evangelical women in New York City founded the Society for the Relief of Poor Widows. And young Quaker women in Philadelphia ran the Society for the Free Instruction of African Females.

Women became active in religion and charitable work partly because they were excluded from other spheres of public life and partly because they formed a substantial majority in many denominations. After 1800 over 70 percent of the members of New England Congregational churches were female. Ministers acknowledged their presence by changing long-standing practices such as gender segregated seating at services and separate prayer meetings for each sex, while evangelical Methodist and Baptist preachers actively encouraged mixed seating and praying. "Our prayer meetings have been one of the greatest means of the conversion of souls," a minister in central New York reported in the 1820s, "especially those in which brothers and sisters have prayed together."

Far from promoting promiscuity as critics feared, these new practices were accompanied by greater moral self-discipline. Absorbing the principle of female virtue, many young women and the men who courted them postponed sexual intercourse until after marriage—a form of self-restraint uncommon in the eighteenth century. In Hingham, Massachusetts, and many other New England towns about 30 percent of the women who married between 1750 and 1800 had borne a child within eight months of their wedding day. By the 1820s the proportion had dropped to 15 percent.

Nevertheless, as women exercised their new social power, their religious activities and organizations were scrutinized and sometimes seen as subversive of social order. Many laymen resented the clergy's emphasis on women's moral superiority, and the religious and social activism that sprang from it. "Women have a different calling," one man argued. "They are neither required nor permitted to be exhorters or leaders in public assemblies. . . . That they be chaste, keepers at home is the Apostle's direction." Despite such criticism by the 1820s mothers throughout the United States had founded local maternal associations to encourage Christian child rearing. Newsletters such as *Mother's Magazine* were widely read in hundreds of small towns and villages, giving women a sense of shared purpose and identity as women.

Religious activism also advanced female education. Churches established scores of seminaries and academies where girls from the middling classes received sound intellectual training and moral instruction. Emma Willard, the first American to advocate higher education for women, opened the Middlebury Female Seminary in Vermont in 1814 and later founded girls' schools in Waterford and Troy, New York. Women educated in these seminaries and academies gradually displaced men as public school teachers. By the 1820s women taught the summer session in many schools; in the following decade they took on the more demanding winter term as well. Women were able to usurp these formerly male roles because women had few other opportunities and would therefore accept lower pay than men. Female schoolteachers earned from $12 to $14 per month with room and board—less than a farm laborer. However, as schoolteachers women had an acknowledged place in public life, one that had been beyond their reach in colonial and Revolutionary times. Here too, the Second Great Awakening had transformed the scope of women's lives. Just as the ideology of democratic republicanism had expanded voting rights and the political influence of ordinary men in the North, so the values of Christian repub-

T I M E L I N E

1782	St. Jean de Crèvecoeur's *Letters from an American Farmer*		Chesapeake blacks adopt Protestant beliefs.
1787	Benjamin Rush's *Thoughts on Female Education*	**1807**	New Jersey excludes propertied women from suffrage.
1790s	Second Great Awakening begins. Parents limit family size. "Republican motherhood" defined	**1809**	Washington Irving's *Diedrich Knickerbocker's History of New York*
		1810s	Expansion of suffrage for men
1800	Gabriel Prosser's rebellion in Virginia		Slavery defended as a "necessary evil"
1800s	Rise of sentimentalism and republican marriage system		Expansion of cotton South and domestic slave trade
	Women's religious activism and female academies	**1819–1821**	Conflict over admission of Missouri as a slave state ends with the Missouri Compromise.
	Spread of evangelical Baptists and Methodists		
	Religious benevolence linked with social reform	**1820s**	Reform of public education Women become schoolteachers.

licanism had encouraged women to take a more active role in the affairs of their communities.

In the South evangelical religion played a very different role. Initially revivalism was a disruptive force; by proclaiming the spiritual equality of all people—women and blacks as well as white men—it threatened the traditional authority wielded by husbands and planters and incurred their wrath. In response Methodist and Baptist preachers adapted the social content of their religious message so that it supported the rule of yeomen patriarchs and slaveowning planters. "We hold that a Christian slave must be submissive, faithful, and obedient," a Methodist Conference proclaimed, while a Baptist minister declared that a man was naturally at "the head of the woman." Ultimately Christian republicanism in the South added a sacred dimension to the ideology of aristocratic republicanism, while in the North it pushed forward the movement toward a democratic republican society.

For Further Exploration

For an intimate portrayal of family life on the Maine frontier, see Laurel Thatcher Ulrich, *A Midwife's Tale: The Life of Martha Ballard* (1990), which has also been made into a PBS dramatic documentary, *A Midwife's Tale* (1.5 hours). Additional materials on Ballard's experiences and women's lives are available on the web at <http://www.pbs.org/amex/midwife> and <http://www.DoHistory.org>. Jan Lewis's *The Pursuit of Happiness: Family and Values in Jefferson's Virginia* (1983) explores the domestic and emotional lives of the paternalistic slaveowning gentry of the late eighteenth century in the upper South, while Stephanie McCurry's *Masters of Small Worlds: Yeomen Households, Gender Relations, and the Political Culture of the Antebellum South Carolina Low Country* (1995) offers a brilliant analysis of yeomen families. In *The Ruling Race: A History of American Slaveholders* (1982) James Oakes argues that by the nineteenth century most slaveholders had become ruthless profit-seeking entrepreneurs.

Two stimulating analyses of the changing character of slavery and African American society are Ira Berlin, *Many Thousands Gone: The First Two Centuries of Slavery in North America* (1998), and Peter Kolchin, *American Slavery, 1619–1877* (1993). Douglas R. Egerton, *Gabriel's Rebellion: The Virginia Slave Conspiracies of 1800 and 1802* (1995), traces the political and economic causes of Gabriel's movement and its near success. For primary documents that illustrate the ways in which African Americans acquired and transformed the doctrines and beliefs of Protestant Christianity, log on to "Documenting the American South: The Church in the Southern Black Community," at <http://metalab.unc.edu/docsouth>.

In *The Democratization of American Christianity* (1987) Nathan Hatch traces the impact of evangelical Protestantism on the life and politics of the early republic. Bernard Weisberger, *They Gathered at the River* (1958), narrates the coming of the Second Great Awakening in engaging and witty prose, offers dramatic portraits of revivalists such as Charles Grandison Finney, and explores the many links between religious enthusiasm and social reform.

Part Three

ECONOMIC REVOLUTION AND SECTIONAL STRIFE

1820–1877

	ECONOMY	SOCIETY	GOVERNMENT
	The Economic Revolution Begins	A New Class Structure Emerges	Creating a Democratic Polity
1820	• Waltham textile factory (1814) • Erie Canal completed (1825)	• Business class emerges. • Rural women and girls recruited as factory workers.	• Universal white male suffrage • Rise of Jackson and Democratic Party
1830	• Protective tariffs aid owners and workers. • Panic of 1837 • U.S. textile makers outcompete British.	• Mechanics form craft unions. • Depression shatters labor movement.	• Anti-Masonic movement • Whig Party formed (1834); Second Party System emerges
1840	• Irish join labor force. • *Commonwealth v. Hunt* (1842) legalizes unions. • Manufacturing grows.	• Working-class districts emerge in cities. • Irish immigration accelerates.	• Log Cabin campaign mobilizes voters. • Antislavery parties: Liberty and Free Soil
1850	• Growth of cotton output in South and railroads in North and Midwest • Panic of 1857	• Expansion of farm society into Midwest and Far West • Free labor ideology justifies inequality.	• Whig Party disintegrates; Republican Party founded (1854): Third Party System
1860	• Northern war industries thrive. • Republicans enact Homestead Act, aid to railroads, high tariffs.	• Emancipation Proclamation (1863) • Free blacks struggle for control of land.	• Thirteenth Amendment (1865) ends slavery; Fourteenth Amendment (1868) extends legal and political rights.
1870	• Panic of 1873	• Rise of sharecropping in the South	• Fifteenth Amendment extends vote to black men (1870).

CULTURE	SECTIONALISM
REFORMING PEOPLE AND INSTITUTIONS	FROM COMPROMISE TO CIVIL WAR AND RECONSTRUCTION
• American Colonization Society (1817) • "Benevolent" Reform • Revivalist Charles Finney	• Missouri Compromise (1820) • David Walker's *Appeal to the Colored Race* (1829)
• Joseph Smith founds Mormonism. • Female Moral Reform Society (1834) • Temperance crusade	• Nullifications crisis (1832) • W. L. Garrison forms American Anti-Slavery Society (1833)
• Fourierist and other communal settlements founded • Seneca Falls convention (1848)	• Mexican War and Wilmot Proviso (1846) increase sectional conflict.
• Harriet Beecher Stowe's *Uncle Tom's Cabin* (1852) • Anti-immigrant nativist movement	• Compromise of 1850 • Kansas-Nebraska Act (1854) • *Dred Scott* decision (1857)
• U.S. Sanitary Commission and American Red Cross founded	• South Carolina secedes (1860). • Confederate States of America (1861–1865)
• African Americans create schools and institutions.	• Compromise of 1877 ends Reconstruction.

Between 1820 and 1877 the United States changed from a predominantly agricultural society into one of the world's most powerful industrial economies. This profound transformation began slowly in the Northeast and then accelerated after 1830, affecting every aspect of life in the northern and midwestern states and bringing major changes to the South as well.

Two interrelated economic revolutions—in manufacturing and in commerce—transformed the productive system. Factory owners used high-speed machines and new methods of labor discipline to boost production while enterprising merchants employed a newly built network of canals and railroads to create a vast national market. The share of the nation's wealth produced by the industrial sector rose from less than 5 percent in 1820 to more than 30 percent in 1877.

This new economic system spurred the creation of a class-based society. A wealthy elite of merchants, manufacturers, bankers, and other entrepreneurs emerged at the top of the social order and tried to maintain social stability through a paternalistic program of religious reform. However, an urban middle class with a distinct material and religious culture grew in size and political importance. Equally striking was the growing number of propertyless workers, many of them immigrants from Germany and Ireland, who labored for wages in the new factories and built the new canals and railroads. By 1860 half the nation's free workers labored for wages, and wealth had become concentrated in the hands of relatively few families.

The character of the emerging economic and social system affected the style and the substance of politics. The widespread ownership of property helped to spur the extension of the franchise, creating an open, democratic policy. Farmers, workers, and entrepreneurs demanded favors from politicians—improved transportation, shorter workdays, special corporate charters—and Catholic immigrants from Ireland and Germany entered the political arena to safeguard their religion and culture. Led by Andrew Jackson, the Democratic Party advanced the interests of southern planters, urban workers, and

immigrants and carried through a political and constitutional revolution that cut the scope of governmental authority on both the national and state levels. To compete with the Democrats, the Whig Party (and beginning in the 1850s the Republican Party) promoted social reform and a vision of commerce as reducing class barriers and allowing a high rate of individual social mobility. The result was a two-party system that engaged the energies of the electorate and unified the fragmented social order.

During these years a series of reform movements, many with religious roots and goals, swept across America. Dedicated men and women preached the gospel of temperance, Sunday observance, prison reform, and dozens of other causes. A few visionaries created utopian communities in rural areas of the Midwest, but most radical activists worked within American society. Two of their major movements were for equal rights for women and the abolition of racial slavery. During the 1840s and 1850s antislavery advocates turned to political action, campaigning for "free soil" in the western territories and alleging that the "Slave Power" threatened free labor and republican values.

These economic, political, and cultural changes combined to sharpen sectional divisions: the North and Midwest developed into diversified societies—rural and urban, farming and manufacturing—based on free labor, whereas the South remained a rural, slaveholding society dependent on the export of cotton and other staple crops. Following the conquest of vast western territories during the war with Mexico, northern and southern politicians vigorously debated whether these lands would be open to slavery. On the election of Republican Abraham Lincoln as president in 1860, the Southern states seceded from the Union, sparking a bloody four-year civil war. Because of its new industrial technology and the mass mobilization of economic resources and armies, the North emerged victorious only after each side endured unprecedented casualties and costs.

The fruits of victory were substantial. During Reconstruction the Republican Party ended slavery and imposed its economic policies and constitutional doctrines on the nation. However, the effort by Radical Republicans to extend full democratic rights to the former slaves elicited massive resistance from white southerners, and Northern leaders and voters lacked the will to undertake the fundamental transformation of a South that would have been required to provide African Americans with the full benefits of freedom.

Chapter 10

THE ECONOMIC REVOLUTION
1820–1860

[In America] all is circulation, motion, and boiling agitation . . .
enterprise follows enterprise [and] riches and poverty follow. . . .
— MICHEL CHEVALIER, FRENCH VISITOR, 1839

In 1804 life suddenly turned grim for eleven-year-old Chauncey Jerome. Following the death of his farmer-blacksmith father Jerome was hired out as an indentured servant to a farmer. Aware that few farmers "would treat a poor boy like a human being," Jerome instead bought out his indenture by finding a job making dials for clocks and eventually ended up working as a journeyman for Eli Terry. A manufacturing wizard, Terry had turned Litchfield, Connecticut, into the clockmaking center of the United States by designing an enormously popular desk-model clock with brass parts. Jerome followed in Terry's footsteps, setting up his own clock business in 1816. By organizing work more efficiently and using new machines to make interchangeable metal parts, Jerome drove down the price of a simple clock from $20 to $5 and then to less than $2. By the 1840s he was selling his clocks in England, the center of the Industrial Revolution; two decades later his workers were turning out 200,000 clocks a year, helping the United States to become a major manufacturing nation.

The French aristocrat Alexis de Tocqueville captured a key feature of Chauncy Jerome's experience and the American economic revolution in his treatise *Democracy in America* (1835). "What most astonishes me," he remarked after a two-year stay in the United States, "is not so much the marvelous grandeur of some undertakings, as the innumerable magnitude of small ones." The individual efforts of tens of thousands of artisan-inventors like Terry and Jerome had helped to propel the country into a new economic era. As the editor of *Niles Weekly Register* put it, there was an "almost universal ambition to get forward."

Not all Americans embraced the new ethic of enterprise, and many who did failed to share in the new prosperity. The Industrial Revolution and the Market Revolution created a class-divided society that challenged the founders' vision of an agricultural republic with few distinctions of wealth or power. As the philosopher Ralph Waldo Emerson warned in 1839, "The invasion of Nature by Trade with its

Money, its Credit, its Steam, [and] its Railroad threatens to . . . establish a new, universal Monarchy."

The Coming of Industry: Northeastern Manufacturing

Together, the Industrial Revolution and the Market Revolution created a new economy. Industrialization came to the United States after 1790 as American merchants and manufacturers increased the output of goods by reorganizing work and building factories. The rapid construction of turnpikes, canals, and railroads by state governments and private entrepreneurs allowed those products to be sold throughout the land. Thanks to these innovations the average per capita wealth of Americans increased by nearly 1 percent per year—30 percent over the course of a generation. Goods that once had been luxury items became part of everyday life.

DIVISION OF LABOR AND THE FACTORY

This impressive gain in output stemmed initially from changes in the organization of production. During the 1820s and 1830s merchants and manufacturers increased output in the shoe industry through a more efficient "division of labor." The employers hired journeymen and set them to work in central shops cutting leather into soles and uppers. They sent out the uppers to shoe binders, usually women who worked at home sewing in fabric linings. Finally, the manufacturers had other journeymen assemble the shoes in small shops and return them to the central shop for inspection and packing. The new system made the manufacturer into a powerful "shoe boss" and eroded the workers' control over the pace and conditions of labor. "I guess you won't catch me to do that little thing again," vowed one Massachusetts binder. Whatever the cost to workers, the division of labor dramatically increased the output of shoes while cutting their price.

For tasks that were not suited to the outwork system, entrepreneurs created an even more important new organization, the modern factory. As in the traditional artisan economy, they concentrated production under one roof but now divided the work into specialized tasks performed by different individuals. For example, in the 1830s Cincinnati merchants built slaughterhouses that rationalized the process of butchering hogs. A simple system of overhead rails moved the carcasses past workers who had specific tasks: splitting the animals, removing various organs, and trimming the carcasses before packers stuffed them in barrels and pickled them. The system was efficient and quick—sixty hogs per hour—and by the 1840s Cincinnati was butchering so many hogs that the city became known as "Porkopolis."

Some factories boasted impressive new technology. The prolific Delaware inventor Oliver Evans built a highly automated flourmill driven by waterpower. His machinery lifted the grain to the top of the mill, cleaned the grain as it fell into hoppers, ground it into flour, conveyed the flour back to the top of the mill, and

Pork Packing in Cincinnati

The only modern technology in this Cincinnati pork packing plant was the overhead pulley system that carried hog carcasses past the workers. The plant's efficiency came from organization, a division of labor so that each worker performed a specific task. Such plants pioneered the design of the moving assembly lines that Henry Ford used in his automobile factories in the early twentieth century. (Cincinnati Historical Society)

then cooled the flour during its descent into barrels. Evans's factory, remarked one observer, "was as full of machinery as the case of a watch." It needed only six men to mill 100,000 bushels of grain a year.

Subsequently, manufacturers made use of newly improved stationary steam engines to power their mills. They also extended the use of power-driven machines and assembly lines from the processing of agricultural goods—pork, leather, wool, cotton—to the manufacturing of goods and machines made of metal. Cyrus McCormick of Chicago developed power-driven conveyor belts to assemble reapers, and Samuel Colt built an assembly-line factory in Hartford, Connecticut, to produce his invention—the "six-shooter" revolver, as it became known. As a team of British observers noted with admiration, many American products were made "in large factories, with machinery applied to almost every process, the extreme subdivision of labor, and all reduced to an almost perfect system of manufacture."

THE TEXTILE INDUSTRY AND BRITISH COMPETITION

As textile manufacturers adopted new machinery and the division of labor, they achieved dramatic gains in productivity (output per worker). To protect its industrial leadership Britain prohibited the export of textile machinery and the emigration of mechanics who knew how to build it. Lured by high wages or offers of partnerships, thousands of British mechanics disguised themselves as ordinary laborers and set sail for the United States. By 1812 there were more than 300 British mechanics at work in the Philadelphia area alone.

The most important was Samuel Slater, who came to America in 1789 after working for Richard Arkwright, the inventor and operator of the most advanced machinery for spinning cotton. Having memorized the design of Arkwright's machinery, the young Slater introduced his innovations in merchant Moses Brown's cotton mill in Providence, Rhode Island. The opening of Slater's factory in 1790 marks the advent of the American Industrial Revolution.

In competing with British mills American manufacturers had one major advantage: an abundance of natural resources. America's rich agriculture produced a wealth of cotton and wool, and from Maine to Delaware its rivers provided a cheap source of energy. As rivers cascaded downhill from the Appalachian foothills to the Atlantic coastal plain, they were easily harnessed to run power machinery. All along this fall line industrial villages and towns sprang up.

Nevertheless, the British producers easily undersold their American competitors. Thanks to cheap shipping and lower interest rates in Britain, they could import raw cotton from the United States, manufacture it into cloth, and then ship the textiles back across the Atlantic. Moreover, because British companies were better established, they could engage in cutthroat competition, cutting prices briefly but sharply to drive the newer American firms out of business. The most

A New England Textile Village, 1822

Because the first textile mills used waterpower, the American Industrial Revolution began in small rural settlements, like that shown in Francis Alexander's painting of Globe Village on the Blackstone River in Massachusetts. (Jacob Edwards Library, Southbridge, MA)

important British advantage was cheap labor. Britain had a larger population—about 12.6 million in 1810 compared with 7.3 million Americans—and thousands of landless laborers who were willing to take low-paying factory jobs. Since unskilled American workers could obtain good pay for farm or construction work, American manufacturers had to pay them higher wages.

To offset these British advantages American entrepreneurs sought assistance from the federal government. In 1816 Congress passed a tariff that gave manufacturers protection from low-cost imports of cotton cloth. New protective legislation in 1824 levied a tax of 35 percent on imported iron products, higher-grade woolen and cotton textiles, and various agricultural products, and the rate rose to 50 percent in 1828. But in 1833, under pressure from southern planters, western farmers, and urban consumers—who wanted to buy inexpensive manufactures—Congress began to reduce tariffs (see Chapter 11), causing some American textile firms to go out of business.

American producers adopted two other strategies to compete with their British rivals. First they improved on British technology. In 1811 Francis Cabot Lowell, a wealthy Boston merchant, spent a holiday touring British textile mills. A well-educated and charming young man, he flattered his hosts by asking a great many questions, but his easy manner hid a serious purpose. Lowell secretly made detailed drawings of power machinery, and Paul Moody, an experienced American mechanic, then copied the machines and made improvements. In 1814 Lowell joined two other merchants, Nathan Appleton and Patrick Tracy Jackson, to form the Boston Manufacturing Company. Raising the staggering sum of $400,000, they built a textile plant in Waltham, Massachusetts, on the Charles River. The Waltham factory was the first in America to perform all the operations of cloth making under one roof. Thanks to Moody's improvements, Waltham's power looms operated at higher speeds than British looms and needed fewer workers.

The second American strategy was to find less expensive workers. In the 1820s the Boston Manufacturing Company pioneered a manufacturing system that became known as the Waltham plan. The company recruited thousands of farm girls and women, who would work at low wages, as textile operatives. To attract these workers, the company provided boardinghouses and cultural activities such as evening lectures. The mill owners reassured anxious parents by enforcing strict curfews, prohibiting alcoholic beverages, and requiring regular church attendance. At Lowell (1822), Chicopee (1823), and other sites in Massachusetts and New Hampshire, the Company built new cotton factories on the Waltham plan; other Boston-owned firms quickly followed suit.

By the early 1830s more than 40,000 young women were working in textile mills. One of them, Lucy Larcom of Lowell, Massachusetts, became an operative when she was eleven so that she would not be "a trouble or burden or expense" to her widowed mother. Many women sent their savings home to help their fathers pay off farm mortgages, defray the cost of schooling for their brothers, or accumulate a dowry for themselves. Women textile operatives often found their work

---

A New England Mill Worker

SARAH RICE

S arah Rice had to defy her father to take a job tending looms in a mill in Masonville, Connecticut. Her letters explain both the financial advantages of factory labor over work as a domestic servant and its toll on her health. Operatives in New England worked an average of 12 hours a day, six days a week, 309 days a year; in addition to Sundays, they had three days off: Fast Day in the spring, the Fourth of July, and Thanksgiving.

Masonville Feb 23d 1845

Dear Father

I now take my pen in hand to let you know where I am. I have been waiting perhaps longer than I ought to without leting you know where I am yet I had a reason for so doing . . . knowing that you was dolefully prejudiced against a Cotton Factory, and being no less prejudiced myself I thought it best to wait and see how I prospered. . . .

To be sure it is a noisy place and we are confined more than I like to be but I do not wear out my clothes and shoes as I do when I do house work. If I can make 2 dollars per week beside my board and save my clothes and shoes I think it will be better than to do housework for nine shillings [$1.12] I mean for a year or two. I should not like to spend my days in a mill . . . because I like a Farm to well for that.

Millbury [Massachusetts] Sept 14th 1845

You surely cannot blame me for leaving the factory so long as I realised that it was killing me to work in it. Could you have seen me att the time or a week before I came away you would [have] advised me as many others did to leave immediately. I realise that if I lose my health which is all I possess on earth . . . that I shall be in a sad condition.

SOURCE: Gary Kulik, Roger Parks, Theodore Z. Penn, eds., *The New England Mill Village, 1790–1860* (Cambridge, MA: MIT Press, 1982), pp. 389–90.

---

oppressive and took periodic breaks before moving to another mill, but many gained a new sense of freedom and autonomy (see American Voices, "A New England Mill Worker"). "Don't I feel independent!" a mill worker wrote to her sister in the 1840s. "The thought that I am living on no one is a happy one indeed to me."

The owners of the Boston Manufacturing Company were even happier. By combining improved technology, female labor, and tariff protection, they could sell cheap textiles for a lower price than their British rivals could. They also had an advantage over textile manufacturers in New York and Pennsylvania, where farm workers were better paid than in New England and textile wages consequently were higher. Manufacturers in those states pursued a different strategy, modifying traditional technology to produce higher-quality cloth, also with good results. In 1825

A Mill Girl, c. 1850

This fine daguerreotype (an early form of photography) shows a neatly dressed textile worker about twelve years old. Labor in the mill has taken a toll on her spirit and body: the young girl's eyes and mouth show little joy or life and her hands are rough and swollen. She probably worked either as a knotter, tying broken threads on spinning jennies, or a warper, straightening out the strands of cotton or wool as they entered the loom. (Jack Naylor Collection)

Thomas Jefferson, once a critic of industrialization, expressed his pride in the American achievement: "Our manufacturers are now very nearly on a footing with those of England."

AMERICAN MECHANICS AND TECHNOLOGICAL INNOVATION

By the 1820s American-born craftsmen had replaced British immigrants at the cutting edge of technological innovation. Although few craftsmen had a formal education and once had been viewed as "mean" or even "servile" workers, they now claimed respect as "men professing an ingenious art." In 1837 one such inventor, Richard Garsed, experimented with improvements on power looms in his father's factory and in three years nearly doubled their speed. By 1846 Garsed had patented a cam and harness device that allowed elaborately figured fabrics such as damask to be woven by machine.

In the Philadelphia region the most important inventors came from the remarkable Sellars family. Samuel Sellars Jr. invented a machine for twisting worsted woolen yarn. His son John devised more efficient ways of using waterpower to run the family's sawmills and built a machine to weave wire sieves. John's sons and grandsons built machine shops that turned out a variety of new products: riveted leather fire hoses, papermaking equipment, and eventually locomotives. In 1824 the Sellars and other mechanics founded the Franklin Institute in Philadelphia. Named after Benjamin Franklin, whom the mechanics admired for his scientific accomplishments and idealization of hard work, the institute fostered a sense of professional identity. The Franklin Institute published a journal; provided high school–level instruction in mechanics, chemistry, mathematics, and mechanical drawing; and organized annual fairs to exhibit the most advanced products. Craftsmen in Ohio and other states soon established their own mechanics institutes, which played a crucial role in diffusing technical knowledge and encouraging innovation. Around 1820 the United States Patent Office issued about 200 patents on new inventions each year, mostly to gentlemen and merchants. By 1850 it was awarding 1,000 patents annually, mostly to mechanics, and by 1860 over 4,000.

During these years American mechanics pioneered the development of machine tools—machines for making other machines—thus facilitating the rapid spread of the Industrial Revolution. Mechanics in the textile industry invented lathes, planers, and boring machines that made standardized parts, making it possible to manufacture new spinning jennies and weaving looms at a low cost and to repair broken machines. Moreover, this machinery was precise enough in design and construction to operate at higher speeds than British equipment.

Technological innovation swept through the rest of American manufacturing, with especially important advances coming in the firearms industry. To fill large-scale contracts for guns from the federal government, Eli Whitney and his coworkers in Connecticut developed machine tools that produced parts that were interchangeable and precision-crafted. After Whitney's death his partner, John H. Hall, an engineer at the federal armory at Harpers Ferry, Virginia, built a series of sixteen special-purpose lathes to make a gun stock out of sawn lumber and an array of machine tools to work metal: turret lathes, milling machines, and precision grinders. Thereafter, manufacturers could use those machine tools to produce complicated machinery with great speed, at low cost, and in large quantities.

With this expansion in the availability of machines, the American Industrial Revolution came of age. The sheer volume of output caused some products—Remington rifles, Singer sewing machines, and Yale locks—to become household names in the United States and abroad. After showing their machine-tooled goods at the Crystal Palace Exhibition in London in 1851 (the first major international display of industrial goods), these American businesses built factories in Great Britain and soon dominated many European markets.

WAGE WORKERS AND THE LABOR MOVEMENT

As the Industrial Revolution gathered momentum, it changed the nature of work and of workers' lives. Each decade, more and more white Americans ceased to be self-employed and took jobs as wage-earning workers. They had little security of employment or control over their working conditions.

Some wageworkers worked as journeymen in traditional crafts, such as the building trades. These carpenters, housepainters, stonecutters, masons, nailers, and cabinetmakers had valuable skills and a strong sense of craft identity. Consequently, they were able to form unions and bargain with the master artisans who employed them. The journeymen's main concern was the increasing length of the workday, which deprived them of time to spend with their families or improve their education. The traditional workday for artisans had averaged about twelve hours, including breaks for meals. By the 1820s masters were demanding a longer day during the summer, when it stayed light longer, while paying journeymen the old daily rate. In response, 600 carpenters in Boston went on strike in 1825, demanding a ten-hour day, 6 A.M. to 6 P.M. with an hour each for breakfast and dinner. Although the Boston protest failed, two years later journeymen carpenters in Philadelphia won a similar strike and then helped found the Mechanics' Union of Trade Associations. This citywide organization of fifty unions and 10,000 Philadelphia wage-earners set forth a broad program of reform, demanding "a just balance of power . . . between all the various classes." To secure this goal in 1828 the Philadelphia artisans founded the Working Men's Party, which campaigned for the abolition of banks, equal taxation, and a universal system of public education. By the mid-1830s skilled building-trades workers had forced many urban employers to accept a ten-hour workday and persuaded President Andrew Jackson to establish a ten-hour day at the Philadelphia navy yard.

Artisans whose occupations were threatened by industrialization were less successful. As machines changed the nature of their work, shoemakers, hatters, printers, furniture makers, and weavers faced declining incomes, unemployment, and loss of status. To avoid the regimentation of factory work some artisans moved to small towns or set up specialized shops. In New York City 800 highly skilled cabinetmakers worked in artisanlike shops that made fashionable or custom-made products. In status and income they outranked a much larger group of 3,200 semitrained workers—derogatively called "botches"—who turned out cheap, mass-produced furniture.

In many industries factory workers banded together to form craft unions to seek higher pay and better conditions. In 1830 in Lynn, Massachusetts, journeymen shoemakers founded a Mutual Benefit Society that quickly grew into a national union and formed local federations with other craft unions. In 1834 federations from Boston to Philadelphia formed the National Trades' Union, the first national union of different trades.

Union leaders mounted a critique of the new industrial order. Afraid that workers were becoming "slaves to a monied aristocracy," they condemned the new outwork and factory systems in which "capital and labor stand opposed." To restore a just society, they devised a *labor theory of value,* arguing that the price of a product should reflect the labor required to make it and should be paid primarily to the artisan or farmer who produced it, to "enable him to live as comfortably as others." Appealing to the spirit of the American Revolution, which had destroyed the aristocracy of birth, they called for a new revolution to destroy the aristocracy of capital. Armed with this artisan-republican ideology, in 1836 union men organized nearly fifty strikes for higher wages.

Agitation for workers' rights prompted strikes by women textile operatives. Competition in the industry was fierce because the output of cotton cloth increased at a rate of 5 percent a year while its price fell by more than 1 percent a year. To ward off bankruptcy employers reduced workers' wages and imposed more stringent work rules. In 1828 women mill workers in Dover, New Hampshire, struck against new rules, winning some relief; six years later more than 800 Dover women walked out to protest wage cuts. In Lowell, Massachusetts, 2,000 women operatives backed a strike by withdrawing their savings from an employer-owned bank. The *Boston Transcript* reported that "one of the leaders mounted a pump, and made a flaming . . . speech on the rights of women and the iniquities of the 'monied aristocracy.'" When conditions did not improve, young New England women refused to enter the mills, and impoverished Irish (and later French Canadian) immigrants took their places. Many of the new textile workers were men, foreshadowing the emergence of a predominately male system of factory labor (see Chapter 17).

By the 1850s workers faced yet another threat to their jobs. As machines produced more goods, the supply of available products exceeded the demand for them, prompting employers to lay off or dismiss workers. One episode of overproduction preceded the Panic of 1857—a financial crisis sparked by excess railroad investments—and resulted in a major recession. Unemployment rose to 10 percent, reminding Americans of the social costs of the new—and otherwise very successful—system of industrial production.

The Expansion of Markets

As American factories and farms turned out more goods, merchants and legislators sought faster and cheaper ways to get those products to consumers—setting in motion the Market Revolution. Beginning in the 1820s they promoted the construction of a massive system of canals and roads to link the Atlantic coast states with those in the trans-Appalachian West. By 1860 nearly one-third of the nation's people lived in the midwestern states (the five states carved out of the Northwest Territory—Ohio, Indiana, Illinois, Michigan, and Wisconsin—along with Missouri, Iowa, and Minnesota), where they created a complex society and economy that increasingly resembled that of the Northeast.

MIGRATION TO THE SOUTHWEST AND THE MIDWEST

After 1820 vast numbers of men and women migrated to the west, following in the footsteps of the thousands who had already left the seaboard states (see Map 10.1). Abandoned farms and homes dotted the countryside of the Carolinas, Vermont,

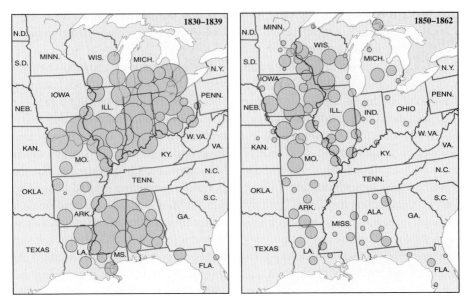

M A P 10.1
Western Land Sales, 1830s and 1850s

The federal government opened land offices along the frontier to sell farmland to settlers. Each circle centers on a land office, and the size of the circle reflects the relative amount of land sold at that office. In the 1830s land sales boomed in the Old Northwest (especially Indiana, Michigan, and Illinois) and in the Old Southwest (Alabama and Mississippi). By the 1850s the demand for land centered in the upper Mississippi River Valley (particularly Iowa and Wisconsin).

and New Hampshire. "It is useless to seek to excite patriotic emotions" for one's state of birth, complained an easterner, "when self-interest speaks so loudly." Some migrant families wanted to acquire enough land to settle their children on nearby farms, recreating traditional rural communities. Others were more entrepreneurial and hoped for greater profits from the fertile soil of the West.

As in the past the new pioneers migrated in three great streams. In the South plantation owners encouraged by the voracious demand for raw cotton moved more slaves into the Old Southwest (see Chapter 8), expanding the cotton kingdom in Louisiana, Mississippi, and Alabama, and pushing on to Missouri (1821) and Arkansas (1836). "The Alabama Feaver rages here with great violence," a North Carolina planter remarked, "and has carried off vast numbers of our Citizens."

Small-scale farmers from the upper South, especially Virginia and Kentucky, created a second stream as they crossed the Ohio River into the Northwest Territory. Some of these migrants were fleeing planter-dominated slave states. In a free community, thought Peter Cartwright, a Methodist lay preacher from southwestern Kentucky, "I would be entirely clear of the evil of slavery . . . [and] could raise my children to work where work was not thought a degradation." These southerners introduced corn and hog farming to the southern regions of Ohio, Indiana, and Illinois.

A third stream of migrants continued to flow from the overcrowded farms of New England. Thousands of settlers poured first into upstate New York and then into the fertile farmlands of the Old Northwest, establishing wheat farms throughout the Great Lakes Basin: northern Ohio, northern Illinois, Michigan (admitted in 1837), Iowa (1846), and Wisconsin (1848).

To meet the demand for cheap land, in 1820 Congress reduced the price of federal land from \$2.00 an acre to \$1.25—just enough to cover the cost of surveying and sale. For \$100 a farmer could buy 80 acres, the minimum required under federal law. Many American families saved enough in a few years to make the minimum purchase and used money from the sale of an old farm to finance the move. By 1860 the population center of American society had shifted significantly to the west.

THE TRANSPORTATION REVOLUTION FORGES REGIONAL TIES

To enhance the "common-wealth" of their citizens the federal and state governments took measures to create a larger market. Since the 1790s they had chartered private companies to build toll-charging turnpikes in well-populated areas and subsidized road construction in the West. The most significant feat was the National Road, which started in Cumberland, Maryland, passed Wheeling (then in Virginia) in 1818, crossed the Ohio River in 1833, and reached Vandalia, Illinois, in 1839 (see Map 10.2). The National Road and other interregional highways mostly carried migrants and their heavily loaded wagons to the West and herds of livestock to the East; road travel was too slow and expensive to serve as a means of carrying manufactured goods and farm crops.

To exchange these goods Americans developed a water-borne transportation system of unprecedented size, complexity, and cost, beginning with the Erie Canal. When the New York legislature approved the building of the canal in 1817, no artificial waterway in the United States was longer than 28 miles—a reflection of their huge capital cost and the lack of American engineering expertise. The New York project had three things in its favor: the vigorous support of New York City merchants, who wanted access to western markets; the backing of New York's governor, DeWitt Clinton, who persuaded the legislature to finance the waterway from tax revenues, tolls, and bond sales to foreign investors; and the relative gentleness of the terrain west of Albany. Even so, the task was enormous. Workers—many of them Irish immigrants—had to dig out millions of cubic yards of soil, quarry thousands of tons of rock to build huge locks to raise and lower boats, and construct vast reservoirs to ensure a steady supply of water. The first great engineering project in American history, the Erie Canal altered the ecology and the economy of an entire region.

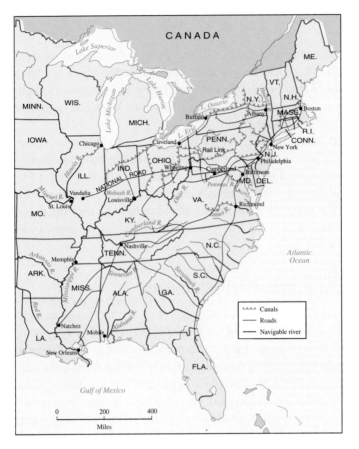

M A P 10.2
The Transportation Revolution: Roads and Canals, 1820–1850

By 1850 the United States had an efficient transportation system based on roads, natural waterways, and canals. Short canals and navigable rivers carried cotton, tobacco, and other products from the upcountry of the seaboard states into the Atlantic commercial system. Major canals—the Erie, Chesapeake and Ohio, and Pennsylvania Mainline—linked major seaport cities to the vast trans-Appalachian region, and a set of regional canals connected most of the Great Lakes region to the Ohio and Mississippi Rivers and New Orleans.

The Erie Canal was an instant success. The first section, a stretch of 75 miles opened in 1819, immediately generated enough revenue to repay its cost. When the canal was completed in 1825, a 40-foot-wide ribbon of water stretched 364 miles from the Lake Erie port of Buffalo to Albany, where it linked up with the Hudson River for a 150-mile trip to New York City. One-hundred-ton freight barges pulled by two horses moved along the canal at a steady 24 miles a day, greatly accelerating the flow of goods and cutting transportation costs. On New York's roads it took four horses to pull a 1-ton wagon 12 miles in a day.

The Erie Canal brought prosperity to central and western New York, carrying wheat and meat from farming communities in the interior to eastern cities and foreign markets. In 1818 the mills in Rochester had processed only 26,000 barrels of flour from the wheat grown by nearby farmers; ten years later the number soared to 200,000 barrels, and in 1840 to 500,000 barrels. After a trip on the canal the novelist Nathaniel Hawthorne suggested that its water "must be the most fertilizing of all fluids, for it causes towns with their masses of brick and stone, their churches and theaters, their business and hubbub, their luxury and refinement, their gay dames and polished citizens, to spring up." The canal also linked the economies of the Northeast and the Midwest. Northeastern manufacturers provided clothing, boots, and farm equipment to farm families in the Great Lakes Basin and the Ohio Valley. In payment the farmers sent grain, cattle, and hogs as well as raw materials (such as leather, wool, and hemp) to the East.

The spectacular benefits of the Erie Canal prompted a national canal boom (see Map 10.2). Civic and business leaders in Philadelphia and Baltimore proposed their own waterways to compete for the trade of the West. Copying New York's fiscal innovations they persuaded their state governments to invest directly in canal companies or force state-chartered banks to do so. They also won state guarantees for their bonds, thereby encouraging British and Dutch investors to buy them. Indeed, foreign investors provided almost three-quarters of the $400 million invested in canals by 1840. Soon these waterways connected the Midwest with the great port cities of New York (via the Erie and Pennsylvania Canals) and New Orleans (via the Ohio and Mississippi Rivers).

The steamboat, another product of the industrial age, ensured the success of this vast transportation system. The engineer-inventor Robert Fulton had built the first American steamboat, the *Clermont,* which he navigated up the Hudson in 1807. However, the first steamboats consumed huge amounts of wood or coal and could not navigate shallow western rivers. During the 1820s engineers broadened the hulls of these boats, thereby enlarging their cargo capacity and giving them a shallower draft. This improved design cut the cost of upstream river transport in half and dramatically increased the flow of goods, people, and news into the interior. In 1830 a traveler or a letter from New York could go by water to Buffalo and Pittsburgh in less than a week and to Detroit and St. Louis in two weeks. Thirty years earlier the same journeys, by road or sail, had taken twice as long.

The rapid emergence of this national system of transportation was encouraged by the Supreme Court headed by John Marshall, which struck down state controls over interstate commerce. In the crucial case of *Gibbons v. Ogden* (1824) the Court voided a New York law that created a monopoly on steamboat travel into New York City by ruling that the federal government had paramount authority over interstate commerce (see Chapter 8). This decision meant that no local or state monopolies—or tariffs—would impede the flow of goods and services across the nation.

Another product of industrial technology—the railroad—created close ties between the Northeast and the Midwest (see Map 10.3). As late as 1852 canals were

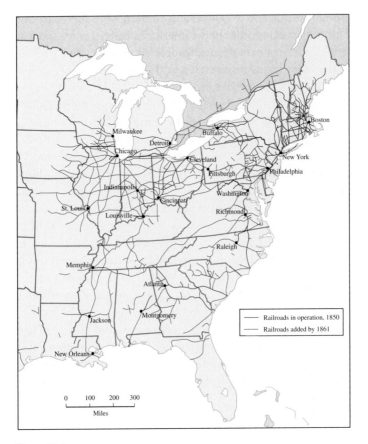

MAP 10.3
Railroads of the North and South, 1850–1860

In the decade before the Civil War the rapid construction of railroads provided the Northeast and the Midwest with extensive and dense transportation systems that stimulated economic development. The South built a much simpler system. In all regions railroad lines used different track gauges, hindering the efficient flow of goods (and, during the Civil War, of military supplies).

carrying twice the tonnage of railroads, but over the next six years track mileage increased dramatically and railroads became the main carriers of freight. The Erie Railroad, the Pennsylvania Railroad, and other trunk lines connected New York City, Philadelphia, and Boston to Cleveland and Chicago, serviced by a vast network of locomotive and freight car repair shops. Each year more and more midwestern grain moved east by rail rather than south by barge down the Ohio and Mississippi Rivers.

Tied to one another by the steel rails that ran along the route of New England migration, the Midwest and the Northeast increasingly resembled each other in ethnic composition, cultural values, and technical skills. The first migrants to the Midwest had relied on manufactured goods made in Britain or in the Northeast. They bought high-quality shovels and spades fabricated at the Delaware Iron Works, axes forged in Connecticut factories, and steel horseshoes manufactured in Troy, New York. By the 1830s midwestern entrepreneurs were producing many of these goods. As a blacksmith in Grand Detour, Illinois, John Deere made his first steel plow out of old saws in 1837; ten years later he opened a factory in Moline that used mass-production techniques. His steel plows, superior in strength to the cast-iron model developed earlier in New York by Jethro Wood, soon dominated the midwestern market. Other midwestern companies—McCormick and Hussey—mass-produced self-raking reapers that allowed a farmer to harvest twelve acres of grain a day (rather than the two or three acres he could cut by hand).

The maritime commercial links between the Northeast and the South did not produce a similar social and economic order in those regions. Southern investors concentrated their resources in cotton and slaves; by the 1840s the South was producing more than two-thirds of the world's cotton and accounted for almost two-thirds of the total value of American exports. Planters used the profits from the cotton trade to buy manufactures from the Northeast and Britain; only Richmond, Virginia, developed as an important industrial center. Lacking cities, factories, and highly trained workers, the South remained a predominantly agricultural economy and did not provide a majority of its people with a rising standard of living. In 1860 the per capita income was $141 in the North but only $103 in the South. The national system of commerce had accentuated the agricultural character of the South even as it helped to create a diversified economy in the Northeast and the Midwest.

THE GROWTH OF CITIES AND TOWNS

The expansion of industry and trade in the 1830s led to a dramatic increase in the urban population. In 1820 there were only 58 towns in the nation with more than 2,500 inhabitants; by 1840 there were 126, located mostly in the Northeast and Midwest. During those two decades the total number of urban residents grew fourfold, from 443,000 to 1,844,000.

The most rapid growth occurred in the new industrial towns that sprang up along the fall line. In 1822 the Boston Manufacturing Company built a new complex of mills in East Chelmsford, Massachusetts, quickly transforming the sleepy Merrimack River village into the bustling town of Lowell. Hartford, Connecticut, Trenton, New Jersey, and Wilmington, Delaware, also became urban centers as mill owners exploited their water power and recruited workers from the surrounding countryside.

Western commercial cities such as New Orleans, Pittsburgh, Cincinnati, and Louisville grew almost as rapidly. The initial expansion of these cities resulted from their location at points where goods were transferred from one mode of transport, such as canal boats or farmers' wagons, to another, such as steamboats or sailing vessels. As the midwestern population grew during the 1830s and 1840s, St. Louis,

Rochester, Buffalo, and Detroit emerged as dynamic centers of commerce. Merchants and bankers settled there, developing the marketing, provisioning, and financial services that were essential to farmers and small-town merchants in the hinterland.

Within a few decades these western commercial hubs—joined by Cleveland and Chicago—became manufacturing centers as well. Exploiting these cities' location as key junctions for railroad lines and steamboats, entrepreneurs established flour mills, packing plants, and docks, and provided work for hundreds of artisans and laborers. In 1846 Cyrus McCormick moved his reaper factory from western Virginia to Chicago to be closer to his midwestern customers. St. Louis and Chicago were the fastest-growing boom towns, and by 1860 had become the nation's third and fourth largest cities, respectively, after New York and Philadelphia.

Yet the old Atlantic seaports—Boston, Philadelphia, Baltimore, Charleston, and especially New York—remained important for their foreign commerce and increasingly as centers of finance and manufacturing. In 1817 New York merchants founded the New York Stock Exchange, which soon became the nation's chief market for securities. The New York metropolis grew at a phenomenal rate, diversifying into small-scale manufacturing and becoming the center of the ready-made clothing industry, which relied on the labor of thousands of low-paid seamstresses. "The wholesale clothing establishments are . . . absorbing the business of the country," a "Country Tailor" complained to the *New York Tribune,* "casting many an honest and hardworking man out of employment [and allowing] . . . the large cities to swallow up the small towns."

New York's growth stemmed primarily from its control of foreign trade. It had the best harbor in the United States, and ocean-going vessels could sail or steam up the Hudson River to Albany and the Erie Canal. The city's merchants exploited these natural advantages. In 1818 four Quaker merchants founded the Black Ball Line, a service that operated on a regular schedule and carried cargo, people, and mail between New York and the European ports of Liverpool, London, and Le Havre. New York merchants also gained an unassailable lead in commerce with the newly independent Latin American nations of Brazil, Peru, and Venezuela. New York–based traders also took over the cotton trade by offering finance, insurance, and shipping to cotton exporters in southern ports. And, by persuading the state government to build the Erie Canal, the city's merchants acquired a dominant position in the export of western grain to European markets. By 1840 the port of New York handled almost two-thirds of foreign imports and almost half of all foreign trade.

Changes in the Social Structure

The Industrial and Market Revolutions transformed the material lives of many Americans, allowing them to live in larger houses, cook on iron stoves, and wear better-made clothes. But the new economic order created distinct social classes: a wealthy industrial and commercial elite, a substantial urban middle class, and a mass of propertyless wage earners. By creating a class-divided society industrialization posed a momentous challenge to American republican ideals.

THE BUSINESS ELITE

Before industrialization white American society had been divided into various ranks, with "notables" ruling over the "lower orders." But in rural society the different ranks shared a common culture: gentlemen farmers talked easily with yeomen about crop yields, while their wives conversed about the art of quilting. In the South humble tenants and aristocratic slaveowners shared the same amusements: gambling, cockfighting, and horse racing. Rich and poor attended the same Quaker meetinghouse or Presbyterian church. "Almost everyone eats, drinks, and dresses in the same way," a European visitor to Hartford, Connecticut, reported in 1798, "and one can see the most obvious inequality only in the dwellings."

The Industrial Revolution shattered this traditional order and created a society of classes, each with its own culture. The new economic system pulled many Americans into cities and made a few of them—the business elite of merchants, manufacturers, bankers, and landlords—very rich. In 1800 the top 10 percent of the nation's families owned about 40 percent of the wealth; by 1860 the wealthiest 10 percent owned nearly 70 percent. In the cities the richest 1 percent of the population held more than 40 percent of all tangible property—such as land and buildings—and an even higher share of intangible property—such as stocks and bonds.

Government tax policies allowed this accumulation of wealth. The U.S. Treasury raised most of its revenue from tariffs—taxes on imported goods such as textiles that were purchased mostly by ordinary citizens. State and local governments also favored the wealthier classes. They usually taxed real estate and tangible personal property (such as furniture, tools, and machinery) but almost never taxed the stocks and bonds owned by the rich or the inheritances they passed on to their children.

Over time the wealthiest families consciously set themselves apart. Master artisans had labored side by side with journeymen and apprentices in small shops, but merchants and manufacturers were managers, issuing orders to hundreds of outworkers or factory operatives. Similarly, by the 1830s most employers had stopped providing their workers with housing and had moved themselves to distinct upper-class neighborhoods. Many American cities became class-segregated communities.

THE MIDDLE CLASS

Standing between wealthy owners and entrepreneurs at one end of the social spectrum and nonpropertied wage-earners at the other was a growing middle class. In the words of a Boston printer and publisher, the "middling class" was made up of "the farmers, the mechanics, the manufacturers, the traders, who carry on professionally the ordinary operations of buying, selling, and exchanging merchandize." As cities and industry expanded, other professional groups—such as building contractors, lawyers, and surveyors—found their services in great demand and financially profitable. Middle-class business owners, employees, and professionals were most numerous in the Northeast, where they numbered about 30 percent of the population in 1840, but they could be found in every American town and village, even in the agrarian South.

The size, wealth, and cultural influence of the middle class continued to grow, fueled by a dramatic rise in prosperity. Between 1830 and the Panic of 1857, the per capita income of Americans increased by about 2.5 percent a year, a remarkable rate that the United States has never since matched. This surge in income, along with the availability of inexpensive mass-produced goods, facilitated the creation of a distinct middle-class culture, especially in urban areas of the Northeast. Middle-class husbands had sufficient earnings so that their wives did not have to seek paid work. Typically these men saved about 15 percent of their income, depositing it in banks and then using it to buy a well-built house in a "respectable part of town." They purchased handsome clothes for themselves and their families and drove about town in smart carriages. Their wives and daughters were literate and accomplished, buying books and pianos as well as commodious furniture for their front parlors. And they filled their residences with the products of industrial technology: furnaces that heated water for bathing and for radiators that warmed entire rooms; stoves with ovens, including broilers and movable grates; treadle-operated sewing machines; and iceboxes, which ice-company wagons filled daily, to preserve perishable food.

If material comfort was one distinguishing mark of the middle class, moral and mental discipline was another. Seeking to pass on their status to their children, successful parents usually provided them with a high school education (in an era when most white children received only five years of schooling). Ambitious parents were equally concerned with their children's character and stressed discipline, morality, and hard work. Puritans and other American Protestants had long believed that work in an earthly "calling" was a duty people owed to God. Now the business elite and the middle class gave this idea a secular twist: they celebrated work as socially beneficial, the key to a higher standard of living for the nation and social mobility for the individual.

Benjamin Franklin gave classical expression to the secular work ethic in his *Autobiography,* which was published in full in 1818 and immediately found a huge audience. Heeding Franklin's suggestion that an industrious man would become a rich one, tens of thousands of young American men worked hard, saved their money, adopted temperate habits, and practiced honesty in their business dealings. Countless magazines, children's books, self-help manuals, and novels taught the same lessons. The ideal of the "self-made man" became a central theme of American popular culture. Just as a rural-producer ethic had united the social ranks in

Middle-Class Family Life, 1836

The family of Azariah Caverly boasted many of the amenities of middle-class life—handsome clothes, finely decorated furniture, and a striking floor covering. Revealing the social conventions of the time, the husband and his son hold a newspaper and a square, symbolizing the worlds of commerce and industry, while the wife and her daughter are pictured next to a Bible, indicating their domestic and moral vocation. (New York State Historical Society, Cooperstown, New York. Photo: Richard Walker)

pre-1800 America, this new goal of personal achievement and social mobility tied together the upper and middle classes of the new industrializing society.

THE NEW URBAN POOR

As thoughtful members of the business elite surveyed the emerging social landscape, they suggested that a yeomanlike society made up of independent families no longer seemed possible or even advisable. "Entire independence ought not to be wished for," Ithamar A. Beard, the paymaster of the Hamilton Manufacturing Company, told a mechanics' association in 1827. "In large manufacturing towns, many more must fill subordinate stations and must be under the immediate direction and control of a master or superintendent, than in the farming towns."

Beard had a point. By 1840 as many as half the nation's free workers were laboring for others rather than for themselves. The bottom 10 percent of this wage-earning labor force consisted of casual workers—those hired on a short-term basis for the most arduous jobs. Poor women washed clothes, while their husbands and sons carried lumber and bricks for construction projects, loaded ships and wagons, and dug out dirt and stones to build canals. Most casual laborers owned little property except the clothes they wore. During business depressions they bore the brunt of unemployment, and even in the best of times their jobs were unpredictable, seasonal, and dangerous.

Other laborers had greater security of employment, but few were prospering. In Massachusetts in 1825 the daily wage of an unskilled worker was about two-thirds that of a mechanic; two decades later it was less than half as much. The 18,000 women who made men's clothing in New York City in the 1850s were even worse off, averaging less than $80 a year. These meager wages paid for food and rent and not much more, so many wage-earners were unable to take advantage of the rapidly falling prices of manufactured goods. Only the most fortunate working families could afford to educate their children, pay the fees required for an apprenticeship, or accumulate small dowries so that their daughters could marry men with better prospects. Most families sent their children out to work, and the death of one of the parents often threw the survivors into dire poverty. As a charity worker noted, "What can a bereaved widow do, with 5 or 6 little children, destitute of every means of support but what her own hands can furnish (which in a general way does not amount to more than 25 cents a day)."

By the 1830s most urban factory workers and unskilled laborers resided in well-defined neighborhoods. Single men and women lived in large, crowded boarding-houses, while families inhabited tiny apartments carved out of the living quarters, basements, and attics of small houses. As urban populations soared, developers squeezed a number of buildings, interspersed with outhouses and connected by foul-smelling courtyards, onto a single lot.

Living in such distressing conditions, many wage-earners turned to the dubious solace of alcohol. Alcohol had long been an integral part of American life; beer and rum had lubricated ceremonies, work breaks, barn-raisings, and games. But during the 1820s urban wage-earners led Americans to new heights of alcohol consumption. Aiding them were western farmers, who distilled corn and rye into gin and whiskey as a low-cost way to get their grain to market. By 1830 the per capita consumption of liquor had risen to more than 5 gallons a year, over three times present-day levels.

Drinking patterns changed as well. Workers in many craft unions "swore off" liquor, convinced that it would undermine their skilled work as well as their health and finances. But other workers began to drink on the job—and not just during the traditional 11 A.M. and 4 P.M. "refreshers." Journeymen used apprentices to smuggle whiskey into shops, and then, as one baker recalled, "One man was stationed at the window to watch, while the rest drank." Grogshops and tippling houses appeared on almost every block in working-class districts. The saloons became focal points for crimes, including assault and vandalism, and urban disorder. Fueled by unrestrained drinking, a fistfight among young men one night could turn into a brawl the second night and a full-scale riot the third. The urban police forces, consisting of low-paid watchmen and untrained constables, were unable to contain the lawlessness.

THE BENEVOLENT EMPIRE

The disorder and lawlessness among urban wage-earners sparked concern among well-to-do Americans. Inspired by the religious ideal of benevolence—doing good for the less fortunate—they created a number of organizations that historians refer to collectively as the "Benevolent Empire." During the 1820s Congregational and Presbyterian ministers united with like-minded merchants and their wives to launch a program of social reform and regulation. Their purpose, announced Presbyterian minister Lyman Beecher of Boston, was to restore "the moral government of God." The reformers introduced new forms of moral discipline into their own lives and tried to infuse them into the lives of working people. They would regulate popular behavior—by persuasion if possible, by law if necessary.

Although the Benevolent Empire targeted age-old evils such as drunkenness, prostitution, and crime, its methods were new. Instead of relying on church sermons and moral suasion by community leaders, the reformers set out to institutionalize charity and combat evil in a systematic fashion. They established large-scale organizations—the Prison Discipline Society and the American Society for the Promotion of Temperance, among many others. Each had a managing staff, a network of volunteers and chapters, and a newspaper.

Together, these groups set out to improve society. First they encouraged people to lead well-disciplined lives, campaigning for temperance in drinking habits and an end to prostitution. Beyond that they persuaded local governments to ban carnivals of drink and dancing, such as the Negro Election Day festivities in New England, which had been enjoyed by whites as well as blacks. Second, they created new institutions to control people who were threats to society and to assist those who were unable to handle their own affairs. Reformers provided homes of refuge for the abandoned children of the poor, removed the insane from isolation in attics and cellars and placed them in newly built asylums, and campaigned for an end to corporal punishment for criminals and for their rehabilitation through moral training in penitentiaries.

Women played an increasingly active role in the Benevolent Empire. Since the 1790s upper-class women had sponsored a number of charitable organizations, such as the Society for the Relief of Poor Widows with Small Children, founded in New York by Isabella Graham, a devout Presbyterian widow. By the 1820s Graham's society was assisting hundreds of widows and their children in New York City. Her daughter, Joanna Bethune, set up other charitable institutions, including the Orphan Asylum Society and the Society for the Promotion of Industry, which found hundreds of poor women jobs as spinners and seamstresses.

Some reformers came to believe that one of the greatest threats to the "moral government of God" was the decline of the traditional sabbath. As the pace of commercial activity accelerated after 1820, merchants and shippers began to conduct business on Sunday, since they did not want their goods and equipment to lie idle one day in every seven. To restore traditional values, in 1828 Lyman Beecher and other ministers formed the General Union for Promoting the Observance of the Christian Sabbath. General Union chapters sprang up—usually with women's auxiliaries—from Maine to the Ohio Valley. Seeking a symbolic issue to rally Christians to their cause, the General Union focused on a law Congress had enacted in 1810 allowing mail to be transported—though not delivered—on Sunday. To secure its repeal the Union adopted the tactics of a political party, organizing rallies and circulating petitions. Its members also boycotted shipping companies that did business on the sabbath and campaigned for municipal laws forbidding games and festivals on the Lord's day.

Not everyone agreed with the program of the Benevolent Empire. Men who labored twelve or fourteen hours a day for six days a week refused to spend their one day of leisure in meditation and prayer. Shipping company managers demanded that the Erie Canal provide lockkeepers on Sundays and joined those Americans who argued that using boycotts and laws to enforce morality was "contrary to the free spirit of our institutions." And when the evangelical reformers proposed to teach Christianity to slaves, many white southerners were outraged. Such popular resistance or indifference limited the success of the Benevolent Empire. A different kind of message was required if religious reformers were to do more than preach to the already converted and discipline the already disciplined.

REVIVALISM AND REFORM

It was the Presbyterian minister Charles Grandison Finney who brought just such a message to Americans. Finney was not part of the traditional religious elite. Born into a poor farmer family in Connecticut, he hoped to join the new middle class as a lawyer. But in 1823 Finney underwent an intense conversion experience and decided to become a minister. Beginning in towns along the Erie Canal the young minister conducted emotional revival meetings that stressed conversion rather than instruction; what counted for Finney was the will to be saved. He maintained that God would welcome any sinner who submitted to the Holy Spirit. Finney's ministry drew on—and greatly accelerated—the Second Great Awakening, the wave of Protestant revivalism that had begun after the Revolution (see Chapter 9).

Finney's message that "God has made man a moral free agent" able to *choose* salvation was particularly attractive to members of the new middle class, who had already chosen to improve their material lives. But he became famous for converting those at the ends of the social spectrum: the haughty rich, who had placed themselves above God, and the abject poor, who seemed lost to drink, sloth, and misbehavior. His goal was to humble the pride of the rich and relieve the shame of the poor by celebrating their common fellowship in Christ and identifying them spiritually with earnest, pious middle-class respectability.

Finney's most spectacular triumph came in 1830, when he moved his revivals from small towns to Rochester, New York, a major Erie Canal city. For six months he preached every day and added a new tactic—group prayer meetings in family homes—in which women played an active role. Finney's wife, Lydia, and other pious middle-class women carried the message to the wives of the unconverted, often while their disapproving husbands were at work. Soon, one convert reported, "You could not go upon the street and hear any conversation, except upon religion."

Finney won over the influential merchants and manufacturers of Rochester, who pledged to reform their lives and those of their workers. They would attend church, join the "Cold Water" movement by giving up intoxicating beverages, and work steady hours. To encourage their employees to follow suit, wealthy businessmen founded a new Free Presbyterian Church—"free" because members did not have to pay for pew space. Other evangelical Protestants founded two similar churches to serve canal laborers, transients, and the settled poor. To reinforce the work of the churches, Rochester's business elite established a savings bank to encourage thrift, Sunday schools for poor children, and the Female Charitable Society to provide relief for the families of the unemployed.

Revivalists in cities and towns from New England to the Midwest duplicated the success of the Protestant crusade in Rochester. Dozens of younger ministers—Baptist and Methodist as well as Congregationalist and Presbyterian—adopted Finney's evangelical message and techniques. In New York City, where Finney established himself after leaving Rochester, the wealthy silk merchants Arthur and Lewis Tappan founded a magazine, *The Christian Evangelist,* that promoted his ideas across the country. The success of the revival "has been so general and thorough," concluded a General Assembly of Presbyterians, "that the whole customs of society have changed."

The temperance movement proved to be the most effective arena for national evangelical reform. In 1832 evangelicals gained control of the American Temperance Society; within a few years it had grown to 2,000 chapters with more than 200,000 members. The society adapted the methods that had worked so well in the revivals—group confession and prayer, a focus on the family and the spiritual role of women, and sudden, emotional conversion—and took them into virtually every town in the North and rural hamlet in the South. On one day in New York City in 1841, 4,000 people took the temperance "pledge" (see American Voices, "The Demon Rum"). The average annual consumption of spirits fell from about 5 gallons per person in 1830 to about 2 gallons in 1845.

Evangelical reformers reinforced the traditional moral foundations of the American work ethic. Laziness and drinking could not be cured by Benjamin Franklin's patient methods of self-discipline, they argued. Instead, people had to experience the profound change of heart achieved only in religious conversion. Then even the poorest family could look forward to a prosperous new life. Through such

The Demon Rum

JOHN GOUGH

J ohn Gough (1817–1886) was twelve years old when his impoverished English parents sent him to America, where he found work as a bookbinder in New York City—and eventually turned to drink. In 1842, at age twenty-five, Gough converted to temperance. For the next four decades he used his eloquence as a lecturer to command high fees and persuade thousands to join the temperance movement.

Will it be believed that I again sought refuge in rum? Yet so it was. Scarcely had I recovered from the fright, than I sent out, procured a pint of rum, and drank it all in less than an hour. And now came upon me many terrible sensations. Cramps attacked me in my limbs, which racked me with agony; and my temples throbbed as if they would burst. . . . Then came on the drunkard's remorseless torturer—delirium tremens, in all its terrors, attacked me. For three days I endured more agony than pen could describe. . . . I was at one time surrounded by millions of monstrous spiders, that crawled slowly over every limb, whilst the beaded drops of perspiration would start to my brow, and my limbs would shiver until the bed rattled. . . . I was falling—falling swiftly as an arrow—far down into some terrible abyss. . . .

By the mercy of God, I survived this awful seizure; and when I rose, a weak, broken-down man, and surveyed my ghastly features in the glass, I thought of my mother, and asked myself how I had obeyed the instructions received from her lips. . . . Oh! how keen were my rebukes; and, in the excitement of the moment, I resolved to lead a better life, and abstain from the accursed cup.

For about a month, terrified by what I had suffered, I adhered to my resolution; then my wife came home, and, in my joy at her return, I flung my good resolutions to the wind, and, foolishly fancying that I could now restrain my appetite . . . I took a glass of brandy. That glass aroused the slumbering demon, who would not be satisfied by so tiny a libation. . . . The night of my wife's return, I went to bed intoxicated.

SOURCE: David Brion Davis, ed., *Antebellum American Culture: An Interpretive Anthology* (Lexington, MA: Heath, 1979), pp. 402–03.

means evangelical Protestantism reinforced the sense of common identity between the business elite and the middle class and implanted a commitment to individual enterprise and moral discipline among many wage-earners. Religion and the ideology of social mobility served as powerful cement, holding society together in the face of the massive changes brought by the spread of industrial enterprise and the market economy.

IMMIGRATION AND CULTURAL CONFLICT

Between 1840 and 1860 about 2 million Irish immigrants, 1.5 million Germans, and 750,000 Britons poured into the United States, placing new strains on the American social order. Most immigrants avoided the South because they opposed slavery, shunned blacks, or feared competition from enslaved workers. Many German migrants moved to states in the Midwest such as Wisconsin, Iowa, and Missouri, where they made up a majority of the settlers in many areas, while other Germans and most of the Irish settled in the Northeast, where by 1860 they accounted for nearly one-third of white adults.

The most prosperous immigrants were the British, many of whom were professionals, propertied farmers, and skilled workers. Likewise, the majority of German immigrants came from farming and artisan families and could afford to buy land in America. The poorest migrants were peasants and laborers from Ireland, who fled from a famine caused by severe overpopulation and devastating blight on the potato crop. Arriving in dire poverty Irish peasants found new homes in the cities of New England and New York, taking low-skilled, low-paying jobs as laborers in factories and on construction projects and as servants in private residences. Many Irish immigrants lived in crowded tenements with primitive sanitation systems and were the first to die when epidemics swept through American cities. In the summer of 1849 a cholera epidemic took the lives of thousands in St. Louis and New York, mostly poor immigrants.

In times of hardship and sorrow immigrants turned to their churches. Many Germans and virtually all the Irish were devout Catholics, and they fueled the growth of the Catholic Church. In the 1840s there were 16 Catholic dioceses and 700 churches in the United States, and the number increased to 45 dioceses and 3,000 churches by 1860. Under the guidance of their priests and bishops the Irish built an impressive network of institutions: charitable societies, orphanages, militia companies, parochial schools, and political organizations that helped them maintain their cultural identity.

When the first Irish immigrants arrived in the 1830s, they were greeted by a rash of anti-Catholic publications. One of the most militant critics of Catholicism was Samuel F. B. Morse (who would later make the first commercial adaptation of the telegraph). In 1834 Morse published *Foreign Conspiracy against the Liberties of the United States,* which warned of a Catholic threat to American republican institutions. Morse believed that Catholic immigrants would obey the dictates of Pope Pius IX, who had condemned republicanism as a false political ideology based on the sovereignty of the people rather than the sovereignty of God. Republican-minded Protestants of many denominations shared Morse's fears, and *Foreign Conspiracy* became their textbook.

The social tensions stemming from industrialization intensified anti-Catholic sentiment. Unemployed Protestant mechanics and factory workers joined mobs that attacked Catholics; other Protestants organized Native American Clubs, which called for limits on immigration, the restriction of public office to native-born citizens, and the exclusive use of the Protestant version of the Bible in public schools. Many reformers supported the anti-Catholic movement for reasons of public policy—to prevent the diversion of tax resources to Catholic schools and to oppose alcoholic abuse by many Irish men.

In almost every large northeastern city religious and cultural conflicts led in violence. In 1834 in Charlestown, Massachusetts, a quarrel between Catholic laborers repairing a convent owned by the Ursuline order of nuns and Protestant workers in a neighboring brickyard turned into a full-scale riot and the burning of the convent. In Philadelphia the violence peaked in 1844 when the Catholic bishop persuaded public school officials to use the Catholic as well as the Protestant ver-

An Anti-Catholic Riot

When riots against Irish Catholics broke out in Philadelphia in 1844, the governor of Pennsylvania called out the militia to protect Catholic churches and residential neighborhoods. In the foreground two Protestant rioters, depicted by the artist as well-dressed gentlemen, attack an Irish family with sticks, while in the background the militia exchanges musket fire with other members of the mob. (Library Company of Philadelphia)

TIMELINE

1790 Samuel Slater opens a spinning mill in Providence, Rhode Island.	**1824** *Gibbons v. Ogden* promotes interstate trade.
1807 Robert Fulton launches the *Clermont*, the first American steamboat.	**1830s** Growth of commercial cities Labor movement gains strength Class-segregated cities Expansion of temperance movement Charles Grandison Finney leads revivals.
1814 Boston Manufacturing Company opens a cotton mill in Waltham, Massachusetts.	
1817 Erie Canal begun; completed in 1825	
1818 Benjamin Franklin's *Autobiography* published.	**1837** John Deere invents the steel plow. Panic of 1837; seven-year recession begins.
1820 Minimum price of federal land reduced to $1.25 per acre	**1840s–1850s** Irish and German immigration Expansion of railroads Rise of machine tool industry
1820s New England women become textile operatives. Building workers seek a ten-hour day. Rise of the Benevolent Empire	

sion of the Bible. Anti-Irish rioting incited by the city's Native American Clubs lasted for two months and escalated into open warfare between Protestants and the Pennsylvania militia.

Thus, even as economic revolution brought prosperity to many Americans, it divided the society along the lines of class and, by encouraging the influx of immigrants, created new ethnic and religious tensions. Differences of class and culture now split the North in much the same way that race and class had long divided the South. Yet overall the majority of white Americans shared a common commitment to a dynamic economic system based on private property and a vibrant political culture of democratic republicanism.

For Further Exploration

Stuart Weems Bruchey, *Enterprise: The Dynamic Economy of a Free People* (1990), offers a panoramic history of America's economy and explains its legal and political context. Another broad study is Charles C. Sellers, *The Market Revolution: Jacksonian America, 1815–1846* (1991), which focuses on social and cultural change and underlines the tensions between market capitalism and democratic politics. David Freeman Hawke, *Nuts and Bolts of the Past: A History of American Technology, 1776–1860* (1988), offers an entertaining account of technical progress and the often eccentric inventors who made it possible.

Stephen Aron, *How the West Was Lost: The Transformation of Kentucky from Daniel Boone to Henry Clay* (1996), explores the drama of economic and political conflict in the trans-Appalachian West, while Peter Way, *Common Labor: Workers and the Digging of North American Canals, 1780–1860* (1993), describes the deprivation and anger experienced by the men who dug the western canals. The appearance of a new urban society forms the background of Stuart M. Blumin's study of *The Emergence of the Middle Class: Social Experience in the American City, 1760–1900* (1989). In *Home and Work: Housework, Wages and the Ideology of Labor in the Early Republic* (1990), Jeanne Boydston takes a critical look at the impact of the market revolution and urban life on women's lives. W. J. Rorabaugh, *The Alcoholic Republic, an American Tradition* (1979), describes a society awash in liquor and the efforts of the temperance reformers to do something about it.

For the settlement of the Great Lakes region, log on to "Pioneering the Upper Midwest: Books from Michigan, Minnesota, and Wisconsin, 1820–1910" at <http://memory.loc.gov/ammem/umhtml/umhome.html>, for the full text of first-person accounts, biographies, and promotional literature from the collections of the Library of Congress. An excellent tool for tracking social changes is the United States Historical Census Data Browser <http://fisher.lib.virginia.edu/census>, which has mined the censuses (especially the rich returns for 1850 and 1860) for information on race, slavery, immigration, religion, and other topics.

Chapter 11

A DEMOCRATIC REVOLUTION
1820–1844

A Representative Democracy Is The Ordinance Of God.
—Petition for a new Virginia Constitution, 1815

If Americans believed their political institutions were ordained by God, visiting Europeans thought them the work of the Devil. "The gentlemen spit, talk of elections and the price of produce, and spit again," Mrs. Frances Trollope reported in *The Domestic Manners of the Americans* (1832). In her view American politics was the sport of party hacks who reeked of "whiskey and onions." Other European visitors used more refined language but they found little to praise. Harriet Martineau was "deeply disgusted" by the "prostitution of moral sentiment, the claptrap of praise and pathos" uttered by a leading Massachusetts politician, while Basil Hall could only shake his head in astonishment at the shallow arguments, the "conclusions in which nothing was concluded," that were advanced by the inept "farmers, shopkeepers, and country lawyers" who sat in the New York assembly.

The verdict was unanimous and negative. As the French aristocrat Alexis de Tocqueville put it in *Democracy in America* (1835): "the most able men in the United States are very rarely placed at the head of affairs," a result he ascribed to the character of democracy itself. Ordinary citizens were jealous of their intellectual superiors and so refused to elect them to office; moreover, most voters had little time to consider important policy issues and so they "assent to the clamor of a mountebank [charlatan] who knows the secret of stimulating [their] tastes."

The Europeans were witnesses to the unfolding of a Democratic Revolution in the United States. In the early years of the nation the slogan had been *republicanism,* rule by property owning "men of TALENTS and VIRTUE." By the 1820s and 1830s the watchword was becoming *democracy,* power exercised by party politicians elected by the people as a whole. "That the majority should govern was a fundamental maxim in all free governments," declared Martin Van Buren, the most talented of the new breed of middle-class professional politicians that had taken over the halls of government. The new party politicians were often crude and usually self-interested, but by uniting ordinary Americans in "election fever," they held together an increasingly fragmented social order.

The Rise of Popular Politics, 1820–1829

Expansion of the franchise was the most dramatic expression of the democratic revolution. Beginning in the late 1810s the states revised their constitutions to eliminate property qualifications, giving the franchise to nearly every farmer and wage earner. Nowhere else in the world did ordinary men have so much political power; in England, even after passage of the Reform Bill of 1832, only 600,000 out of 6 million men—a mere 10 percent—had the right to vote.

THE DECLINE OF THE NOTABLES AND THE RISE OF PARTIES

In America's traditional agricultural society wealthy notables—northern landlords, slaveowning planters, and seaport merchants—dominated the political system. As former Supreme Court Justice John Jay put it in 1810, "Those who own the country are the most fit persons to participate in the government of it." The notables managed local elections by building up an "interest": lending money to small farmers, giving business to storekeepers and artisans, and treating their workers and tenants to rum at election time. An outlay of £5 [about $20] for refreshments, according to an experienced poll watcher, "may produce about 100 votes." As Martin Van Buren, whose father was a tavern keeper, knew from personal experience, this gentry-dominated system excluded men of modest means who lacked wealth and "the aid of powerful family connections."

The first assaults on the traditional order in which ordinary people deferred to their social "betters" came in the Midwest and Southwest. As smallholding farmers and ambitious laborers settled the trans-Appalachian region, they broke free of control by the gentry; "no white man or woman will bear being called a servant," reported a traveler in Ohio. The constitutions of the new states of Indiana (1816), Illinois (1818), and Alabama (1819) prescribed a broad male franchise. Armed with the vote ordinary citizens usually elected middling men to local and state offices. A well-to-do migrant in Illinois was surprised to find that his plowman "was a colonel of militia, and a member of the legislature." Once in public office men from modest backgrounds listened to the demands of their ordinary constituents, enacting laws that restricted imprisonment for debt and kept taxes low.

To deter migration to the western states and unrest at home the elites who ran most eastern legislatures grudgingly accepted a broader franchise. Reformers in Maryland condemned property qualifications as a "tyranny" that endowed "one class of men with privileges which are denied to another," and so in 1810 the legislature extended the vote to all adult white men. By the mid-1820s only a few states—North Carolina, Virginia, Rhode Island—required the ownership of freehold property for voting. Others, such as Ohio and Louisiana, limited suffrage to men who paid taxes or served in the militia, but a majority of the states had instituted universal white manhood suffrage. Between 1818 and 1821 the eastern states of Connecticut, Massachusetts, and New York revised their entire constitutions, reapportioning legislatures on the basis of population and instituting more democratic forms of local government, such as the election (rather than the appointment) of judges and justices of the peace.

The politics of democracy was more complex and contentious than the politics of deference. Powerful entrepreneurs and speculators—notables and self-made men alike—demanded government assistance for their business enterprises and paid bribes to legislators to get it. Bankers sought charters and opposed limits on interest rates, while land speculators demanded the eviction of squatters and the building of roads and canals to enhance the value of their holdings. Other Americans turned to politics to advance religious and cultural causes. In 1828 evangelical Presbyterians in Utica, New York, campaigned for town ordinances to restrict secular activities on Sunday; in response a member of the local Universalist church attacked this effort at coercive reform and called for "Religious Liberty."

Political parties allowed the voices of such ordinary voters and interest groups to be heard. The founders of the American republic had condemned political "factions" and "parties" as antirepublican and refused to give parties a role in the new constitutional system. But as the power of notables declined, the political party emerged as the organizing force in the American system of government. The new parties were disciplined groups run by professional politicians from middle-class backgrounds, especially lawyers and journalists. To some observers the parties resembled the mechanical innovations of the Industrial Revolution, political "machines" that, like a well-designed textile loom, wove the diverse threads of social groups and economic interests into an elaborate tapestry—a coherent legislative program.

Martin Van Buren of New York was the chief architect—and advocate—of the emerging system of party government. Between 1817 and 1821 Van Buren created the first statewide political machine, the Albany Regency; a few years later he organized the first nationwide political party, the Jacksonian Democrats. Van Buren repudiated the republican principle that political parties were dangerous to the commonwealth. Indeed, he argued, the opposite was true: "All men of sense know that political parties are inseparable from free government" because they checked the government's "disposition to abuse power . . . [and] the passions, the ambition, and the usurpations of individuals."

One key to Van Buren's success as a politician was his systematic use of the *Albany Argus* and other party newspapers to promote a platform and drum up the vote. Patronage was even more important, for the awarding of state jobs gave Van Buren a greater "interest" than any landed notable—some 6,000 appointments to the legal bureaucracy of New York (judges, justices of the peace, sheriffs, deed commissioners, and coroners) carrying salaries and fees worth $1 million. Finally, Van Buren insisted on party discipline, requiring state legislators to follow the majority decisions of a party meeting, or *caucus.* On one crucial occasion, Van Buren pleaded with seventeen legislators to "magnanimously sacrifice individual preferences for the general good" and rewarded their party loyalty with patronage and a formal banquet where, an observer wrote, they were treated with "something approaching divine honors."

THE ELECTION OF 1824

The advance of political democracy disrupted the old system of national politics managed by leading notables. The aristocratic Federalist Party virtually disappeared, and the Republican Party broke up into competing factions. As the election of 1824 approached, no fewer than five candidates, all calling themselves Republicans, campaigned for the presidency. Three were veterans of President James Monroe's cabinet: Secretary of State John Quincy Adams, the son of John Adams; Secretary of War John C. Calhoun; and Secretary of the Treasury William H. Crawford. The fourth candidate was Henry Clay of Kentucky, the dynamic speaker of the House of Representatives, and the fifth was General Andrew Jackson, now a senator from Tennessee. Although a caucus of the Republicans in Congress had selected Crawford as the "official" nominee, the other candidates refused to accept that result.

Instead they introduced democracy to national politics by seeking support among ordinary voters. Thanks to democratic reforms, eighteen of the twenty-four states used popular elections (rather than a vote of the state legislature) to choose members of the electoral college. Thus, in three-quarters of the states the contest for the presidency depended directly on the votes of ordinary men.

The battle was closely fought. Thanks to his diplomatic success as secretary of state, John Quincy Adams enjoyed national recognition. Henry Clay framed his candidacy around the American System, a national program of tariffs and internal improvements to promote economic growth. Rejecting Clay's plan for an activist central government, William Crawford of Georgia promised strong support for the rights of the states, a position that enhanced his popularity in the South. Recognizing Crawford's strength in his home region, John C. Calhoun of South Carolina switched to the vice-presidential race and endorsed Andrew Jackson for the presidency.

As the hero of the Battle of New Orleans Jackson surged to prominence on the wave of nationalistic pride that flowed from the War of 1812. Born in the Carolina backcountry, Jackson had settled in Nashville, Tennessee, where he had formed ties to influential families through his marriage and his career as an attorney, cotton planter, and slaveowner. His reputation as a man of civic virtue and "plain solid republican utility" attracted many voters, and his rise from common origins fit the tenor of the new democratic age. Nominated for the presidency by the Tennessee legislature Jackson soon commanded nationwide support.

Still, Jackson's strong showing surprised most political leaders. He received 99 electoral votes; Adams, 84 votes; Crawford (having suffered a stroke during the campaign), 41; and Clay, 37 (Map 11.1). Since no candidate had received an absolute majority, the Constitution specified that the House of Representatives would choose

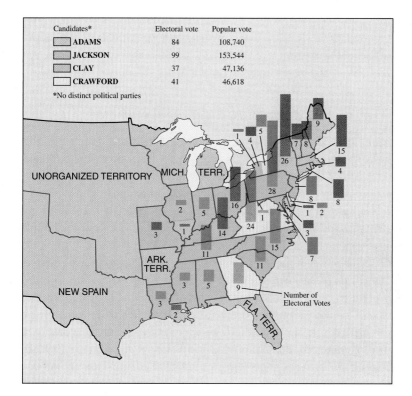

Candidates*	Electoral vote	Popular vote
ADAMS	84	108,740
JACKSON	99	153,544
CLAY	37	47,136
CRAWFORD	41	46,618

*No distinct political parties

MAP 11.1
The Election of 1824

In 1824 voting reflected regional allegiances. John Quincy Adams captured every electoral vote in New England and most of those in New York, home to many New England migrants. Henry Clay captured the western states of Ohio and Kentucky, and William Crawford garnered his votes in the South. Only Andrew Jackson claimed a national constituency, winning Pennsylvania and New Jersey in the East, Indiana and Illinois in the Midwest, and most of the South. In this last presidential election of the predemocratic era only 356,000 Americans voted, about 27 percent of the eligible electorate.

the president from among the three leading contenders. This procedure hurt Jackson, as many congressmen were horrified at the thought of a rough-hewn westerner in the White House and feared that this "military chieftain" would become a political tyrant. Personally out of the race Henry Clay used his powers as speaker to thwart Jackson's election. By the time the House met in February 1825, Clay had assembled a coalition of congressmen from New England and the Ohio Valley that voted Adams into the presidency. Adams showed his gratitude by appointing Clay secretary of state, the traditional steppingstone to the presidency.

Clay's appointment was a fatal mistake for both men. John C. Calhoun accused Adams of thwarting the popular will by using "the power and patronage of the

Executive" to select his successor. It was, he wrote, "the most dangerous stab, which the liberty of this country has yet received." Jacksonians in Congress, their numbers increased by the election results, condemned Clay for arranging this "corrupt bargain" and vowed he would never become president.

THE LAST NOTABLE PRESIDENT: JOHN QUINCY ADAMS

As president Adams called for bold national leadership. "The moral purpose of the Creator," he told Congress, was to use the president and every other public official to "improve the conditions of himself and his fellow men." To that end Adams embraced the American System of national economic development proposed by Henry Clay: (1) a protective tariff to stimulate manufacturing, (2) federally subsidized internal improvements (roads and canals) to aid commerce, and (3) a national bank to provide a uniform currency and control credit.

Adams's policies favored the business elite of the Northeast and also assisted entrepreneurs and commercial farmers in the Midwest. They won little support among southern planters, who opposed tariffs, and among smallholding farmers, who feared powerful banks. From his deathbed Thomas Jefferson condemned Adams for promoting "a single and splendid government of [a monied] aristocracy . . . riding and ruling over the plundered ploughman and beggared yeomanry." Other politicians objected on constitutional grounds. In 1817 President Madison had vetoed a Bonus Bill, proposed by Henry Clay and John C. Calhoun, that would have used the federal government's income from the Second Bank of the United States to fund internal improvement projects in the various states. Madison had argued that such projects exceeded the national government's constitutional powers, a sentiment that was widely shared. Most Americans believed that the state governments should assume the primary responsibility for economic development. A hostile Congress defeated most of Adams's ambitious proposals, approving only a few navigation improvements and a short extension of the National Road from Wheeling, Virginia, into Ohio.

The most far-reaching battle of the Adams administration came over tariffs. In 1824 a new tariff had imposed a protective tax of 35 percent on imported manufactures—iron goods and woolen and cotton cloth—and Adams and Clay wanted even higher duties to protect Pennsylvania and New England producers. When Van Buren and his Jacksonian allies took control of Congress in 1827, they also supported higher tariffs but for different reasons. By imposing tariffs on imported raw materials, such as wool and hemp, Van Buren hoped to win the support of farmers in New York, Ohio, and Kentucky for Jackson's presidential candidacy in 1828. "I fear this tariff thing," remarked Thomas Cooper of South Carolina, "by some strange mechanical contrivance . . . it will be changed into a machine for manufacturing Presidents, instead of broadcloths, and bed blankets." Disregarding southern opposition, northern Jacksonians enacted the Tariff of 1828, which raised duties on both raw materials and manufactures.

John Quincy Adams (1767–1848)

This famous daguerreotype of Adams, taken about 1843, conveys his rigid personality and high moral standards, attributes that hindered his effectiveness as president but contributed to his success as an anti-slavery congressman in the 1840s. (Metropolitan Museum of Art. Gift of I. N. Phelps Stokes, Edward S. Hawes, Mary Hawes, Marion Augusta Hawes)

The new tariff enraged the South, which gained nothing from the new legislation. As the world's cheapest producer of raw cotton, the South did not need a protective tariff, and by raising the price of British manufactures, the tariff cost southern planters about $100 million a year. Now they had to buy either higher-cost American textiles and iron goods, thus enriching northeastern businesses and workers, or highly taxed British goods, thus paying the cost of the national government. This was "little less than legalized pillage" declared an Alabama legislator, a "Tariff of Abominations."

"THE DEMOCRACY" AND THE ELECTION OF 1828

Despite the Jacksonians' support for the tariff, most southerners blamed President Adams for the new act and refused to support his bid for a second term. Adams had already offended expansionist-minded southern whites by supporting the land rights of Native Americans. In 1825 U.S. commissioners had secured a treaty from one faction of Creeks that ceded the remaining Creek lands in Georgia to the United States. When the Creek National Council repudiated the treaty as fraudulent, Adams called for new negotiations. In response Governor George M. Troup vowed to take the lands by force. Troup attacked the president as a "public enemy . . . the un-blushing ally of the savages" and persuaded Congress to extinguish Creek land titles, which forced most Creeks to leave the state.

Elsewhere in the nation Adams's primary weakness was political. He was the last notable to serve in the White House, and he acted the part: aloof, haughty, pa-ternalistic. Ignoring his waning popularity, Adams failed to use patronage to reward his supporters and to oust officeholders who opposed him. In 1828 Adams "stood" for reelection, telling supporters, "If my country wants my services, she must ask for them."

Martin Van Buren and the professional politicians handling Jackson's campaign had no reservations about "running" for office. Now a U.S. senator, Van Buren cre-ated the first national campaign organization. His goal was to recreate the old Jef-fersonian coalition, uniting northern farmers and artisans (the "plain Republicans of the North") with the southern slaveowners and planters who had voted Jefferson, Madison, and Monroe into the presidency. John C. Calhoun, Jackson's semiofficial running mate, brought his South Carolina allies into Van Buren's party, and Jack-son's close friends in Tennessee rallied voters in the Old Southwest to the cause. Di-rected by Van Buren, state politicians orchestrated a massive newspaper campaign; in New York fifty newspapers declared their support for Jackson on the same day. Local Jacksonians organized mass meetings, torchlight parades, and barbecues to excite public interest. They celebrated Jackson's frontier origins and his rise to fame without the advantages of birth, education, or political intrigue. Old Hickory—the nickname came from the toughest American hardwood tree—was a "natural" aris-tocrat, a self-made man. "Jackson for ever!" was their cry.

Initially the Jacksonians called themselves Democratic-Republicans, but as the campaign wore on, they became Democrats or "the Democracy." The name con-veyed their message. The republic, Jacksonians charged, had been corrupted by "spe-cial privilege" and corporate interests that they would root out and replace by rule of the majority—the democracy. "Equality among the people in the rights con-ferred by government," Jackson would declare, was the "great radical principle of freedom."

Jackson's message appealed to a variety of social groups. His hostility to spe-cial privileges for business corporations and to Clay's American System won sup-port among urban workers and artisans in the Northeast who felt threatened by industrialization. In the Southeast and the Midwest Old Hickory's well-known animus toward Native Americans reassured white farmers who favored Indian re-moval. On the controversial Tariff of Abominations, Jackson benefited from the fi-nancial boost it gave to Pennsylvania ironworkers and New York farmers, but he declared his personal preference for a "judicious" tariff, thus appealing for south-ern votes by suggesting that the existing rates were too high.

The Democrats' strategy of seeking votes from a wide variety of social and eco-nomic groups worked like a charm. In 1824 only about a fourth of the eligible electorate had voted; in 1828 more than half went to the polls, and they voted overwhelmingly for Jackson. The senator from Tennessee received 178 of 261 electoral votes and became the first president from a western state, indeed from any state other than Virginia and Massachusetts. The massive outpouring of popular support for Jackson frightened the northern business elite. When the new president came to Washington, warned ex-Federalist Daniel Webster, he would "bring a breeze with him. Which way it will blow, I cannot tell. . . . My fear is stronger than my hope." Watching an unruly crowd clamber over the elegant furniture in the White House to shake the hand of the newly inaugurated president, Supreme Court Justice Joseph Story lamented that "the reign of King 'Mob' seemed triumphant" (see American Voices, "Republican Majesty and Mobs").

The Jacksonian Presidency, 1829–1837

Political democracy—a broad franchise, a disciplined political party, and policies tailored to specific social groups—had carried Andrew Jackson to the presidency. Jackson used his popular mandate to enhance the authority of the president, destroy the nationalistic American System of Adams and Clay, and ordain a new ideology for the Democracy. As an Ohio supporter outlined Jackson's vision: "the Sovereignty of the People, the Rights of the States, and a Light and Simple [national] Government."

JACKSON'S AGENDA: PATRONAGE AND POLICY

To decide policy, Jackson relied primarily on an informal group of advisers, his so-called Kitchen Cabinet. Its most influential members were Francis Preston Blair of Kentucky, who edited the *Washington Globe;* Amos Kendall, also from Kentucky, who helped Jackson write his public papers; Roger B. Taney of Maryland, who became attorney general and then chief justice of the United States; and, the most influential, Secretary of State Martin Van Buren.

Following Van Buren's example in New York, Jackson used patronage to create a loyal and disciplined national party. He insisted on rotation in office: when a new administration came to power, bureaucrats would have to leave government service and return "to making a living as other people do." Dismissing the argument that forced rotation would eliminate expertise, Jackson suggested that most public duties were "so plain and simple that men of intelligence may readily qualify themselves for their performance." William L. Marcy, a New York Jacksonian, put it more bluntly: government jobs were like the spoils of war, and there was "nothing wrong in the rule that to the victor belong the spoils of the enemy." Using the spoils system Jackson dispensed government jobs to aid his friends and win support for his legislative program.

AMERICAN VOICES

Republican Majesty and Mobs

MARGARET BAYARD SMITH

*A*s Andrew Jackson ascended to the presidency in 1829, he seemed to many observers to *threaten the established political and social system. Writing to her son the Washington socialite Margaret Bayard Smith revealed a mixture of pride and anxiety about the coming of popular democracy.*

The inauguration . . . an imposing and majestic spectacle. . . . Thousands and thousands of people, without distinction of rank, collected in an immense mass around the Capitol, silent, orderly, and tranquil, with their eyes fixed on the front of the Capitol, waiting the appearance of the president. . . . The door from the Rotunda opens, preceded by the marshall surrounded by the judges of the Supreme Court, the old man [President Jackson] with his grey hair, that crown of glory, advances, bows to the people, who greet him with a shout that rends the air.

After reading his speech, the oath was administered to him by the chief justice. The marshall presented the Bible. The president took it from his hand, pressed his lips to it, laid it reverently down, then bowed again to the people—Yes, to the people in all their majesty—and had the spectacle closed here, even Europeans must have acknowledged that a free people, collected in their might, silent and tranquil, restrained solely by a moral power, without a shadow around of military force, was majesty, rising to sublimity, and far surpassing the majesty of Kings and Princes, surrounded with armies and glittering in gold. . . .

[But at the reception that followed,] what a scene did we witness!! The *Majesty of the People* had disappeared, and a rabble, a mob . . . scrambling, fighting, romping . . . [crowded around] the President, [who,] after having literally been nearly pressed to death . . . escaped to his lodgings at Gadsby's. Cut glass and bone china to the amount of several thousand dollars had been broken in the struggle to get refreshments. . . . Ladies and gentlemen only had been expected at this [reception], not the people *en masse*. . . . The . . . rabble in the president's house brought to my mind descriptions I had read of the mobs in the Tuileries and at Versailles [during the French Revolution].

SOURCE: M. B. Smith to Mrs. Kirkpatrick, 11 March 1829, in Galliard Hunt, ed., *The First Forty Years of Washington Society . . . the Family Letters of Mrs. Samuel Harrison Smith . . .* (New York, 1906), pp. 290–97.

Jackson's main priority was to destroy Clay's American System. Maintaining that the "voice of the people" called for "economy in the expenditures of the Government," Jackson rejected federal support for transportation projects. In 1830 he vetoed four internal improvement bills, including an extension of the National Road, arguing in part that because the proposed extension would lie entirely within

President Andrew Jackson, 1830

The new president came to Washington with a well-deserved reputation as an aggressive Indian fighter and dangerous military chieftain. But in this "official" portrait of 1830 he appears "presidential"—his dress and posture (and the artist's composition) creating an image of a calm and deliberate statesman. Subsequent events would show that Jackson had not lost his hard-edged personality. (Library of Congress)

Kentucky, it amounted to "an infringement of the reserved powers of states." Then Jackson turned his attention to two complex and equally politically charged parts of the American System: protective tariffs and the national bank.

THE TARIFF AND NULLIFICATION

The Tariff of 1828 had helped Jackson win the presidency, but it saddled him with a major political crisis. The fiercest opposition to the tariff was in South Carolina, where slaveowners suffered from chronic insecurity. South Carolina was the only state with an African American majority—56 percent of the population in 1830— which made it more like Jamaica or Barbados than the rest of the South. Like white planters in the West Indies South Carolina slaveowners lived in fear of a black rebellion. They also worried about laws that would abolish slavery. The British Parliament was about to end slavery in the West Indies (and did so in August 1833), and South Carolina planters worried that the U.S. government might do the same. "If the general government shall continue to stretch their powers," a southern congressman had warned as early as 1818, antislavery societies "will undoubtedly put them to try the question of emancipation." To prevent that development South Carolina politicians tried to limit the power of the central government and chose the tariff as their target.

The crisis began in 1832, when tariff advocates in Congress ignored southern warnings that they were "endangering the Union" and refused to lower the duties imposed by the Tariff of Abominations. In November leading South Carolinians called a state convention, which boldly adopted an Ordinance of Nullification. The Ordinance declared the tariffs of 1828 and 1832 null and void, forbade the collection of those duties in the state after February 1, 1833, and threatened secession if the federal government tried to collect them.

South Carolina's act of nullification rested on the constitutional arguments developed in a tract published in 1828, *The South Carolina Exposition and Protest.* Written anonymously by Vice President John C. Calhoun, the *Exposition* denied that majority rule lay at the heart of republican government. "Constitutional government and the government of a majority are utterly incompatible," Calhoun wrote. "An unchecked majority is a despotism." To devise a mechanism to check congressional majorities Calhoun turned to the arguments advanced by Jefferson and Madison in the Kentucky and Virginia resolutions of 1798. Developing a constitutional theory that states' rights advocates would use well into the twentieth century, Calhoun maintained that the U.S. Constitution had been ratified by the people in state conventions. Consequently, he argued, a state convention could determine whether or not a congressional law was unconstitutional and declare it null and void within the state's borders.

Although Jackson wanted to limit the powers of the national government, he believed it should be done through the existing constitutional system. Confronting Calhoun at a banquet, Jackson publicly repudiated his vice president's ideas by proposing a formal toast: "Our Federal Union—it must be preserved." Two years later the president's response to South Carolina's Nullification Ordinance was equally forthright. "Disunion by armed force is treason," he declared in December 1832. Appealing to patriotism Jackson asserted that nullification violated the Constitution and was "unauthorized by its spirit, inconsistent with every principle on which it is founded, and destructive of the great object for which it was formed." At Jackson's request, Congress passed a Force Bill early in 1833 authorizing him to use the army and navy to compel obedience. Simultaneously, Jackson met South Carolina's objections to the tariff by winning new legislation for a compromise Tariff Act that provided for a gradual reduction in duties. By 1842 import taxes would revert to the modest levels set in 1816, and another part of Clay's American System would be eliminated.

The compromise worked. Having won a gradual reduction in rates, the South Carolina convention rescinded its nullification of the tariff (while defiantly nullifying the now-meaningless Force Act). Jackson was satisfied. He had upheld the principle that no state could nullify a law of the United States, a position that

Abraham Lincoln would embrace in defense of the Union during the secession crisis of 1861.

THE BANK WAR

In the middle of the tariff crisis Jackson faced a major challenge from the supporters of the Second Bank of the United States. The Second Bank stood at the center of the American financial system. A privately managed entity, it had operated since 1816 under a twenty-year charter from the federal government, which owned 20 percent of its stock. Its most important role was to stabilize the nation's money supply. Most American money consisted of notes—in effect, paper money—issued by state-chartered banks. The banks promised to redeem the notes on demand with "hard" money—that is, gold or silver coins (also known as *specie*). By collecting those notes and regularly demanding specie the Second Bank kept the state banks from issuing too many notes, preventing monetary inflation and higher prices.

During the prosperous 1820s the Second Bank had maintained monetary stability and restrained expansion-minded banks in the western states, forcing some to close. This policy was welcomed by bankers and entrepreneurs in Boston, New York, and Philadelphia, whose capital was underwriting economic development, but aroused popular hostility. Most Americans did not understand the regulatory role of the Second Bank and feared its ability to force bank closures, which left ordinary citizens holding worthless paper notes. Some wealthy Americans also opposed the Second Bank and resented the financial power wielded by its president, Nicholas Biddle. New York bankers wanted the specie owned by the federal government to be deposited in their institutions rather than in the Second Bank. Likewise, expansion-minded bankers in western cities, including friends of Jackson in Nashville, wanted to escape supervision by a central bank.

But it was a political miscalculation by the supporters of the Second Bank that brought about its downfall. In 1832 Jackson's opponents in Congress, led by Henry Clay and Daniel Webster, persuaded Biddle to request an early recharter of the Bank. They had the votes to get a rechartering bill through Congress and hoped to lure Jackson into a veto that would split the Democrats just before the 1832 elections.

Jackson turned the tables on Clay and Webster. He vetoed the bank bill and became a public hero by justifying his action in a masterful public statement. His veto message blended constitutional arguments with class rhetoric and patriotic fervor. Taking Jefferson's position he declared that Congress had no constitutional authority to charter a national bank, which was "subversive of the rights of the States." Then, using the rhetoric of the American Revolution, he attacked the Second Bank as "dangerous to the liberties of the people," a nest of special privilege and monopoly power that promoted "the advancement of the few at the expense of the many . . . the farmers, mechanics, and laborers." Finally, the president evoked patriotism by pointing out that British aristocrats owned much of the Bank's stock; any such powerful institution should be "purely American," he declared.

Jackson's attack on the Bank carried him to victory in the presidential election of 1832. He jettisoned Calhoun as a running mate because of the South Carolinian's support for nullification and his refusal to welcome Peggy Eaton, a cabinet wife accused of sexual improprieties, into Washington society. As his new vice president, Jackson chose his longtime political ally, Martin Van Buren. Together Old Hickory and "Little Van" overwhelmed Henry Clay, who headed the National Republican ticket, by 219 to 49 electoral votes. Jackson's most fervent supporters were farmers and workers whose lives had been disrupted by price fluctuations or falling wages. But many Jacksonians were promoters of economic growth. State bankers welcomed the demise of the Second Bank, and thousands of middle-class Americans—lawyers, clerks, shopkeepers, artisans—cheered his attacks on privileged corporations. They wanted equal opportunity to rise in the world.

Immediately after his reelection Jackson launched a new attack on the Second Bank, which still had four years left on its charter. He appointed Roger B. Taney, a strong opponent of corporate privilege, secretary of the Treasury and had him withdraw the government's gold and silver from the Bank and deposit it in state institutions, which critics called his "pet banks." To justify this abrupt (and probably illegal) act Jackson claimed that the recent election had given him a mandate to destroy the Second Bank. It was the first time a president had claimed that victory at the polls allowed him to act independently of Congress.

The "Bank War" escalated. In March 1834 Jackson's opponents in the Senate passed a resolution written by Henry Clay censuring the president and warning of despotism: "We are in the midst of a revolution, hitherto bloodless, but rapidly descending towards a total change of the pure republican character of the Government, and the concentration of all power in the hands of one man." But Jackson and Taney continued to oppose the Second Bank, and in 1836 it became a state-chartered bank in Pennsylvania, still a wealthy institution but one without public responsibilities.

Jackson had destroyed both national banking—the creation of Alexander Hamilton—and the American System of protective tariffs and internal improvements favored by John Quincy Adams and Henry Clay. The result was a profound change in the policies and powers of the national government. "All is gone," observed a Washington newspaper correspondent. "All is gone, which the General Government was instituted to create and preserve."

Jackson's legacy as chief executive, like that of every great president, was complex and rich. By destroying the American System, he disrupted the movement toward stronger central direction of American life and reinvigorated the Jeffersonian tradition of limited, frugal government. Having redefined the character of the Union, he firmly defended it during the nullification crisis, threatening the use of military force to uphold laws enacted by the national legislature. Finally, Jackson greatly expanded the authority of the nation's chief executive, using the rhetoric of popular sovereignty to declare that "the President is the direct representative of the American people."

INDIAN REMOVAL

The status of the Native American peoples was as difficult a political issue as the tariff and the Bank, and it also raised issues of federal versus state power. In the late 1820s white voices throughout the western states and territories called for the re-settlement of Indians to the west of the Mississippi River. Many eastern whites, including those sympathetic to the Native American peoples, also favored removal; in their view resettlement would preserve traditional cultures of the Indians and protect them from direct competition with whites.

Jackson endorsed Indian removal in his first inaugural address in 1829 and quickly began to implement it. The Old Southwest was the home of the so-called Five Civilized Tribes: the Cherokees and Creeks in Georgia, Tennessee, and Alabama; the Chickasaws and Choctaws in Mississippi and Alabama; and the Seminoles in Florida. During the War of 1812 Jackson's expeditions had forced the Creeks to re-linquish millions of acres. But Indian peoples still controlled vast tracts of land, and some of them had adopted European institutions and values. By the 1820s the mixed-blood Cherokees had created a centralized political system, a thriving agricultural economy, and a wealthy slaveowning class of cotton planters. Both the mixed-blood Christians and the full-blood traditionalists were determined to retain their ancestral lands. In 1827 the Cherokee adopted a constitution and pro-claimed themselves a separate nation within the United States.

The Cherokees' preferences carried no weight with the Georgia legislature, which in 1802 had given up land claims in the West in return for a federal promise to extinguish Indian land holdings in the state. It declared that the Cherokees were merely tenants on state-owned land. Nor did the Cherokees' claims impress Jackson, who had been a committed Indian fighter (and alleged Indian hater; see Chapter 8). On becoming president he threw his support to Georgia, withdrawing the federal troops that had protected Indian enclaves there and in Alabama and Mississippi; the states, he argued, were sovereign within their borders.

Jackson then pushed through Congress the Indian Removal Act of 1830, which provided territory in present-day Oklahoma and Kansas to Native Americans who would give up their ancestral holdings. To persuade Indians to move to the new lands, government officials promised them that they "can live upon it, they and all their children, as long as grass grows and water runs." When Chief Black Hawk and his Sauk and Fox followers refused to move from rich farmland along the Missis-sippi River in western Illinois, in 1832 Jackson sent troops to expel them (see Amer-ican Voices, "A Sacred Reverence for Our Lands"). Rejecting Black Hawk's offer to surrender, the American army pursued him into the Wisconsin Territory and, in the brutal eight-hour-long Bad Axe Massacre, killed 850 of Black Hawk's 1,000 warriors. Over the next five years diplomatic pressure and military power forced

AMERICAN VOICES

A Sacred Reverence for Our Lands

BLACK HAWK

*B*lack Hawk (1767–1838), or Makataimeshekiakiak, was a chief of the Sauk and Fox. In 1833 he dictated his life story to a government interpreter, and a young newspaper editor published it. Here Black Hawk describes the coming of white settlers to his village, near present-day Rock Island, Illinois, and his decision to resist removal to lands west of the Mississippi River.

We had about eight hundred acres in cultivation. The land around our village . . . was covered with bluegrass, which made excellent pasture for our horses. . . . The rapids of Rock river furnished us with an abundance of excellent fish, and the land, being good, never failed to produce good crops of corn, beans, pumpkins, and squashes. We always had plenty—our children never cried with hunger, nor our people were never in want. Here our village had stood for more than a hundred years.

[In 1828] Nothing was now talked of but leaving our village. Ke-o-kuck [the principal chief] had been persuaded to consent to . . . remove to the west side of the Mississippi. . . . [I] raised the standard of opposition to Ke-o-kuck, with full determination not to leave my village. . . . I was of the opinion that the white people had plenty of land and would never take our village from us. . . .

During the [following] winter, I received information that three families of whites had arrived at our village and destroyed some of our lodges, and were making fences and dividing our corn-fields for their own use. . . . [Some weeks later] others had come, and that the greater part of our corn-fields had been enclosed. . . . The white people brought whiskey into our village, made people drunk, and cheated them out of their homes, guns, and [beaver] traps!

That fall [1829] I paid a visit to the agent, before we started to our hunting grounds. . . . He said that the land on which our village stood was now ordered to be sold to individuals; and that, when sold, *our right* to remain, by treaty, would be at an end. . . . I refused . . . to quit my village. It was here, that I was born—and here lie the bones of many friends and relatives. For this spot I felt a sacred reverence, and never could consent to leave it, without being forced therefrom.

SOURCE: David Jackson, ed., *Black Hawk, An Autobiography* (Urbana: University of Illinois Press, 1964), pp. 88–113.

seventy Indian peoples to sign treaties and move west of the Mississippi. Those agreements exchanged 100 million acres of land in the East for $68 million and 32 million acres in the West.

In the meantime the Cherokees had carried their case to the Supreme Court, claiming the status of a "foreign nation" under the U.S. Constitution. In *Cherokee*

Nation v. Georgia (1831) Chief Justice John Marshall denied their claim to national independence. Speaking for a majority of the justices Marshall declared that Indian peoples enjoyed only partial autonomy and were "domestic dependent nations." However, in *Worcester v. Georgia* (1832) Marshall sided with the Cherokees, voiding Georgia's extension of state law over them and holding that Indian nations were "distinct political communities, having territorial boundaries, within which their authority is exclusive ... [and this is] guaranteed by the United States." When Jackson heard the outcome, he reputedly responded, "John Marshall has made his decision; now let him enforce it."

Rather than protecting the Cherokees' territory, Jackson moved purposefully to take it from them. U.S. Commissioners signed a removal treaty with a minority faction and insisted that all Cherokees abide by it. By the deadline in May 1838 only 2,000 of the 17,000 Cherokees had departed. During the summer, Martin Van Buren, who had succeeded Jackson as president, ordered General Winfield Scott to enforce the treaty. Scott's army rounded up about 14,000 Cherokees and forcibly marched

Black Hawk (1767–1838)

George Catlin (1796–1872) painted many Indians, depicting them in realistic and dignified poses. His portrait of Black Hawk, rendered when the Indian leader was about sixty years old, shows a man who has endured the vicissitudes of life and was the stronger because of these experiences. To resist the Indian Removal Act Black Hawk mobilized Sauk and Fox warriors of Illinois, declaring, "It was here that I was born—and here lie the bones of many friends and relatives, I . . . could never consent to leave it." (Thomas Gilcrease Institute of American History and Art)

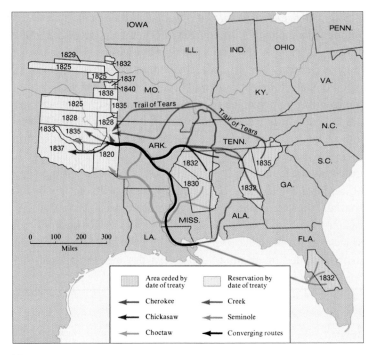

MAP 11.2
The Removal of Native Americans, 1820–1840

Between 1820 and 1840 the U.S. government concluded treaties with Native American peoples in the East, giving them designated tracts of land west of the Mississippi River. During the 1830s the Five Civilized Tribes of the Old Southwest (the Cherokee, Chickasaw, Choctaw, Creek, and Seminole) were forced to move to these reservations in the Indian Territory, the present-day state of Oklahoma; other eastern tribes were settled in Kansas.

them 1,200 miles to the new Indian Territory, an arduous journey they remembered as the Trail of Tears (Map 11.2). Along the way 3,000 Indians died of starvation and exposure. Because the Creeks, Chickasaws, and Choctaws had moved west of the Mississippi, the only remaining Indian people in the Old Southwest were the Seminoles in Florida. Aided by runaway slaves who had married into the tribe, a portion of the Seminoles fought a successful guerrilla war during the 1840s and remained in Florida. They were the exceptions. The national government had asserted its control over most eastern Indian peoples and forced their removal to the West.

THE JACKSONIAN IMPACT

Jacksonian Democrats used their political power to infuse American institutions with their principles. Following the death in 1835 of John Marshall, Jackson appointed Roger B. Taney as chief justice of the Supreme Court. During his long tenure

(1835–1864), Taney persuaded the Court to give constitutional legitimacy to Jackson's policies of antimonopoly and states' rights. Thus in the landmark case of *Charles River Bridge Co. v. Warren Bridge Co.* (1837) Taney undermined the legal position of chartered corporations by ruling that the legislative charter held by the Charles River Bridge Company did not convey a monopoly because an exclusive right was not explicitly stated in the charter. Consequently, the Massachusetts legislature retained the power to charter a competing bridge company. As Taney put it: "While the rights of private property are sacredly guarded, we must not forget that the community also has rights." This decision qualified John Marshall's interpretation of the contract clause in *Dartmouth College v. Woodward* (1819), which had emphasized the binding nature of public charters and had limited the power of states to alter or repeal them (see Chapter 8). It also encouraged competitive enterprise, opening the way for legislatures to charter railroads that would compete with existing canal and turnpike companies.

Other decisions by the Taney Court retreated from Marshall's nationalist interpretation of the commerce clause and enhanced the regulatory role of state governments. For example, in *Mayor of New York v. Miln* (1837) the Taney Court ruled that New York State could use its "police power" to inspect the health of arriving immigrants. The Taney Court also restored to the states some of the economic powers they had exercised before 1787. In *Briscoe v. Bank of Kentucky* (1837) the Court approved the issuance of currency by a bank owned and controlled by the state of Kentucky, ruling that it did not violate the provision (in Article I, Section 10, of the U.S. Constitution) that forbade states from issuing "bills of credit."

Jacksonian Democrats in the various states mounted their own constitutional revolution. Extending the democratic upsurge of the previous decades, between 1830 and 1860 twenty states called conventions to revise their basic charters. Most states extended the vote to all white men and reapportioned their legislatures on the basis of population. The new documents also brought government "near to the people" by mandating the election, rather than appointment, of most officials, including sheriffs, justices of the peace, and judges. By inserting Jacksonian ideals into the new constitutions, the delegates changed their basic character from "republican" governments that undertook public projects to "liberal" regimes that limited the power of the state. Thus most Jacksonian-era constitutions prohibited states from granting exclusive charters to corporations or extending loans or credit guarantees to private businesses. "If there is any danger to be feared in . . . government," declared a New Jersey Democrat, "it is the danger of associated wealth, with special privileges." The new state constitutions also protected taxpayers by setting strict limits on state debts and encouraging judges to enforce them. As a New York reformer put it, "We will not trust the legislature with the power of creating indefinite mortgages on the people's property." Just as Jackson had destroyed the American System's government subsidies on the national level, so his disciples in the states undermined the "commonwealth" philosophy of using chartered corporations and state funds to promote economic development. Declaring that "the world is governed too much," Jacksonians embraced a small-government, laissez-faire out-look. The first American "populists," they attacked government-granted special privileges and celebrated the power of ordinary people to make decisions in the marketplace and the voting booth.

Class, Culture, and the Second Party System

The rise of the Democracy and Jackson's tumultuous presidency sparked the creation in the mid-1830s of a second national party—the Whigs. For the next two decades Whigs and Democrats dominated American politics, forming what historians call the Second Party System. Many evangelical Protestants became Whigs, while most Catholics and nonevangelical Protestants joined the Democrats. The two parties competed fiercely for votes, debating issues of economic policy, class power, and moral reform and offering Americans a clear choice between political programs.

THE WHIG WORLDVIEW

The Whig Party began in Congress in 1834, when opponents of Andrew Jackson banded together to protest his policies and high-handed actions. They took the name Whigs to identify themselves with the pre-Revolutionary American and British parties—also called Whigs—that had opposed the arbitrary actions of British monarchs. The congressional Whigs charged that "King Andrew I" had violated the Constitution through "executive usurpation." Led by Senators Webster of Massachusetts, Clay of Kentucky, and Calhoun of South Carolina, the Whigs gradually elaborated their political vision. Beginning in the congressional elections of 1834 they sought votes especially among evangelical Protestants and upwardly mobile middle- and working-class citizens in the North. Their goal, like that of the Federalists of the 1790s, was a political world dominated by men of ability and wealth; unlike the Federalists, the Whig elite would be chosen by talent, not birth.

The Whigs celebrated the role played by enterprising entrepreneurs and activist governments in increasing the nation's wealth. Arguing that the Industrial Revolution had increased social harmony, they welcomed the investments of "moneyed capitalists" as providing the poor with jobs, "bread, clothing and homes." Whig Congressman Edward Everett told a Fourth of July crowd in Lowell, Massachusetts, that there was a "holy alliance" among laborers, owners, and governments. Many workers agreed, especially those holding jobs in the New England textile factories and Pennsylvania iron mills that benefited from state subsidies and protective tariffs. To continue economic progress Everett and northern Whigs called for a return to the American System of Henry Clay and John Quincy Adams.

Southern Whigs had a different perspective. They condemned Jackson's "executive usurpation" and advocated economic development, but they did not share the northern Whigs' support for high tariffs and social mobility. Indeed, Calhoun argued that the northern Whig ideal of equal opportunity was contradicted by the reality of slavery and industrial wage labor. "A conflict between labor and capital" was inevitable, Calhoun argued, urging southern slaveowners and northern factory owners to unite against their common foe: the working class of enslaved blacks and propertyless whites.

Most Whig leaders rejected Calhoun's class-conscious vision. "A clear and well-defined line between capital and labor" might fit the slave South or class-ridden Europe, Daniel Webster conceded, but in the North "this distinction grows less and less definite as commerce advances." Webster focused on the growing size and affluence of the northern middle class. Indeed, in the election of 1834 the Whigs won a majority in the House of Representatives by appealing to middling groups—the prosperous farmers, small-town merchants, and skilled industrial workers in New England, New York, and the new communities along the Great Lakes. Those voters were attracted to the Whigs' ideology of individual mobility and commitment to moral reform. Many of them had previously been Anti-Masons, members of a powerful but short-lived political movement directed against the secret Order of Freemasonry. Picking up on Anti-Masonic themes—temperance, equality of opportunity, evangelical religious values—Whigs favored legal curbs on the sale of alcohol and local bylaws that preserved Sunday as a day of worship. The Whigs also won congressional seats in the Ohio and Mississippi Valleys, where farmers, bankers, and shopkeepers favored Henry Clay's policies for governmental subsidies for roads, canals, and bridges.

Support for the Whigs in the South was fragmentary and rested on the appeal of specific policies rather than agreement with the Whigs' social vision. For example, many yeomen whites in the backcountry voted Whig to break the grip over state politics held by low-country planters, most of whom were Democrats. Yet a significant minority of wealthy planters became Whigs, especially those who had investments in railroads and banks or sold their cotton to New York merchants. Finally, some states' rights Democrats in Virginia and South Carolina condemned Andrew Jackson's crusade against nullification and, so like John C. Calhoun, joined the Whigs.

In the election of 1836 the Whigs faced Martin Van Buren, the architect of the Democratic Party and Jackson's handpicked successor. Van Buren emphasized his opposition to the American System and support for "equal rights." He also promised to preserve liberty, declaring himself an "uncompromising opponent" of those Whigs who wanted to use government power to uphold the sabbath, prohibit the sale of alcoholic beverages, or abolish slavery. "The government is best which governs least" became his motto.

To oppose Van Buren the Whigs ran four regional candidates, hoping to garner enough electoral votes to throw the contest into the House of Representatives, which they controlled. The plan failed. The Whig tally—73 electoral votes collected by William Henry Harrison of Ohio, 26 by Hugh L. White of Tennessee, 14 by Daniel

Webster of New Hampshire, and 11 by W. P. Magnum of Georgia—fell far short of Van Buren's 170 votes. Still, the size of the popular vote for the four Whig candidates—49 percent of the total—showed that the party's message of economic improvement and moral uplift appealed not only to middle-class Americans but also to farmers and workers with little or no property.

LABOR POLITICS AND THE DEPRESSION OF 1837–1843

In seeking the votes of workers, Whigs had to compete with the workingmen's parties that had sprung up in fifteen states between 1827 and 1833. Rising prices and stagnant wages had lowered the standard of living of many urban artisans and wage earners, who feared what they called "the glaring inequality of society." To redress this inequality the Working Men's Party in New York City demanded the abolition of private banks, chartered monopolies, and imprisonment for debt. The Philadelphia Working Men's Party demanded higher taxes on the wealthy and in 1834 persuaded the Pennsylvania legislature to authorize free, tax-supported schools so that workers' children could advance into the ranks of the propertied classes.

The workingmen's parties embraced the ideology of artisan republicanism. Their goal was a society in which (as the radical thinker Orestes Brownson put it) there would be no dependent wage-earners and "all men will be independent proprietors, working on their own capitals, on their own farms, or in their own shops." This vision led the Working Men's Parties, like the Democratic Party, to demand equal rights and attack legislation that created chartered corporations and monopolistic banks "for the benefit of the rich and the oppression of the poor." "The only safeguard against oppression," argued William Leggett, a leading member of the New York Loco-Foco (Equal Rights) Party, "is a system of legislation which leaves to all the free exercise of their talents and industry." At first the workingmen's parties did well in urban areas, but divisions over policy and voter apathy soon took a toll. By the mid-1830s most politically active workers had joined the Democratic Party, trying to win its support for their program of opposition to protective tariffs and the taxation of the stocks and bonds owned by wealthy capitalists.

Taking advantage of the economic boom of the early 1830s, which increased the demand for skilled labor, workers formed unions to bargain for higher wages and organized General Trade Union federations in New York City and Philadelphia. Employers responded to the workers' demands by attacking the union movement. In 1836 clothing manufacturers in New York City agreed not to hire workers belonging to the Union Trade Society of Journeymen Tailors and circulated a list—a so-called *blacklist*—of its members. The employers also brought lawsuits to overturn *closed-shop* agreements that required them to hire only union members. They argued that such contracts violated the common law and legislative statutes that prohibited "conspiracies" in restraint of trade.

Judges usually agreed. In 1835 the New York Supreme Court found that a shoemaker's union in Geneva had illegally caused "an industrious man" to be "driven out of employment." "It is important to the best interests of society that the price of labor be left to regulate itself," the court declared. When a court in New York City upheld a conspiracy verdict against a tailors' union, a crowd of 27,000 people demonstrated outside city hall, and tailors circulated handbills proclaiming that the "Freemen of the North are now on a level with the slaves of the South." In 1836 popular demonstrations prompted local juries to acquit shoemakers in Hudson, New York, carpet makers in Thompsonville, Connecticut, and plasterers in Philadelphia of similar conspiracy charges. The resistance of workers and their supporters had preserved the unions from legal attack.

At this juncture the Panic of 1837 threw the American economy into disarray. The Panic began early in the year, when the Bank of England, needing to boost the British economy, sharply curtailed the flow of money and credit to the United States. For the previous decade and a half British manufacturers and investors had stimulated the American economy, providing southern planters with credit to expand cotton production and purchasing millions of dollars of canal bonds in northern states. As the British economy faltered, textile mills cut their purchases of raw cotton from the South, causing its price to collapse from 20 cents a pound to 10 cents or less. Deprived of British funds American planters, merchants, and canal corporations had to withdraw specie from domestic banks to pay their foreign loans and commercial debts.

This drain of gold and silver set off a general financial crisis. On May 8 the Dry Dock Bank of New York City closed its doors, and panicked depositors withdrew more than $2 million in coin from other city banks, forcing them to suspend all payments in specie. Within two weeks every bank in the United States had followed suit, shocking high-flying entrepreneurs and ordinary citizens and sending the economy into a steep decline. "This sudden overthrow of the commercial credit and honor of the nation" had a "stunning effect," observed Henry Fox, the British minister in Washington. "The conquest of the land by a foreign power could hardly have produced a more general sense of humiliation and grief." The crisis engulfed state governments, as tax revenues and canal tolls fell. Nine states defaulted on bonds issued to finance canal building; others declared a moratorium on debt payments, undermining the confidence of British investors and cutting the flow of capital. Bumper crops during the late 1830s drove down cotton prices even further, bringing more bankruptcies.

The American economy fell into a deep depression. By 1843 canal construction had dropped 90 percent and prices nearly 50 percent; unemployment rose, reaching almost 20 percent of the workforce in seaports and industrial centers. From his pulpit, minister Henry Ward Beecher described a land "filled with lamentation . . . its inhabitants wandering like bereaved citizens among the ruins of an earthquake, mourning for children, for houses crushed, and property buried forever."

By creating a surplus of skilled workers the depression devastated the labor movement. In 1837, 6,000 masons, carpenters, and other building-trade workers lost their jobs in New York City, depleting the membership of unions and

The Panic of 1837

Thousands of workers, including this carpenter, lost their jobs during the panic and the subsequent depression, threatening their families with disaster. "I'm so hungry," says one child, while the landlord stands at the door, eviction notice in hand. By placing portraits of Jackson and Van Buren on the wall, the artist implicitly blames them for the family's suffering and encourages workers to turn away from the Democratic Party. (Library of Congress)

destroying their bargaining power. By 1843 most local unions and all the national labor organizations had disappeared, along with their newspapers and other publications.

However, two events during the depression years improved the long-term prospects of the labor movement. One was a major legal victory. In *Commonwealth v. Hunt* (1842) a case decided by the Massachusetts Supreme Judicial Court, Chief Justice Lemuel Shaw upheld the rights of workers to form unions and enforce a closed shop. Shaw, one of the great jurists of the nineteenth century, overturned common-law precedents by making two critical rulings: (1) a union was not an inherently illegal organization, and (2) union members could legally attempt to enforce a closed shop, even by striking. Courts in other states generally accepted Shaw's opinion, but judges (who were mostly Whigs) found other methods, such as court injunctions, to restrict strikes and boycotts. Labor's second success was political. Continuing Jackson's effort to attract workers to the Democratic Party, in 1840 President Van Buren signed an executive order establishing a ten-hour day for all federal employees. Significantly, this achievement came after the unions had been defeated in the marketplace, underlining the fact that the workers' struggle—like conflicts over tariffs, banks, and internal improvements—had moved into the political arena.

"TIPPECANOE AND TYLER TOO!"

The depression had a major impact on American politics. Few people understood the complex workings of the international economy, and so many Americans blamed the Democrats for their economic woes. In particular, they derided Jackson for destroying the Second Bank and for issuing the Specie Circular of 1836, which required western settlers to use gold and silver coins to pay for land purchases. Not realizing that shipment of specie to Britain (to pay off past debts) was the main cause of the financial panic, the Whigs blamed Jackson's policies.

The public turned its anger on Van Buren, who entered office just as the panic began. Ignoring the pleas of influential bankers, the new president refused to revoke the Specie Circular or take other actions that might reverse the downturn. Holding to his philosophy of limited government Van Buren advised Congress that "the less government interferes with private pursuits the better for the general prosperity." As the depression continued, this laissez-faire outlook commanded less and less political support. Worse, Van Buren's major piece of economic legislation, the Independent Treasury Act of 1840, actually delayed recovery. The act pulled federal specie out of Jackson's "pet banks" (which had used it to back loans) and placed it in government vaults (where it did no economic good at all). Whatever its value in placing the nation's financial reserves above politics, the Independent Treasury did little to enhance Van Buren's popularity.

Determined to exploit Van Buren's weakness, in 1840 the Whigs organized their first national convention and nominated William Henry Harrison of Ohio for president and John Tyler of Virginia for vice president. A military hero of the Battle of Tippecanoe and the War of 1812, Harrison was well advanced in age (sixty-eight) and had little political experience. But the Whig leaders in Congress, Clay and Webster, did not want a strong president; they planned to have Harrison rubber-stamp their program for protective tariffs and a national bank. Party strategists such as Thurlow Weed of New York had chosen Harrison primarily because of his military record and western background, promoting him as the Whig version of Andrew Jackson. An unpretentious, amiable man, Harrison warmed to that task, telling voters that Whig policies were "the only means, under Heaven, by which a poor industrious man may become a rich man without bowing to colossal wealth."

Panic and depression stacked the political cards against Van Buren, but the contest itself turned as much on style as on substance. It became the great "log-cabin" campaign—the first occasion on which two well-organized parties competed for the loyalties of a mass electorate. One result was a new political style of festive celebrations. Whig pamphleteering, songfests, parades, and well-orchestrated mass meetings dominated the contest, drawing new voters and new social groups into the political arena. Whig speakers assailed "Martin Van Ruin" as a manipulative politician with aristocratic tastes—a devotee of fancy wines and elegant clothes, as indeed he was. With less candor they praised Harrison, actually the son of a wealthy planter who had signed the Declaration of Independence, as a self-made soldier and statesman who lived in a simple log cabin and enjoyed hard cider, a drink of the common man.

The Whigs boosted their electoral hopes by welcoming women to their festivities. Previously women had been systematically excluded not only from voting and jury duty but also from nearly every other aspect of political life, even marching in July 4 and Washington's Birthday parades. Jacksonian Democrats celebrated politics as a "manly" affair, likening women who ventured into the political arena to the ordinary run of "public" women—the prostitutes who plied their trade in the-

The Log-Cabin Campaign, 1840

Under the Second Party System politics became more responsive to the popular will as ordinary people voted for candidates who shared their values and lifestyles. The barrels of hard cider surrounding this campaign banner depict the drink of the common man (not the wines favored by Martin Van Buren), while the picture falsely portrays William Henry Harrison as a poor frontier farmer in a log cabin. (New-York Historical Society)

aters and other public places. But the Whigs recognized that women from Yankee families, a core Whig constituency, were deeply involved in religious revivalism, the temperance movement, and other benevolent activities. And so in October 1840 Daniel Webster addressed a special meeting of 1,200 Whig women, perhaps the first mass meeting of women in American politics. Noting women's benevolent efforts, Webster praised their moral perceptions as "both quicker and juster" than those of men and identified their concerns with the Whig programs for moral reform.

"This way of making politicians of their women is something new under the sun," noted one Democrat, worried that it would bring more Whig men to the polls. More than 80 percent of the eligible voters cast ballots in 1840 (up from less than 60 percent in 1832 and 1836). Heeding the Whig slogan "Tippecanoe and Tyler Too," they voted Harrison into the White House and gave the Whigs a majority in Congress.

The Whig triumph was short-lived. One month after his inauguration Harrison died of pneumonia, and the nation got "Tyler Too." Vice President John Tyler of Virginia, who became president, had joined the Whig Party primarily because he opposed Jackson's stance against nullification. On economic issues Tyler was more like a Democrat, sharing Jackson's hostility to the Second Bank and the American System. Consequently, he vetoed bills that would have raised tariffs and created a new national bank. Also like Jackson, Tyler favored the common man and the rapid settlement of the West. He approved the Preemption Act of 1841, which helped cash-poor settlers by allowing them to stake a free claim to 160 acres of federal land. By building a house and cultivating the land, they could purchase the property later at the standard price of $1.25 an acre.

The split between Tyler and the Whigs allowed the Democrats to regroup. The party vigorously recruited supporters among subsistence farmers in the North and smallholding planters in the South. It cultivated the votes of the urban working class and was particularly successful among Irish and German Catholic immigrants—whose numbers had increased rapidly during the 1830s—supporting their demands for religious and cultural freedom. Thanks to these recruits, the Democrats remained the majority party in most parts of the nation. Their program of equal rights, states' rights, and cultural liberty was more attractive than the Whig platform of economic nationalism, moral reform, and individual mobility.

The continuing struggle between Whigs and Democrats, each claiming to speak for "the people," completed the Democratic Revolution that European visitors found so troubling. The new system perpetuated many problematic practices—denying women, Indians, and most African Americans an effective voice in political life—and introduced a few more, such as the spoils system and a coarser standard of public debate. Yet the United States now boasted universal suffrage for white men as well as a highly organized system of representative government that was responsive to ordinary citizens. In their scope and significance for American life these political innovations matched the economic advances of the industrial and market revolutions.

T I M E L I N E

1810s	Revised state constitutions broaden male suffrage. Van Buren creates a disciplined party in New York.		South Carolina nullifies Tariff of 1832. Frances Trollope's *The Domestic Manners of the Americans*
1825	John Quincy Adams elected president by House and advocates Henry Clay's American System.	**1833**	Force Bill and compromise Tariff Act
		1834	Whig Party formed by Henry Clay, John C. Calhoun, and Daniel Webster
1827–1833	Working Men's Parties organized	**1835**	Roger B. Taney named chief justice of U.S. Supreme Court Alexis de Tocqueville's *Democracy in America*
1828	Tariff of Abominations Andrew Jackson elected president *The South Carolina Exposition and Protest* challenges legitimacy of national legislation.	**1837**	*Charles River Bridge Co. v. Warren Bridge Co.* weakens legal privileges of chartered corporations. Panic of 1837 begins depression of 1837–1843.
1830	Jackson vetoes extension of National Road. Indian Removal Act	**1838**	Cherokee Trail of Tears
1831	*Cherokee Nation v. Georgia* denies Cherokee claim of national independence.	**1840**	Log-cabin campaign
		1841	John Tyler succeeds William Henry Harrison as president. Preemption Act
1832	*Worcester v. Georgia* upholds political authority of Indian communities. Expulsion of Sauk and Fox; Bad Axe Massacre Jackson vetoes rechartering of Second Bank.	**1842**	*Commonwealth v. Hunt* legitimizes trade unions.

For Further Exploration

George Dangerfield, *The Era of Good Feelings* (1952), is the classic study of American politics between 1815 and 1828 and offers a fascinating, detailed panorama of the period and the administration of John Quincy Adams. Two concise and well-written surveys of the Jacksonian era are Harry L. Watson, *Liberty and Power: The Politics of Jacksonian America* (1990), which emphasizes the importance of republican ideology and the market revolution, and Daniel Feller, *The Jacksonian Promise: America, 1815–1840* (1995), which underlines the tremendous optimism of the period as well as conflicting views of the nation's destiny. In *The Idea of a Party System* (1969) Richard Hofstadter lucidly explains the traditional opposition to parties and their triumphant entry into America politics.

Robert V. Remini, *The Life of Andrew Jackson* (1988), highlights Jackson's triumphs without neglecting his shortcomings. The brutal impact of Jackson's Indian policy is brought to life in Robert J. Conley, *Mountain Windsong: A Novel of the Trail of Tears* (1995). Major L. Wilson, *The Presidency of Martin Van Buren* (1984), provides a shrewd assessment of the man and his policies. The political ideology and politics of the laboring population is the focus of Sean Wilentz, *Chants Democratic: New York City and the Rise of the American Working Class, 1788–1850* (1986).

Alexis de Tocqueville's classic, *Democracy in America* (1835), should be sampled for its insights into the character of American society and political institutions. The book is available on line accompanied by an excellent exhibit explaining Tocqueville's trip to the United States and a collection of essays complementing his study, at <http://xroads.virginia.edu/~hyper/detoc/home.html>. For a brief treatment of the life of Andrew Jackson and some of his important state papers, log on to the Revolution to Reconstruction site at the University of Groningen in the Netherlands at <http://odur.let.rug.nl/~usa/P/aj7/aj7.htm>. For material on the Cherokees, see the websites prepared by Ken Martin, a tribal member of the Cherokee Nation of Oklahoma, <http://pages.tca.net/martikw/default.html>, and by Golden Ink in North Georgia, <http://ngeorgia.com/history/findex.html>.

Chapter 12

RELIGION AND REFORM
1820–1860

A peaceable man can hardly venture to eat or drink, . . . to correct
his child or kiss his wife, without obtaining the permission . . . of
some moral or other reform society.
— ORESTES BROWNSON, 1838

"The spirit of reform is in every place," the children of legal reformer
David Dudley Field wrote in their handwritten monthly "Gazette" in 1842:

the labourer with a family says "reform the common schools"; the merchant
and the planter say, "reform the tariff"; the lawyer "reform the laws," the politician "reform the government," the abolitionist "reform the slave laws," the
moralist "reform intemperance," . . . the ladies wish their legal privileges
extended, and in short, the whole country is wanting reform.

Like many Americans the young Field children sensed that a whirlwind of political change in 1830s had transformed the way people thought about themselves as
individuals and as a society. It encouraged men and women to believe that they
could improve not just their personal lives but society as a whole. Some dedicated
themselves to societal reform. Beginning as an antislavery advocate William Lloyd
Garrison went on to embrace women's rights, pacifism, and the abolition of prisons. Such individuals, the Unitarian minister Henry W. Bellows warned, were ob-
sessed, pursuing "an object, which in its very nature is unattainable—the perpetual
improvement of the outward condition."

Many obstacles stood in the reformers' quest for a better society. The American
social order was still rigidly divided by race and gender as well as wealth and religious belief. Moreover, recent social changes imposed new burdens on some individuals even as they improved the condition of others. Thus the new industrial and
market economy imposed new forms of social control on many workers, such as
gang labor for enslaved African Americans and a strict work routine for factory
operatives. In fact the first wave of American "improvers," the benevolent reformers of the 1820s, seized on social discipline as the answer to the nation's ills, cham-

338

pioning regular church attendance, temperance, and the strict moral codes of the evangelical churches.

Then in the 1830s and 1840s a more powerful wave of reform spilled out of these conservative religious channels and washed over American society, threatening to submerge traditional values and institutions. Mostly middle-class northerners and midwesterners in origin, the new reformers propounded a bewildering assortment of radical ideals—extreme individualism, common ownership of property, the immediate emancipation of slaves, and sexual equality—and demanded action to satisfy their visions. The result was a far-reaching intellectual and cultural debate that challenged the premises of the American social order. As a fearful southerner saw it, the goal of the reformers was a world in which there would be "No-Marriage, No-Religion, No-Private Property, No-Law and No Government."

Individualism

In 1835 Alexis de Tocqueville coined the word *individualism* to describe Americans as a people who were "no longer attached to each other by any tie of caste, class, association, or family." Unlike Tocqueville, who feared the disintegration of society, the New England transcendentalist Ralph Waldo Emerson (1803–1882) celebrated this liberation of the individual from traditional social and institutional constraints. Emerson's vision of individual freedom balanced by personal responsibility influenced thousands of ordinary Americans and a generation of important artists and writers.

EMERSON AND TRANSCENDENTALISM

Emerson was the leading spokesman for transcendentalism, an intellectual movement rooted in the religious soil of New England. Its first advocates were spiritually inclined young men, often Unitarian ministers from well-to-do New England families, who questioned the constraints imposed by their Puritan heritage. For inspiration they turned to Europe, drawing on a new conception of self and society known as Romanticism. Romantic thinkers, such as the English poet Samuel Taylor Coleridge, rejected the ordered, rational world of the eighteenth-century Enlightenment. Instead they tried to capture the passionate character of the human spirit and sought deeper insights into the mysteries of existence. Drawing on ideas borrowed from the German philosopher Immanuel Kant, English romantics and Unitarian radicals believed that behind the concrete world of the senses was an ideal world. To reach this deeper reality people had to "transcend," or go beyond, the rational ways in which they normally comprehended the world. By tapping mysterious intuitive powers people could soar beyond the limits of ordinary experience and gain mystical knowledge of ultimate and eternal things.

Emerson had followed in the footsteps of his father and become a Unitarian minister, thus placing himself outside the religious mainstream. Unlike most Christians Unitarians held that God was a single being and not a trinity of Father, Son, and Holy Spirit. In 1832 Emerson moved still further from orthodox Christianity, resigning his Boston pulpit and rejecting organized religion in favor of individual moral insight. Moving to Concord, Massachusetts, he turned to writing essays and lecturing. His subject was what he called "the infinitude of the private man," the idea of the radically free individual.

The young philosopher saw people as being trapped in inherited customs and institutions. They wore the ideas of people from earlier times—the tenets of New England Calvinism, for example—as a kind of "faded masquerade" and needed to shed those values and practices. "What is a man born for but to be a Reformer, a Remaker of what man has made?" he asked. For Emerson an individual's remaking depended on the discovery of his or her own "original relation with Nature," an insight that would lead to a mystical private union with the "currents of Universal Being." The ideal setting for such a discovery was solitude under an open sky, among nature's rocks and trees.

Emerson's genius lay in his capacity to translate abstract ideas into examples that made sense to ordinary middle-class Americans. His essays and lectures conveyed the message that all nature was saturated with the presence of God—a pantheistic spiritual outlook that departed from traditional Christian doctrine and underlay his attack on organized religion. Emerson also criticized the new industrial society, predicting that a preoccupation with work, profits, and the consumption of factory-made goods would drain the nation's spiritual energy. "Things are in the saddle," Emerson wrote, "and ride mankind."

The transcendentalist message of inner change and self-realization reached hundreds of thousands of people, primarily through Emerson's writings and lectures. Public lectures had become a spectacularly successful new way of spreading information and fostering discussion among the middle classes. Beginning in 1826 the American Lyceum attempted to "promote the general diffusion of knowledge" by organizing lecture tours by all sorts of speakers—poets, preachers, scientists, reformers—and soon achieved great popularity, especially in the North and Midwest. In 1839, 137 local Lyceum groups in Massachusetts invited lecturers to their towns during the fall and winter to speak to more than 33,000 subscribers. Among the hundreds of lecturers on the Lyceum circuit, Emerson was the most popular. Between 1833 and 1860 he gave 1,500 lectures in more than 300 towns in twenty states.

Emerson's celebration of the individual who was liberated from traditional social restraints but self-disciplined and responsible, tapped currents that already ran deep in his middle-class audiences. The publication of Benjamin Franklin's *Autobiography* in 1818 had given Americans a down-to-earth model of an individual seeking "moral perfection" through self-discipline and self-improvement. Charles

***The Founder of
Transcendentalism***

As this painting of Ralph
Waldo Emerson reveals, the
young New England
philosopher was an attractive man, his face brimming
with confidence and opti-
mism. Because of his radiant
personality Emerson deeply
influenced dozens of influential writers, artists, and
scholars and enjoyed great
success as a lecturer among
the emerging middle class.

(Artist unknown, The Metropolitan
Museum of Art, Bequest of Chester
Dale, 1962 [64.97.4])

Grandison Finney's account of his conversion experience in 1823 also pointed in
Emersonian directions. Finney, the foremost business-class evangelist, pictured his
conversion as a mystical union of an individual, alone in the woods, with God. And
the great revivalist's message, like that of Emerson, affirmed the importance of
individual action. As Finney put it, "God has made man a moral free agent," thus
endowing individuals with the ability—and the responsibility—to determine their
spiritual fate.

EMERSON'S LITERARY INFLUENCE

Emerson took as one of his tasks the remaking of American literature. In an address entitled "The American Scholar" (1837) the philosopher issued a literary
declaration of independence from the "courtly muse" of old Europe. He urged
American writers to celebrate democracy and individual freedom and find

inspiration not in the doings and sayings of aristocratic courts but in the "familiar, the low . . . the milk in the pan; the ballad in the street; the news of the boat; the glance of the eye; the form and gait of the body."

A young New England intellectual, Henry David Thoreau (1817–1862), heeded Emerson's call by turning to the American environment for inspiration. In 1845, prompted by his beloved brother's death, Thoreau turned away from society and embraced self-reliance and the natural world, building a cabin at the edge of Walden Pond near Concord, Massachusetts, and living alone there for two years. In 1854 he published *Walden, Or Life in the Woods,* an account of his spiritual search for meaning beyond the artificiality of life in a "civilized" society:

> I went to the woods because I wished to live deliberately, to front only the essential facts of life, and see if I could not learn what it had to teach, and not, when I came to die, discover that I had not lived.

Although Thoreau's book had little impact outside transcendentalist circles during his lifetime, *Walden* has become an essential text of American literature and an inspiration to those who reject the dictates of society. Its most famous metaphor provides an enduring justification for independent thinking: "If a man does not keep pace with his companions, perhaps it is because he hears a different drummer." Beginning from this premise, Thoreau became an advocate for social nonconformity and a philosopher of civil disobedience.

As Thoreau sought independence and self-realization for men, Margaret Fuller (1810–1850) explored the possibilities of freedom for women. Born into a wealthy Boston family, Fuller learned to read the classic works of literature in six languages and educated her four siblings. After teaching in a girls' school she became interested in Emerson's ideas and in 1839 began a transcendental "conversation," or discussion group, for educated Boston women. Soon Fuller was editing the leading transcendentalist journal, the *Dial,* and in 1844 she published *Woman in the Nineteenth Century,* which proclaimed that a "new era" was coming in the relations between men and women.

Fuller's philosophy began with the transcendental belief that women, like men, had a mystical relationship with God that gave them identity and dignity. It followed that every woman deserved psychological and social independence—the ability "to grow, as an intellect to discern, as a soul to live freely and unimpeded." Thus, she declared, "We would have every arbitrary barrier thrown down" and "every path laid open to Woman as freely as to Man." Embracing that vision, Fuller became the literary critic of the *New York Tribune* and went to Italy to report on the Revolution of 1848. Her adventurous life brought an early death; returning to the United States at the age of forty, she drowned in a shipwreck. But Fuller's example and writings inspired a rising generation of women reformers.

Another writer who responded to Emerson's call was the poet Walt Whitman (1819–1892). Whitman said that when he first encountered Emerson, he had been "simmering, simmering." Then Emerson "brought me to a boil." Whitman had been a teacher, a journalist, an editor of the *Brooklyn Eagle* and other newspapers, and an active publicist for the Democratic Party. But it was poetry that was the "direction of his dreams." In *Leaves of Grass,* first published in 1855 and constantly revised and expanded for almost four decades afterward, he recorded his attempt to pass a number of "invisible boundaries": between solitude and community, between prose and poetry, and even between the living and the dead.

At the center of *Leaves of Grass* is the individual—the figure of the poet, "I, Walt." He begins alone: "I celebrate myself, and sing myself." But because he has what Emerson called an "original relation" with nature, Whitman claims not solitude but perfect communion with others: "For every atom belonging to me as good belongs to you." Whitman was celebrating democracy as well as himself, arguing that a poet could claim a profoundly intimate, mystical relationship with a mass audience. For Emerson, Thoreau, and Fuller the individual had a divine spark. For Whitman the individual had actually become divine.

The transcendentalists were not naive optimists. Whitman wrote about human suffering with passion, and Emerson's accounts of the exhilaration that could come in natural settings were tinged with anxiety. "I am glad," he said, "to the brink of fear." Thoreau's gloomy judgment of everyday life is well known: "The mass of men lead lives of quiet desperation." Still, such dark murmurings were muted in their work, woven into triumphant and expansive assertions that nothing was impossible for an individual who could break free from tradition, law, and other social restraints and discover an "original relation with Nature."

Emerson's writings also influenced two great novelists, Nathaniel Hawthorne and Herman Melville, who had more pessimistic visions. They addressed the opposition between individual transcendence and the legitimate requirements of social order, discipline, and responsibility. Both sounded powerful warnings that unfettered egoism could destroy individuals and those around them. Hawthorne's most brilliant exploration of the theme of excessive individualism appeared in his novel *The Scarlet Letter* (1850). The two main characters, Hester Prynne and Arthur Dimmesdale, challenge their seventeenth-century New England community in the most blatant way—by committing adultery and producing a child. The result of their assertion of individual freedom from social discipline is not liberation but degradation—condemnation by the community.

Melville explored the limits of individualism in even more extreme and tragic terms and emerged as a scathing critic of transcendentalism. He made his most powerful statement in *Moby Dick* (1851), the story of Captain Ahab's obsessive hunt for a mysterious white whale that brings death not only to Ahab but to all but one of his crew. Here the quest for spiritual meaning in nature brings death, not transcendence, to the liberated individual who lacks inner discipline and self-restraint.

Moby Dick was a commercial failure. The middle-class audience that was the primary target of American publishers was unwilling to follow Melville into the dark, dangerous realms of individualism gone mad. Readers also were unenthusiastic about Thoreau's advocacy of civil disobedience and Whitman's boundless claims for a mystical union between the man of genius and the democratic mass. What American readers emphatically preferred were the more modest examples of individualism offered by Emerson.

BROOK FARM

To escape the constraints of life in industrializing America transcendentalists and other radical reformers created ideal communities, or *utopias*. They hoped that these planned societies, which organized life in new ways, would allow members to realize their spiritual and moral potential. The most important communal experiment of the transcendentalists was Brook Farm, founded in 1841. Free from the tension and demands of an urban competitive society, its members hoped to develop their minds and souls and uplift society through inspiration. The Brook Farmers supported themselves by selling milk, vegetables, and hay for cash but organized their farming so that they could remain relatively independent of the market, with its competitive pressures and cycles of boom and bust.

The intellectual life at Brook Farm was electric. Hawthorne lived there for a time and later used the setting for *The Blithedale Romance* (1852). All the major transcendentalists, including Emerson, Thoreau, and Fuller, were residents or frequent visitors. A former member recalled that they "inspired the young with a passion for study, and the middle-aged with deference and admiration, while we all breathed the intellectual grace that pervaded the atmosphere." Music, dancing, games, plays, parties, picnics, and dramatic readings filled the leisure hours.

If Brook Farm offered intellectual fulfillment, it failed to achieve economic sustainability. At first most of its members were ministers, teachers, writers, and students who had few productive skills; to succeed it needed practical men and women. A reorganization in 1844 attracted more farmers and artisans but yielded only marginal economic gains. And these changes resulted in a more disciplined routine that, as one resident put it, suppressed "the joyous spirit of youth." After a devastating fire in 1846 the organizers disbanded and sold the farm.

After the failure of Brook Farm the transcendentalists abandoned their attempts to fashion a new system of social organization. Most accepted the brute reality of industrial society and tried to reform it, especially through the education of workers. However, the passion of the transcendentalists for individual freedom and social progress lived on in the movement to abolish slavery, which many of them joined.

Communalism

Even as Brook Farm faded, thousands of Americans joined other communal settlements during the 1840s, primarily in the rural areas of the Northeast and Midwest (see Map 12.1). Most communalists were ordinary farmers and artisans

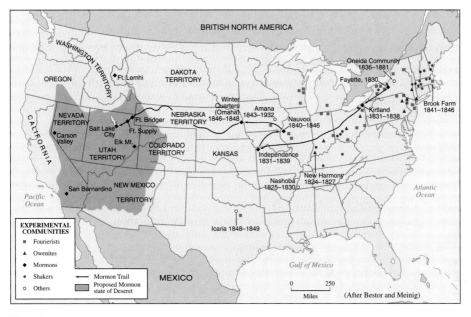

M A P 12.1
Major Communal Experiments before 1860

The United States was a vast land, so experimental communities had no difficulty finding sub-stantial tracts of land in the East as well as the Midwest. Because of their opposition to slav-ery, most communalists avoided the South. Those Mormons who in the mid-1840s followed Brigham Young into the Salt Lake Basin (in what was then Mexican territory) formed the largest and most enduring communal society.

seeking refuge and security from the seven-year economic depression that had begun with the Panic of 1837. But these rural utopias were also symbols of social protest. By organizing themselves along socialist lines with common ownership of property, or by experimenting with unconventional forms of marriage and family life, they questioned acquisitive capitalist values and traditional gender roles.

THE SHAKERS

The Shakers, whose origins dated back to the Revolutionary era, were the first suc-cessful American communal movement. In 1770 Ann Lee Stanley (Mother Ann), a young cook in Manchester, England, had a vision that she was an incarnation of Christ; four years later she led a band of eight followers to America, where they es-tablished a church near Albany, New York. Because of the ecstatic dances that be-came part of their worship, the sect became known as "Shaking Quakers" or, more simply, "Shakers." After Mother Ann's death the Shakers decided to withdraw from the evils of the world into strictly run communities of believers. They embraced the common ownership of property, accepted strict government by the church, and pledged to abstain from alcohol, tobacco, politics, and war. Shakers also eliminated marriage and made a commitment to celibacy, in accordance with Mother Ann's testimony against "the lustful gratifications of the flesh as the source and foundation of human corruption."

The Shakers believed that God was "a dual person, male and female" and that Mother Ann represented God's female element. These doctrines provided the underpinning for their attempt to eliminate distinctions between the sexes. In practice Shakers maintained a traditional division of labor between men and women except in community governance, which in both its religious and its economic aspects, was undertaken by both women and men, the Eldresses and Elders.

Beginning in 1787 Shakers founded twenty communities, mostly in New England, New York, and Ohio. Their agriculture and crafts, especially furniture making, acquired a reputation for quality that enabled most of these communities to become self-sustaining and even comfortable. Thanks to this economic success and their ideology of sexual equality, Shaker communities attracted more than 3,000 converts during the 1830s, with women outnumbering men more than two to one. Because Shakers had no children of their own, they had to rely on converts and the adoption of young orphans to replenish their numbers. As these sources dried up in the 1840s and 1850s, the communities stopped growing and eventually began to decline. By the end of the nineteenth century most Shaker communities had virtually disappeared, leaving as their material legacy a distinctive and much-imitated furniture style.

THE FOURIERIST PHALANXES

The rise of the American Fourierist movement in the 1840s was one cause of the Shakers' decline. Charles Fourier (1777–1837) was a French utopian reformer who devised an eight-stage theory of social evolution, predicting the imminent decline of individualism and capitalism. As interpreted by his idealistic American disciple Arthur Brisbane, Fourierism would complete "our great political movement of 1776" through new social institutions that would end the "menial and slavish system of Hired Labor or Labor for Wages." In the place of capitalist waged labor there would be cooperative work in groups called *phalanxes*. The members of a phalanx would be its shareholders; they would own all its property in common, including stores and a bank as well as a school and a library. Fourier and Brisbane saw the phalanx as a practical, more humane alternative to the emerging capitalist society and one that would liberate women as well as men. "In society as it is now constituted," Brisbane wrote, "Woman is subjected to unremitting and slavish domestic

A Shaker Community

Like all Shaker communities, the settlement at Poland Hill, Maine, painted by Joshua H. Bussell around 1850, was built on a regular gridlike plan. There was a large dwelling for communal living, surrounded by various workshops and farm buildings. The design of the architecture, like that of Shaker furniture, was plain and sparse.

(Collection of the United Society of Shakers, Sabbathday Lake, Maine)

duties"; in the "new Social Order . . . based upon Associated households" women's domestic labor would be shared with men.

Brisbane skillfully promoted Fourier's ideas in his influential book *The Social Destiny of Man* (1840), a regular column in Horace Greeley's *New York Tribune,* and hundreds of lectures, many of them in towns along the Erie Canal. These ideas found a receptive audience among educated farmers and craftsmen, who yearned for economic stability and communal solidarity in the wake of the Panic of 1837. In the 1840s Brisbane and his followers started nearly 100 cooperative communities, mostly in the western New York and the midwestern states of Ohio, Michigan, and Wisconsin, but almost all were unable to support themselves and quickly collapsed. Despite its failure to establish viable communities the Fourierist movement underscored both the extent of the social dislocation caused by the economic depression and the difficulty of establishing a utopian community in the absence of charismatic leaders or a compelling religious vision.

NOYES AND THE ONEIDA COMMUNITY

The radical minister John Humphrey Noyes (1811–1886) was both charismatic and deeply religious. He believed that the Fourierists had failed because their communities lacked the strong religious ethic required for sustained altruism and cooperation and pointed to the success of the Shakers, praising them as the true "pioneers of modern Socialism." Noyes was also attracted by the Shakers' marriageless society and set about creating a community that defined sexuality and gender roles in radically new ways.

Noyes was a well-to-do graduate of Dartmouth College in New Hampshire who was inspired to join the ministry by the preaching of Charles Finney. When Noyes was expelled from his Congregational Church for unorthodox doctrines, he became a leader of "perfectionism." Perfectionism was an evangelical movement that attracted thousands of followers during the 1830s, primarily among religiously minded New Englanders who had settled in New York. Perfectionists believed that the Second Coming of Christ had already occurred and that people could therefore aspire to perfection in their earthly lives, attaining complete freedom from sin. Unlike most perfectionists (who lived conventional personal lives), Noyes believed that the major barrier to achieving this ideal state was marriage, which did not exist in heaven and should not exist on earth. "Exclusiveness, jealousy, quarreling have no place at the marriage supper of the Lamb," Noyes wrote. He wanted to reform marriage to liberate individuals from sin, as had the Shakers, but his solution was dramatically different: instead of Shaker celibacy, Noyes and his followers embraced *complex marriage*—all the members of his community were married to one another.

Complex marriage was a complex doctrine designed to attain various social goals. Noyes rejected monogamy partly because he wished to free women from being regarded (as they were by custom and by common law) as the property of their husbands. To give women even more freedom he sought to limit childbirth by urging men to have intercourse without orgasm and established community nurseries for those children they did have. By freeing women from endless childbearing and childraising Noyes hoped to help them become full and equal members of the community. To symbolize their equality with men the women cut their hair short and wore pantaloons under their calf-length skirts.

In the 1830s Noyes gathered his followers in his hometown of Putney, Vermont, but local opposition to the practice of complex marriage prompted him to move the community to Oneida, New York, in 1848. By the mid-1850s more than 200 people were living at Oneida, and it became financially self-sufficient when the inventor of a highly successful steel animal trap joined the community. With the profits from the production of traps Oneida diversified into making silverware. After Noyes fled to Canada in 1879 to avoid prosecution for adultery, the community abandoned complex marriage and founded a joint-stock silver manufacturing company, the Oneida Community, Ltd., which survived well into the twentieth century.

As with the Shakers and Fourierists, the historical significance of Noyes and his followers does not lie in their numbers, which were small, or in their fine crafts. Rather, they were important because they set up alternative communities that rejected certain social and sexual divisions of the emergent capitalist industrial society.

THE MORMON EXPERIENCE

The Shakers and the Oneidians challenged marriage and family life—two of the most deeply rooted institutions in American society—but their small communities aroused little hostility. The Mormons, or the Church of Jesus Christ of Latter-Day Saints, provoked much more animosity because of their equally controversial doctrines and their success in attracting thousands of members.

Like many social movements of the era Mormonism emerged from the religious ferment among families of Puritan descent who lived along the Erie Canal. The founder of the Mormon Church was Joseph Smith (1805–1844), a vigorous, powerful individual. Born in Vermont, he moved at the age of ten with his very religious but rather poor farming and shopkeeping family to Palmyra in central New York. In a series of religious experiences that began in 1820, Smith came to believe that God had singled him out to receive a special revelation of divine truth. In 1830 he published *The Book of Mormon,* claiming he had translated it from ancient hieroglyphics on gold plates shown to him by an angel named Moroni. Seeing himself as a prophet to a sinful, excessively individualistic society, Smith affirmed traditional patriarchal authority within the family and church control over many aspects of life. Like many Protestant ministers he encouraged his followers to work hard, save their earnings, and become entrepreneurs—practices central to success in the age of capitalist markets and factories. Unlike those ministers Smith placed equal emphasis on a communal framework that would protect the Mormon "New Jerusalem" from individualism and outside threats. His goal was a church-directed society that would inspire moral perfection.

Smith struggled for years to establish a secure home for his new religion. Facing persecution from anti-Mormons, Smith and his growing congregation trekked west, eventually settling in Nauvoo, Illinois, a town they founded on the Mississippi River. By the early 1840s Nauvoo had become the largest utopian community in the United States, with 30,000 inhabitants. The rigid discipline and secrecy of the Mormons, along with their prosperity, hostility to other sects, and bloc voting in Illinois elections, fueled resentment among their neighbors. This resentment turned to overt hostility when Smith refused to abide by any Illinois law that he did not approve, asked Congress to turn Nauvoo into a federal territory, and in 1844 declared himself a candidate for president of the United States (see American Voices, "An Illinois 'Jeffersonian' Attacks the Mormons").

An Illinois "Jeffersonian" Attacks the Mormons

*T*he solidarity of the Mormon community enraged many Illinois residents, who feared the power of the nearly independent city-state at Nauvoo and the 2,000-strong "Legion" of armed men organized as a defense force by Joseph Smith. This anonymous letter, probably written by a leading anti-Mormon editor who then published it in his own newspaper, proposes that the Mormons be forcibly expelled from the state.

Mr. Editor,
     . . . It is a low pitiable contemptable kind of electioneering, that old Tom Jefferson would have been ashamed of—when a body of men acting under the garb of religion (as the Mormons themselves say they are) shall decide our elections and act together as a body politically, we might as well bid a final farewell to our liberties and the common rights of man.

     Now Sir, under all these circumstances, it is high time that every individual should come out and clearly define the position that he occupies. I too am an Anti-Mormon both in principle and in practice. . . . Mr. Editor when I speak harshly of the Mormons . . . I do not mean every individual that advocates the Mormon cause. By no means; that there are some good, law-abiding peaceable citizens belonging to the Mormon profession I verily believe . . . but I am opposed to them because of the unprincipled manner in which the leaders of that fanatical sect, set at defiance the laws of the land . . . (as was the case in Missouri) claiming to be the chosen people of God; not subject to the laws of the state in any respect whatever, and receiving revelations direct from Heaven almost daily commanding them to take the property of the older citizens of the county and confiscate it to the use of the Mormon church. . . .

     It was for the commission of such deeds . . . that finally led to their expulsion from that state, and one of the brightest pages in the history of Missouri is that, on which is written "Governor Boggs's exterminating order" directing that the lawless rabble should be driven beyond the limits of the state, or exterminated at their own option. They chose the former, [which was] a most unfortunate thing for the state of Illinois.

SOURCE: David Brion Davis, *Antebellum America: An Interpretive Anthology* (Lexington, MA: Heath, 1979), pp. 226–27.

     Moreover, Smith had received a new revelation that justified *polygamy*—a man having more than one wife at the same time. A few Mormon leaders began to practice polygamy, dividing the community from within, while Christian outrage encouraged assaults from without. In 1844 Smith was arrested and charged with treason for allegedly conspiring with foreign powers to create a Mormon colony in

Mexico. An anti-Mormon mob stormed the jail where Smith and his brother were being held in Carthage, Illinois, and murdered them.

Now led by Brigham Young the Mormon elders sought religious freedom by leaving the United States. In 1846 Young began a phased migration of more than 10,000 people across the Great Plains into Mexican territory. (Many of the migrants accepted the practice of polygamy; those who remained in the United States did not. Led by Smith's son, Joseph Smith III, they formed the Reorganized Church of Jesus Christ of Latter-Day Saints and remained in the Midwest.) Young's party eventually reached the Great Salt Lake Valley. Using communal labor and an elaborate irrigation system based on communal water rights, the Mormon pioneers transformed the region. They quickly spread planned agricultural communities along the base of the Wasatch Range in present-day Utah.

When the United States acquired the region from Mexico in 1848 (see Chapter 13), Congress rejected a Mormon petition to create a new state, Deseret, stretching all the way to Los Angeles. Instead, it set up the much smaller Utah Territory in 1850, with Young as territorial governor. In 1858 President James Buchanan removed Young from the governorship and, responding to pressure from Christian churches to eliminate polygamy, sent a small army to Salt Lake City. However, the

A Mormon Man and His Wives

Only a minority of Mormon men in Utah had more than one wife, and only a few had as many as this homesteader, who profited sexually and financially from their presence. The cabin, although cramped for such a large family, is well built, with a brick chimney and—a luxury for any pioneer home—a glass window. (Library of Congress)

"Mormon War" proved bloodless. Fearing that the forced abolition of polygamy would serve as a precedent for the ending of slavery, Buchanan withdrew the troops. The national government did not succeed in pressuring the Utah Mormons to outlaw polygamy until 1890, six years before Utah became a state.

Mormons in both Utah and the Midwest had succeeded where other social experiments and utopian communities had failed. They endorsed the private ownership of property and encouraged individualistic economic enterprise, accepting the entrepreneurial spirit of market society. But Mormon leaders resolutely used strict religious controls to create disciplined communities and patriarchal families, reaffirming values inherited from the eighteenth century. This blend of economic innovation, social conservatism, and hierarchical leadership created a prosperous church with a strong missionary impulse.

Abolitionism

In most cities and farm villages the communalists attracted far less attention than the abolitionists, whose demand for an immediate end to racial slavery led to fierce political debates, riots, and sectional conflict. Like other reform movements, abolitionism drew on the religious energy and ideas generated by the Second Great Awakening, which altered the attitude of many northern and midwestern whites toward the South's "peculiar institution." Early nineteenth-century reformers had criticized human bondage as contrary to the tenets of republicanism and liberty. Now abolitionists condemned slavery as a sin and saw it as their moral duty to end this violation of God's law.

AFRICAN COLONIZATION

By 1820 republican-minded reformers had prevented the expansion of slavery into the states of the Old Northwest and had persuaded the northern states to provide for gradual emancipation. They had also induced Congress to outlaw the importation of enslaved Africans and, in the Missouri Compromise, to prohibit slavery in most of the Louisiana Purchase. But the most difficult problem remained untouched: ending slavery in the South and the border states of Kentucky, Tennessee, and Missouri.

In 1817 the founders of the American Colonization Society, which included President James Monroe and Henry Clay, thought they had the answer. Slaveowners would gradually emancipate their slaves—some 1.5 million people in 1820—and the Society would arrange for their resettlement in Africa. The Society's leaders believed, as Clay put it, that racial bondage had placed his state of Kentucky and the other slaveholding states "in the rear of our neighbors . . . in the state of agriculture, the progress of manufactures, the advance of improvement, and the general prosperity of society."

Slavery had to go, as did the freed slaves. Emancipation without colonization, the influential Kentucky Congressman predicted, "would be followed by instantaneous collisions between the two races, which would break out into a civil war that would end in the extermination or subjugation of the one race or the other." Northerners who joined the Colonization Society had much the same outlook. They regarded the 250,000 free blacks in the northern states as "notoriously ignorant, degraded and miserable, mentally diseased, brokenspirited," as one Society report put it. Hoping to create a "white man's country," what they wanted was "African removal."

The American Colonization Society was a dismal failure. Despite appeals to wealthy individuals, churches, and state governments, it raised enough money to purchase freedom for only a few hundred slaves. Moreover, most free blacks rejected colonization, agreeing with Bishop Richard Allen of the African Methodist Episcopal Church that "this land which we have watered with our tears and our blood is now our mother country." Three thousand African Americans met in Philadelphia's Bethel Church to condemn colonization, declaring that their goal was to advance in American society using "those opportunities . . . which the Constitution and the laws allow to all." And they refused to support the only African American newspaper, *Freedom's Journal* (founded in 1827), once it endorsed colonization, causing it to collapse in 1829. Lacking significant support from either blacks or whites, the Society transported only 6,000 African Americans to Liberia, a colony it established on the west coast of Africa.

SLAVE REBELLION

Having rejected colonization, free blacks demanded an end to slavery. To build support for emancipation, African American leaders tried to "uplift" the black masses by stressing "respectability": temperance, sabbath keeping, and education. To achieve these goals they helped to create an impressive number of churches, schools, and benevolent associations. But some whites felt threatened by this quest for respectability, and in the mid-1820s led mobs against blacks in New Haven, Boston, and Pittsburgh.

Partly in response to these attacks, in 1829 David Walker published a stirring pamphlet entitled *An Appeal . . . to the Colored Citizens.* A free black from North Carolina who had moved to Boston, Walker used the pamphlet to ridicule the "colonizing trick" and the religious pretensions of bigoted whites in the North and slaveholders in the South. He justified slave rebellion, warning white Americans that the slaves would revolt if justice was delayed. "We must and shall be free. . . . And woe, woe, will be it to you if we have to obtain our freedom by fighting. . . . I do declare that one good black man can put to death six white men." Walker's *Appeal* quickly went through three printings and began to reach free blacks in the South. In 1830 Walker and other African American activists called a national convention in Philadelphia. The delegates did not adopt Walker's radical position but urged free

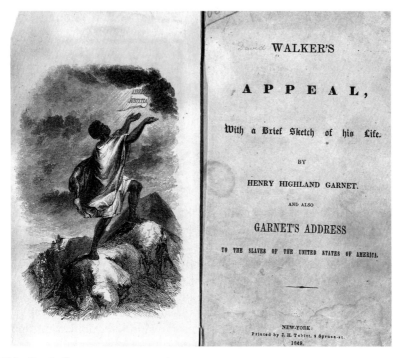

WALKER'S

APPEAL,

With a Brief Sketch of his Life.

BY

HENRY HIGHLAND GARNET.

AND ALSO

GARNET'S ADDRESS

TO THE SLAVES OF THE UNITED STATES OF AMERICA.

NEW-YORK:
Printed by J. H. Tobitt, 9 Spruce-st.
1848.

A Call for Revolution

David Walker (1785–1830) used his own savings to publish the *Appeal to the Colored Citizens of the World,* a learned and passionate attack against racial slavery. In the *Appeal,* published in 1829, Walker depicts Christ as an avenging "God of justice and of armies" and raises the banner of slave rebellion. A year later he was found in his shop, dead from unknown causes. (Library of Congress)

blacks to use every legal means to improve the condition of their race and asked for divine assistance in breaking "the shackles of slavery."

As Walker was calling for violent black rebellion from Boston, Nat Turner, a slave in Southampton County, Virginia, staged a bloody revolt—a coincidence that had far-reaching consequences. As a child Turner had taught himself to read and had hoped to be emancipated, but a new master forced him into field work and another master separated him from his wife. Turner became deeply spiritual, seeing visions and concluding that he might have been chosen to carry Christ's burden of suffering in a race war. Taking an eclipse of the sun as an omen, Turner plotted with a handful of relatives and close friends to meet the masters' terror with violence of their own. In August 1831 his men killed almost sixty whites, in many cases dismembering and decapitating them. Turner hoped that a vast army of slaves would rally to his cause, but he had mustered only sixty men by the time a white militia dispersed his poorly armed and exhausted followers. Vengeful whites now took slaves' lives at random. One company of cavalry killed forty in two days, putting the heads of fifteen on poles to warn "all those who should undertake a similar plot." Fifty slaves were prosecuted, and twenty were hanged. After hiding for nearly two months Turner was captured and hanged, still identifying his mission with Christ's.

Deeply shaken by Turner's rebellion, the Virginia legislature debated a bill providing for gradual emancipation and colonization. When the bill was rejected in 1832 by a vote of seventy-three to fifty-eight, the possibility that southern planters would legislate an end to slavery faded forever. Instead, the southern states marched down another path, toughening their slave codes, limiting the movement of slaves, and prohibiting anyone from teaching them to read. They would meet Walker's radical *Appeal* with radical measures of their own.

GARRISON AND EVANGELICAL ABOLITIONISM

Frightened by the prospect of a bloody racial revolution and inspired by the antislavery efforts of free blacks, a dedicated cadre of northern and midwestern evangelical whites launched a moral crusade to abolish slavery. Previously Quakers, along with some Methodists and Baptists, had freed their slaves and campaigned for gradual emancipation in the North. Now radical Christian abolitionists demanded that southerners free their slaves immediately. The issue was absolute: if the slaveowners did not repent and allow slaves their God-given status as free moral agents, the evangelical abolitionists believed, they faced the prospect of revolution in this world and damnation in the next.

The most uncompromising leader of the abolitionist movement was William Lloyd Garrison (1805–1879). A Massachusetts-born printer, Garrison had collaborated in Baltimore during the 1820s with a Quaker, Benjamin Lundy, who published the *Genius of Universal Emancipation,* the leading antislavery newspaper of the decade. In 1830 Garrison went to jail for seven weeks for libeling a New England merchant engaged in the domestic slave trade. Garrison went on to found his own antislavery weekly, *The Liberator,* in Boston in 1831. The next year he spearheaded the formation of the New England Anti-Slavery Society.

From the outset *The Liberator* took a radical stance. Garrison condemned the American Colonization Society, charging that its real aim was to strengthen slavery by removing troublesome African Americans who were already free. He attacked the U.S. Constitution for its implicit acceptance of racial bondage, labeling it "a covenant with death, an agreement with Hell." And he demanded the immediate abolition of slavery without reimbursement for slaveholders. As time went on, Garrison concluded that slavery was a sign of deep corruption infesting all American institutions and called for comprehensive reform of society.

Theodore Dwight Weld, who joined Garrison as a leading abolitionist, came to the movement from the religious revivals of the 1830s. The son of a Congregationalist minister and inspired by Charles Finney, Weld became an advocate of temperance and educational reform. Turning to abolitionism, he worked in northern

Presbyterian and Congregational churches, preaching the moral responsibility of all Americans for the denial of liberty to slaves. In 1834 Weld inspired a group of students at Lane Theological Seminary in Cincinnati to form an antislavery society. Weld's crusade gathered force, buttressed by the theological arguments he advanced in *The Bible against Slavery* (1837). Collaborating closely with Weld were Angelina Grimké, whom he married in 1838, and her sister, Sarah. The Grimkés had left their father's South Carolina slave plantation and converted to Quakerism and abolitionism in Philadelphia.

Weld and the Grimkés provided the abolitionist movement with a mass of evidence in *American Slavery as It Is: Testimony of a Thousand Witnesses* (1839). The book set out to answer a simple question—"What is the actual condition of the slaves in the United States?"—with evidence from southern newspapers and firsthand testimonies. In one account, Angelina Grimké told of a treadmill that slaveowners used for punishment: "One poor girl, [who was] sent there to be flogged, and who was accordingly stripped naked and whipped, showed me the deep gashes on her back—I might have laid my whole finger in them—*large pieces of flesh had actually been cut out by the torturing lash.*" The book sold over 100,000 copies in its first year alone.

In 1833 Weld, Garrison, Arthur and Lewis Tappan, and sixty other delegates, black and white, met in Philadelphia to establish the American Anti-Slavery Society. The Society received financial support from the Tappans, wealthy merchants in New York City. Women abolitionists quickly established their own organizations, such as the Philadelphia Female Anti-Slavery Society, founded by Lucretia Mott in 1833, and the Anti-Slavery Conventions of American Women, formed by a network of local societies in the late 1830s. The women's societies raised money for *The Liberator* and were a major force in the movement, especially in the farm villages and rural areas of the Midwest, distributing abolitionist literature and collecting tens of thousands of signatures on antislavery petitions.

Abolitionist leaders developed a three-pronged plan of attack, beginning with an appeal to public opinion. To foster intense public condemnation of slavery they adopted the tactics of the religious revivalists: large rallies led by stirring speakers, constant agitation by local antislavery chapters, and home visits by agents of the movement. The abolitionists also used the latest techniques of mass communication. Assisted by new steam-powered printing presses, the American Anti-Slavery Society distributed more than 100,000 pieces of literature in 1834. In 1835 the Society launched its "great postal campaign," which flooded the nation, including the South, with a million abolitionist pamphlets. In July 1835 alone abolitionists mailed more than 175,000 items at the New York City post office.

The abolitionists' second strategy was to assist the African Americans who fled from slavery. Those blacks who lived near a free state had the greatest chance of success, but fugitives from plantations deeper in the South received aid from the "underground railroad," an informal network of whites and free blacks in Richmond, Charleston, and other southern cities. In Baltimore a free African

American sailor lent his identification papers to the future abolitionist Frederick Douglass, who used them to escape to New York. Many escaped slaves, such as Harriet Tubman, returned repeatedly to the South, risking reenslavement or death to help others escape. Thanks to the "railroad" by the 1840s about 1,000 African Americans reached freedom in the North each year.

There they faced an uncertain future. Whites in the northern and midwestern states did not support civic equality for free blacks. Five New England states extended suffrage to African American men, while six northern and midwestern states changed their constitutions to deny them the franchise. Moreover, the Fugitive Slave Law (1793) allowed masters and hired slave-catchers to capture suspected fugitives and carry them back to bondage. To thwart these efforts white abolitionists in northern cities joined with crowds of free blacks to seize recaptured slaves and drive slave-catchers out of town.

Third, the abolitionists sought support from state and national legislators. In 1835 the American Anti-Slavery Society encouraged local chapters and members to bombard Congress with petitions demanding the abolition of slavery in the District of Columbia, an end to the domestic slave trade, and a ban on the admission of new slave states. By 1838 petitions with nearly 500,000 signatures had arrived in Washington.

This agitation drew thousands of middle-class men and women to abolitionism. During the 1830s the number of local abolitionist societies grew swiftly, from about 200 in 1835 to more than 500 in 1836 and nearly 2,000 by 1840—when they had nearly 200,000 members, including many leading transcendentalists. Emerson condemned American society for tolerating slavery; Thoreau was even more assertive. Seeing the Mexican War as an attempt to extend slavery, in 1846 he refused to pay his taxes and submitted to arrest. Two years later he published an anonymous essay entitled "Civil Disobedience" that outlined how individuals, by resisting governments because of loyalty to a higher moral law, could redeem themselves and the state. "A minority is powerless while it conforms to the majority," Thoreau declared, but it becomes "irresistible when it clogs by its whole weight."

OPPOSITION AND INTERNAL CONFLICT

As Thoreau recognized, the abolitionist crusade had won the wholehearted allegiance of only a small minority. Perhaps 10 percent of northerners and midwesterners strongly supported the movement; another 20 percent were sympathetic to its goals. But its opponents were much more numerous and no less aggressive. Men of wealth feared that the abolitionist attack on slave property might become a general assault on all property rights; tradition-minded clergymen condemned the public roles assumed by abolitionist women; and northern merchants and textile manufacturers rallied to the support of their white customers and suppliers in the South. Northern wage-earners feared that freed slaves would work for subsistence wages and take their jobs. Finally, whites almost universally opposed the prospect of "amalgamation"—racial mixing and intermarriage—that Garrison seemed to support.

Moved by such sentiments, northern opponents of abolitionism, often led by "gentlemen of property and standing," turned to violence. In 1833 an antiabolitionist mob of 1,500 New Yorkers stormed a church in search of Garrison and Arthur Tappan, and in 1834 a group of laborers vandalized and set fire to Lewis Tappan's house. Another white mob swept through Philadelphia's African American neighborhoods, clubbing and stoning residents, destroying homes and churches, and forcing crowds of black women and children to flee the city. In 1835 in Utica, New York, a group of lawyers, local politicians, merchants, and bankers broke up an abolitionist convention and beat several delegates. Two years later in Alton, Illinois, a mob shot and killed an abolitionist editor, Elijah P. Lovejoy. By raising the issues of emancipation and racial equality the abolitionists had shattered the possibility of a biracial middle class in the North open to "respectable" African Americans and encouraged whites—and blacks—to identify across class lines with those of their own race.

Racial solidarity was particularly strong in the South, where whites reacted to abolitionism with fury. Southern legislatures banned the movement and passed resolutions demanding that northern states follow suit. The Georgia legislature offered a $5,000 reward to anyone who would kidnap Garrison and bring him South to be tried for inciting rebellion. In Nashville vigilantes whipped a northern college student for distributing abolitionist pamphlets, and a mob in Charleston attacked the post office and destroyed sacks of abolitionist mail. After 1835 southern postmasters simply refused to deliver mail suspected to be of abolitionist origin.

Politicians joined the fray. President Andrew Jackson, though a radical on many issues, was a slaveowner and a firm supporter of the southern social order. Jackson privately approved of South Carolina's removal of abolitionist pamphlets from the U.S. mail, and in 1835 he asked Congress to restrict the use of the mails by abolitionist groups. Congress did not comply, but in 1836 the House of Representatives adopted the so-called *gag rule*. Under this rule, which remained in force until 1844, antislavery petitions were automatically tabled when they were received so that they could not become the subjects of debate in the House.

Assailed from outside abolitionists were also divided among themselves. Many antislavery clergymen denounced the public lecturing to mixed audiences by the Grimké sisters and other women as "promiscuous" and immoral. Other supporters denied any intention to promote race-mixing through marriage; others abandoned the Anti-Slavery Society because of Garrison's advocacy of further social reforms.

Indeed, Garrison had broadened his agenda and now supported pacifism and the abolition of prisons and asylums. Arguing that "our object is universal emancipation, to redeem women as well as men from a servile to an equal condition," he demanded that the American Anti-Slavery Society retain a broad platform that supported women's rights. At the convention of the American Anti-Slavery Society in 1840 Garrison precipitated a split with more conservative abolitionists by insisting on equal participation by women and helping to elect Abby Kelley to the organization's business committee. When the movement split, Kelley, Lucretia Mott, and Elizabeth Cady Stanton remained with Garrison in the American Anti-Slavery Society. They recruited new women agents, including Lucy Stone, to proclaim the common interests of enslaved blacks and free women.

Garrison's opponents founded a new organization, the American and Foreign Anti-Slavery Society, which received financial backing from Lewis Tappan. Its members worked through their churches to win public support for practical measures against slavery. Other abolitionists turned to electoral politics, establishing the Liberty Party and nominating James G. Birney for president in 1840. Birney was a former Alabama slaveowner who had been converted to abolitionism by Theodore Weld and had founded an antislavery newspaper in Cincinnati. Birney and the Liberty Party argued that the Constitution did not recognize slavery; that the Fifth Amendment, by barring any congressional deprivation of "life, liberty, or property," prevented the federal government from supporting slavery; and that slaves became automatically free when they entered areas of federal authority, such as the District of Columbia and national territories. But Birney won few votes in the election of 1840, and the future of the party and political abolitionism appeared dim.

Coming hard on the heels of popular violence and political suppression, these schisms and electoral failures stunned the abolitionist movement. It had attracted the energies and ideas of thousands of evangelical Protestants, moral reformers, and transcendentalists. But the abolitionists had aroused the hostility of a substantial majority of the white population. "When we first unfurled the banner of *The Liberator*," Garrison admitted in 1837, ". . . it did not occur to us that nearly every religious sect, and every political party would side with the oppressor."

The Women's Movement

The prominence of women among the abolitionists was the product of a broad shift in American culture. After the American Revolution women began to play a small role in public life, joining religious revivals and reform movements such as the temperance crusade. But it was the public activities of abolitionist women that created great controversy over gender issues and made some reformers into advocates for women's rights. They argued that women had rights as individuals and within marriage that were equal to those of men.

ORIGINS OF THE WOMEN'S MOVEMENT

During the American Revolution, upper-class women had raised the issue of greater legal rights for married women but won only a slightly enhanced status as "republican mothers." Subsequently the economic revolution presented young farm women with new opportunities for factory labor but imposed new constraints on middle-class married women, reinforcing their confinement to a "separate sphere." Rather than working as household producers (the traditional roles of the wives of farmers and artisans), middle-class women became full-time providers of household services, such as child care. But many of these middle-class women achieved greater authority within their families by joining religious revivals and becoming guardians of morality. Such activities bolstered their self-esteem and encouraged wives to enlarge their influence over all areas of family life, including the timing of pregnancies. Publications such as *Godey's Lady's Book* and Catharine Beecher's *Treatise on Domestic Economy* (1841) taught women how to make their homes more efficient and moral and justified a life of middle-class domesticity.

For most middle-class women a greater influence over family life was enough, but some women used their newfound religious authority to increase their involvement outside the home. Moral reform was among the first of their efforts in the public arena. In 1834 a group of middle-class women founded the New York Female Moral Reform Society and elected Lydia Finney, the wife of the evangelical minister Charles Finney, as its president. Its goals were to end prostitution, redeem "fallen" women, and protect single women from moral corruption. By 1840 it had grown into a national association, the American Female Moral Reform Society, with 555 chapters and 40,000 members throughout the North and Midwest. Employing only women as its agents, bookkeepers, and staff, the society attempted to provide moral "government" for factory girls, seamstresses, clerks, and servants who lived away from their families. Women reformers even visited brothels, where they sang hymns, offered prayers, searched for runaway girls, and noted the names of clients. They also founded homes of refuge for prostitutes and homeless women and won the passage of laws regulating men's sexual behavior—including making seduction a crime—in Massachusetts in 1846 and New York in 1848.

Women also turned their energies to the reform of social institutions, working to improve conditions in almshouses, asylums, hospitals, and jails, which grew in number in the 1830s and 1840s. The Massachusetts reformer Dorothea Dix was a leader in these efforts. Outraged that insane women were jailed alongside criminals, Dix persuaded the Massachusetts legislature to expand the state hospital to accommodate the poor and mentally ill. Dix carried her message to other states, persuading legislatures to expand their public hospitals, and nearly secured congressional legislation that would have set aside 12.5 million acres of public land to support asylums for the insane.

Both as reformers and as teachers northern women played a major role in education. From Maine to Wisconsin women vigorously supported the movement led by Horace Mann to increase the number of public elementary schools and improve their quality. As secretary of the newly created Massachusetts Board of Education from 1837 to 1848, Mann lengthened the school year; established teaching standards in reading, writing, and arithmetic; and improved instruction by recruiting well-educated women as teachers. The intellectual leader of the new corps of women educators was Catharine Beecher, who founded academies for young women in Hartford and Cincinnati. In a series of publications Beecher argued that "energetic and benevolent women" were the best qualified to impart moral and intellectual instruction to the young. By the 1850s most teachers were women both because school boards heeded Beecher's arguments and because women could be paid less than men.

ABOLITIONISM AND WOMEN

The public accomplishments of moral reformers such as Dix and Beecher inspired other women to assume public roles in the movement to end slavery. During the Revolutionary era Quaker women in Philadelphia had established schools for freed slaves, and subsequently many Baptist and Methodist women in the upper South endorsed religious arguments against slavery. When William Lloyd Garrison began his radical campaign for abolition, a few women rallied to his cause. One of the first Garrisonian abolitionists was Maria W. Stewart, an African American who spoke to mixed audiences of men and women in Boston in the early 1830s. As the abolitionist movement mushroomed, scores of white women delivered lectures condemning slavery and thousands more conducted home "visitations" to win converts.

Influenced by abolitionist ideas and their own experience of discrimination, a few women challenged the subordinate status of their sex. The most famous were Angelina and Sarah Grimké. When some Congregationalist clergymen demanded in 1836 that they cease lecturing on slavery to mixed male and female audiences, Sarah Grimké turned to the Christian Bible for justification: "The Lord Jesus defines the duties of his followers in his Sermon on the Mount . . . without any reference to sex or condition," she wrote. "Men and women are CREATED EQUAL! They are both moral and accountable beings and whatever is right for man to do is right for woman." In a debate with Catharine Beecher (who wanted women to exercise power through their domestic activities) Angelina Grimké pushed the argument beyond religion, using Enlightenment principles to claim equal civic rights for women:

> It is a woman's right to have a voice in all the laws and regulations by which she is governed, whether in Church or State. . . . The present arrangements of society, on these points are a violation of human rights, a rank usurpation of power, a violent seizure and confiscation of what is sacredly and inalienably hers.

By 1840 the Grimkés were asserting that traditional gender roles amounted to the "domestic slavery" of women.

Not all abolitionist women shared that exact view, but many soon were using the abolitionist movement as a launching point from which to address the

Sojourner Truth

Few women had as interesting a life as Sojourner Truth. Born as Isabella in Dutch-speaking rural New York about 1797, she labored as a slave until 1827. Following a religious vision, Isabella moved to New York City, learned English, and worked for deeply religious—and ultimately fanatical—Christian merchants. Seeking spiritual enlightenment in 1843 she took the name "Sojourner Truth" and left New York. After briefly joining the Millerites (who believed the world would end in 1844) Truth became famous as a forceful speaker on behalf of abolitionism and women's rights. This photograph, taken when she was in her seventies, suggests Truth's powerful personal presence. (Massachusetts Historical Society)

condition of their sex. The most prominent example was the novelist Harriet Beecher Stowe, who in the novel *Uncle Tom's Cabin* (1852) charged that among the greatest moral failings of slavery was its destruction of the slave family and the degradation of slave women. Sojourner Truth, a former slave who lectured to both antislavery and women's rights conventions, hammered home the point that women slaves were denied both basic human rights and the protected separate sphere enjoyed by free women. "I have ploughed and planted and gathered into barns, and no man could head me—and ain't I a woman?" she asked. Drawn into public life

A Farm Woman Defends the Grimké Sisters

KEZIAH KENDALL

*T*he New England lecture tour of the Grimké sisters sparked a huge outcry, including a lecture on "The Legal Rights of Women," by Simon Greenleaf, Royall Professor of Law at Harvard College. Replying to Greenleaf's advocacy of a restricted role for women, Keziah Kendall—possibly the fictional creation of a contemporary women's rights advocate—penned the following letter.

My name is Keziah Kendall. I live not many miles from Cambridge, on a farm with two sisters, one older, one younger than myself. I am thirty two. Our parents and only brother are dead—we have a good estate—comfortable house—nice barn, garden, orchard &c and money in the bank besides. . . . Under these circumstances the whole responsibility of our property, not less than twenty five thousand dollars rest upon me.

Well—our milkman brought word when he came from market that you were a going to lecture on the legal rights of women, and so I thought I would go and learn. Now I hope you wont think me bold when I say, I did not like that lecture much . . . [because] there was nothing in it but what every body knows. . . .

What I wanted to know, was good reasons for some of those laws that I cant account for. . . . One Lyceum lecture that I heard in C[ambridge] stated that the Americans went to war with the British, because they were taxed without being represented in Parliament. Now we [women] are taxed every year to the full amount of every dollar we possess— town, county, state taxes—taxes for land, for movable, for money and all. Now I don't want to [become a legislative] representative . . . any more than I do to be a "constable or a sheriff," but I have no voice about public improvements, and I don't see the justice of being taxed any more than the "revolutionary heroes" did.

Nor do I think we are treated as Christian women ought to be, according to the Bible rule of doing to others as you would others should do unto you. . . . Another thing . . . women have joined the Antislavery societies, and why? Women are kept for slaves as well as men—it is a common cause, deny the justice of it, who can! To be sure I do not wish to go about lecturing like the Misses Grimkie, but I have not the knowledge they have, and I verily believe that if I had been brought up among slaves as they were . . . I should run the venture of your displeasure, and that of a good many others like you.

SOURCE: Dianne Avery and Alfred S. Konefsky, "The Daughters of Job: Property Rights and Women's Lives in Mid-Nineteenth-Century Massachusetts," *Law and History Review*, 10 (Fall 1992), pp. 323–56.

by abolitionism, thousands of northern and midwestern women had become firm advocates of greater rights not only for African Americans but also for white women (see American Voices, "A Farm Woman Defends the Grimké Sisters").

THE PROGRAM OF SENECA FALLS

The commitment to full civil equality for women emerged during the 1840s as activists devised a pragmatic program of reform. While championing the rights of women, they did not challenge the institution of marriage or even the conventional division of labor within the family. Instead, harking back to the efforts of Abigail Adams and other Revolutionary era women, they tried to strengthen the legal rights of married women, especially with respect to property. In 1848 New York adopted legislation giving married women greater control over their own property, and similar laws were enacted in fourteen other states. Affluent men provided crucial support for this legislation. They wanted to protect their wives' assets in case their own businesses went into bankruptcy and to guard against dissolute sons-in-law who might waste their daughters' inheritances.

To advance the nascent women's movement Elizabeth Cady Stanton and Lucretia Mott, who had become friends at the World Anti-Slavery Convention in London in 1840, organized a gathering in Seneca Falls in central New York in 1848. The group, composed mostly of men and women from the immediate area, outlined for the first time a coherent program for women's equality. Taking the republican ideology of the Declaration of Independence as a starting point, the group declared that "all men and women are created equal" but that "the history of mankind is a history of repeated injuries and usurpations on the part of man toward woman, having in direct object the establishment of an absolute tyranny over her." To persuade Americans to right this long-standing wrong, they resolved to "use every instrumentality within our power.... We shall employ agents, circulate tracts, petition the State and national legislatures, and endeavor to enlist the pulpit and the press on our behalf." By staking out claims for equality for women in public life, the Seneca Falls activists repudiated the idea that the assignment of separate spheres for men and women was the natural order of society.

Although most men dismissed the Seneca Falls Declaration as nonsense, it drew women—and a few radical men—into the movement. In 1850 the first national women's rights convention in Worcester, Massachusetts, began to hammer out a reform program. Local and state conventions of women called on churches to revise concepts of female inferiority in their theology and worked for legal changes that would allow married women to control their property and earnings, guarantee the custody rights of mothers in the event of divorce or the father's death, and ensure women's right to sue and testify in court. Finally, and above all else, they began a concerted campaign to win the vote for women. In 1851 the national convention of women declared that suffrage was "the corner-stone of this enterprise, since we do not seek to protect woman, but rather to place her in a position to protect herself."

The struggle for legislation required leaders who had talents as organizers and lobbyists. The most prominent political operative was Susan B. Anthony (1820–1906). Anthony came from a Quaker family and as a young woman had been ac-

Susan B. Anthony, circa 1850

As a child, Susan B. Anthony worked on the Rochester, New York, farm of her father, a failed textile manufacturer. During the Civil War she showed her organizational skills as the founder (with Elizabeth Cady Stanton) of the National Women's Loyal League, which promoted the cause of women's suffrage and gathered 400,000 signatures in favor of a constitutional amendment prohibiting slavery. (Courtesy Meserve-Kunhardt Collection, Mt. Kisco, NY)

tive in temperance and antislavery efforts. Her experience in the temperance movement, Anthony explained, had taught her "the great evil of woman's utter dependence on man." In 1851 she joined the movement for women's rights and forged an enduring friendship with Elizabeth Cady Stanton. Anthony created a network of political "captains," all women, who relentlessly lobbied the legislature in New York and other states. In 1860 her efforts culminated in a New York law granting women the right to collect and spend their own wages (which fathers or husbands previously could insist on controlling), bring suit in court, and, if widowed, acquire full control of the property they had brought to the marriage. Such successes would provide the basis for more aggressive reform attempts after the Civil War.

The attack by women's rights activists against the traditional legal and social prerogatives of husbands, like the abolitionists' assault on the power and property of southern slaveholders, prompted many Americans to fear that social reform might not perfect their society but destroy it. The various movements for reform, begun with such confidence and religious zeal, had raised legal and political issues that threatened the fabric of society and the unity of the nation.

TIMELINE

1817	American Colonization Society founded	1841	Transcendentalists found Brook Farm.
1829	David Walker's *Appeal . . . to the Colored Citizens* advocates slave rebellion.		Dorothea Dix promotes hospitals for the insane.
1830	Joseph Smith's *The Book of Mormon*	1844	Margaret Fuller's *Woman in the Nineteenth Century*
1831	William Lloyd Garrison begins publishing *The Liberator.* Nat Turner's rebellion	1845	Henry David Thoreau withdraws to Walden Pond.
1832	Ralph Waldo Emerson rejects organized religion and embraces transcendentalism.	1846	Mormons begin trek to Salt Lake.
		1848	John Humphrey Noyes founds Oneida Community. Seneca Falls meeting on women's rights
1833	American Anti-Slavery Society founded		
1834	New York Female Moral Reform Society established	1850	Nathaniel Hawthorne's *The Scarlet Letter*
1835	Abolitionist mail campaign; antiabolitionist riots	1851	Herman Melville's *Moby Dick* Susan B. Anthony joins movement for women's rights.
1836	House of Representatives adopts a gag rule against antislavery petitions. Grimké sisters defend public roles for women.	1852	Harriet Beecher Stowe's *Uncle Tom's Cabin*
		1855	Walt Whitman's *Leaves of Grass*
1840	Liberty Party runs James G. Birney for president.	1858	The "Mormon War"
1840s	Creation of Fourierist communities		

For Further Exploration

Ronald Walters, *American Reformers, 1815–1860* (1978), offers a succinct discussion of the major antebellum reform movements. Robert H. Abzug, *Cosmos Crumbling: American Reform and the Religious Imagination* (1994), demonstrates the religious roots of the reform impulse and provides profiles of leading activists. David S. Reynolds, *Walt Whitman's America: A Cultural Biography* (1995), is a comprehensive study of the poet and nineteenth-century society. Charles Capper, *Margaret Fuller: An American Romantic Life* (1992), provides an illuminating analysis of Fuller's intellectual milieu. Fuller was the inspiration for the character of Zenobia in Nathaniel Hawthorne's *The Blithedale Romance* (1852), which reflects his life at Brook Farm and touches on many issues (and fads) of the day, including communalism and mesmerism. For a study of religious utopianism gone mad, see Paul E. Johnson and Sean Wilentz, *The Kingdom of Matthias: A Story of Sex and Salvation in Nineteenth-Century America* (1995).

James B. Stewart, *Holy Warriors: The Abolitionists and American Slavery* (1976), places the Garrisonian movement in a broader social and economic context. Stephen B. Oates, *The Fires of Jubilee: Nat Turner's Fierce Rebellion* (1975), is a short and imaginative narrative of the life of the insurrectionist, while the *Narrative of the Life of Frederick Douglass, An American Slave, Written by Himself*, is a literary and social masterpiece. For antiabolitionism, see the probing studies by Leonard L. Richards, *"Gentlemen of Property and Standing": Anti-Abolition Mobs in Jacksonian America* (1970), and David Roetiger, *The Wages of Whiteness* (1995).

Mary Ryan, *Women in Public: Between Banners and Ballots, 1825–1880* (1990), explores the limits on women's civic activities, and Eleanor Flexner, *Century of Struggle* (1959), narrates the history of the women's movement. The PBS video directed by Ken Burns, *Not for Ourselves Alone: The Story of Elizabeth Cady Stanton and Susan B. Anthony* (3 hours), presents a comprehensive view of the first generation of activists.

"Women and Social Movements in the United States, 1830–1930," at <http://womhist.binghamton.edu./>, prepared by Kathryn Kish Sklar and Thomas Dublin, provides a fine introductory essay and an extensive selection of primary documents. Additional source materials (newspapers and periodicals, with an index to articles and contributors) for the period 1830 to 1877 are available through Cornell University's "Making of America" project at <http://moa.cit.cornell.edu/> and its companion site at the University of Michigan at <http://moa.umdl.umich.edu/>.

Chapter 13

THE CRISIS OF THE UNION
1844–1860

This government was made by our fathers, by white men for the
benefit of white men and their posterity forever.

—Stephen Douglas, 1858

During the 1850s the crusaders in the temperance and antislavery movements faced off against the defenders of traditional rights. The resulting struggle was nowhere more intense than in South Carolina. When local temperance activists demanded a law like that in Maine to prohibit the sale of intoxicants, Randolph Turner was outraged: any such "legislation upon Liquor would cast a shade on my character which as a Caucassian (sic) and a white man, I am not willing to bear." A candidate for the South Carolina assembly, Turner vowed to shoulder his musket and, along with "hundreds of men in this district, . . . fight for individual rights, as well as State Rights." In Washington Congressman Preston Brooks and other South Carolinians battled against abolitionists to defend "Southern Rights." In an inflammatory speech in 1856, Senator Charles Sumner of Massachusetts denounced the South and accused Senator Andrew P. Butler of South Carolina of having taken "the harlot slavery" as his mistress. Outraged by Sumner's verbal attack on his uncle, Brooks accosted the Massachusetts senator at his desk and beat him unconscious with a walking cane. As Brooks struck down Sumner in Washington, Axalla Hoole of South Carolina and other proslavery migrants leveled their guns at an armed force of abolitionist settlers in the Kansas Territory. Passion and violence had replaced political compromise as the hallmark of American public life.

The pivotal events that sparked much of the political violence of the 1850s were the admission of Texas to the Union in 1845 and the war with Mexico that followed. But the ultimate causes lay deep in the process of economic and cultural change that had widened the long-standing differences between North and South—sectional differences that were increasingly *felt*, especially in the South. As John C. Calhoun warned in 1850, white southerners feared the North's wealth, political power, and moral righteousness, especially its "long-continued agitation of the slavery question." A massive surge of westward migration accentuated the importance of those divisions. Many Americans believed that the nation's "Manifest Destiny" was to extend republican institutions to the Pacific Ocean. But whose republican institutions: those of the slaveholding South or those of the reform-minded North and Midwest? The answer would determine the future of the nation.

Manifest Destiny

For nearly a generation after the Missouri Compromise of 1820 the two major political parties prevented another confrontation over slavery by devising programs that were national in appeal. But the compromise worked only so long as the territory of the United States remained unchanged, and by the 1840s the nation was on the move.

THE INDEPENDENCE OF TEXAS

During the 1830s, as northeastern farmers and European migrants were settling the Midwest, migrants from the Ohio Valley and the South were claiming the best lands in Arkansas and southern Missouri, pushing just beyond their western boundaries to the ninety-fifth meridian of longitude. Beyond this north-south line stretched the semiarid Great Plains. In 1820 an army explorer, Major Stephen H. Long, had described the area between the Missouri River and the Rocky Mountains as a Great American Desert, "almost wholly unfit for cultivation." Sharing this assumption, land-hungry American planters looked southward toward the Mexican province of Texas.

Texas had long been a zone of conflict between European nations. During the eighteenth century the Spanish had used Texas as a buffer against the French. After the Louisiana Purchase in 1803 Texas became Spain's buffer against Americans. Although adventurers from the United States did arrive, the Adams-Onís treaty of 1819 guaranteed Spanish sovereignty over Texas.

After winning independence from Spain in 1821 the Mexican government encouraged settlement by its own citizens and migrants from the United States. To win the allegiance of the Americans officials granted them some of the best land (see Map 13.1). One early grantee was Moses Austin, whose son Stephen F. Austin later acquired about 180,000 acres, which he sold to new migrants. The Americans did not assimilate Mexican culture and in 1829 won special exemption from a law ending slavery in Mexico. By 1835, 27,000 white Americans and their 3,000 African American slaves were raising cotton and cattle in eastern and central Texas; they far outnumbered the 3,000 Mexican residents, most of whom lived in the southwestern towns of Goliad and San Antonio.

When the Mexican government began to assert control over Texas in the mid-1830s, the Americans split into two groups. The "peace party," led by Stephen Austin and other longtime settlers, worked to win more self-government for the province, while the "war party," led by recent smallholder migrants from Georgia, demanded independence. Austin won significant concessions from Mexican authorities, but

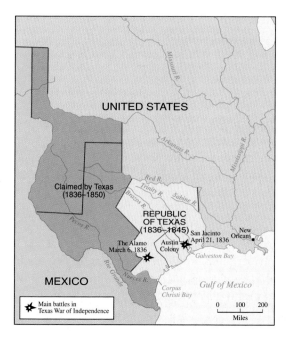

MAP 13.1
American Settlement in Texas,
1821–1850

In 1821 Stephen F. Austin established the first organized Anglo-
American settlement in Texas on
land granted to his father by the
Mexican authorities. By 1835 he
had issued land titles to more than
1,000 families, who grew cotton
and exported it from Corpus
Christi Bay and Galveston Bay. At
the time of rebellion in 1836 there
were nearly 30,000 Americans in
Texas; anticipating a flood of settlers, the new Texas republic
claimed all Mexican lands east of
the Rio Grande.

these were nullified by the new president, General Antonio López de Santa Anna.
A strong nationalist, Santa Anna appointed a military commandant for Texas,
prompting the American war party to provoke a rebellion that most of the American settlers ultimately supported. On March 2, 1836, the rebels proclaimed the independence of Texas and adopted a constitution legalizing slavery.

Santa Anna vowed to put down the rebellion. On March 6 his army wiped out
the rebel garrison defending the Alamo in San Antonio and soon thereafter captured the settlement of Goliad (see American Voices, "A Mexican View of the
Battle of the Alamo"). With these victories Santa Anna thought he had crushed the
rebellion, but the battle of the Alamo had captured the attention of New Orleans
and New York newspapers. Their correspondents romanticized the heroism of the
Texans at the Alamo and the deaths of the folk heroes Davy Crockett and Jim Bowie.
Using strong anti-Catholic rhetoric the newspapers described the Mexicans as tyrannical butchers in the service of the pope. Thousands of American adventurers, lured
by Texan offers of land bounties, flocked in from neighboring states. Reinforced by
the new arrivals and led by General Sam Houston, in April 1836 the rebels routed
the Mexicans in the Battle of San Jacinto, establishing de facto independence. The
Mexican government refused to recognize the new republic but abandoned efforts
to reconquer it.

The Texans immediately voted by plebiscite for annexation by the United States,
but Presidents Andrew Jackson and Martin Van Buren refused to act. They knew
that adding Texas as a slave state would divide the Democratic Party and the nation and almost certainly lead to war with Mexico.

SIEGE OF THE ALAMO.

Assault on the Alamo

After a thirteen-day siege, a Mexican army of 4,000 stormed the small mission on March 6, 1836. "The first to climb were thrown down by bayonets . . . or by pistol fire," reported a Mexican officer, and it took the attackers a half hour of continuous assaults to gain control of the wall. The battle took the lives of all 250 American defenders; the Mexicans suffered 1,500 dead or wounded. (Archives Division, Texas State Library)

THE PUSH TO THE PACIFIC: OREGON AND CALIFORNIA

The annexation of Texas became a more pressing issue in the 1840s, as American expansionists developed continental ambitions. Those dreams were captured by the term *Manifest Destiny*, coined in 1845 by John L. O'Sullivan, the editor of the *Democratic Review*. As O'Sullivan put it, "Our manifest destiny is to overspread the continent allotted by Providence for the free development of our yearly multiplying millions." Behind the rhetoric of Manifest Destiny was a sense of cultural and even racial superiority; "inferior" peoples—such as Native Americans and Mexicans—were to be brought under American dominion, taught about republican forms of government, and converted to Protestantism.

Already many residents of the Ohio River Valley were casting their eyes westward to the fertile valleys of the Oregon Country. This region stretched along the Pacific Coast from the forty-second parallel in the south (the border with Mexican California) to the fifty-fourth in the north (54° 40′, the border with Russian Alaska) and was claimed by both Great Britain and the United States. Since 1818

AMERICAN VOICES

A Mexican View of the Battle of the Alamo

COLONEL JOSÉ ENRIQUE DE LA PEÑA

*I*n February 1836 a Mexican army led by General Antonio López de Santa Anna laid siege to the Alamo, an old San Antonio mission held by about 250 Americans commanded by William B. Travis. Colonel Peña, a Mexican officer, recorded a dramatic and critical-minded account of the ensuing events.

Our commander [president-general Santa Anna] became more furious when he saw that the enemy resisted the idea of surrender. He believed as others did that the fame and honor of the army were compromised the longer the enemy lived. . . . But prudent men . . . were of the opinion that victory over a handful of men concentrated in the Alamo did not call for a great sacrifice. In fact, it was necessary only to await the artillery's arrival . . . for these to surrender. . . .

Travis's resistance was on the verge of being overcome, for several days his followers had been urging him to surrender, giving the lack of food and the scarcity of munitions as reasons . . . on the 5th he promised them if no help arrived on that day they would surrender the next day or would try to escape under the cover of darkness. . . . It was said as a fact . . . that the president-general knew of Travis's decision, and it was for this reason that he precipitated the assault, because he wanted to create a sensation and would have regretted taking the Alamo without clamor and without bloodshed, for some believed that without these there is no glory.

The columns, bravely storming the fort in the midst of a terrible shower of bullets and cannon-fire, had reached the base of the walls. . . . A lively rifle fire coming from the roof . . . caused painful havoc. . . . [Finally] our soldiers, some stimulated by courage and others by fury, burst into the quarters. . . . Our losses were grievous . . . [but] a horrible carnage [of the Americans] took place. . . . This scene of extermination went on for an hour before the curtain of death covered and ended it. . . . The taking of the Alamo was not considered a happy event, but rather a defeat that saddened us all.

SOURCE: José Enrique de la Peña, *With Santa Anna in Texas: A Personal Narrative of the Revolution*, trans. Carmen Perry (College Station: Texas A&M University Press, 1975), pp. 40–57.

a British-American convention had allowed both Britons and Americans to settle anywhere in the disputed region. The British-run Hudson's Bay Company developed a lucrative fur trade north of the Columbia River, while several hundred Americans settled to the south, mostly in the Willamette Valley. On the basis of this settlement the United States established a claim to the zone between the forty-second parallel and the Columbia River (see Map 13.2).

In 1842 American interest in Oregon increased dramatically. Navy lieutenant Charles Wilkes published glowing reports of the potential harbors he had found in the area of Puget Sound, news of great interest to New England merchants plying the China trade. In the same year a party of a hundred settlers journeyed along the Oregon Trail that fur traders and explorers had blazed through the Great Plains and the Rocky Mountains (see Map 13.3). Their reports told of a mild climate and fertile soil.

"Oregon fever" suddenly raged. In May 1843 over a thousand men, women, and children gathered in Independence, Missouri, for the trek to Oregon. The migrants were mostly farming and trading families from Missouri, Kentucky, and Tennessee. They had more than 100 wagons and 5,000 oxen and cattle. With military-style organization, the pioneers overcame flooding streams, dust storms, dying livestock, and encounters with Indians. After a journey of six months they reached the Willamette Valley, more than 2,000 miles across the continent. During the next two seasons another 5,000 people reached Oregon.

By 1860 about 350,000 Americans had braved the Oregon Trail. Over 34,000 of them died in the effort, mostly from disease and exposure; 400 deaths came from

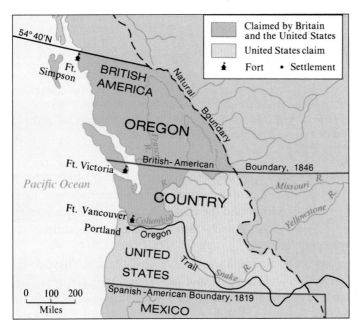

M A P 13.2
Territorial Conflict in Oregon, 1819–1846

As thousands of American settlers poured into the so-called Oregon Country in the early 1840s, British authorities tried to confine them south of the Columbia River. But the migrants—and fervent midwestern expansionists—asserted that American (and British) citizens could settle anywhere in the territory. In 1846 British and American diplomats resolved the dispute by drawing the boundary at the forty-ninth parallel.

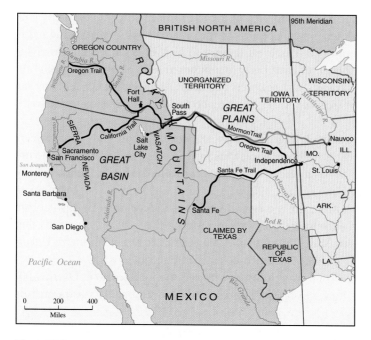

MAP 13.3
Settlement of the Trans-Missouri West

In the 1840s tens of thousands of Americans crossed the Great Plains in huge wagon trains. The Mormons settled in the Salt Lake Basin; other pioneers pressed on to Mexican California and the Oregon Country. There was remarkably little crime on these treks because most migrants were deeply religious or were committed to the rule of Anglo-American law, which they enforced through political compacts and self-created institutions.

Indian attacks. The walking migrants wore 3-foot-deep paths, and their wagons carved 5-foot-deep ruts, across sandstone formations in southern Wyoming—tracks that are visible today. Women found the trail especially difficult, for it exaggerated the authority of their husbands and added to their traditional chores the labor of driving wagons and animals.

Some pioneers ended up in the Mexican province of California. They left the Oregon Trail at the Snake River and struggled southward down the California Trail, settling in the interior valley along the Sacramento River. California had been the remotest corner of Spain's American empire, and Spain had established a significant foothold there only in the 1770s, when it built a chain of coastal missions and presidios along the coast (see Chapter 8). New England merchants soon struck up trade with the settlers in California, buying sea otter pelts that they carried to China. Commerce increased after Mexico won independence. To promote California's development the new Mexican government took over the California missions, liberating more than 20,000 Indians who worked on them, and promoted large-scale cattle ranching.

The rise of cattle ranching had created a new society and economy. While some mission Indians joined native American peoples in the interior, many remained in the coastal region. They intermarried with the local *mestizos* (Mexicans of mixed Spanish and Indian ancestry) and worked as laborers and cowboys. New England merchants carried the leather and tallow produced on the large California ranches to the booming Massachusetts boot and shoe industry. To handle the increased business New England firms dispatched dozens of resident agents to California. Unlike the American settlers in Texas many of those New Englanders assimilated Mexican culture. They married into the families of the elite Mexicans—the *Californios*—and adopted their dress, manners, outlook, and Catholic religion. A crucial exception was Thomas Oliver Larkin, the most successful merchant in Monterey. Larkin established a close working relationship with Mexican authorities, but he remained an American citizen and plotted for the peaceful annexation of California to the United States.

Like Larkin, American settlers in the Sacramento Valley had no desire to assimilate into Mexican society. Their legal standing was uncertain because they had received dubious land grants or had squatted without any title. They hoped to emulate the Americans in Texas by colonizing the country, overwhelming what they regarded as an inferior culture, and seeking annexation by the United States. However, these settlers numbered only about 700 in the early 1840s, compared to the coastal population of 7,000 Mexicans and 300 American traders.

A Californio *Patriarch*

Mariano Guadalupe Vallejo was descended from a Spanish family that had lived—and prospered—in Mexico since the Spanish Conquest. He served in California as a military officer and in the 1820s acquired 270,000 acres of land in the Sonoma Valley north of San Francisco. The father of nine children, Vallejo presents himself in this photograph as a proud patriarch, surrounded by two daughters and three granddaughters. During the American takeover in 1846 he was imprisoned for a short period but then lived out his life in California, gradually losing most of his vast holdings.
(Courtesy of the Bancroft Library, University of California, Berkeley)

THE FATEFUL ELECTION OF 1844

The election of 1844 determined the course of the American government's policy toward California, Oregon, and Texas. Since 1836, when Texas requested annexation, some southern leaders had favored territorial expansion to extend the slave system. They had been opposed not only by cautious party politicians and northern abolitionists but also, southerners came to think, by British antislavery advocates. In 1839 Britain and France had intervened in Mexico to force it to pay its foreign debts, and there were rumors that Britain wanted California as payment. Southern leaders also believed that Britain was encouraging Texas to remain independent and had designs on Spanish Cuba, which some southerners wanted to annex. To thwart any such British schemes southern expansionists demanded the immediate annexation of Texas.

At this moment "Oregon fever" and Manifest Destiny altered the political and diplomatic landscape in the North. In 1843 Americans throughout the Ohio Valley and the Great Lakes states called on the federal government to renounce the joint occupation of Oregon. Democrats and Whigs jointly organized "Oregon conventions," and in July a bipartisan national convention demanded that the United States seize Oregon all the way to 54° 40′ north latitude, the southern limit of Russian Alaska.

Now that northerners were demanding expansion southern Democrats could champion the annexation of Texas without threatening party unity. President John Tyler, disowned by the Whigs because of his opposition to Henry Clay's nationalist economic program, hoped to win reelection in 1844 as a Democrat. To curry favor among expansionists Tyler proposed both the annexation of Texas and the seizure of Oregon to the 54° 40′ line. In April 1844 Tyler and John C. Calhoun, his new secretary of state, submitted to the Senate a treaty to annex Texas. The treaty was opposed by two other leaders with presidential ambitions: the Democrat Martin Van Buren and the Whig Henry Clay, who knew annexation would alienate many northern voters. At their urging Whigs and northern Democrats united to defeat the treaty.

Texas became the central issue in the election. The Democrats passed over Tyler, whom they did not trust, and Van Buren, whom southern Democrats despised for his opposition to annexation. They selected former Governor James K. Polk of Tennessee, a slaveowner who was Andrew Jackson's personal favorite and who carried the nickname "Young Hickory." Unimpressive in appearance, Polk was a man of iron will and boundless ambition for the nation. He called for the annexation of Texas and taking all of Oregon. "Fifty-four forty or fight!" became the patriotic cry of his campaign.

The Whigs nominated Henry Clay, who once again championed his American System of internal improvements, high tariffs, and national banking. Initially Clay dodged the issue of Texas, finally suggesting that he might support annexation. His position disappointed thousands of northern Whigs and Democrats who opposed any expansion of slavery. Rather than vote for Clay, some antislavery advocates supported the Liberty Party's candidate, James G. Birney of Kentucky. Birney won less than 3 percent of the popular vote but probably took enough votes from Clay in New York to cause him to lose that state by 5,000 votes. By taking New York's 36 electoral votes, Polk won by a margin of 170 to 105 in the electoral college.

After Polk's victory congressional Democrats closed ranks and moved immediately to bring Texas into the Union. Unable to secure a two-thirds majority in the Senate for a treaty with the Texas Republic, they approved annexation by a joint resolution of Congress, which required only a majority vote in each house. Polk's strategy of linking Texas and Oregon had been successful.

War, Expansion, and Slavery, 1846–1850

James K. Polk and the Democrats had swept to victory in 1844 by promising the immediate annexation of Texas and laying claim to all of Oregon. But Polk had even greater territorial ambitions: he wanted all of Mexico between Texas and the Pacific Ocean and was prepared to go to war to get it. What he was not prepared for, though he should have been, was the major crisis over slavery unleashed by the success of his expansionist dreams.

THE WAR WITH MEXICO, 1846–1848

Mexico had not prospered in the twenty-five years since it won independence from Spain in 1821. Its population remained small at 7 million people, and its stagnant economy yielded only modest tax revenue, which was eaten up by interest payments on foreign debt and a bloated government bureaucracy. Consequently, the Mexican republic lacked the money and people to settle its distant northern provinces. The Spanish-speaking population of California and New Mexico remained small— about 75,000 in 1840—and contributed little to the national economy. Still, the Mexican government was determined to retain all its historical territories, and when the breakaway Texas Republic accepted American statehood on July 4, 1845, Mexico broke off diplomatic relations with the United States.

President James Polk viewed that action as a great opportunity and had already devised a secret plan to acquire Mexico's far northern provinces. To intimidate the Mexican government he ordered General Zachary Taylor and an American army of 2,000 soldiers to occupy the disputed lands between the Nueces River (the historical boundary of the Mexican province of Texas) and the Rio Grande, which the expansionist-minded Texas Republic had claimed as its southern and western border (see Map 13.1). Then Polk launched a diplomatic initiative, dispatching John Slidell on a secret mission to Mexico City. Slidell was instructed to secure Mexico's acceptance of the Rio Grande boundary and buy the Mexican provinces of New Mexico and California, paying as much as $30 million. When Slidell arrived in December 1845, Mexican officials refused to see him, declaring that the American annexation of Texas was illegal.

Anticipating the failure of Slidell's mission, Polk had already embarked on an alternative plan to take California. The president's strategy was to foment a revolution that, as in Texas, would lead to the creation of an independent republic and a request for annexation. In October 1845 he had Secretary of State James Buchanan advise Thomas O. Larkin, who had become the U.S. consul in the port of Monterey, to encourage leading Mexican residents to declare independence and support peaceful annexation. To add military muscle to any uprising Polk sent orders to American naval commanders in the Pacific to seize San Francisco Bay and California's coastal towns in the event of war. The president also had the War Department dispatch Captain John C. Frémont and an "exploring" party of heavily armed soldiers deep into Mexican territory. By December 1845 Frémont had reached California's Sacramento Valley.

Events now moved quickly toward war. When Polk learned of the failure of Slidell's mission, he ordered General Taylor to build a fort near the Rio Grande, hoping to incite an armed response by Mexico. As Ulysses S. Grant, a young officer serving with Taylor, said much later, "We were sent to provoke a fight, but it was essential that Mexico should commence it." When Mexican and American forces clashed near the Rio Grande in May 1846, Polk delivered the war message he had drafted long before, saying that Mexico "has passed the boundary of the United States, has invaded our territory, and shed American blood upon the American soil." Ignoring Whig pleas for a peaceful resolution of the dispute the Democratic majority in Congress voted for war with Mexico, unleashing large and almost hysterical demonstrations of popular support. To avoid a simultaneous war with Britain over Oregon the president retreated from his campaign pledge of "fifty-four forty or fight" and accepted a British proposal to divide the Oregon region at the forty-ninth parallel.

As the Senate ratified the Oregon Treaty with Great Britain in June 1846, fighting broke out in California between American naval forces and Mexican authorities. Naval commander John Sloat landed 250 marines and seamen in Monterey and declared that California "henceforward will be a portion of the United States." American settlers in the interior staged a revolt and, supported by Frémont's forces, captured the town of Sonoma. To ensure American control of California Polk ordered army units to capture Santa Fe in New Mexico and march to the Pacific Ocean. Despite stiff resistance from the Mexicans American forces secured control of all of California early in 1847.

Zachary Taylor's army in Texas had been equally successful. In May 1846 the American forces had crossed the Rio Grande, occupied Matamoros, and after a fierce six-day battle in September took the interior town of Monterrey. Two months later a U.S. naval squadron in the Gulf of Mexico seized Tampico, Mexico's second most important port. By the end of 1846 the United States controlled much of north-eastern Mexico.

Polk expected that these American victories in Texas, New Mexico, California, and northern Mexico would prompt the Mexicans to sue for peace, but he had underrated their national pride and the determination of President Santa Anna. Santa Anna went on the offensive, attacking the depleted units of Zachary Taylor at Buena Vista in February 1847. Only superior artillery enabled Taylor to eke out a victory and hold the American line in northeastern Mexico.

To bring Santa Anna to terms Polk accepted the plan devised by General Winfield Scott to strike deep into the heart of Mexico. In March 1847 Scott captured the port of Veracruz and began the 260-mile march to Mexico City. Leading Scott's 14,000 troops was a cadre of talented West Point officers who would become famous in the Civil War: Robert E. Lee, George Meade, and P.G.T. Beauregard. Scott's troops crushed Santa Anna's attempt to block their march at Cerro Gordo and after inflicting heavy losses on the Mexican army at the Battle of Churubusco seized Mexico City in September 1847. Santa Anna was overthrown, and the new Mexican government agreed to make peace. The war was finally over.

A DIVISIVE VICTORY

Initially many Americans viewed the war with Mexico as a noble struggle to extend American republican institutions, but the conflict quickly became politically divisive. A few Whigs, such as Charles Francis Adams of Massachusetts and Joshua Giddings of Ohio, had opposed the war from the beginning on moral grounds (and became known as "conscience Whigs"), viewing it as a conspiracy to add new slave states in the West. They argued that the expansion of slavery would jeopardize the Jeffersonian ideal of a yeoman freeholder society and ensure control of the federal government by slaveholding Democrats. These antislavery Whigs grew bolder after the elections of 1846, which gave their party control of Congress.

Polk's expansionist policy split the Democrats into sectional factions. In August 1846 David Wilmot, a Democratic representative from Pennsylvania, proposed a simple amendment to a military appropriations bill to prohibit slavery in any new territories acquired from Mexico. This amendment, known as the Wilmot Proviso, quickly became a rallying point for antislavery northerners. In the House the Democratic supporters of Martin Van Buren joined forces with antislavery Whigs to pass the Proviso. The Senate, dominated by southerners and proslavery northern Democrats, killed it.

In this heated atmosphere the most fervent Democrat expansionists became even more aggressive. Polk, Secretary of State Buchanan, and Senators Stephen A. Douglas of Illinois and Jefferson Davis of Mississippi wanted the United States to take at least part of Mexico south of the Rio Grande. But some southerners worried that the United States could not absorb the Mexicans and feared that a longer war would augment the power of the federal government. John C. Calhoun supported taking only California and New Mexico, the most sparsely populated areas of Mexico.

To reunify the Democratic Party before the next election Polk and Buchanan abandoned their expansionist dreams in Mexico and accepted Calhoun's policy. In February 1848 Polk signed the Treaty of Guadalupe Hidalgo, in which the United States agreed to pay Mexico $15 million in return for more than one-third of its territory: Texas north of the Rio Grande, New Mexico, and California (see Map 13.4). The United States also agreed to assume all the claims of its citizens, totaling $3.2 million, against the Mexican government. The Senate ratified the treaty in March 1848.

The passions aroused by the war dominated the election of 1848. The Wilmot Proviso had energized abolitionists who had been seeking a legislative solution to the problem of slavery, and the Senate's refusal to pass it alarmed them. Antislavery advocates now claimed that southern planters and their northern business allies had entered into a massive "Slave Power" conspiracy to expand the bounds of

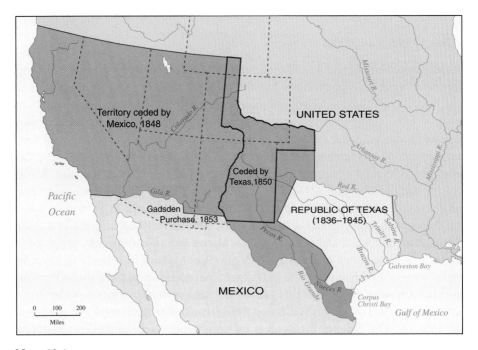

M A P 13.4
The Mexican Cession, 1848–1853

In the Treaty of Guadalupe Hidalgo (1848) and the Gadsden Purchase (1853) Mexico ceded to the United States its vast northern territories—the present-day states of California, Nevada, Utah, Arizona, New Mexico, and half of Colorado and Texas. These new territories, President Polk boasted to Congress, "constitute of themselves a country large enough for a great empire, and the acquisition is second in importance only to that of Louisiana in 1803."

slavery. To defeat this alleged plan a significant number of northerners joined a new "free-soil" movement. The free-soilers abandoned the Liberty Party's focus on the sinfulness of slavery and the natural rights of African Americans. Instead they depicted slavery as a threat to republican institutions and yeoman farming. This shift in emphasis—toward keeping the West open for settlement by white families and away from freeing slaves—led the radical abolitionist William Lloyd Garrison to denounce free-soil doctrine as racist "whitemanism."

Despite Garrison's hostility the new political approach worked. The Wilmot Proviso's call for free soil was the first antislavery proposal to attract broad popular support. Hundreds of women in the Great Lakes states joined female free-soil organizations formed by the American and Foreign Anti-Slavery Society. Frederick Douglass, the foremost black abolitionist, also endorsed free soil, seeing it as the best way to provoke a political struggle between the North and the South that would overthrow slavery.

The conflict over slavery took a toll on Polk and the Democratic Party. Opposed by free-soilers and exhausted by his rigorous dawn-to-midnight work regime, Polk declined to run for a second term and died three months after leaving office. The Democrats nominated Senator Lewis Cass of Michigan, an avid expansionist who had advocated buying Cuba, annexing Mexico's Yucatan Peninsula, and taking all of Oregon. To maintain party unity Cass was deliberately vague on the question of slavery in the West. He promoted a new idea—squatter sovereignty—that would give settlers in each territory the power to determine its status as free or slave.

Cass's political ingenuity failed to hold the party together. Demanding unambiguous opposition to the expansion of slavery, some northern Democrats joined the newly formed Free Soil Party, which nominated Martin Van Buren for president. Van Buren's conversion to free soil was genuine, but he also wanted to punish southern Democrats for having denied him the presidential nomination in 1844. To attract Whig votes the Free Soil Party chose conscience Whig Charles Francis Adams as its candidate for vice president.

To avoid similar divisions the Whigs nominated General Zachary Taylor. Taylor was a southerner and a Louisiana slaveowner, but he had not taken a position on the politically charged issue of slavery in the territories. Equally important the general's exploits during the War with Mexico had made him a popular hero. Known as "Old Rough and Ready," Taylor possessed a common touch that had won him the affection of his troops. "Our Commander on the Rio Grande," wrote Walt Whitman, "emulates the Great Commander of our revolution"—George Washington.

In 1848, as in 1840, running a military hero worked for the Whigs but only barely. Taylor and his vice-presidential running mate Millard Fillmore took 47 percent of the popular vote against 42 percent for Cass, but the margin in the electoral college was thin: 163 to 127. The Free Soil ticket of Van Buren and Adams made the difference in the election, winning 10 percent of the popular vote and depriving the Democrats of enough votes in New York to cost Cass that state and the presidency. The popularity of the Wilmot Proviso had changed the dynamics of American politics.

1850: CRISIS AND COMPROMISE

Even before President Taylor took office, events in California sparked a major political crisis that threatened the Union. In January 1848 workmen building a mill for John A. Sutter discovered flakes of gold in the Sierra Nevada foothills in northern California. Sutter was a Swiss immigrant who arrived in California in 1839, became a Mexican citizen, and established an estate in the Sacramento Valley. He tried to keep the discovery a secret, but by May Americans from San Francisco were pouring into the foothills. When President Polk confirmed the discovery in December, the gold rush was on. By January 1849 sixty-one crowded ships had departed from northeastern ports to sail around Cape Horn for San Francisco, and by May, 12,000 wagons had crossed the Missouri River, also bound for the gold fields. In 1849 alone more than 80,000 migrants—the "forty-niners"—arrived in California.

California Prospectors

Beginning in 1849 thousands of fortune seekers from all parts of the world converged on the California gold fields. By 1852 the state had 200,000 residents, including 25,000 Chinese, many of whom worked as wage laborers in the gold fields, and thousands of African Americans, both enslaved and free. These 1852 prospectors at Head of Auburn Ravine are using a primitive technique—panning—to separate gold from sand and gravel.

(Courtesy of the California History Room, California State Library, Sacramento, CA)

The rapid influx of settlers revived the national debate over free soil. The forty-niners, who lived in crowded, chaotic towns and mining camps, demanded the formation of a territorial government to protect their lives and property. To avoid an extended debate over slavery President Taylor advised the Californians to apply for statehood immediately, and in November 1849 they ratified a state constitution that prohibited slavery. Few of the many southerners who flocked to the gold fields or to San Francisco owned slaves or wanted to. For his part Taylor wanted to attract Free Soilers and northern Democrats into the Whig Party and urged Congress to admit California as a free state.

Southern politicians were alarmed by the swift victory of the antislavery forces in California. Not only had a valuable area been lost to free soil, but the admission of California would threaten the carefully maintained balance in the Senate. In 1845 the entry of Texas and Florida had raised the total of slave states to fifteen, against thirteen free states. However, the entry of Iowa in 1846 and Wisconsin in 1848 had reestablished the balance. Now southern leaders feared that admitting California as a free state would place their section at a political disadvantage from which it would never recover. They decided to block its entry unless the federal government guaranteed the future of slavery.

The resulting impasse produced long and passionate debates in Congress. As usual John C. Calhoun took the most extreme states'-rights position, warning of possible secession by the slave states and civil war. To avoid that outcome he proposed that slavery be guaranteed in all the territories and that a constitutional amendment be adopted to create a permanent balance of power between the sections. In making these proposals Calhoun advanced the radically new constitutional doctrine that Congress had no constitutional authority to regulate slavery in the territories. This argument ran counter to a half century of practice. Congress had prohibited slavery in the Northwest Territory in 1787 and in most of the Louisiana Purchase in the Missouri Compromise in 1821.

While Calhoun's new doctrine won support in the Deep South, many southerners were prepared to accept a more moderate position: an extension of the Missouri Compromise line to the Pacific Ocean. This extension would guarantee slaveowners access to some western territory, including a separate state in southern California. Some northern Democrats, including former Secretary of State James Buchanan, also favored this plan as a way to resolve the crisis.

A third alternative was squatter sovereignty, the plan advanced by Lewis Cass in 1848 and now championed by Democratic Senator Stephen Douglas of Illinois. Douglas called his plan "popular sovereignty" to emphasize its roots in republican ideology, and it had considerable appeal. Popular sovereignty would place decisions about slavery in the hands of local settlers and their territorial governments, removing the explosive issue from national politics. However, popular sovereignty was a vague and slippery concept: could slavery be accepted or banned when the territory was first organized or only when it framed a constitution and applied for statehood?

Antislavery advocates were unwilling to accept any plan that involved the expansion of slavery. In 1850 Senator Salmon P. Chase of Ohio, elected by a Democratic–Free Soil coalition, and Senator William H. Seward, a New York Whig, urged federal authorities to contain slavery and then extinguish it completely. Condemning slavery as "morally unjust, politically unwise, and socially pernicious" and invoking "a higher law than the Constitution," Seward demanded bold action to protect freedom, "the common heritage of mankind."

Standing on the brink of disaster, senior Whigs and Democrats desperately sought a compromise to preserve the Union. Through a long, complex legislative process the Whig leaders Henry Clay and Daniel Webster and the Democrat Stephen A. Douglas organized a complex package of six laws known collectively as the Compromise of 1850. To mollify the South the Compromise included a new Fugitive Slave Act allowing slaveowners to use federal magistrates to return runaway slaves. To satisfy the North the Compromise admitted California as a free state, resolved a boundary dispute between New Mexico and Texas in favor of New Mexico, and abolished the slave trade (but not slavery) in the District of Columbia. Finally, the Compromise organized the rest of the lands acquired from Mexico into the territories of New Mexico and Utah on the basis of popular sovereignty (see Map 13.5).

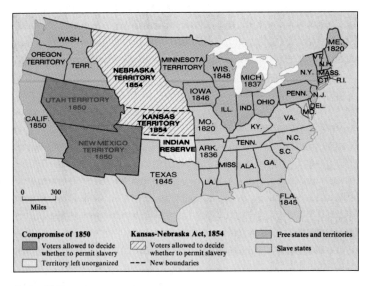

MAP 13.5

The Compromise of 1850 and the Kansas-Nebraska Act of 1854

Vast territories were at stake in the contest over the extension of slavery. The Compromise of 1850 resolved the status of lands in the Far West: California would be a free state, and the settlers of the Utah and New Mexico territories would decide their own fate. In 1854 the implementation of popular sovereignty in Kansas sparked a bitter local war between the advocates of free soil and slavery, revealing a fatal flaw in the concept.

The Compromise averted a secession crisis in 1850—but only barely. In the midst of the struggle the governor of South Carolina declared that there was not "the slightest doubt" that his state would secede. He and other "fire-eaters" in Georgia, Mississippi, and Alabama organized special conventions to protect "Southern Rights" and demand secession. To persuade the convention delegates to support the Compromise moderate southern politicians agreed to support secession in the future if Congress abolished slavery anywhere or refused to grant statehood to a territory with a proslavery constitution. Lacking sufficient support, the "fire-eaters" drew back from secession, averting a constitutional crisis. The fact that the Compromise of 1850 elicited such a passionately negative response throughout the Deep South—and among many northern Whigs and Free Soilers as well—did not augur well for its success.

The End of the Second Party System, 1850–1858

The architects of the Compromise of 1850 hoped that their agreement would resolve the issue of slavery for a generation. Their hopes were quickly dashed. Demanding freedom for fugitive slaves and free soil in the West, some northerners undermined the Compromise, while some southerners plotted to expand slavery in the West and the Caribbean. These disputes destroyed the Second Party System, deepening the crisis of the Union.

RESISTANCE TO THE FUGITIVE SLAVE ACT

The most controversial element of the Compromise proved to be the Fugitive Slave Act. Under its terms federal judges or special commissioners in the northern states determined the status of blacks who were accused of being runaway slaves. The accused blacks were denied jury trials and even the right to testify. Because federal marshals were legally required to support slave-catchers, the new legislation was effective, and about 200 fugitives (as well as some free blacks) were sent to the South and enslaved.

The plight of runaways and the appearance of slave-catchers aroused popular hostility in the North and Midwest, and free blacks and abolitionists defied the new law. In October 1850 Boston abolitionists helped two slaves escape to freedom and drove a Georgia slave-catcher out of town. A year later rioters in Syracuse, New York, broke into a courthouse to free a fugitive slave. Abandoning pacifism, Frederick Douglass declared that "the only way to make a Fugitive Slave Law a dead letter is to make half a dozen or more dead kidnappers." As if in response, in September 1851 a deadly confrontation took place in the Quaker village of Christiana, Pennsylvania. About twenty African Americans exchanged gunfire with a group of slave-catchers from Maryland, killing two of them. Federal marshals arrested thirty-six

Uncle Tom's Cabin, 1852

The cover of this "Young Folks Edition" of *Uncle Tom's Cabin* shows Tom as a well-dressed and kindly older man, reading the Bible to Little Eva, whom he has saved from drowning. Like the book's text, this image offered whites a sympathetic view of African Americans, challenging generations of negative stereotypes.

(The Charles L. Blockson Afro-American Collection, Temple University)

blacks and four whites and had them indicted for treason for defying the law. But a jury acquitted one defendant, and northern public opinion forced the government to drop its charges against the rest.

Harriet Beecher Stowe's abolitionist novel, *Uncle Tom's Cabin* (1852), increased northern opposition to the Fugitive Slave Act. By translating the moral principles of abolitionism into heartrending personal situations, Beecher's novel evoked empathy and outrage throughout the North. Responding to popular sentiment, northern legislatures challenged federal authority by enacting personal-liberty laws that extended legal rights to accused fugitives. In 1857 the Wisconsin Supreme Court went even further, ruling in *Ableman v. Booth* that the Fugitive Slave Act could not be enforced in Wisconsin because it violated the Constitution and contesting the power of the federal courts to review their decision. When the case was considered by the U.S. Supreme Court in 1859, Chief Justice Taney led a unanimous court in affirming the supremacy of federal over state courts—a position that has stood the test of time—and upheld the constitutionality of the Fugitive Slave Act. By that time popular opposition had made it impossible to catch fugitive blacks. As Douglass had hoped, the act had become a "dead letter."

THE WHIGS' DECLINE AND THE DEMOCRATS' DIPLOMACY

The conflict over fugitive slaves split the Whig Party, which went into the election of 1852 weakened by the death of Henry Clay, one of its greatest leaders. Rejecting Millard Fillmore, who had become president on the death of Zachary Taylor, the Whigs nominated General Winfield Scott, another hero of the war with Mexico. But about a third of southern Whigs refused to support Scott because northern members of the party refused to support slavery; they threw their support to the Democrats.

The Democrats too were divided. Southerners wanted a candidate who would support Calhoun's position that all territories should be open to slavery. But northern and midwestern Democrats advocated the principle of popular sovereignty, as did the three leading candidates—Lewis Cass of Michigan, Stephen Douglas of Illinois, and James Buchanan of Pennsylvania. At the national convention no candidate could secure the necessary two-thirds majority. Exhausted after forty-eight ballots, the convention settled on a compromise nominee, Franklin Pierce of New Hampshire, a congenial man reputed to be sympathetic to the South.

The Democrats' cautious strategy paid off, and they swept the election. Pleased by the admission of California as a free state, Martin Van Buren and many other Free Soilers voted for Pierce, reuniting the Democratic Party. Conversely, the election fragmented the Whig Party into sectional wings; it would never again wage a national campaign.

As president, Pierce pursued an expansionist foreign policy. To assist northern merchants he sent a mission to Japan to negotiate a commercial treaty. Pierce was even more solicitous of southern interests. To resolve a dispute over the southern boundary of New Mexico the president revived Polk's plan to annex a large amount of territory south of the Rio Grande and named James Gadsden as his negotiator. Mexican officials rejected Pierce's annexation bid but agreed to sell a small amount of land that Gadsden, a railroad promoter, wanted to construct a southern-based transcontinental railroad to the Pacific (see Map 13.4).

Pierce's most dramatic foreign policy initiative came in the Caribbean. Southern expansionists had already funded three clandestine military expeditions to Spanish Cuba, where they hoped to prod the slaveowning elite into declaring independence and then joining the Union. In 1853 Pierce covertly supported a new Cuban expedition led by John A. Quitman, a former governor of Mississippi. While Quitman was building up his forces, the Pierce administration threatened war with Spain over the seizure of an American ship, demanding an apology and a large indemnity. But when northern Democrats in Congress refused to support this aggressive diplomacy, Pierce and Secretary of State William L. Marcy had to back down. Still determined to seize Cuba, Marcy tried to buy the island from Spain and then prompted American diplomats in Europe to pressure Pierce to seize it. In the Ostend Manifesto (1854), the diplomats declared that the United States would be justified in seizing Cuba "by every law, human and Divine." Quickly leaked to the press by antiexpansionists, the Ostend Manifesto triggered a new wave of northern resentment against the South and forced Pierce to halt his efforts. But his expansionist policy had already revived northern fears of a "Slave Power" conspiracy.

THE KANSAS-NEBRASKA ACT AND
THE RISE OF NEW PARTIES

In the wake of the Ostend Manifesto a new struggle over westward expansion enflamed sectional divisions. Because the Missouri Compromise prohibited slavery in the Louisiana Purchase north of 36° 30', southern senators had delayed the political organization of that area. But westward-looking residents of the Ohio River Valley and the upper South demanded its settlement, and Senator Stephen A. Douglas of Illinois became their spokesman, in part because he supported a northern transcontinental railroad from Chicago to California. In 1854 Douglas introduced a bill to extinguish Native American rights on the central Plains and organize a large territory to be called Nebraska. Because Nebraska was north of 36° 30', it would be a free territory.

Douglas's bill conflicted with the plans of southern senators, who wanted to extend slavery throughout the Louisiana Purchase and, like James Gadsden, hoped that a southern city—New Orleans, Memphis, or St. Louis—would become the eastern terminus of a transcontinental railroad. To win southern support for the organization of Nebraska Douglas made two major concessions. First, he amended his bill so that it explicitly repealed the Missouri Compromise and organized the region on the basis of popular sovereignty. Second Douglas agreed to the formation of two new territories, Nebraska and Kansas, giving slaveholders a chance to dominate the settlement of Kansas, the more southern territory (see Map 13.5). To win northern and midwestern support for this scheme Douglas argued that Kansas would be settled primarily by nonslaveholders because its climate and terrain were not suited to plantation agriculture. Supported primarily by southern representatives, the Kansas-Nebraska Act passed in May 1854.

The Kansas-Nebraska Act proved to be the last nail in the coffin of the Second Party System. Abolitionists and free-soilers denounced the act, calling it "part of a great scheme for extending and perpetuating supremacy of the slave power." Antislavery northern Whigs and "Anti-Nebraska" Democrats abandoned their respective parties to create a new party, taking the Jeffersonian name Republican. Emphasizing uncompromising opposition to the expansion of slavery, the Republicans ran a slate of candidates, primarily in the Midwest, in the congressional election of 1854.

Like most American parties, the Republican Party was a coalition of diverse groups—Free Soilers, antislavery Democrats, conscience Whigs—but its founders shared a distinct vision. They opposed slavery because it degraded manual labor, creating poor black and white workers who were subservient to wealthy landlords. In contrast, Republicans such as Senator Thaddeus Stevens of Pennsylvania celebrated the moral virtues of a society based on "the middling classes who own the soil and work it with their own hands." Abraham Lincoln, an Illinois Whig who became a Republican, articulated the party's vision of social mobility. "There is no permanent class of hired laborers among us," he argued, and every man had a chance to become a property owner. In the face of increasing class divisions in the industrializing North and Midwest, Lincoln and his fellow Republicans asserted the values of republican freedom and individual enterprise.

Competing for Whig and Democratic votes was another new party, the American, or "Know-Nothing," Party. The American Party had its origins in the anti-immigrant and anti-Catholic organizations of the 1840s (see Chapter 10). In 1850 these secret societies banded together as the Order of the Star-Spangled Banner; a year later they formed the American Party. The secrecy-conscious members sometimes answered outsiders' questions by saying "I know nothing," giving the party its nickname, but its program was far from secret. Know-Nothings hoped to unite native-born Protestants against the "alien menace" of Irish and German Catholics, banning further immigration and instituting literacy tests for voting. In 1854 the Know-Nothings gained control of the state governments of Massachusetts and Pennsylvania and, allied with the Whigs, commanded a majority in the U.S. House of Representatives. The emergence of a new major party led by nativists suddenly became a real possibility.

At the same time, the results of the Kansas-Nebraska Act were creating a new political crisis. In 1854 thousands of settlers rushed into the Kansas Territory, putting Douglas's theory of popular sovereignty to the test. On the side of slavery Senator David R. Atchison of Missouri organized residents of his state to cross into Kansas and vote in crucial elections. Opposing him were agents of the abolitionist New England Emigrant Aid Society, which colonized Kansas with free-soilers. In March 1855 the Pierce administration recognized the territorial legislature in Lecompton, Kansas, which had been elected largely by border-crossing Missourians and had adopted proslavery legislation, but free-soilers rejected the legitimacy of the territorial government.

In May 1856 both sides turned to violence (see American Voices, "'Bleeding Kansas': A Southern View"). A proslavery gang, 700 strong, sacked the free-soil town of Lawrence, destroying two newspaper offices, looting stores, and burning down buildings. The attack enraged John Brown, an abolitionist from New York and Ohio, whose free-state militia force arrived too late to save the town. Brown was a complex man with a checkered past. Born in 1800, he had started more than twenty businesses in six states and had often been sued by his creditors. Nonetheless, he had an intelligence and a moral intensity that won the trust of influential people, including leading abolitionists. Taking vengeance for the sack of Lawrence, he and a few followers murdered and mutilated five proslavery settlers. We must "fight fire with fire" and "strike terror in the hearts of the proslavery people," Brown declared. The sack of Lawrence and the "Pottawatomie massacre," as the killings became known, initiated a guerrilla war in Kansas that cost about 200 lives.

"Bleeding Kansas": A Southern View

AXALLA JOHN HOOLE

*E arly in 1856 Axalla John Hoole and his bride left South Carolina to support the South-
ern cause while building a new life in Kansas. These letters show that things went badly
from the start and only got worse; after eighteen months the Hooles returned to South Carolina. A Confederate militia captain, Axalla Hoole died in the Battle of Chickamauga in September 1863.*

Kansas City, Missouri, Apl. 3d., 1856

My Dear Brother . . .

The Missourians . . . are very sanguine about Kansas being a slave state & I have heard
some of them say it shall be . . . but generally speaking, I have not met with the reception
which I expected. Everyone seems bent on the Almighty Dollar, and as a general thing that
seems to be their only thought. . . .

Lecompton, K.T., Sept. 12, 1856

My Dear Mother . . .

I have been unwell ever since the 9th of July. . . . I thought of going to work in a few
days, when the Abolitionists broke out and I have had to stand guard of nights when I
ought to have been in bed, took cold which . . . caused diarrhea. . . . Betsie is well—

You perceive from the heading of this that I am now in Lecompton, almost all of the
Proslavery party between this place and Lawrence are here. We brought our families here,
as we thought that we would be better able to defend ourselves. . . . Lane [and a Free State
army] came against us last Friday (a week ago to-day). As it happened we had about 400
men with two cannon . . . but we were acting on the defensive, and did not think it prudent to commence the engagement.

Douglas, K.T., July the 5th., 1857

Dear Sister . . .

I fear, Sister, that [our] coming here will do no good at last, as I begin to think that this
will be made a Free State at last. 'Tis true we have elected Proslavery men to draft a state
constitution, but I feel pretty certain, if it is put to a vote of the people, it will be rejected,
as I feel pretty confident that they have a majority here at this time. The South has ceased
all efforts, while the North is redoubling her exertions. . . .

SOURCE: William Stanley Hoole, ed., "A Southerner's Viewpoint of the Kansas Situation, 1856–1857,"
Kansas Historical Quarterly (1934), vol. 3: pp. 43–68, 145–71, passim.

BUCHANAN'S FAILED PRESIDENCY

The violence in Kansas dominated the presidential election of 1856. The Democrats reaffirmed their support for popular sovereignty and the Kansas-Nebraska Act and nominated James Buchanan of Pennsylvania. A tall, dignified figure of sixty-four, Buchanan was an experienced but unimaginative and timid politician.

The two-year-old Republican Party counted on anger over "Bleeding Kansas" to boost its fortunes. The party's platform denounced the Kansas-Nebraska Act and, alleging a "Slave Power" conspiracy, insisted that the federal government prohibit slavery in all the territories. The platform also called for federal subsidies to transcontinental railroads, reviving the element of the Whig economic program that was most popular among midwestern Democrats. For president the Republicans nominated Colonel John C. Frémont, a free-soiler famous for his role in the conquest of California.

The American Party entered the election with high hopes, but it quickly split into sectional factions over Kansas. The Republicans cleverly maneuvered the northern faction into endorsing Frémont and won the support of many Know-Nothing workingmen by adding anti-Catholic nativism to its program of high tariffs on foreign manufactures. As a Pennsylvania congressman declared, "Let our motto be, protection to everything American, against everything foreign," while in New York Republicans worked "to cement into a harmonious mass . . . all of the Anti-Slavery, Anti-Popery and Anti-Whiskey" voters. The southern faction of the American Party nominated former president Millard Fillmore, who won 21 percent of the national vote but only 8 electoral votes.

James Buchanan, the Democrat, won the three-way race. He drew 1.8 million votes (45 percent) to 1.3 million (33 percent) for Frémont. Frémont demonstrated the appeal of the new Republican Party in the North by carrying eleven free states with 114 electoral votes. Buchanan took only five free states, and a small shift of the popular vote to Frémont in Illinois and Pennsylvania would have cost Buchanan the presidency.

The dramatic restructuring of parties was now apparent. With the collapse of the Know-Nothings, the Republicans had replaced the Whigs as the second major party. Because the Republicans had no support in the South, a victory for the new party in the next presidential election might mean the end of the Union. The fate of the republic hinged on the ability of President Buchanan to defuse the passions of the past decade and achieve a new compromise that would protect free soil in the West and slavery in the South.

Events—and his own values and weaknesses—conspired against Buchanan. Although Congress had long regulated slavery in the territories, its constitutional authority to do so had never been tested in the courts. In 1856 the case of Dred Scott reached the Supreme Court. Scott was an enslaved African American who had lived for a time with his master, an army surgeon, in the free state of Illinois and at Fort Snelling, then in the Wisconsin Territory, where the Northwest Ordinance (1787) prohibited slavery. In his suit Scott claimed that his residence in a free state and a free territory had made him free. In March 1857, after Buchanan had pressured several justices, the Court announced its decision in *Dred Scott v. Sandford.*

Seven members of the Court concurred on one critical point: Scott remained a slave. But they could not agree on the legal issues, and each justice wrote a separate opinion. In the most influential opinion, Chief Justice Roger B. Taney of Maryland declared that African Americans, slave or free, could not be citizens of the United States and that Scott therefore had no right to sue in federal court. That argument was controversial enough, since free African Americans could be citizens of a state. But Taney went on to make two even more controversial points. First, he repeated John C. Calhoun's argument that because the Fifth Amendment prohibited the taking of property without due process of law, Congress could not prevent southern citizens from taking their slave "property" into the territories or owning it there. Therefore, the chief justice concluded, the Northwest Ordinance and the Missouri Compromise—which prohibited slavery in the territories—had never been constitutional. Second, Taney declared that Congress could not give to territorial governments any powers that Congress itself did not possess. Since Congress had no authority to prohibit slavery in a territory, neither did a territorial government. Thus Taney endorsed Calhoun's interpretation of popular sovereignty: only when settlers wrote a constitution and requested statehood could they prohibit slavery. In a single stroke a Democrat-dominated Supreme Court had declared the Republicans' antislavery platform unconstitutional, a decision the Republicans could never accept. Led by Senator William H. Seward of New York, they accused the Supreme Court and President Buchanan of participating in the "Slave Power" conspiracy.

Buchanan then made things worse. In early 1858 he recommended the admission of Kansas as a slave state under the Lecompton constitution. Many observers—including the Democrat Stephen Douglas—believed that the constitution had been enacted by fraudulent means. Angered that Buchanan would not permit a referendum in Kansas on the constitution, Douglas broke with the president and his southern allies and persuaded Congress to deny statehood to Kansas. (Kansas would enter the Union as a free state in 1861.) By pursuing a proslavery agenda—first in the *Dred Scott* decision and then in Kansas—Buchanan had split his party and the nation.

Abraham Lincoln and the Republican Triumph, 1858–1860

The crisis of the Union intensified as the national Democratic Party fragmented into sectional factions and the Republicans gained the support of a majority of northern voters. During this transition Abraham Lincoln emerged as the pivotal figure in American politics, the only Republican leader whose policies and temperament might have saved the Union. But few southerners trusted Lincoln, and his election threatened to unleash the secessionist movement that had menaced the nation since 1850.

LINCOLN'S EARLY CAREER

The rise of the middle class in the small towns of the Ohio River Valley shaped Lincoln's early career. He came from an illiterate farming family of modest means that had moved from Kentucky, where Lincoln was born in 1809, to Indiana and then Illinois. In 1831 Lincoln rejected the farmer's life of his father and became a store clerk in New Salem, Illinois. Socially ambitious, Lincoln sought entry into the middle class, joining the New Salem Debating Society and reading Shakespeare and other literary works.

Lincoln's ambition was "a little engine that knew no rest," as a close associate later remarked. Admitted to the bar in 1837, Lincoln moved to Springfield, the small country town that had become the new state capital. There he met Mary Todd, the cultured daughter of a Kentucky banker; they married in 1842. The couple were a picture in contrasts. Her tastes were aristocratic; his were humble. She was volatile; he was easygoing. Bouts of depression, which plagued Lincoln throughout his life, tried her patience and tested his character. Entering political life, Lincoln served four terms as a Whig in the Illinois assembly, where he promoted education, state banking, and internal improvements such as canals and railroads. In 1846 Lincoln won election to Congress.

As a member of Congress during the war with Mexico, Lincoln had to take a stand on the contentious issue of slavery. He had long felt that slavery was unjust but had little sympathy for abolitionism and did not believe that the federal government had the constitutional authority to tamper with slavery in the South. Lincoln took the middle ground. He supported military appropriations for Polk's war in Mexico but voted for the Wilmot Proviso. He also proposed the gradual compensated emancipation of slaves in the District of Columbia. Lincoln argued that such measures—firm opposition to the expansion of slavery, gradual emancipation, and the colonization of freed slaves in Africa and elsewhere—represented the only practical way to address the issue. But his ideas were derided by both abolitionists and proslavery activists. Dismayed, Lincoln withdrew from politics and devoted his energies to a lucrative legal practice representing railroads and manufacturers.

Lincoln returned to the political fray after the passage of Stephen Douglas's Kansas-Nebraska Act. Attacking Douglas's doctrine of popular sovereignty, Lincoln articulated a clear position on slavery. He would not threaten the institution in areas where it existed but would use the authority of the national government to exclude it from the territories. Beyond that, Lincoln expressed his conviction that the nation must eventually cut out slavery like a "cancer."

Abandoning the Whig Party in favor of the Republicans, Lincoln soon emerged as their leader in Illinois. Campaigning for the U.S. Senate against Stephen Douglas in 1858, Lincoln alerted his audiences to the dangers of the "Slave Power" conspiracy. He warned that the proslavery Supreme Court might soon declare that the Constitution "does not permit a state to exclude slavery from its limits," just as it had decided (in *Dred Scott*) that "neither Congress nor the territorial legislature can do it." In that event, he continued, "we shall awake to the reality . . . that the Supreme Court has made Illinois a slave state." This fear informed Lincoln's famous "House Divided" speech. Quoting from the Bible, "A house divided against itself cannot stand," he predicted a constitutional crisis: "I believe this government cannot endure permanently half slave and half free. . . . It will become all one thing, or all the other."

THE REPUBLICAN POLITICIAN

Lincoln's 1858 duel with Stephen Douglas for the U.S. Senate attracted national interest because of Douglas's prominence and Lincoln's reputation as a formidable speaker. During a series of seven debates Douglas declared his support for white supremacy and attacked Lincoln for his alleged belief in "negro equality." Put on the defensive by Douglas's racist tactics, Lincoln advocated economic opportunity for blacks (but not equal political rights) and asked Douglas how he could accept the *Dred Scott* decision (which protected slaveowners' property in the territories) and at the same time advocate popular sovereignty. Douglas responded with the so-called Freeport Doctrine, asserting that settlers could exclude slavery simply by not adopting local legislation to protect it. Douglas's statement upset both proslavery advocates, who feared they would be denied the victory won in the *Dred Scott* decision, and abolitionists, who were not convinced that local regulations would halt the expansion of slavery. Nonetheless, the Democrats carried Illinois, and the state legislature reelected Douglas to the U.S. Senate. Yet Lincoln had established himself as a national leader, and the Republican Party, by winning control of the House of Representatives in the election of 1858, had moved a step closer to national power.

In the wake of Republican gains southern Democrats divided into two groups. Moderates such as Senator Jefferson Davis of Mississippi, who were known as Southern Rights Democrats, pursued the traditional policy of seeking ironclad commitments to protect slavery in the territories. Radicals such as Robert Barnwell Rhett of South Carolina and William Lowndes Yancey of Alabama actively promoted secession.

Radical northerners played into their hands. In 1858 Senator William Seward declared that freedom and slavery were locked in "an irrepressible conflict." In October 1859 the militant abolitionist John Brown led eighteen heavily armed black and white men in a raid that temporarily seized the federal arsenal at Harpers Ferry, Virginia. Brown's explicit purpose was to provide arms for a slave rebellion that

Abraham Lincoln and Stephen Douglas, 1860

When Douglas and Lincoln squared off in the presidential election of 1860, they distributed thousands of silk campaign-ribbons bearing their portraits and signatures. The well-known photographer Matthew Brady took pictures and retouched the images to make them more flattering—smoothing out Lincoln's gaunt and well-lined face and slimming down Douglas's ample cheeks.
(Collection of Janice L. and David J. Frent)

would establish an African American state in the South. Republican leaders disavowed Brown's raid, but Democrats called his plot "a natural, logical, inevitable result of the doctrines and teachings of the Republican party." Fueling the Democratic charges were letters that linked six leading abolitionists to the financing of Brown's raid. Brown was charged with treason, sentenced to death, and hanged— only to be praised by reformer Henry David Thoreau as "an angel of light." Slaveholders were horrified by northern admiration of Brown and looked toward the future with fear. "The aim of the present black republican organization is the destruction of the social system of the Southern States, without regard to consequences," warned one newspaper.

Nor could the South count on the Democratic Party to protect its interests. At the April 1860 party convention northern Democrats rejected Jefferson Davis's program to protect slavery in the territories, prompting the delegates from eight southern states to leave the hall. At a second Democratic convention in Baltimore northern and western delegates nominated Douglas; southern Democrats met separately and nominated Buchanan's vice president, John C. Breckinridge of Kentucky. The Democratic Party had broken into two sectional factions.

The Republicans sensed victory. They courted white voters by opposing both slavery and racial equality: "Missouri for white men and white men for Missouri," declared that state's Republican platform. On the national level the Republican convention chose Lincoln as its presidential candidate. Lincoln's position on slavery was more moderate than that of the best-known Republicans, Senator William H. Seward of New York and Salmon P. Chase of Ohio, who demanded its abolition. Lincoln also conveyed a compelling egalitarian image that appealed to smallholding farmers and wage earners. And Lincoln's home territory—the rapidly growing Midwest—was crucial in the competition between Democrats and Republicans. The Republican platform followed Lincoln's views and struck a moderate tone, upholding free soil in the West and denying the right of states to secede but ruling out direct interference with slavery in the South. In addition, the platform endorsed the old Whig program of economic development, which had gained increasing support in the Midwest, especially after the Panic of 1857.

The Republican strategy was successful. Lincoln received only 40 percent of the popular vote but won every northern and western state except New Jersey and garnered a majority in the electoral college. Douglas took 30 percent of the total vote, drawing support from all regions except the South, but won electoral votes only in Missouri and New Jersey. Breckinridge captured every state in the Deep South as well as Delaware, Maryland, and North Carolina, while John Bell, a former Tennessee Whig who became the nominee of the compromise-seeking Constitutional Union Party, carried the upper South states where the Whigs had been strongest: Kentucky, Tennessee, and Virginia.

The Republicans had united the Northeast, the Midwest, and the Far West behind free soil and had seized national power. To many southerners it now seemed time to think carefully about the meaning of Lincoln's words of 1858 that the Union must "become all one thing, or all the other."

For Further Exploration

Patricia Nelson Limerick, *The Legacy of Conquest: The Unbroken Past of the American West* (1989), provides a sharply written interpretation of the struggle among individuals, groups, and nations for control of the resources of the vast region. David Potter, *The Impending Crisis, 1848–1861* (1976), presents a lucid and detailed account of the political history of the years leading up to the Civil War, while the classic study by Avery Craven, *The Growth of Southern Nationalism* (1953), traces the emergence of sectional feeling and stresses the importance of John Brown's raid in the southern movement toward secession. For an eloquent discussion of the ideology and politics of the Republican Party, see Eric Foner, *Free Soil, Free Labor, Free Men* (1970). Michael Holt's *The Crisis of the 1850s* (1978) shows how the loss of morale among voters and the collapse of the Second-Party System allowed sectional rivalries to engulf the nation in war. For an incisive treatment of Lincoln's personal and political life, see Stephen Oates, *With Malice Toward None: A Life of Abraham Lincoln* (1977).

A fine video documentary, *The West* (6 hours), by Ken Burns and Stephen Ives has a useful website—"New Perspectives on the West" at <http://www.pbs.org/thewest>—that

T I M E L I N E

1820s	Growth of cattle ranching in Mexican California		Fugitive Slave Act antagonizes northern abolitionists.
1821	Mexico wins independence from Spain.	1851	American (Know-Nothing) Party formed
1836	Texas proclaims independence from Mexico.	1852	Harriet Beecher Stowe's *Uncle Tom's Cabin*
1842	Overland migration to Oregon begins.	1854	Ostend Manifesto
1845	John O'Sullivan coins term *Manifest Destiny*. Texas Republic admitted to Union as slave state		Kansas-Nebraska Act Republican Party formed
		1856	"Bleeding Kansas" devastated by guerrilla war, showing problems in Douglas's scheme of popular sovereignty
1846	War with Mexico begins. Treaty with Britain divides Oregon Country at 49th parallel. Wilmot Proviso to prohibit slavery in annexed Mexican territories dies in Congress.	1857	*Dred Scott v. Sandford* allows slavery in territories.
		1858	James Buchanan backs Lecompton constitution. Lincoln-Douglas debates
1848	Gold discovered in California In Treaty of Guadalupe Hidalgo Mexico cedes Texas, New Mexico, and California to U.S. Free Soil Party organized	1859	John Brown's raid on Harpers Ferry
		1860	Abraham Lincoln elected president in four-way contest
1850	Compromise of 1850 seeks to preserve Union.		

includes a good collection of maps, biographical essays, original documents, and images. The PBS documentary *The U.S.-Mexican War* (4 hours) and its website at <http://www.pbs.org/usmexicanwar> view the war both from the American and the Mexican perspectives, drawing on the expertise of historians from each country. "*Uncle Tom's Cabin* and American Culture: A Multi-Media Archive" at <http://jefferson.village.virginia.edu/utc/> is an extremely rich website that explores the literary and cultural context of the time through essays, original documents, and recordings of minstrel music.

Chapter 14

TWO SOCIETIES AT WAR
1861–1865

Our fathers made this country, we their children are to save it.
—Enlistee, 12th Ohio Regiment, Union Army, 1861

"What a scene it was," the Union soldier Elisha Hunt Rhodes wrote in his diary as the battle of Gettysburg ended in 1863. "Oh the dead and the dying on this bloody field." The passions kindled by Southern Rights and American nationalism had inspired thousands of men to die in battle, and the slaughter would continue for two more years. "What is this all about?" asked Confederate lieutenant R. M. Collins at the end of another gruesome battle. "Why is it that 200,000 men of one blood and tongue . . . [should be] seeking one another's lives? We could settle our differences by compromising and all be at home in ten days." But there was no compromise—not in 1861 or even in 1865.

To explain why the war was fought—and fought to the bitter end—is not simple, but racial slavery is an important part of the answer. For political leaders in the South the Republican victory in 1860 presented a clear and immediate danger to their way of life. They knew that Lincoln regarded slavery as morally wrong and that the Republicans would prevent the extension of slavery into the territories and might well attack the institution in the South. Soon, a southern senator warned, "cohorts of Federal office-holders, Abolitionists, may be sent into [our] midst" to mobilize the African American population. The result, he and many others predicted, would be waves of bloody slave revolts and the prospect of racial intermixture. "Better, far better! [to] endure all horrors of civil war," declared a Confederate recruit from Virginia, "than to see the dusky sons of Ham leading the fair daughters of the South to the altar." To save slavery and white supremacy radical southern leaders embarked on the dangerous journey of secession.

But Lincoln and the North would not let them go in peace. In a world still ruled by kings and princes they believed that the dissolution of the American Union would endanger forever the principle of a republican government based on majority rule, constitutional procedures, and democratic elections. "We cannot escape history," the new president declared. "We shall nobly save, or meanly loose, the last best, hope of earth." As a young Union army recruit from Ohio put the issue, "If our institutions prove a failure . . . of what value will be house, family, or friends?"

And so came the Civil War. Called the "War Between the States" by southerners and the "War of the Rebellion" by northerners, the struggle went on until the great issues of the Union and of slavery had been resolved once and for all. The cost was incredibly high: more lives lost than in all the nation's subsequent wars put together and a century-long legacy of bitterness between the triumphant North and the vanquished South.

Secession and Military Stalemate, 1861–1862

After Lincoln's election in November 1860 secessionist fervor swept through the Deep South. In the four months before Lincoln's inauguration in March 1861 political leaders in Washington struggled to forge a new compromise that (like those of 1787, 1821, and 1850) would preserve the Union.

CHOOSING SIDES

The movement toward secession was most rapid in South Carolina—the home of Calhoun, nullification, and the Southern Radical movement. Robert Barnwell Rhett and other South Carolina fire-eaters had been planning for secession since 1850 and now called a convention to achieve their goal. On December 20 the convention voted unanimously to dissolve "the union now subsisting between South Carolina and other States."

Moving quickly, fire-eaters elsewhere in the Deep South called similar conventions and organized vigilante groups and militia. In early January, amid an atmosphere of public celebration, Mississippi enacted a secession ordinance. Within a month Florida, Alabama, Georgia, Louisiana, and Texas had also left the Union (see Map 14.1). In early February the jubilant secessionists met in Montgomery, Alabama, to proclaim a new nation—the Confederate States of America. They adopted a provisional constitution and named Jefferson Davis, a former U.S. senator and secretary of war, as provisional president.

Secessionist fervor was less intense in the eight slave states of the upper South (Virginia, Delaware, Maryland, North Carolina, Kentucky, Tennessee, Missouri, and Arkansas), where there were fewer slaves and yeomen farmers had greater political power. In January 1861 the legislatures of Virginia and Tennessee voted to resist any federal invasion but went no further. Seeking a compromise that would restore the Union, upper South leaders proposed federal guarantees for slavery in the states where it existed.

Meanwhile, the Union government floundered. In his last message to Congress in December 1860 President Buchanan declared secession illegal but said that the federal government lacked the authority to restore the Union by force. South Carolina immediately claimed that Buchanan's message implicitly recognized its independence and demanded the surrender of Fort Sumter, a federal garrison in

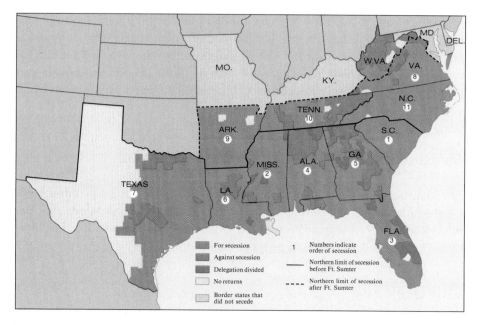

MAP 14.1
The Process of Secession, 1860–1861

The states with the highest concentration of slaves (see Map 9.2) led the secessionist movement. After the attack on Fort Sumter they were joined by the states of the upper South. Yeomen farmers in Tennessee and the backcountry of Alabama, Georgia, and Virginia opposed secession but, except in the future state of West Virginia, generally rallied to the Confederate cause and until 1864 supported the war effort.

Charleston harbor. Reluctant to turn over federal property, Buchanan tested the secessionists' resolve by ordering an unarmed merchant ship to resupply the fort. When the South Carolinians fired on the ship, Buchanan backed down, refusing to order the navy to escort it into the harbor.

As the crisis continued, Buchanan urged Congress to find a compromise. The proposal that received the most support was submitted by Senator John J. Crittenden of Kentucky, who hoped to follow in the footsteps of his mentor, Henry Clay, and devise a compromise similar to that of 1850. Crittenden advanced a two-part plan. First he proposed—and won congressional approval for—a constitutional amendment that would permanently protect slavery from federal interference in any state where it presently existed. Second, to deal with the territories, he called for the westward extension of the Missouri Compromise line (36° 30' north) to the California border, with slavery barred north of the line and protected to the south— including any territories "hereafter acquired." After consulting with President-elect Lincoln, congressional Republicans rejected this part of Crittenden's plan. Lincoln was determined to uphold the doctrine of free soil and feared that extending the

Missouri Compromise line would encourage the South to embark on new imperialist adventures in Mexico, the Caribbean, and Latin America.

In his inaugural address on March 4, 1861, Lincoln carefully balanced a call for reconciliation with a firm commitment to the Union. He promised to permit slavery in states where it existed but stood firm for free soil in the territories. Most important, he stated that secession was illegal and that acts of violence against the Union constituted insurrection. He announced his intention to enforce federal law throughout the United States and—of particular relevance to Fort Sumter—to hold federal property in the seceded states. The choice was the South's: return to the Union or face war.

The decision came quickly. Within a month of Lincoln's inauguration the garrison at Fort Sumter urgently needed supplies. To maintain his credibility the new president dispatched a relief expedition, promising that it would not land troops or arms unless the rebels disrupted the delivery of food and medicine. Jefferson Davis and his government welcomed Lincoln's decision, believing that a confrontation would turn the wavering upper South against the North and win foreign support for the Confederate cause. Resolving to take the fort immediately, Davis demanded its surrender. When Major Robert Anderson refused to comply, the Confederate forces opened fire on April 12, forcing the surrender of the Fort two days later. The next day Lincoln called 75,000 state militiamen into federal service for ninety days to put down an insurrection "too powerful to be suppressed by the ordinary course of judicial proceedings." All talk of compromise was past.

Northerners responded to Lincoln's call to arms with enthusiasm. Asked to provide thirteen regiments of volunteers, Republican Governor William Dennison of Ohio sent twenty. "The lion in us is thoroughly roused," he explained. Many northern Democrats were equally committed to the Union cause. As Stephen Douglas declared six weeks before his death: "Every man must be for the United States or against it. There can be no neutrals in this war, only patriots—or traitors."

The white residents of the upper South now had to choose between the Union and the Confederacy, and their decision was crucial. Those eight states accounted for two-thirds of the South's white population, more than three-fourths of its industrial production, and well over half its food and fuel. They were home to many of the nation's best military leaders, including Colonel Robert E. Lee of Virginia, a career officer whom General-in-Chief Winfield Scott recommended to Lincoln as field commander of the new Union army. And they were geographically strategic. Kentucky, with its 500-mile border on the Ohio River, was essential to the movement of troops and supplies. Maryland was vital to the Union's security because it surrounded the nation's capital on the north.

The weight of history decided the outcome in Virginia, the original home of American slavery. Three days after the fall of Fort Sumter a Virginia convention passed an ordinance of secession by a vote of eighty-eight to fifty-five. The dissenting votes came mainly from the yeoman-dominated northwestern counties (see Map 14.1); elsewhere in Virginia whites rallied to the Confederate cause. Refusing

Scott's offer to command the Union troops, Robert E. Lee resigned from the army. "Save in defense of my native state," Lee told Scott, "I never desire again to draw my sword." Arkansas, Tennessee, and North Carolina quickly joined Virginia in the Confederacy.

Lincoln moved aggressively to hold the rest of the upper South. In May he ordered General George B. McClellan to take control of northwestern Virginia, thus securing the railway line between Washington and the Ohio Valley. In October voters there overwhelmingly approved the creation of a new state, West Virginia, which was admitted to the Union in 1863. The Union cause also triumphed in Delaware but it was much less popular in Maryland, where slavery was well entrenched. A pro-Confederate mob attacked Massachusetts troops marching between railroad stations in Baltimore, causing the war's first combat deaths: four soldiers and twelve civilians. When other Maryland secessionists destroyed railroad bridges and telegraph lines, Lincoln ordered military occupation of the state and imprisoned suspected secessionists, including members of the state legislature. He released them only in November 1861, after Unionists had gained control of the Maryland legislature.

In Missouri the key to communications and trade on the Missouri and upper Mississippi Rivers, Lincoln mobilized support among the large German American community. In July a force of German American militia defeated Confederate sympathizers commanded by the governor. Despite continuing raids by Confederate guerrilla bands led by William Quantrill and Jesse and Frank James, the Union retained control of Missouri.

In Kentucky secessionist and Unionist sentiment was evenly balanced, so Lincoln moved cautiously. He waited until August, when Unionists took control of the state government, before ordering federal troops to cut Kentucky's thriving export trade in horses, mules, whiskey, and foodstuffs. When the Confederacy responded to this cut-off by moving troops into Kentucky, the Unionist legislature asked for federal protection. In September Illinois volunteers under the command of the relatively unknown brigadier general Ulysses S. Grant crossed the Ohio River and drove out the Confederates. Of the eight states of the upper South, Lincoln had kept four (Delaware, Maryland, Kentucky, and Missouri) and a portion of a fifth (western Virginia) in the Union.

SETTING OBJECTIVES AND DEVISING STRATEGIES

After secession Confederate leaders called on their people to defend the independence of the new nation. At his inauguration in February 1861 Jefferson Davis identified the Confederate cause with that of the American Revolution; like their grandfathers, white southerners were fighting against tyranny and for the "sacred right of self-government." As Davis put it, the Confederacy sought "no conquest, no aggrandizement, no concession of any kind from the states with which we were lately confederated; all we ask is to be let alone." The decision to focus on the defense of the Confederacy (and not to conquer western territories) gave southern leaders a strong advantage: they needed only a military stalemate to guarantee independence.

Lincoln made his first major statement on Union goals and strategy in a speech to Congress on July 4, 1861. He portrayed secession as an attack on popular government, America's great contribution to world history, telling his audience that the issue was simple: "Whether a constitutional republic, or a democracy—a government of the people, by the same people—can or cannot maintain its territorial integrity against its domestic foes." Only by crushing the rebellion could the nation preserve its principles. Lincoln therefore rejected General Winfield Scott's plan to use economic sanctions and a naval blockade to persuade the Confederates to return to the Union. Instead, the president called for an aggressive military strategy and insisted on a policy of unconditional surrender.

The president knew that the northern public wanted a strike toward Richmond, the Confederate capital, and he hoped an early victory would end the rebellion. He therefore dispatched General Irwin McDowell and an army of 30,000 men to attack P.G.T. Beauregard's force of 20,000 troops at Manassas, a major rail junction in Virginia 30 miles southwest of Washington. McDowell attacked strongly on July 21 near Manassas Creek (also called Bull Run), but panic swept through his troops during a Confederate counterattack. For the first time Union soldiers heard the hair-raising rebel yell. "The peculiar corkscrew sensation that it sends down your backbone under these circumstances can never be told," one Union veteran wrote. "You have to feel it." McDowell's troops retreated in disarray to Washington, along with the many civilians who had come to observe the battle. The victorious Confederate troops also dispersed, confused and without the wagons and supplies they needed to pursue McDowell's army.

It was now clear that the rebellion would not be easily crushed. To bolster northern morale, shattered by the rout at Bull Run, Lincoln replaced McDowell with General George B. McClellan and signed bills for the enlistment of an additional million men, who would serve for three years in the newly created Army of the Potomac. A cautious military engineer, McClellan spent the winter of 1861 to 1862 training raw recruits, and in 1862 he launched the first major offensive of the war, a thrust toward Richmond. In a maneuver that required skillful logistics, the Union general transported about 100,000 troops by boat down the Potomac River and Chesapeake Bay and then up the peninsula between the York and James Rivers toward the South's capital. But McClellan moved slowly, despite Lincoln's advice to "strike a blow" quickly, allowing the Confederates to mount a counterstroke. In May a Confederate army under Thomas J. ("Stonewall") Jackson marched rapidly north up the Shenandoah Valley in western Virginia, threatening Washington. To head off the danger Lincoln diverted 30,000 troops from McClellan's army, but Jackson, a brilliant general, defeated three Union armies in the valley. Then Jackson joined the Confederates' formidable commanding general, Robert E. Lee, who had confronted McClellan outside Richmond. Lee launched a ferocious attack that lasted for seven days (June 25 to July 1), suffering heavy casualties (20,000 to the Union's 10,000). But McClellan failed to exploit his advantage, refusing to renew the offensive unless he received fresh troops. Lincoln ordered the withdrawal of the Army of the Potomac, and Richmond remained secure.

Lee promptly went on the offensive, hoping for victories that would humiliate Lincoln's government. Joining with Jackson in northern Virginia, Lee routed a Union army in the Second Battle of Bull Run (August 1862) and then struck north through western Maryland, where he met with near disaster. When Lee divided his force—sending Jackson to capture Harpers Ferry in West Virginia—a copy of his orders fell into McClellan's hands. But the Union general again failed to pursue his advantage, delaying his attack until Lee's depleted army had occupied a strong defensive position behind Antietam Creek, near Sharpsburg, Maryland. Outnumbered 87,000 to 50,000, Lee desperately fought off McClellan's attacks. Just as Union regiments were about to overwhelm his right flank, Jackson's troops arrived, saving the Confederates from a major defeat. Appalled by Union casualties, McClellan let Lee retreat to Virginia.

The fighting at Antietam was savage. A Wisconsin officer described his men as "loading and firing with demoniacal fury and shouting and laughing hysterically." At a critical point in the battle a sunken road, nicknamed Bloody Lane, was filled with Confederate bodies two and three deep, and the attacking Union troops knelt on "this ghastly flooring" to shoot at the retreating Confederates. The battle at Antietam on September 17, 1862, remains the bloodiest single day in U.S. military history. Together the Confederate and Union dead numbered 4,800 and the wounded 18,500, of whom 3,000 soon died. (In comparison, 6,000 Americans were wounded or killed on D-Day, which began the invasion of Nazi-occupied France, in World War II.)

In public Lincoln declared Antietam a victory, but privately he declared that McClellan should have fought Lee to the finish. A masterful organizer of men and supplies, McClellan lacked the stomach for an all-out attack. Dismissing McClellan, Lincoln began a long search for an effective replacement. His first choice was Ambrose E. Burnside, who proved to be more daring but less competent. In December, after heavy losses in futile attacks against well-entrenched Confederate forces at Fredericksburg, Virginia, Burnside resigned his command and Lincoln replaced him with Joseph ("Fighting Joe") Hooker. As 1862 ended, the Confederates had some reason to be content: the war in the East was a stalemate.

In the West Union forces had been more successful (see Map 14.2). Their goal was to control the Ohio, Mississippi, and Missouri Rivers, dividing the Confederacy and reducing the mobility of its armies. The decision of Kentucky not to join the rebellion had already given the Union dominance in the Ohio River Valley. In 1862 the Union army launched a series of highly innovative land and water operations to gain control of the Tennessee and Mississippi Rivers as well. In the north, General Ulysses S. Grant used riverboats clad with iron plates to take Fort Henry on the Tennessee River and Fort Donelson on the Cumberland. Grant then moved south

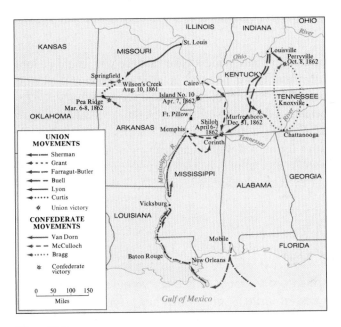

M A P 14.2
The Western Campaigns, 1861–1862

As the Civil War intensified during the course of 1861, Union and Confederate military and naval forces fought to control the great valleys of the Ohio, Tennessee, and Mississippi Rivers. By the end of 1862 Union forces had achieved dominance over most of these crucial transportation routes, allowing them to keep Missouri in the Union, drive Confederate armies out of Kentucky and half of Tennessee, and capture New Orleans. With their victory at Shiloh (along the Tennessee River), northern forces carried the war to the borders of the states of the Deep South.

along the Tennessee to seize critical railroad lines. A Confederate army under Albert Sidney Johnston and P.G.T. Beauregard caught Grant by surprise on April 6 near a small log church named Shiloh. Grant relentlessly threw troops into the battle, forcing a Confederate withdrawal the following day but taking huge casualties. Grant described a large field "so covered with dead that it would have been possible to walk over the clearing in any direction, stepping on dead bodies, without a foot touching the ground." The cost in lives was high, but Lincoln was pleased. "What I want . . . is generals who will fight battles and win victories." Grant had done that, creating military momentum for the Union in the West.

Three weeks later Union naval forces commanded by David G. Farragut struck from the south, moving through the Mississippi Delta from the Gulf of Mexico to capture New Orleans. The Union now held the South's financial center and largest city as well as a major base for future naval operations. Union victories in the West had thus significantly undermined Confederate strength in the Mississippi Valley.

Toward Total War

The carnage at Antietam and Shiloh had made it clear that the war would be long and costly. After Shiloh, Grant later noted, he "gave up all idea of saving the Union except by complete conquest." The conflict became a total war—arraying the entire resources of the two societies against each other and eventually resulting in warfare against enemy civilians. Aided by a strong party and a talented cabinet, Lincoln skillfully mobilized the North for all-out war, organizing an effective central government. Jefferson Davis was less successful in harnessing the resources of the South because the eleven states of the Confederacy remained deeply suspicious of centralized rule.

MOBILIZING ARMIES AND CIVILIANS

Initially, patriotic fervor filled both armies with eager volunteers. The call for soldiers was especially successful in the South, which had a strong military tradition and an ample supply of trained officers. But the initial surge of enlistments fell off as the people saw the realities of war: heavy losses to disease and dreadful battlefield carnage. Soon both governments faced the necessity of forced enlistment (see American Voices, "A Doctor on the Health and Patriotism of Union Recruits").

The Confederacy was the first to act. In April 1862, after the defeat at Shiloh, the Confederate Congress imposed the first legally binding draft in American history. One law extended all existing enlistments for the duration of the war; another required three years of military service from all able-bodied men between the ages of eighteen and thirty-five. In September, after the heavy casualties at Antietam, the age limit was raised to forty-five. The Confederate draft had two loopholes. First, it exempted one white man—either the planter or an overseer—for each twenty slaves, allowing men on large plantations to avoid military service. Second, drafted men could hire substitutes. Before this provision was repealed in 1864, the price for a substitute had risen to $300 in gold, about three times the annual wages of a skilled worker. Laborers and yeomen farmers angrily complained that it was "a rich man's war and a poor man's fight."

Consequently, some southerners refused to serve, and the Confederate government lacked the power to compel them. Because the Confederate constitution vested sovereignty in the individual states, strong governors such as Joseph Brown of Georgia and Zebulon Vance of North Carolina simply ignored Davis's first draft call in early 1862. Elsewhere state judges issued writs of habeas corpus (a legal process designed to protect people from arbitrary arrest) and ordered the Confederate army to release protesting draftees. Reluctantly the Confederate Congress overrode the judges' authority to free conscripted men, enabling the Confederacy to keep substantial armies in the field well into 1864.

AMERICAN VOICES

A Doctor on the Health and Patriotism of Union Recruits

HORACE O. CRANE

*D*r. *Horace O. Crane was an army medical examiner for the Union army in Wisconsin. In the following report to his superiors, he dissected the various reasons that men tried to avoid service in the Union army. Nonetheless, Wisconsin provided more Union soldiers (in relation to population) than almost any other state, in part because many of its people were native-born American Protestants who strongly opposed slavery.*

While on duty [in Wisconsin] . . . I examined fourteen thousand one hundred and sixty-five men, mostly enrolled or drafted men, nearly all of whom claimed severe indisposition of some kind. . . .

A large preponderance of this [examined] population is foreign, representing every state and duchy in Europe. They subsist by the cultivation of small farms and the manufacture of lumber and shingles from their pine-forests. Necessity compels them to be industrious, but they are usually very poor and ignorant, mostly Roman Catholics, and as such generally *hostile to the conscription act.* . . . Demagogues, interested in preserving their [Democratic] party ascendancy, have educated this people to believe that the war was not only useless and cruel, but that its effect would be to finally subvert their civil and political privileges.

The frauds practiced by enrolled and drafted men are so numerous and varied as to require the utmost vigilance on the part of the surgeon. . . . [For example:] Alleged blindness of the right eye is very common; the pupil often appearing fully and apparently permanently dilated. . . . Some of these men had *belladonna* [a poison plant that causes dilation] upon their persons at the time of the examination, which they had been using freely. . . .

Occupation, in this district, is of far greater importance in the selection of recruits than locality. . . . The lumbermen (unless they have hernia) are universally good recruits, having abundance of vitality, with muscles well developed; they are a brave, cheerful, and hardy class. In one sub-district is a large tannery, and a boot and shoe manufactory . . . ; of these mechanics, nearly sixty-five percent, were discharged from enrollment, *before the draft*, for physical disability [because of] . . . organic disease of heart or lungs. . . . From four years' experience . . . I am decidedly of opinion that the . . . descendants of the early settlers of New England, New York, Pennsylvania, and Ohio, where physical development and courage are combined with intelligence and patriotism, make the best soldiers the world has ever seen.

SOURCE: Peter T. Harstad, ed., "A Civil War Examiner: The Report of Dr. Horace O. Crane," *Wisconsin Magazine of History* 48 (Spring 1965), pp. 226–31.

The Union government took a more authoritarian stance toward potential foes and ordinary citizens. To prevent opposition to the war Lincoln suspended habeas corpus and over the course of the war imprisoned about 15,000 Confederate sympathizers without trial. The president also extended martial law to civilians who discouraged enlistment or resisted the draft, making them subject to military courts rather than local juries. This firm policy had the desired effect. The Militia Act of 1862 set a quota of volunteers for each state, which was increased by the Enrollment Act of 1863. States and towns enticed volunteers with cash bounties, prompting the enlistment or reenlistment of almost a million men. As in the South wealthy men could avoid the draft by providing a substitute or paying a $300 commutation, or exemption, fee.

The Enrollment Act sparked significant opposition, as thousands of recent immigrants refused to serve in the Union army, saying it was not their fight. Northern Democrats exploited this resentment by charging that Lincoln was drafting poor whites to free the slaves and flood the cities with black laborers. Some Democrats opposed the war, believing that the South should be allowed to secede; others simply wanted to protect the interests of immigrants, most of whom were Democratic voters. In July 1863 hostility to the draft and to African Americans spilled onto the streets of New York City. For five days immigrant Irish and German workers ran rampant, burning draft offices, sacking the homes of important Republicans, and attacking the police. The rioters lynched and mutilated a dozen African Americans, drove hundreds of black families from their homes, and burned down the Colored Orphan Asylum. Lincoln rushed in Union troops, who killed more than a hundred rioters and suppressed the insurrection.

The Union government's determination to wage total war won greater support among native-born citizens. In 1861 prominent New Yorkers established the United States Sanitary Commission. Its task was to provide medical services and prevent deaths from disease, which accounted for three-fourths of the casualties in the recently concluded Crimean War between Britain and Russia. Through its network of 7,000 local auxiliaries, the Sanitary Commission gathered supplies; distributed clothing, food, and medicine to the army; improved the sanitary standards of camp life; and recruited battlefield nurses and doctors for the Union Army Medical Bureau. These efforts were not consistently successful. Diseases—dysentery, typhoid, and malaria as well as childhood viruses such as mumps and measles, to which many rural men had not developed an immunity—killed about 250,000 Union soldiers, about twice the number who died in combat. Still, because of better sanitation and high-quality food the mortality rate among Union troops from disease and wounds was substantially lower than that in other major nineteenth-century wars. Confederate soldiers were less fortunate. Although thousands of white women volunteered as nurses, the Confederate health system was poorly organized. Thousands of southern soldiers contracted scurvy because of the lack of vitamin C in their diets, and they died from camp diseases at higher rates than did Union soldiers.

Draft Riots in New York City

The Enrollment Act of 1863 enraged many workers who opposed the war, especially recent Irish and German immigrants. In July in New York City they took out their anger on free blacks in a week-long riot. As the club-waving mob hangs an African American, three other blacks escape by climbing over a fence. The violence against African Americans received wide publicity (this engraving appeared in the *Illustrated London News* on August 8, 1863) and prompted many northerners to increase their support for the war effort.
(Culver Pictures)

Women took a leading role in the Sanitary Commission and other wartime agencies. As superintendent of female nurses, Dorothea Dix became the first woman to receive a major federal appointment. Dix used her influence to combat the prejudice against women treating men, opening a new occupation to women. Thousands of educated Union women also joined the war effort as clerks in the expanding governmental bureaucracy, while in the South women staffed the efficient Confederate postal service. Indeed, in both sections millions of women assumed new economic responsibilities and worked with far greater intensity. They took over many farm tasks previously done by men and went to work in schools and textile, clothing, and shoe factories. A number of women even took on military duties as spies, scouts, and (disguised as men) soldiers. As the nurse Clara Barton, who later founded the American Red Cross, recalled, "At the war's end, woman was at least fifty years in advance of the normal position which continued peace would have assigned her."

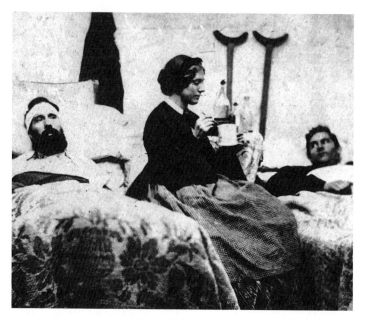

Hospital Nursing

Working as nurses in chaotic battlefront hospitals, thousands of Union and Confederate women gained firsthand experience of the horrors of war. But a sense of calm prevails in this behind-the-lines Union hospital in Nashville, Tennessee, as nurse Anne Belle tends to the needs of those recovering from their wounds. Most nurses were unpaid volunteers, cooking and cleaning for their patients as well as tending to their injuries.
(Massachusetts Commandery Military Order of the Loyal Legion and the U.S. Army Military History Institute)

MOBILIZING RESOURCES

Wars are usually won by the side with superior resources and economic organization, and in this regard the Union entered the war with a distinct advantage. With nearly two-thirds of the American people, about two-thirds of the nation's railroad mileage, and nearly 90 percent of American industrial output, the North's economy was far superior to the South's. The North had an especially great advantage in the manufacture of cannon and rifles because many of its arms factories were equipped for mass production.

But the Confederate position was far from weak. Virginia, North Carolina, and Tennessee had substantial industrial capacity. Richmond, with its Tredegar Iron Works, was an important industrial center, and in 1861 the Confederacy transported to Richmond the gun-making machinery from the U.S. armory at Harpers Ferry. The production of the Richmond armory, the purchase of Enfield rifles from Britain, and the capture of 100,000 Union guns enabled the Confederacy to provide every infantryman with a modern rifle-musket by 1863.

Moreover, with 3 million slaves, the Confederacy commanded an enormous workforce. Kept in the fields by their masters, slaves produced food for the army and cotton for export. Confederate leaders counted on "King Cotton" to provide revenue to purchase clothes, boots, blankets, and weapons from abroad. They also counted on cotton as a diplomatic weapon, hoping that the British, who depended on the South to supply their textile factories, would grant diplomatic recognition and provide military aid. Although the British government never recognized the Confederacy as an independent nation, it regarded the conflict as a war (rather than a domestic insurrection), thereby giving the rebels the status of a belligerent power with the right under international law to borrow money and purchase weapons. Thus the odds did not necessarily favor the Union, despite its superior resources.

The outcome depended on the success of the rival governments in mobilizing their societies. To build political support for their party and boost industrial output, Lincoln and the Republicans enacted the program of national mercantilism previously advocated by Henry Clay and the Whig Party. First the Republicans raised tariffs, winning praise from northeastern manufacturers and laborers who feared competition from cheap foreign goods. Then Secretary of the Treasury Salmon P. Chase created a national banking system—an important element of every modern centralized government—by linking thousands of local banks. This integrated system was far more effective in raising capital and controlling inflation than earlier efforts by the First and Second Banks of the United States had been. Finally, the Lincoln administration devised a far-reaching system of internal improvements. In 1862 the Republican Congress began to build transcontinental railroads, chartering the Union Pacific and Central Pacific railways and subsidizing them lavishly. It gave them 20 square miles of federal land for every mile of track they put down and in 1864 provided a similar subsidy to the Northern Pacific. In addition, the Republicans moved aggressively to provide northern farmers with "free land" in the West. The Homestead Act of 1862 gave heads of families or individuals age twenty-one or older the title to 160 acres of public land after five years of residence and improvement. This economic program sustained the allegiance of many northerners to the Republican Party while bolstering the Union's ability to fight the war.

In contrast, the Confederate government had a much less coherent economic policy. True to its states'-rights philosophy the Confederacy left most economic matters in the hands of the state governments. But as the realities of total war became clear, the Davis administration took some extraordinary measures: it built and operated shipyards, armories, foundries, and textile mills; commandeered food and scarce raw materials such as coal, iron, copper, and lead; requisitioned slaves to work on fortifications; and exercised direct control over foreign trade. As the war wore on, ordinary southern citizens resented these measures, especially in areas where Confederate leaders failed to manage wartime shortages. To sustain the war effort they increasingly counted on racial solidarity: Jefferson Davis warned whites that a

Union victory would destroy slavery "and reduce the whites to the degraded position of the African race."

For both the North and the South the cost of fighting a total war was enormous. In the Union government spending shot up from less than 2 percent of gross national product to about 15 percent. To meet those expenses the Republicans established a powerful modern state that raised money in three ways. First the government increased revenue by increasing tariffs on consumer goods and imposing direct taxes on business corporations, large inheritances, and incomes. These levies paid for about 20 percent of the cost of the war. The sale of Treasury bonds financed another 65 percent of the northern war effort. Led by Jay Cooke, a Philadelphia banker, the Treasury used newspaper advertisements and 2,500 subagents to persuade nearly a million northern families to buy war bonds. In addition, the National Banking Acts of 1863 and 1864 essentially forced state banks to accept a national charter and to purchase Treasury bonds.

The Union financed the remaining cost of the war by printing paper money beginning in 1862 and requiring the public to accept it as legal tender. By the end of the war there were nearly $450 million of these "greenbacks" in circulation. Unlike the "Continentals" issued during the War for Independence, the greenbacks depreciated only moderately, primarily because they funded only about 15 percent of wartime expenses (as opposed to 80 percent in the Revolutionary War). By imposing broad-based taxes, borrowing from the middle classes, and creating a national monetary system, the Union government had created the financial foundations of a modern nation-state.

The financial demands on the South were just as great, but it lacked a powerful central government that could tax and borrow. The Confederate Congress fiercely opposed taxes on cotton exports and slaves, the most valuable property of wealthy planters. Taxes fell primarily on urban middle-class and nonslaveholding yeomen farm families, who often refused to pay. Consequently, the Confederacy covered less than 5 percent of its expenditures through taxation. The government paid for another 35 percent by borrowing, although many wealthy planters refused to buy large quantities of Confederate bonds, and foreign bankers were equally wary.

Thus the Confederacy was forced to finance about 60 percent of its expenses with unbacked paper money. The flood of currency created a spectacular inflation, which was compounded by the widespread circulation of counterfeit Confederate notes. As the huge supply of money (and shortages of goods) caused food prices to soar, riots broke out in more than a dozen southern cities and towns. In Richmond several hundred women broke into bakeries, crying, "Our children are starving while the rich roll in wealth." By the spring of 1865 prices had risen to ninety-two times their 1861 levels. Inflation not only undermined civilian morale but also prompted farmers to refuse Confederate money. Supply officers had to seize what they needed, offering payment in worthless IOUs. Fearful of a strong government and taxation, the Confederacy was forced to violate the property rights of its citizens to sustain the war.

The Turning Point: 1863

By 1863 the Lincoln administration had mobilized northern society, creating a complex war machine and a coherent financial system. "Little by little," the young diplomat Henry Adams noted at his post in London, "one began to feel that, behind the chaos in Washington power was taking shape; that it was massed and guided as it had not been before." Slowly but surely the tide of battle shifted toward the Union.

EMANCIPATION

From the beginning of the conflict antislavery Republicans had tried to persuade their party to make abolition a Union war aim. They based their argument not just on morality but on "military necessity," pointing out that slave-grown crops sustained the Confederate war effort. As Frederick Douglass put it, "the very stomach of this rebellion is the Negro in the form of a slave. Arrest that hoe in the hands of the Negro, and you smite the rebellion in the very seat of its life." As war casualties mounted in 1862, Lincoln and some Republican leaders accepted Douglass's argument and began to redefine the war as a struggle against slavery—the cornerstone of southern society.

But it was enslaved African Americans who forced the issue by seizing freedom for themselves. Exploiting the disorder of wartime tens of thousands of slaves escaped and sought refuge behind Union lines. The first Union official to confront this issue was General Benjamin Butler. When three slaves reached his camp on the Virginia coast in May 1861, he labeled them "contraband of war" and refused to return them to their owner. His term stuck, and for the rest of the war slaves behind Union lines were known as *contrabands*. Within a few months a thousand contrabands were camping with Butler's army. To define their status and undermine the Confederate war effort, in August 1861 Congress passed the First Confiscation Act, which authorized the seizure of all property—including slaves—used to support the rebellion.

Radical Republicans, who had long condemned slavery, now saw a way to use the war to end it. By the spring of 1862 leading Radicals—Treasury secretary Chase; Charles Sumner, chair of the Senate Committee on Foreign Relations; and Thaddeus Stevens, chair of the House Ways and Means Committee—had pushed moderate Republicans toward abolition. In April Congress enacted legislation ending slavery in the District of Columbia, with compensation for owners. In June it outlawed slavery in the federal territories, finally enacting the Wilmot Proviso and the Republicans' free-soil policy. And in July Congress passed the radical Second Confiscation Act, which, overriding the property rights of Confederate slaveowners, declared "forever free" all fugitive slaves and all slaves captured by the Union army.

Lincoln now seized the initiative from the radicals. In July 1862 he prepared a general proclamation of emancipation and, viewing the battle of Antietam as "an indication of the Divine Will," issued it on September 22, 1862. Based on the president's war powers the proclamation declared Lincoln's intention to free the slaves in all states still in rebellion on January 1, 1863. The seceding states had a hundred days to preserve slavery by returning to the Union. None chose to do so.

The proclamation was politically astute. Because Lincoln needed to keep the loyalty of the border states still in the Union, he left slavery intact there. He also wanted to win the allegiance of the areas occupied by Union armies—western and central Tennessee, western Virginia, and southern Louisiana, including New Orleans—so he left slavery untouched there. Consequently, because Lincoln's order of course would not be followed within the Confederacy, the Emancipation Proclamation did not free a single slave. Yet it dramatically changed the nature of the conflict. Union troops became agents of liberation, transforming the struggle to preserve the Union into (as Lincoln put it) a war of "subjugation" in which "the old South is to be destroyed and replaced by new propositions and ideas."

As a war aim emancipation was extremely controversial. During the congressional election of 1862 the Democrats denounced emancipation as unconstitutional, warned of slave uprisings and massive bloodshed in the South, and claimed that a "black flood" would wash away the jobs of northern workers. Democrat Horatio Seymour won the governorship of New York by declaring that if abolition was the purpose of the war, the South should not be conquered. Other Democrats swept to victory in New York, Pennsylvania, Ohio, and Illinois, and the party gained thirty-four seats in Congress. However, the Republicans still held a twenty-five-seat majority in the House and had gained five seats in the Senate. Lincoln refused to retreat. On New Year's Day 1863 he signed the Emancipation Proclamation. To reassure northerners who sympathized with the South or feared race warfare, Lincoln urged slaves to "abstain from all violence." But he now justified emancipation as an "act of justice." "If my name ever goes into history," he said, "it was for this act."

VICKSBURG AND GETTYSBURG

The fate of the proclamation would depend on the success of Union armies and the Republicans' ability to win support for their program. The outlook was not encouraging. Not only had Democrats registered gains in the election of 1862; there was increased popular support for Democrats who favored a negotiated peace. Two brilliant victories by Lee, whose army defeated Hooker's forces at Fredericksburg (December 1862) and Chancellorsville, Virginia (May 1863), caused further erosion of northern support for the war, as did rumors of a new draft.

At this crucial juncture General Grant mounted a major offensive in the West designed to split the Confederacy in two. Grant drove south along the west bank of the Mississippi and then moved his troops across the river near Vicksburg, Mississippi, where he defeated two Confederate armies and laid siege to the city. After repelling Union assaults for six weeks the exhausted and starving Vicksburg garrison surrendered on July 4, 1863. Five days later Union forces took Port Hudson, Louisiana, establishing Union control of the Mississippi. Grant had taken 31,000 prisoners, cut off Louisiana, Arkansas, and Texas from the rest of the Confederacy, and prompted hundreds of slaves to desert their plantations.

Grant's initial advance down the Mississippi had created an argument over strategy within the Confederate leadership. Davis and other civilian leaders wanted to throw in reinforcements to defend Vicksburg and send troops to Tennessee to draw Grant out of Mississippi. But Lee, buoyed by his recent victories over Hooker, favored a new invasion of the North. He argued that a military thrust into the free states would relieve the pressure on Vicksburg by drawing the Union armies east. Beyond that Lee hoped for a major victory that would undermine northern support for the war.

Lee won out. In June 1863 he maneuvered his army north through Maryland into Pennsylvania. The Union's Army of the Potomac moved along with him, positioning itself between Lee and Washington. The two great armies met in an accidental but decisive confrontation at Gettysburg, Pennsylvania (see Map 14.3). On the first day of battle, July 1, Lee drove the Union's advance guard to the south of town. There General George G. Meade, who had just taken over command of the Union forces from Hooker, placed his troops in well-defended hilltop positions and

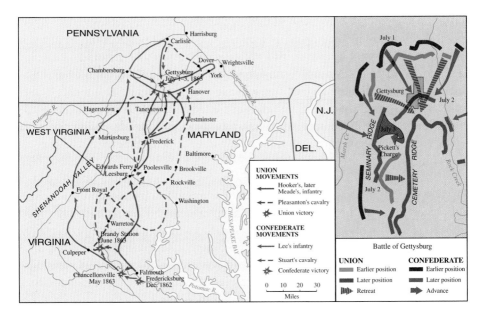

MAP 14.3
The Battle of Gettysburg, 1863

After Lee's victory at Chancellorsville, Virginia, in May the two armies jockeyed for position as the Confederate forces moved northward. At Gettysburg the Union army commanded by General George Meade emerged victorious primarily because it was much larger than the Confederate force and held well-fortified positions along Cemetery Ridge, which gave its units a major tactical advantage.

called up reinforcements. By the morning of the second day Meade had 90,000 troops to Lee's 75,000. Aware that he was outnumbered but bent on victory, Lee attacked both of Meade's flanks but failed to turn them. General Richard B. Ewell, assigned to attack the Union right, was unwilling to risk his men in an all-out assault, and General Longstreet, on the Union left, was unable to dislodge Meade's forces from Little Round Top.

On July 3 Lee decided to attempt a frontal assault on the center of the Union lines. He felt this might be his last chance to inflict a crushing defeat on the North, and he had enormous confidence in his troops. After the heaviest artillery barrage of the war Lee ordered 14,000 men under General George E. Pickett to take Cemetery Ridge. But Meade had reinforced the center of his line with artillery and his best troops. When Pickett's men charged across a mile of open terrain, they were met by massive fire; thousands were killed, wounded, or captured. By the end of the battle Lee had suffered 28,000 casualties, one-third of the Army of Northern Virginia, and Meade had 23,000 killed or wounded, making Gettysburg the most lethal battle of the Civil War.

Gettysburg was a great Union victory; never again would a southern army invade the North. Shocked by the bloodletting, Meade allowed the remaining Confederate soldiers to escape, thus losing an opportunity to end the war. "As it is," Lincoln brooded, "the war will be prolonged indefinitely." Nonetheless, the victories at Gettysburg and at Vicksburg were a major turning point in the conflict. In the fall of 1863 Republicans reaped political gains from those victories by sweeping state and local elections in Pennsylvania, Ohio, and New York. In the South the military setbacks accentuated war weariness. The Confederate elections of 1863 went sharply against the politicians who supported Jefferson Davis, and a large minority in the new Confederate Congress was outspokenly hostile to his policies. A few advocated peace negotiations, and many more criticized the ineffectiveness of the war effort.

Vicksburg and Gettysburg also represented a great diplomatic victory for the North, ending the Confederacy's prospect of winning foreign recognition and acquiring advanced weapons. In 1862 British shipbuilders had begun to supply armed cruisers to the Confederacy, and one of them, the *Alabama,* had sunk or captured more than a hundred Union merchant ships. Union diplomats in London despaired of preventing the scheduled delivery of two more ironclad cruisers in mid-1863. But news of the Union victories changed everything, and the American minister persuaded the British government to impound the ships.

Moreover, cotton had not become a diplomatic weapon, as the South had hoped. British manufacturers had stockpiled raw cotton before the war, and when those stocks were depleted, they found new sources in Egypt and India. Equally important, the dependence of British consumers on cheap wheat from the North deterred the government from supporting the Confederacy. Finally, British workers and reformers were enthusiastic champions of abolition, which the Emancipation Proclamation had established as a Union war aim. The results at Vicksburg and

Gettysburg confirmed British neutrality by demonstrating the military might of the Union. The British did not want to risk Canada or their merchant marine by provoking a strong, well-armed United States.

The Union Victorious, 1864–1865

The Union victories of 1863 made it clear that the South could not win the war on the battlefield, but the Confederacy still hoped for a stalemate and a negotiated peace. Lincoln and his generals faced the daunting task of winning a quick and decisive military victory; otherwise a majority of northern voters might well desert the Republican Party and its policies.

SOLDIERS AND STRATEGY

Free African Americans and fugitive slaves had tried to enlist in the Union army as early as 1861, and the black abolitionist Frederick Douglass had embraced their cause: "Once let the black man get upon his person the brass letters, 'U.S.' . . . a musket on his shoulder and bullets in his pockets, and there is no power on earth which can deny that he has earned the right to citizenship in the United States." Such an outcome frightened many northern whites, who were determined to keep blacks subjugated. Moreover, most Union generals doubted that former slaves would make good soldiers, and so the Lincoln administration initially refused to consider blacks for military service.

The Emancipation Proclamation changed popular thinking and military policy. If blacks were to benefit from a Union victory, some northern whites argued, they should share in the fighting and dying. The valor exhibited by the first African American regiments also influenced northern opinion. In January 1863 Thomas Wentworth Higginson, the white abolitionist commander of the First South Carolina (Black) Volunteers, wrote a glowing newspaper account of their military prowess: "No officer in this regiment now doubts that the key to the successful prosecution of the war lies in the unlimited employment of black troops." The War Department authorized the enlistment of free blacks and contraband slaves, and as white resistance to conscription increased, the Lincoln administration recruited as many African Americans as it could. Without black soldiers, the president suggested in the autumn of 1864, "we would be compelled to abandon the war in three weeks." By the spring of 1865 there were nearly 200,000 African American soldiers and sailors.

Military service did not end racial discrimination. Black soldiers served under white officers in segregated regiments and were used primarily to build fortifications, garrison forts, and guard supply lines. At first they were paid less than white soldiers ($7 versus $13 per month), and only a few were promoted to higher ranks. Despite such treatment African Americans volunteered for military service in

Black Soldiers in the Union Army

Tens of thousands of African Americans volunteered for military service and a chance to fight for the freedom of their people. These proud soldiers were members of the 107th Colored Infantry, stationed at Fort Corcoran near Washington, D.C. In January 1865 their regiment participated in the daring capture of Fort Fisher, which protected Wilmington, North Carolina, the last Confederate port open to blockade runners. (Library of Congress)

disproportionate numbers and diligently served the Union cause. They knew they were fighting for freedom and the possibility of a new social order. "Hello, Massa," said one black soldier to his former master, who had been taken prisoner. "Bottom rail on top dis time." The worst fears of the secessionists had come true: through the agency of the Union army blacks had enlisted in a great rebellion against slavery.

As African Americans joined the ranks, Lincoln finally found a commanding general in whom he had confidence. In March 1864 he put General Ulysses S. Grant in charge of all the Union armies and wholeheartedly approved Grant's plan to advance simultaneously against all the major Confederate forces—a strategy he had long favored. Both the general and the president wanted a decisive victory before the election of 1864.

As the successful western campaigns of 1863 showed, Grant understood how to fight a modern war—a war relying on industrial technology and directed at an entire society. At Vicksburg he had besieged an entire city and forced its surrender. A few months later, in November 1863, he had used the North's superior technology, utilizing railroad transport to charge to the rescue of a Union army near Chattanooga, Tennessee, and drive an invading Confederate army back into Georgia. Moreover, Grant was willing to accept heavy casualties in assaults on strongly defended positions, abandoning the caution of earlier Union commanders. Their attempts "to conserve life" had in fact prolonged the war, Grant argued. But Grant's aggressive tactics earned him a reputation as a butcher both of his own men and of enemy armies, which he pursued relentlessly. Finally, to crush the South's will to resist, the new Union commander was willing to terrorize the civilian population.

In May 1864 Grant ordered major new offensives on two fronts. Personally taking charge of the 115,000-strong Army of the Potomac, he set out to destroy Lee's force of 75,000 troops in Virginia. Simultaneously he instructed General William Tecumseh Sherman, who shared his views on warfare, to invade Georgia and take Atlanta. As Sherman prepared for battle, he wrote that "all that has gone before is mere skirmish. The war now begins."

Grant advanced toward Richmond, hoping to force Lee to fight in open fields, where the Union's superior manpower and artillery could prevail. Lee, remembering Gettysburg, maintained strong defensive positions, attacking only when he held a tactical advantage. He seized such opportunities twice, winning narrow victories in the battles of the Wilderness on May 5–7 and Spotsylvania Court House on May 8–12. Nevertheless Grant drove on toward Richmond (see Map 14.4). In early June he attacked Lee at Cold Harbor but withdrew after losing 7,000 men in a frontal assault. Grant had severely eroded Lee's forces, which had suffered 31,000 casualties, but Union losses were even higher at 55,000 men.

William Tecumseh Sherman

Sherman was a nervous man who smoked cigars and talked continuously, a journalist noted, his fingers constantly "twitching his red whiskers—his coat buttons—playing a tattoo on the table—or running through his hair." But he was a decisive general who commanded the loyalty of his troops and dealt a devastating blow to the Confederacy. (Library of Congress)

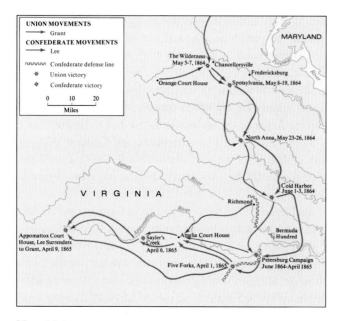

MAP 14.4
The Closing Virginia Campaigns, 1864–1865

During the last eight months of 1864 the armies of Grant and Lee were locked in a deadly dance across the Virginia countryside. By threatening Lee's lines of communication, Grant attempted to lure him into open battle. But Lee avoided a major test of strength, falling back and taking defensive positions that forced the Union army to undertake protracted sieges. As the number of casualties mounted, northern support for the war declined dramatically.

The fighting took a heavy psychological toll. "Many a man has gone crazy since this campaign began from the terrible pressure on mind and body," complained a Union officer. Previous battles had lasted only a few days and had been separated by long intervals. But in this campaign Grant's relentless advance and Lee's defensive tactics produced sustained fighting and grueling attrition. In June Grant pulled some of his troops away from Richmond to lay siege to Petersburg, an important railroad center. Protracted trench warfare, which foreshadowed that of World War I, made the spade as important as the sword. Union and Confederate soldiers built complex networks of trenches, tunnels, and artillery emplacements for almost 50 miles around Richmond and Petersburg. An officer described the continuous artillery firing and sniping as "living night and day within the 'valley of the shadow of death.'" The stress was especially great for the outnumbered Confederate troops, who spent months in the muddy, sickening trenches without rotation to the rear. As time passed, Lincoln and Grant felt pressures of their own; the enormous casualties and continued military stalemate threatened Lincoln with defeat in the November election.

The outlook for the Republicans worsened in July 1864, when a raid by Jubal Early's cavalry near Washington forced Grant to divert his best troops from the

Petersburg campaign. To punish farmers in the Shenandoah Valley, who provided a base for Early and food for Lee's army, Grant ordered General Philip H. Sheridan to turn the region into "a barren waste." Through the fall Sheridan's troops conducted a scorched-earth campaign, destroying grain supplies, barns, farming implements, and gristmills. This terrorism went beyond the military norms of the day, for most officers regarded civilians as noncombatants and feared that punishing them would erode military discipline. But Grant's decision to carry the war to Confederate civilians had changed the definition of conventional warfare.

THE ELECTION OF 1864 AND SHERMAN'S MARCH TO THE SEA

As the siege at Petersburg dragged on, Lincoln's reelection hopes came to rest on General William Sherman in Georgia. Sherman had gradually penetrated to within about 30 miles of Atlanta, a great railway hub that lay at the heart of the Confederacy. Although his army outnumbered that of General Joseph E. Johnston 90,000 to 60,000, he avoided a direct attack and slowly pried the Confederates out of one defensive position after another. Finally, on June 27 at Kennesaw Mountain Sherman engaged Johnston in a set battle, in which Sherman suffered 3,000 casualties while inflicting only about 600. By late July the Union general had laid siege to Atlanta on the north, but the next month brought little gain. Like Grant, Sherman seemed bogged down in a hopeless campaign.

Meanwhile, the presidential campaign of 1864 was well under way. In June the Republican convention endorsed Lincoln's war measures, demanded the unconditional surrender of the Confederacy, and called for a constitutional amendment to abolish slavery. To attract Democratic support the party temporarily renamed itself the National Union Party and nominated Andrew Johnson, a Unionist Tennessee Democrat, for vice president. The Democratic convention met in late August and nominated General George B. McClellan. The delegates declared their opposition to emancipation and divided over continuing the war. By threatening to bolt the convention the "Peace Democrats" forced through a platform calling for "a cessation of hostilities" and a convention to restore peace "on the basis of the Federal Union." Although personally a "War Democrat" McClellan promised if elected to recommend an immediate armistice and a peace convention. Rejoicing in "the first ray of real light I have seen since the war began," Confederate Vice President Alexander Stephens declared that if Atlanta and Richmond held out, Lincoln could be defeated and then northern Democrats could be persuaded to accept an independent Confederacy.

But on September 2 Atlanta fell. In a stunning move Sherman pulled his troops from the trenches and swept around the city to destroy its roads and rail links to the rest of the Confederacy, forcing its surrender. In her diary Mary Chestnut, a slaveowning plantation mistress, despaired of victory: "We are going to be wiped off the earth." Amid the 100-gun salutes in northern cities that greeted the news of

Atlanta in Ruins

As the Confederate army retreated from Atlanta, it blew up manufacturing facilities and munitions factories to keep them out of Union hands. Sherman's forces destroyed the remaining industries, including the roundhouse and car repair sheds of the Georgia Central Railroad. The devastation of Atlanta and southern Georgia during Sherman's "march to the sea" was a severe blow to Confederate morale. (Library of Congress)

Sherman's victory, McClellan repudiated the Democratic peace platform. But Republicans charged that he was still a peace candidate and attacked Peace Democrats as "copperheads" (a poisonous snake) who were hatching treasonous plots.

Sherman's success in Georgia gave Lincoln a clear-cut victory in November. He took 212 of 233 electoral votes, winning 55 percent of the popular vote in the free and border states and carrying all states except Delaware, Kentucky, and New Jersey. Republicans won 145 of the 185 seats in the House of Representatives and increased their Senate majority to 42 of 52 seats. Many of those victories came from the votes of Union troops, most of whom wanted the war to continue until the Confederacy met every Union demand, including emancipation.

Already the pace of legal emancipation had accelerated. In 1864 Maryland and Missouri amended their constitutions to free their slaves, and the three occupied states of Tennessee, Arkansas, and Louisiana followed suit. Abolitionists still worried that the Emancipation Proclamation, based on the president's wartime powers, would lose its force at the end of the war and that southern states would reestablish slavery. Urged on by Lincoln the Republican-dominated Congress took a major step to guarantee black freedom. On January 31, 1865, it approved the Thirteenth Amendment, which prohibited slavery throughout the United States, and sent it to the states for ratification. Slavery was nearly dead.

And so was the Confederacy. After the capture of Atlanta Sherman declined to follow the retreating Confederate army into Tennessee and decided on a bold strategy. Rather than spread his troops dangerously thin by protecting supply lines to the rear, he would "cut a swath through to the sea," living off the land. To persuade Lincoln and Grant to approve this unconventional plan Sherman pointed out that such a march would devastate Georgia and score a major psychological victory. It would be "a demonstration to the world, foreign and domestic, that we have a power [Jefferson] Davis cannot resist."

Sherman carried out the concept of total war he and Sheridan had pioneered: destruction of the enemy's economic resources and will to resist. "We are not only fighting hostile armies," Sherman wrote, "but a hostile people, and must make old and young, rich and poor, feel the hard hand of war." He left Atlanta in flames and during his 300-mile march to the sea destroyed railroads, property, and supplies (see Map 14.5). A Union veteran wrote that "[we] destroyed all we could not eat,

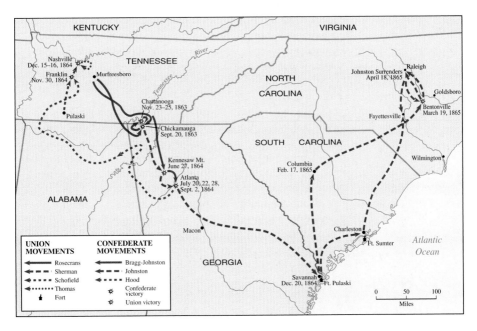

MAP 14.5
Sherman's March through the Confederacy, 1864–1865

The Union victory in November 1863 at Chattanooga, Tennessee (on that state's border with Georgia), was almost as critical as those in July at Gettysburg and Vicksburg. Having already split the Confederacy along the Mississippi, the Union was now in position to divide it again by driving through Georgia to the sea. After capturing Atlanta in September 1864, Sherman relied on other Union armies to repulse General John B. Hood's invasion of Tennessee, and swept to the Atlantic.

AMERICAN VOICES

Sherman's March through Georgia

Dolly Summer Lunt

"We must make old and young, rich and poor, feel the hand of war," General William Tecumseh Sherman wrote to General Grant late in 1864. A few weeks later Dolly Summer Lunt of Covington, Georgia, found out what he meant. Born in Maine in 1817, Dolly Summer came south to teach school, married a slaveowner, and, following his death, ran the family's plantation. Her Wartime Journal describes its destruction by Sherman's army.

November 19, 1864

Slept in my clothes last night, as I heard that the Yankees went to neighbor Montgomery's on Thursday night at one o'clock, searched his house, drank his wine, and took his money and valuables. As we were not disturbed, I walked after breakfast . . . up to Mr. Joe Perry's, my nearest neighbor, where the Yankees were yesterday. Saw Mrs. Laura [Perry] in the road surrounded by her children . . . looking for her husband. . . . Before we were done talking, up came Joe and Jim Perry from their hiding-place. Jim was very much excited. Happening to turn and look behind, as we stood there, I saw some blue-coats coming down the hill. Jim immediately raised his gun, swearing he should kill them anyhow.

"No, don't" said I, and ran home as fast as I could.

I could hear them cry "Halt! Halt!" and their guns went off in quick succession. Oh God, the time of trial has come. . . .

I hastened back to my frightened servants [slaves] and told them they had better hide, and then went back to the gate to claim protection and a guard. But like demons they [Sherman's troops] rushed in! . . . The thousand pounds of meat in my smokehouse is gone in a twinkling, my flour, my meat, my lard, butter, eggs . . . all gone. My eighteen fat turkeys, hens, chickens . . . are shot down in my yard and hunted as if they were rebels themselves. Utterly powerless I ran out and appealed to the guard.

"I cannot help you, Madam; it is orders." . . .

Sherman himself and a greater portion of his army passed my house that day . . . ; they tore down my garden palings, made a road through my back-yard and lot field . . . desolating my home—wantonly doing it when there was no necessity for it.

Such a day, if I live to the age of Methuselah, may God spare me from ever seeing again!

As night drew its sable curtains around us, the heavens from every point were lit up with flames from burning buildings.

SOURCE: *Eyewitnesses and Others: Readings in American History* (New York: Holt, Rinehart and Winston, 1995), vol. 1: pp. 413–17.

stole their niggers, burned their cotton & gins, spilled their sorghum, burned & twisted their R.Roads and raised Hell generally" (see American Voices, "Sherman's March through Georgia"). The havoc so demoralized Confederate soldiers that many deserted and fled home to protect their farms and families. When Sherman reached Savannah, Georgia, in mid-December, the 10,000 Confederate defenders left without a fight.

In February 1865 Sherman invaded South Carolina. He planned to link up with Grant at Petersburg and along the way punish the state where secession had begun. "The truth is," Sherman wrote, "the whole army is burning with an insatiable desire to wreak vengeance upon South Carolina." His troops cut a comparatively narrow swath across the state but ravaged the countryside even more thoroughly than they had in Georgia. By March Sherman had reached North Carolina and was on the verge of linking up with Grant and crushing Lee's army.

Sherman's march exposed an internal Confederate weakness: rising class resentment on the part of poor whites. Long angered by the "twenty-negro" exemption from military service given to slaveowners and fearing that the Confederacy was doomed, ordinary southern farmers resisted military service. "It is no longer a reproach to be known as a deserter," a Confederate officer in South Carolina complained in late 1863. By early 1865 the Confederacy was experiencing such a severe manpower crisis that its leaders decided to take an extreme measure: arming the slaves. Urged on by Lee the Confederate Congress voted to enlist black soldiers; Davis issued an executive order granting freedom to all blacks who served in the Confederate army. But the war ended too soon to reveal whether any slaves would have fought for the Confederacy.

The symbolic end of the war took place in Virginia. In April 1865 Grant finally forced Lee into a showdown by gaining control of the crucial railroad junction at Petersburg and cutting off his supplies. Lee abandoned the defense of Richmond and turned west, hoping to join up with Confederate forces in North Carolina. While Lincoln visited the ruins of the Confederate capital, mobbed by joyful former slaves, Grant cut off Lee's escape route. On April 9, almost precisely four years after the attack on Fort Sumter, Lee surrendered to Grant at Appomattox Court House, Virginia. In accepting the surrender of the Confederate general Grant set a tone of generosity, allowing Lee's men to take their horses home for spring planting. By May 26 all the Confederate generals had ceased to fight, and the Confederate army and government simply dissolved (see Map 14.6).

The armies of the Union had destroyed the Confederacy and much of the South's economy. Its factories, warehouses, and railroads were in ruins, as were many of its farms and some of its most important cities. Almost 260,000 Confederate soldiers had paid for secession with their lives. Most significant, the Union had been preserved and slavery destroyed. But the cost of victory was enormous in money, resources, and lives. Over 360,000 Union soldiers were dead, and hundreds of thousands were maimed and crippled. The hard and bitter war was over, and a reunited nation turned to the tasks of peace. These were to be equally hard and bitter.

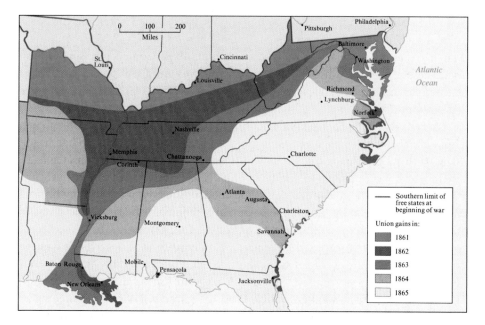

M A P 14.6
The Conquest of the South, 1861–1865

It took four years for the Union army to occupy the territory of the Confederacy, and much of the South remained under Confederate control until the last year of the war. Most of the Union's victories came on the western front, where its domination of strategic lines of communication—the Ohio and Mississippi Rivers and important railroad lines—allowed it to mount large-scale attacks against Confederate armies.

For Further Exploration

Charles P. Roland, *An American Iliad: The Story of the Civil War* (1991), is an excellent brief survey, while James M. McPherson, *The Battle Cry of Freedom* (1988), offers a fine synthesis of the coming of the conflict and the wartime years. For a lucid description of the complex mixture of goals, personalities, and accident that precipitated the conflict, read Richard Current, *Lincoln and the First Shot* (1963). John Hope Franklin, *The Emancipation Proclamation* (1963), explains the background of Lincoln's edict and its impact in the United States and other nations.

Nancy Scott Anderson and Dwight Anderson, *The Generals: Ulysses S. Grant and Robert E. Lee* (1988), is a vivid popular account of their personal histories and military exploits. James M. McPherson, *For Cause and Comrades: Why Men Fought in the Civil War* (1997), draws on the letters of ordinary soldiers to explain their extraordinary commitment to the cause of the Union and Confederacy. For experiences of black soldiers told in their own words, see Ira Berlin et al., eds., *Freedom's Soldiers: The Black Military Experience in the Civil War* (1998). Earl J. Hess, *The Union Soldier in Battle: Enduring the Ordeal of Combat* (1997),

TIMELINE

1861	Confederate States of America formed (February 4)	1863	Lincoln signs Emancipation Proclamation (January 1).
	Abraham Lincoln inaugurated (March 4)		Enrollment Act begins conscription in North; riots in New York City (July).
	Confederates fire on Fort Sumter (April 12).		Union victories at Battles of Gettysburg (July 1–3) and Vicksburg (July 4)
	Virginia secession (April 17) leads upper South out of Union.	1864	General Ulysses S. Grant given charge of all Union armies (March)
	General Benjamin Butler declares runaway slaves "contraband of war" (May).		Grant advances on Richmond (May).
	Union forces routed at first Battle of Bull Run (July 21)		General William Tecumseh Sherman invades Georgia (May).
1862	Congress begins to print "greenbacks."		Sherman takes Atlanta (September 2).
	Homestead Act		Lincoln reelected (November)
	Federal aid to transcontinental railroads		Sherman marches through Georgia (November and December).
	Battle of Shiloh (April 6–7) advances Union cause in West.	1865	Congress approves Thirteenth Amendment, which outlaws slavery (January).
	Confederacy introduces conscription.		Robert E. Lee surrenders at Appomattox Court House, Virginia (April 9).
	Battle of Antietam (September 17) halts Confederate offensive.		
	Lincoln issues preliminary Emancipation Proclamation (September 22).		

presents a vivid and convincing account of the heat, smell, sounds, and feel of battle, as does Michael Sharra's *Killer Angels* (1974), a masterful novel of the battle of Gettysburg.

Peter Quinn's novel, *Banished Children of Eve* (1994), recounts the New York City draft riots from an Irish American perspective. *Mary Chesnut's Civil War,* edited by C. Vann Woodward (1981), is the diary of a planter's wife that provides a witty and incisive view of southern society.

Two award-winning websites treat the events of these years. "The Valley of the Shadow" at <http://jefferson.village.virginia.edu/vshadow2/> traces the experiences of two communities—one northern, one southern—during the prewar era using a multitude of hyperlinked sources, including newspaper, letters, diaries, photographs, and maps. "The Freedmen and Southern Society Project" at <http://www.inform.umd.edu/ARHU/Depts/History/Freedman/home.html> captures the drama of war and emancipation in the words of the participants: liberated slaves and defeated masters, soldiers and civilians, common folk and leaders.

Chapter 15

RECONSTRUCTION
1865–1877

I felt like a bird out of a cage. Amen. Amen. Amen. I could hardly
ask to feel any better than I did that day.

—HOUSTON H. HOLLOWAY, A FORMER SLAVE
RECALLING HIS EMANCIPATION IN 1865

In his second inaugural address, President Lincoln spoke of the need
to "bind up the nation's wounds." No one knew better than Lincoln how daunting
a task that would be. Foremost, of course, were the terms on which the rebellious
states would be restored to the Union. But America's Civil War had opened more
fundamental questions. Slavery was finished. That much was certain. But what system of labor should replace plantation slavery? What rights should the freedmen
be accorded beyond emancipation itself? How far should the federal government
go to settle these questions? And who should decide—the president or Congress?

While the war was still on, the North began to grope for answers. Taking the
initiative, Lincoln in December 1863 offered a general amnesty to all but high-
ranking Confederates willing to pledge loyalty to the Union and abolish slavery.
When 10 percent of a state's 1860 voters had taken this oath, they could organize
a new government and be restored to the Union. Only states under military occupation—Louisiana, Arkansas, and Tennessee—took advantage of Lincoln's generous offer. Although it reflected Lincoln's conciliatory bent, his Ten Percent Plan was
really aimed at subverting the southern war effort.

What it also did, however, was to reveal the rocky road that lay ahead for Reconstruction. Thus, in Louisiana sugar planters used the restored government to
regain control over the freed slaves, employing curfew laws to restrict their movements and vagrancy regulations to force them back to work. But the Louisiana
freedmen fought back. Led by the well-established free-black community of New
Orleans, they began to agitate for political rights. No less than their former masters, former slaves intended to be actors in the savage drama of Reconstruction.

With the struggle in Louisiana in mind, congressional Republicans proposed a
stricter substitute for Lincoln's Ten Percent Plan. The initiative came from the Radical wing—those bent on a stern peace and full rights for the freedmen—but with
broad support among congressional Republicans generally. The Wade-Davis Bill,
passed on July 2, 1864, laid down, as conditions for the restoration of the rebellious

states to the Union, an oath of allegiance by a majority of each state's adult white men, new state governments formed and operated only by those who had never carried arms against the Union, and permanent loss of voting rights by Confederate leaders. The Wade-Davis Bill served notice that the congressional Republicans were not about to hand reconstruction policy over to the president.

Lincoln was not perturbed. Rather than openly challenging Congress, he executed a "pocket" veto of the Wade-Davis Bill by not signing it before Congress adjourned. At the same time he initiated informal talks with congressional leaders aimed at finding a common ground. The last speech he ever delivered, on April 11, 1865, demonstrated Lincoln's cautious realism. Reconstruction, he pleaded, had to be regarded as a practical, not a theoretical, problem. It could be solved only if Republicans remained united, even if that meant compromising, and only if the defeated South gave its consent, even if that meant forgiveness. What the speech showed, above all, was Lincoln's sense of the fluidity of events, of policy toward the South as an evolving, not a fixed, position.

What course Reconstruction might have taken had Lincoln lived is one of the unanswerable questions of American history. On April 14, 1865—five days after Lee's surrender at Appomattox—Lincoln was shot in the head at Ford's Theater in Washington by a wild-eyed actor named John Wilkes Booth. Ironically, Lincoln might have been spared if the war had dragged on longer, for Booth and his Confederate associates had originally plotted to kidnap the president to force a negotiated settlement. Without regaining consciousness, Lincoln died on April 15.

With one stroke John Wilkes Booth had sent Lincoln to martyrdom, hardened many northerners against the South, and handed the presidency to a man utterly lacking in Lincoln's moral sense and political judgment, Vice President Andrew Johnson.

Presidential Reconstruction

At the end of the Civil War, a big constitutional question remained in dispute—whether, on seceding, the Confederate states had legally left the Union. If so, then they became conquered territory whose fate could be decided only by Congress. If not, if even in rebellion they remained states of the Union, then the terms for their restoration might appropriately be left to the president. This was Andrew Johnson's view, and by an accident of timing he was free to act on it: under leisurely rules that went back to the early republic, the 39th Congress elected in November 1864 was not scheduled to convene until December 1865.

JOHNSON'S INITIATIVE

Andrew Johnson was a self-made man from the hills of eastern Tennessee. A Jacksonian Democrat, he saw himself as the champion of the common man. He hated what he called the "bloated, corrupt aristocracy" of the Northeast, and he was

Andrew Johnson

The president was not an easy man.
This photograph of Andrew Johnson
(1808–1875) conveys some of the
personal qualities that contributed so
centrally to his failure to reach an
agreement with Republicans on a
program of moderate reconstruction.
(Library of Congress)

equally disdainful of the wealthy planters, whom he blamed for the poverty of the
South's small farmers. It was poor whites he championed; Johnson, a slaveholder
himself, had little sympathy for the enslaved blacks. His political career had taken
him to the U.S. Senate, where he remained when the war broke out, loyal to the
Union. After federal forces captured Nashville, he became Tennessee's military governor. The Republicans nominated him in 1864 for vice president in an effort to
promote wartime political unity and to court southern Unionists.

In May 1865, just a month after Lincoln's death, Johnson executed his own plan
for restoration. He offered amnesty to all southerners who took an oath of allegiance to the Constitution, except for high-ranking Confederate officials and
wealthy property owners, whom he held responsible for secession. Such persons
could be pardoned only by the president. Johnson appointed provisional governors
for the southern states and, as conditions for their restoration, required only that
they revoke their ordinances of secession, repudiate their Confederate debt, and ratify the Thirteenth Amendment, which abolished slavery. Within months all the former Confederate states had met Johnson's requirements for rejoining the Union
and had functioning, elected governments.

At first Republicans responded favorably. The moderates among them were
sympathetic to Johnson's states-rights argument that it was for the states, not the
federal government, to decide what civil and political rights the freedmen should
have. Even the Radicals held their fire. They liked the stern treatment of Confederate leaders, and they hoped that the restored governments would show good faith
by generous treatment of the freed slaves.

Nothing of the sort happened. The South lay in ruins. But white southerners
held fast to the old order. The newly seated legislatures moved to restore slavery in

all but name. They enacted laws—known as Black Codes—designed to drive the former slaves back to the plantations and deny them elementary civil rights. The new governments had been formed mostly by southern Unionists, but when it came to racial attitudes, not a lot distinguished these loyalists from the Confederates. The latter, moreover, soon filtered back into the corridors of power. Despite his hard words against them, Johnson forgave ex-Confederate leaders easily so long as he got the satisfaction of making them submit to his personal authority.

His perceived indulgence of their efforts to restore white supremacy emboldened the former Confederates. They packed the delegations to the new Congress with old comrades—nine members of the Confederate Congress, seven former officials of Confederate state governments, four generals and four colonels, and even the vice president of the Confederacy, Alexander Stephens. For Republicans, this was the last straw.

Under the Constitution, Congress is "the judge of the elections, returns and qualifications of its members" (Article 1, Section 5). With this power, the Republican majorities in both houses refused to admit the southern delegations when Congress convened in early December 1865. Although relations with the president had already cooled, the Republicans assumed he would cooperate with them in formulating the new terms on which the South would be readmitted to Congress. To that end, a House-Senate committee—the Joint Committee on Reconstruction—was formed and began public hearings on conditions in the South.

In response, the southern states backed away from the most flagrant of the Black Codes, replacing them with nonracial ordinances whose effect was the same: in practice, they applied to blacks, not to whites. On top of that, a wave of violence erupted across the South against the freedmen. Listening to the graphic testimony of officials, observers and victims, Republicans concluded that the South had embarked on a concerted effort to circumvent the Thirteenth Amendment. The only possible response was for the federal government to intervene.

Back in March 1865, before adjourning, the 38th Congress had established the Freedmen's Bureau to provide emergency aid to former slaves during the chaotic period between war and peace. Now in early 1866, under the leadership of the moderate Republican senator Lyman Trumbull, chairman of the Judiciary Committee, Congress voted to extend the Bureau's life, gave it federal funding for the first time, and authorized its agents to investigate cases of discrimination against blacks.

More extraordinary was Trumbull's proposal for a Civil Rights Bill, declaring all persons born in the United States to be citizens and guaranteeing them—without regard to race—equal rights of contract, of access to the courts, and of protection of persons and property. Trumbull's bill nullified all state laws depriving citizens of these rights, authorized U.S. attorneys to bring enforcement suits in the federal courts, and provided for fines and imprisonment for violators, including public officials. Provoked by an unrepentant South, Republicans of the most moderate persuasion demanded that the federal government accept responsibility for securing the basic civil rights of the freedmen.

ACTING ON FREEDOM

While Congress debated, African Americans acted on their own idea of freedom. News of emancipation left them exultant and hopeful. Freedom meant many things—the reuniting of separated families, the end of punishment by the lash, the ability to move around, the opportunity to begin schools and churches, and, not least, the chance to engage in politics. Across the South, freed slaves held mass meetings, paraded, and formed organizations. Topmost among their demands were equality before the law and the right to vote—"an essential and inseparable element of self-government."

First of all, however, came economic independence, which emancipated blacks believed was the basis for true freedom. During the Civil War they had acted on this assumption whenever Union armies drew near. In the chaotic final months of the war, as plantation owners fled Union forces, freedmen seized control of land where they could. Most famously, General William T. Sherman reserved vast tracts of coastal lands in Georgia and South Carolina—the Sea Islands and the abandoned plantations within 30 miles of the coast—for liberated blacks and settled them on 40-acre tracts. Sherman wanted only to shift the responsibility for the refugees from his army as it marched across the lower South. But the freedmen assumed that Sherman's order meant that the land would be theirs. When the war ended, resettlement became the responsibility of the Freedmen's Bureau, which was charged with distributing confiscated land to "loyal refugees and freedmen." Many black families stayed expectantly on their old plantations. When the South Carolina

Schoolhouse, Port Hudson, Louisiana

This was probably the first schoolhouse built for freedmen by Union forces. In front, African American soldiers from the Port Hudson "Corps d'Afrique" pose with their textbooks. It stood to reason that former slaves who had taken up arms should be first to receive the education so coveted by all freedmen. (Chicago Historical Society)

planter Thomas Pinckney returned, his freed slaves told him, "We ain't going nowhere. We are going to work right here on the land where we were born and what belongs to us."

Johnson's amnesty plan, entitling pardoned Confederates to recover confiscated property, shattered these hopes. In October 1865 President Johnson ordered General Oliver O. Howard, head of the Freedmen's Bureau, to tell Sea Island blacks that they would have to surrender the land they occupied. When Howard reluctantly obeyed, the dispossessed farmers protested: "Why do you take away our lands? You take them from us who have always been true, always true to the Government! You give them to our all-time enemies! That is not right!" (see American Voices, "A Plea for Land"). In the Sea Islands and elsewhere, former slaves resisted efforts to remove them. Led by black veterans of the Union army, they fought pitched battles with plantation owners and bands of former Confederate soldiers. Generally, the local whites prevailed in this land war.

As planters prepared for a new growing season, a great struggle took shape over the labor system that would replace slavery. Convinced that blacks needed supervision, planters insisted on retaining the gang labor of the past, only now with wages replacing the food, clothing, and shelter that their slaves had previously received. The Freedmen's Bureau, although watchful against too exploitative labor contracts, sided with the planters. The Bureau, anxious that former slaves be weaned from the habits of dependency, saw the planters' offer of wage work as a halfstep to independence. But the blacks knew better. It was not only their unequal bargaining power they worried about or even that their former masters' real desire was to reenslave them under the guise of "free" contracts. In their eyes, the condition of wage labor was itself debasing. The rural South was not like the North, where working for wages was the norm and qualified a man as independent. In the South, selling one's labor to another—and in particular, selling one's labor to work another's land—implied not freedom but dependency. To be a "freeman"—a fully empowered citizen—meant heading a household, owning some property, conducting one's own affairs.

So the issue of wage labor cut to the very core of the former slaves' struggle for freedom. Nothing had been more horrifying than the fact that as slaves their persons had been the property of others. In a famous oration celebrating emancipation, the Reverend Henry M. Turner spoke bitterly of the time when his people had "no security of domestic happiness," when "our wives were sold and husbands bought, children were begotten and enslaved by their fathers." That was why formalizing marriage was so urgent a matter after emancipation and why, when hard-pressed planters demanded that freedwomen go back into the fields, they resisted so resolutely. "I seen on some plantations," one former slave recounted, "where the white men would . . . tell colored men that their wives and children could not live on their places unless they worked in the fields. The colored men [answered that] whenever they wanted their wives to work they would tell them themselves; and if he could not rule his own domestic affairs on that place he would leave it and go someplace else."

AMERICAN VOICES
A Plea for Land

*F*ollowing is a painfully written letter by the freed slaves of Edisto Island to President
Andrew Johnson, pleading for a reversal of his order that the lands they now worked be
returned to the plantation owners.

Edisto Island S.C. Oct 28th, 1865.
To the President of these United States. We the freedmen Of Edisto Island South Carolina
have learned . . . with deep sorrow and Painful hearts of the possibility of government
restoring These lands to the former owners. . . . Here is where secession was born and Nurtured Here is where we have toiled nearly all Our lives as slaves and were treated like dumb
Driven cattle. This is our home, we have made These lands what they are. . . . Shall not we
who Are freedmen and have always been true to this Union have the same rights as are
enjoyed by Others? Have we broken any Law of these United States? have we forfeited our
rights of property In Land?—If not then! are not our rights as A free people and good citizens of these United States To be considered before the rights of those who were Found
in rebellion against this good and just Government. . . . And we who have been abused
and oppressed For many long years But be subject To the will of these large Land owners?
God forbid.
   . . . We the freedmen of this Island and the State of South Carolina—Do hereby petition to you as the President of these United States, that some provisions be made by which
Every colored man can purchase land. and Hold as his own. We wish to have A home if It
be but A few acres. . . . May God bless you in the Administration of your duties as the President Of these United States is the humble prayer Of us all.—

	In behalf of the Freedmen
	Henry Bram
Committee	Ishmael. Moultrie
	yates. Sampson

SOURCE: Eileen Boris and Nelson Lichtenstein, eds., *Major Problems in the History of American Workers: Documents and Essays* (Lexington, MA: Heath, 1990), pp. 137–39.

The reader will see the irony in this definition of freedom: it assumed the wife's
subordinate role and designated her labor as the husband's property. But if that was
the price of freedom, freedwomen were prepared to pay it. Far better to take a chance
with their own men than with their former masters.

Many freedpeople voted with their feet, abandoning their old plantations and
seeking better lives and more freedom in the towns and cities of the South. Those
who remained in the countryside refused to work the cotton fields under the hated
gang labor or negotiated tenaciously over the terms of their labor contracts. Whatever system of labor finally might emerge, it was clear that the freedmen and their
families would never settle for anything resembling the old plantation system.

The efforts of former slaves to control their own lives ran counter to deeply entrenched white attitudes. "The destiny of the black race," asserted one Texan, could be summarized "in one sentence—subordination to the white race." Southern whites, a Freedmen's Bureau official observed, could not "conceive of the negro having any rights at all." And when freedmen resisted, white retribution was swift and often terrible. The toll of murdered and beaten blacks mounted into untold thousands. The governments established under Johnson's plan put the stamp of legality on the pervasive efforts to enforce white supremacy. Blacks "would be *just as well* off with no law at all or no Government," concluded a Freedmen's Bureau agent, as with the justice they got under the restored white rule.

In this unequal struggle, blacks turned to Washington. "We stood by the government when it wanted help," a black Mississippian wrote President Johnson. "Now . . . will it stand by us?"

CONGRESS VERSUS PRESIDENT

Andrew Johnson was not, alas, the man to ask. In February 1866 he vetoed the Freedmen's Bureau Bill, declaring it unconstitutional because Congress lacked authority to provide a "system for the support of indigent people" and because the states most directly affected by its provisions were not yet represented in Congress. The Bureau was an "immense patronage," showering benefits on blacks never granted to "our own people." Republicans could not muster enough votes to override his veto. A month later, in a further rebuff to his critics, Johnson vetoed Trumbull's Civil Rights Bill, again arguing that federal protection of black civil rights constituted "a stride toward centralization." His racism, hitherto muted, now blazed forth. In his view, granting blacks the privileges of citizenship was discriminatory, operating "in favor of the colored and against the white race" and fraught with evil consequences, including racial mixing.

Galvanized by Johnson's attack on the Civil Rights Bill, the Republicans went into action. In early April they got the necessary two-thirds majorities in both Houses and enacted the Civil Rights Act of 1866. This was a truly historic event, the first time Congress had prevailed over a presidential veto on a major piece of legislation. The Republican resolve was reinforced by news of mounting violence in the South, culminating in three days of bloody rioting in Memphis. In July an angry Congress renewed the Freedmen's Bureau over a second Johnson veto.

Anxious to consolidate their gains, Republicans moved to enshrine black civil rights in an amendment to the Constitution. The heart of the Fourteenth Amendment was Section 1, which declared that "all persons born or naturalized in the United States" were citizens. No state could abridge "the privileges or immunities of citizens of the United States," deprive "any person of life, liberty, or property, without due process of law," or deny anyone "the equal protection of the laws." These phrases were vague, intentionally so, but they established the constitutionality of the Civil Rights Act and, more important, the basis on which the courts and

Congress could over time erect an enforceable standard of equality before the law in the states.

For the moment, however, the Fourteenth Amendment was most important for its impact on national politics. With the 1866 congressional elections approaching, Johnson somehow figured he had a winning issue in the Fourteenth Amendment. He urged the states not to ratify it. Months earlier, Johnson had begun to maneuver politically against the Republicans, aiming to build a coalition of white southerners, northern Democrats, and conservative Republicans under the banner of National Union. Any hope of creating a new national party, however, was shattered by Johnson's intemperate behavior and by escalating violence in the South. A dissension-ridden National Union convention in July ended inconclusively, and Johnson's campaign against the Fourteenth Amendment became, effectively, a campaign for the Democratic Party.

Republicans responded furiously, unveiling an attack that would become known as "waving the bloody shirt." The Democrats were traitors, charged Indiana governor Oliver Morton; their party was "a common sewer and loathesome receptacle into which is emptied every element of treason." In late August Johnson embarked on a disastrous "swing around the circle"—a railroad tour from Washington to Chicago and St. Louis and back. It was unprecedented for a president to campaign personally for his party, and Johnson made matters worse by engaging in shouting matches with hecklers and insulting the hostile crowds.

The 1866 congressional elections inflicted a humiliating defeat on Johnson. The Republicans won a three-to-one majority in Congress, so that, to begin with, the Republicans considered themselves "masters of the situation," free to proceed "entirely regardless of [Johnson's] opinions or wishes." As a referendum on the Fourteenth Amendment, moreover, the election registered overwhelming popular support for securing the civil rights of the former slaves. The Republican Party emerged with a new sense of unity—a unity coalescing not at the center but on the left, around the unbending program of the Radical minority.

The Radicals represented the abolitionist strain within the Republican Party. Most of them hailed from New England or from the area of the upper Midwest settled by New Englanders. In the Senate they were led by Charles Sumner of Massachusetts; in the House, by Thaddeus Stevens from Pennsylvania. For them, Reconstruction was never primarily about restoring the Union but about remaking southern society. "The foundations of their institutions . . . must be broken up and relaid," declared Stevens, "or all our blood and treasure will have been spent in vain."

Only a handful went as far as Stevens in demanding that the plantations be treated as "forfeited estates of the enemy" and broken up into small farms for the former slaves. About protecting the civil rights of the freedmen and granting them the suffrage, however, there was agreement. In this endeavor Radicals had no qualms about using the powers of the federal government. Nor were there qualms about being aggressively partisan. The Radicals regarded the Republican Party as the instrument of the Lord and black votes as the means by which the party would bring about the regeneration of the South.

At first, in the months after Appomattox, few but the Radicals imagined that so extreme a program had any chance of enactment. Black suffrage especially seemed beyond reach, since the northern states themselves (except in New England) denied blacks the vote at this time. And yet, as fury mounted against the intransigent South, Republicans became ever more radicalized until, in the wake of the smashing victory of 1866, they embraced the Radicals' vision of a reconstructed South.

Radical Reconstruction

Afterward thoughtful southerners admitted that the South had brought radical Reconstruction on itself. "We had, in 1865, a white man's government in Alabama," remarked the man who had been Johnson's provisional governor, "but we lost it." The state's "great blunder" was not to "have at once taken the negro right under the protection of the laws." Remarkably, the South remained defiant even after the 1866 congressional elections. Every state legislature (excepting Tennessee) rejected the Fourteenth Amendment, mostly by virtual acclamation. It was as if they could not imagine that governments installed under the presidential imprimatur and fully functioning might be swept away. But that, in fact, is just what the Republicans intended to do.

CONGRESS TAKES COMMAND

The Reconstruction Act of 1867, enacted in March, organized the South as a conquered land, dividing it (with the exception of Tennessee) into five military districts, each under the command of a Union general (see Map 15.1). The price for reentering the Union was granting the vote to the freedmen and disenfranchising the South's prewar political class. Each military commander was ordered to register all eligible adult men (black as well as white), supervise the election of state conventions, and make certain that the new constitutions guaranteed black suffrage. Congress would readmit a state to the Union if its voters ratified the state constitution, if that document proved acceptable to Congress, and if the new state legislature approved the Fourteenth Amendment (thereby ensuring the three-fourths of the states need for ratification). Johnson vetoed the act, but Congress overrode the veto.

Republicans also restricted President Johnson's room for maneuver. The Tenure of Office Act, companion legislation to the Reconstruction Act, ordered the president not to remove without Senate consent any official whose appointment had required Senate confirmation. Congress chiefly wanted to protect Secretary of War Edwin M. Stanton, a Lincoln hold-over and the only member of Johnson's cabinet who favored radical Reconstruction. In his position Stanton could do much

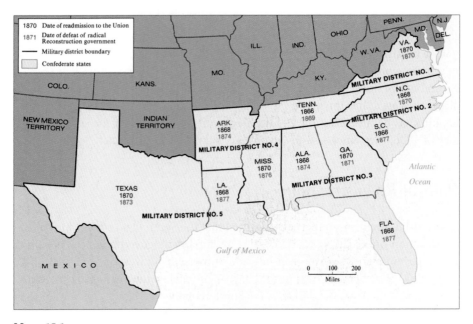

MAP 15.1
Reconstruction

The federal government organized the Confederate states into five military districts during radical Reconstruction. For each state the first date indicates when that state was readmitted to the Union; the second date shows when radical Republicans lost control of the state government. All the ex-Confederate states rejoined the Union from 1868 to 1870, but the periods of radical rule varied widely. Radicals lasted only a few months in Virginia; they held on until the end of Reconstruction in Louisiana, Florida, and South Carolina.

to prevent Johnson from frustrating the goals of Reconstruction. The law also required the president to issue all orders to the army through its commanding general, Ulysses S. Grant. In effect, Congress was attempting to reconstruct the presidency as well as the South.

Seemingly defeated, Johnson appointed generals recommended by Stanton to command the five military districts in the South. But he was just biding his time. In August 1867, after Congress had adjourned, he "suspended" Stanton and replaced him with Grant, believing that the general would be a good soldier and follow orders. Next Johnson replaced four of the commanding generals, including Philip H. Sheridan, Grant's favorite cavalry general. Johnson, however, had misjudged Grant, who publicly registered his opposition to the president's machinations. When the Senate reconvened in the fall, it overruled Stanton's suspension. Grant, now an open enemy of Johnson's, resigned so that Stanton could resume his office.

On February 21, 1868, Johnson dismissed Stanton. The feisty secretary of war barricaded his office and refused to admit the replacement Johnson had appointed.

Resistance in the South

This engraving, entitled *If He Is a Union Man or Freedman: Verdict, Hang the D—Yankee and Nigger,* appeared in *Harper's Weekly* on March 23, 1867, just as the Reconstruction Act was being adopted. Thomas Nast's cartoon encapsulated the outrage at the South's murderous intransigence that led even moderate Republicans to support radical Reconstruction.

(Library of Congress)

Three days later, House Republicans introduced articles of impeachment against President Johnson, employing the power of the Congress under the Constitution to remove high federal officers guilty of "Treason, Bribery, or other high Crimes and Misdemeanors." The House overwhelmingly approved eleven counts of presidential misconduct, nine of which dealt with violations of the Tenure of Office Act.

The case went to the Senate, which acts as the court in impeachment cases, with Chief Justice Salmon P. Chase presiding. After an eleven-week trial, thirty-five senators on May 15 voted for conviction, one vote short of the two-thirds majority required. Seven moderate Republicans broke ranks, voting for acquittal along with twelve Democrats. Congress had removed federal judges from office but never a president. The reluctant Republicans were overwhelmed by the drastic nature of the attack on Johnson. They felt the Tenure of Office Act that Johnson had violated was of dubious validity (in fact, it was subsequently declared unconstitutional by the Supreme Court). The real issue was a political dispute, and removing a president for disagreeing with Congress seemed too extreme, too threatening to the constitutional system of checks and balances, even for the sake of punishing Johnson.

Even without being convicted, however, Johnson had been defanged. For the remainder of his term he was helpless to alter the course of Reconstruction.

The impeachment controversy made Grant, already the North's most popular war hero, a Republican hero as well, and he easily won the party's presidential nomination in 1868. In the fall campaign he supported radical Reconstruction, but he also urged reconciliation between the sections. His Democratic opponent was Horatio Seymour, a former governor of New York and a Peace Democrat who almost declined the nomination, certain that the Democrats could not overcome the stigma of being the party of the disloyal South.

As Seymour feared, the Republicans waved the bloody shirt, stirring up old wartime emotions against the Democrats to great effect. Grant won about the same share of the northern vote (55 percent) that Lincoln had won in 1864 and received 214 of 294 electoral votes. The Republicans also retained two-thirds majorities in both houses of Congress.

In the wake of their smashing victory, the Republicans quickly produced the last major piece of Reconstruction legislation—the Fifteenth Amendment, which forbade either the federal government or the states from denying citizens the right to vote on the basis of race, color, or "previous condition of servitude." The amendment left room for poll taxes and property or literacy tests that could be used to discourage blacks from voting. But its authors did not want to alienate northern states that already relied on such qualifications to keep immigrants and the "unworthy" poor from the polls. A California senator warned that in his state, with its rabidly anti-Chinese sentiment (see Chapter 16), any restriction on that power would "kill our party as dead as a stone."

Despite grumbling by Radical Republicans, the amendment passed without modification in February 1869. Congress required the states still under federal control—Virginia, Mississippi, Texas, and Georgia—to ratify it as a condition of being readmitted to the Union. A year later the Fifteenth Amendment became part of the Constitution.

WOMAN SUFFRAGE DENIED

If the Fifteenth Amendment troubled some proponents of black suffrage, this was nothing as compared to the outrage felt by women's rights advocates. They had fought the good fight for the abolition of slavery for so many years, only to be abandoned by their male allies when their chance finally came; all it would have taken was one more word in the Fifteenth Amendment, so that the protected categories for voting would have read "race, color, *sex,* or previous condition of servitude." Leading suffragists such as Susan B. Anthony and Elizabeth Cady Stanton did not want to hear from Radical Republicans that this was "the Negro's hour" and that women would have to wait for another day. How could the suffrage be granted to former slaves, Elizabeth Cady Stanton demanded, but not to them?

In her despair, Stanton lashed out in ugly terms against "Patrick and Sambo and Hans and Ung Tung," men ignorant of the Declaration of Independence and yet entitled to vote, while the best and most accomplished of American women remained voteless. In 1869 the annual meeting of the Equal Rights Association, the lead organization in the struggle for the rights of blacks and women, broke up in acrimony, and Stanton and Anthony came out against the Fifteenth Amendment.

At this searing moment, a schism opened in the ranks of the women's movement. The majority, led by Lucy Stone and Julia Ward Howe, reconciled themselves to disappointment and accepted the priority of black suffrage. Organized into the American Woman Suffrage Association, these moderates remained allied to the Republican Party in the forlorn hope that once Reconstruction had been settled, it would be time for the woman's vote. The Stanton-Anthony group, however, struck out in a new direction. Stanton declared that woman "must not put her trust in man" in fighting for her rights. The new organization she headed, the New York–based National Women Suffrage Association, accepted only women, focused exclusively on women's rights, and resolutely took up the battle for a federal woman suffrage amendment.

The fracturing of the women's movement obscured the common ground the two sides shared. Both now realized that a broader popular constituency had to be built beyond the small elite of evangelical reformers who had founded the movement. Both elevated suffrage into the preeminent women's issue. And both were energized by a shared anger not evident in earlier times. "If I were to give vent to all my pent-up wrath concerning the subordination of woman," Lydia Maria Child wrote to the Republican warhorse Charles Sumner in 1872, "I might frighten *you*. . . . Suffice it, therefore, to say, either the theory of our government is *false*, or women have the right to vote." If radical Reconstruction seemed a barren time for women's rights, in fact it had planted the seeds of the modern feminist movement.

THE SOUTH UNDER RADICAL RECONSTRUCTION

Between 1868 and 1871 all the southern states met the congressional stipulations and rejoined the Union. Protected by federal troops and encouraged by northern party leaders, Republican organizations took hold across the South and won control of the newly established Reconstruction governments. These Republican administrations remained in power for periods ranging from a few months in Virginia to nine years in South Carolina, Louisiana, and Florida. Their core support came from African Americans, who constituted a majority of registered voters in Alabama, Florida, South Carolina, Mississippi, and Louisiana and nearly a majority in Georgia, Virginia, and North Carolina.

The southern whites who became Republicans faced the scorn of Democratic former Confederates, who mocked them as *scalawags*—an ancient Scots-Irish term for runty, worthless animals. Whites who had come from the North they denounced as *carpetbaggers*—self-seeking interlopers who carried all their property in cheap cloth suitcases called carpetbags. Such labels glossed over the actual diversity of these groups.

Some carpetbaggers, while motivated by personal gain, also brought capital and skills. Others were Union army veterans taken with the South—its climate, people, and economic opportunities. And interspersed with the self-seekers were many idealists anxious to advance the cause of emancipation.

The scalawags were even more diverse. Some were former slaveowners, ex-Whigs and even ex-Democrats, drawn to Republicanism as the best way to attract northern capital to southern railroads, mines, and factories. In southwest Texas, the large population of Germans was strongly Republican. They sent to Congress Edward Degener, an immigrant and a San Antonio grocer whom Confederate authorities had imprisoned and whose sons had been executed for treason. But most numerous among the scalawags were yeomen farmers from the backcountry who wanted to rid the South of its slaveholding aristocracy. Scalawags had generally fought against (or at least refused to support) the Confederacy; they believed that slavery had victimized whites as well as blacks. "Now is the time," a Georgia scalawag wrote, "for every man to come out and speak his principles publickly and vote for liberty as we have been in bondage long enough."

The Democrats' scorn for black political leaders as ignorant and impressionable field hands was just as ill-founded. The first African American leaders in the South came from an elite of blacks free before the Civil War. They were joined by northern blacks who moved south when radical Reconstruction offered the prospect of meaningful freedom. Some had fought in the antislavery crusade or were Union army veterans; a number were employed by the Freedmen's Bureau or northern missionary societies. Others had escaped from slavery and were returning home, like Blanche K. Bruce, who first taught school in Missouri and then in 1874 became Mississippi's second black U.S. senator.

With the formation of the reconstructed Republican governments, this diverse group of ministers, artisans, shopkeepers, and former soldiers reached out to the freedmen. African American speakers, some financed by the Republican Party, fanned out into the old plantation districts and recruited freed slaves for leadership roles. Still, few among these former slaves had been field hands; most had been preachers or artisans. The literacy of one freedman, Thomas Allen, who was a Baptist minister and shoemaker, helped him win election to the Georgia legislature. "In my county," he recalled, "the colored people came to me for instructions, and I gave them the best instructions I could. I took the *New York Tribune* and other papers, and in that way I found out a great deal, and I told them whatever I thought was right."

Although never proportionate to their size in the population, black office holders held positions of importance throughout the South. In South Carolina African Americans occupied a majority of the seats in one house of the state legislature in 1868. They were heavily represented in states' executive offices, elected three members of Congress, and won a place on the state supreme court. Over the entire course

THE FIRST COLORED SENATOR AND REPRESENTATIVES.
In the 41st and 42nd Congress of the United States.

African American Congressional Delegation, 1872

This Currier and Ives lithograph celebrates one of the notable achievements of radical Reconstruction—the representation that former slaves won, however briefly, in the U.S. Congress. Hiram Revels of Mississippi, the Senate's first African American member, is seated at the extreme left. (Granger Collection)

of Reconstruction twenty African Americans served in the executive branch as governor, lieutenant governor, secretary of state, treasurer, or superintendent of education, more than 600 served as state legislators, and sixteen as Congressmen.

The Republicans who took office had ambitious plans for a reconstructed South. They wanted to end its dependence on cotton agriculture and build instead an industrial economy like the North's. They fell short of achieving this vision but accomplished more than their critics gave them credit for.

The Republicans modernized state constitutions, eliminated property qualifications for the vote, and made more offices elective. They attended especially to the personal freedom of the former slaves, sweeping out the shadow Black Codes that imposed labor discipline on them and limited their mobility. Women also benefited from the Republican defense of personal liberty. Nearly all the new constitutions expanded the rights of married women, enabling them to hold property and personal earnings independent of their husbands. Republican social programs called for hospitals, more humane penitentiaries, and asylums for orphans and the insane.

Reconstruction governments built roads in areas where roads had never existed. They poured money into reviving the region's railroad network. And they did all this without federal financing.

To pay for their ambitious programs, the Republicans copied taxes that Jacksonian reformers had earlier introduced in the North—in particular, general property taxes applying not only to real estate but to personal wealth. The goal was to force planters to pay their fair share of taxes and to force uncultivated land onto the market. In many plantation counties, especially in South Carolina, Louisiana, and Mississippi, former slaves served as tax assessors and collectors, administering the taxation of their onetime owners.

Increasing tax revenues never managed to offset the burgeoning obligations undertaken by the Reconstruction governments. State debts mounted rapidly, and as interest payments on bonds fell into arrears, public credit collapsed. On top of that, much of the spending was wasted or ended in the pockets of state officials. Corruption was endemic to American politics, present in the southern states before the Republicans came on the scene and rampant everywhere in this era, not least in the Grant administration itself. Still, in the free-spending atmosphere of the early Republican regimes, corruption was especially widespread and damaging to the cause of radical Reconstruction.

Nothing, however, could dim the achievement in public education. Here the South had lagged woefully; only Tennessee had a system of public schooling before the Civil War. Republican state governments vowed to make up for lost time, viewing education as the foundation for a democratic order. African Americans of all ages rushed to attend the newly established schools, even when they had to pay tuition. An elderly man in Mississippi explained his desire to go to school: "Ole missus used to read the good book [the Bible] to us . . . on Sunday evenin's, but she mostly read dem places where it says, 'Servants obey your masters.' . . . Now we is free, there's heaps of tings in that old book we is just suffering to learn." By 1875 about half of all the children in Florida, Mississippi, and South Carolina were in classrooms.

The building of schools was part of a larger effort by African Americans to fortify the institutions that had sustained their spirit during the days of slavery. Religious belief had struck deep roots in nineteenth-century slave society. Now, in freedom, the African Americans left the white-dominated congregations, where they had been relegated to segregated balconies and denied any voice in church governance, and built churches of their own. These churches joined together to form African American versions of the Southern Methodist and Southern Baptist denominations, including, most prominently, the National Baptist Convention and the African Methodist Episcopal Church. Everywhere, the robust new churches served not only as places of worship but as schools, social centers, and political meeting halls.

Black ministers were community leaders and often political officeholders. As Charles H. Pearce, a Methodist minister in Florida, declared, "A man in this State cannot do his whole duty as a minister except he looks out for the political interests of his people." Calling for the brotherhood of man and the special destiny of the former slaves as the "Children of Israel," black ministers provided a powerful religious underpinning for the Republican politics of their congregations.

SHARECROPPING

In the meantime, the freedmen were locked in a great economic struggle with their former owners. In 1869 South Carolina established a land commission empowered to buy property and resell it on easy terms to the landless. In this way about 14,000 black families acquired farms. South Carolina's land distribution plan showed what was possible, but it was the exception, not the rule. Despite a lot of rhetoric, Republican regimes elsewhere did little to help the freedmen fulfill their dreams of becoming independent farmers. Federal efforts proved equally feeble. The Southern Homestead Act of 1866 offered 80-acre grants to settlers, limited for the first year to freedmen and southern Unionists. The advantage was mostly symbolic, however, since the public land made available to homesteaders was off the beaten track in swampy, infertile parts of the lower South and since homesteaders lacked the resources to get started. Only about 1,000 homesteading families finally succeeded.

There was no reversing President Johnson's order restoring confiscated lands to the former Confederates. Property rights, it seemed, trumped everything else, even for most radical Republicans. The Freedmen's Bureau, which had earlier championed the land claims of former slaves, now devoted itself to teaching them how to be good agricultural laborers.

So while they yearned for farms of their own, most freedmen started out landless and with no option but to labor for their former owners. But not, they vowed, under the conditions of slavery—no gang work, no overseers, no fines or punishments, no regulation of their private lives or personal freedom. In certain parts of the agricultural South—for example, on the great sugar plantations of Louisiana taken over after the war by northern investors—wage work became the norm. The problem was that cotton planters lacked the money to pay wages, at least not until the crop came in, and sometimes, in lieu of a straight wage, they offered a share of the crop. As a *wage,* this was a bad deal for the freedmen, but if they could be paid in shares for their work, why could they not pay in shares to rent the land they worked?

This form of share tenantry, already familiar in parts of the white South, freedmen now seized on for the independence it offered them. Planters resisted, believing, as one wrote, that "wages are the only successful system of controlling hands." But in a battle of wills that broke out across the cotton South, the planters yielded to "the inveterate prejudices of the freedmen, who desire to be masters of their own time."

Thus there sprang up the distinctive laboring system for cotton agriculture—*sharecropping,* in which the freedmen worked as tenant farmers, exchanging their labor for the use of land, house, implements, sometimes seed and fertilizer, typically turning over half to two-thirds of their harvested crops to the landlord (see Map 15.2). The sharecropping system joined laborers and the owners of land and capital in a common sharing of risks and returns. But it was a very unequal relationship, given the force of southern law and custom on the white landowner's side and given the sharecroppers' dire economic circumstances. Starting out in poverty, they had no way of making it through the first growing season without borrowing for food and supplies.

Country storekeepers stepped in. Bankrolled by their northern suppliers, they "furnished" the sharecropper and took as collateral a *lien* on the crop, effectively assuming ownership of the cropper's share. Under lien laws passed after radical Reconstruction collapsed, sharecroppers received only the proceeds that remained after their debts had been paid. Once indebted at one store, the sharecropper was no longer free to shop around and became an easy target for exorbitant prices, unfair interest rates, and crooked bookkeeping. As cotton prices declined during the 1870s, more and more sharecroppers failed to settle accounts and fell into permanent debt.

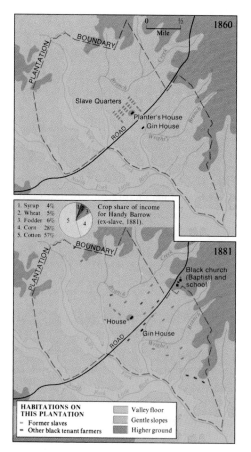

MAP 15.2

The Barrow Plantation, 1860 and 1881

Comparing the 1860 map of this central Georgia plantation with the 1881 map reveals the changing patterns of black residence and farming. In 1860 the slave quarters were clustered near the planter's house, which sat on a small hilltop. The sharecroppers of 1881 built cabins along the spurs or ridges of land between the streams, scattering their community over the plantation. A black church and school were built by this date. A typical sharecropper on the plantation earned most of his income from growing cotton.

Sharecropping

This sharecropping family seems proud of its new cabin and crop of cotton, which it planted in every available bit of ground. But the presence of the white landlord in the background suggests that sharecropping was only a limited kind of economic freedom. (Brown Brothers)

And if the merchant was also the landowner or conspired with the landowner, the debt became a pretext for forced labor, or *peonage,* although evidence now suggests that sharecroppers generally managed to pull up stakes and move on once things became hopeless. Sharecroppers always thought twice about moving, however, because part of their "capital" was being known and well-reputed in their communities. Freedmen who lacked that local standing generally found sharecropping hard going and ended up in the ranks of agricultural laborers.

In the face of all this adversity, the freedpeople struggled to better themselves. The fact that it enabled *family* struggle was, in truth, the saving advantage of sharecropping because it mobilized husbands and wives in common enterprise while shielding both from personal subordination to whites. The trouble with sharecropping, grumbled one planter, was that "it makes the laborer too independent; he becomes a partner, and has to be consulted." By the end of Reconstruction, about one-quarter of sharecropping families had managed to save enough to rent with cash payments, and eventually black farmers owned about a third of the land they cultivated—but rarely the best land and usually at a cost greater than its fertility warranted.

For the freedmen, sharecropping was not the worst choice; it certainly beat wage work for their former owners. But for southern agriculture, the costs were devastating. Sharecropping committed the South inflexibly to cotton, despite soil depletion and unprofitable prices. Crop diversification declined, costing the South its self-sufficiency in grains and livestock. And with farms leased year to year, the tenant had little incentive to improve the property. The crop-lien system lined merchants' pockets with unearned profits that might otherwise have gone into agricultural improvement. The result was a stagnant farm economy, blighting the South's future and condemning it to economic backwardness—a kind of retribution, in fact, for the fresh injustices visited on the people it had once enslaved.

The Undoing of Reconstruction

Former Confederates were blind to the benefits of radical Reconstruction. Indeed, no amount of achievement could have persuaded them that it was anything but an abomination, undertaken without their consent and intended to deny them their rightful place in southern society. Led by the planters, former Confederates staged a massive counterrevolution—one designed to "redeem" the South and restore them to political power under the banner of the Democratic Party. But the Redeemers could not have succeeded on their own. They needed the complicity of the North. The undoing of Reconstruction is as much about northern acquiescence as it is about southern resistance.

COUNTERREVOLUTION

Insofar as they could win at the ballot box, the Democrats took that route. They worked hard to get former Confederates restored to the rolls of registered voters, they appealed to racial solidarity and southern patriotism, and they campaigned against black rule as a threat to white supremacy. But force was equally acceptable. Throughout the Deep South, especially where black voters were heavily concentrated, former Confederate planters and their supporters organized secret societies and waged campaigns of terror against blacks and their white allies.

The most widespread of these groups, the Ku Klux Klan, first appeared in 1866 as a Tennessee social club but quickly became a paramilitary force under Nathan Bedford Forrest, the Confederacy's most decorated cavalry general. Forrest was notorious for a wartime incident at Fort Pillow, Tennessee, when his troops massacred African American soldiers after they had surrendered.

By 1870 the Klan was operating almost everywhere in the South as an armed force serving the Democratic Party. The Klan murdered and whipped Republican politicians, burned black schools and churches, and attacked party gatherings (see American Voices, "The Intimidation of Black Voters"). In October 1870 a group of Klansmen assaulted a Republican rally in Eutaw, Alabama, killing four African Americans and wounding fifty-four. Such terrorist tactics enabled the Democrats to seize power in Georgia and North Carolina in 1870 and make substantial gains

Klan Portrait, 1868

Two armed Klansmen from Alabama
pose proudly in their disguises.
Northern audiences saw a lithograph
based on this photograph in *Harper's
Weekly* in December 1868.
(Rutherford B. Hayes Presidential Center,
Spiegel Grove, Fremont, Ohio)

elsewhere. An African American politician in North Carolina wrote, "Our former
masters are fast taking the reins of government."

Congress responded by passing enforcement legislation, including the Ku Klux
Klan Act of 1871, authorizing President Grant to use federal prosecutions, military
force, and martial law to suppress conspiracies to deprive citizens of the right to
vote, hold office, serve on juries, and enjoy equal protection of the law. Federal
agents penetrated the Klan and gathered evidence that provided the basis for widespread arrests; federal grand juries indicted more than 3,000 Klansmen. In South
Carolina, where the Klan was most deeply entrenched, federal troops occupied nine
counties, driving as many as 2,000 Klansmen from the state.

The Grant administration's assault on the Klan raised the spirits of southern
Republicans, but it also emphasized how dependent they were on the federal government. The potency of the Ku Klux Klan Act, a Mississippi Republican wrote,
"derived alone from its source" in the federal government. "No such law could be
enforced by state authority, the local power being too weak." If Republicans were
to prevail over former Confederate terrorists, they needed what one carpetbagger
described as "steady, unswerving power from without."

AMERICAN VOICES

The Intimidation of Black Voters

Harriet Hernandes

*T*he following testimony was given in 1871 by Harriet Hernandes, a black resident of Spartanburg, South Carolina, to the Joint Congressional Select Committee investigating conditions in the South. The terrorizing of black women through rape and other forms of physical violence was among the means of oppression used by the Ku Klux Klan.

Question: How old are you?
Answer: Going on thirty-four years. . . .
Q: Are you married or single?
A: Married.
Q: Did the Ku-Klux come to your house at any time?
A: Yes, sir; twice. . . .
Q: Go on to the second time. . . .
A: They came in; I was lying in bed. Says he, "Come out here, sir; come out here, sir!" They took me out of bed; they would not let me get out, but they took me up in their arms and toted me out—me and my daughter Lucy. He struck me on the forehead with a pistol, and here is the scar above my eye now. Says he, "Damn you, fall." I fell. Says he, "Damn you, get up." I got up. Says he, "Damn you, get over this fence!" and he kicked me over when I went to get over; and then he went on to a brush pile, and they laid us right down there, both together. They laid us down twenty yards apart, I reckon. They had dragged and beat us along. They struck me right on top of my head, and I thought they had killed me; and I said, "Lord o'mercy, don't, don't kill my child!" He gave me a lick on the head, and it liked to have killed me; I saw stars. He threw my arm over my head so I could not do anything with it for three weeks, and there are great knots on my wrist now.
Q: What did they say this was for?
A: They said, "You can tell your husband that when we see him we are going to kill him. . . ."
Q: Did they say why they wanted to kill him?
A: They said, "He voted the radical ticket [slate of candidates], didn't he?" I said, "Yes," that very way. . . .
Q: When did [your husband] get back home after this whipping? He was not at home, was he?
A: He was lying out; he couldn't stay at home, bless your soul! . . .
Q: Has he been afraid for any length of time?
A: He has been afraid ever since last October. He has been lying out. He has not laid in the house ten nights since October.
Q: Is that the situation of the colored people down there to any extent?
A: That is the way they all have to do—men and women both.
Q: What are they afraid of?
A: Of being killed or whipped to death.
Q: What has made them afraid?

A: Because men that voted radical tickets they took the spite out on the women when they could get at them.
Q: How many colored people have been whipped in that neighborhood?
A: It is all of them, mighty near.

SOURCE: *Report of the Joint Congressional Select Committee to Inquire into the Condition of Affairs in the Late Insurrectionary States, House Reports*, 42d Cong., 2d sess. (Washington, DC: U.S. Government Printing Office, 1972), vol. 5, South Carolina, December 19, 1871.

But northern Republicans were growing weary of Reconstruction and the bloodshed it seemed to produce. Although reelected handily in 1872, Grant did not see his victory as a mandate for an endless war against the white South. Prosecuting Klansmen under the enforcement acts was an uphill battle. U.S. attorneys usually faced all-white juries, and the Justice Department lacked the resources to prosecute effectively. After 1872, prosecutions dropped off, and many Klansmen received hasty pardons; only a small fraction served significant prison terms.

The faltering zeal for Reconstruction stemmed from more than discouragement about prosecuting the Klan, however. The worst depression in the nation's history struck in 1873, and the North became preoccupied with its own economic problems. Northern business interests complained that the turmoil of Reconstruction retarded the South's economic recovery and harmed their investment opportunities. Sympathy for the freedmen also began to wane. The North was flooded with one-sided, often racist reports, such as James M. Pike's *The Prostrate State* (1873), describing extravagant, corrupt Republican rule and a South in the grip of "a mass of black barbarism." In the 1874 elections, the Republicans suffered a crushing defeat, losing control of the House of Representatives for the first time since secession and also losing seven normally Republican states to the Democrats. For party strategists, the political costs in a disillusioned North began to outweigh their hopes for a Republican-dominated South.

In a kind of self-fulfilling prophesy, the unwillingness of the Grant administration to shore up Reconstruction guaranteed that it would fail. Republican governments that were denied federal help found themselves overwhelmed by massive resistance from former Confederates. Democrats overthrew Republican governments in Texas in 1873, in Alabama and Arkansas in 1874, and in Mississippi in 1875.

The Mississippi campaign showed all too clearly what the Republicans were up against. As elections neared in 1875, paramilitary groups such as the Rifle Clubs and Red Shirts operated openly. Often local Democrats paraded armed, as if they were militia companies. They identified black leaders in assassination lists called "dead-books," broke up Republican meetings, provoked rioting that left hundreds of African Americans dead, and threatened voters, who still lacked the protection of the secret ballot. Mississippi's Republican governor, Adelbert Ames, a Congressional Medal of Honor winner from Maine, appealed to President Grant for federal troops, but Grant refused. Ames then contemplated organizing a state militia but ultimately decided against it, believing that only blacks would join and that the state would be plunged into racial war. Brandishing their guns and stuffing the ballot boxs, the Redeemers swept the 1875 elections and took command of Mississippi. Facing impeachment by the new Democratic legislature, Governor Ames resigned his office and returned to the North.

THE POLITICAL CRISIS OF 1877

Northerners were not much troubled by the South's counterrevolution. National politics had moved on, and other concerns absorbed voters. Foremost was the stench of scandal that hung over the White House. In 1875 Grant's secretary of the treasury, Benjamin Bristow, exposed the so-called Whiskey Ring, a network of distillers and government agents who had defrauded the U.S. Treasury of millions of dollars of excise taxes on liquor. The ringleader was a Grant appointee, and Grant's own private secretary, Orville Babcock, had a hand in the thievery. The others went to prison, but Grant stood by Babcock, possibly perjuring himself to save his secretary. On top of this, the economic depression deepened. Grant's administration responded ineffectually, rebuffing the pleas of debtors for relief by increasing the money supply (see Chapter 18).

Among the casualties of the bad economy was the Freedman's Savings and Trust Company, which had been sponsored by the Freedmen's Bureau and held the small deposits of thousands of former slaves. When the bank failed in 1874, Congress refused to compensate the depositors, and many lost their life savings. In denying the depositors' pleas, Congress was signaling that Reconstruction had lost its moral claim on the country.

Abandoning Grant, the Republicans in 1876 nominated Rutherford B. Hayes, governor of Ohio, a colorless figure but untainted by corruption, or by strong convictions—in a word, a safe man. His Democratic opponent was Samuel J. Tilden, governor of New York, a wealthy lawyer with ties to Wall Street and a reform reputation for helping to break the hold of the thieving Tweed Ring over New York City politics. The Democrat Tilden favored "home rule" for the South, but so, more discretely, did the Republican Hayes. Reconstruction actually did not figure prominently in the campaign and was mostly subsumed under broader Democratic charges of "corrupt centralism" and "incapacity, waste, and fraud." By now, Republicans had written off the South and scarcely campaigned there. They paid little attention to the states still ruled by Reconstruction governments—Florida, South Carolina, and Louisiana.

Once the returns started coming in on election night, however, those three states began to loom very large indeed. Tilden led in the popular vote, and with victories in key northern states, he seemed headed for the White House. But sleepless politicians at Republican headquarters realized that if they kept Florida, South Carolina, and Louisiana, Hayes would win by a single electoral vote. The campaigns in those states had been bitterly fought, with the same kinds of Democratic assaults on blacks that had overturned Republican regimes everywhere else in the South. But Republicans still controlled the election machinery in those states, and citing Democratic fraud and intimidation they could certify Republican victories. Late on election night the audacious announcement came forth from Republican headquarters: Hayes had carried the three southern states and won the election. But newly elected Democratic officials in the three states also sent in electoral votes for Tilden. When Congress met in early 1877, it faced two sets of electoral votes from those states.

The Constitution did not provide for this contingency. All it said was that the President of the Senate (in 1877, a Republican) opens the electoral certificates before the House (Democratic) and the Senate (Republican) and that "The votes shall then be counted." An air of crisis gripped the country. There was talk of inside deals, of a new election, even of a violent coup and civil war. Just in case, the commander of the army, General William T. Sherman, deployed four artillery companies in Washington. Finally, Congress decided to appoint an electoral commission to settle the question. The commission included seven Republicans, seven Democrats, and, as the deciding member, David Davis, a Supreme Court justice not known to have fixed party loyalties. But Davis disqualified himself by accepting an Illinois seat in the Senate. He was replaced by Republican Justice Joseph P. Bradley, and by a vote of 8 to 7, the commission awarded the disputed votes to Hayes.

Outraged Democrats had one more trick up their sleeves. They controlled the House, and they set about stalling a final count of the electoral votes so as to prevent Hayes's inauguration on March 4, 1877. But a week earlier, secret talks had begun between southern Democrats and Ohio Republicans representing Hayes. Other issues may have been on the table, but the main thing was the situation in South Carolina and Louisiana, where rival governments were encamped at the state capitols, with federal soldiers holding the Democrats at bay. Exactly what deal was struck or how involved Hayes himself was will probably never be known, but on March 1 the House Democrats suddenly ended their filibuster, the ceremonial counting of votes went forward, and Hayes was inaugurated on schedule. He soon ordered the Union troops back to their barracks, and the Republican regimes in South Carolina and Louisiana fell. Reconstruction had ended.

In 1877 political leaders on all sides seemed ready to say that what Lincoln had called "the work" was complete. But for the freedmen, the work had only begun. Reconstruction turned out to have been a magnificent aberration, a magnum jump beyond what most white Americans actually felt was due their black fellow citizens. Redemption represented a sad falling back to the norm. Still, something real had been achieved—three rights-defining amendments to the Constitution, some elbow room to advance economically, and, not least, a stubborn confidence among

T I M E L I N E

1863 Lincoln's Ten Percent Plan	**1870** Ku Klux Klan at peak of power
1864 Wade-Davis Bill "pocket"-vetoed by Lincoln.	Congress responds with Enforcement Acts.
1865 Freedmen's Bureau established	Fifteenth Amendment ratified
Lincoln assassinated	**1872** Grant reelected president.
Andrew Johnson becomes President and implements his restoration plan.	**1873** Panic of 1873 ushers in depression of 1873–77.
1866 Civil Rights Act passes over Johnson's veto.	**1874** Democrats gain majority in House of Representatives.
Johnson makes disastrous "swing around the circle."	**1875** Whiskey Ring scandal undermines Grant administration.
Congressional elections repudiate Johnson.	**1876** Disputed presidential election
1867 Reconstruction Acts	**1877** Congressional compromise makes Rutherford B. Hayes president.
1868 Impeachment crisis	Reconstruction ends.
Fourteenth Amendment ratified	
Ulysses S. Grant elected president	

blacks that by their own efforts they could lift themselves up. Things would, in fact, get worse before they got better, but the work of Reconstruction was imperishable and could never be erased.

For Further Exploration

The best current book on Reconstruction is Eric Foner's major synthesis, *Reconstruction: America's Unfinished Revolution, 1863–1877* (1988), available also in a shorter version. *Black Reconstruction in America* (1935), by the African American activist and scholar W. E. B. Du Bois, deserves attention as the first book to challenge traditional racist interpretations of Reconstruction and stress the role of blacks in their own emancipation. For the presidential phase of Reconstruction, see Dan T. Carter, *When the War Was Over: The Failure of Self-Reconstruction in the South, 1865–1867* (1985). On the freedmen, Leon F. Litwack, *Been in the Storm So Long: The Aftermath of Slavery* (1979), provides a stirring account. More recent emancipation studies emphasize slavery as a labor system: Julie Saville, *The Work of Reconstruction; From Slave to Wage Laborer in South Carolina, 1860–1870* (1994), and Amy Dru Stanley, *From Bondage to Contract* (1999), which expands the discussion to show what the onset of wage labor meant for freedwomen. Eric Foner, *Nothing But Freedom: Emancipation and Its Legacy* (1983), helpfully places emancipation in a comparative context. William S. McFeely, *Grant: A Biography* (1981), deftly explains the politics of Reconstruction. The emergence of the sharecropping system is explored in Gavin Wright, *Old South, New South* (1986), and Edward Royce *The Origins of Southern Sharecropping* (1993). On the Compromise of 1877, see C. Vann Woodward's classic *Reunion and Reaction* (1956). Two informative websites are <http://womhis .binghampton.edu/intro.htm>, which deals with northern women who assisted the freed-people, and <1cweb2.loc.gov/ammen/aaohtml/aollist.html>, which provides Library of Congress documents and illustrations on African Americans during Reconstruction.

DOCUMENTS

THE DECLARATION OF INDEPENDENCE

The Unanimous Declaration of the Thirteen United States of America

When in the Course of human events, it becomes necessary for one people to dissolve the political bands which have connected them with another, and to assume among the Powers of the earth, the separate and equal station to which the Laws of Nature and of Nature's God entitle them, a decent respect to the opinions of mankind requires that they should declare the causes which impel them to the separation.

We hold these truths to be self-evident, that all men are created equal, that they are endowed by their Creator with certain unalienable rights, that among these are Life, Liberty, and the pursuit of Happiness. That to secure these rights, Governments are instituted among Men, deriving their just powers from the consent of the governed. That whenever any Form of Government becomes destructive of these ends, it is the Right of the People to alter or to abolish it, and to institute new Government, laying its foundation on such principles and organizing its powers in such form, as to them shall seem most likely to effect their Safety and Happiness. Prudence, indeed, will dictate that Governments long established should not be changed for light and transient causes; and accordingly all experience hath shown, that mankind are more disposed to suffer, while evils are sufferable, than to right themselves by abolishing the forms to which they are accustomed. But when a long train of abuses and usurpations, pursuing invariably the same Object evinces a design to reduce them under absolute Despotism, it is their right, it is their duty, to throw off such Government, and to provide new Guards for their future security. —Such has been the patient sufferance of these Colonies; and such is now the necessity which constrains them to alter their former Systems of Government. The history of the present King of Great Britain is a history of repeated injuries and usurpations, all having in direct object the establishment of an absolute Tyranny over these States. To prove this, let Facts be submitted to a candid world.

He has refused his Assent to Laws, the most wholesome and necessary for the public good.

He has forbidden his Governors to pass Laws of immediate and pressing importance, unless suspended in their operation till his Assent should be obtained; and, when so suspended, he has utterly neglected to attend to them.

He has refused to pass other Laws for the accommodation of large districts of people, unless those people would relinquish the right of Representation in the Legislature, a right inestimable to them and formidable to tyrants only.

He has called together legislative bodies at places unusual, uncomfortable, and distant from the depository of their public Records, for the sole purpose of fatiguing them into compliance with his measures.

He has dissolved Representative Houses repeatedly, for opposing with manly firmness his invasions on the rights of the people.

He has refused for a long time, after such dissolutions, to cause others to be elected; whereby the Legislative powers, incapable of Annihilation, have returned to the People at large for their exercise; the State remaining in the mean time exposed to all the dangers of invasion from without and convulsions within.

He has endeavoured to prevent the population of these States; for that purpose obstructing the Laws of Naturalization of Foreigners; refusing to pass others to encourage their migrations hither, and raising the conditions of new Appropriations of Lands.

He has obstructed the Administration of Justice, by refusing his Assent to Laws for establishing Judiciary powers.

He has made Judges dependent on his Will alone, for the tenure of their offices, and the amount and payment of their salaries.

He has erected a multitude of New Offices, and sent hither swarms of Officers to harass our People, and eat out their substance.

He has kept among us, in times of peace, Standing Armies without the Consent of our legislature.

He has combined with others to subject us to a jurisdiction foreign to our constitution, and unacknowledged by our laws; giving his Assent to their Acts of pretended Legislation:

For quartering large bodies of armed troops among us:

For protecting them, by a mock Trial, from Punishment for any Murders which they should commit on the Inhabitants of these States:

For cutting off our Trade with all parts of the world:

For imposing taxes on us without our Consent:

For depriving us of many cases, of the benefits of Trial by jury:

For transporting us beyond Seas to be tried for pretended offences:

For abolishing the free System of English Laws in a neighbouring Province, establishing therein an Arbitrary government, and enlarging its Boundaries so as to render it at once an example and fit instrument for introducing the same absolute rule into these Colonies:

For taking away our Charters, abolishing our most valuable Laws, and altering fundamentally the Forms of our Governments:

For suspending our own Legislatures, and declaring themselves invested with Power to legislate for us in all cases whatsoever.

He has abdicated Government here, by declaring us out of his Protection and waging War against us.

He has plundered our seas, ravaged our Coasts, burnt our towns, and destroyed the lives of our people.

He is at this time transporting large armies of foreign mercenaries to compleat the works of death, desolation, and tyranny, already begun with circumstances of Cruelty & perfidy scarcely paralleled in the most barbarous ages, and totally unworthy the Head of a civilized nation.

He has constrained our fellow Citizens taken Captive on the high Seas to bear Arms against their Country, to become the executioners of their friends and Brethren, or to fall themselves by their Hands.

He has excited domestic insurrections amongst us, and has endeavoured to bring on the inhabitants of our frontiers, the merciless Indian Savages, whose known rule of warfare, is an undistinguished destruction of all ages, sexes, and conditions.

In every stage of these Oppressions We have Petitioned for Redress in the most humble terms: Our repeated petitions have been answered only by repeated injury. A Prince, whose character is thus marked by every act which may define a Tyrant, is unfit to be the ruler of a free people.

Nor have We been wanting in attention to our British brethren. We have warned them from time to time of attempts by their legislature to extend an unwarrantable jurisdiction over us. We have reminded them of the circumstances of our emigration and settlement here. We have appealed to their native justice and magnanimity, and we have conjured them by the ties of our common kindred to disavow these usurpations, which, would inevitably interrupt our connections and correspondence. They too have been deaf to the voice of justice and of consanguinity. We must, therefore, acquiesce in the necessity, which denounces our Separation, and hold them, as we hold the rest of mankind, Enemies in War, in Peace Friends.

We, therefore, the Representatives of the United States of America, in General Congress, Assembled, appealing to the Supreme Judge of the world for the rectitude of our intentions, do, in the Name, and by Authority of the good People of these Colonies, solemnly publish and declare, That these United Colonies are, and of Right ought to be FREE AND INDE-PENDENT STATES; that they are Absolved from all Allegiance to the British Crown, and that all political connection between them and the State of Great Britain, is and ought to be totally dissolved; and that as Free and Independent States, they have full Power to levy War, conclude Peace, contract Alliances, establish Commerce, and to do all other Acts and Things which Independent States may of right do. And for the support of this Declaration, with a firm reliance on the Protection of Divine Providence, we mutually pledge to each other our Lives, our Fortunes, and our sacred Honor.

John Hancock

Button Gwinnett	George Wythe	James Wilson	Josiah Bartlett
Lyman Hall	Richard Henry Lee	Geo. Ross	Wm. Whipple
Geo. Walton	Th. Jefferson	Caesar Rodney	Saml. Adams
Wm. Hooper	Benja. Harrison	Geo. Read	John Adams
Joseph Hewes	Thos. Nelson, Jr.	Thos. M'Kean	Robt. Treat Paine
John Penn	Francis Lightfoot Lee	Wm. Floyd	Elbridge Gerry
Edward Rutledge	Carter Braxton	Phil. Livingston	Step. Hopkins
Thos. Heyward, Junr.	Robt. Morris	Frans. Lewis	William Ellery
Thomas Lynch, Junr.	Benjamin Rush	Lewis Morris	Roger Sherman
Arthur Middleton	Benja. Franklin	Richd. Stockton	Sam'el Hunington
Samuel Chase	John Morton	Jno. Witherspoon	Wm. Williams
Wm. Paca	Geo. Clymer	Fras. Hopkinson	Oliver Wolcott
Thos. Stone	Jas. Smith	John Hart	Matthew Thornton
Charles Carroll	Geo. Taylor	Abra. Clark	
of Carrollton			

THE ARTICLES OF CONFEDERATION AND PERPETUAL UNION

Between the states of New Hampshire, Massachusetts Bay, Rhode Island and Providence Plantations, Connecticut, New York, New Jersey, Pennsylvania, Delaware, Maryland, Virginia, North Carolina, South Carolina, Georgia.*

ARTICLE 1.

The stile of this confederacy shall be "The United States of America."

ARTICLE 2.

Each State retains its sovereignty, freedom and independence, and every power, jurisdiction, and right, which is not by this confederation expressly delegated to the United States, in Congress assembled.

ARTICLE 3.

The said states hereby severally enter into a firm league of friendship with each other for their common defence, the security of their liberties and their mutual and general welfare; binding themselves to assist each other against all force offered to, or attacks made upon them, or any of them, on account of religion, sovereignty, trade, or any other pretence whatever.

ARTICLE 4.

The better to secure and perpetuate mutual friendship and intercourse among the people of the different states in this union, the free inhabitants of each of these states, paupers, vagabonds, and fugitives from justice excepted, shall be entitled to all privileges and immunities of free citizens in the several states; and the people of each State shall have free ingress and regress to and from any other State, and shall enjoy therein all the privileges of trade and commerce, subject to the same duties, impositions, and restrictions, as the inhabitants thereof respectively; provided, that such restrictions shall not extend so far as to prevent the removal of property, imported into any State, to any other State of which the owner is an inhabitant; provided also, that no imposition, duties, or restriction, shall be laid by any State on the property of the United States, or either of them.

If any person guilty of, or charged with treason, felony, or other high misdemeanor in any State, shall flee from justice and be found in any of the United States, he shall, upon demand of the governor or executive power of the State from which he fled, be delivered up and removed to the State having jurisdiction of his offence.

Full faith and credit shall be given in each of these states to the records, acts, and judicial proceedings of the courts and magistrates of every other State.

---

*This copy of the final draft of the Articles of Confederation is taken from the *Journals*, 9:907–25, November 15, 1777.

ARTICLE 5.

For the more convenient management of the general interests of the United States, delegates shall be annually appointed, in such manner as the legislature of each State shall direct, to meet in Congress, on the 1st Monday in November in every year, with a power reserved to each State to recall its delegates, or any of them, at any time within the year, and to send others in their stead for the remainder of the year.

No State shall be represented in Congress by less than two, nor by more than seven members; and no person shall be capable of being a delegate for more than three years in any term of six years; nor shall any person, being a delegate, be capable of holding any office under the United States, for which he, or any other for his benefit, receives any salary, fees, or emolument of any kind.

Each State shall maintain its own delegates in a meeting of the states, and while they act as members of the committee of the states.

In determining questions in the United States, in Congress assembled, each State shall have one vote.

Freedom of speech and debate in Congress shall not be impeached or questioned in any court or place out of Congress: and the members of Congress shall be protected in their persons from arrests and imprisonments, during the time of their going to and from, and attendance on Congress, except for treason, felony, or breach of the peace.

ARTICLE 6.

No State, without the consent of the United States, in Congress assembled, shall send any embassy to, or receive any embassy from, or enter into any conference, agreement, alliance, or treaty with any king, prince, or state; nor shall any person, holding any office of profit or trust under the United States, or any of them, accept of any present, emolument, office or title, of any kind whatever, from any king, prince, or foreign state; nor shall the United States, in Congress assembled, or any of them, grant any title of nobility.

No two or more states shall enter into any treaty, confederation, or alliance, whatever, between them, without the consent of the United States, in Congress assembled, specifying accurately the purposes for which the same is to be entered into, and how long it shall continue.

No state shall lay any imposts or duties which may interfere with any stipulations in treaties entered into by the United States, in Congress assembled, with any king, prince, or state, in pursuance of any treaties already proposed by Congress to the courts of France and Spain.

No vessels of war shall be kept up in time of peace by any State, except such number only as shall be deemed necessary by the United States, in Congress assembled, for the defence of such State or its trade; nor shall any body of forces be kept up by any State, in time of peace, except such number only as, in the judgment of the United States, in Congress assembled, shall be deemed requisite to garrison the forts necessary for the defence of such State; but every State shall always keep up a well regulated and disciplined militia, sufficiently armed and accoutred, and shall provide, and constantly have ready for use, in public stores, a due number of field pieces and tents, and a proper quantity of arms, ammunition and camp equipage.

No State shall engage in any war without the consent of the United States, in Congress assembled, unless such State be actually invaded by enemies, or shall have received certain advice of a resolution being formed by some nation of Indians to invade such State, and the danger is so imminent as not to admit of a delay till the United States, in Congress assembled, can be consulted; nor shall any State grant commissions to any ships or vessels of war, nor letters of marque or reprisal, except it be after a declaration of war by the United States, in Congress assembled, and then only against the kingdom or state, and the subjects thereof, against which war has been so declared, and under such regulations as shall be established by the United States, in Congress assembled, unless such State be infested by pirates, in which case vessels of war may be fitted out for that occasion, and kept so long as the danger shall continue, or until the United States, in Congress assembled, shall determine otherwise.

ARTICLE 7.

When land forces are raised by any State for the common defence, all officers of or under the rank of colonel, shall be appointed by the legislature of each State respectively, by whom such forces shall be raised, or in such manner as such State shall direct; and all vacancies shall be filled up by the State which first made the appointment.

ARTICLE 8.

All charges of war and all other expences, that shall be incurred for the common defence or general welfare, and allowed by the United States, in Congress assembled, shall be defrayed out of a common treasury, which shall be supplied by the several states, in proportion to the value of all land within each State, granted to or surveyed for any person, as such land and the buildings and improvements thereon shall be estimated according to such mode as the United States, in Congress assembled, shall, from time to time, direct and appoint.

 The taxes for paying that proportion shall be laid and levied by the authority and direction of the legislatures of the several states, within the time agreed upon by the United States, in Congress assembled.

ARTICLE 9.

The United States, in Congress assembled, shall have the sole and exclusive right and power of determining on peace and war, except in the cases mentioned in the 6th article; of sending and receiving ambassadors; entering into treaties and alliances, provided that no treaty of commerce shall be made, whereby the legislative power of the respective states shall be restrained from imposing such imposts and duties on foreigners as their own people are subjected to, or from prohibiting the exportation or importation of any species of goods or commodities whatsoever; of establishing rules for deciding, in all cases, what captures on land or water shall be legal, and in what manner prizes, taken by land or naval forces in the service of the United States, shall be divided or appropriated; or granting letters of marque and reprisal in times of peace; appointing courts for the trial of piracies and felonies committed on the high seas, and establishing courts for receiving and determining, finally, appeals in all cases of captures; provided, that no member of Congress shall be appointed a judge of any of the said courts.

 The United States, in Congress assembled, shall also be the last resort on appeal in all disputes and differences now subsisting, or that hereafter may arise between two or more states concerning boundary, jurisdiction or any other cause whatever; which authority shall always be exercised in the manner following: whenever the legislative or executive authority, or lawful agent of any State, in controversy with another, shall present a petition to Congress, stating the matter in question, and praying for a hearing, notice thereof shall be given, by order of Congress, to the legislative of executive authority of the other State in controversy, and a day assigned for the appearance of the parties by their lawful agents, who shall then be directed to appoint, by joint consent, commissioners or judges to constitute a court for hearing and determining the matter in question; but, if they cannot agree, Congress shall name three persons out of each of the United States, and from the list of such persons each party shall alternately strike out one, the petitioners beginning, until the number shall be reduced to thirteen; and from that number not less than seven, nor more than nine names, as Congress shall direct, shall, in the presence of Congress, be drawn out by lot; and the persons whose names shall be so drawn, or any five of them, shall be commissioners or judges to hear and finally determine the controversy, so always as a major part of the judges who shall hear the cause shall agree in the determination; and if either party shall neglect to attend at the day appointed, without shewing reasons which Congress shall judge sufficient, or, being present, shall refuse to strike, the Congress shall proceed to nominate three persons out of each State, and the secretary of Congress shall strike in behalf of such party absent or refusing; and the judgment and sentence of the court to be appointed, in the manner before prescribed, shall be final and conclusive; and if any of the parties shall refuse to submit to the authority of such court, or to appear or defend their claim or cause, the court shall nevertheless proceed to pronounce sentence or judgment, which shall, in like manner, be final and decisive, the judgment or sentence and other proceedings begin, in either case, transmitted to Congress, and lodged among the acts of Congress for the security of the parties concerned: provided, that every commissioner, before he sits in judgment, shall take an oath, to be administered by one of the judges of the supreme or superior court of the State where the cause shall be tried, "well and truly to hear and determine the matter in question, according to the best of his judgment, without favour, affection, or hope of reward:" provided, also, that no State shall be deprived of territory for the benefit of the United States.

All controversies concerning the private right of soil, claimed under different grants of two or more states, whose jurisdictions, as they may respect such lands and the states which passed such grants, are adjusted, the said grants, or either of them, being at the same time claimed to have originated antecedent to such settlement of jurisdiction, shall, on the petition of either party to the Congress of the United States, be finally determined, as near as may be, in the same manner as is before prescribed for deciding disputes respecting territorial jurisdiction between different states.

The United States, in Congress assembled, shall also have the sole and exclusive right and power of regulating the alloy and value of coin struck by their own authority, or by that of the respective states; fixing the standard of weights and measures throughout the United States; regulating the trade and managing all affairs with the Indians not members of any of the states; provided that the legislative right of any State within its own limits be not infringed or violated; establishing and regulating post offices from one State to another throughout all the United States, and exacting such postage on the papers passing through the same as may be requisite to defray the expences of the said office; appointing all officers of the land forces in the service of the United States, excepting regimental officers; appointing all the officers of the naval forces, and commissioning all officers whatever in the service of the United States; making rules for the government and regulation of the said land and naval forces, and directing their operations.

The United States, in Congress assembled, shall have authority to appoint a committee to sit in the recess of Congress, to be denominated "a Committee of the States," and to consist of one delegate from each State, and to appoint such other committees and civil officers as may be necessary for managing the general affairs of the United States, under their direction; to appoint one of their number to preside; provided that no person be allowed to serve in the office of president more than one year in any term of three years; to ascertain the necessary sums of money to be raised for the service of the United States, and to appropriate and apply the same for defraying the public expences; to borrow money or emit bills on the credit of the United States, transmitting, every half year, to the respective states, an account of the sums of money so borrowed or emitted; to build and equip a navy; to agree upon the number of land forces, and to make requisitions from each State for in quota, in proportion to the number of white inhabitants in such State; which requisitions shall be binding; and thereupon, the legislature of each State shall appoint the regimental officers, raise the men, and cloathe, arm, and equip them in a soldier-like manner, at the expence of the United States; and the officers and men so cloathed, armed, and equipped, shall march to the place appointed and within the time agreed on by the United States, in Congress assembled; but if the United States, in Congress assembled, shall, on consideration of circumstances, judge proper that any State should not raise men, or should raise a smaller number than its quota, and that any other State should raise a greater number of men than the quota threof, such extra number shall be raised, officered, cloathed, armed, and equipped in the same manner as the quota of such State, unless the legislature of such State shall judge that such extra number cannot be safely spared out of the same, in which case they shall raise, officer, cloathe, arm, and equip as many of such extra number as they judge can be safely spared. And the officers and men so cloathed, armed, and equipped, shall march to the place appointed and within the time agreed on by the United States, in Congress assembled.

The United States, in Congress assembled, shall never engage in a war, nor grant letters of marque and reprisal in time of peace, nor enter into any treaties or alliances, nor coin money, nor regulate the value thereof, nor ascertain the sums and expences necessary for the defence and welfare of the United States, or any of them: nor emit bills, nor borrow money on the credit of the United States, nor appropriate money, nor agree upon the number of vessels of war to be built or purchased, or the number of land or sea forces to be raised, nor appoint a commander in chief of the army or navy, unless nine states assent to the same; nor shall a question on any other point, except for adjourning from day to day, be determined, unless by the votes of a majority of the United States, in Congress assembled.

The Congress of the United States shall have power to adjourn to any time within the year, and to any place within the United States, so that no period of adjournment be for a longer duration than the space of six months, and shall publish the journal of their proceedings monthly, except such parts thereof, relating to treaties, alliances or military operations, as, in their judgment, require secrecy; and the yeas and nays of the delegates of each State on any question shall be entered on the journal, when it is desired by any delegate; and the delegates of a State, or any of them, at his, or their request, shall be furnished with a transcript of the said journal, except such parts as are above excepted, to lay before the legislatures of the several states.

ARTICLE 10.

The committee of the states, or any nine of them, shall be authorized to execute, in the recess of Congress, such of the powers of Congress as the United States, in Congress assembled, by the consent of nine states, shall, from time to time, think expedient to vest them with; provided, that no power be delegated to the said committee, for the exercise of which, by the articles of confederation, the voice of nine states, in the Congress of the United States assembled, is requisite.

ARTICLE 11.

Canada acceding to this confederation, and joining in the measures of the United States, shall be admitted into and entitled to all the advantages of this union; but no other colony shall be admitted into the same, unless such admission be agreed to by nine states.

ARTICLE 12.

All bills of credit emitted, monies borrowed and debts contracted by, or under the authority of Congress before the assembling of the United States, in pursuance of the present confederation, shall be deemed and considered as a charge against the United States, for payment and satisfaction whereof the said United States and the public faith are hereby solemnly pledged.

ARTICLE 13.

Every State shall abide by the determinations of the United States, in Congress assembled, on all questions which, by this confederation, are submitted to them. And the articles of this confederation shall be inviolably observed by every State, and the union shall be perpetual; nor shall any alteration at any time hereafter be made in any of them, unless such alteration be agreed to in a Congress of the United States, and be afterwards confirmed by the legislatures of every State.

These articles shall be proposed to the legislatures of all the United States, to be considered, and if approved of by them, they are advised to authorize their delegates to ratify the same in the Congress of the United States; which being done, the same shall become conclusive.

THE CONSTITUTION OF THE UNITED STATES

We the People of the United States, in Order to form a more perfect Union, establish Justice, insure domestic Tranquility, provide for the common defence, promote the general Welfare, and secure the Blessings of Liberty to ourselves and our Posterity, do ordain and establish this Constitution for the United States of America.

ARTICLE I

Section 1
All legislative Powers herein granted shall be vested in a Congress of the United States, which shall consist of a Senate and a House of Representatives.

Section 2
The House of Representatives shall be composed of Members chosen every second Year by the People of the several States, and the Electors in each State shall have the Qualifications requisite for Electors of the most numerous Branch of the State Legislature.

No Person shall be a Representative who shall not have attained to the Age of twenty-five Years, and been seven Years a Citizen of the United States, and who shall not, when elected, be an Inhabitant of that State in which he shall be chosen.

Representatives and direct Taxes shall be apportioned among the several States which may be included within this Union, according to their respective Numbers, *which shall be determined by adding to the whole Number of free Persons, including those bound to Service for a Term of Years, and excluding Indians not taxed, three fifths of all other Persons.** The actual Enumeration shall be made within three Years after the first Meeting of the Congress of the United States, and within every subsequent Term of ten Years, in such Manner as they shall by Law direct. The Number of Representatives shall not exceed one for every thirty Thousand, but each State shall have at Least one Representative; and *until such enumeration shall be made, the State of New Hampshire shall be entitled to chuse three, Massachusetts eight, Rhode Island and Providence Plantations one, Connecticut five, New-York six, New Jersey four, Pennsylvania eight, Delaware one, Maryland six, Virginia ten, North Carolina five, South Carolina five, and Georgia three.*

When vacancies happen in the Representation from any State, the Executive Authority thereof shall issue Writs of Election to fill such Vacancies.

The House of Representatives shall chuse their Speaker and other Officers; and shall have the sole Power of Impeachment.

Section 3
The Senate of the United States shall be composed of two Senators from each State, *chosen by the Legislature thereof,*† for six Years; and each Senator shall have one Vote.

Immediately after they shall be assembled in Consequence of the first Election, they shall be divided as equally as may be into three Classes. The Seats of the Senators of the first

---

Note: The Constitution became effective March 4, 1789. Provisions in italics have been changed by constitutional amendment.

*Changed by Section 2 of the Fourteenth Amendment.

†Changed by Section 1 of the Seventeenth Amendment.

Class shall be vacated at the Expiration of the second Year, of the second Class at the Expiration of the fourth Year, and of the third Class at the Expiration of the sixth Year, so that one-third may be chosen every second Year; *and if Vacancies happen by Resignation, or otherwise, during the Recess of the Legislature of any State, the Executive thereof may make temporary Appointments until the next Meeting of the Legislature, which shall then fill such Vacancies.**

No person shall be a Senator who shall not have attained to the Age of thirty Years, and been nine Years a Citizen of the United States, and who shall not, when elected, be an Inhabitant of that State for which he shall be chosen.

The Vice President of the United States shall be President of the Senate, but shall have no Vote, unless they be equally divided.

The Senate shall chuse their other Officers, and also a President pro tempore, in the absence of the Vice President, or when he shall exercise the Office of President of the United States.

The Senate shall have the sole Power to try all Impeachments. When sitting for that Purpose, they shall be on Oath or Affirmation. When the President of the United States is tried, the Chief Justice shall preside: And no Person shall be convicted without the Concurrence of two thirds of the Members present.

Judgment in Cases of Impeachment shall not extend further than to removal from Office, and disqualification to hold and enjoy any Office of honor, Trust or Profit under the United States: but the Party convicted shall nevertheless be liable and subject to Indictment, Trial, Judgment and Punishment, according to Law.

Section 4

The Times, Places and Manner of holding Elections for Senators and Representatives, shall be prescribed in each State by the Legislature thereof, but the Congress may at any time by Law make or alter such Regulations, except as to the Places of Chusing Senators.

The Congress shall assemble at least once in every Year, and such Meeting *shall be on the first Monday in December, unless they shall by Law appoint a different Day.*†

Section 5

Each House shall be the Judge of the Elections, Returns and Qualifications of its own Members, and a Majority of each shall constitute a Quorum to do Business; but a smaller number may adjourn from day to day, and may be authorized to compel the Attendance of absent Members, in such Manner, and under such Penalties, as each House may provide.

Each House may determine the Rules of its Proceedings, punish its Members for disorderly Behavior, and, with the Concurrence of two thirds, expel a Member.

Each House shall keep a Journal of its Proceedings, and from time to time publish the same, excepting such Parts as may in their Judgment require Secrecy; and the Yeas and Nays of the Members of either House on any question shall, at the Desire of one-fifth of those Present, be entered on the Journal.

---

*Changed by Clause 2 of the Seventeenth Amendment.

†Changed by Section 2 of the Twentieth Amendment.

Neither House, during the Session of Congress, shall, without the Consent of the other, adjourn for more than three days, nor to any other Place than that in which the two Houses shall be sitting.

Section 6

The Senators and Representatives shall receive a Compensation for their Services, to be ascertained by Law, and paid out of the Treasury of the United States. They shall in all Cases, except Treason, Felony and Breach of the Peace, be privileged from Arrest during their Attendance at the Session of their respective Houses, and in going to and returning from the same; and for any Speech or Debate in either House, they shall not be questioned in any other Place.

No Senator or Representative shall, during the Time for which he was elected, be appointed to any civil Office under the Authority of the United States, which shall have been created, or the Emoluments whereof shall have been increased, during such time; and no Person holding any Office under the United States, shall be a Member of either House during his Continuance in Office.

Section 7

All Bills for raising Revenue shall originate in the House of Representatives; but the Senate may propose or concur with Amendments as on other Bills.

Every Bill which shall have passed the House of Representatives and the Senate, shall, before it becomes a Law, be presented to the President of the United States; If he approve he shall sign it, but if not he shall return it, with his Objections to that House in which it shall have originated, who shall enter the Objections at large on their Journal, and proceed to reconsider it. If after such Reconsideration two thirds of that House shall agree to pass the Bill, it shall be sent, together with the Objections, to the other House, by which it shall likewise be reconsidered, and if approved by two thirds of that House, it shall become a Law. But in all such Cases the Votes of both Houses shall be determined by Yeas and Nays, and the Names of the Persons voting for and against the Bill shall be entered on the Journal of each House respectively. If any Bill shall not be returned by the President within ten Days (Sundays excepted) after it shall have been presented to him, the Same shall be a Law, in like Manner as if he had signed it, unless the Congress by their Adjournment prevent its Return, in which Case it shall not be a Law.

Every Order, Resolution, or Vote to which the Concurrence of the Senate and the House of Representatives may be necessary (except on a question of Adjournment) shall be presented to the President of the United States; and before the Same shall take Effect, shall be approved by him, or being disapproved by him, shall be repassed by two thirds of the Senate and House of Representatives, according to the Rules and Limitations prescribed in the Case of a Bill.

Section 8

The Congress shall have Power To lay and collect Taxes, Duties, Imposts and Excises, to pay the Debts and provide for the common Defence and general Welfare of the United States; but all Duties, Imposts and Excises shall be uniform throughout the United States;

To borrow money on the credit of the United States;

To regulate Commerce with foreign Nations, and among the several States, and with the Indian Tribes;

To establish an uniform Rule of Naturalization, and uniform Laws on the subject of Bankruptcies throughout the United States;

To coin Money, regulate the Value thereof, and of foreign Coin, and fix the Standard of Weights and Measures;

To provide for the Punishment of counterfeiting the Securities and current Coin of the United States;

To establish Post Offices and post Roads;

To promote the Progress of Science and useful Arts, by securing for limited Times to Authors and Inventors the exclusive Right to their respective Writings and Discoveries;

To constitute Tribunals inferior to the supreme Court;

To define and punish Piracies and Felonies committed on the high Seas, and Offenses against the Law of Nations;

To declare War, grant Letters of Marque and Reprisal, and make Rules concerning Captures on Land and Water;

To raise and support Armies, but no Appropriation of Money to that Use shall be for a longer Term than two Years;

To provide and maintain a Navy;

To make Rules for the Government and Regulation of the land and naval Forces;

To provide for calling forth the Militia to execute the Laws of the Union, suppress Insurrections and repel Invasions;

To provide for organizing, arming, and disciplining the Militia, and for governing such Part of them as may be employed in the Service of the United States, reserving to the States respectively, the Appointment of the Officers, and the Authority of training the Militia according to the discipline prescribed by Congress;

To exercise exclusive Legislation in all Cases whatsoever, over such District (not exceeding ten Miles square) as may, by Cession of particular States, and the acceptance of Congress, become the Seat of Government of the United States, and to exercise like Authority over all Places purchased by the Consent of the Legislature of the State in which the Same shall be, for the Erection of Forts, Magazines, Arsenals, dock-Yards, and other needful Buildings;—And

To make all Laws which shall be necessary and proper for carrying into Execution the foregoing Powers, and all other Powers vested by this Constitution in the Government of the United States, or in any Department or Officer thereof.

Section 9

The Migration or Importation of such Persons as any of the States now existing shall think proper to admit, shall not be prohibited by the Congress prior to the Year one thousand eight hundred and eight but a tax or duty may be imposed on such Importation, not exceeding ten dollars for each Person.

The privilege of the Writ of Habeas Corpus shall not be suspended, unless when in Cases of Rebellion or Invasion the public Safety may require it.

No Bill of Attainder or ex post facto Law shall be passed.

No capitation, or other direct, Tax shall be laid, unless in Proportion to the Census or Enumeration herein before directed to be taken.*

---

*Changed by the Sixteenth Amendment.

No Tax or Duty shall be laid on Articles exported from any State.

No Preference shall be given by any Regulation of Commerce or Revenue to the Ports of one State over those of another: nor shall Vessels bound to, or from, one State, be obliged to enter, clear, or pay Duties in another.

No Money shall be drawn from the Treasury, but in Consequence of Appropriations made by law; and a regular Statement and Account of the Receipts and Expenditures of all public Money shall be published from time to time.

No Title of Nobility shall be granted by the United States: And no Person holding any Office of Profit or Trust under them, shall, without the Consent of the Congress, accept of any present, Emolument, Office, or Title, of any kind whatever, from any King, Prince, or foreign State.

Section 10

No State shall enter into any Treaty, Alliance, or Confederation; grant Letters of Marque and Reprisal; coin Money; emit Bills of Credit; make any Thing but gold and silver Coin a Tender in Payment of Debts; pass any Bill of Attainder, ex post facto Law, or Law impairing the Obligation of Contracts, or grant any Title of Nobility.

No State shall, without the Consent of the Congress, lay any Imposts or Duties on Imports or Exports, except what may be absolutely necessary for executing its inspection Laws: and the net Produce of all Duties and Imposts, laid by any State on Imports or Exports, shall be for the Use of the Treasury of the United States; and all such Laws shall be subject to the Revision and Control of the Congress.

No State shall, without the Consent of the Congress, lay any duty of Tonnage, keep Troops, or Ships of War in time of Peace, enter into any Agreement or Compact with another State, or with a foreign Power, or engage in War, unless actually invaded, or in such imminent Danger as will not admit of delay.

ARTICLE II

Section 1

The executive Power shall be vested in a President of the United States of America. He shall hold his Office during the Term of four Years, and, together with the Vice President, chosen for the same Term, be elected, as follows:

Each State shall appoint, in such Manner as the Legislature thereof may direct, a Number of Electors, equal to the whole Number of Senators and Representatives to which the State may be entitled in the Congress; but no Senator or Representative, or Person holding an Office of Trust or Profit under the United States, shall be appointed an Elector.

The Electors shall meet in their respective States, and vote by Ballot for two Persons, of whom one at least shall not be an Inhabitant of the same State with themselves. And they shall make a List of all the Persons voted for, and of the Number of Votes for each; which List they shall sign and certify, and transmit sealed to the Seat of the Government of the United States, directed to the President of the Senate. The President of the Senate shall, in the Presence of the Senate and House of Representatives, open all the Certificates, and the Votes shall then be counted. The Person having the greatest Number of Votes shall be the President, if such Number be a Majority of the whole Number of Electors appointed; and if there be more than one who have such Majority, and have an equal Number of Votes, then the House of Representatives shall immediately chuse by Ballot one of them for President; and if no Person have a Ma-

jority, then from the five highest on the List the said House shall in like Manner chuse the President. But in chusing the President, the Votes shall be taken by States, the Representation from each State having one Vote; a quorum for this Purpose shall consist of a Member or Members from two thirds of the States, and a Majority of all the States shall be necessary to a Choice. In every Case, after the Choice of the President, the Person having the greatest Number of Votes of the Electors shall be the Vice President. But if there should remain two or more who have equal Votes, the Senate shall chuse from them by Ballot the Vice President.*

The Congress may determine the Time of chusing the Electors, and the Day on which they shall give their Votes; which Day shall be the same throughout the United States.

No Person except a natural born Citizen, or a Citizen of the United States, at the time of the Adoption of this Constitution, shall be eligible to the Office of President; neither shall any Person be eligible to that Office who shall not have attained to the Age of thirty five Years, and been fourteen years a Resident within the United States.

In Case of the Removal of the President from Office, or of his Death, Resignation, or Inability to discharge the Powers and Duties of the said Office, the same shall devolve on the Vice President, *and the Congress may by Law provide for the Case of Removal, Death, Resignation, or Inability, both of the President and Vice President, declaring what Officer shall then act as President, and such Officer shall act accordingly, until the Disability be removed, or a President shall be elected.*†

The President shall, at stated Times, receive for his Services a Compensation, which shall neither be increased nor diminished during the Period for which he shall have been elected, and he shall not receive within that Period any other Emolument from the United States, or any of them.

Before he enter on the Execution of his Office, he shall take the following Oath or Affirmation:—"I do solemnly swear (or affirm) that I will faithfully execute the Office of President of the United States, and will to the best of my Ability, preserve, protect and defend the Constitution of the United States."

Section 2

The President shall be Commander in Chief of the Army and Navy of the United States, and of the Militia of the several States, when called into the actual Service of the United States; he may require the Opinion, in writing, of the principal Officer in each of the executive Departments, upon any Subject relating to the Duties of their respective Offices, and he shall have Power to Grant Reprieves and pardons for Offences against the United States, except in Cases of Impeachment.

He shall have Power, by and with the Advice and Consent of the Senate, to make Treaties, provided two thirds of the Senators present concur; and he shall nominate, and by and with the Advice and Consent of the Senate, shall appoint Ambassadors, other public Ministers and Consuls, Judges of the supreme Court, and all other Officers of the United States, whose Appointments are not herein otherwise provided for, and which shall be established by Law: but the Congress may by Law vest the Appointment of such inferior Officers, as they think proper, in the President alone, in the Courts of Law, or in the Heads of Departments.

---

*Superseded by the Twelfth Amendment.

†Modified by the Twenty-Fifth Amendment.

The President shall have Power to fill up all Vacancies that may happen during the Recess of the Senate, by granting Commissions which shall expire at the End of their next Session.

Section 3

He shall from time to time give to the Congress Information of the State of the Union, and recommend to their Consideration such Measures as he shall judge necessary and expedient; he may, on extraordinary Occasions, convene both Houses, or either of them, and in Case of Disagreement between them, with Respect to the Time of Adjournment, he may adjourn them to such Time as he shall think proper; he shall receive Ambassadors and other public Ministers; he shall take Care that the Laws be faithfully executed, and shall Commission all the Officers of the United States.

Section 4

The President, Vice President and all civil Officers of the United States, shall be removed from Office on Impeachment for, and Conviction of, Treason, Bribery, or other high Crimes and Misdemeanors.

ARTICLE III

Section 1

The judicial Power of the United States, shall be vested in one supreme Court, and in such inferior Courts as the Congress may from time to time ordain and establish. The Judges, both of the supreme and inferior courts, shall hold their Offices during good Behaviour, and shall, at stated Times, receive for their Services a Compensation, which shall not be diminished during their Continuance in Office.

Section 2

The judicial Power shall extend to all Cases, in Law and Equity, arising under this Constitution, the Laws of the United States, and Treaties made, or which shall be made, under their Authority;—to all Cases affecting Ambassadors, other public Ministers and Consuls;—to all Cases of admiralty and maritime Jurisdiction;—to Controversies to which the United States shall be a Party;—to Controversies between two or more States;—*between a State and Citizens of another State,**—between Citizens of different States;—between Citizens of the same State claiming Lands under Grants of different States, and between a State, or the Citizens thereof, and foreign States, Citizens or Subjects.

In all Cases affecting Ambassadors, other public Ministers and Consuls, and those in which a State shall be Party, the supreme Court shall have original Jurisdiction. In all the other Cases before mentioned, the supreme Court shall have appellate Jurisdiction, both as to Law and Fact, with such Exceptions, and under such Regulations as the Congress shall make.

---

*Restricted by the Eleventh Amendment.

The trial of all Crimes, except in Cases of Impeachment, shall be by Jury; and such Trial shall be held in the State where said Crimes shall have been committed; but when not committed within any State, the Trial shall be at such Place or Places as the Congress may by Law have directed.

Section 3

Treason against the United States, shall consist only in levying War against them, or in adhering to their Enemies, giving them Aid and Comfort. No Person shall be convicted of Treason unless on the Testimony of two Witnesses to the same overt Act, or on Confession in open Court.

The Congress shall have Power to declare the Punishment of Treason, but no Attainder of Treason shall work Corruption of Blood, or Forefeiture except during the Life of the Person attainted.

ARTICLE IV

Section 1

Full Faith and Credit shall be given in each State to the public Acts, Records, and judicial Proceedings of every other State. And the Congress may by general Laws prescribe the Manner in which such Acts, Records, and Proceedings shall be proved, and the Effect thereof.

Section 2

The Citizens of each State shall be entitled to all Privileges and Immunities of Citizens in the several States.

A Person charged in any State with Treason, Felony, or other Crime, who shall flee from Justice, and be found in another State, shall on demand of the executive Authority of the State from which he fled, be delivered up, to be removed to the State having Jurisdiction of the Crime.

No Person held to Service or Labour in one State, under the Laws thereof, escaping into another, shall, in Consequence of any Law or Regulation therein, be discharged from such Service or Labour, but shall be delivered up on Claim of the Party to whom such Service or Labour may be due.*

Section 3

New States may be admitted by the Congress into this Union; but no new State shall be formed or erected within the Jurisdiction of any other State; nor any State be formed by the Junction of two or more States, or parts of States, without the Consent of the Legislatures of the States concerned as well as of the Congress.

The Congress shall have Power to dispose of and make all needful Rules and Regulations respecting the Territory or other Property belonging to the United States; and nothing in this Constitution shall be so construed as to Prejudice any Claims of the United States, or of any particular State.

---

*Superseded by the Thirteenth Amendment.

Section 4

The United States shall guarantee to every State in this Union a Republican Form of Government, and shall protect each of them against Invasion; and on Application of the Legislature, or of the Executive (when the Legislature cannot be convened) against domestic Violence.

ARTICLE V

The Congress, whenever two thirds of both Houses shall deem it necessary, shall propose Amendments to this Constitution, or, on the Application of the Legislatures of two thirds of the several States, shall call a Convention for proposing Amendments, which, in either Case, shall be valid to all Intents and Purposes, as Part of this Constitution, when ratified by the Legislatures of three fourths of the several States, or by Conventions in three fourths thereof, as the one or the other Mode of Ratification may be proposed by the Congress; Provided that no Amendment which may be made prior to the Year One thousand eight hundred and eight shall in any Manner affect the first and fourth Clauses in the Ninth Section of the first Article; and that no State, without its Consent, shall be deprived of its equal Suffrage in the Senate.

ARTICLE VI

All Debts contracted and Engagements entered into, before the Adoption of this Constitution, shall be as valid against the United States under this Constitution, as under the Confederation.

This Constitution, and the Laws of the United States which shall be made in Pursuance thereof; and all Treaties made, or which shall be made, under the Authority of the United States, shall be the supreme Law of the Land; and the Judges in every State shall be bound thereby, any Thing in the Constitution or Laws of any State to the Contrary notwithstanding.

The Senators and Representatives before mentioned, and the Members of the several State Legislatures, and all executive and judicial Officers, both of the United States and of the several States, shall be bound by Oath or Affirmation, to support this Constitution; but no religious Test shall ever be required as a Qualification to any Office or public Trust under the United States.

ARTICLE VII

The Ratification of the Conventions of nine States shall be sufficient for the Establishment of this Constitution between the States so ratifying the Same.

Done in Convention by the Unanimous Consent of the States present the Seventeenth Day of September in the Year of our Lord one thousand seven hundred and Eighty seven and of the Independence of the United States of America the Twelfth. In Witness whereof We have hereunto subscribed our Names.

Go. Washington

President and deputy from Virginia

New Hampshire
John Langdon
Nicholas Gilman

Massachusetts
Nathaniel Gorham
Rufus King

Connecticut
Wm. Saml. Johnson
Roger Sherman

New York
Alexander Hamilton

New Jersey
Wil. Livingston
David Brearley
Wm. Paterson
Jona. Dayton

Pennsylvania
B. Franklin
Thomas Mifflin
Robt. Morris
Geo. Clymer
Thos. FitzSimons
Jared Ingersoll
James Wilson
Gouv. Morris

Delaware
Geo. Read
Gunning Bedford jun
John Dickenson
Richard Bassett
Jaco. Broom

Maryland
James McHenry
Dan. of St. Thos. Jenifer
Danl. Carroll

Virginia
John Blair
James Madison, Jr.

North Carolina
Wm. Blount
Richd. Dobbs Spaight
Hu Williamson

South Carolina
J. Rutledge
Charles Cotesworth
   Pickney
Pierce Butler

Georgia
William Few
Abr. Baldwin

AMENDMENTS TO THE CONSTITUTION

AMENDMENT I [1791]*

Congress shall make no law respecting an establishment of religion, or prohibiting the free exercise thereof; or abridging the freedom of speech, or of the press; or the right of the people peaceably to assembley, and to petition the Government for a redress of grievances.

AMENDMENT II [1791]

A well regulated Militia, being necessary to the security of a free State, the right of the people to keep and bear Arms shall not be infringed.

AMENDMENT III [1791]

No Soldier shall, in time of peace, be quartered in any house, without the consent of the Owner, nor in time of war, but in a manner to be prescribed by law.

AMENDMENT IV [1791]

The right of the people to be secure in their persons, houses, papers, and effects, against unreasonable searches and seizures, shall not be violated, and no Warrants shall issue, but upon probable cause, supported by Oath or affirmation, and particularly describing the place to be searched, and the persons or things to be seized.

AMENDMENT V [1791]

No person shall be held to answer for a capital or otherwise infamous crime, unless on a presentment or indictment of a Grand Jury, except in cases arising in the land or naval forces, or in the Militia, when in actual service in time of War or public danger; nor shall any person be subject for the same offence to be twice put in jeopardy of life or limb; nor shall be compelled in any criminal case to be a witness against himself, nor be deprived of life, liberty, or property, without due process of law; nor shall private property be taken for public use, without just compensation.

AMENDMENT VI [1791]

In all criminal prosecutions, the accused shall enjoy the right to a speedy and public trial, by an impartial jury of the State and district wherein the crime shall have been committed, which district shall have been previously ascertained by law, and to be informed of the nature and cause of the accusation; to be confronted with the witnesses against him; to have compulsory process for obtaining witnesses in his favor, and to have the Assistance of Counsel for his defence.

---

*The dates in brackets indicate when the amendments were ratified.

AMENDMENT VII [1791]

In suits at common law, where the value in controversy shall exceed twenty dollars, the right of trial by jury shall be preserved, and no fact tried by a jury, shall be otherwise reexamined in any Court of the United States, than according to the Rules of the common law.

AMENDMENT VIII [1791]

Excessive bail shall not be required, nor excessive fines imposed, nor cruel and unusual punishments inflicted.

AMENDMENT IX [1791]

The enumeration in the Constitution, of certain rights, shall not be construed to deny or disparage others retained by the people.

AMENDMENT X [1791]

The powers not delegated to the United States by the Constitution, nor prohibited by it to the States, are reserved to the States respectively, or to the people.

AMENDMENT XI [1798]

The Judicial power of the United States shall not be construed to extend to any suit in law or equity, commenced or prosecuted against one of the United States by Citizens of another State, or by Citizens or subjects of any foreign state.

AMENDMENT XII [1804]

The Electors shall meet in their respective States and vote by ballot for President and Vice-President, one of whom, at least, shall not be an inhabitant of the same State with themselves; they shall name in their ballots the person voted for as President, and in distinct ballots the person voted for as Vice-President, and they shall make distinct lists of all persons voted for as President, and of all persons voted for as Vice-President, and of the number of votes for each, which lists they shall sign and certify, and transmit sealed to the seat of the government of the United States, directed to the President of the Senate;—the President of the Senate shall, in the presence of the Senate and House of Representatives, open all the certificates and the votes shall then be counted;—The person having the greatest number of votes for President, shall be the President, if such number be a majority of the whole number of Electors appointed; and if no person have such majority, then from the persons having the highest numbers not exceeding three on the list of those voted for as President, the House of Representatives shall choose immediately, by ballot, the President. But in choosing the President, the votes shall be taken by States, the representation from each State having one vote; a quorum for this purpose shall consist of a member or members from two-thirds of the States, and a majority of all the States shall be necessary to a choice. And if the House of Representatives shall not choose a President whenever the right of choice shall devolve upon them, before *the fourth day of March* next following, then the Vice-President shall act as President, as in the case of the death or other constitutional disability of the President.*—The person having the greatest number of votes as Vice-President, shall be the Vice-President, if such number be a majority of the whole number of Electors appointed, and if no person have a majority, then from the two highest numbers on the list, the Senate shall choose the Vice-President; a quorum for the purpose shall consist of two-thirds of the whole number of Senators, and a majority of the whole number shall be necessary to a choice. But no person constitutionally ineligible to the office of President shall be eligible to that of Vice-President of the United States.

AMENDMENT XIII [1865]

Section 1
Neither slavery nor involuntary servitude, except as a punishment for crime whereof the party shall have been duly convicted, shall exist within the United States, or any place subject to their jurisdiction.

Section 2
Congress shall have power to enforce this article by appropriate legislation.

AMENDMENT XIV [1868]

Section 1
All persons born or naturalized in the United States, and subject to the jurisdiction thereof, are citizens of the United States and of the State wherein they reside. No State shall make or enforce any law which shall abridge the privileges or immunities of citizens of the United States; nor shall any State deprive any person of life, liberty, or property, without due process of law; nor deny to any person within its jurisdiction the equal protection of the laws.

Section 2
Representatives shall be apportioned among the several States according to their respective numbers, counting the whole number of persons in each State, excluding Indians not taxed. But when the right to vote at any election for the choice of electors for President and Vice-President of the United States, Representatives in Congress, the Executive and Judicial officers of a State, or the members of the Legislature thereof, is denied to any of the male inhabitants of such State, being twenty-one years of age, and citizens of the United States, or in any way abridged, except for participation in rebellion, or other crime, the basis of representation therein shall be reduced in the proportion which the number of such male citizens shall bear to the whole number of male citizens twenty-one years of age in such State.

Section 3
No person shall be a Senator or Representative in Congress, or elector of President and Vice-President, or hold any office, civil or military, under the United States, or under any State,

*Superseded by Section 3 of the Twentieth Amendment.

who, having previously taken an oath, as a member of Congress, or as an officer of the United States, or as a member of any State legislature, or as an executive or judicial officer of any State, to support the Constitution of the United States, shall have engaged in insurrection or rebellion against the same, or given aid or comfort to the enemies thereof. Congress may by a vote of two-thirds of each house, remove such disability.

Section 4
The validity of the public debt of the United States, authorized by law, including debts incurred for payment of pensions and bounties for services in suppressing insurrection or rebellion, shall not be questioned. But neither the United States nor any State shall assume or pay any debt or obligation incurred in aid of insurrection or rebellion against the United States, or any claim for the loss or emancipation of any slave; but all such debts, obligations and claims shall be held illegal and void.

Section 5
The Congress shall have power to enforce, by appropriate legislation, the provisions of this article.

Amendment XV [1870]

Section 1
The right of citizens of the United States to vote shall not be denied or abridged by the United States or by any State on account of race, color, or previous condition of servitude—

Section 2
The Congress shall have power to enforce this article by appropriate legislation.

Amendment XVI [1913]

The Congress shall have power to lay and collect taxes on incomes, from whatever source derived, without apportionment among the several States, and without regard to any census or enumeration.

Amendment XVII [1913]

The Senate of the United States shall be composed of two Senators from each State, elected by the people thereof, for six years; and each Senator shall have one vote. The electors in each State shall have the qualifications requisite for electors of the most numerous branch of the State legislatures.

When vacancies happen in the representation of any State in the Senate, the executive authority of such State shall issue writs of election to fill such vacancies: *Provided,* That the legislature of any State may empower the executive thereof to make temporary appointments until the people fill the vacancies by election as the legislature may direct.

This amendment shall not be so construed as to affect the election or term of any Senator chosen before it becomes valid as part of the Constitution.

AMENDMENT XVIII [1919]

Section 1
After one year from the ratification of this article the manufacture, sale, or transportation of intoxicating liquors within, the importation thereof into, or the exportation thereof from the United States and all territory subject to the jurisdiction hereof for beverage purposes hereby prohibited.

Section 2
The Congress and the several States shall have concurrent power to enforce this article by appropriate legislation.

Section 3
This article shall be inoperative unless it shall have been ratified as an amendment to the Constitution by the legislatures of the several States, as provided by the Constitution, within seven years from the date of submission hereof to the States by the Congress.*

AMENDMENT XIX [1920]

The right of citizens of the United States to vote shall not be denied or abridged by the United States or by any State on account of sex.
      Congress shall have power to enforce this article by appropriate legislation.

AMENDMENT XX [1933]

Section 1
The terms of the President and Vice-President shall end at noon on the 20th day of January, and the terms of Senators and Representatives at noon on the 3d day of January, of the years in which such terms would have ended if this article had not been ratified; and the terms of their successors shall then begin.

Section 2
The Congress shall assemble at least once in every year, and such meeting shall begin at noon on the 3d day of January, unless they shall by law appoint a different day.

Section 3
If, at the time fixed for the beginning of the term of the President, the President elect shall have died, the Vice-President elect shall become President. If a President shall not have been chosen before the time fixed for the beginning of his term, or if the President elect shall have failed to qualify, then the Vice-President elect shall act as President until a President shall have qualified; and the Congress may by law provide for the case wherein neither a President elect nor a Vice-President elect shall have qualified, declaring who shall then act

---

*Repealed by Section 1 of the Twenty-First Amendment.

as President, or the manner in which one who is to act shall be selected, and such person shall act accordingly until a President or Vice-President shall have qualified.

Section 4
The Congress may by law provide for the case of the death of any of the persons from whom the House of Representatives may choose a President whenever the right of choice shall have devolved upon them, and for the case of the death of any of the persons from whom the Senate may choose a Vice-President whenever the right of choice shall have devolved upon them.

Section 5
Sections 1 and 2 shall take effect on the 15th day of October following the ratification of this article.

Section 6
This article shall be inoperative unless it shall have been ratified as an amendment to the Constitution by the legislatures of three-fourths of the several States within seven years from the date of its submission.

AMENDMENT XXI [1933]

Section 1
The eighteenth article of amendment to the Constitution of the United States is hereby repealed.

Section 2
The transportation or importation into any State, Territory, or possession of the United States for delivery or use therein of intoxicating liquors, in violation of the laws thereof, is hereby prohibited.

Section 3
This article shall be inoperative unless it shall have been ratified as an amendment to the Constitution by conventions in the several States, as provided in the Constitution, within seven years from the date of submission hereof to the States by the Congress.

AMENDMENT XXII [1951]

Section 1
No person shall be elected to the office of President more than twice, and no person who has held the office of President, or acted as President, for more than two years of a term to which some other person was elected President shall be elected to the office of the President more than once. But this Article shall not apply to any person holding the office of President when this Article was proposed by the Congress, and shall not prevent any person who may be holding the office of President, or acting as President, during the term within which this Article becomes operative from holding the office of the President or acting as President during the remainder of such term.

Section 2

This article shall be inoperative unless it shall have been ratified as an amendment to the Constitution by the legislatures of three-fourths of the several States within seven years from the date of its submission to the States by the Congress.

AMENDMENT XXIII [1961]

Section 1

The District constituting the seat of Government of the United States shall appoint in such manner as the Congress may direct:

A number of electors of President and Vice-President equal to the whole number of Senators and Representatives in Congress to which the District would be entitled if it were a State, but in no event more than the least populous State; they shall be in addition to those appointed by the States, but they shall be considered, for the purposes of the election of President and Vice-President, to be electors appointed by a State; and they shall meet in the District and perform such duties as provided by the twelfth article of amendment.

Section 2

The Congress shall have power to enforce this article by appropriate legislation.

AMENDMENT XXIV [1964]

Section 1

The right of citizens of the United States to vote in any primary or other election for President or Vice-President, for electors for President or Vice-President, or for Senator or Representative in Congress, shall not be denied or abridged by the United States or any State by reason of failure to pay any poll tax or other tax.

Section 2

The Congress shall have power to enforce this article by appropriate legislation.

AMENDMENT XXV [1967]

Section 1

In case of the removal of the President from office or of his death or resignation, the Vice-President shall become President.

Section 2

Whenever there is a vacancy in the office of the Vice-President, the President shall nominate a Vice-President who shall take office upon confirmation by a majority vote of both houses of Congress.

Section 3

Whenever the President transmits to the President pro tempore of the Senate and the Speaker of the House of Representatives his written declaration that he is unable to discharge the powers and duties of his office, and until he transmits to them a written declaration to the contrary, such powers and duties shall be discharged by the Vice-President as Acting President.

Section 4
Whenever the Vice-President and a majority of either the principal officers of the executive departments or of such other body as Congress may by law provide, transmit to the President pro tempore of the Senate and the Speaker of the House of Representatives their written declaration that the President is unable to discharge the powers and duties of his office, the Vice-President shall immediately assume the powers and duties of the office as Acting President.

Thereafter, when the President transmits to the President pro tempore of the Senate and the Speaker of the House of Representatives his written declaration that no inability exists, he shall resume the powers and duties of his office unless the Vice-President and a majority of either the principal officers of the executive department or of such other body as Congress may by law provide, transmit within four days to the President pro tempore of the Senate and the Speaker of the House of Representatives their written declaration that the President is unable to discharge the powers and duties of his office. Thereupon Congress shall decide the issue, assembling within forty-eight hours for that purpose if not in session. If the Congress, within twenty-one days after receipt of the latter written declaration, or, if Congress is not in session, within twenty-one days after Congress is required to assemble, determines by two-thirds vote of both Houses that the President is unable to discharge the powers and duties of his office, the Vice-President shall continue to discharge the same as Acting President; otherwise, the President shall resume the powers and duties of his office.

Amendment XXVI [1971]

Section 1
The right of citizens of the United States, who are eighteen years of age or older, to vote shall not be denied or abridged by the United States or by any state on account of age.

Section 2
The Congress shall have power to enforce this article by appropriate legislation.

Amendment XXVII [1992]

No law varying the compensation for services of the Senators and Representatives, shall take effect, until an election of Representatives shall have intervened.

APPENDIX

Territorial Expansion			
Territory	Date Acquired	Square Miles	How Acquired
Original states and territories	1783	888,685	Treaty of Paris
Louisiana Purchase	1803	827,192	Purchased from France
Florida	1819	72,003	Adams-Onís Treaty
Texas	1845	390,143	Annexation of independent country
Oregon	1846	285,580	Oregon Boundary Treaty
Mexican cession	1848	529,017	Treaty of Guadalupe Hidalgo
Gadsden Purchase	1853	29,640	Purchased from Mexico
Midway Islands	1867	2	Annexation of uninhabited islands
Alaska	1867	589,757	Purchased from Russia
Hawaii	1898	6,450	Annexation of independent country
Wake Island	1898	3	Annexation of uninhabited island
Puerto Rico	1899	3,435	Treaty of Paris
Guam	1899	212	Treaty of Paris
The Philippines	1899–1946	115,600	Treaty of Paris; granted independence
American Samoa	1900	76	Treaty with Germany and Great Britain
Panama Canal Zone	1904–1978	553	Hay–Bunau-Varilla Treaty
U.S. Virgin Islands	1917	133	Purchased from Denmark
Trust Territory of the Pacific Islands*	1947	717	United Nations Trusteeship

*A number of these islands have recently been granted independence: Federated States of Micronesia, 1990; Marshall Islands, 1991; Palau, 1994.

The Labor Force (thousands of workers)

Year	Agriculture	Mining	Manufacturing	Construction	Trade	Other	Total
1810	1,950	11	75	—	—	294	2,330
1840	3,570	32	500	290	350	918	5,660
1850	4,520	102	1,200	410	530	1,488	8,250
1860	5,880	176	1,530	520	890	2,114	11,110
1870	6,790	180	2,470	780	1,310	1,400	12,930
1880	8,920	280	3,290	900	1,930	2,070	17,390
1890	9,960	440	4,390	1,510	2,960	4,060	23,320
1900	11,680	637	5,895	1,665	3,970	5,223	29,070
1910	11,770	1,068	8,332	1,949	5,320	9,041	37,480
1920	10,790	1,180	11,190	1,233	5,845	11,372	41,610
1930	10,560	1,009	9,884	1,988	8,122	17,267	48,830
1940	9,575	925	11,309	1,876	9,328	23,277	56,290
1950	7,870	901	15,648	3,029	12,152	25,870	65,470
1960	5,970	709	17,145	3,640	14,051	32,545	74,060
1970	3,463	516	20,746	4,818	15,008	34,127	78,678
1980	3,364	979	21,942	6,215	20,191	46,612	99,303
1990	3,186	730	21,184	7,696	24,269	60,849	118,793
1998	3,378	620	20,733	8,518	27,203	71,011	131,463

SOURCE: *Historical Statistics of the United States, Colonial Times to 1970* (1975), 139; *Statistical Abstract of the United States,* 2000, Table 672.

Changing Labor Patterns

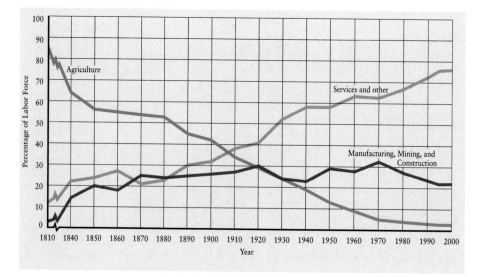

SOURCE: *Historical Statistics of the United States, Colonial Times to 1970* (1975), 139; *Statistical Abstract of the United States,* 2000, Table 672.

American Population

Year	Population	Percent Increase	Year	Population	Percent Increase
1610	350	—	1810	7,239,881	36.4
1620	2,300	557.1	1820	9,638,453	33.1
1630	4,600	100.0	1830	12,866,020	33.5
1640	26,600	478.3	1840	17,069,453	32.7
1650	50,400	90.8	1850	23,191,876	35.9
1660	75,100	49.0	1860	31,443,321	35.6
1670	111,900	49.0	1870	39,818,449	26.6
1680	151,500	35.4	1880	50,155,783	26.0
1690	210,400	38.9	1890	62,947,714	25.5
1700	250,900	19.2	1900	75,994,575	20.7
1710	331,700	32.2	1910	91,972,266	21.0
1720	466,200	40.5	1920	105,710,620	14.9
1730	629,400	35.0	1930	122,775,046	16.1
1740	905,600	43.9	1940	131,669,275	7.2
1750	1,170,800	29.3	1950	150,697,361	14.5
1760	1,593,600	36.1	1960	179,323,175	19.0
1770	2,148,100	34.8	1970	203,235,298	13.3
1780	2,780,400	29.4	1980	226,545,805	11.5
1790	3,929,214	41.3	1990	248,709,873	9.8
1800	5,308,483	35.1	2000	281,421,906	13.2

Note: These figures largely ignore the Native American population. Census takers never made any effort to count the Native American population that lived outside their political jurisdictions and compiled only casual and incomplete enumerations of those living within their jurisdictions until 1890. In that year the federal government attempted a full count of the Indian population: the Census found 125,719 Indians in 1890, compared with only 12,543 in 1870 and 33,985 in 1880.

SOURCE: *Historical Statistics of the United States, Colonial Times to 1970* (1975); *Statistical Abstract of the United States,* 1999; Bureau of the Census, 2001 <http://blue.census.gov/dmd/www/resapport/states/unitedstates.pdf>.

Presidential Elections

Year	Candidates	Parties	Percentage of Popular Vote	Electoral Vote	Percentage of Voter Participation
1789	**George Washington**	No party designations	*	69	
	John Adams†			34	
	Other candidates			35	
1792	**George Washington**	No party designations		132	
	John Adams			77	
	George Clinton			50	
	Other candidates			5	
1796	**John Adams**	Federalist		71	
	Thomas Jefferson	Democratic-Republican		68	
	Thomas Pinckney	Federalist		59	
	Aaron Burr	Democratic-Republican		30	
	Other candidates			48	
1800	**Thomas Jefferson**	Democratic-Republican		73	
	Aaron Burr	Democratic-Republican		73	
	John Adams	Federalist		65	
	Charles C. Pinckney	Federalist		64	
	John Jay	Federalist		1	
1804	**Thomas Jefferson**	Democratic-Republican		162	
	Charles C. Pinckney	Federalist		14	
1808	**James Madison**	Democratic-Republican		122	
	Charles C. Pinckney	Federalist		47	
	George Clinton	Democratic-Republican		6	
1812	**James Madison**	Democratic-Republican		128	
	De Witt Clinton	Federalist		89	
1816	**James Monroe**	Democratic-Republican		183	
	Rufus King	Federalist		34	
1820	**James Monroe**	Democratic-Republican		231	
	John Quincy Adams	Independent Republican		1	
1824	**John Quincy Adams**	Democratic-Republican	30.5	84	26.9
	Andrew Jackson	Democratic-Republican	43.1	99	
	Henry Clay	Democratic-Republican	13.2	37	
	William H. Crawford	Democratic-Republican	13.1	41	
1828	**Andrew Jackson**	Democratic	56.0	178	57.6
	John Quincy Adams	National Republican	44.0	83	
1832	**Andrew Jackson**	Democratic	54.5	219	55.4
	Henry Clay	National Republican	37.5	49	
	William Wirt	Anti-Masonic	8.0	7	
	John Floyd	Democratic	‡	11	
1836	**Martin Van Buren**	Democratic	50.9	170	57.8
	William H. Harrison	Whig		73	
	Hugh L. White	Whig		26	
	Daniel Webster	Whig	49.1	14	
	W. P. Mangum	Whig		11	
1840	**William H. Harrison**	Whig	53.1	234	80.2
	Martin Van Buren	Democratic	46.9	60	

*Prior to 1824, most presidential electors were chosen by state legislators rather than by popular vote.
†Before the Twelfth Amendment was passed in 1804, the electoral college voted for two presidential candidates; the runner-up became vice president.
‡Percentages below 2.5 have been omitted. Hence the percentage of popular vote might not total 100 percent.

Year	Candidates	Parties	Percentage of Popular Vote	Electoral Vote	Percentage of Voter Participation
1844	**James K. Polk**	Democratic	49.6	170	78.9
	Henry Clay	Whig	48.1	105	
	James G. Birney	Liberty	2.3		
1848	**Zachary Taylor**	Whig	47.4	163	72.7
	Lewis Cass	Democratic	42.5	127	
	Martin Van Buren	Free Soil	10.1		
1852	**Franklin Pierce**	Democratic	50.9	254	69.6
	Winfield Scott	Whig	44.1	42	
	John P. Hale	Free Soil	5.0		
1856	**James Buchanan**	Democratic	45.3	174	78.9
	John C. Frémont	Republican	33.1	114	
	Millard Fillmore	American	21.6	8	
1860	**Abraham Lincoln**	Republican	39.8	180	81.2
	Stephen A. Douglas	Democratic	29.5	12	
	John C. Breckinridge	Democratic	18.1	72	
	John Bell	Constitutional Union	12.6	39	
1864	**Abraham Lincoln**	Republican	55.0	212	73.8
	George B. McClellan	Democratic	45.0	21	
1868	**Ulysses S. Grant**	Republican	52.7	214	78.1
	Horatio Seymour	Democratic	47.3	80	
1872	**Ulysses S. Grant**	Republican	55.6	286	71.3
	Horace Greeley	Democratic	43.9		
1876	**Rutherford B. Hayes**	Republican	48.0	185	81.8
	Samuel J. Tilden	Democratic	51.0	184	
1880	**James A. Garfield**	Republican	48.5	214	79.4
	Winfield S. Hancock	Democratic	48.1	155	
	James B. Weaver	Greenback-Labor	3.4		
1884	**Grover Cleveland**	Democratic	48.5	219	77.5
	James G. Blaine	Republican	48.2	182	
1888	**Benjamin Harrison**	Republican	47.9	233	79.3
	Grover Cleveland	Democratic	48.6	168	
1892	**Grover Cleveland**	Democratic	46.1	277	74.7
	Benjamin Harrison	Republican	43.0	145	
	James B. Weaver	People's	8.5	22	
1896	**William McKinley**	Republican	51.1	271	79.3
	William J. Bryan	Democratic	47.7	176	
1900	**William McKinley**	Republican	51.7	292	73.2
	William J. Bryan	Democratic; Populist	45.5	155	
1904	**Theodore Roosevelt**	Republican	57.4	336	65.2
	Alton B. Parker	Democratic	37.6	140	
	Eugene V. Debs	Socialist	3.0		
1908	**William H. Taft**	Republican	51.6	321	65.4
	William J. Bryan	Democratic	43.1	162	
	Eugene V. Debs	Socialist	2.8		
1912	**Woodrow Wilson**	Democratic	41.9	435	58.8
	Theodore Roosevelt	Progressive	27.4	88	
	William H. Taft	Republican	23.2	8	
1916	**Woodrow Wilson**	Democratic	49.4	277	61.6
	Charles E. Hughes	Republican	46.2	254	
	A.L. Benson	Socialist	3.2		

Year	Candidates	Parties	Percentage of Popular Vote	Electoral Vote	Percentage of Voter Participation
1920	**Warren G. Harding**	Republican	60.4	404	49.2
	James M. Cox	Democratic	34.2	127	
	Eugene V. Debs	Socialist	3.4		
1924	**Calvin Coolidge**	Republican	54.0	382	48.9
	John W. Davis	Democratic	28.8	136	
	Robert M. La Follette	Progressive	16.6	13	
1928	**Herbert C. Hoover**	Republican	58.2	444	56.9
	Alfred E. Smith	Democratic	40.9	87	
1932	**Franklin D. Roosevelt**	Democratic	57.4	472	56.9
	Herbert C. Hoover	Republican	39.7	59	
1936	**Franklin D. Roosevelt**	Democratic	60.8	523	61.0
	Alfred M. Landon	Republican	36.5	8	
1940	**Franklin D. Roosevelt**	Democratic	54.8	449	62.5
	Wendell L. Willkie	Republican	44.8	82	
1944	**Franklin D. Roosevelt**	Democratic	53.5	432	55.9
	Thomas E. Dewey	Republican	46.0	99	
1948	**Harry S Truman**	Democratic	49.6	303	53.0
	Thomas E. Dewey	Republican	45.1	189	
1952	**Dwight D. Eisenhower**	Republican	55.1	442	63.3
	Adlai E. Stevenson	Democratic	44.4	89	
1956	**Dwight D. Eisenhower**	Republican	57.6	457	60.6
	Adlai E. Stevenson	Democratic	42.1	73	
1960	**John F. Kennedy**	Democratic	49.7	303	64.0
	Richard M. Nixon	Republican	49.5	219	
1964	**Lyndon B. Johnson**	Democratic	61.1	486	61.7
	Barry M. Goldwater	Republican	38.5	52	
1968	**Richard M. Nixon**	Republican	43.4	301	60.6
	Hubert H. Humphrey	Democratic	42.7	191	
	George C. Wallace	American Independent	13.5	46	
1972	**Richard M. Nixon**	Republican	60.7	520	55.5
	George S. McGovern	Democratic	37.5	17	
1976	**Jimmy Carter**	Democratic	50.1	297	54.3
	Gerald R. Ford	Republican	48.0	240	
1980	**Ronald W. Reagan**	Republican	50.7	489	53.0
	Jimmy Carter	Democratic	41.0	49	
	John B. Anderson	Independent	6.6	0	
1984	**Ronald W. Reagan**	Republican	58.4	525	52.9
	Walter F. Mondale	Democratic	41.6	13	
1988	**George H. W. Bush**	Republican	53.4	426	50.3
	Michael Dukakis	Democratic	45.6	111*	
1992	**William J. Clinton**	Democratic	43.7	370	55.1
	George H. W. Bush	Republican	38.0	168	
	H. Ross Perot	Independent	19.0	0	
1996	**William J. Clinton**	Democratic	49	379	49.0
	Robert J. Dole	Republican	41	159	
	H. Ross Perot	Reform	8	0	
2000	**George W. Bush**	Republican	47.9	271	N.A.
	Albert A. Gore	Democratic	48.4	266†	
	Ralph Nader	Green Party	2.7		

*One Dukakis elector cast a vote for Lloyd Bentsen.
†One Gore elector abstained.

CREDITS

CHAPTER 1

"Aztec Elders Describe the Spanish Conquest." Excerpt from *The Florentine Codex: General History of the Thiggs of New Spain,* translated by Arthur J. O. Anderson and Charles E. Dibble. Copyright © 1975 by the University of Utah Press and the School of American Research. Reprinted courtesy of the University of Utah Press.

CHAPTER 2

Excerpt from *The Unredeemed Captive: A Family Story from Early America* by John Demos. Copyright © 1994 by John Demos. Reprinted with the permission of Alfred A. Knopf, a division of Random House, Inc.

CHAPTER 4

"Runaway Servants and Slaves." Excerpt from *Blacks Who Stole Themselves: Advertisements for Runaways* in the Pennsylvania Gazette, *1728–1790* by Billy G. Smith and Richard Wojtowicz. Copyright © 1989 University of Pennsylvania Press. Reprinted with the permission of the publisher.

"The Power of a Preacher." Excerpt from *English Historical Documents Vol. IX: American Colonial Documents to 1776,* edited by Merrill Jensen. Copyright © 1955 by Oxford University Press, Inc.

CHAPTER 8

"The Battle of Tippecanoe." Excerpt from "Shabonne's Account of Tippecanoe" in *Indiana Magazine of History* 18 (December 1921): 355–59, edited by Wesley Whickar. Reprinted with permission from the Indiana Historical Society.

CHAPTER 10

"A New England Mill Worker." Excerpt from *The New England Mill Village, 1790–1860* by Gary Kulik, Roger Parks, Theodore Z. Penn, editors. Copyright © 1982 by MIT Press. Reprinted with permission of MIT Press.

CHAPTER 12

"An Illinois 'Jeffersonian' Attacks the Mormons." Excerpt from *Antebellum America: An Interpretive Anthology* by David Brion Davis, editor. Copyright © 1997 by David Brion Davis. Reprinted with permission of the author. Now published by Pennsylvania State University Press.

"A Farm Woman Defends the Grimké Sisters." Excerpt from "The Daughters of Job: Property Rights and Women's Lives in Mid-Nineteenth-Century Massachusetts" by Dianne Avery and Alfred S. Konefsky in *Law and History Review* 10 (Fall 1992): 323–56. From Box 3, folder 10, Simon Greenleaf Papers, Harvard Law School Library. Reprinted with permission of the publisher.

CHAPTER 13

"A Mexican View of the Battle of the Alamo." Excerpt from *With Santa Anna in Texas: A Personal Narrative of the Revolution* by José Enrique de la Peña, translated by Carmen Perry. Copyright © 1975 Carmen Perry. Reprinted with permission from Texas A & M University Press.

CHAPTER 14

"Sherman's March through Georgia." Excerpt from *Eyewitnesses and Others: Readings in American History,* vol. 1 (1995). Copyright © 1995 Holt, Rinehart and Winston. Reprinted with permission.

INDEX

Note: Italic letters following page numbers refer to illustrations (*i*), maps (*m*), tables (*t*) and figures (*f*).